The British School Film

Stephen Glynn

The British School Film

From Tom Brown to Harry Potter

Representations of Secondary Education in British Cinema

palgrave
macmillan

Stephen Glynn
Oakham, Leicestershire
United Kingdom

ISBN 978-1-137-55886-2   ISBN 978-1-137-55887-9   (eBook)
DOI 10.1057/978-1-137-55887-9

Library of Congress Control Number: 2016948744

Printed on acid-free paper

This Palgrave Macmillan imprint is published by Springer Nature
The registered company is Macmillan Publishers Ltd. London

ACKNOWLEDGEMENTS

This book is informed by my thirty years plus as a secondary school teacher, 'the noblest calling a man can follow' (Discuss). My decades observing 'real' staffroom colleagues have allowed a fuller understanding of their 'reel' counterparts discussed herein; the same holds for the pupils in my charge – I've taught thousands of them, thousands of them...and half of them boys. This book acknowledges them all.

Outside of school, my thanks to Felicity Plester and the staff at Palgrave for their wise counsel on this project. My thanks also to Steve Chibnall for allowing access to his 'old school' stash of trade magazines, to Tim O'Sullivan for his recommended reading list, and to Basil Glynn and Jeongmee Kim for helping me to access 'new school' online resources. Huge thanks to my mother and father, who believed in education and made of me a Grammar School boy (with serendipity at Michael Balcon's alma mater). Finally, as ever, my greatest thanks to Sarah and Roz, always voicing common sense amidst the educational jargon: with them I have enjoyed the happiest days of my life.

CONTENTS

LIST OF FIGURES

PART I

Introduction

CHAPTER 1

The School Film: A British Genre?

1 INDUCTION

In 1994, the British Film Institute commissioned a documentary series on national cinemas to commemorate the centenary of the motion picture industry. The opening instalment, entrusted to Leicester-born director Stephen Frears, begins by quoting François Truffaut on 'a certain incompatibility between the terms "cinema" and "Britain"' (1978: 140). Retorting over the title-card with a robust 'well, bollocks to Truffaut!', *Typically British* (Channel 4, 2 September 1994), Frears' 'Personal History of British Cinema', commences with a sequence of clips from British school films, each showing a teacher either promising to cane or soundly caning a pupil. First to account is *Goodbye, Mr. Chips* (1939) where the ferociously hirsute Headmaster (Lyn Harding) informs a cowering class of his intention to thrash them all: 'You will present yourselves at my study tomorrow afternoon, in alphabetical order at intervals of three minutes, starting at three o'clock. I believe I can promise you that I have lost none of my vigour!' Perhaps not, but maybe there was a leniency in the announced timing since, to 'really tell this story', Frears next avails himself of an archive Alfred Hitchcock interview. 'At college', Hitchcock recalls with his distinctive laconic delivery, 'the method of punishment was rather a dramatic thing, I felt: if one had not done one's prep, the form master would say "Go for three!" Going for three, that was a sentence. And it was a sentence as though it were spoken by a judge.' Frears explains how Hitchcock's teachers would tell him on a Monday that he

© The Editor(s) (if applicable) and The Author(s) 2016
S. Glynn, *The British School Film*,
DOI 10.1057/978-1-137-55887-9_1

was going to be beaten on a Friday and concludes: 'that's how he learnt about suspense'. As we reflect on that (frequently cited) formative connection with Hitchcock's own 'masters of suspense' at his Jesuit boarding school, St Ignatius College, London (Russell Taylor 1978: 29–30; McGilligan 2003: 18–20), we cut to *Housemaster* (1938) where Otto Kruger takes two canes from his office cupboard and tests them to decide which would—at the appointed hour—have greater purchase (Fig. 1.1). While Frears recollects how his class would gather every Saturday afternoon to watch films that 'the school thought appropriate for children to watch: George Formby; Will Hay; typically British films, often about school itself', we witness Alastair Sim beating a pupil in *The Happiest Days of Your Life* (1950) and a similar scene from *The Guinea Pig* (1948) where Leicester's finest, Richard Attenborough, is caned for burning the toast. As Frears recounts that the first film he saw at school was *Boys Will Be Boys* (1935), the extract shown reverses the power dynamics, with headmaster

Fig. 1.1   'If you can wait and not be tired by waiting'

Hay being tossed on a blanket by his pupils outside the school gates—'in that very British, benign sort of way', Frears notes. The sequence ends with Frears recalling the British school film on which he worked as Assistant Director, Lindsay Anderson's *If....* (1968). This was much less benign: as the rebellious Crusaders (Malcolm McDowell and Christine Noonan) take aim from the roof tops of Cheltenham College, Frears concludes: 'We *shot* the headmaster in *If....*!'

It is a striking montage, and its central trope is as old as British cinema itself. In *The School Master's Portrait* (Bamforth, 1898) a disorderly pupil is discovered drawing cartoons of his teacher on the blackboard, and is soundly caned: film over. It is also a deep-seated montage: as well as comprising a demotic dismissal of Truffaut's celebrated insult, Frears' filmography of flagellation raises a second, earthy, Anglo-Saxon finger, again across the Channel, to Jacques Rivette who explained his neighbouring nation's mediocrity thus: 'British cinema is a genre cinema, but one where the genre has no genuine roots' (1985 [1957]: 32). Wrong, Rivette! So argues Mark Sinker who, in his monograph on *If....,* emphasises the appositeness of Frears' headmagisterial exposition: 'The boarding school story *is* a British genre, with genuine roots: central to the Romance of Empire, its history as a genre—both literary and otherwise—is a map of the fortunes of Empire, from mid-life crisis, to zenith to dismantlement' (2004: 20). There is more, it seems, to this catalogue of canings than a Midlander's cinematic nostalgia. Time to define our terminology.

2   Lessons in Genre

Can we talk of a British school film genre? Genre *tout court* is a troublesome constant in film studies. Is it a theoretical concept of analysis or a function of industry and market forces? Is it best assessed as a product or process? At its most reductive a film genre can be adjudged to display distinct narrative patterns and a secure iconography: 'Put simply, genre movies are those commercial feature films which, through repetition and variation, tell familiar stories with familiar characters in familiar situations' (Grant 2007: 1). Many of the films under examination here clearly possess common properties, telling of errant pupils (or staff) finding their way to an acceptance of societal norms in a visual cadre of classrooms, common rooms, playing fields, gowns, mortarboards and, enduringly it seems, canes.[1] Genres, though, are seldom well-behaved: for Steve Neale they 'are not to be seen as forms of textual codifications, but as systems of orientations, expectations and conventions that circulate between industry, text and subject' (1980: 19). It is a useful enlargement of scope and this study will replicate such a tripartite structure for its case studies, investigating production histories, the film 'texts' themselves, and their consumption both critical and commercial. Categorisation is further complicated since films often demonstrate varying degrees of overlap, aka 'generic hybridity'. Many of the films treated here could equally, if not primarily, be classified as examples of comedy or tragedy, the musical or horror film, social realism or romantic drama. Or multiples thereof: *To Sir, With Love* (1967) is a 'Swinging London' musical drama—and a school film; *Never Let Me Go* (2010) is a dystopian sci-fi romance—and a school film. Moreover, a genre study must investigate its intertextual relationship with other media. Film is rarely generically pure, evident if we consider the medium's derivative entertainment heritage (Hayward 1996: 161), and pertinent for this genre study would be music hall, theatre, newspaper cartoons, television series and, especially, the novel. Steve Neale contends that film constantly refers to itself as a cross-media generic formation (1980: 62) and this will be explored for the British school film which is composed of several 'intertexts' that rework, extend and transform the norms that codify it.

A further problematising factor is that genre is never 'the simple reproduction of a formalistic model, but always the performance of a politically and historically significant and constrained social process' (Threadgold 1989: 109). Many commentators see mass media genres as 'reflecting' or 're-presenting' values dominant at the time of their production and dissemination. John Fiske, for instance, contends that generic conventions 'embody the crucial ideological concerns of the time in which they are popular' (1987: 110), while their evolution indicates for Leo Braudy how they serve as a 'barometer' of the socio-cultural concerns of cinema audiences (1992: 431). Such an approach operates with the belief that the culture itself is the prime 'author' of the text since filmmakers can only work the representational conventions available within that culture. Thus, through its study of a discrete film genre, this book also functions as a work of social history. This holds whatever a film's temporal placement since, as Pierre Sorlin has explained, 'we can only understand characters and events in historical films by referring to the years in which those films were produced' (1980: 83): hence *Another Country* (1984), though set in a boys' public school of the early 1930s, reveals as much of the 'heritage' and homophobic values permeating Thatcherite Britain as does the explicit professional aspirations of a mid-1980s co-educational secondary modern headmaster in *Clockwise* (1986).

The near-concurrent commissioning of these two films demonstrates how school life is both a common and singular experience. As James Hilton wrote in his 1938 follow-up to *Goodbye, Mr. Chips*: 'Schooling is perhaps the most universal of all experiences, but it is also one of the most individual… No two schools are alike, but more than that—the school with two hundred pupils is really two hundred schools, and among them, almost certainly, are somebody's long remembered heaven and somebody else's hell' (1938: 11–12). The happiest days of your life? It is the sorrow that often predominates. In the course of a personal selection of the world's 'top ten' school films, Peter Bradshaw questions why more, if not all films, are not set in schools: 'For many, it's the most intensely felt period of their lives: more emotionally raw and vivid and painfully real than anything in adult existence. It's a period when we are judged with terrifying candour and finality, when we will be exposed to adult emotions but without the adult prerogatives, adult status, and the adult carapace of worldly wisdom that protect us from humiliation. Who cannot close their eyes and mentally walk, in cinematic detail, down every corridor of their old school?' As with Frears, Bradshaw homes in on Britain's caning trope, again choosing *If….* and musing on the scene where Malcolm McDowell's character awaits a caning from the privileged prefectorial oligarchy: 'McDowell is caught between gloweringly accepting his fate, and ferociously realising that he doesn't have to accept it. They are just boys like him—how dare they presume to beat him?' (Fig. 1.2). For Bradshaw 'this is the sixth-form crisis writ large: a growing and overwhelming sense of your own possibilities as an adult, yet still treated as a child' ('Starring You and Me', *Guardian*, 24 February 2004). The scene highlights both the individual and the general, the way a school setting frequently underpins a troublesome 'coming of age' story, a site for the British *bildungsfilme*. On this theme, Josephine May notes how, especially with the increased secularisation of society, the individual's rites of passage to adulthood, once signalled through traditional 'staged' religious ceremonies and processes, have largely been transferred to education, with the leaving of school now arguably the primary marker of the closing of childhood (2013: 5). In *Tell England* (1931) the inexpressive Edwardian father invites his son, on leaving school and entering army training, into his study for a drink: this formal familial gesture has few words but intense emotion and signifies the son's ascent to man's estate. This study will demonstrate how British cinema has long been keen

Fig. 1.2   School—the new religious rite of passage

to explore this transitional temporal and spatial terrain: a trend intensified since the 1950s when unprecedented challenges from suburbanisation, television and other leisure pursuits led film studios to target the remaining youthful market by drawing on aspects of teenage culture and catering for teenage interests, tastes and concerns. This newly important cinematic audience was coupled with an increased school attendance beyond the compulsory age of 16, a demographic that helped to render depictions of schools other than those in the private sector both financially and ideologically viable.

3   Lessons in Nationhood

While acknowledging this expedient commercial exploitation of market segmentation, the school narrative allows filmmakers to comment on explicit educational and broader socio-cultural issues. This study answers

Bradshaw's question by showing that British filmmakers and studios *have* consistently presented cinematic discussions of schools, pupils and teachers, encompassing issues such as the nature of 'public' (i.e. fee-paying) and state schooling, the values of single-sex and special schooling, the role of male and female teachers in society and culture, and the nature of adolescence itself. Beyond this, often more implicitly, these cinematic representations have addressed issues of gender, race and class, and, more broadly, have broached issues pertinent to British national identity.

'School is the world in miniature', announces headmaster Frank Simmons (Sam Livesey) at the start of *Young Woodley* (1930). It is more commonly interpreted as the nation in miniature, a metonym for the contemporary social situation. Jeffrey Richards evaluates the British public school, as Braudy did for genre, as 'the microcosm of society and a sensitive barometer of change in society', be it the training of an Evangelical middle class, an imperialist elite or a business plutocracy (1988: 181). Tony Garnett, producer of *Kes* (1969), saw the role of post-war comprehensives as to teach their pupils 'the bare necessities to be thrown onto the labour market' as fodder for factories and coalmines (1970: n.p.). Whatever their size or status, as an entity schools are so ubiquitous a part of the everyday fabric of British lives that one rarely stops to consider the various sociocultural meanings that (echoing Bradshaw's 'carapace' metaphor) they are adjudged to carry like 'invisible shells' (Burke and Grosvenor 2008: 188). As such, the reality of and the cultural fabrications around British schools imperceptibly yet significantly shape opinions, expectations and behaviours.

This is school as an ideological commonplace—and the films discussed here thus form an important subset of the diverse and contested notion of British 'national cinema'.[2] Charles Barr, in his pioneering *Ealing Studios*, offered to cut through possible obfuscation by advancing that, 'If national "character" seems an old-fashioned, impressionistic term, it is worth noting that it could perfectly well be replaced by "ideology"' (1977: 108). It is, at best, a quasi-equivalence and, as with genre itself, the nuances of the concept of ideology have since been much debated within film studies. Ideological doctrine contends that the dominant elite not only rules but regulates the way other classes are perceived or represented. The most influential explanation of this theory, notably on Britain's *Screen* magazine, came from the writings of Louis Althusser, who saw the practice of reproducing patterns of social inequality as a matter of collusion rather than imposition and primarily achieved by the reassuringly encompassing nature of 'national identity'. A key strategy by which dominant groups win consent for the institutions through which they rule those without power is by the careful employment of consensual terms such as '*our* government', '*our* economy' and, not least, '*our* schools'. Althusser emphasises the latter: 'one ideological State apparatus certainly had the dominant role' and 'this is the School', functioning to provide pupils with 'a certain amount of "know-how" wrapped in the ruling ideology' (1971: 155). Tim Edensor, in his study of national identity, similarly concludes that it is through the institution of the school that the state most markedly enacts its responsibility of 'enforcing and prioritising specific forms of conduct, of inducing particular kinds of learning experiences, and regulating certain "good" habits amongst its citizens' (2002: 20). British schools, thus, do much more than teach the three 'r's. As both material and cultural entities, they work ideologically, in their formal curriculum and extra-curricular activities as in their overarching practices and value systems, to render coherent and consensual local, national and wider levels of British experience. More than this, because of their ubiquity in society, being so 'naturalised' a concept and so intimately enmeshed in the personal histories of its subjects (not citizens), British schools become accessible institutional structures through which to explore cinematic discussions of the nation.

This constitutes a potent, 'seamless' combination since, as with ideology, mainstream cinema is commonly viewed as functioning consensually in its mediation of hegemonic values. With its habitual employment of a classic realist style, the audience is not aware of how cinema produces meaning, and through this 'invisible' rendering of dominant class interests cinema reveals them again as 'natural' and therefore incontestable, desirable by all. In short, cinema 'puts ideology up on screen' (Hayward 1996: 215). Thus, in film treatments of '*our* schools', the overlaying of subject matter and medium forms a popular and powerful tool of consensual national identity. Such a function was not unknown to those within the film industry: Lorraine Noble, who worked for MGM's writing team at Denham Studios, expressed her hopes for the 'sincere effort' made to provide a portrayal acceptable to the teaching profession with *Goodbye, Mr. Chips*: 'For both film makers and teachers have a vast body of common interest. Both teach and mould the youth of a nation' (1939: 27). This consensus may have been the dominant trope in the British school film throughout the first half of the twentieth century, but ideology, like genre, is never fixed, and its contradictory, contested elements can at times be deduced through close analysis of the film text, exposing an internal criticism which 'cracks the film apart at the seam' (Comolli and Narboni 1977 [1969]: 7).

Thus, even in the doubly hegemonic school film genre, one can follow John Hill in conceiving of 'a national cinema, in the sense of one which works with or addresses nationally specific materials, which is none the less critical of inherited notions of national identity, which does not assume the existence of a unique or unchanging "national culture", and which is quite capable of dealing with social divisions and differences' (1992: 17). Especially in the second half of the century, but with important earlier interpolations (e.g. the safety-valve relief of Will Hay's headmaster) and later eulogies (e.g. the nostalgic mythopoeia of Peter O'Toole's Chipping), British national cinema, and its school film microcosm, have re-presented the diversity of British society, challenging the hegemonic function of our 'imagined community' that, as Andrew Higson points out, 'must be able to hold in place—or specifically to exclude—any number of other experiences of belonging' (1995: 6). As with Britain's educational system and its cinematic history, the British school film will be seen to have two broad types or tiers, polarising around what Thomas Elsaesser has called 'an "official" cinema and an "unofficial" cinema, a respectable cinema and a disreputable one' (1993: 64). Charles Barr noted that, 'if the school in *If....* "is England", then so is that in *The Happiest Days of Your Life*' (1974: 116). This study will explore even wider polarities, with examples ranging from *The Browning Version* (1951) to *The Yellow Teddybears* (1963).

Parameters must be drawn, however. Christine Gledhill counsels that there are no 'rigid rules of inclusion and exclusion' since genres 'are not discrete systems, consisting of a fixed number of listable items' (2008: 254, 259). Yet even, or especially, with a flexible, 'unfixed' model where a *genius loci* allows a secure generic location, pragmatic assumptions will need to operate. This study will examine the cinematic treatment of secondary schools catering for pupils aged 11–18, with pre-11 education possessing a very different set of objectives and methodologies—it thus omits films where pupils are exclusively of junior/prep school age such as *Mandy* (Alexander Mackendrick, 1952) or *A Feast at Midnight* (Justin Hardy, 1994). It also limits itself to films made for theatrical release, omitting television-made fare such as David Leland's 1982 *Tales Out of School* quartet or Jack Rosenthal's *First Love* series, texts which have a different economic, stylistic and exhibition dynamic.[3] Returning finally to the reductive, Alan Williams categorises three 'principal genres' of narrative film, experimental/avant-garde film and documentary (all other categories being 'sub-genres' thereof) (1984: 121–5). This study has limited its scope to fictional narrative films, partly because of the paucity of avant-garde work with a secondary school setting, and partly because documentaries necessitate a different set of generic criteria already rehearsed elsewhere (Renov 1993; Ward 2005), but mainly because the frequency of fictional treatments points to the importance of schooling not only in the everyday rhythms of national life but also, and especially, its immutable place in Britain's social and cultural *imaginary* landscape. The school film's enduring popularity can be deduced from the British Film Institute's 1999 poll to find the top 100 British films of the twentieth century: it featured six secondary school films, of differing types and eras: 94—*The Belles of St. Trinian's* (1954); 72—*Goodbye, Mr. Chips* (1939); 61—*The Loneliness of the Long Distance Runner* (1962); 30—*Gregory's Girl* (1981); 12—*If....* (1968) and, predominant in people's reflections, 7—*Kes* (1969).

4   School Reading List

A bedrock of the British school film, especially in its early phases, is the fictional 'school story'. Ostensibly beginning with Thomas Hughes' *Tom Brown's Schooldays* (1857),[4] a flurry of school-based literature followed, stretching from light-hearted periodicals such as *Magnet* and *Gem* featuring the multi-pseudonymous Frank Richards, critical texts such as Rudyard Kipling's *Stalky and Co.* (1899) and E.M. Forster's *The Longest Journey* (1907) and restorative 'middle-brow' fare such as *Goodbye, Mr. Chips*, all of which mirror the film genre's first phases, while novels such as E.R. Braithwaite's *To Sir, With Love* (1959), Muriel Spark's *The Pride of Miss Jean Brodie* (1961) and Barry Hines' *A Kestrel for a Knave* (1968) would regularly inform its subsequent developments before finding a world-reaching apogee with J.K. Rowling's *Harry Potter* series. The school novel has attracted a relative wealth of critical literature, especially its early public school manifestations. A critical review would award joint school prizes to (film critic) Isabel Quigly's literary investigation *The Heirs of Tom Brown* (1982) and P.W. Musgrave's sociological analysis *From Brown to Bunter* (1985) with Jeffrey Richards commended for his definitive history *Happiest Days: the public schools in English fiction*. While Richards offers a brief evaluation of each case studied novel's film and television versions, this work does not intend to undertake detailed comparisons between source texts and films with the concomitant value judgements rooted in the concept of fidelity. The danger of this approach is to root evaluation in a hierarchical medium specificity that still commonly privileges literature and reading over screen and viewing, highlighting restrictions such as film's inability to convey internal knowledge, how cinematic realism denies the dimension of a reader's imagination, how the voice-over is intrinsically non-cinematic, etc. Such evaluative comparisons constitute a constant feature of contemporary press reviews for the films explored here, but also hold for much current adaptation theory, suggesting a formative literary background or even what Robert Stam has called 'iconophobia', i.e. a 'deeply rooted prejudice against the visual arts' (2004: 5). Even critics that admirably challenge this approach can, at times, become prescriptive, as when Deborah Cartmell and Imelda Whelehan claim that 'The films of Harry Potter can only offer us a pale imitation of the fiction' (2010: 81). While acknowledging that faithfulness matters to many viewers, and that films often foreground their precursor for the associated cultural capital, this study will not restrict its analysis to 'literary' qualities such as narrative and theme and ignore aspects that are essential to film analysis such as genre and star casting, mise-en-scène and music, editing and acting style.

Anthony Lane has confessed to dreading few genres 'more than the teaching movie', largely because 'more often than not, the mechanics of actual teaching are side-lined in favour of a public lecture on Ways to Inspire' ('Academic Questions', *New Yorker*, 4 July 2011). Nonetheless, several academic studies have explored the treatment of educational themes across a range of contemporary media. Front runners here would be Roy Fisher et al.'s *Education in Popular Culture* (2008) which, from a sociology of education perspective, examines how teacher performance, the curriculum and pupil behaviour are mediated in predominantly American (plus some British) popular fiction, film, television and song lyrics. Their investigations explicitly aim to provide a framework through which educators can relate these popular representations to their own professional values and development, and demonstrate how such works interconnect with professional and political discourses about education. Close behind, Ulrike Mietzner et al.'s *Visual History: Images of Education* (2005) concentrates on visual media, ranging from the picture schemes used in Victorian classrooms to contemporary European film representations of schooling. Without presenting an overriding orthodoxy the essays invite theoretical reflection on methodology and modes of representation in the field of the history of education. There exists also a considerable literature with a precise focus on school films, but these are again predominantly written with the emphasis on *school*, i.e. studies that foreground issues of social and pedagogical history, rather than placing the emphasis on *film* and its signifying practices, i.e. an approach highlighting formal aspects and film history. In a British context, school colours would go to Susan Ellsmore's 2005 monograph *Carry on Teachers! Representations of the Teaching Profession in Screen Culture*. Employing American and British films and television series as a source for educational theory, Ellsmore explores the 'reel' teacher as a charismatic figure, uniquely able to address student problems and deprivations to create that special life-changing bond, and contrasts it with the researched reactions and experiences of 'real' classroom practitioners. A broader contextual study of the place of school in a national cinema is found in Josephine May's 2013 *Reel Schools*. Looking at Australian education through the lens of its national cinema, May argues, much as this study will do for Britain, that the cinematic school is a pervasive metaphor for the Australian nation and, alongside commenting on the relationship of schools to the Australian class structure, demonstrates how Australian films about schools have increasingly explored issues of gender, race and ethnicity. Nonetheless, the book foregrounds film as social history: May defines her study as 'not a work of film criticism: it does not focus on or critique the quality of the films it discusses' (2013: 13–14). This study *is* a work of film criticism, and will undertake a complementary aesthetic critique, necessary to its dual investigation of the genre's formal and socio-historical import.

Ellsmore and May are honourable exceptions since, secondly, almost all such literature, whether prioritising historical educational content or modes of cinematic depiction, concentrates on North American schools. These again vary in approach: they include Mary M. Dalton's foregrounding of critical pedagogy in *The Hollywood Curriculum*; the psychological explorations of Jo Keroes' *Tales Out of School*; the cultural studies approach of Henry A. Giroux's *Breaking in to the Movies* and the sociological investigations of Robert C. Bulman's *Hollywood Goes to High School*. There are no extant studies with a dedicated focus on and critical exploration of British secondary education as depicted on film. Of broader works with a discrete section on school films Jeffrey Richards again heads the class with his chapter entitled 'The Old School Tie' in his *Visions of Yesterday*. Here Richards establishes the tenets of a public school education ethos as expounded in both film and literature: sandwiched between page and screen surveys are examples of the public school archetype put to work in an imperial setting, mostly resulting in 'heroic defeat' as in *Scott of the Antarctic* (Charles Frend, 1948). Jim Leach also devotes a chapter to 'The Ruling Class: Ideology and the School Movie' in his *British Film*, an exploration of British cinema in its social, political and cultural contexts. The centrepiece of Leach's survey is a comparison of the extremes of social status and educational provision revealed by *If....* and *Kes*, together resonantly defined as 'Acts of Class Villainy' (2004: 182–98).

5   LEARNING OBJECTIVES

This book will highlight a similar socio-educational polarisation. It explores the cinematic framing of the British educational experience by examining a wide variety of films that feature significant representations of secondary schools and schooling. It explores the ways in which teachers, pupils and schooling in general are represented on the British screen and what these representations signify, both 'wittingly' and 'unwittingly'.[5] Though some of the expedient film groupings may strike one as being as arbitrary as the awarding of Hogwarts house points, this work aims to demonstrate that, for the first half of the twentieth century, British film treatment of education comprised a near-total concentration on the role and (largely positive) value of the fee-paying 'public' school. Later films will more openly problematise school's capacity to be relevant to the lives of its charges and to achieve both local and national goals, often exploring the increasingly unstable role of teachers and articulating contextually generated concerns about the ability not only of its schools but of the nation itself to control and shape social change, embodied in its young. Finally, through the lens of the school film, this study simultaneously offers a historical study of British cinema itself, highlighting its evolving and varying practices of production, exhibition, star-billing and artistic merit.

Class begins.

NOTES

1. On the institutionalisation of corporal punishment in British schools, see Jacob Middleton (2012) 'Spare the Rod'. *History Today*, 62, 11. The practice was only banned in British state schools in 1987.
2. For a full treatment of 'the idea of a National Cinema', see Higson 1996: 4–25
3. For instance, Channel 4's *P'tang, Yang, Kipperbang* (Michael Apted, 1982) was given a limited theatrical release in the summer of 1984: 'The larger dimensions of the cinema screen don't help this romantic comedy', noted Ruth Baumgarten. *Monthly Film Bulletin*, September 1984: 283.

4. The first school story is commonly attributed to Sarah Fielding's *The Governess* (1749). While approximately 60 school stories preceded Hughes' novel, *Tom Brown's Schooldays* 'popularised the genre as a whole'. Robert Kirkpatrick (2000) *The Encyclopaedia of Boys' School Stories*. Farnham: Ashgate: 2.

5. On the distinctions between the intentional and unintentional evidence provided by primary sources, see Arthur Marwick (1989) *The Nature of History*. London: Macmillan: 216–8.

REFERENCES

Althusser, L. (1971) *Lenin and Philosophy and other Essays* (trans. Ben Brewster). New York: Monthly Review Press.

Barr, C. (1974) '"Projecting Britain and the British Character": Ealing Studios'. *Screen*, 15, 1, Spring.

Barr, C. (1977) *Ealing Studios*. London: Cameron and Tayleur.

Braithwaite, E.R. (1959) *To Sir, With Love*. London: Bodley Head.

Braudy, L. (1992) 'From the World in a Frame', in G. Mast, M. Cohen and L. Braudy (eds) *Film Theory and Criticism: Introductory Readings*, 4th edn. New York and Oxford: Oxford University Press.

Bulman, R.C. (2004) *Hollywood Goes to High School: Cinema, Schools and American Culture*. New York: Worth Publishers.

Burke, C. and I. Grosvenor (2008) *School*. London: Reaktion.

Cartmell, D. and I. Whelehan (2010) *Screen Adaptation: Impure Cinema*. London: Palgrave Macmillan.

Comolli, J-L. and P. Narboni (1977 [1969]) *Screen Reader: Cinema / Ideology / Politics* (trans. Susan Bennett). London: Society for Education in Film and Television.

Dalton, M.M. (1999) *The Hollywood Curriculum: Teachers and Teaching in the Movies*. New York: Peter Lang.

Edensor, T. (2002) *National Identity, Popular Culture and Everyday Life*. Oxford: Berg.

Elsaesser, T. (1993) 'Images for Sale: The "New" British Cinema', in L. Friedman (ed.) *British Cinema and Thatcherism*. London: University of London Press.

Fisher, R., A. Harris and C. Jarvis (2008) *Education in Popular Culture: Telling Tales on Teachers and Learners*. London: Routledge.

Fiske, J. (1987) *Television Culture*. London: Routledge.

Garnett, T. (1970) 'The Interview: Tony Garnett'. *Afterimage*, 1.

Giroux, H.A. (2002) *Breaking in to the Movies: Film and the Culture of Politics*. Oxford: Basil Blackwell.

Gledhill, C. (2008) 'Genre', in P. Cook (ed.) *The Cinema Book*, 3rd edn. London, BFI.

Grant, B.K. (2007) *Film Genre: From Iconography to Ideology*. London: Wallflower.

Hayward, S. (1996) *Key Concepts in Cinema Studies*. London: Routledge.

Higson, A. (1995) *Waving the Flag: Constructing a National Cinema in Britain*. Oxford: Oxford University Press.

Higson, A. (1996) 'Space, Place, Spectacle: Landscape and Townscape in the "Kitchen Sink" Film', in A. Higson (ed.) *Dissolving Views: Key Writings on British Cinema*. London: Cassell.

Hill, J. (1992) 'The Issue of National Cinema and British Film Production', in D. Petrie (ed.) *New Questions of British Cinema*. London: BFI.

Hilton, J. (1938) *To You, Mr. Chips*. London: Hodder and Stoughton.

Hines, B. (1968) *A Kestrel for a Knave*. London: Michael Joseph.

Keroes, J. (1999) *Tales Out of School: Gender, Longing and the Teacher in Fiction and Film*. Carbondale: Southern Illinois University Press.

Leach, J. (2004) *British Film*. Cambridge: Cambridge University Press.

May, J. (2013) *Reel Schools: Schooling and the Nation in Australian Cinema*. Bern: Peter Lang.

McGilligan, P. (2003) *Alfred Hitchcock: A Life in Darkness and Light*. New York: Regan Books.

Mietzner, U., K. Myers and N. Peim (eds) (2005) *Visual History: Images of Education*. Bern: Peter Lang.

Musgrave, P.W. (1985) *From Brown to Bunter: Life and Death of the School Story*. London: Routledge and Kegan Paul.

Neale, S. (1980) *Genre*. London: BFI.

Noble, L. (1939) 'Goodbye, Mr. Chips! and farewell, England!'. *Sight and Sound*, 8, 29, Spring.

Quigly, I. (1982) *The Heirs of Tom Brown: The English School Story*. London: Chatto and Windus.

Renov, M. (ed.). (1993) *Theorising Documentary*. London: Routledge.

Richards, J. (1988) *Happiest Days: The public schools in English fiction*. Manchester: Manchester University Press.

Rivette, J. (1985 [1957]) 'Six Characters in Search of Auteurs: A Discussion about French Cinema', *Cahiers du Cinéma*, 71, May, in J. Hillier (ed.) *Cahiers du Cinéma: The 1950s – Neo-Realism, Hollywood, New Wave*. Cambridge MA: Harvard University Press.

Russell Taylor, J. (1978) *Hitch: The Life and Times of Alfred Hitchcock*. London: Faber and Faber.

Sinker, M. (2004) *If.....* London: BFI.

Sorlin, P. (1980) *The Film in History: Restaging the Past*. Oxford: Basil Blackwell.

Stam, R. (2004) 'The Theory and Practice of Adaptation', in R. Stam and A. Raengo (eds) *Literature and Film: A Guide to the Theory and Practice of Film Adaptation*. Oxford: Blackwell.

Threadgold, T. (1989) 'Talking about Genre: Ideologies and Incompatible Discourses'. *Cultural Studies*, 3, 1, January.

Truffaut, F. (1978) *Hitchcock*. London: Paladin.

Ward, P. (2005) *Documentary: The Margins of Reality*. London: Wallflower.

Williams, A. (1984) 'Is a Radical Genre Criticism Possible?'. *Quarterly Review of Film Studies*, 9, 2.

The Early Years Programme (1900–45)

PART II

The Early Years Programme
(1900–45)

CHAPTER 2

The Early Public School Film (1900–1945)

1   First Years

While formal education in Britain can be traced back to church-run schools set up in the latter half of the first millennium such as King's School Canterbury (597) and Sherborne (*c.*710), followed by a 'first wave' of endowed schools such as Winchester (1382), Eton (1440), Harrow and Rugby (both 1567), the British public school system that has monopolised the British screen, and that featured at its most punitive in Frears' opening gambit, came to fruition in the second half of the nineteenth century. This was principally due to Dr Thomas Arnold, Headmaster of Rugby School from 1828 to 1841, who introduced a number of influential reforms that arrested the near-terminal monetary and moral decline of public schools. A corporate identity to school and house, a more adult-supervised prefect system and a curriculum grounded in Chapel and the Classics was the widely followed model for a 'second wave' of fee-paying schools, including Cheltenham (1841), Marlborough (1843) and Haileybury (1862). These institutions emphasised sport and the games ethic, transmuting Arnold's 'Godliness and Good Learning' into the realisation of a 'Muscular Christianity' (Bamford 1967). The quote attributed to Wellington that 'the battle of Waterloo was won upon the playing fields of Eton' is apocryphal, but the new passion for sport—encapsulated in Henry Newbolt's poetic refrain to 'play up, play up, and play the game!'[1]—indisputably dovetailed with the era of British imperialism and public schools became, in Edward Mack's description, 'mints for the coining of Empire-builders'

© The Editor(s) (if applicable) and The Author(s) 2016   21
S. Glynn, *The British School Film*,
DOI 10.1057/978-1-137-55887-9_2

(1938: 400), creating a caste, though short on imagination, expert at giving and taking orders to uphold the 'Pax Britannica'. Jeffrey Richards sees this 'imperial archetype' as sustained by the 'public school code', the result of instilling in pupils 'first, religious and moral principle; second, gentlemanly conduct; third, intellectual ability' (1973: 44). The priorities are significant, fitting in with a long-standing indigenous mistrust of the intellectual: Typically British, one might say.[2]

'With *Tom Brown* the school story as *genre* effectively began' (Richards 1988: 23). The same is true of the British school film, with the first substantively plotted effort again traceable to Rugby for Rex Wilson's 1916 adaptation of Thomas Hughes' enduring novel. As with the written text, though, there were earlier cinema sorties to the classroom. Rachael Low sees it 'in keeping with the premature sophistication of the early cinema that there was never a true film equivalent of [the] *Gem* and *Magnet* form of schoolboy serial literature' (1951: 176). Instead, the first dramatisation of a 'worthy' literary work came with the Gaumont-produced *Dotheboys Hall* or *Nicholas Nickleby* (Alf Collins, UK release November 1903). This single-take, three-minute film presents the re-staging of a well-known scene from Dickens' novel where (inevitably) a pupil is subjected to a caning, the cruel and appropriately titled Wackford Squeers beating young Smike, before the master is himself, in turn, caned by his outraged new assistant, Nickleby. Short 'adaptations' from Dickens were already common, and *Dotheboys Hall* exemplifies how 'in this early period adaptation often meant extreme condensation, in which context the meaning of fragments from longer source-narratives was heavily dependent on intertextual knowledge' (Higson 2002: 59). The canings here constitute a 'cinema of attractions', meaningless without a prior knowledge of the source novel—or else a live theatre 'descriptive talker' or 'lecturer' to explain what is happening on screen (Kember 2013).

The same broadly holds for Wilson's *Tom Brown's Schooldays* (March 1916), produced by the Windsor Film Company, and an example of silent cinema's expansion towards longer, multiple-scene selections from a well-known source text. Though on the cusp of coherence and continuity, cinema here remains a subservient medium, providing a series of moving illustrations to a novel the audience is presumed to know. In this staccato presentation the ten years of Squire's son Tom Brown at Rugby are portrayed first by the actress Joyce Templeton, then Jacks Coleman and Hobbs. The film follows young Tom beginning life at his new school in 1834, excelling in his first game of rugby, being taken

under the wing of new friend Harry East (Mr Johnson) and confronting school bully Flashman (Laurie Leslie). Cutting to his final year at
school, Tom becomes, at the behest of Dr Arnold (Wilfred Benson), the
guardian of shy new arrival Arthur (Eric Barker), a 'chumming' which
completes Tom's maturation as an upstanding young British gentlemen. So far so faithful to Hughes' novel, with character-forming sport,
bedtime prayers and Victorian-style moralising much to the fore. But
writer-director Wilson, undoubtedly mindful of melodrama's success
on the contemporary stage, interpolates a romantic subplot between
Tom and Dr Arnold's daughter, Elsa, plus scenes involving Tom's sister,
Cynthia (Evelyn Boucher), detailing an elopement, paternal disavowal,
widowhood and struggles as a governess to support her son, eventually
revealed as none other than young Arthur.

Tom Brown's Schooldays is curtly dismissed as 'goody-goody' by Rachael
Low (1951: 176). The description may hold true for Tom, with his early
foolishness in the novel here transferred to his sister, but otherwise Low
is a touch harsh. The film is good in striving for historical authenticity,
with period details including a coach identical to that used at Rugby and
the early 'set-piece' rugby match, played according to 1830s rules with
a watching crowd of over 300 schoolboy extras. The film is also good
in effecting an experimentation that pushes at its technological limitations, notably when Tom and Harry's faces appear in the top corners
of the dialogue intertitles and mouth the words written beside them.
Less laudatory though, Wilson's female additions receive scant character development and serve only to reflect differing qualities of the ever-
saintly Master Brown. As David Morrison notes, the most effectively
realised scenes involve Tom fighting and playing rugby and thus 'the
film succeeds best when giving a boys' account of a boys' world' (n.d.).
It is a generic bias that would long endure. Contemporary reviews were
highly commendatory of 'an excellent example of British character building at its best' (*Cinema*, 6 April 1916) and a riposte to the authorities who 'complain of the evil effects of the cinema upon growing boys'
(*Screen*, 15 April 1916). Here instead was a picture of British moral and
physical fortitude to inspire wartime audiences and, alongside their positive evaluations, reviewers were at patriotic pains to point out that 'no-
one was employed in the film who ought to have been in our fighting
forces' and that 'the young actor Jack Hobbs, who presents Tom in the
later scenes, is now in the Army' (*Picture Palace News*, 11 April 1916).
The film's national significance was recognised with a Royal Command

Performance on 24 February 1917, a categorical 'seal of respectability' for the burgeoning British school film genre.

2   HITCHCOCK AND CO.: DOWN WITH SCHOOL!

This generic respectability was deepened with films by two major British directors, each showing the formative influence on young lives of early public school scenes. Alfred Hitchcock realised his theories on the lingering dread of school life with *Downhill* (24 May 1927), produced by Michael Balcon for Gainsborough Pictures. Following Hitchcock's breakthrough critical and commercial success with *The Lodger* (1927), a follow-up vehicle reuniting the director with matinee idol Ivor Novello was secured with the West End play *Down Hill*, co-written by and starring Novello who, though now 35, remained as the schoolboy lead. The film version retained a symbiotic relationship with its source text as, on advertised evenings during its initial London run, an interval allowed Novello and co-star Robin Irvine to enact, front of screen, a key school scene preceding their summons to the headmaster's office.[3] Hitchcock's fifth film begins with wealthy Rodney 'Roddy' Berwick scoring the winning try in a key school rugby match, a prelude to being elected School Captain. Soon after, though, a local waitress (Daisy Jackson) he visited with roommate Tim Wakeley (Irvine) makes a 'serious charge' against him. Out of loyalty to his scholarship-dependent friend, Roddy does not deny the charge and is expelled. Shunned by his peers and berated by his humiliated father, Sir Thomas (Norman McKinnel), Roddy leaves home. He works as a jobbing actor, marries and then loses gold-digging actress Julia Fotheringale (Isabel Jeans), moves to Paris where he becomes a gigolo and ends up delirious in a dockside room in Marseilles. Shipped back to England, his father, now knowing of his son's innocence, welcomes him home. In an Old Boys' rugby match, Roddy scores another try.

Hitchcock biographer John Russell Taylor notes that the director's attitude to public school life is 'seemingly, not over-romantic—this is no starry-eyed *Goodbye, Mr. Chips* view of upper-class youth at school from the viewpoint of the deprived *petit-bourgeois*' (1978: 84). Indeed, the critique is quite damning. *Downhill* opens with the image of a whistle-blowing master, arbiter of the sport-centred public school regime within which Roddy thrives. The all-encompassing horizon-narrowing nature of this 'play-the-game' ideology is highlighted when Roddy, on being informed of his expulsion, can only ask 'Won't I be able to play for the Old Boys,

Fig. 2.1 The master of suspense: 'a sentence as though spoken by a judge'

sir?' (Fig. 2.1). Charles Barr notes the response's function 'of emphasising, and even, by its risibility, subverting the role of the institution from which Roddy is being abruptly cast' (1999: 46). Elsewhere Hitchcock questions public school codes with a knowing if not blatant ('schoolboy'?) visual humour. An early scene cuts from a shot of newly promoted Roddy's cap bearing the school motto, 'Honour', to Tim's identical cap, lying on an open already-sampled box from the bakery where school waitress, Mable (Annette Benson), also works. The box's inscription, that 'Ye Olde Bunne Shoppe' closes on a Wednesday afternoon, implies Tim's current location, while the result of this after-hours entry is Mable's pregnancy, her own 'bunne in the oven'. Roddy's cap appears again when he disconsolately throws it aside as he packs his bags: one friend has lived up to the school motto, the other has not. For Hitchcock, though, the consequences of upholding this public school code of honour are a dire descent, Roddy's literal fall from North to South bringing him to the edge of insanity. While the school scenes such as the visit to the head-master are treated with forward horizontal tracks, Hitchcock marks the expelled pupil's downhill path with a series of visual symbols, pushing a lift's 'down' button, descending a London underground escalator, and finally taking gangways down to the hold of a freighter bound for Blighty. For Raymond Durgnat this cinematic katabatic 'paraphrases that fear of social downfall which existed even more intensely during the economic miseries of the interwar years' (1974: 75). The formalist style, though, is epistemological as much as economic, with uncertainty first visualised as soon as Roddy leaves school: evening dress and camera movements ini-tially intimate that Roddy has become a nightclub patron, then a waiter, before finally revealing him as a dancer in a stage-set musical review. On the boat back home his mental torment is expressed with the film tinted a sickly green (a feature redeployed in *Vertigo* (1956)), while a subjective camera assumes his delirious perspective back in England with buildings and traffic fading in and out of focus, recorded in double and triple expo-sure. The film's structural symmetry, ending with Roddy's acceptance by the Old Boys and scoring another try, implicates the opening school sec-tion in this fevered miasma and questions its validity, its potential verac-ity. Has he learnt nothing in the interim? Indeed, has he really returned? Hitchcock avers working in *Downhill* 'to embody the dream in the reality' (Truffaut 1978: 58) and the happy ending is curt to the point of ironic exaggeration: are the values espoused by public schools themselves an illu-sion, a debilitating and hence dispensable social convenience rather than a life-shaping code of honour?

Downhill is often decried as 'by far the director's most misogynistic work, overflowing with images of women as harpies and betrayers who prey on hopeless young males like Rodney' (Leitch 2002: 85). Mark Duguid shifts some of the blame to Novello, whose source play 'reflects the experiences of a homosexual matinee idol oppressed by unwanted female attention' (n.d.). However, the all-male public school setting is also relevant, with women in serving roles or admitted only on special occasions such as the match-day dinner. The film knows commercially to fetishise Novello's body, showing him stripped to the waist, but when seen by Wakeley's sister, Sybil (Sybil Rhoda), he grabs a towel to conceal his naked chest, revelatory perhaps of the actor's sexually ambiguous public persona, but readable also as a diegetic indication of how public school—and its aching lack of sex education—leaves a young man ill-prepared for the outside world and the attentions of the women he will meet. The trade press voiced the critical consensus: 'It is more by the brilliant treatment of the director and the excellent acting that this film is likely to appeal to the public than by the strength of its story' (*Bioscope*, 26 May 1927). The *Yorkshire Post* demonstrated a commensurate misogyny in pinpointing the plot's principal weakness: 'We are asked to believe that the headmaster of a public school accepts without question the unsupported word of an obvious little minx from a tea shop, accusing his head prefect of having seduced her' (31 May 1927).

The First World Wartime encouragements (and cast exculpation) of *Tom Brown's Schooldays* did not find voice when sound cinema finally arrived. *Tell England* (2 March 1931)—an apposite title for one of Britain's first 'talkies'—centres on the Great War's Gallipoli campaign and was filmed by Anthony Asquith with Gallipoli veteran and location-shooting specialist Geoffrey Barkas. Asquith's father, Herbert, had been Liberal Prime Minister at the time of the Gallipoli landings, a link which drew considerable press attention to the film, while Anthony, ex-Winchester and Oxford, exemplified what Rachael Low termed 'the new generation of well-connected, well-educated young men, who, unlike their parents, were prepared to take films seriously' (1951: 182). Plans to film ex-prep schoolmaster Ernest Raymond's novel began in 1927 and, though delays and the arrival of sound changed the production goals, the film's origins as a silent project can be gleaned from the continued—and highly effective—use of intertitles. These, plus an extensive, at times expressionistic employment of dialogue, sound effects and music create a far more austere work than the source text, suggesting the added thematic influence of Forster's *The Longest Journey* (Richards 1988: 227). Asquith's adaptation for British Instructional Films, reputed for its military re-enactments, emphasised the stress of trench warfare on its public school-trained officers Edgar Doe (Carl Harbord) and Rupert Ray (Tony Bruce): the Kensingstowe School chapters, celebrating the pair's friendship and comprising half of Raymond's novel, are here reduced to a handful of scenes, but remain thematically crucial. A full exposition presents the two upper-middle-class leads in their last days at school, an idyllic time of punting, relaxation and sport, Edgar securing the swimming regatta victory with his superb final leg. However, a poster clearly dates the school relay at 15 July 1914, three weeks before Britain declared war on Germany, and Edgar's sporting celebration, borne aloft by his adoring fellow pupils (including future directors John and Roy Boulting), fades to black and the sound of a tolling bell. It is an abrupt transition, a tonal shift from community to carnage reminiscent of *The*

Deer Hunter (Michael Cimino, 1978), and the majority of the film follows the school chums from enlisting to their posting with the Mediterranean Expeditionary Forces to Gallipoli. There Edgar, his nerves torn by months of inaction followed by the swift slaughter of his men by a Turkish trench mortar, argues with the less articulate Ray: his bitter alcohol-fuelled denunciation of the war—three times he cries that 'I know what I'd like to tell England!—is seemingly validated by an accompanying modernist montage of harrowing battlefield images. His 'un-British' outburst clears the air, however, and the reconciled friends reminisce with flashbacks to their carefree school days. The scene's function, though, is preparatory before retrospective, a reminder that Edgar is a Kensingstowe boy as he recovers his sense of duty and dies the gallant death for which his schooling had prepared him, singlehandedly immobilising the Turkish mortar post. On his deathbed Edgar (schooled in the Classics like his Colonel) translates a Greek passage based on the epitaph of the Spartans of Thermopylae: it is displayed on the wooden cross marking his grave—'Tell England, ye who pass this monument,/We died for her, and here we rest content'. The final image of scores of such graves, viewed impassively by German and Turkish officers and prefaced by an intertitle contextualising how 'On January 8 1916 the last British troops had left the peninsula', leaves unspoken the human cost of a disastrous military campaign.

The film itself was adjudged a success. The *Evening News* wrote that '*Tell England* proves to be one of the two or three outstanding British talkies made so far... It is a brilliant piece of work pictorially and contains many novel and impressive ideas in the use of sound' (31 March 1931). While the graphic documentary-style battle scenes were eulogised, the school-set opening was less well received: Charles Morgan found it 'very weak' but praised the film overall since 'it recognises heroism as a thing of beauty which, even when frustrate, is not vain' (*Times*, 3 March 1931). Does *Tell England*, though, recognise the beauty of such heroism, with Gallipoli a justified sacrifice by the higher classes? An affirmative (if ironised) reading has endured, Jeffrey Richards emphasising the entrenched British trope of 'glorifying patriotic sacrifice and the public school code of the officer and gentleman' (1973: 153), while Alan Burton notes how, 'if modern war is unpleasant, young gentlemen, forged in the public schools, can nonetheless be counted upon to make the ultimate sacrifice and do their duty' (2002: 34). On its release, however, Asquith called his film 'powerful anti-war propaganda' (*Film Weekly*, 7 November 1931) and *Tell England*'s attitude towards the preparation that public schooling provided for foreign slaughter is, at best, ambivalent—as evident in the contrasting deployment of the film's eponymous imperative. Edgar may lead (and die) by example, but elsewhere the officer classes are shown as culpably complacent: dialogue such as 'I shouldn't think there'll be very much trouble' is intercut with, and undercut by, images of Turkish gunners awaiting and mowing down rows of disembarking soldiers. This is not quite the 'beautiful celebration of the public school ethos' as adjudged by Raymond Durgnat (1970: 142). A tension is at play, traceable, at least in part, to the man and his medium, Asquith belonging to an intellectual elite critical of the Great War and its leadership, but working in a popular medium (and with a popular source text) that exerted different, more consensual ideological pressures. Other ideological 'cracks' are textually evident. W.D. Routt has accused *Tell England* of being 'a compounded act of disinheritance' in its removal of the Australasian contribution to the Dardanelles campaign (1994: 66): within the film's narrow national focus, a further disinheritance is evident. The polarities of the British education system come into focus with the caricatured presentation of working-class batman Sims (Lionel Hedges), cheerful, Cockney, illiterate and utterly dispensable. Asked by Rupert to look after Edgar—'Cor bless you, sir, it's all in a day's work'—he is quickly killed, and soon forgotten. Asquith's first talkie unwittingly tells England that one (public school-educated) man's final sacrifice is more glorious than another's.

Though bemoaning its antipodean absences, Routt praises the 'multiple expositions' in *Tell England*, a film he characterises as simultaneously 'artistic, committed, sexy, evil' (1994: 67–8). The penultimate epithet may surprise, but Routt asserts the film's many 'improper' sexual and familial subtexts. The source text has been variously described as a story of '"manly love" or "romantic friendship"' (Richards 1988: 225) or else 'a homo-erotic celebration of middle-class English youth' (Smith 1995: 181), but with schooldays largely erased, one has, in truth, to infer at depth. This is attempted by Charles Silver, for whom the soldiers naming the Turkish mortar post 'Clara' 'suggest[s] a perverse kind of feminine intimacy—probably as much intimacy as his young, upper-class heroes might ever have had, except quite possibly with each other' (2003: 121).

Such 'feminine intimacy' is not ostensibly lacking in *Young Woodley* (2 July 1930), Thomas Bentley's film version for British International Pictures (BIP) of John van Druten's 1925 controversial stage success, initially refused a licence by the Lord Chamberlain due to the piece's unacceptably critical educational subject matter.[4] Its eventual *succès de scandale* made a star of Frank Lawton, who reprised his title role on film, complete with theatrically exaggerated facial and bodily gestures. Jeffrey Richards sees the film as 'typical of the worst kind of early talkie, a straightforward static photographed record of the stage play, further hampered by a clutch of stagey performances directed at an unseen proscenium arch' (1984: 313). This was, in fact, Bentley's second attempt: a 1928 silent version, made for Regal Pictures, fell foul of new technology and never secured a theatrical release. The plot line, evidently risqué for the late-1920s Establishment, has David Woodley, a highly sensitive and versifying prefect in his final term at Mallhowhurst, falling in love with the lonely and receptive headmaster's wife, Laura Simmons (Madeleine Carroll). As they kiss, enter the demon headmaster, with expulsion only prevented by Laura's threat to end their marriage. When Laura plays down the significance of their kiss, Woodley's petulant reaction includes taking the local tea-shop waitress Kitty (René Ray) off into the woods for instantly regretted 'beastly' sex. In a melodramatic finale the taunted Woodley attacks fellow prefect Vining (Billy Milton) with a knife, rendering his expulsion unavoidable: hearing that Laura did love him, Woodley leaves the school in tears, and with sympathy.[5]

Young Woodley's critique of the dominant educational ethos pushes far beyond the ironies at play in *Downfall* and the ambiguity permeating *Tell England*. Simmons, the headmagisterial embodiment of public school values, is consciously portrayed as a dogmatic and insensitive philistine. His by-numbers start-of-term address to 'unselfishness, loyalty, decency, the public school code' is undermined by mocking remarks from the prefect body, an insubordination never exposed as misguided: instead scenes such as Simmons' brusque dismissal of the 'unhealthy poetry' admired by Woodley and Laura further alienate viewer sympathies. In similar vein, the earthy banter and professed promiscuity of Vining are rejected not only by Woodley—'I hate the way he talks about women. I think it's beastly!'—but also by the film which visually and narratively privileges Woodley's courtly compositions and Werther-like romantic love, even if, as with *Downfall*, the lack of sex education is implicitly critiqued. Class and gender depictions also remain troublesome. Well-bred Laura is largely exculpated, her mixed messages to Woodley shown as emanating from an essentially decent woman determined not to mislead her young admirer into ruin whilst fostering positive memories to stave off permanent embitterment. Less laudably, Woodley's 'rebound' relationship with Kitty is narratively motivated solely to occasion the ethereal poet's self-disgust:

she disappears from his thoughts and from the film when 'used'. It is a schoolboy—waitress coupling that will be have to await *If....* for a more egalitarian (and graphic) portrayal.

Further still, the gender–class matrix of *Young Woodley* may, like *Tell England*, be open to 'multiple expositions' and an alternative reading can explain Woodley's wildly differing reactions to physical contact with the finally restrained Laura and fully responsive Kitty. Referencing van Druten's source play, Sean O'Connor points out how 'Characters such as Laura have been positioned in a long line, from Mrs Erlynne [*Lady Windermere's Fan*] to Blanche Dubois [*A Streetcar Named Desire*], as women who "represent" the "tensions and ambiguities of homosexual desire"' (1998: 22). Interpreted thus, Woodley's 'abnormal' love is less a transgression of the boundaries of middle-class respectability than an explanation for why he finds heterosexual lovemaking so repugnant. For John Deeney Laura's parting words to Woodley, 'don't let me spoil love for you'—replicated in the film—'might be offered as evidence of a homosexual subtext, casting her in the role of "outsider", articulating the predicament and complex surrounding homosexuality' (2000: 78). Whatever Woodley's sexual orientation and however coded his crime, the endorsement of the aesthete before the athlete broached a new direction for the British school film. Absent entirely from *Young Woodley* are the already-expected generic tropes: the sage professorial protection, the bonding dormitory japes and, above all, the climactic and character-forging trial by sport—instead Woodley kisses Laura while the whole school are at a largely off-screen cricket match. Alongside its tentative aesthetic and technological solutions to the new sound medium—plus, arguably, the unclear sexual cloaking that 'cracks' the film's third act—this generic innovation may explain why, despite its source text's enticing notoriety and critical praise for the love affair narrated 'with such commendable restraint that its interest never lags' (Morduant Hall, *New York Times*, 27 September 1930), the 'vocalised pictorial version' performed poorly at the box office. As such, *Young Woodley* is the first exemplar of Leo Braudy's reading of genre as a 'social barometer'. A 'sophisticated' West End (and State-Side) audience may have applauded an attack on an ossified British public school ethos, but cinema, arguably a more generalising medium, performs best commercially when adhering to a familiar set of pictorial and plot tropes, symbolic systems and institutional arrangements—and the British public of 1930 was evidently not ready for a serious, heartfelt contestation of the 'top' public school values elsewhere propagated as a powerful constituent of national identity. It would be a lesson well learnt for the remainder of the decade.

3   HILTON AND CO.: HURRAY FOR SCHOOL!

With *Young Woodley*'s transgressions completing a trilogy of dissent, the early school film shifts in focus from pupil to teacher and counters with three affectionate, affirmative studies of men devoting their lives to teaching and personifying the worthy traditions that they instil in their charges: loyalty to the school, ruling with respect not fear, and firm but fair discipline.

Housemaster (Herbert Brenon, 31 January 1938), retrospectively readable as a light-hearted trial-run for *Goodbye, Mr. Chips*, is adapted from Fettes-educated former schoolteacher Ian Hay's successful stage version of his own 1936 comic novel. In the Associated British Picture Corporation (ABPC) film version the eponymous housemaster, Charles Donkin, long-established in his role at Marbledown, is securely played by ex-Hollywood matinee idol Otto Kruger. The main plotline places 'Old Moat' Donkin as the defender of tried-and-trusted tradition against the jarring, unfeeling innovations of recently-appointed headmaster Rev. Edmund Ovington (Kynaston Reeves, reprising his London stage role). Low-level discontent rises to outrage when, ignoring Marbledown's long tradition of rowing, 'the Egg' cancels the school's participation in the annual regatta and puts the entire town out of bounds. Donkin feels compelled to speak up, but when his entire house disobeys the new strictures and offers 'three groans to the Egg', he offers his resignation. In a sensitively underplayed scene, Donkin wanders around the grounds of the school he dearly loves and, in a farewell speech to his bereft pupils, stresses their need to adhere to the precepts of the public school code: 'loyalty, even if sometimes it may be against your convictions'; courtesy, the need to be 'infinitely considerate to other people's feelings'; and thirdly (in what could again count as giving young men mixed messages) 'honesty, always having the courage to speak what one believes'. His homily ends with an application of school conduct to contemporary geopolitical tensions: 'Believe me, of all the methods that have been tried by great men from Machiavelli down to their present day imitators, speaking the truth has always served Man best, and us, as a nation, best.' Far from being undermined as in *Young Woodley*, the denouement to *Housemaster* bears out the veracity of his address—and the benefits of public school networks. Sir Berkeley Nightingale (Cecil Parker), cabinet minister, vice-chair of the school governors and uncle to

Donkin's house-captain, comes to the rescue, engineering a newly created bishopric for Ovington and Donkin succeeding as headmaster. The film ends with the school hall resounding to a hearty rendition of 'Old Acquaintance', showing Marbledown to be back in safe hands: as George Orwell wrote (not uncritically) of the *Gem* and *Magnet* school stories, 'Everything is safe, solid and unquestionable. Everything will be the same for ever and ever' (1970 [1940]: 518).

For Jeffrey Richards Donkin, like Chips, stands for the enduring values of the public school code, each 'a fixed point in a changing world, a reassuring reminder of all that is good in tradition' (1973: 62). This holds for generic tradition too: *Housemaster* returns wholeheartedly to the school film's expected visual, narrative and thematic tropes. The opening montage of cloisters, quad and gateway establishes recognisable terrain (repeated in *Goodbye, Mr. Chips*). On constant show thereafter is the comforting familiarity of house meals, morning prayers with the apposite 'Onward Christian Soldiers', cricket matches and rowing practice (Donkin, an old Blue, advises the school eight), and parties in the dorm after lights out, a diurnal round known in detail by audiences from reading Thomas Hughes or Frank Richards. Little time is given over to lessons, while the requisite canings remain in place with boys and masters understanding their purpose and value. Genre, though, cannot be entirely static, and *Housemaster* again allows its charges a degree of female intimacy. A comic subplot, retained from Hay's source texts, centres on the three daughters of the (recently deceased) woman whom Donkin once loved descending on the school from Paris. With much shrieking and hugging, the Faringdon sisters play havoc with the school rules and the house members' hearts. The younger daughters, tomboy Button (Rosamund Barnes) and glamorous Chris (René Ray again), are catalysts for the house to defy Ovington's diktats. The eldest, 20-year-old Rosemary (Diana Churchill), takes a shine to the shy and wholly unsuccessful junior Science and Music master, Peter 'the Poop' de Pourville (Phillips Holmes): under her influence he grows in self-assertion, gains control over his class (principally by thrashing its ringleader 'until [he] howled for mercy') and, with Donkin's avuncular approval, wins Rosemary's hand in marriage. Though the subplot is often decried (and was mostly cut for the US play release), its romantic slant again serves as a narrative and thematic rehearsal for *Goodbye, Mr. Chips*, demonstrating the value of a lively, loving partner in helping a dedicated but diffident pedagogue to blossom, drawing out the authority and/or compassion necessary to complement dry scholarship.

On its release *Housemaster* was considered a curate's egg, the *Monthly Film Bulletin* (*MFB*) exemplifying the majority response: 'The superb acting of Otto Kruger invests the main theme with a dignity and reality which makes a strange contrast to the spasms of exaggerated and rather tiresome farce' (January 1938: 9). Nonetheless, Hay's knowledge of his environment was seen as a benefit, Basil Wright labelling the film 'a sympathetic and astonishingly accurate picture of public-school life' (*Spectator*, 20 May 1938). This (perceived) quasi-ethnographic educational portrayal appealed State-side: for Frank Nugent *Housemaster* 'caught so well the unconsciously-humorous portrait of the English school boy and his masters wearing the stiff upper lip' that 'we were as annoyed as the headmaster at the feminine intrusions upon a scene, and a plot, that could have been worked out just as easily without them' (*New York Times*, 10 April 1939). *Cherchez la femme*, it seems, even in the school film genre.

3.1   Section Prize Winner: Goodbye, Mr. Chips (1939)

The 1930s American fascination with the peculiarities of British education culminated in the international success of a prestige production by MGM, the 'Tiffany' of US studios. James Hilton's novella of 1934 recounted the teaching career of Chipping who, after meeting and marrying young Katherine while on holiday, blossoms from a rigid Classics master to a much-loved educator and wartime headmaster during his lengthy tenure at the fictional Fenland Brookfield Grammar School.[6] MGM had quickly bought the rights to Hilton's novel but, with Charles Laughton and Myrna Loy slated to play the leads, the project stalled after the death of producer Irving Thalberg in 1936. The next year MGM set up a British production base, both to meet the requirements of the new British quota legislation and to recruit the new raft of talented UK cast and crew (Glancy 1999: 81–3). Artistically, the move also fed into a lengthy Hollywood attraction to Britain's historical hinterland and the studio's first venture, *A Yank at Oxford* (Jack Conway, 1938), narratively enacted America's seduction by the images and ambiance of Britain's long-standing educational establishments. Also in 1938, as a West End theatrical version of Hilton's text opened with Leslie Banks and Constance Cummings as leads, *Goodbye, Mr. Chips* was resurrected as an MGM-British production and assigned to anglophile MGM director Sidney Franklin who, with home-grown writers R.C. Sherriff, Claudine West and Eric Maschwitz, scripted another US paean to traditional British values. Franklin's promotion to a production

role led to Sam Wood, a safe pair of hands at MGM since 1927, being dispatched to England as replacement director, under the guidance of Victor
Saville, MGM-Britain's new head of production. Saville, who vied with
Hitchcock in the early 1930s for the title of Gaumont's foremost director,
had recent experience of school scenes with his *South Riding* (4 January
1938), adapted from Winifred Holtby's popular novel. Rated by the *Daily
Mirror* 'higher than any film ever made here' (5 January 1938), Saville
delivered a wide-canvas melodrama where consensus politics is brokered
in a Yorkshire council by crusading local schoolmistress Sarah Barton
(Edna Best), with hopes for national unity allegorically embodied in the
classroom reconciliation between working-class scholarship girl Lydia
Hardy (Joan Elllum) and local squire's spoilt daughter, Midge Carne
(Glynis Johns) (Richards 1984: 320–2). Under Saville's credible counsel,
Manchester-born Robert Donat, already an international star and signed
to MGM for a lucrative six-picture deal, took the role of Chipping while
London actress Greer Garson landed her first film role as Katherine Ellis.
With Freddie Young as cinematographer, location shooting took place at
Repton School, with interiors, courtyards (and the Austrian Tyrol moun-
tains) filmed at Denham Studios, Buckinghamshire. *Goodbye, Mr. Chips*
premiered in New York on 15 May 1939 and in London on 8 June—
Britain would declare war on Germany on 3 September.

While the plotline remained faithful to its source text, American admiration led to an aggrandisement of setting with Brookfield, in Hilton's
novel no more than 'a good school of the second rank' that turned out
'merchants, manufacturers and professional men' (1934: 18), promoted
by Franklin et al. into one of Britain's top-ranking public schools. This is
clear when the opening shot of the school's imposing buildings closes in
on two masters reading a plaque commemorating its founding: '1492, the
year Columbus discovered America!' one comments, drawing the reply
that 'We're in the heart of England, a heart with a very gentle beat.' A cut
presents this elision of school and nation personified: the eponymous hero
patiently reassuring a new boy aka 'stinker', pointing out an inscription
in the chapel alcove to the pupil's ancestor 'The Duke of Dorset, 1650'
and another reading 'Sir Francis Drake, 1552'. The new boy, and audiences American and British, are being seduced with a thick slice of heritage
(cinema). 'Chips' is next introduced to new and nervous History master
Mr Johnson (David Tree) who inquires after 'the secret' of his success as a
beloved teacher and elder statesman. Chips' reply that it 'took time—too
much time' and that the secret came from 'somebody else' precedes his

return home to prepare Sunday tea and falling asleep, his fireside dream of 58 years' service forming the cinematic flashback that tells his story. This structure is significant as the flashback is a cinematic representation of memory *and* of history: it adds a narrative momentum since it is hermeneutically determined, its motivation being to 'yield a solution to an enigma' (Hayward 1996: 123). This is established by Jackson's enquiry and comes to a 'natural' end when the past has caught up with the present and has *explained* the present state of affairs—why this doddering old man remains so highly regarded. The use of the flashback, though, surpasses the explanation of an individual's longevity. Maureen Turim demonstrates how this structural device is 'naturally' aligned with history because its presentation of a narrative past is often historical in sweep or setting: she further emphasises how, in times of war or tension, the flashback 'serves a prevailing ideology, such as patriotic identification'. Her example is *Napoléon vu par Abel Gance* (1927) where the flashback, because evaluated through a subjective framing of history, works to mythologise the 'great man' (sic) (1989: 18). It may seem a bathetic link from Napoleon to Mr Chips (and from Gance to Sam Wood), but the difference is one of degree rather than of kind. Within the socio-cultural parameters of this genre study, and at a time of concern at the prospect of imminent war with Nazi Germany, Chips is deliberately presented as a man of destiny, a fixed point in a changing pedagogical *and* political landscape, the personification of enduring patrician worth. The film's shifting historical context is presented through montages of pupils processing through 'callover' and discussing events from the Boer War to Louis Bleriot, while Brookfield's pupil continuity is emphasised by employing the same actor (Terry Kilburn) for four generations of the Colley family. The outside and school worlds—the national as a metonym for the individual—also narratively chime: staffroom discussion of a new writer, H.G. Wells—'He'll never come to anything'—leads directly into Chipping's nadir when he is denied a longed-for pastoral promotion.

Throughout change and crisis, in Britain as in Brookfield, the overriding constant is Chipping himself and the Victorian-born values he both embodies and imparts. The 'secret' of Chips' longevity is seen to work, like ideology (and genre), not through imposition but via acquiescence. And like ideology (and genre) this necessitates the ability to adapt and rejuvenate. Chips' educational journey begins disastrously (in the Education Act year of 1870): on taking the lower school 'for preparation'—the same initiation awaits Jackson nearly 60 years later—the boys run riot, causing headmaster Dr Wetherby to intervene (the scene shown in *Typically British*). Chipping determines thereafter to become a strict disciplinarian, but goes too far, losing the respect of the boys (and staff) for keeping the entire class in detention when its star pupil is needed for a vital cricket match—which is lost. Twenty years pass, signalled by the first call-over montage, intercut with further now-inviolable cricket and rugby matches: Chipping sinks into a dull, defeated routine, valued for his discipline but little else. The catalyst for his own re-education comes when, cajoled by German master Max Staefel (Paul Henreid) into taking his maiden European holiday, he meets and marries the vivacious Katherine, the 'someone else' who encourages him into relaxing, telling his dry Latin jokes and, through a fuller manifestation of his care and kindness, winning the confidence and affection of his pupils. The opposite of alienated Laura in *Young Woodley*, Katherine involves herself fully in her older husband's career, bestowing his sobriquet and initiating the 'revolutionary' idea of inviting boys every Sunday for tea, biscuits and informal friendship. With such guidance 'Chips' is reborn as an inspirational teacher, gains the coveted housemaster position and continues with Katherine's radical charter after her death in childbirth, right up to the present and his film-structuring tea-time slumber.

His educational philosophy is explicitly played out when Dr Ralston (Austin Trevor), a new progressive headmaster in the Ovington mould, tries to force Chips and his 'outdated' methodology to retire. Unspoken in the novel, the cinematic Chips expounds his credo in a passionate retort: 'Modern methods! Intensive training! Poppycock! Give a boy a sense of humour and a sense of proportion and he'll stand up to anything!' With Chips' refusal to leave supported by both pupil and governing bodies and with Ralston later admitting his error, Chips' speech and its surrounding validation operate as a staunch defence of the British public school tradition of concentrating on character building in order to turn out gentlemen all-rounders. Crucially, this privileged pedagogy is shown to be benevolent in a belligerent age. An early scene finds Brookfield's Peter Colley scrapping with Perkins, the local greengrocer's boy: Chips insists that they make up and make friends (Fig. 2.2). Later, when Lt Colley (John Mills) sets off for the Great War, it is with the same 'town cheese' as his trusty batman (David Croft, uncredited). In *Tell England* the officer's batman was summarily dispatched, but not here: Colley is killed in action, we learn, trying to rescue the mortally wounded Perkins. With war imminent, the film's explicit message is that we are all in it together:

Fig. 2.2   Chips and cheese

the upper classes care for, and will even sacrifice themselves for, the lower orders. It is an unequivocal endorsement of the public school ethos and, by extension the social status quo. Similarly, the film's wartime sections show Chips—and Britain—at their fighting best. There is fortitude: while shells fall Chips calmly instructs a pupil to continue reciting his Latin. There is fairness: when announcing Brookfield's war losses, Chips names, alongside Colley, the 'enemy' Staefel, felled with his Saxon regiment. And there is firmness: when a pupil labels the masters 'a lot of weak-kneed women' for not being in the army (cf. the 1916 reviews of *Tom Brown's Schooldays*), Chips assures him that all have tried to join—'we take no man unless he has done that'—and then administers the cane, less a punishment for the boy's impertinence than a preparation for his imminent army career: 'You'll need discipline from your men and to get that you must know what discipline means.' His lesson learnt, the contrite youth promises to 'stick in and do [his] share'. MGM's press release stressed how 'all that England is, and stands for, was brought with gracious dignity to the screen in this film version of James Hilton's novel' (*Goodbye, Mr. Chips* publicity package 1939), and the outbreak of the Second World War highlighted the film's patriotic potential. In an early 'Programme for Film Propaganda' the British Ministry of Information emphasised a main theme for cinema as '*What Britain is fighting for*', and listed '*British life and character*, showing our independence, toughness of fibre, sympathy with the underdog, etc. *Goodbye, Mr. Chips* is an obvious example of this kind' (Public Record Office, File INF1/867, September 1939–January 1940). A wartime editorial in *The Listener* similarly lauded the film's propaganda value, stating that 'there must be few Englishmen who can see the film without having their faith in the English ideal strengthened' (25 January 1940).

Goodbye, Mr. Chips was a resounding commercial and critical success. Made for $1.1 million, it took $1.7 million at the US box office, and $1.5 in British and other markets. It was nominated for seven Academy Awards: Production, Director, Actor, Actress, Screenplay, Film Editing and Sound. Competing against *Gone with the Wind* (Victor Fleming, 1939) in all seven categories, Donat beat Clark Gable for Best Actor, though elsewhere British 'toughness of fibre' was needed as Brookfield lost out to Georgia in five other categories. Critical response was also positive. While Graham Greene announced that 'some of us may feel unsympathetic to Mr Chips and the rosy sentimental view of an English public school', he conceded that 'on the whole, sentimentality is ably balanced by humour, the direction and acting are almost everything to be desired' (*Spectator*, 16 June 1939). The *MFB* forgave the film's 'excessive' length 'since all the incidents of school life are so remarkably "right"' and the cast 'combine to bring a book to life with such fidelity as has rarely, if ever, been seen before' (June 1939: 112). Only Peter Galway perceived a less endearing national ideal in the cinematic Chips: 'the popularity of his type is accounted for by two important features of English psychology: their love for mediocrity in high places and their admiration of longevity for its own sake. In Mr Chips there is something of Queen Victoria' (*New Statesman*, 17 June 1939). An enthralled America had no such reservations: Frank Nugent thought that MGM had 'dealt with the chronicle affectionately, almost as though the centuried tradition and ingrained snobbery of the English public school system were our own', and the imported nostalgia passed into personal hinterlands: 'if we never knew a Mr Chips, we should have known him. He belongs to every young man's past' (*New York Times*, 16 May 1939). The affection has continued, in school and on screen: in 1998 Terry Warburton asserted the endurance of 'Mr Chips' as 'a figure of speech representing the traditional "caring" values of teachers' (1998: 254), while the next year *Goodbye, Mr. Chips* became one of the BFI's Top 100 British Films. *Haec olim meminisse iuvabit*, as Chips put it.[7]

The first cycle of the British school film ends where it began, at (a studio-reconstructed) Rugby with a (loose) adaptation of Thomas Hughes' novel. Though Britain was now at war, American attention to—or exploitation of—its future ally's educational past continued as RKO rushed out their version in the wake of the success accorded to *Goodbye, Mr. Chips.* While the financial package behind its production categorises *Tom Brown's School Days* (14 July 1940) as an American film, there is a strong sense of British 'ownership' not only in its subject matter but also in its personnel. It was directed by Buxton-born pacifist-émigré Robert Stevenson, 'the 1930s genre director par excellence in British cinema' (McFarlane 1999: 161), while the cast featured knight of the realm Cedric Hardwicke as Dr Arnold and Freddie Bartholomew in the role of Harry East. Other key roles went overseas: future Harry Aldrich star Jimmy Lydon portrayed Tom Brown, while former Dead End Kid Billy Halop's extra-diegetic 'baggage' as school bully Flashman reinforced Arnold's diegetic maxim that there is 'bullying in every community in every nation'.

This first feature-length version of Hughes' ur-text apes *Goodbye, Mr. Chips* for structure as much as subject matter, beginning at the end as Tom and East's reconciliation at Arnold's funeral leads to a recollection of school careers. A more apposite title would be 'Thomas Arnold's Schooldays' since the ensuing narrative foregrounds major incidents in the life of Rugby's reformist headmaster, showing the fierce resistance he faced in transforming the institution from 'a school of savage barbarians' into one that would 'change the future of Education in England'. Thus, in this culmination of a balancing trilogy of assent, the flashback device again serves to mythologise the 'great man'—as East explicitly labels the Doctor—with Brown essentially Arnold's 'man on the ground', his like-minded surrogate within the school body. Excising entirely the sickly Arthur subplot, Stevenson's retrospectively structured film follows the gruelling trajectory of Tom Brown and Rugby School to its inevitable realisation of Arnold's radical education philosophy. The prevailing culture of 'tyranny' that Arnold and Brown must tackle is portrayed in unflinching detail, as is the sense of despair that pupil ostracism can inflict. Such scenes convincingly convey the necessity to transform these 'nurseries of iniquity and vice', though Arnold's reforms are more debated than dramatised: narratively the violent 'before' wins over the peaceful 'after' with Brown's final three years quickly summarised in a montage of cricket matches, cursory study and his ascension to head of house. The source text's moral emphases remain in scenes where Arnold voices his creed to teach his charges 'to love what is right, to mould them into courageous, god-fearing gentlemen', notably in his opening pulpit address which, validated by a low camera angle and its Chipping senti-ment, topically warns that 'those who are to govern others must first learn to govern themselves'. Britain's critical reception was less validating, Basil Wright forcefully dismissing a 'California' film 'pedalling "more high falu-tin" tommyrot about our public schools' (*Spectator*, 6 September 1940). America was more impressed, *Variety* finding the film 'sympathetically and skilfully made, with many touching moments and an excellent cast' (31 December 1939). The time for fagging and Victorian hagiography had clearly passed, though, as the film bombed at the box office, recording a loss of $110,000. While the 1916 version had been perceived as a fillip to the fighting forces, *Tom Brown's School Days* felt irrelevant—if not impu-dent—and quickly disappeared from cinemas. By now the public school code had lost its invulnerability.

4   THE BOYS' PUBLIC SCHOOL CARNIVALESQUE

George Orwell considers the school story particularly British because the nation's education 'is mainly a matter of status'. He elucidates: 'The most definite dividing line between the petite-bourgeoisie and the working class is that the former pay for their education, and within the bourgeoisie there is another unbridgeable gulf between the "public" school and the "private" school' (1970 [1940]: 518). The latter, aka 'very cheap public schools', afforded the veneer of middle-class respectability but offered a product of doubtful academic pedigree and if the popular reception of *Downhill* and *Young Woodley* demonstrated the enduring untouchabil-ity of top public schools, the cultural depiction of cheaper educational establishments bypassed pastiche straight to parody, becoming a staple of popular comedy. It first came to cinema in the person of Will Hay, already a national celebrity with an act honed over 25 years in music hall and on radio. After three films for BIP, Hay's move to Gainsborough brought to screen his most lauded characterisation, 'the Fourth Form of St. Michael's', wherein a self-important and incompetent schoolmaster is invariably shown up by his more intelligent pupils. Fitting exactly with Orwell's social categorisations, Raymond Durgnat noted in Hay's pedagogical persona 'an amoral and weary indomitability which is at once truly proletarian and truly shabby genteel' (1970: 172).

Boys Will Be Boys (William Beaudine, 9 December 1935), Hay's school screen debut, betrays uncertainty with the new medium by grafting his teacher onto a loose adaptation of the Dr Smart-Allick stories from the 'By the Way' *Daily Express* column of J.B. Morton (aka 'Beachcomber'). The film relates the adventures of Dr Alexander Smart, MA, who becomes headmaster of Narkover School by means of a forged testimonial supplied by Faker Brown (Gordon Harker), a prison inmate and father to the school's head boy, Cyril (Jimmy Hanley). Brown later blackmails Smart into employing him as school porter, an 'insider' position from which he plans to steal a diamond necklace belonging to Narkover's Chair of Governors, Lady Dorking (Norma Varden). Smart's attempts to thwart the scheme culminate in the necklace being hidden in a rugby ball and ruthlessly pursued in the Founders' Day match between the current corrupt Narkovians and a team of hardened criminal Old Boys until it finds its way to the police.

Various publicity strategies perpetuated the work's music hall provenance by encouraging audience interaction: these included a tie-in charity campaign offering those who enrolled as pupils (cost one shilling) a Narkover College Book of Rules, such as rugby players needing to provide their own knuckle-dusters. Even in comic mode, however, a critique of British schooling met with official opposition and *Boys Will Be Boys* was given an 'A' certificate (open to under-16s only if adult-accompanied) by the British Board of Film Censors (BBFC), the *Daily Mail* musing that 'Perhaps it thought that unless some restraining adult influence was imposed upon juvenile beholders of the film, regrettable results might ensue in schools' (17 August 1935). Graham Greene argued it was the film's 'realistic study of our public schools' that spooked the censor (*Spectator*, 23 August 1935), but Hay's work has more habitually attracted the epithet of 'carnivalesque': Marcia Landy sees the school setting as 'a locus for carnival' (1991: 348), while David Sutton adjudges the film 'A wonderfully funny, carnivalesque attack on the institution of an English education' (2000: 131). It is a concept worth exploring, for its applicability both to Hay and the school film genre in general.[8]

The carnivalesque is a cultural theory derived from Soviet critic Mikhail Bakhtin's reading of the French writer Rabelais. Carnival, related to the

Medieval Feast of Fools, was a form of popular 'low' humour allowing for the parody of authority by creating 'a second world and a second life outside officialdom' (Bakhtin 1984b [1965]: 6). As capitalism replaced feudalism carnival as an event metamorphosed into the 'carnivalesque', the carnival spirit in artistic form, but continued the 'long tradition of turning the world upside-down, of symbolically subverting the dominant, ruling hierarchies of social existence' (Crawford 2002: 42–3). This subversion, the ability to crown a fool, has led to carnivalesque discourse being labelled 'a social and political protest' (Kristeva 1980: 65). A reading of the carnivalesque features of *Boys Will Be Boys* would foreground its inversion of the traditional public school practices that fed the accepted tropes in school literature and film. Firstly, Hay himself is 'upside-down', in tenure as in treatment. Where Thomas Arnold succeeded to and at Rugby with the support of upstanding Squire Brown, here the forgery of (the significantly surnamed) Faker Brown secures Smart's headship—the evident crowning of a fool. On arrival it is not the new boy or 'stinker' who, like Tom Brown, is 'hazed', but the new head, his humiliation culminating in a literal inversion when he is blanket-tossed (the scene shown in *Typically British*) until left hanging by his trousers over the school gates. Similarly, during the chaotic closing rugby match Smart swallows the referee's whistle and the boys turn him upside down in order to dislodge it: not only is the individual figure of authority (literally) upended, but the generic communal sanctity of the sports terrain and the code of 'playing the game' are trampled underfoot. Secondly, the carnivalesque 'world upside-down' creates an alternative social space where diverse voices destabilise the authoritative pronouncement of hegemonic forces. This 'joyful relativity of everything' (Bakhtin 1984a [1963]: 125) centres on the film's classroom scenes where the teacher as a repository of knowledge is exposed as a spurious notion: a close-up on his textbook during a lecture on 'Lepidoptera' shows Smart erring on the word's genealogy, while his set-piece routine on 'How high is a Chinaman?/Yes, Howe Hi is a Chinaman' reveals his pupil's semantic superiority. Smart's explanation when caught card-dealing in class—'I wasn't teaching the boys, they were teaching me!'—encapsulates the carnivalesque spirit: that his protest is lost when Hay's sabotaged welcome bouquet reduces the governing body to fits of sneezing, indicates in microcosm how Hay 'flirts with the darker and more subversive aspects of institutional behaviour, which, if tapped, explode' (Landy 1991: 351). Several such incidentals underscore the general. For instance, when Smart discovers that the pupil firing ink pellets is his physical superior, he makes a smaller boy stand up and take the punishment. It succeeds as a comic moment, but chimes also with the narrative drive that sees Faker Brown finally expose scheming governor Colonel Crableigh (Davy Burnaby) as the real jewel thief, thus presenting a wider metaphorical comment on how convicted criminals and 'pillars of the Establishment' are equally self-seeking, though the 'little man' normally takes the blame. There are no messages of loyalty, courtesy and honesty at Narkover: pupils are largely left to fend for themselves, with adult role models invariably avaricious and egotistical. Thirdly, music and mise-en-scène also revel in subverting the dominant style. The school song suggests a future serving His Majesty in means other than imperial: 'We are the boys who soon will be/Known to the dear old C.I.D.', while tablets lining the school cloisters commemorate 'in memoriam' not old Narkovians lost in war but those distinguished in the annals of crime. Like Stevenson's *Tom Brown's School Days*, the film's opening credits pass over the school crest: here its handcuffs and convict arrows honour Narkover's nefarious tradition while underneath runs the school motto 'Quid Pro Quo'—the classical icon elsewhere idealising education now has its nakedly commercial imperative writ large. Indeed, language is throughout duplicitous, Hay's convincing Lady Dorking that the graffitied phrase 'Smart Alec is a gump' signifies 'a friend in need' subverts preconceived connections between being upper-class and well-educated.

Not all of the comedy in *Boys Will Be Boys* can be construed as 'carnivalesque', however. While excess is a film constant, a key aspect of the carnivalesque is what Bakhtin terms 'grotesque realism' (1984b [1965]: 18), a style that transgresses the boundaries between the enduring work of art and quotidian corporeal life. Smart's bodily weaknesses are highlighted in his frequent receipt of physical blows, but the more *grotesque* aspects, the orifices' practices, do not feature in Hay's work as they will, for example, in later Carry On and St Trinian's films. The final item on the Founders' Day menu, 'nuts', disappears with a loud belch and Lady Dorking may flirtatiously ask to be Smart's 'gump', but sex? For Ray Seaton and Roy Martin 'the question, while watching a Hay comedy, does not arise any more than it does in a boys' comic paper' (they also note Hay's fondness for Frank Richards' stories) (1978: 88), and the absence, not only of romance but any inkling of sexual attraction, links to a lack of the bodily imperative—in thought, word or deed. When the colonel bewails his broken watch, presented by the 'Old Berkeley Hunt', the Cockney rhyming slang passes without diegetic comment or reaction: Smart's opening anatomy lesson is conducted with 'Napoleon', a model skeleton—there are no sins of the flesh here.

More fundamentally, one could argue the extent to which any alternative ideological interpretation can be made of the carnival/esque: how can it offer rebellion when those exercising social control demarcate both its timing and duration? For Umberto Eco the 'diabolic trick' is that 'carnival can exist only as *authorised* transgression', reminding all 'of the existence of the rule': as such it functions as a safety-valve rather than a vehicle for subversion and 'is only an instrument of social control and can never be a form of social criticism' (1984: 6–7). In this vein Sue Harper sees Hay's films as establishing 'a comforting locale where the central myths of the culture can be rehearsed and recognised' and dealt with 'in a confident and unproblematic manner' (1997: 86). However, if *Boys Will Be Boys* is a permissible rupture of hegemony, one could further speculate quite why the initial censors were so nervous. The final scenes here are pertinent, and problematic: with Smart again blanket-tossed, the film fails to provide a restoration of social/school order, pointedly withholding a validating authority and respectability for Smart who, one surmises, will be even more indebted to Faker Brown for exposing Crableigh. This ending is not strictly carnivalesque since it is not strictly contained, thus rendering it potentially more genuinely subversive. The same holds true for character. As headmaster, Smart is initially a prickly, small-scale authoritarian, unpleasantly spluttering as he bluffs his way out of situations escaping his minimal control. By the end, though, he has won audience sympathy, principally because he can never fully mask his essentially childish nature: rather than exert discipline, he prefers to play games with his pupils, be it rugby or surreptitious rounds of banker with the sixth-form. While *Boys Will Be Boys* breaks with the established public school code in *not* inculcating gentlemanly godliness and selfless service to the nation, it also breaks with carnival in revealing the ultimate deception that is adulthood and its concomitant social order. This absence of personal maturation and refusal of closure may well explain the film's non-'U' certification: worryingly, boys will be boys, whatever their age or status.

Critical opinion was mixed. Bakhtin entitled one of his Rabelais chapters 'the language of the marketplace' to emphasise carnival's opposition to the discrete spaces of serious art, and several (high-end) critics considered *Boys Will Be Boys* wrongly sited, the *Times* regretting not just the 'heavy-handed humour' but how 'the prolonged verbal by-play of Mr Will Hay's famous music-hall act seem[s] to have had considerable difficulty in meeting the demands of a more exacting medium' (19 August 1935). *The Cinema*, by contrast, considered it 'one of the funniest films ever made in this country' (26 July 1935); the *Sunday Express*, though noting that 'it is letting our public schools down', also approved of 'a very funny comedy' and, with carnivalesque inversion, advised that 'Every schoolboy should take his parents to see it' (18 August 1935). More than enough did to secure a second appointment.

4.1   *Section Prize Winner:* Good Morning, Boys *(1937)*

After two further Beaudine films Hay's seedy schoolmaster returned to the cinema, now minus the 'Beachcomber' filter. Working from Anthony Kimmins' original story initially entitled 'The Fifth Form at St Michael's', this would prove the first of Hay's eight collaborations with French-born Charterhouse-educated Marcel Varnel, now Gainsborough's resident comedy director and adept at adapting variety and radio stars' routines for cinema with a fast, free-ranging technique, while directors-in-waiting Val Guest and Frank Launder respectively contributed screenplay/dialogue and script-editing. On screen, 21-year-old Lilli Palmer, fresh from Hitchcock's *Secret Agent* (1936), was cast as Yvette, an unusually glamorous co-star for a Hay film, while the pupil ranks foregrounded regular Bunter-esque side-kick Graham Moffatt as class leader Albert Brown, the foil for Hay's set-pieces. Public school and Paris filming took from mid-October to December 1936 at Gainsborough's Islington Studios after which, alongside a nationwide publicity tour by Hay and Palmer, audience interaction was again encouraged with the sale of ancillary merchandise, ranging from an astrological Twisterism Chart—St Michael's advance on Pelmanism—to a Palmer-modelled woman's hat with mortarboard design. *Good Morning, Boys* went on general release on 5 April 1937, though for its 26 July American opening it was (confusingly) retitled *Where There's A Will*. The film begins with a new Chair of Governors, Colonel Willoughby-Gore (Peter Gawthorne), inspecting the school and demanding the resignation of its headmaster, now named Dr Benjamin Twist. Twist defends his educational methods (cue product placement for his astrological chart) and is given one last chance to demonstrate what his pupils can do at the inter-school examinations in London. A briefcase mix-up supplies Twist with the papers in advance, the boys emerge as academic champions in French and receive an invitation to Paris from France's ministry of education. There the school inadvertently assist a gang, led by pupil parent and safe-cracker Arty Jones (Mark Daly) alongside nightclub chanteuse Yvette, in stealing the *Mona Lisa* from the Louvre. When the boys realise what has happened, they come to Twist's rescue, exposing the thieves and returning the picture at the ministry reception.

Good Morning, Boys is readable as a rerun of *Boys Will Be Boys*: Hay is again the bumbling pedagogue amidst roguish pupils and hardened criminals. There is again an affluent governess, Lady Bagshott (Martita Hunt), on Hay's side, a gruff colonel against him, and a parent chasing a priceless artefact. Once more the plot motor allows space for Hay to provide his audience with well-known sketches from his stage act—'What is the unit of electricity?/A unit of electricity is a watt'—alongside moments of purely physical humour, as in the fine silent scene when a contact man, successive pupils and finally Twist all try to point out the thief's son in class. As one might expect from a 'retest', the results generally surpass the first effort, especially in writing and direction. The film also more precisely situates Orwell's social divisions and St Michael's status: Twist's pretentions to knowledge, undermined by his malapropisms, primer French phrases and vernacular lapses, expose him/Hay as a class act in all senses of the term; when he finally defines the unit of electricity as an ohm (not a 'watt/ what') and asks Albert to confirm the definition, the pupil's reply that 'it's a place there's no place like' drops not just an aitch but another clear class signifier, problematising Sue Harper's reading that Hay's films 'carefully avoid a class-based explanation of the world' (1997: 86).

In a contemporary interview Hay emphasised the licence of laughter provided by his films' 'second world and second life' (*Good Morning, Boys Press Book* 1937: 15) and his second school film offers more assured refinements of the carnivalesque 'world upside-down' discourse than *Boys Will Be Boys*. When Twist demotes a pupil only to be told he is already at the bottom of the class, his retort is to 'go to the top and remember you're a lap behind', while the classroom obfuscation normally played out on the teacher is passed upwards when Twist hoodwinks Willoughby-Gore, transforming 'Honest' Albert's bookmakers' odds into a history lesson on pikemen at Agincourt, its ingenuity drawing a ripple of diegetic class applause. *Good Morning, Boys* also offers a pointed parody of the imperial trope, the expectations of Willoughby-Gore—'late of the Indian Army'— for a curriculum based on a factual knowledge of Empire ridiculed when his class question to name six animals found on the subcontinent is eventually answered with 'a tiger and five elephants'. Public school as a mint to coin Empire-builders is further mocked with the incompetent Officer Training Corps drilling, the colonel's exasperated command to 'slope' (arms) leading to a hurried dispersal of the ranks—a 'sloping off'. The educational satire broadens as the London competition exposes a national system run by incompetents, with exam papers lost, cheating undetected and pedantic questioning, all predicated on 'the smug view that winning a prize demonstrates the possession of knowledge' (Landy 1991: 350).

Bakhtin adumbrated his theories of the carnivalesque in a study of Dostoevsky, several of which can be applied to *Good Morning, Boys*. Central to the film's crime plot is 'profanation', with the 'decrowning' theft of the *Mona Lisa*, amongst the reigning icons of the Western cultural tradition, allowing a broad 'playing with the symbols of higher authority' (Bakhtin 1984a [1963]: 125). An earlier 'profanation' is effected, however, on the enduring cinematic symbol of British educational discipline. It is a momentary scene, but Twist's tampered cane connotes not just the emasculation of the individual (Hay's son—in his only screen appearance—being the putative recipient adds further Freudian ramifications) but a (literal) breaking with the generic sanctity of that most 'typically British' of educational exchanges: as stated by William Hay Jr of his punishment, 'it's not cricket' (Fig. 2.3). Carnival's allowance for unusual combinations

Fig. 2.3   The Cane Mutiny

is felicitously translated as '*mésalliances*' since St Michael's visit to France facilitates the rupture of 'all things that were once self-enclosed, disunified, distanced from one another by a non-carnivalistic hierarchical worldview', notably 'the lofty with the low, the great with the insignificant, the wise with the stupid' (Bakhtin 1984a [1963]: 125). The film's *mésalliance* of British youth with the French 'other' promises a stereotypical exposure to emotional and sexual excess, but this too is frequently overturned. Steven Allen notes 'an inversion of the stereotype's properties' so that 'the most pronounced qualities of being French become admirable, or at least have a positive influence through being turned back on the British social types to reveal their flaws' (2010: 443). Thus almost all the main players become positive catalysts to 'loosen up', as Yvette sings, the limitations of British reserve. The 'grotesque realism', absent from *Boys Will Be Boys*, is now plentifully evident, with the pupils quickly 'at home' in the fleshpots of Paris and sexually knowing, as in Albert's reference to Yvette as Twist's 'little bit of homework'. Again the boys are teaching the master: Twist's liaison with Yvette could never be a prelude to the libidinous undoing of an educator as in *Der Blaue Engel/The Blue Angel* (Josef von Sternberg, 1930), his answer to Yvette on the women in his life—'twelve cooks in three months'—revealing the continued asexual Hay persona. While *Housemaster* and *Goodbye, Mr. Chips* enlist the engagement to a good woman, the making of a schoolmaster is here pursuant on his entrapment by a *femme fatale*.

Not that Twist would understand the term. The insularity of Britain's educational system is mocked with Twist telling his charges that 'This is an English Schools' examination, so French won't be necessary.' Such ideological isolation is reinforced by St Michael's being, like many public schools, rurally situated, while its Blackmoor (Dartmoor) placement and the ease with which Jones moves there from the adjacent prison intimates the interchangeability/comparability of institutions. Culturally adrift in Paris, Twist confuses the *Mona Lisa* with the song 'Mona the Moocher', while a pupil, asked about the Louvre's collection, asserts that 'I didn't give anything!' The class(room) divisions transform, however, with exposure to the greater (low cultural) freedoms of Paris. French stereotypes crystallise in the louche nightclub to which Twist follows the inquisitive boys, only to be compromised by Yvette's 'innocent kiss' and plentiful alcohol. Pointedly, this is where the boys first rally round Twist and effect his escape, while on hearing of Twist's intended resignation Albert's rallying call not to 'see the old man done down by a load of crooks' draws an approving chorus of 'up the school!' and the class, now fully cognisant of the value of 'proper' behavioural codes, expose the real perpetrators and return the painting. The nightclub where this understanding begins is aptly named the 'Cuisine du Diable' since it functions as the locale for Eco's 'diabolic trick' of ensuring the reinstatement of rule. Differences have been lived out and consensus found: Twist is no paragon of pedagogical virtue but his failings are slight when compared to others' material avarice (Peter Godfrey's gangleader Cliquot) or intellectual arrogance (Charles Hawtrey's scholar Septimus). This is less a plague on town and gown than a minor public school coming to know its place in the scheme of things, and such a submission to authority may explain why, for David Sutton, the boys 'are not quite the young monsters of Narkover, and the film, though very funny, lacks some of the bite of *Boys Will Be Boys*' (2000: 132). Indeed not: St Michael's ultimate growth into a defence of property and justice renders the film more fully a carnivalesque text than its predecessor since an *authorised* carnival is achieved, with social and school order fully restored. There was no need here for the censors' intervention.

The public were equally pleased and *Good Morning, Boys* featured among the top 30 British box-office successes of 1937. Press divisions, though, remained unresolved. Paul Dein was effusive: '*Good Morning, Boys* happens to be louder and funnier than any film that Mr Hay has made. Were there three Mr Hays, England would have its Marx Brothers' (*Sunday Referee*, 4 February 1937). The schoolroom scenes were mostly graded higher than the Paris escapades, *Film Weekly* adjudging the first half 'thoroughly good, typically British entertainment; and the film would probably have been better as a whole if it had adhered to this form of humour throughout' (13 February 1937). Some, though, were already baulking at schoolmaster comedies: 'in spite of good gags, a neat plot and cast-iron laughs, it all seems vaguely familiar—Something new, please!' pleaded the *Daily Express* (12 February 1937).

The settings would be new, but Benjamin Twist continued to blag his way through British cinema: when sacked from St Michaels', mistaken identity landed him the position of prison governor in *Convict* 99, before masquerading as a History professor when duped onto an American-bound liner in *Hey! Hey! USA* (both Marcel Varnel, 1938). Three films on and Hay returned to the classroom, now in the unfamiliar setting of Ealing Studios under producer Michael Balcon. With shooting delayed by the 1940 blitzkrieg on London, *The Ghost of St. Michael's* (Marcel Varnel, 19 May 1941), featured Hay as William Lamb, new Science master at St

Michael's, now evacuated to Dunbain Castle on the Isle of Skye. Lamb (to the slaughter?) is victim to practical jokes from his pupils, notably ring-leader Percy Thorne (26-year-old Charles Hawtrey), and is concerned to find an old rival, Humphries (Raymond Huntley), on the staff. As recounted by crazed porter Jamie (John Laurie), the ancient pile is haunted by a ghost whose appearance accompanies the death of members of staff. Such a fate duly befalls headmaster Dr Winter (Felix Aylmer) and his successor, Humphries. The staff suspect each other, but, with the latest head Hilary Teasdale (Claude Hulbert) set up as decoy, the legend is exposed as a cover for the formidable matron Mrs Wigmore (Elliott Mason) and Jamie, German spies installed in the castle to contact U-boats.

Though Ealing provided a step up from Gainsborough in production values, *The Ghost at St. Michael's* is generally considered overplotted to make an ideal Hay vehicle. Nonetheless, the school setting allows a reprise of his monumental ignorance and bluff, and a rerun of music hall set-pieces as in the 'What's the matter with your grammar?/She was alright the last time I saw her' exchange with the habitually sharper student. It also provides two scenes of carnivalesque disorder and loss of dignity: a Physics lesson where Percy goads Lamb into demonstrating the laws of gravity with a Tower of Pisa pile of chairs, on which Hay is perched precariously when the headmaster enters; and a dormitory party for Hallowe'en where Lamb gets drunk on whisky which he believes is lemonade and does a tipsy act before a scandalised Humphries. Overall, though, the narrative and thematic 'inversion' of *The Ghost of St. Michael's* seeks not an undermining of society but the quasi-propagandistic upholding of national interests with Lamb called out of retirement to 'teach for victory' and facing specific enemy targets. This was a time for projecting a patriotic consensus cinema, so problems of dishonesty, incompetence and corruption could not now be allegorised and institutionalised. As such, *The Ghost of St. Michael's* fits snugly within Balcon and Ealing's wartime entertainment remit for 'indirect propaganda attesting to the exhilaration and efficiency of working together' (Kardish 1984: 56). This motivates the film's *formal* transgression when, in its final seconds, the fourth wall breaks between phantom fiction and wartime reality as the sound of bagpipes segues into an all-clear siren: Twist turns and addresses the audience—and fellow actor Hulbert—with 'You can go home now if you like. Come on, Claude.' The inclusive nature of Carnival, which exists 'without a division into performers and spectators' since all 'live in it', is here, through the national 'escapist' medium of cinema, finally, achieved: but rather than an authorised Carnival, it is war-torn Britain that demolishes all divisions, suspending 'hierarchical structure and all the forms of terror, reverence, piety and etiquette connected with it' (Bakhtin 1984a [1963]: 122). The film connected well enough to ensure its effectiveness at the box office. The *MFB* lauded its technical professionalism—'A good story, well directed, with first-class photography and sound and as admirable a cast as could be found'—but was more circumspect regarding the comedy: 'If you like Will Hay's humour, you will like this film' (February 1941: 14). As with *Good Morning, Boys* the generic hybridity was regretted: 'Hay's schoolmaster sequences are in good old tradition and amuse, but the more hectic spy-chasing and murderer-detecting tend to be a little too puerile' (*Picturegoer*, 22 February 1941).

Undeterred, Hay's professorial persona continued to fight the good fight. In *The Goose Steps Out* (Basil Dearden, Will Hay, August 1942) he dons a Nazi uniform, with schoolmaster William Potts masquerading as his exact double, German super-spy Herr Muller: his pupils, including Hawtrey and Peter Ustinov, are young Brownshirts receiving instruction on how to behave in England. Potts/Muller shows them the correct gesture of ceremonial address, a V-sign that the class assiduously practise before a giant portrait of the Fuhrer. It is a successful scene but, for Seaton and Martin, overall 'it is a laboured comedy, and best excused as Hay's contribution to the war effort' (1978: 171). Post-war, education would of necessity become more serious.

NOTES

1. Newbolt's *Vitaï Lampada* (1892) relates how a Clifton College schoolboy, later a soldier in the Sudan, learns selfless devotion to duty through playing cricket on the College Close.

2. In Hughes' novel (1930 [1857]) Squire Brown asserts that he sent his son to school not 'to make himself a good scholar' but only so 'he might turn out a brave, helpful, truth-telling Englishman and a gentleman and a Christian.' London: Nelson: 47.

3. Few saw the cross-media experiment as successful: 'Mr Ivor Novello is excellent as himself, but he is never so much like a schoolboy as when he appears in person in an interpolated scene. This scene... seemed to interest the audience, but the advisability of mingling the two forms of entertainment seems very doubtful.' *Times*, 12 October 1927.

4. The Lord Chamberlain condemned the play as 'an attack upon the public school system, liable to cause offence to scholastic bodies and pain to parents and guardians'. J. van Druten (1938) *The Way to the Present: A Personal Record*. London: Michael Joseph: 266.

5. *Young Woodley*'s premise was reworked in Robert Anderson's 1953 Broadway hit *Tea and Sympathy*, with housemaster's wife Laura now sleeping with a pupil to allay his fears after homosexual taunts—it was again banned by Britain's Lord Chamberlain. A film version, with Deborah Kerr and without the homosexuality, was directed by Vincente Minnelli in 1956.

6. W.H. Balgarnie, long-serving master at the Leys School, Cambridge (1900–1930), is, alongside Hilton's headmaster father, the acknowledged model for Chipping.

7. 'In the future it will please us to remember all this.' The phrase, taken from Vergil's *Aeneid, Book 1*, is offered by Chips to Katherine at the conclusion of their European holiday.

8. For a full film application of Bakhtin's theories, see Robert Stam (1982) *Subversive Pleasures: Bakhtin, Cultural Criticism, and Film*. Baltimore: John Hopkins University Press.

REFERENCES

Allen, S. (2010) 'A French Exchange: Education as the Cultural Interface in British Comedies'. *Journal of British Cinema and Television*, 7, 3.

Bakhtin, M. (1984a [1963]) *Problems of Dostoevsky's Poetics* (trans. Caryl Emerson). Manchester: Manchester University Press.

Bakhtin, M. (1984b [1965]) *Rabelais and his World* (trans. Helene Iswolsky). Bloomington: Indiana University Press.

Bamford, T. (1974) *The Rise of the Public School*. London: Nelson.

Barr, C. (1999) *English Hitchcock*. Moffat: Cameron and Hollis.

Burton, A. (2002) 'Death or Glory? The Great War in British film', in C. Monk and A. Sergeant (eds) *British Historical Cinema*. London: Routledge.

Crawford, P. (2002) *Politics and History in William Golding: The World Turned Upside Down*. Columbia: University of Missouri Press.

Deeney, J. (2000) 'When men were men and women were women', in C. Barker and M.B. Gale (eds) *British Theatre Between the Wars, 1918–1939*. Cambridge: Cambridge University Press.

Durgnat, R. (1970) *A Mirror for England: British Movies from Austerity to Affluence*. London: Faber and Faber.

Durgnat, R. (1974) *The Strange Case of Alfred Hitchcock*. London: Faber and Faber.

Eco, U. (1984) 'The Frames of Comic Freedom', in T. Seboek (ed.) *Carnival!*. Berlin: Mouton Publishing.

Glancy, H.M. (1999) *When Hollywood Loved Britain: The Hollywood 'British' Film 1939–1945*. Manchester: Manchester University Press.

Harper, S. (1997) '"Nothing to Beat the Hay Diet": Comedy at Gaumont and Gainsborough', in P. Cook (ed.) *Gainsborough Pictures*. London: Cassell.

Hayward, S. (1996) *Key Concepts in Cinema Studies*. London: Routledge.

Higson, A. (2002) 'Cecil Hepworth, *Alice in Wonderland* and the Development of the Narrative Film', in A. Higson (ed.) *Young and Innocent? The Cinema in Britain 1896–1930*. Exeter: University of Exeter Press.

Hilton, J. (1934) *Goodbye, Mr. Chips*. London: Hodder and Stoughton.

Kardish, L. (1984) 'Michael Balcon and the Idea of a National Cinema', in G. Brown and L. Kardish, *Michael Balcon: The Pursuit of British Cinema*. New York: Museum of Modern Art.

Kember, J. (2013) 'Professional Lecturing in Early British Film Shows', in J. Brown and A. Davidson (eds) *The Sounds of the Silents in Britain*. Oxford: Oxford University Press.

Kristeva, J. (1980) *Desire in Language: A Semiotic Approach to Literature and Art*. New York: Columbia University Press.

Landy, M. (1991) *British Genres: Cinema and Society, 1930–1960*. Princeton, NJ: Princeton University Press.

Leitch, T. (2002) *Encyclopedia of Alfred Hitchcock*. New York: Checkmark Books.

Low, R. (1951) *History of the British Film, 1914–1918*. London: George Allen and Unwin.

Mack, E.C. (1938) *Public Schools and British Opinion, 1780–1860*. London: Methuen.

McFarlane, B. (1999) 'Jack of All Trades: Robert Stevenson', in J. Richards (ed.) *The Unknown 1930s: An alternative history of the British cinema, 1929–1939*. London: I.B. Tauris.

O'Connor, S. (1998) *Straight Acting: Popular Gay Drama from Wilde to Rattigan*. London: Cassell.

Orwell, G. (1970 [1940]) 'Boys' Weeklies', in *The Collected Essays, Journalism and Letters, 1*. Harmondsworth. Penguin.

Richards, J. (1973) *Visions of Yesterday*. London: Routledge and Kegan Paul.

Richards, J. (1984) *The Age of the Dream Palace: Cinema and Society in Britain 1930–1939*. London: Routledge and Kegan Paul.

Richards, J. (1988) *Happiest Days: The public schools in English fiction*. Manchester: Manchester University Press.

Routt, W.D. (1994) 'Some early British films considered in the light of early Australian production'. *Metro*, Summer.

Russell Taylor, J. (1978) *Hitch: The Life and Times of Alfred Hitchcock*. London: aber and Faber.

Seaton, R. and R. Martin (1978) *Good Morning Boys: Will Hay, Master of Comedy.* London: Barrie and Jenkins.

Silver, C. (2003) 'King and Country', in M. Mandy and A. Monda (eds) *The Hidden God: Film and Faith.* New York: Museum of Modern Art.

Smith, M. (1995) 'The war and British culture', in S. Constantine (ed.) *The First World War in British History.* London: Edward Arnold.

Sutton, D. (2000) *A Chorus of Raspberries: British Film Comedy 1929–1939.* Exeter: University of Exeter Press.

Truffaut, F. (1978) *Hitchcock.* London: Paladin.

Turim, M. (1989) *Flashbacks in Film: Memory and History.* London: Routledge.

Warburton, T. (1998) 'Cartoons and Teachers: Mediated visual images as data', in J. Prosser (ed.) *Image-Based Research: A Sourcebook for Qualitative Researchers.* London: Falmer Press.

The Middle Years Programme (1945–70)

CHAPTER 3

The Post-War Public School Film (1945–70)

1   THE RIGHT STUFF

The Education Act of 1944 (aka the Butler Act) finally provided a nation-wide system of free, compulsory schooling from age five to 15, with a change of school at 11. Whilst overall a laudably progressive programme, underpinned by the principle that 'the nature of a child's education should be based on his capacity and promise and not by the circumstances of his parent' (Board of Education 1943: 7), it nonetheless received consider-able criticism for its continued divisiveness, firstly for sending the 'top' 20 per cent of children to grammar school with the Eleven Plus-failing majority consigned to local technical colleges or secondary moderns,[1] but mainly for refusing to dismantle private education. Instead, the concurrent 1944 Fleming Report recommended a degree of integration by awarding up to a quarter of public school places to suitably 'qualified' state school children: thus began 'assisted places', an arguably disingenuous scheme to placate left-wing objections that public school elitism was at variance with the social cohesion created by the war and that its outdated ethos had contributed to the war's disastrous early course (Barber 1994: 49–56). The scheme would never thrive, local authorities prioritising expenditure elsewhere, but it attracted the early attention of British stage and screen.

© The Editor(s) (if applicable) and The Author(s) 2016   59
S. Glynn, *The British School Film*,
DOI 10.1057/978-1-137-55887-9_3

1.1   Section Prize Winner: The Guinea Pig *(1948)*

Sherborne-educated Warren Chetham-Strode's 1946 play *The Guinea Pig*, directly inspired by the Fleming Report, traced the uneasy passage of Cockney council schoolboy Jack Read through the fictional Saintbury public school. A successful two-year West End run led to an American stage production (retitled *The Outsider*) and a film contract with Pilgrim Pictures. The project was entrusted to the Charterhouse-educated twin Boulting brothers, with Roy directing and John as producer. Their film output, notably *Fame is the Spur* (1947), an adaptation of Howard Spring's novel and a thinly-veiled portrait of the first Labour Party Prime Minister Ramsay MacDonald, identified the brothers with the ideals of the post-war Labour government and *The Guinea Pig* had strong Labour credentials: Bernard Miles, whose Pilgrim production *Chance of a Lifetime* (1950) would focus on unionised workers running a factory (and fail to find a major circuit backer), worked with Chetham-Strode and Roy Boulting on the screenplay—and played Mr Read, father of the Fleming 'guinea pig' pupil. This was played by 24-year-old Richard Attenborough, fresh from his triumph as Pinky Brown in John Boulting's *Brighton Rock* (1947), while Cecil Trouncer and Robyn Flemyng reprised their stage roles as pivotal schoolmasters. With Gilbert Taylor working his first film as cinematographer, exteriors were shot at Sherborne School, Dorset, with sets at MGM-Britain's Borehamwood studios modelled directly on Chetham-Strode's alma mater. The film premiered in London on 27 October 1948 and New York on 30 April 1949.

The Guinea Pig sets out to examine the role of the public school in the post-war British society being forged by the new Labour government. In this less deferential climate, where the cosy certainties of *Goodbye, Mr. Chips* were ceding to *Browning Version* representations of bleakness and repression, the Boultings' film is, in all senses, the 'guinea pig' in the middle, at pains to provide arguments both for and against the Fleming experiment, articulated in familiar generic patterning by two schoolmasters representing traditional and progressive educational philosophies. In the Donkin/Chips corner is Lloyd Hartley, MA (Trouncer), Latin teacher, elderly housemaster and staunch traditionalist, influentially sceptical of class integration. His need to retire with heart trouble may, as with Crocker-Harris, suggest the natural ending of an era, but the national benefits of such pedagogy are emphasised in a central chapel scene where peace celebrations pan to the shrine for 12 Old Boys who gave their lives in the Battle of Britain. In the

Ralston/Ovington corner, but with a different power dynamic, is Nigel Lorraine (Flemyng), new History master and house tutor, the young and idealistic meritocrat open to affirmative action: though Hartley's junior, his credentials are generically impeccable as an ex-army officer and Oxford rugby Blue who also served and sacrificed, losing a leg in the war. Their differences of opinion, centred on Jack Read and the Fleming scheme's potentialities, ape *Housemaster* with Lorraine offering his resignation after Hartley accuses him of disloyalty. The dialectic is reiterated at trustee level where discussions on the War Memorial Fund separate the progressive headmaster, Stringer (Anthony Nicholls), looking to fund academic scholarships, from the (elderly) governors, led by the Bishop (*Housemaster*'s Kynaston Reeves), who prefer a new school hall and fear that bursaries will 'lower the tone'. Both conflicts are resolved by an engineered epiphany, Lorraine's invitation for Jack's parents to visit the school dispelling some of the prejudicial mist, while Hartley's valedictory walk alights on the inscription of founder Thomas Wolsey's 1520 bequest for '*Twenty boyes being sonnes of poore townsmen of Saintbury to be maintained out of the foundation of the schoole.*' With the boost of a musical crescendo, Hartley is reminded of the reason for the creation of public schools, and his intervention in support of Stringer both carries the scholarship proposal and ensures Jack's future. With reconciliation complete, Hartley asks Lorraine to succeed him as housemaster, confident that he can introduce necessary reforms within a cadre of continuity. The new unity is sealed by Lorraine's engagement to Hartley's daughter Lynne (Sheila Sim) who may in reverie quote Newbolt's 'Clifton Chapel' but who reveals herself another 'revolutionary' woman encouraging her fiancé's meliorist philosophy.

Interwoven with debates on the Fleming scheme's methods is the school life of the eponymous Guinea Pig. Jack's 'Pilgrim's Progress' follows the standard generic pattern of early alienation, mid-career peer bonding amidst sporting success, culminating in the upper-school inculcation of self-reliance and duty to others. New, though, is the thorny issue of class. This is established when Jack's revelation of state school provenance reduces the Saintbury-bound train carriage to disapproving silence. The habitual school-setting montage is then predominantly presented from Jack's point of view, a high angle shot down on his upturned face emphasising the buildings' intimidating nature, though the pastoral score reassuringly anchors Saintbury in Britain's socio-cultural tradition. Mocked for his accent, attitudes and, not least, his admiration for his father's footballing honours—'no decent chap talks about soccer at a rugby school, do they?'—Jack's misery culminates at the Founder's Ceremony where his refusal to bow before the statue of Henry VIII and receive what he terms 'a kicking up the arse'[2] causes such peer outrage that he is dumped in a freshly-filled rubbish box (Fig. 3.1). Hartley, sharing their disgust, openly despairs at making of Fleming's experiment 'a decent, self-respecting Saintburian'. As ostracised as Stevenson's Tom Brown, Jack remains only after Lorraine's cogent evaluation of Saintbury as 'a New World' of opportunity, reinforced with empathetic essay assignments on Sir Francis Drake and the *Golden Hinde*. Persuaded not to 'run away from life', to stand up for what he believes in, but to understand that the other boys are not 'snobs', just 'brought up differently' (another example of advice difficult to equate with the evidence presented), he settles down to learn the workings of Latin and rugby, fagging and the obligatory canings from staff and sixth-formers (the latter featuring in Frears' generic montage).

Fig. 3.1   Ra-ra-ra, we're going to smash the oik!

His muted defence of Saintbury to his parents at Christmas illustrates his incipient 'moulding', cemented when he settles grievances with early nemesis and 'ruinous smear' Tracey (Tim Bateson) in gentlemanly fashion via a school gym boxing match rather than a common-room fist-fight. The boys become good friends, the lesson is learnt of the need for rules and ritual, and by the film's end Jack is a fully paid-up member of the educated elite, recipient of the new school bursary to Cambridge and, on seeing Hartley dishevelled after a final day 'ragging', declaring with admiration: 'gosh, sir, jolly good show!'

Though Richard Attenborough contended that the film was 'an *attack* on the class system' (McFarlane 1992: 16), it is hard to read *The Guinea Pig* as anything other than a palliative to the enduring institution of the British public school: for Marcia Landy 'the film is most revealing in its exposure of its recuperative strategies' and 'Jack, the guinea pig, is exemplary of the possibilities for bourgeoisification of the working class' (1991: 445). What militates against *both* these claims is that Jack, for all his initial 'Cockney sparrer' affectation, is not working class at all but a product of the post-war aspirational lower-middle class. Jack's father, an ex-sergeant major, is the proud owner of a tobacconist's in Walthamstow, securely placing him as a Thatcherite *avant la lettre* who shares Hartley's reactionary opinions: both see the need for deference to authority and the merits of stern discipline, and Read Snr, equating the roles of housemaster and sergeant major as taking raw recruits to 'make them into men', thanks Hartley (and Saintbury) for teaching team spirit, self-confidence and manners, 'things which they don't learn at other places'. It is the Arnoldian value code in every detail. Add in the readiness of Mrs Read (Joan Hickson) to work to pay for Jack's university studies, and there is little sense of radical class conflict in this family. Rather, the film offers 'a conflict not between two *different* ideological positions, but between two different articulations of what is at base the *same* ideological position' (Petley 2000: 21). In keeping with the Fleming Report's intentions, *The Guinea Pig* extends the Victorian principle of enabling a rapprochement between the aspiring middle class and the adaptive upper class in order to consolidate a single ruling elite. It also retains for a 'new world' scenario the narrative arc of a *Stalky and Co.*: the audience learns, like Jack, that all the fagging and flogging is justified as a training ground for the new technocracy that will lead Britain and what remains of its Empire. *Plus ça change…*

The Guinea Pig was unanimously praised for its direction and acting. The *MFB* noted 'some very smooth, sometimes amusing, somewhat thought-provoking entertainment' (November 1948: 155), though the nature of the thoughts provoked depended on the political affiliations of its reviewers. The conservative *Daily Graphic* was confident that 'you'll agree with me that there's a lot to be said for English public school system' (24 October 1948). Not so the communist *Daily Worker*: 'the film takes for granted the inherent superiority of the public school... While (gently) criticising snobbery, the film itself reeks of snobbery, and its patronising attitude to the "guinea pig" and his parents is as insufferable as it is unintentional' (25 October 1948). The liberal-leaning *Manchester Guardian* saw both sides of the argument: 'This is not, goodness knows, the first film about a British public school, but it is the first of them to be so truthful... And when one hears the film (like the play from which it was adapted) damned both for brandishing the "old school tie" and for being "socialist propaganda", then one is inclined to believe that it has, indeed, found the just, truthful, middle way' (25 October 1948). The *Sunday Times* also caught the consensual approach: 'the piece has two morals. The first, that the public schools should unbend a bit... The second, that the Common Boy has something to learn even from the nobs' (24 October 1948).

This hegemonic stance, that with mutual understanding all would be well with the public school system and therefore beyond, continued with a third film reworking of Thomas Hughes' generic foundation stone. An up-market move for George Minter's Renown production company, *Tom Brown's Schooldays* (Gordon Parry, May 1951), surviving an 'ungentlemanly' opportunistic re-release of the 1940 RKO film, pointedly presented itself in its opening credits as 'an Authentic British Film Version', made with the full co-operation of Rugby School. This authenticity ranged visually from the school hall's 'open plan' lessons to the (widely reported) reconstruction of a period-accurate rugby ball, while its narrative fidelity followed the plot development (excised from Stevenson and afforded melodramatic family connections in Wilson) where Dr Arnold (Robert Newton) asks Tom Brown (John Howard Davies) to 'mentor' the sickly, fatherless George Arthur (Glyn Dearman), leading to persistent conflicts with school bully Flashman (John Forrest, previously Jack's friendly mentor Fitch in *The Guinea Pig*).

Sue Harper and Vincent Porter considered *Tom Brown's Schooldays* 'a coherent attempt to situate the male public-school ethic at the very heart of national identity' (2003: 163) and, for all its costume drama and sports field emphases—Tom's early try-saving tackle proves that 'he's made of the right stuff'—Parry's version chimes heavily with *The Guinea Pig*. It offers thematic and structural parallels, with staged battles between a rump of reactionary masters committed to a tradition stultified by social conformism and prejudice—Flashman cannot be bad, they argue, since he comes from British East India Company people!—and those supportive of the Doctor's programme of moral and academic modernisation. It also shares incipient post-war concerns over disruptive male youth—this version's focus lies less with the Doctor or Brown than Flashman's proficiency at 'hazing' younger pupils—and expresses the benefits, for both individual and society, of a benign and nurturing environment. Allied to this, *Tom Brown's Schooldays* brings into sharper relief than afforded by the Boultings' class-centred film the benefits of female input to the hypermasculine public school universe—the 'Katherine Ellis effect' writ large. In *The Guinea Pig* the reformist principles of the female-named Lorraine were fuelled by Hartley's daughter, Lynne; the boys cheered Mrs Hartley (Edith Sharpe) for being 'a mother and a friend'; even Jack's teasing during his first vacation—'fancy making boys do the housework! Do you wear an apron?'—suggested a flexibility in gender roles clouded by rigid fagging rituals. More explicitly, in *Tom Brown's Schooldays* Arnold's struggle to reform Rugby's institutionalised tyranny and class prejudice is shaped by Mrs Arnold (Diana Wynyard) who, part of a holy trinity with Mrs Brown (Kathleen Byron) and Mrs Arthur (Rachel Gurney), leavens the headmaster's liberal but manly ethics with a compassionate maternality: Brown's duty to care for Arthur includes not just 'paternal' protection but 'maternal' companionship—or 'wet nursing' as teased by his friends; when Arnold has Arthur round for tea, the boy is framed between the headmaster's two young daughters offering strawberries and sympathy; motherhood is so narratively valorised that the cynical atheism of 'Scud' East (John Charlesworth) is traced to his own maternal abandonment. At a time of post-war reconstruction, the school as a surrogate family is foregrounded as the instrument for the amelioration—or overpowering—of adolescent behaviour (whatever the class) potentially disruptive to accepted societal norms. Critical reception was less nurturing, however, of a film 'all too genteelly proud of its brutalities' (*New Statesman*, 21 April 1951), and with 'no hint of the development from adolescence to maturity' (*Evening Standard*, 12 April 1951).

Whither the public schoolboy's formative structure and sense of adventure? The revisiting of the Second World War in 1950s cinema abandoned collective heroism for the revisionist celebration of individual heroism, invariably of public school-educated men. Raymond Durgnat sees the

CO–junior officer relationship of these films as paternal, reminiscent of the symbolic father–son drink shared in *Tell England* (1970: 140). It can equally be viewed as professorial, with British war films of the era invariably including headmagisterial commanding officers exercising a benign control over their prefectorial officer cadets. In what had latterly become exclusively an officers' war, emotional reserve in the face of mortal danger, coupled with the social and sporting ethos of the public school code, was everywhere on show, resonating further with intertextual school film-casting connotations. The enclosed world of prisoner of war films most completely fostered the replication of public school dynamics, as in *The Wooden Horse* (Jack Lee, 1950) with Leo Genn, and *The Colditz Story* (Guy Hamilton, 1955) with John Mills. Andy Medhurst (a touch harshly) dismisses the latter as 'a Billy Bunter story where Mr Quelch is a Nazi' and the war 'just a backdrop for masculine high jinks, a stirring test of strength and ingenuity' (1984: 35). If so minded, the same accusation could hold for *Angels One Five* (George More O'Ferrall, 1952) and the apotheosis of the genre, *The Dam Busters* (Michael Anderson, 1955), which modulates between 'typical' public school repression and cathartic homoerotic horseplay—'Come on, chaps: off with their trousers!' is the call from the officers' mess as one squadron looks to debag another. Elsewhere, the surprise in witnessing a pillar of stoic service emotionally overcome, as with Redgrave in *The Browning Version*, prepared for the breakdown of Jack Hawkins' Lt Commander Ericson before his first lieutenant Lockhart (Donald Sinden) in *The Cruel Sea* (Charles Frend, 1953).

For Neil Rattigan the 1950s war film, the decade's British generic mainstay, was a 'reflection of the last ditch effort by the dominant class to maintain its hegemony by re-writing the history of the celluloid war in its own favour' (1994: 150). Fast-forward to the end of the decade and the effort has been abandoned: the majority may have 'never had it so good', but the decent chaps who won the war had now lost their social function. Andrew Roberts notes how two military dramas replicate *Mr. Perrin and Mr. Traill* 'in depicting men whose essential immaturity is fostered by institutionalisation' (*Sight and Sound*, 17, 8, August 2007: 49). In *Tunes of Glory* (Ronald Neame, 1960) Alec Guinness plays Jock Sinclair, self-made major and self-satisfied bully who, in the cloistered environment of a Scottish military regiment, savours the social and psychological destruction of his new commanding officer, Lt Col Basil Barrow (John Mills again). In more comedic mode, *The League of Gentlemen* (Basil Dearden, 1960) has Jack Hawkins now the decommissioned Colonel Hyde who determines that his fellow former-officers, including Richard Attenborough's Lexy, need structure to obviate their decommissioned anomie, and so billets them in his country pile to plan a bank robbery with military precision. 'It's just like being back at school!' exclaims ex-Captain Stevens (Kieron Moore), cashiered for homosexual offences, when shown his sleeping quarters. 'I sincerely hope not!' replies his startled room-mate.

2   THE WRONG WOMAN

School may function as a metaphor for the national welfare, but as an enclosed, often enervated environment, it is also a fertile site for particular crimes of person or passion. Immediate pre-war cinematic teachers were largely respected as selfless defenders of tradition; post-war, however, the carapace more repeatedly cracked. *Take My Life* (Ronald Neame, May 1947), a British noir adapted from Winston Graham's story, finds its murder motive on school grounds. The search by opera star Philippa Talbot (Greta Gynt) to prove her husband innocent of killing his ex-girlfriend Elizabeth (Rosalie Crutchley) leads her to the isolated Penmair School in Scotland and a tense school tour with headmaster Sidney Fleming (Marius Goring), the real murderer of Elizabeth, his wife, whose vindictive divorce threats jeopardised his career—'the only thing in the world that matters to me', he avers passionately. The flip-side to the constructive partnerships lauded in *Goodbye, Mr. Chips* etc., the 'little tin god with his wonderful gift for teaching', as Elizabeth taunts him, is here undone by his love for the wrong woman. Widely praised—'this is the way to make a thriller and it's a great satisfaction to know that its British', enthused the *Sunday Dispatch* (25 May 1947)—the site work of Goring and Gynt proved a successful rehearsal for the first in a run of films where the supportive environments of a Brookfield or Marbledown, centres of a hierarchical society moulding the youth of its landed and warrior gentry, are replaced by representations of the public school, and especially its staffroom, as a site of bitterness and imprisonment, a new 'metaphor for a wider world of lovelessness, cruelty and repression' (Richards 1988: 262).

The source text for *Mr. Perrin and Mr. Traill* (Lawrence Huntington, 25 August 1948), written by Hugh Walpole in 1911 and 'the first successful novel about adults in a public school' (Quigly 1982: 182), was so obviously a *roman à clef* of Walpole's teaching career at Epsom College that the school ostracised him for 30 years, while *Housemaster* author Ian Hay decried 'the sort of realism which leaves nothing unphotographed' and strongly advised it not be recommended to schoolmasters (1914: 141–2). Two Cities Films, renowned for unifying wartime productions such as *This Happy Breed* (David Lean, 1944), reflected a shifting social barometer by optioning the rights to photograph Walpole's fractious fiction, updated to the present in L.A.G. Strong's 'A' certificated adaptation and given a star casting with youthful idealist David Traill played by Powell and Pressburger regular David Farrar, while the aging failure Vincent Perrin was taken by the normally urbane Marius Goring, again paired with Greta Gynt. The film, set at Banfield's College, a public school on the Cornish coast steadily losing cast through the tyrannical leadership of Mr Moy-Thompson (Raymond Huntley), pitches the instantly popular new sports master Traill against a jealous staffroom and especially against Perrin, senior housemaster but a crushed acolyte of the headmaster. Traill's announcement of his engagement to the woman Perrin secretly loves, doctor's assistant Isobel Lester (Gynt), breaks Perrin's sanity and leads him, in a literal cliff-hanger climax, to lose his life after attempting first to stab and then rescue Traill from the incoming tide.

Unlike several entries in the British school film genre, *Mr. Perrin and Mr. Traill* is an aesthetically accomplished work, with a provocative narrative, first-class characterisation, authentic dialogue, and shrewd, empathetic direction: Anthony Slide assesses it 'one of the best studies of English public school life, particularly of the relationship between the masters and the headmaster' (1985: 70). The minutiae of public school life are well observed, as are the tensions, professional and sexual, that Huntington captures in a series of tightly composed confrontations, skilfully lit by cinematographer Max Greene. Before any national metaphors, the senior common room here functions as a mirror of the pupils' domain, with a sadistic head bullying from above and inducing a constant jostling for position amongst a set of deeply frustrated men, their early professional ideals long moribund, constrained by their isolated environment and by each other. Moy-Thompson fuels their guilt and emasculation, pointing out how, unlike them, Traill served in the war, 'doing a man's work, playing a man's part in the fighting services'. The private sphere offers scant consolation as every school marriage is loveless, the wives as withered and poisonously rumour-mongering as their husbands. Rather than inculcating any 'toughness of fibre' the pupil body is equally constrained, with Traill derided for placing a 'wretched, nervous, shrinking' boy in the rugby team so that his courage can develop. The school's Prize Day speech from visitor Sir Joshua Varley (Finlay Currie) is as replete with the empty platitudes of the public school code as Frank Simmons' opening remarks in *Young Woodley*—'it is the proud boast of our British schools that we breed not brains but character!'—and supports the view of resident cynic Birkland (Edward Chapman) that Banfield's is 'like a decaying tooth: it doesn't trouble you much once the nerve's dead'. Here, though, the roots are examined, and prepare for the more severe school renderings of *If…..*

Much as Chipping is the embodiment of Brookfield, so Perrin is Banfield's personified, the school's falling numbers and 'stinking' reputation under Moy-Thompson mirrored by the teacher's (effectively nuanced) psychological decline and his increasingly strident responses to Traill: when the new man overrides a Perrin detention so pet pupil Rogers (Donald Barclay) can play in a rugby match, Perrin accuses him of looking to 'subvert authority, or to turn Banfield's College into a bear garden'. Pre-war staff conflicts over educational philosophy had sided with the elder statesman and proven the merits of retaining all that is good in tradition—thus Donkin wins over Ovington, Chips over Ralston—but no longer. The redundant lineage is given an explicit visual coding by presenting Goring's Perrin very much in the image of Robert Donat's Chipping with greying hair, rough moustache and fusty clothing. The imagery here accentuates a fossilised inflexibility: Perrin, an unloved pedantic disciplinarian unable to inspire his pupils, is trapped on the trajectory that Chipping's career would have followed without that rejuvenating 'someone else'. The timings are pointedly equivalent: Chips had been 20 years at Brookfield when he met Katherine; Perrin has 21 years' service at Banfield's when he is beaten to Isobel's affections. The film's final image of Rogers shouting 'Goodbye, Pompo' into the master's room cements the generic intertextuality. The work's title and examination of an educated man's descent into criminal schizophrenia also suggest a pedagogical overlaying of the Dr Jekyll and Mr Hyde paradigm and Traill can be read as Perrin's alter-ego: both teach Mathematics and work in the same house, but Traill, at ease with Isobel, popular with the boys and unfazed by Moy-Thompson, is the man and master that Perrin subconsciously wishes he could have been. The division can also be applied to sexuality: Walpole was gay and his novel is interpreted as having a gay subtext (Quigly 1982: 182), and while the film omits Perrin's final kissing of Traill's hand and Isobel's Edwardian *garçonne* appearance and manner, its emotional dynamics can still support a gay reading. Perrin's cliff-top stammering of his grievances to Traill— 'Taken away everything that makes life endurable… Used to like teaching. Taken away Rogers… Took away Miss Lester'—can imply that Perrin loves Traill, is jealous of his attentions to the real or/and coded 'boy' and finally sacrifices himself so Traill can enjoy unhindered his new relationship. The internal struggles to 'do right' or cede to his repressed passions are narrativised when a sleepwalking Perrin wakes, horrified, just as he has reached Traill's bedside, and visualised when Perrin's disintegrating mental state, supported by an agitated musical score and mise-en-scène foregrounding a cracked lightshade and encroaching darkness, makes him see, in place of the solicitous school chaplain, a goading, laughing Traill. Such scenes bear interpretation as a coded homosexual dilemma—a conflict that, in the film's (and novel's) terms, can only be resolved by death. Fear as much as pettiness may finally explain his unyielding refusal to share with Traill the communal bathroom—Perrin literally in the closet. Contemporary reviews were equally divided, lauding a 'capital pedagogic atmosphere' (*Daily Herald*, 27 August 1948) or else lamenting 'a kind of "period caricature"' (*Manchester Guardian*, 28 August 1948). Britain's trade press liked how 'This picture, at once noble and mean, warm and frigid, funny and austere, carefully mirrors and analyses the psychology of the schoolmaster' and evaluated it 'Without question, the best school yarn since *Goodbye, Mr. Chips*' (*Kinematograph Weekly*, 19 August 1948). America's *Newsweek* went even further: perhaps influenced by Traill's final denunciation of the 'torment' wrought by Moy-Thompson, its conclusion that, 'in its basic intent *Mr. Perrin and Mr. Traill* resembles the brilliant Swedish study of faculty neurosis, *Torment* [(Alf Sjoberg, 1944)]' (31 January 1949), placed Banfield's alongside Bergman.[3]

2.1   Section Prize Winner: The Browning Version *(1951)*

Providing Traill with an updated backstory whilst leaving Perrin with the values of a Victorian pedagogue doubly stacked the odds in Huntington's film. A more contemporary source text—and value system—was provided by Terence Rattigan, whose successful one-act play *The Browning Version* premiered in September 1948 with Eric Portman and Mary Ellis in the leads. Based on an incident from Rattigan's Harrow schooldays when a stern Classics master, J.W. Coke Norris, received a pupil's leaving gift with scant gratitude, the imaginative extrapolation of a life of emotional repression resonated with the playwright's current position as a homosexual in fashionable London. Anthony Asquith, having just filmed Rattigan's *The Winslow Boy* (1948), was immediately interested, though finding backers for such downbeat material proved difficult, Two Cities/Javelin eventually picking up the film rights with Rattigan adapting his own play. At Asquith's behest, Andrew Crocker-Harris was played by (former Modern Languages teacher) Michael Redgrave, while cast as his wife Millie was Jean Kent (after Margaret Lockwood declined the part). The play adhered to the 'three unities' of time, place and action, unfolding entirely in the drawing-room of Crocker-Harris' school cottage on a late-July evening: the film version opens this out, permitting a visual display of the generic rhythms and rituals of public school life including morning chapel, cricket and Prize Day, adds a 20-minute exposition to sketch in the main protagonists and, most controversially, changes the ending by allowing Crocker-Harris to deliver a valedictory speech. Filmed at Pinewood Studios with school exteriors shot at Sherborne, *The Browning Version* premiered in London on 13 March and New York on 29 October 1951: for most overseas markets it was retitled *The Shadow of a Man*. In the film Andrew Crocker-Harris is enduring his last day after 18 years as Classics master, ill-health having compelled him to retire early and work instead at a private 'crammer'—a 'school for backward boys'. He knows he has been a failure in his relationships with his pupils, colleagues, and wife: the boys see him only as a petty tyrant; the headmaster Frobisher (Wilfrid Hyde-White) denies him a pension; his younger, serially unfaithful wife is having an affair with the pointedly named Science master, Frank Hunter (Nigel Patrick). The cold, unsympathetic manner that Crocker-Harris has established to withstand these humiliations suddenly cracks when a pupil, Taplow (Brian Smith), brings him a farewell present—Robert Browning's version of the *Agamemnon* bearing the inscription that 'God from afar looks graciously upon a gentle master'. Newly decisive, Crocker-Harris leaves his wife, defies the headmaster by speaking last at Prize Day, and wins sympathetic applause after confessing to all his regret at 'degrading the noblest calling a man can follow, the care and moulding of the young'.

The Browning Version is today highly regarded: for Bruce Eder it 'could be the best adaptation of a modern play ever done to the screen' (DVD commentary, Criterion Collection, 2007). Key to this reputation is Redgrave's towering central performance, for Raymond Durgnat 'derived surely, from the most meticulous observation of the mannerisms of an almost vanished pedagogic type—the classical pedant whose very mouth closes like a cane' (1970: 191–2). In its generic context, the film offers another study in the devalued cultural currency of the post-war public school and of its staff as incorporating national values. The belittling parallels with the titular Greek tragedy where Agamemnon is murdered by his wife Clytemnestra and her lover—Hunter's warning to Crocker-Harris that his wife is 'out to kill' him is effected at an emotional level with her bitter undermining of Taplow's motives—are entirely lost on Crocker-Harris whose pedagogy has rendered Greek tragedy, for him and for his pupils, an arid exercise in construing before a passionate and 'timeless' work relatable to life as lived. Crocker-Harris may evoke bathetic classical echoes, but he is no Chipping, growing into personal veneration and professional fulfilment through a loving companionship. Instead, in its realisation of a teacher's wasted life *The Browning Version* operates as a deliberate antithesis to the earlier Donat vehicle with pupil cruelty to an unloved master—narratively broached but quickly erased with Chipping—now in full and enduring focus. *Mr. Perrin and Mr. Traill* made visual references to Chipping in its antiphonal presentation: here the riposte is explicitly articulated, Millie contrasting her husband's ignominious departure with that undoubtedly awaiting his successor, Gilbert (Ronald Howard)—'it'll be roses, roses all the way, and tears and cheers and "Goodbye, Mr. Chips"'. Intertextual markers abound: for instance, we learn that Crocker-Harris, a Classicist like Chips, also met his future wife while on a walking tour (as in Hilton's novel) in the Lake District. The results, though, are explicitly divergent with Crocker-Harris' professional failure rooted in his failed marriage, Millie's open affair(s) prompting her husband's emotional withdrawal into the role of school timetabler and his concomitant obsession with punctuality.

There are less dialectic differences, however, especially at the chalk-face. Whereas *Goodbye, Mr. Chips*, like *Housemaster*, offered set-piece debates on shifting educational patterns, *The Browning Version* effects a visual contrast of classroom practice, intercut scenes reinforcing the growing tension between the conformity, ritual and tradition with which Crocker-Harris is identified, and less prescribed parameters of social and educational behaviour exemplified by Hunter and his pupil-centred methodology. In Hunter's brightly lit Chemistry class, the teacher engages informally with his 'young budding Einsteins' who gather round the cluttered front desk and laugh loudly at shared jokes in a shared space before leaving early. By contrast, the Classics classroom is dark, the pupils sitting immobile and uninterested in regimented rows until the appointed hour, while Crocker-Harris, ensconced behind his high desk, dominates the tensely silent space. Gilbert's (callow) criticism of such rigid authority, declaring that his search for 'human nature' is not to be found in Latin verses, is patronisingly dismissed by Crocker-Harris: 'Ah, the modern psychological method'. The mise-en-scène, however, counters their mutual contempt: exemplifying the psychological dysfunctionality that has bled from private into professional spheres, the blackboard beside them bears an *Agamemnon* extract describing Menelaus' all-too-human despair on being abandoned by his wife Helen.[4] Similarly, for all its life and laughter, the headmaster (whose skills in corporate management before pedagogy again prepares the ground for *If….*) disapproves of Hunter's lessons for having 'no sense of discipline': his caveat more explicitly articulates underlying tensions centred on shifting stances towards authority, and realigns the classroom scenes as an ambivalent instance of how 'The irretrievable loss of a sense of national identity is played out in the post-war films' (Landy 1991: 49).

While *The Browning Version* is ambivalent towards 'modern' educational practices, its gender depictions betray an unreconstructed cultural misogyny. With the castrating Millie ostracised for exercising agency over her sexual desires, the film ostensibly displaces blame onto the adulterous woman, 'thus reinforcing the exclusive masculine codes of the public school' (Leach 2004: 188). Again, though, the sexuality of the film's creators, Asquith, Rattigan and the bisexual Redgrave invites more veiled or 'paraphrased' interpretations that can mitigate the miserabilist portrayal of Millie.[5] Crocker-Harris' subject, Classics, is resonant with an 'openly erotic homosexual literature' (Gathorne-Hardy 1979: 215) and his discussion with Hunter of 'two kinds of love', diegetically referencing the heterosexual couple's intellectual and physical incompatibility, is also readable as signifying 'the love that dare not speak its name', with Millie's viperish character articulating a coded critique of heteronormativity. This can be further construed with Crocker-Harris' 'conversion', initiated by his relationship with an admiring pupil. Taplow, who like Rogers with Perrin is alone in his regard for 'the Crock', has stronger associations with his teacher in the film version: when his private-tuition enthusiasm for the *Agamemnon*'s 'more lurid aspects of dramaturgy' elicits Crocker-Harris' confession of his own youthful free translation, the exchange's shot and counter-shot editing intimates a growing bond inevitably smothered in more public situations. That a young boy is the vehicle for restoring Crocker-Harris' sense of manhood intimates that sexuality rather than pedagogical shortcomings is the underlying cause of his unhappiness and that, 'If the film exposes his repression as sexual, it also suggests that his pedantic relationship to the young men he teaches has been, like his marriage, a defence against his desires' (Landy 1991: 280) (Fig. 3.2). His farewell speech can thus be read as 'a memorable and moving "coming out" statement' (Bourne 1996: 101).

Fig. 3.2　Crocker-Harris and Greek love

The cinematic expansion of the play has been considered a semantic shrinking, with metaphor ceding to mimesis: 'By opening out to include the life of the whole school and the Crocker-Harris's relations with other members of the staff the film undermines the universal implications of Crocker-Harris's tragedy, narrowing attention onto his role as a master of a public school' (Darlow and Hodson 1979: 160). Others argue that the film reveals 'an inevitable association between the failure of human relationships and the ritual and politics of the educational system in which they are embedded' (Leach 2004: 188). Whether the teacher has failed the system or vice versa, *The Browning Version* both dramatises and ironises the British myth of stoical acceptance: this may not render it 'universal', but it foregrounds the experiences of the British middle to upper-middle classes and the film ends not with a complete Chips-style professional redemption—despite the rousing Beethoven that accompanies his walk to the school gates Crocker-Harris is too old for that—but with another vestige of the imperial public school archetype evident in films such as

Scott of the Antarctic, the very British concept of the 'heroic defeat'. With this confirming national tone, *The Browning Version* was feted in overseas film festivals: Redgrave won Best Actor and Rattigan Best Screenplay at the 1951 Cannes Film Festival, while the film itself, nominated for the Palme d'Or, won a Bronze Bear at the Berlin Film Festival. At home the *Daily Mirror* considered it 'a superb British film' that 'out-chips *Mr. Chips*' with Redgrave 'giving one of the greatest performances ever seen in films' (16 March 1957). The review was unusual in focusing solely on film referents: with so recent a source text, much critical response centred on the adaptation, and the demerits of its additions. C.A. Lejeune lambasted 'a valedictory address that must have alarmed more parents, and embarrassed more boys and masters, than any words ever uttered on the occasion of a public school leaving ceremony' and berated how Crocker-Harris 'alienates our sympathy by pleading for it so abjectly' in a film version where 'nothing is left to the imagination' (*Observer*, 18 March 1951). America was also underwhelmed: John McCarthy saw it 'steer a nice course between the treacly nonsense of *Goodbye, Mr Chips* and the beat-him-when-he-sneezes rules of *Tom Brown's School Days*', but adjudged it 'no movie at all but an extraordinarily clever enlarged photograph of an inconsiderable play' (*New Yorker*, 3 November 1951).

3   THE HAY SCHOOL

Magic in school is not entirely the preserve of J.K. Rowling and Harry Potter: a forerunner can be found in *Vice Versa*, the 1882 novel written by F. Anstey (aka Thomas Anstey Guthrie), where pompous Victorian stockbroker Paul Bultitude, the unwitting possessor of an Indian stone with magical properties, wishes himself into the place of his reluctant boarding-school-bound son Dick, who eagerly reciprocates. In their new bodies and environments hilarity ensues, and when both return to their rightful states a fuller mutual understanding strengthens family bonds. A first screen version from London Film Productions (March 1916), directed by the prolific Maurice Elvey, featured a tour de force from Edward O'Neill as fearsome headmaster Dr Grimstone. Post-war, Will Hay alumnus Peter Ustinov rewrote and directed *Vice Versa* (28 January 1948) for Two Cities. The film's credit-titles, with lantern slides occasionally inserted upside-down, introduced Roger Livesey and debutant Anthony Newley as father and son. Following their switch of bodies but not of nature, a divergent carnivalesque ensues as firm patron Dick indulges in drinking lemonade, ruins a football game and organises children's parties while pupil Paul smokes cigars and voices his reactionary views on child-rearing, much to the consternation of cane-wielding Grimstone (James Robertson Justice) and his daughter, Dulcie (Petula Clark), prior recipient of Dick's adolescent affections. The body-swap inverts social space and instigates ameliorative family dialogue, while the 'adult' pupil's school antics could, at a pinch, be seen to offer transgressive play on sexual exploitation as a young boy chases a mature maid around the house: overall, though, the societal and sexual politics remain resolutely Victorian with Robert Eddison's high camp Mr Blinkhorn and Kay Walsh's vampish Fanny Verlane overwhelming a limp Boer War satire. The class and classroom politics are, Raymond Durgnat notes, similarly outdated, since 'By 1945 the educational tone has completely shifted away from the thunderous and paranoid authoritarianism of a Grimsdyke' (sic) (1970: 115). Whether nostalgia for an age of stable social order or 'a burlesque of the book, with additions designed to make us laugh at those foolish Victorians' (*MFB*, January 1948: 17), the *Daily Graphic* found *Vice Versa* 'to have scarcely any connection with true cinema' (30 January 1948) and it performed indifferently at the box office.

Generic retrospection remained a post-war staple, however, and the ghost of Will Hay returned in the shape of Cockney comedian Ronald Shiner with *Top of the Form* (John Paddy Carstairs, February 1953), a straight remake of *Good Morning, Boys*. 'Straight' in the sense of an exact copy of public school setting, plot and characterisation (Shiner at least changes his name to Professor Ronnie Fortescue and prior profession to bookmaker); 'straight' in not securing a West End premiere and going straight to the suburban rounds; 'straight' also in the sense of lacking in humour. Such, at least, was the view of the *MFB* for whom 'The comedy, poorly scripted, is slow and unfunny, and depends mainly on slapstick and slap and tickle' (April 1953: 57). Another misguided attempt at media transposition emerged with the small independent Adelphi Films' production of *Fun at St. Fanny's* (Maurice Elvey 40 years on, January 1956). Comedian Douglas Robinson's persona of Cardew 'The Cad' of St Fanny's School had become a post-war radio and comic-strip regular, though the film gave top billing to television star Fred Emney as devious headmaster Dr Septimus Jankers, an evident extrapolation of Hay's gambling-obsessed dispenser of bogus information, while Claude Hulbert's ineffectual Mr Winkle added a casting connection to St Michael's. Seaming a long-exhausted vein of corny puns and variety-style set pieces, the cursory plotline has Cardew a 25-year-old serial year-repeating pupil at St Fanny's and heir to a fortune which passes to the school should he be expelled. Jankers, in serious debt to his bookmakers, devises a plan to plant a stolen painting on the 'Cad'—another Hay steal—and thus expedite his expulsion: it is foiled by bookmaker's sister, Maisie (Vera Day), who (incredulously) falls in love with Cardew. More Calvary than Carnival, the film, released without a major circuit deal, was crucified by the press, Alan Brien berating 'Some of the rottenest chestnuts I have had thrown at me in twenty years' (*Evening Standard*, 15 December 1955), though Roy Nash admitted a grudging, quasi-patriotic admiration for 'the British school joke stretched almost to infinity' (*Star*, 16 December 1955).

Undeterred, along came another tall tale set in another impecunious academy 'for the sons of gentlefolk'. *Bottoms Up!* (Mario Zampi, 18 April 1960) was another series adaptation, now of the immensely popular BBC television Jimmy Edwards vehicle *Whack-O!* (1956–60), where the failing Chiselbury academy served predominantly as a motor for the ill-conceived money-making schemes of bewhiskered and cane-wielding headmaster 'Professor' James Edwards, MA (applied for)—think Phil Silvers' Sergeant Bilko in gown and mortarboard. The film finds Edwards, faced with dismissal, claiming to host a refuge-seeking Eastern Prince, a role feigned by Cecil Biggs (Melvyn Hayes), free-loading son of the inevitable money-owed bookmaker. The plan goes awry when the real Prince Hassan (Paul Castaldini) is posted by the Foreign Office and Cecil is mistakenly kidnapped by enemy agents. Meanwhile Edwards must contend with an anti-caning pupil rebellion, organised with military precision by bishop's son Wendover (John Mitchell). The rebellion is survived, the Prince's safety secured, and Edwards is covered in glory.

Resolutely 'residual' for content and character,[6] the plot of *Bottoms Up!* is an amalgam of the television series' opening 1956 episode, 'The School Strike,' and the post-imperial exploitation/xenophobia first seen in *The Belles of St. Trinian's*, while its leads are a throwback to the late-1930s, with Chair of Governors, Lady Gore-Willoughby (Martita Hunt), a reverse-named homage to *Good Morning, Boys*' Colonel and Edwards a more hirsute—and flagellomaniacal—Will Hay principal. A sequence featuring an elongated cane and purpose-built platform for mass public canings grotesquely extends the genre's corporal punishment trope to breaking point (Fig. 3.3); the resultant pupil uprising, resolved only by major concessions, equally prolongs the generic carnivalesque. The film's title reassuringly conveys the headmaster's pre-existent penchant for canings and alcohol, and offers a sexual connotation impossible on television—publicity posters foregrounded, in basque and mortarboard, the school's

Fig. 3.3   The eponymous breaking point

'blond-bombshell' matron (Vanda Hudson)—but the film itself remains as chaste as an edition of *Magnet*. *Bottoms Up!* is, however, significantly 'emergent' in its use of source text. The television sitcom film adaptation or 'spin off', for Andrew Higson an 'important if under-valued' strand in British cinema (1994: 233), is a low-budget domestically-marketed production strategy largely associated with the 1970s, but it can be traced back to three outriders over a decade earlier: *I Only Arsked* (Montgomery Tully, 1958), *Inn for Trouble* (C.M. Pennington-Richards, 1960) and, bringing up the rear, *Bottoms Up!*. The press mostly warmed to the film's 'breezy, good-humoured fun' that 'debunks the snobbish English private school system without malice' (*Kinematograph Weekly*, 10 March 1960): Alexander Walker noted that 'you cannot really take it out on a film which has the nerve to rhyme "gaudeamus" with "pyjamas"' (*Evening Standard*, 10 March 1960); William Whitebait could, lamenting a television transfer 'bogged down in the push-over routines that will finally close cinemas' (*New Statesman*, 19 March 1960).

The strain continued, nonetheless. The Boulting brothers' 'evangelical' *Guinea Pig* period ceded from the mid-1950s to comedies such as their satirical *I'm All Right, Jack* (1959): hot on its (high) heels came *A French Mistress* (19 September 1960), made for British Lion and based on Robert Monro's successful stage farce. The plot turns on John Crane, MA (Cecil Parker), headmaster at Melbury Boys Public School, hastily appointing, sight unseen, a new French teacher: 'he' turns out to be glamorous Mlle Madeleine Lafarge (Agnès Laurent). Her appearance, soon in tennis shorts or bikini, occasions an unprecedented popularity for French and a heart's desire for both head boy Edmonds (Scot Finch) and the head's son, sports master Colin (Ian Bannen). However, fearing she is his daughter from a past affair, Crane Snr insists on Madeleine's departure: cue a pupil strike led by Edmonds and the threat to burn down the school gymnasium. The boy's blimpish Colonel father (Thorley Walters), Chair of Governors, calls an emergency meeting, the head's fears prove groundless and Madeleine stays—but the gym still burns down. *A French Mistress* has been read as socially 'emergent' in charting 'the shift from quasi-Victorian values to the new sexual openness, focusing along the way upon the guilt and confusion attendant in the transition' (Wells 2000: 62). In its school generic context, Madeleine's geographical and gendered 'otherness' allows an 'objective' critique of British education, highlighted by her confusion that her own professional and personal integrity, supposedly the raison d'être of a public school upbringing, occasions such Dionysian abandon amongst this Arnoldian league of gentlemen. Aesthetically, however, the film is relaxedly 'residual', full of schoolboy innuendo: this begins with the opening credits, labelling expected British male types such as deputy head Robert Martin (James Robertson Justice)—'His pupils are the "beat" generation—well beaten'; it continues with the pupils, outraged at the prospect of a (mature) woman teacher, preparing signs reading 'You can't can-can here' and (intertextually) 'We're all right, Jacqueline!' The arrival of the Bardotesque Lafarge instantly changes Melbury to a locus for carnival as men and boys, in *Housemaster*-style, forsake their code and principles, resorting to voyeurism, erotic poetry and even—heavens above!—cutting cricket practice. That Colonel Edmonds is central to solving the sexual complexities—'your mouth doesn't water for a peach unless the fruit is displayed in an attractive manner', he offers at one point—suggests a denouement that moulds difference into an unreconstructed patriarchal public school ethos, rather like *The Guinea Pig*. However, race and gender make their gentle mark, and *A French Mistress* ultimately escapes the carnivalesque since its subversion is not totally annulled: Steven Allen notes how 'active protest, long associated with the French, has replaced the placards that greeted her arrival' (2010: 455), and while it is excessive to see Melbury's gym burning as presaging 1968's student riots and *If....*, it adds a Nero-esque ambivalence to the colonel's closing self-satisfaction. The critical reception showed scant *entente cordiale* with only *The Times* supporting 'a Good Farcical Comedy' (3 September 1960): *Kinematograph Weekly* termed it a '*Whack-O!* cum *Young Woodley* comedy' and 'far from consistently funny', especially in its 'hint at possible incest' (5 September 1960), while the *MFB* pleaded for 'some relation to contemporary English life' and concluded that 'It is time surely that we pensioned off, even in farce, these phoney English public schools, fire-eating colonels, bird-watching vicars, sporty cane-brandishers and all the other dearly loved images of "the English as they see themselves"' (October 1960: 142).

It was not to happen. ABPC's *Tamahine* (Philip Leacock, 18 July 1963), based on Thelma Niklaus' novel, offers a near-exact re-run of the Boultings' farce, replacing the European with an Oriental 'other'. When her ex-pat father dies, 17-year-old half-Polynesian Tamahine (the 'Chinese Bardot' Nancy Kwan) is sent to England to stay with her uncle Charles Poole (Dennis Price), headmaster of the prestigious Hallow Boys Public School. Her exotic beauty and uninhibited behaviour, parading in her underwear, placing a chamber-pot on the steeple and, worst of all, excelling on Sports Day, create the expected institutional upheaval: she undermines Poole's confidence in what he comes to term the 'pompous' tenets of his school, causes Art master Tim Clove (Derek Nimmo) to rethink his proposed marriage to Poole's daughter Diana (Justine Lord), and distracts Poole's infatuated seventh-form son Richard (the 32-year-old John Fraser) from his studies. The racial stereotyping of South Pacific promiscuity (and mockery of the eastern accent in the school's title?) is, in mitigation, matched by the depiction of joylessly repressed British academia. Again some pre-Anderson public school satire gently strikes, notably Tamahine's innocent questioning of how Officer Cadet training squares with the message of the school chaplain. And as with French mistress Madeline, Tamahine's carnivalesque influence escapes a full resolution: while Clove confirms that Diana is the woman he loves and Richard marries Tamahine and stays on as headmaster-elect with his dutifully supportive child-rearing wife, Poole, convinced by his niece's Polynesian message of freedom, disappears for a free-loving Gauguin-esque existence on her native island—a match again on cultural exchanges. The film's tagline ran 'She loved the whole form—and they loved hers!', but the critics proved more resistant, either regretting 'a potentially good satirical idea, whose edge is taken off by its subservience to the rules and conventions of British light comedy' (*Financial Times*, 19 July 1963), or castigating a 'thin, depressingly familiar and weakly scripted story' that retained 'a certain faint, nostalgic charm (sports day, tea on the lawn, punting on the river etc.)' (*MFB*, July 1963: 133–4). Though residual before emergent fare, such insistent female disruption brings a delayed entry to girls' schools on film.

4   THE GIRLS' PUBLIC SCHOOL CARNIVALESQUE

Few girls' schools existed before the late nineteenth century: Roedean (1885) first followed the boys' model, and set the trend for subsequent girls' public school curricula and values. As with boys' education, a variety of establishments functioned under the 'public school' umbrella, including home, suburban and finishing schools. Again the cheaper alternatives to full-boarding serviced the needs of the expanding middle classes: they were often family run, and for girls emphasised a more 'feminine' curriculum of arts and music; they also served as the setting for most cinematic treatments.

The earliest cinematic trope, the misbehaving pupil, can be seen, in works such as *Girls Indulging in a Pillow Fight* (Warwick Trading Company, 1901), *Rebellious Schoolgirls* and *Schoolgirl Rebels* (Hepworth 1907 and 1915), to have made intermittent modulations into faintly eroticised displays of feminine disorder. The interwar years saw no serious film treatment of female secondary education though music hall eventually crept behind the doors of girls' public schools. The best was *Things Are Looking Up* (Albert de Courville, April 1935), a Gaumont-British vehicle for stage and revue star Cicely Courtneidge replete with carnivalesque potential in its role swaps and settings, centred on staff before student misbehaviour. When Bertha Fytte, mistress at Miss MacTavish's School for Young Ladies, elopes overnight with the wrestler from a travelling circus, her identical twin sister, Cicely, the circus proprietor, steps in until Bertha can be found, keeping the affair from the school authorities. Far less strict than her cantankerous sister and with little interest (or ability) in Latin or geometry, Cicely captivates the pupils—her circus animal impressions in Natural History have them in hysterics—and, with the headmistress due to retire, sufficiently impresses her colleagues for the returning and now-wiser Bertha to inherit the top job. The invasion of the school domain by the 'second world' of the circus brings into play a comportment that, through humour and chaos, subverts and liberates the prim and over-formal assumptions of the dominant style and, in allowing a realisation of the benefits of a ludic and loving approach to pedagogy, creates an alternative social space where the pupil voice carries weight: an (uncredited) debutante Vivien Leigh affirms she will leave unless Miss Fytte is made the new headmistress. While Courtneidge's comedic eccentricities of gait highlight her difference from normative notions of femininity, here Cicely's romance with the music teacher Van Gaard (William Gargan) allows her to escape her usual 'desexualised "aunt" figure' (Sutton 2000: 202). There is no sign, however, of Bakhtin's 'grotesque realism' with sex removed off-screen in Bertha's elopement with the 'Big Black Fox': nor the conspiratorial salaciousness promised by the casting of music hall star Max Miller who, yet to gain his own, more libidinous comedy vehicles with Warner, ambles through another toned-down character part; instead, *Things Are Looking Up* remains with Courtneidge's 'wholesome, cheerful fooling' (Low 1985: 138). While Stephen Shafer posits that the film's very title would have 'helped public spirits in general during troubled times' (2003: 134), contemporary reviews found little to praise beyond the lead's talents: for *Film Weekly* 'Miss Courtneidge triumphantly proves herself capable of putting over a one-woman farce with very little assistance from anybody' (19 April 1935). Such female self-sufficiency—even here compromised by her character's rare romance—would prove rare in the cinematic classroom.

Two male-led, lower-grade efforts sandwiched Courtneidge's film. *Girls, Please!* (Jack Raymond, July 1934), made for Herbert Wilcox' British and Dominions company, starred Yorkshire's chubby stage-star Sydney Howard as the Physical Education teacher Trampleasure at Highleigh Girls School. Left in charge when headmistress Miss Prout (Lena Halliday) is called away, Trampleasure is faced with the concerted attempts of new pupil Renée van Hoffenheim (Jane Baxter) to elope with her beau Jim Arundel (Edward Underdown). Howard's frantic efforts to thwart the young couple's plans and maintain school dignity rehearse several tropes later foregrounded in the genre: combatting a St Trinian's-esque class revolt; resisting the nubile new French mistress—Jim's sister Ann (Meriel Forbes) in disguise; and, especially, dressing up as Prout to impress a (bogus) school inspector. All ends well as Trampleasure and Ann persuade Renée's father

(*Good Morning, Boys*' Peter Gawthorne) to agree to the marriage. It was considered 'an amusing farce, spoilt only by a number of unnecessarily suggestive lines' (*MFB*, August 1934: 57). In similar vein was *Please Teacher* (Stafford Dickins, 2 August 1937), an ABPC vehicle for diminutive song and dance funny-man Bobby Howes. Based on a play by K.R.G. Browne, Tommy Deacon (Howes) learns that a gift bequeathed by his aunt is hidden in her house in a bust of Napoleon. On finding that the house has become a girls' private school, Tommy pretends to be brother to a sixth-form pupil in order to gain admission. Howes is soon spilling his heart in song to his supposed sister (the ubiquitous René Ray) and is pursued by a Chinaman (future Brookfield head, Lyn Harding) who wants back a stolen jewelled cup that Anne's real brother sent to the school. The negligible plot is the pretext for a succession of comic and musical interludes, as when Tommy, caught in the girls' dormitory, stages a gravity-defying sleepwalking masquerade. While accepted as 'very good fun', it was emphasised that the film's events and settings 'not unnaturally, bear little resemblance to any conceivable school' (*MFB*, February 1937: 30).

The girls' school film reappeared post-war, via France, in Pinnacle Productions' *The Romantic Age* (Edmond T. Gréville, 29 November 1949). Awarded a restrictive 'A' certificate in Britain and less coyly retitled *Naughty Arlette* for its American release, the film, based on the 1946 French novel *Lycée des Jeunes Filles* by Serge Véber, centres on middle-aged Arnold Dickson (Hugh Williams) who becomes the first male teacher at Lyttleton Hall Girls Finishing School where his daughter Julie (Petula Clark) also enrols as a pupil. As revenge for a perceived classroom slight, 'sophisticated' (and over-accented) French student Arlette Tessereau (24-year-old Mai Zetterling) sets about seducing her new teacher who is soon ready to jettison his career and marriage until Julie shames him out of his infatuation. *The Romantic Age* exhibits a carnivalesque inversion of social norms in the daughter's containment of her father's desires, and in the exasperated butler's final (and fetishistic) spanking of the putative *femme fatale* with her hairbrush. The corrective is earlier threatened by Arnold's wife, Helen (Margot Grahame): her exasperated cry that 'if the consequences weren't so serious, it would be laughable' is true of the film itself, a tonally uncertain, broken-backed affair. The comedy of its early scenes fits ill with the dark tone of its climax: when the camera cuts to a rain-spattered puddle as Arlette finally seduces Arnold on a nature ramble, classroom banter and dormitory dares switch to a barely disguised terror at the destructive potential of post-war liberated female teenage sexuality, especially on a man of 'the romantic age', defined by the knowing girls as one who 'stops trying to dodge temptation and starts checking out if he's missed any'. Intertextually, the film offers greater consistency: chronologically situated mid-way between *Good Morning, Boys* and *A French Mistress*, each film manifests a mistrust of the French for their overt sexuality, seemingly synonymous in British eyes with a duplicitous and dangerous 'otherness'. The film itself met with manifest mistrust, the *Manchester Guardian* calling it 'one of those works which people will remember when they are trying to decide which was the worst film of the year' (3 December 1949).

Concurrent and contrasting with this French temptation, the Northern music hall tradition returned to the cinematic classroom as George Minter's Renown, before moving up-market with Tom Brown, released *Old Mother Riley, Headmistress* (John Harlow, January 1950), the thir- teenth (and penultimate) Nettlefold Studios' programme filler featur- ing 'pantomime dame' Arthur Lucan. Here Lucan's Irish washerwoman sees daughter Kitty (real-life wife Kitty McShane) lose her job as a Music teacher at the exclusive St Mildred's School for Young Ladies. In the way of these films, Mother Riley comes into an inheritance, buys the school and reinstates (the clearly incompetent) Kitty, though the narrative pat- terns of renunciatory maternal melodrama are quickly inverted as Mother Riley clearly has the better time. Cue high jinks as Lucan, in trademark poke-bonnet, shawl and button-boots, throws him/herself into the new role, be it taking gym lessons, playing 'The Minstrel Boy' on a haunted piano or cheating at the customary Sports Day finale. Here is *prima facie* a clear carnivalesque paradigm in its employment of the female figure of misrule, with 'otherness' enthroned and its principles enhanced, leading to refreshed social arrangements. And yet, for all Lucan's promise of class and gender fluidity, the slapstick humour is circumscribed by a finish- ing school's gendered curriculum of sport, French and music—the latter showcasing, according to the film's parochial poster, 'the world famous Luton Girls' Choir'. Jeffrey Richards saw in the interwar heyday of Old Mother Riley's 'body-language gone berserk' an 'outward and visible sign of her refusal to be cowed or to conform' (1984: 298), but a clear refusal *of* disunity is here displayed in an unintentionally sour scene where a girl is 'playfully' bullied for not matching the conventional beauty of her peers. And while (a genuinely Old) Mother Riley cavorting in a gymslip amongst a class of teenage girls in gym shorts may 'promise' an eroticised if not quasi-perverted transgression, it takes special pleading to adjudge the resultant chaos as even a tepid warm-up for later schoolgirl fantasy outlets. Nonetheless, moderate Lucan's cross-dressing principal and you have a ready template for Alastair Sim and the St Trinian's cycle, brought to screen by the genre's new boys, Frank Launder and Sidney Gilliat.

4.1   Section Prize Winner: The Happiest Days of Your Life (1950)

Charterhouse-educated John Dighton, Will Hay's co-scriptwriter on *The Ghost of St. Michael's*, had further mined school themes with his Ealing adaptation of *The Life and Adventures of Nicholas Nickleby* (Alberto Cavalcanti, 12 March 1947): a brief sojourn at Dotheboys Hall is effectively realised, with sets modelled on the Yorkshire school that originally inspired Dickens, while Alfred Drayton and Sybil Thorndike offer engagingly repellent portrayals of Wackford and Mrs Squeers, but overall it was thought that 'Director and adaptor have only partially succeeded in the conjurer's task of getting a quart into a pint pot' (*MFB*, March 1947: 35). Dighton fared better with an original stage piece: revisiting recent confusions in the wartime relocation of British schools, his 1948 farce *The Happiest Days of Your Life* ran in London for over 600 performances. Treating the accidental billeting of a girls' school on a boys' establishment, the warring heads were first played by Margaret Rutherford and George Howe. Its success led to a television version (BBC, 11 October, 1949) with Hermione Baddeley and Denys Blakelock locking horns, and attracted the attention of Launder and Gilliat's production company, Individual Pictures, who quickly secured filming rights. Expanding the role of the headmaster, renamed Wetherby Pond, Dighton adapted his play with Launder who directed and shared production duties with his long-established working partner, Gilliat. The pair had a track record of finely crafted satire and films built on group dynamics: they also had form with the subject matter—alongside scripting *Good Morning, Boys*, their accomplished panorama of British society *The Rake's Progress* (Gilliat, 1945) had sharply lampooned the legacy of a public school education and the concomitant class-ridden attitudes that allowed a raffish elite to survive through nurtured bravado and family ties. Casting also proved propitious: in particular, the back catalogue of sexless, celibate parts for the retained Rutherford and seedy, celibate roles for the newly appointed Alastair Sim made them ideal as Miss Whitchurch and Wetherby Pond, the elders of their respective tribes, while notable support came from Joyce Grenfell as the amorous Miss Gossage and

Richard Wattis as the reluctant Billings. The 12 weeks' filming took place at Hammersmith's Riverside Studios with location shooting at Langley Court Girls' School, Hampshire; distributed by British Lion, the film went on general release on 10 April 1950. *Happiest Days* relates how a mix-up at Whitehall's Schools Resettlement Department results in St Swithin's School for Girls being billeted on Nutbourne College, a minor boys' public school in rural Hampshire. While the pupils establish a 'rough and ready harmony', the two heads battle fiercely for supremacy until forced to work together by simultaneous inspections; one from a group of concerned St Swithin's parents, the other by governors of the august boys-only establishment to which Pond has applied as head. Cue an elaborate operation to keep the tours, and sexes apart; frantic classroom and sports field changes finally unravel when a governor leaves the tour and encounters a pitched battle between rugby and lacrosse teams. Pond and Whitchurch, exasperated at increasing educational interference, make a pact to emigrate to Africa.

Happiest Days is accepted as an artistic triumph: for Geoff Brown it is 'a well-nigh perfect example of farce balanced by sprightly dialogue, with superlative character comedians enjoying their choicest parts' (1977: 19). It is also seen as sharing not just cast members but many of the values of Ealing comedies. Marcia Landy specifies how 'The Ealing Comedies and the films of Launder and Gilliat, at their best, are carnivalesque' because 'they focus on dominant social institutions—the public school, the world of commerce and industry, political parties—and turn them on their head' with 'eruptions of physical and psychic energy' (1991: 333). Here, though, lies a clear difference in degree: as Bruce Babington notes, 'Ealing's much-noted suppression of sexuality was an implicit value, but in *The Happiest Days of Your Life* it is articulated at the centre of the narrative' (2002: 153). Launder's film foregrounds what is largely latent not just in Ealing but in almost all previous British school films, from *Young Woodley* through to *The Romantic Age*, and offers instead an open exploration of education's fear of 'energy eruptions', namely its pupils' burgeoning sexuality. The battle of the sexes that follows the forced entry of Miss Whitchurch and Co. is thus a manic, carnivalesque magnification of the disruption caused by the Faringdon sisters in *Housemaster*. Each side defends its position with the language of incipient moral decay: Whitchurch warns her staff that 'we are moving in a descending spiral of iniquity', while Pond describes the girls' billeting as 'an appalling sexual aberration' and his rival as an apocalyptic she-beast who 'spawns her young all over the building'. Pond's fears bleed into his lessons as he pointedly asks his sixth-form class to parse a sentence by John Knox: 'The first blast of the trumpet against the monstrous regiment of women'.[7] The boys applaud the misogynistic call to arms, but immediate interruptions—passing girls in gym shorts, a female political candidate at the door, a bed kicked by a girl collapsing loudly and finally a boy-girl group collision on the stairs—cause the lesson's abandonment and adumbrate the new regime: boys distracted from their studies and disrupted in their passage through 'their' school (and their lives thereafter); females disrupting the male staff's teaching schedules, taking over their sleeping quarters, advancing egalitarian ideals. Pond's 'trumpet blast' returns to taunt him at the end of the film: when the Ministry's new batch of children arrive and dance in carnivalesque abandon around the aghast head teachers, one blows a bugle right into his face. Long before this, though, the initially opposed principals have discovered that they share 'old school' educational beliefs: Pond, for all his brow-beaten intolerance, looks to offer at least the appearance of an education fit for young 'gentlemen'; Whitchurch, for all her predication of female superiority, bases her curriculum on educating girls to be proper wives, and anchors her school nomenclature in patriarchal culture, the male-titled St Swithin's structured into houses named after Byron, Tennyson and Shelley. Above all, these elderly celibates are of one mind, not only to perpetuate an education system based on earlier clearly-defined class and gender divisions, but principally to suppress any signs of sexuality in their charges.

The war, however, has changed the entire socio-sexual landscape—the start of term, September 1949, is pointedly anniversarial. Pond's declaration of a 'monstrous *regiment*' evokes not just his overcrowded school but recent nationwide shifts in gender roles and outlook, notably the 'mobile women' celebrated in Launder and Gilliat's *Millions Like Us* (1943) and *Two Thousand Women* (1944). References to the Second World War and, by extension, the cherished antebellum education system, pervade the film, from the 'left, right' quasi-militaristic arrival complete with brass scoring of St Swithin's pupils at Nutbourne, through raffish teacher Hyde-Brown (Guy Middleton) seeking to impress Senior Biology girls with embellished RAF adventures, to the heads' unified fight against the invading forces of inspection, replaying the nation's finest hour with synchronised watches, campaign plans and orders to 'fall out'. Rather than exposing superannuated educators behind the times, however, the touring parties' reactions clarify that Pond and Whitchurch accurately represent their constituencies: as Harper and Porter note, the film 'used laughter to negotiate the fears of parents and governors about the replacement of single-sex education by co-educational schools' (2003: 254). Try as they might, however, Pond and Whitchurch cannot prevent sexuality from rearing its ugly head—at visual, verbal, narrative and characterisation levels. The visual relates predominantly to Pond: when overwhelmed by female staff in his office, he fearfully retreats to the corner, the priapic candlesticks on his sideboard, either side of a (wryly observed) ornamental sailor bestriding a phallic cannon, constituting his sole defence (Fig. 3.4); his school's motto, 'Guard Thine Honour', proudly displayed, takes on a new—and sexual—meaning with a new clientele. The verbal relates largely to Whitchurch: her reply to worried parents that 'we are bedding down very nicely, considering a certain amount of hugger-mugger' assumes a sheen of sexual euphemism rather than Shakespearian erudition; her commentary on the school butterfly collection—'Priscilla Johnson was romping in a haystack when that Bastard Purple alighted on her, but she had him in the killing bottle in a flash'—needs little Freudian gloss on castration complexes and articulates with unwitting forcefulness the natural dangers of adolescence.

Fig. 3.4   A tactical retreat from the 'monstrous regiment of women'

Significantly, the children are far more secure in their cloaked use of sexual language: the parents of Angela (Patricia Owens) are oblivious to her innuendo as, during a History lesson, she proudly claims to be no longer weak with 'dates'. Narratively, the whole situation works against sexual segregation, the most 'hugger-mugger' manoeuvre making boys and girls swap places in the same beds for sick-bay inspections—a literal 'bedding down'. The differences of sexual nature and nurture are played out in the segregated school tours which, with increasing frenzy, identify the polarised subjects and sports, skills and values stereotypically associated with each school (science and algebra vs drama and eurhythmy; rugby posts vs lacrosse goals; navel cadets vs needlework; 'Billy Boy' vs 'Nymphs and Shepherds'). The divide, however, is ultimately undermined by their arch exponents, the heads themselves: during the tour Whitchurch backheels a pair of rugby boots with such force that they open a pin-up-covered locker, while Pond camply justifies the presence of crêpe-de-chine underwear in a boy's desk. Throughout the 'revacuation' Whitchurch manifests more traditionally assigned 'masculine' qualities in her no-nonsense, proactive stance, with Pond more 'feminine' in his arch, hysterical responses: hence, when planning their inspection campaign, Whitchurch 'naturally' sits down in the 'male' position of organiser while Pond, perched on the desk with pen and paper, gravitates to the 'female' role of secretary.

Oblivious to their own gender-role hybridity, the peace—and peace at such as cost: 'That's what comes of nationalising the railways!', Pond exclaims as girls' trunks arrive at Nutbourne—is evidently no place for this imperial pair who 'cannot but burlesque the serious thematics of the public school as synecdoche for the nation struggling for redefinition in the face of social change' (Babington 2002: 159). The serious thematics remain, however. Indicative of the precarity facing smaller rural private schools in the immediate post-war age of austerity, Nutbourne is shown to be failing even before the girls' arrival: Billings' tour for new English teacher Tassell (John Bentley) offers no Brookfield-style paean to the 'noble' pile's history and tradition: 'According to history it goes back to Henry VIII: according to the bank it goes back to them—unless Pond keeps up with his payments.' St Swithin's, we learn, is faring little better, overdependent on overseas pupils and paranoid of terminal bad publicity. Charles Barr has interpreted *The Ladykillers* (Alexander Mackendrick, 1955) as an allegory of post-war British society, with the eponymous gang, representatives of the post-war Labour government, defeated by their 'internecine quarrels' and by the old lady, representing the 'paralysing charisma of the "natural" governing class' which, in 1951, would return to power just as austerity ended (1977: 171). Here, a year before that political sea change, Nutbourne College is similarly readable as a microcosm of the nation embodying Labour's declining popularity, especially from a struggling middle class frustrated at continued penury and unceasing demands for further sacrifice. Still more is asked when Whitehall compounds its original error by billeting on Nutbourne a fully co-educational school: here, it seems, the barbarians are not just at the gates but in the grounds, busloads of ill-disciplined working-class children with ineffectual (and bearded) teachers, clearly a 'progressive school' where, Tassell conjectures, 'the kids throw inkpots'. This 'emergent' New Society is all too much for the 'residual' Pond and Whitchurch who, in a fully appeased and platonic partnership, agree to leave for Tanganyika where Whitchurch's brother is 'growing groundnuts' and traditional British public school values, structured on single-sex education, still apply.[8] The imperial concept of 'Pax Britannica' now survives solely 'in the outposts' which formerly provided a large percentage of St Swithin's boarding clientele: post-war it is for export only. Harper and Porter adjudge Launder's film a 'forward-looking' comedy that 'poked fun at the surviving rigidities of pre-war social attitudes' (2003: 254). It concludes, though, not with an image of resigned heads or rebellious newcomers: instead, after the camera lifts for the final credits to the heavens—the only site for the senexes' social and educational ideals?—it descends on the playing fields where the school's ration-book-resourceful porter Rainbow (Edward Rigby) and his youthful assistant are seen collapsed under the frequently-removed rugby posts. This ending, with the working class crushed under bureaucratic demands and counter-demands, seems distinctly backward-looking, an indication of *enduring* rigidities of authority and a post-carnivalesque return to the status quo. With the proletariat as overworked as the middle classes are frustrated, the Attlee government's egalitarian imperative would also imminently, inevitably collapse.

Unlike existing governments, *Happiest Days* proved hugely popular, coming second amongst British films (behind Basil Dearden's *The Blue Lamp*) and fifth overall in the box-office takings for 1950. There were some critical reservations for a script that 'squeezed every drop of laughter out of a situation which is about as thin as a Third Form pun' (*Standard*, 9 March 1950), but the majority vote was affirmative, overjoyed that 'here at last we have a polished British comedy that has pace and wit and style' (*Observer*, 12 March 1950). Praise was fulsome: the *Sunday Chronicle* saw in the two school heads 'potentially the best mixed comedy partnership since Groucho Marx and Margaret Dumont'; the *News of the World* lauded 'one of the funniest films for years'; the *Sunday Dispatch* heralded 'the maddest, merriest school story of all' (all 12 March 1950).

The critical and commercial success of *Happiest Days* made a follow-up inevitable, and a suitable vehicle was found in Ronald Searle's 'St Trinian's' cartoon series. Inspired by the Perse Girls School, Cambridge and named from St Trinnean's progressive girls' school in Edinburgh (1922–46), Searle's time as a Japanese prisoner of war caused a temporary hiatus but temperamentally informed his subsequent drawings of demonic, gin-swigging boarding school girls (Searle 1959: 16). Although the St Trinian's characters had been eliminated with a nuclear explosion in 1953, Searle agreed terms to a film adaptation for which he would provide credit sequence and film poster backgrounds—and have a walk-on part as a parent. *The Belles of St. Trinian's* (Launder, 15 November 1954) was scripted by Launder and Gilliat with regular contributor Val Valentine, while Malcolm Arnold composed the music. In a piece of counter-intuitive but inspired casting, Alastair Sim was retained from *Happiest Days* and given the part of the headmistress, Miss Millicent Fritton, as well as playing her black sheep brother, Clarence. Joyce Grenfell, Guy Middleton and Richard Wattis also returned, joined by a plethora of British comedy talent, including Hermione Baddeley, Beryl Reid, George Cole and Sid James—plus early pupil roles for Belinda Lee, Shirley Eaton and Carol White. Shot at Shepperton Studios, the film, granted a 'U' certificate at home, was banned to children by the South African censor. *The Belles* begins with the Arabian Sultan of Makyad (Eric Pohlmann) sending his daughter, Fatima (Lorna Henderson), to St Trinian's School for Young Girls, mainly because of its proximity to his horse stables. The school is in serious debt, and headmistress-proprietress Fritton feels constrained to accept back expelled arsonist Arabella (Vivienne Martin), daughter to her bookmaker brother Clarence. On discovering the quality of the sultan's horse Arab Boy, Clarence, having backed heavily elsewhere, arranges for it to be kidnapped by his daughter's sixth-form gang, but they are thwarted by the fourth-form whose money, like Miss Fritton's and the entire school funds, is on Arab Boy: he wins the race and St Trinian's is saved.

Essentially a 'spin-off' project—continuity with *Happiest Days* is established when the first girl off the school bus blows a bugle for another 'monstrous regiment of women'—*The Belles of St. Trinian's* has become arguably the best-known Launder and Gilliat film, voted onto the BFI's top 100 list and an American cult favourite. Beyond the screen, just as

'Chips' is an enduring sobriquet for male teacher longevity, 'St Trinian's' has become ready media shorthand for female pupil disruption.[9] In academic writing, the film is again seen as possessing 'a carnival atmosphere in which morality, sexuality, and all social conventions are turned on their head' (Landy 1991: 364). This carnivalesque potential is set up in the film's very title, a parody of the sentimental *The Bells of St. Mary's* (Leo McCarey, 1945) starring Bing Crosby's school-saving Father O'Malley. Inverting Hollywood's warm fug of divine providence, Launder's titular pun connotes both a set of fourth-form middle-class delinquents (closest to Scarfe's ink drawings) heedless of school or church bells, and head-turning sexually precocious 'sixth'-form belles, highly sexualised in their short skirts, stockings and suspenders. For Mary Cadogan the film's racehorse plot was 'a virtual inversion of typical girl's comic strip involving... mystery and detection' (1986: 233). It also vigorously inverts the narrative and thematic tropes of the classic British school film. Citing Durgnat's observation that 'girls don't quite fit the public school spirit, they're marginal, slightly free, and, therefore, sinister' (1970: 148), Landy opines that 'The girls' school setting seems more appropriate to puncture public school myths and avoids direct comparisons' (1991: 365). One could object firstly that such pronouncements, like the film itself, replicate a set of patriarchal assumptions; secondly *The Belles* offers plentiful direct comparison, notably with Will Hay's films for curriculum and conduct. Geography lessons identify French wine-growing districts while 'Advanced Chemistry' is given over to producing bootleg gin. Absent as with Hay is any inkling of a benign and professional adult presence: a permanent local advert offers unreferenced employment, with Science teacher Miss Wilson (Reid) admitting to 'not one single jolly qualification'. Absent too is any view of childhood as a time of innocence: the school motto, 'In Flagrante Delicto', matches Narkover in its Latin knowingness, but adds a sexual undertone absent from the Hay universe. Other vices, gambling, smoking and drinking are afforded similar tacit approval, while the generic sanctity of school sport is again roughed up in the lacrosse cup final. Not only does the match descend into a fighting free-for-all with referees and rivals knocked out but, reminiscent of 'Honest Albert', a girl has a blackboard pitch-side with regularly updated match odds.

Sim's headmistress presents a female equivalent to Hay's headmaster with her shabby gentility and bursarial burdens, though time has wrought a greater disillusion, Fritton blaming the war for replacing 'good manners and good taste' with the 'black market values' embodied in her twin brother.

Her diatribe invites socio-historical alongside metaphorical interpretations for St Trinian's representation of national decline and disrupted social order: for Geoff Brown 'the hideous schoolgirls are the right age to be the grown-up results of the wartime babies—the "good citizens" of the future—which Alastair Sim's doctor mused on at the end of *Waterloo Road* [(Gilliat, 1945)]' (1977: 19); for Bruce Babington, the plot's pronounced Arab element 'reflects the Near East post-imperial problems plaguing Britain and reminds viewers of Britain's diminished status' (2002: 171). The only signs here of Empire are the ornamental shields and spears used by the fourth-form in their bid to rescue Arab Boy. Similarly, St Trinian's repositions the post-war male, Fritton warning how an earlier 'gay arcadia of happy girlhood' has become more pragmatic: 'in other schools, girls are sent out quite unprepared into a merciless world, but when our girls leave here, it is the merciless world which has to be prepared'. This 'jolly relativity' extends from gender to class, revealing, as with *Boys Will Be Boys*, little difference in outlook between the bastions of social authority and the 'little folk' like spiv Flash Harry (Cole) or Clarence's bookmaking fraternity: Manton Bassett (Wattis) from HM's School Inspectorate is functionally impotent and happy to 'go native' in St Trinian's summer house; Police Superintendent Kemp Bird (Lloyd Lamble) encapsulates unregulated incompetence and nepotism, while his undercover girlfriend Sgt Ruby Gates (Grenfell) is earnest but emotionally stunted, a perpetual 'girl guide'. Even that glue of the nation, the middle-class family, is exposed: 'it may not be Roedean or Cheltenham, but it has its points', a mother over-protests, sacrificing her daughter to a cheap reputation-saving alternative to 'common' state education.

Finally, like Cicely Courtneidge Sim plays both a headmistress and her twin, but with two obvious differences: socially things are not looking up, and sexually Sim is cross-dressing. Three times, as Fritton shows her operational prowess against the sixth-form barricades, Flash Harry calls out 'what a Dame!'—a diegetic expression of his respect *and* an extradiegetic reminder that this is a man in a dress (Fig. 3.5). How one responds to this rests entirely on how convincing one finds Sim's portrayal. Distinct from the drag queen, usually a gay male song-and-dance performance that works to conceal masculinity and thus 'interrogates the meaning of both gender and sexual identity' (Baker 1994: 18), 'the dame is never effeminate; she is never merely a drag artist, since she always retains her male identity' (Ackroyd 1979: 102). If one determines that Sim's persona can, on occasions, override an awareness of transvestism (hence Flash Harry's exclamations?), the role can be interpreted as calling attention to sexual

Fig. 3.5   What a Dame! Sim in his/her pomp

difference, undermining, even mocking prevailing conceptions of femininity as exclusively biological. As such, it anticipates discourses on sexuality
and gender identity, notably Judith Butler who asserts that 'There is no
gender identity behind the expression of gender... identity is performa-
tively constituted by the very expressions that are said to be its results'
(1993: 25). If, however, one finds that Sim offers a 'transparent' panto-
mimic portrayal, never disguising the 'fact' that he is a man impersonating
a woman (hence the contemporary critical silence on Sim's casting?), then
Fritton is *not* a conscious site for the subversive destabilising of sex and
gender boundaries and instead, like Lucan's Old Mother Riley, *he* reaffirms
an audience's cultural capital that identifies with patriarchal and heteronor-
mative representations of society—a case of carnival-light, perhaps.

The Belles repeated the commercial success of Happiest Days, becoming
the third most popular British film at the 1954 box office. For the critics
adaptation was, as ever, prioritised, the *MFB* enthusing how 'every corner,
as in Searle's own drawings, has been filled with wildly imaginative images

and incidents' (October 1954: 142); C.A. Lejeune, by contrast, found 'nothing in Mr Launder's work to equal, let alone develop, the effect of Ronald Searle's wiry line' (*Observer*, 3 October 1954). Overall, opinion was equally divided: academia hailed 'possibly the boldest, broadest, burlesque feature ever seen' (*Sight and Sound*, 24, 2, October 1954: 91) and America welcomed 'a funny antic as delicate as a hotfoot and as trenchant as a Mack Sennett comedy' (*New York Times*, 23 December 1954). Leonard Mosley, however, finding 'the plot thin and the dialogue dull', offered a revealing educational condemnation: 'Send the makers of this film to a grammar school, but tell them they only just escaped landing in a secondary modern' (*Daily Express*, 30 September 1954).

A franchise had been established and three further films, helmed by Launder, followed at regular intervals. *Blue Murder at St. Trinian's* (31 March 1958) kept the same key players and added a British Lion slogan: 'the Horror film with the "U" certificate'. With Miss Fritton enjoying 'Her Majesty's Pleasure', her stern Australian replacement, Dame Maud Hackshaw (Judith Furse), is quickly taken prisoner by the girls and, with some violent trickery, the school win a trip to Rome where Flash Harry has promised to let wealthy bride-seeking Prince Bruno (Guido Lorraine) look over St Trinian's sixth-form belles. Setting off in two charabancs, the girls leave a trail of destruction, thwart a stowaway jewel thief, and carry back the reward money to a grateful freshly-released Miss Fritton. As well as adding Roman staging, *Blue Murder* gave St Trinian's a school song, its message 'the complete antithesis of those advocated by Thomas Arnold for a boys' public school' (Harper and Porter 2003: 259). Sentiments such as 'The battle's to the strongest, might is always right,/Trample on the weakest, glory in their plight' intimate not just the setting of the sun on a scholastic credo of duty but a rising egotism to parallel emergent consumerist Britain. The film is also much more sexually pragmatic (evident with the casting of 'new girls' like the model Sabrina). Christine Geraghty argues that 1950s British cinema 'provides evidence of a strong resistance to the notion of the new woman and an inability to imagine her as any kind of modern heroine' (2000: 159). The male-fantasy attire and the girls' willingness to sell themselves to Prince Bruno are not promising material for progressive gender portrayals, but St Trinian's sixth-form are not typically 'silly and vindictive or valorised and saintly' females (159) and, just as cross-dressing is epistemological in asking us if we desire the surface or the essence, so *Blue Murder* can be read as indicative of the less subservient 1950s woman's unscrupulous use of her sexual appeal to make her mark in a patriarchal society. While these tendentious thematics may be 'new', the film's plot-line justifies the title *Good Morning, Girls* as St Trinian's cheat their way through a UNESCO school competition and win a European tour culminating in a water polo match in Rome. It even has a pupil's criminal father, 'Gelignite' Joe Mangan (Lionel Jeffries), hiding out with the girls and hiding his loot in the water polo ball. The formula, though doubly second-hand, still succeeded and *Blue Murder*'s own reward money put it in the top ten earners for 1958. However, apart from Dilys Powell, who pronounced 'the inventions of this heartless assault on the social conscience' to be 'a still funnier result' than *Belles* (*Sunday Times*, 22 December 1957), the critical majority found only diminishing returns and condemned how *Blue Murder* 'flogs the joke about fiendish schoolgirls hard enough to warrant an investigation by the NSPCC' (*Sunday Express*, 22 December 1957).

The Pure Hell of St. Trinian's (23 January 1961) has the Academy for Young Ladies, arraigned at the Old Bailey for burning down their school, placed in joint charge of progressive educationalist Professor Canford (Cecil Parker), newly arrived from the University of Baghdad, and headmistress Harker-Packer (Irene Handl), recently discharged from a mental institution. Canford, however, is in the pay of an Emir (Elwyn Brook-Jones) seeking wives for his sons, and his sixth-form cultural tour of Greece is another front to sell the girls into wedlock. Pursued by Flash Harry (Cole), policewoman Ruby Gates (Grenfell) plus Culpepper-Brown (Eric Barker) and Butters (Thorley Walters) from the Ministry of Education, it is ultimately the stowaway and (presaging *If....*) Bren-gun-toting fourth-formers who rescue the girls from 'a fate worse than death': safely back in England, the pupils celebrate by setting fire to their new school. A corollary to the sorely missed Miss Fritton, this entry jettisons the key contrast of staff at least feigning a moral example for their resistant charges. The pupils' role is here greatly reduced, with the action centred on untrustworthy and, in a new world order where the girls' abduction to Arabia risks 'another Suez Crisis', by increasingly underfunded and disempowered adult authorities—an Honorary British Consul must moonlight as a Hotpoint dealer, while an army major, undoubtedly public school-trained in readiness for colonial service, supervises a Mobile Bath Unit. Cleanliness, though, is also sorely missing. A case could (just about) be made for the girls in *Blue Murder*, willing participants in their 'school' trip overseas, maintaining a progressive agency over their sexual desires: *Pure Hell*, though, constitutes an unpleasant regression, the storyline exploiting its older pupils as objects of commodity display and exchange. This is not just a post-imperial inversion with a British public school now pimping its duped charges to an Arab harem; the opening decision of Judge Stanton (Raymond Huntley) to spare the girls from approved schools is based not on any liberal educational agenda but on his libidinous desire for leggy sixth-former Rosalie (Julie Alexander). All the film's females are sexualised, be it through intent, Grenfell continuing as the frustrated Sergeant, or intertexuality, the fourth-form fire-brand named Lolita Chatterley (Ann Wain). A broad and peripatetic farce full of teenage reification and casual racism, not even Gilliat agreed with Launder's assessment that 'This was perhaps the most intellectual of the St. Trinian's films' (Brown 1977: 146). Although another box-office success, *Pure Hell* was the only St Trinian's film financially not to exceed its predecessor and the critics largely sided with Gilliat. *Kinematograph Weekly* found the ridicule too scattergun: 'the book is thrown at public schools, Government education authorities, the police and the army, but with not too sure an aim' (22 December 1960), while America's *Time* thought (ungallantly) that 'now the joke is as mouldy as the girls—theatre owners will be well-advised to put the fans on' (29 September 1961).

In Part Four, *The Great St. Trinian's Train Robbery* (4 April 1966), the school's move into Hamingwell Grange country mansion is facilitated by the affair between new headmistress Amber Spottiswood (Dora Bryan) and new Labour Minister for Schools (Raymond Huntley). However, (male) mail train robbers have just hidden £2.5 million under the ballroom stage and gang leader Alphonse Askett (Frankie Howerd), enrolling his daughters to case the school, organises a Parents' Day retrieval of the money: discovered by Flash Harry, Amber and the pupils, a prolonged train chase concludes with the money recovered and St Trinian's honoured as national heroines. Although connections to Ronald Scarfe's source cartoons again cease at the credit sequence and the girls are mere extras filling runaway trains, *Train Robbery* at least returns to its iconographic school location and revives generic themes, notably the near synonymy of criminal and public school classes, and generic tropes such as the chaotic Parents' Day and unreliable staff—Spottiswood collects her deputy head (Barbara Couper) from Holloway Prison and Art mistress (Margaret Nolan) from a strip club. Its opening also offers an educational topicality: Harold Wilson's 1964 Labour victory ended 13 years of Conservative rule and here holds out the promise for the beleaguered Ministry of Education of the abolition of public schools—and therefore St Trinian's. All begins well as Uppingham,

Westminster and St Paul's are listed as 'the type of school that belongs to the past', while all London schools will become 'one gigantic comprehensive'; however, the Ministry's key target is not just spared but granted an £80,000 government fund with Huntley's figure of the Establishment, as in *Pure Hell*, led astray by the figure of a St Trinian. Educational satire cedes thereafter to wider social events and cinematic genres. The Minister's corrupting liaison faintly echoes the Profumo affair that broke on 22 March 1963,[10] while the film eponymously references the 'Great Train Robbery' of a Royal Mail train on 8 August 1963. The daring theft, lengthy sentences and subsequent prison escapes captured the British imagination: it is referenced in the Beatles' *Help!* (Richard Lester, 1965) and, alongside its crime genre tropes, *Train Robbery*, like *Help!*, looks to parody the new James Bond franchise, as with the plethora of gadgetry in Alphonse's salon employed to communicate with the Voice, the gang's unseen Blofeld-like mastermind. The choice of Voice, Stratford Johns, best known as Detective Inspector Charlie Barlow in *Z-Cars* (BBC, 12 series, 1962–78), is an effective casting against type, and a similar carnivalesque is evident both in the solution to the crime—train robbers may defeat the law but not schoolgirls—and in the bestowal of 300 MBEs to St Trinian's, again Beatle-flavoured in the 'unjustified' award of honours by a Wilson administration keen to be seen as youth oriented—'Thousands Return Their Medals!' and '"A Diabolical Liberty" says Ringo', run the film's newspaper headlines. However, in parodying crimes now three years past, *Train Robbery*, though the first colour St Trinian's film, seems unprepared for the less monochrome, more permissive culture of the mid-1960s: Flash Harry now has 'trend-setter' long hair and a Donovan-style cap but still sports his spiv moustache and Malcolm Arnold leitmotiv; the train chase features new diesel-powered models yet also a hand-cranked inspection trolley redolent of silent comedy. Conversely, long gone are the old regulars and their 'endearing eccentricity' (Grenfell refused to return), yielding to a stream of Carry On-style 'smutty innuendo': for Robert Murphy, 'Like 1960s town planning, which pulled down friendly terraces and replaced them with shopping precincts and high-rise flats, it now seems a dreadful mistake' (1992: 252). Not a financial mistake, though. The film's shift in generic emphasis can be seen in trade reviews, eschewing school metaphors in adjudging the film a 'certain money-stealer' (*Kine Weekly*, 10 March 1966). They were right: *Train Robbery* landed the franchise's top financial returns and reached 1966s top 15 for UK box office earners. While critics lamented a continued decline in quality, Kenneth Tynan offered an explanation: 'With the passage of time, permissive education has eroded the St. Trinian's joke: what was once the comic exception is swiftly becoming the rule. Reality is overtaking Searle's fantasy' (*Observer*, 13 March 1966). It is a representational battle that would continue to the decade's end.

5 (POETIC) REALISM AND TINSEL

The road to ruin is paved with good intentions? *Escapade* (Philip Leacock, 22 August 1955), adapted pseudonymously by Hollywood-blacklisted Donald Ogden Stewart from the West End play by Roger MacDougall, concerns priggish schoolteacher John Hampton (John Mills) who campaigns so ardently for world peace that his family life unravels: neglected wife Stella (Yvonne Mitchell) seeks a separation, while their three sons misbehave so badly at boarding school that expulsion is mooted, amidst comic interludes, by headmaster Dr Skillingsworth (Alastair Sim). The boys resolve both family and wider discord by absconding, stealing a plane and flying to a four-power summit in Vienna where the eldest Icarus presents their father's views via a petition signed by children from all over Britain. Contextually polarising opinion—the *Daily Worker*, lauding the sentiments, thought it 'one escapade which deserves full marks instead of a caning' (30 July 1955); the *Observer*, lamenting the settings, concluded that 'they just don't add up to a convincing picture of life in an English boarding school, or for that matter anywhere' (31 July 1955)—*Escapade* textually manifests a politico-collegiate doubleness to prefigure *If….*, wittingly in Leacock's avowed intention to show that 'to be a pacifist you really had to be a fighter' (McFarlane 1992: 156), unwittingly as its comic tone and very title undermine the boys' militant pacifism. Raymond Durgnat termed *Escapade* a 'lonely harbinger of student CND direct action' (1970: 86): it stands in a similar prescient position to late-1960s schoolroom radicalism.

Before Anderson's bullet-fire, the British public school—and its construction of masculinity—kept a foothold in (late) Swinging Sixties cinema courtesy of American funding. In Universal's *I'll Never Forget What's 'Isname* (Michael Winner, 18 December 1967), 32-year-old successful television advertising agent Michael Quint (Oliver Reed) tries—and ultimately fails—to turn his back on the rat race. In an early sequence, Quint returns to his former public school for a reunion, only to find the bullies regrouping to 'hunt' an old victim, Eldrich (Roland Curram): when Quint intervenes he is held by others and beaten up by prime class bully Maccabee (Harvey Hall). This sadistic scene externalises a series of dreams/flashbacks, intimating Quint's schoolboy traumas to be causally linked to his current personal and professional malaise, much as high capitalist practice is permanently predicated on school-inculcated bully-boy tactics. Confused when viewed as a whole, the *MFB* nonetheless noted a 'cold eye for human frailty' and the 'identification of old school tie sentiments with the worst in human hypocrisy and degradation' (January 1968: 5). In similar vein, Fox's updated adaptation of Evelyn Waugh's 1928 debut novel, *Decline and Fall (...of a Birdwatcher)* (John Krish, 25 September 1968), follows the adventures of ingénu Paul Pennyfeather (Robin Phillips), unjustly sent down from Oxford when caught in a compromising position while out birdwatching. His spell at Llanabba Castle, a dubious Welsh public school kept afloat by devious headmaster Dr Fagan (a final role for Donald Wolfit) with a Dickensian staffroom of social degenerates, is the first step in a 'Downhill' trajectory towards (involuntary) white slave trafficking and subsequent imprisonment—where he is reunited with two former Llanabba colleagues. Overall a hit-and-miss satire of the public school imperial code, the *Sunday Telegraph* argued that the Llanabba section 'maintains a gruesome humour partly because the joke isn't about education, but about the idiocies of those caught up in its practice' (29 September 1968). Neither the system nor its practitioners would escape censure for long.

5.1   *The Public School Film Victor Ludorum:* If.... *(1968)*

If.... is, for this writer, the *Citizen Kane* of the British school film,[11] the summation of the genre to date and the portrayal informing its future developments. It is also the entry that has received the fullest critical attention, mostly centred on a synchronic contextualisation for Britain's prime cinematic contribution to 1960s counterculture (Sinker 2004; Sutton 2005). This section, while acknowledging that importance, seeks to place the film in its equally significant diachronic generic context as a British school film.

The film's lengthy birth pangs are well documented (Sherwin 1996; Lambert 2000). The earliest version of what eventually became *If....* dates back to May 1960, when Oxford undergraduates David Sherwin and John Howlett completed 'Crusaders', a splenetic revenge fantasy on their alma mater, Tonbridge School in Kent. Years of rejection followed with one producer decrying 'the most evil and perverted script' he had ever read:

'it must never see the light of day' (Sherwin 1996: 4). Nicholas Ray, who directed the writers' favourite film *Rebel Without A Cause* (1955), admired their like-minded concept but thought it needed a British director. In 1965 ex-Ealing editor Seth Holt expressed an interest but counselled the inside knowledge of a public school man, and recommended out-of-work Cheltenham College-educated Lindsay Anderson. Stalwart of the Royal Court Theatre, champion of Free Cinema and debut director of the nail in New Wave's coffin, *This Sporting Life* (1963), Anderson, 'unarguably an auteur' (Russell Taylor 1975: 69), was also a polemic critic who, in a 1957 manifesto, had declared that British cinema, 'dedicated to an out-of-date, exhausted national ideal', reflected 'one of the most class-conscious societies in the world'—a fault he placed largely on 'our upper-class system of education' (2004: 234–5). He readily accepted the 'Crusaders' project, but demanded a complete rewrite. This new direction, moving from British realism to Brechtian epic, alienated Holt and Howlett, but two months' concerted effort, Anderson broadly focusing on scene and shape with Sherwin on dialogue, produced an acceptable draft by mid-May 1967.[12] Again rejection ensued, until Anderson's chance encounter with actor/director Albert Finney facilitated a pitch to his newly founded Memorial Enterprises: Finney's business partner, Michael Medwin, agreed to co-produce with Anderson, but at a time when Labour-led debates on the inequalities of British education threw a renewed focus on the place of the British public school, their Establishment-debunking project still failed to find British backers. America's CBS came forward but, without explanation, withdrew six weeks before shooting was due to begin. Paramount stepped in with $500,000/£220,000 to save the project, sight unseen, reputedly because its new owner, billionaire tycoon Charles Bluhdorn, was married to a Finney fan. Anderson, a former head of house who, for all his vituperative criticism, enjoyed a 'love–hate relationship with tradition' (Armes 1975: 275), wanted strongly to film at his old school, so Sherwin doctored the script, including a suitably public school/patriotic title change inspired by Kipling's 1895 poem on the stoicism needed for adulthood, to earn Cheltenham's consent. Seeking actors closer to *Kes* than *The Guinea Pig*, press ads drew 5000 amateur applicants but only unearthed Philip Bagenal as the stargazing Peanuts. More profitably, Anderson auditioned several of the new breed of actors moving into the West End: this yielded the film-debut casting of 24-year-old Malcolm McDowell in the lead role of Mick Travis, plus Oxford undergraduate David Wood and Cheltenham old boy Richard Warwick as his fellow Crusaders, Johnny and

Wallace. With Czech New Wave cameraman Miroslav Ondríček in place as director of photography, filming began on Cheltenham's rugby fields on 28 January 1968 and continued until Easter—the College receiving a daily facility payment of £1000. Additional scenes, including showers and beatings, were shot at Aldenham School, Elstree and London's Merton Park Studios. As anti-Vietnam student uprisings and political assassinations spread across the Summer of Hate, Anderson and David Gladwell spent four months editing the footage down to its final 111 minutes. Always expecting an 'X' certificate, censorship issues were relatively minor and, in a landmark judgement, a supportive BBFC Secretary John Trevelyan allowed the full-frontal view of a naked female as housemaster's wife Mrs Kemp (Mary MacLeod) wanders through the dormitories. Paramount were less supportive of the final film, but *Barbarella* (Roger Vadim, 1968) had performed so poorly at their Piccadilly Circus cinema that it was pulled after a fortnight and *If....*, largely to complete the company's annual Eady quota, plugged the gap, premiering on 17 December 1968. Concerted lobbying, plus £40,000 takings by the New Year, persuaded ABC to grant a January national release. *If....* debuted in New York on 9 March 1969 and limited US distribution followed.

Any narrative summary is problematic. The film *shows* the start of term as the boys of College House—itself a metonym for the unnamed school—settle into the routine of chapel, lessons and games; junior boys, known as 'Scum', attend the house prefects aka 'Whips'. One afternoon, while the school is watching the compulsory rugby match, lower sixth-formers Mick and Johnny escape into town, steal a showroom motorbike and ride to a roadside café where Mick cavorts with the girl behind the counter (Christine Noonan). Back at school a beating and enforced cold shower by head of house Rowntree (Robert Swann) proves the tipping point for the frequently punished Mick who mingles blood with his friends in a ceremony of solidarity against authority. During a Cadet Corps field exercise Mick shoots and bayonets the school chaplain (Geoffrey Chater), but the headmaster (Peter Jeffrey) offers the rebels a chance at redemption. Assigned to clearing junk beneath College Hall, they discover a forgotten stash of arms and ammunition. On Founder's Day, as guest of honour General Denson (Anthony Nicholls) addresses the school, smoke emerges from beneath the stage. Boys, parents, masters and guests rush out into the quad and are met with a hail of gunfire from Mick and his allies, now including the girl from the café. The headmaster steps forward and is shot down; the general leads a counter-attack.

This summarises what we see, but it may not 'really' exist. While *If....* functions predominantly within the realist tradition—Anderson's uncomplicated shooting style is relatively 'classic', tracking on movement with close-ups for emphasis and the camera sill in medium shot for action scenes—a mimetic reading is frequently undercut, either by intertextual references—either Hitchcockian, as with Mick's first appearance with black hat and scarf-hidden face replicating Ivor Novello in *The Lodger*, or home-grown, with junior pupil Machin (Richard Davies) sharing surnames with Richard Harris' lead in *This Sporting Life*—or, more explicitly, by European influences. Anderson has extolled his 'healthy' use of Brechtian alienation devices (2004: 121): some are wholly achieved, as in the film's division into eight title-carded chapters; some are exaggerated—the appearance of the murdered chaplain from the drawer in the headmaster's office is often seen as 'a mistake' (Sutton 2005: 76), a stylistic aberration drawing too much attention to itself;[13] some grew from expediency—with the small lighting budget Ondříček could not guarantee colour consistency for the chapel scenes, initiating 11 further monochrome-shot sequences. Such distancing devices work to instil a receptive questioning of the film by foregrounding the process of its production, theoretically allowing a dispassionate observation and evaluation of societal machinations. As much as distanciation, however, the film seeks disorientation, evident in the equally acknowledged influence of Jean Vigo's *Zéro de Conduite/Zero for Conduct* (1933), a quasi-surrealist film about life at a boys' boarding school. Alongside its Speech Day protest where the French boys throw tin cans and shoes at their teachers, visual echoes of Vigo's somersaulting pupils can be seen in *If....*'s gym scene featuring Wallace's slow-motion acrobatics. Vigo's main influence, though, is structural: Anderson arranged a viewing early in the production process so Sherwin and Howlett would understand his search for a scene succession devoid of clear narrative connection, a 'poetic' structure notably achieved in the first half of *If....* where several scenes could be shuffled without harming the overall thematic drive. Both influences cohere in the film's 'random' scattering of potential fantasy sequences—the chaplain in the drawer, the naked girl in the café, the housemaster's wife in the dorm, potentially capable of extrapolation to the motorbike theft and even the violent ending: the absence of any clear delineation from scenes of accepted diegetic reality enacts, like Hitchcock in *Downhill*, Anderson's problematisation of the distinction between constructed images and 'truthful' actuality.[14] For Elizabeth Sussex this creates a flexible viewing strategy as the film's 'threshold between fantasy and reality' becomes 'something that must vary according to how

much reality the spectator can bear': in this way 'the film's supreme achievement is in enabling audiences to interpret it according to their own ideas of
what is real' (1969: 83). Thus one can read the avant-garde Crusaders as
agents of a present tense Paris-style revolution, or, if that is too 'real' to bear,
as a conditional tense Home Counties allegory, a warning of what could
happen 'if....'—the word appearing bottom right in the film's closing title-
card. It is a doubleness, a resistance to definitive interpretation, that perme-
ates every aspect of *If....*, even the original promotional quad poster that,
over film stills grouped in the shape of a hand grenade, presented Janus-
faced images of Travis, the tail-coated schoolboy with his books and the
leather-jacketed machine-gun-wielding rebel.

For all its recognised overseas-indebted formalism, *If....* equally foregrounds a perspective on the ideology and iconography of the British
school film. The Summer '68 student protests brought audiences to *If....*
frontloaded with countercultural expectations, and the relatively youthful headmaster, his specialist subject the modish Business Management,
promises contemporaneity as he offers his prefects self-satisfied sound-
bites on national attitudes to schooling—'Education in Britain is a nubile
Cinderella, sparsely clad and much interfered with'[15]—and its future
requirements—'everything from pop music to pig farming, from atom
power stations to mini-skirts'. His pally and 'progressive' speech clashes
stridently, however, with his immediate environment: 'establishment' shots
of the school with its manicured lawns, stained-glass windows, portraits of
past headmasters and current pupils in tail-coated uniforms all betoken an
Establishment entrenched in British educational traditions both systemic
and cinematic. In 'reality' much of the surrounding ritual had softened
since the writers' schooldays, but Anderson's intention of presenting a
national metaphor rather than a documentarist's memoir—'Any school—
particularly any boarding school—is a microcosm', he emphasised at the
time (2004: 112)—is textually signalled from the headmaster's (zeug-
matic) opening address: 'College is a symbol of many things: scholarship,
integrity in public office, high standards in the television and entertainment worlds, huge sacrifice in Britain's wars...'—and underlined when
sadistic Whip Denson (Hugh Thomas) taunts Travis: 'I serve the nation.
You haven't the slightest idea what that means, have you?' The metaphor
is visually discernible from College House colours, with ties, scarves and
rugby kit all bearing a Union Jack red, white and blue—and is explicitly
revealed when the final chapter begins with a close-up of the British flag,
a zoom-out locating it atop College House's tower.

Throughout *If....* exploits and intensifies habitual tropes of the school film genre, both serious and comic. The role and rank of staff are deftly exposed. We endure, as with Simmons in *Young Woodley*, the platitudinous address from housemaster Kemp (Arthur Lowe) about how 'We are your new family. And you must expect the rough and tumble that goes with any family life.' We follow, as in *Goodbye, Mr. Chips*, the induction of a new master, here paralleled with pupil life as we encounter the equally spartan abode of John Thomas (Ben Aris)—its soullessness announced by the rattle of a shilling into the gas meter's empty tray—and witness his equally inferior status to the Whips—reprimanded by Denson for being out late. This subservient ranking extends to all staff, evident from the first evening meal where Kemp retreats to his fruit dessert while the Whips map out College House discipline: as in *Tom Brown's Schooldays*, the school is run by its prefects, Rowntree's opening, counter-intuitive command to 'Run in the corridor!' highlighting the unfettered authority of this privileged elite, paisley-waistcoated guardians of an enduringly sadistic 'Pax Britannica'. In keeping with traditional public school priorities, we see little classroom teaching or learning: indeed, intellectual achievement is despised, with Peanuts marginalised for his science skills and everywhere the Whips smothering initiative—'it is not up to you to think', Rowntree tells his 'fag', Philips (Rupert Webster). The staff, when not abusers, are anonymous, so fully socialised that the ironic deployment of the opening quotation from Proverbs 4:7 on the 'getting of wisdom' is apparent long before the (over-signified) metaphor of stultification, a pickled foetus, is discovered by the Crusaders under the school stage. False hope is offered in the first lesson from the dishevelled History master (Graham Crowden): riding his bicycle into the classroom, opening the window unBrodie-like wide to let in some 'freedom' and praising Travis' work all suggest a like-minded maverick misfit, but class indifference to Socratic questions on the nature of his subject—individual agency versus technological determinism—occasions a bathetic decline into standard hegemonic fare on nationalism, warfare, and an essay on George III. Sport instils more active pupil engagement: nonetheless, in reverse momentum, the character-building discipline and xenophobia it purposefully instils is softened by the scene where Thomas, taking junior rugby, picks up the ball and is playfully pulled to the ground; though a minor-key moment, it suggests a warmer bonding of the school body, more Will Hay than Tom Brown. A text (from Plato's *Republic*) translated in senior Greek class—'We also said that we must conduct the children to war on horseback'—is realised when the chaplain embodies Tamahine's public school paradox by leading Cadet Corps manoeuvres, while Peanuts teaches the bayonet-practising juniors a quasi-Orwellian 'Yell of Hate' (Hedling 1998: 95). This is the 'core' education of College—*sed miles, sed pro patria* (Cheltenham too had a strong military tradition). Morning chapel readings—'That ye may live and go in and possess the land, which the Lord God of Fathers giveth unto you' and 'The Son of God goes forth to war... a kingly crown to wear'—reinforce the imperial trope of Britain's 'divine' proprietorial rights, as does 'national hero and old boy' General Denson's Founder's Day speech—largely a rehash of Dr Arnold's pulpit address in Stevenson's *Tom Brown's School Days*—extoling the responsibilities of privilege, the need to learn 'the habit of obedience, how to give orders and how to take them' and the imperative to fight to preserve the 'freedoms' of class and tradition. Acknowledging global changes since the First World War, he counters the headmaster's progressive mantra in promising that College, like 'England, our England, doesn't change so easily'. Spoken before 'Your Royal highness, my Lord Bishop, my lords, ladies and gentlemen', such a message (literally) smokes out the reactionary ruling matrix of (public school-educated) state, church and military. This ideological subsuming, in word and deed, succeeds because its realisation is predicated on self-governing pupil agency before adult interference. The arcane school argot that inculcates both sexism (local girls are 'town tarts') and elitism (grammar schoolboys are 'smudges', all others 'oiks') must be learnt by heart and, like the 'Yell of Hate', be delivered with style. The school's brutal internal social strata, evident in the first evening's bathroom bullying of 'Fatso's blubber', is intensified as the Scottish Biles (Brian Pettifer) is debagged and stuffed head-first down the toilet bowl—not just another cruel carnivaleseque but an 'absurdist metaphor for the brainwashing that the boys endure' (Hedling 1998: 84). Biles' polite request to recover his clothes reveals his cowed complicity with his own oppression, his 'successful' integration.

For Jeffrey Richards and Anthony Aldgate *If....* 'brilliantly recreates the enclosed, all male world of the public school. It lays bare the process by which the system produces an authoritarian elite to govern the country, deals with dissidents and induces unthinking conformism' (1983: 147). Governance will be the (post-)imperial right of Roundtree (we hear of his summer in India) and his fellow Whips—the terminology pointedly overlays their common-room psycho-sexual practices with parliamentary ritual. Mick's excessive punishments provoke his increasingly open dissidence, from hidden facial hair (grown during a summer absorbing London's burgeoning counterculture), through bedroom posters of Che Guevara, Lenin and Geronimo, to final rooftop rebellion, acting out his early Guy Fawkes sobriquet and realising 'the rage that simmers beneath the slapstick: St Trinian's with live ammunition and real death' (Sutton 2005: 78). The conformism is provided via the generic staple of following a new boy and his 'moulding'. Amidst the first day bustle the camera settles on Jute (Sean Bury), his sneering reception from Biles succinctly conveying the psychological realism of the bullied bullying in turn. For Paul Sutton the film largely abandons Jute after the first quarter: 'he is sucked into the system so much so that he almost "disappears", reduced to a non-speaking "extra" on the edge of the frame' (2005: 49). Almost, but not quite: such unobtrusive assimilation is the salient point as Jute, the Tom Brown of College House, importantly provides the dialectic socio-sexual corrective to Mick's increasing marginalisation. Jute begins in social isolation, mistakenly addressing the prefects as 'sir', frantically seeking the right page in his hymnal, struggling to execute a 'through vault' in PE and having his nipple tweaked in class by the sadistic chaplain; he grows in confidence, bypassing Biles as he acquires the requisite school ritual and terminology and, like Brown, plays an active part in a key rugby match, earning the acceptance of his peers; he learns to use his looks, coquettishly returning the chaplain's pulpit stare and earning the acceptance of the school's hierarchy as he is entrusted with carrying a College trophy, before finally, as altar boy, taking a central role in the Founder's Day celebration of the traditional values that Mick by now seems intent on destroying.

Or does he? Travis and friends, with their credo that 'violence and revolution are the only pure acts', their collaged pin-ups of black freedom fighters and constant playing of the 'Sanctus' from the Congolese *Missa Luba*, can readily be identified with Third World resistance to imperial order and interpreted as teenage Marxist-Leninist refuseniks at war with the school/society that 'created' them. The young are often considered conservative, however, and Anderson himself termed Travis and Co. as, 'without knowing it, old-fashioned boys' and 'traditionalists', acting from an 'outraged dignity' and 'sense of fair play' (2004: 122–3), a reading sustainable if one's viewing strategy interprets as earnest patriotism—rather than Errol Flynn playacting—the trio's swearing of blood brotherhood and their fencing match citations of 'England, Awake!' and 'Some love England and her honour yet!'[16] Such jingoistic invocations would then chime with General's Denson's speech and situate the boys in the lineage of Hartley, Chipping and Donkin as essentialist opponents of a new headmaster's evolutionary philosophy. A doubleness can thus be read into the film's very title, signifying as an ironic dismantling of Kipling's support for Empire-coining education, and/or an allusion to the honest heroism of boys 'becoming men' and heroically fighting for their beliefs, here for endangered Arnoldian orthodoxies—thus portraying hardened versions of the three brothers in *Escapade*. Perhaps their stance ultimately exposes the final identicalness of political extremes: David Spiers thought that 'The fascist implications of the theme of the film are made even more disturbing coming as they do from somebody who has always aligned himself with the left' (*Screen*, 10, 2, March–April 1969: 89); David Sherwin drew comparisons with Buchner's *Woyzeck*: 'This is what society does to good people and people who want to be free. This is what happens to Mick. He becomes as evil and terrible as the headmaster or the general' (*Sight and Sound*, 37, 3, Summer 1968: 130–1) (Fig. 3.6).

What, though, of sexual politics? Anderson stressed how 'the impulse to freedom finds expression in emotional relationships as well as in action'

Fig. 3.6   A girl and a gun: Cinemarxism or a Kipling marksman?

(*Times*, 29 November 1969) and, most explicitly, *If....* extrapolates the British school film genre's persistent atmosphere of repression and sublimation. College House's power base is highlighted in trading over fetishised pretty-boy Philips: after being chastised by Rowntree (with gay-sourced terminology) as a 'sod' and 'lazy little bugger', he is 'given' to the over-protesting but clearly infatuated 'Purity' Denson. The Whip's passion is unrequited, however, as Philips intently watches Wallace (peacock-)perform on the gym's high bar, a male gaze that leads *If....* into finally taking the school genre beyond the 'homosexual flirtatiousness', 'multiple expositions' and repressed subtexts raging from *Young Woodley* to *The Browning Version* when, in Chapter VI, accompanied by the musical theme employed in the sexualised gym and café scenes, the camera tracks along the junior dorm before stopping at the bed where Philips is asleep—alongside Wallace. College is not entirely male, however. Throughout its generic history the influence of women on the boys' public school had been double-edged: disruptive, as when the Faringdon sisters come to Marbledown; defining, as with Brookfield's transformation under Katherine Ellis. When term starts, junior pupils complain at the banning of nearby Springfield girls from the school orchestra—'their breasts were getting too big: temptations of the devil'—here, clearly, it's not 'Great to Be Young'; at dinner Mick knowingly offers a nervous Mrs Kemp a phallic-shaped sauce bottle; his dalliance with the café girl acts out textually the lion and tigress predators from his study collage, savage appetites freed from the rigidities of civilisation/school, but also replays intertextually the 'beastly' sex with Kitty in *Young Woodley* and the waitress in *Downhill*. For all its male posturing, however, the greatest belligerence in *If....* is ultimately manifested by its female trio: it is the girl, the only working-class 'interloper' in the Crusaders, who shoots the headmaster through the head; against her, and bracketing the film, Matron (Mona Washbourne)'s early rugby match entreaty for College to 'Fight! Fight!', spat out with clenched fists and pure hatred, is terminally realised as Mrs Machin picks up a machine-gun and leads the counter-attack, screaming 'Bastards! Bastards!' Johnny's horoscope reading from *Women's Own* 'to resist any temptation to go into war' proves accurate as, more fiercely than her playing-field-trained charges, Mother England/Britannia battles to defend her own.

Profiting from serendipitous, globally resonating political events, *If....* became, after the US-targeted *To Sir, With Love*, the highest-grossing British school film export. By Christmas 1971 Paramount had made over $1.7 million in the United States, New York alone yielding more than Britain's entire return of $470,000: riot-friendly France brought in $430,000. The British trade press found *If....* 'a very individual film' that 'nearly bestrides the chasm between popular choice and the fancy of the eggheads' (*Kine Weekly*, 21 December 1968: 19), an evaluation borne out by a further doubleness evident in its critical receptions. With some exceptions, the 'popular' press adjudged the film exclusively as, in Ernest Betts' words, 'a terrific swipe at the public school system' (*People*, 22 December 1968): Felix Barker called it 'a savage attack on the public schools... witty, venomous, exaggerated but with a deadly underlying truth' (*Evening News*, 19 December 1968), while Madeleine Harmsworth saw it as 'exploding a bomb under the English public school, blowing it to bits and showing these privileged one-sexed places for what many people believe they are, unhealthy breeding grounds of snobbery, homosexuality and sadism' (*Sunday Mirror*, 22 December 1968). The 'egghead' journals and broadsheets, however, mostly accepted Anderson's wider intent, termed by John Russell Taylor a 'rich, complex, obscure metaphor on the way we live now' (*Times*, 20 December 1968): for the *MFB* 'The public school in *If....*, neither real nor imaginary, is the perfect metaphor for the established system all but a few of us continue to accept' (February 1969: 26), while Dilys Powell thought it 'not just about an imaginary public school. It is about the rigid ideas and the authoritarian society which Mr Anderson and his collaborators see rooted in the public school' (*Sunday Times*, 22 December 1968). However the focus was perceived, the result was largely lauded: Penelope Mortimer proclaimed the film a 'masterwork... a tremendous artistic success' and played on Kipling: 'If... you can make a film opposed to all commercial concepts, and make a success of it, you probably have a touch of genius, my son' (*Observer*, 22 December 1968); for Nina Hibben 'the devastating view it gives of the cruel traditions which go into the shaping of the ruling class' rendered it the 'best and most significant film of the Sixties' (*Morning Star*, 20 December 1968). There were dissenters, though: Patrick Gibbs was unconvinced by its 'public school parody', seeing little originality in setting such an 'inventive and well organised satire' in a public school where, for over 50 years, 'the fire has been continuous and withering' (*Daily Telegraph*, 20 December 1968); most resistant was Eric Rhode who called *If....* 'the most hating film I know of', a 'spewing' Anderson's 'working out of personal grudges and resentments in terms of social conflict', and 'so nightmarish and humourless that it becomes risible, a picture so unreal that it should play into the hands of the public school lobby' (*Listener*, 26 December 1968). America was similarly divided: Wilfrid Sheed found that *If....*, 'unlike many school movies, is witty and literate and betrays signs of education' (*Esquire*, May 1969); Pauline Kael, however, bracketed the film with *Easy Rider* (Dennis Hopper, 1969) and *Medium Cool* (Haskell Wexler, 1969) as examples of a 'self-serving negativism' little better than the clichéd happy endings of classic Hollywood: 'the audience is probably just as much aware of the manipulation for the sake of beautiful violent imagery… and it probably knows that these apocalyptic finishes are just as much a con' (*New Yorker*, 15 March 1969). Not so the Cannes Film Festival, which awarded *If….* the Palme d'Or for 1969—in spite of efforts by the (public school-educated) British ambassador to France to have it withdrawn for being an 'insult to the nation' (Sherwin 1996: 31); nor BAFTA, who nominated both Anderson and Sherwin. In 1999 the BFI placed *If….* at number 12 in its 'Best 100 British Films': with time, it seems, wisdom has been got, and with it understanding.

Anderson admitted the ultimate futility of the Crusaders' actions: 'The world rallies, as it always will, and brings its overwhelming firepower to bear on the man who says "No"' (2004: 123). And rally it did: the 1970 re-election of the Conservatives took the heat off the public school system and *Goodbye, Mr. Chips* (Herbert Ross, 5 November 1969), a film about a man saved by saying 'I do', in retrospect seems more educationally prescient. Plans by MGM to make a musical version of James Hilton's (or rather Sam Wood's) text, first mooted in 1964, came to fruition amidst the late-1960s trend for major US investment in British-based musicals. A $9 million production and publicity budget, 21 weeks of filming on over 50 major sets at Sherborne School, Pompeii and Borehamwood Studios with a company numbering over 200, all indicate the most lavish attention thus far to a British school film. Several casting changes finally alighted on high-profile Peter O'Toole and genre regular Petula Clark as the Chippings, while (now Sir) Michael Redgrave returned to public school life as Brookfield's headmaster. Terence Rattigan's screenplay made several departures from Hilton's source novella, beginning the film with Arthur Chipping already a long-established member of staff, maintaining his mid-life marriage for 20 years and advancing the story from the original's 1896–1933 timespan to a more contemporary 1924–69. The musical element of the film, if not always achieved, offers a bold formal experimentation, with the 12 songs of (UCS-educated) Leslie Bricusse and American John Williams' underscore discreetly withdrawn and, often interrupted by dialogue, working as a stream-of-consciousness counterpoint to the narrative, while the stylised emotion, traditionally expressed in elaborate dance numbers, yields to Oswald Morris' hyperactive cinematic choreography. However, modish camera moves speeding across the set or subtly examining actors' features collide, not only with a narrative doggedly refusing to bend to anything approximating a Swinging Sixties idiom, but especially with a mise-en-scène which, replicating the 1939 version's myriad shots of Brookfield highlighting unproblematised privilege and heritage, militates against contemporaneity. It is, at least initially, an appropriate environment for the unpopular and ossified Chipping who, retreating behind Latin declensions and dry definitions of 'duty', remains a figure of Victorian propriety. Less wittingly, gender depictions are no more modernised as all changes for Chips with the love of a good woman, willing to sacrifice her career for that of her husband. Katherine's expanded role and 'troubled past'—she is here a London stage-starlet with a stream of past love affairs—show her to be outwardly 'devil-may-care' in her flaunting of conventions but even her proactive pursuit of Chips, declaring her love in the successful 'Walk Through the World' number, reveals her as inwardly desirous of the expected gender staples of family life and social security, less a modern hedonistic soubrette than a good post-imperialist wife.[17] Indeed, rather than a marriage of opposites, the film singularly provides the archetypal English pedagogue with a complementary Mother England partner, a musical Mrs Machin: in her 1920s 'London is London' number Katherine appears seated on a pedestal as Britannia; when in Pompeii she tells Chips that her real name is 'Brisket', he replies with relief: 'charmingly Anglo-Saxon!'; she dies not in childbirth but doing her patriotic wartime duty, entertaining the troops in a RAF concert hall hit by a V-1 flying bomb. The American critic Roger Ebert thought that, 'By modernizing the action, Rattigan has made it possible for the movie to mirror changes in the English class structure during the two decades when it was most obviously becoming obsolete' (*Chicago Sun-Times*, 19 November 1969). It is hard, though, to equate this social reading with the film on view: as much as Katherine teaches Chips to care more openly for his charges, he instructs her in the ways of 'decent' high-bourgeois society. Rattigan's writing of a happy and mutually supportive teacher marriage might orientate *Goodbye, Mr. Chips* as a counterbalance to his earlier *The Browning Version*, but the greater focus on Katherine makes it rather a distaff staffroom variant on *The Guinea Pig*, with Katherine's social malleability measurable against the staged appearances of her friend, Ursula (Siân Phillips), written in to add an 'untutored' theatrical earthiness. Even so, Katherine's inescapable baggage, her lack of birth pedigree and 'class', repeatedly deprives Chipping of his coveted headship: a tobacconist's 'guinea pig' son may get to Cambridge, but 20 years on *Goodbye, Mr. Chips* reaffirms, in class and gender terms, the enduring *exclusive* institution of the British public school, its timely punitive buzz-bomb sparing any sustained investigation of the social awkwardness subsequent to the war-time expediency of a music hall singer's social elevation.

Katherine is central to this ideologically retrenched iteration of Hilton's source text. Alongside her set-piece and ruminative musical intermissions, her 15-years Brookfield stint shifts the film's emphasis from Chips' professional to his marital devotion, demonstrated in several scenes where 'unsuitability doesn't prevail over love'. The habitual montage, in Wood's version a succession of call-overs, here covers the married couple's maturing love—when discussing their childless marriage, it is Katherine who first comments that 'I've hundreds of children, all of them boys.' A film lasting over 2.5 hours contains plentiful musical padding but few of the generic tropes associated with the British school film: in the briefest echo of *Young Woodley* a final-year pupil develops a crush on his beloved 'Katherine', though Chipping seems more shocked by the form of address than the affection; a rivalry between vocational Chips and his careerist junior Baxter (Jack Hedley) barely sketches the opposing philosophies played out in *Housemaster* and Wood's version; the Founder's Day 'Schooldays' number includes the rosily reductive reference: 'Have you guessed that I'll miss my School days,/My Tom Brown's tomfool days'. Otherwise classroom practice is even less seen or discussed than in *If....* as, rather than tracing the realisation of a good teacher from a rigid pedant, Katherine's placement of a flower on Chipping's classroom desk instantly symbolises his growth into popularity, a troublingly simplistic equating of likeability *tout court* with quality teaching. Only the closing reel and Chips' emotionally delivered—and received—retirement speech focuses on the pedagogical, concluding with a firm Arnoldian endorsement that 'we did teach them one thing: how to behave to each other'. Chipping *as* Brookfield is then visualised when, standing in the courtyard while pupils pass at call-over, the camera pulls back until Chips is lost amidst the young boys and antique buildings: as Richards notes, 'He is, as it were, being absorbed into the fabric of the place' (1973: 60).

Goodbye, Mr. Chips, however, now seemed out of place—and time: like many US-funded prestige 'blockbusters', 'caught up on the production escalator operating in Britain in the last few years of the 1960s boom' (Walker 1974: 443), it was a hefty box-office failure and as such a key contributor to the demise of Hollywood financing of British cinema. Still, the US industry admired the film, O'Toole winning a Golden Globe and receiving his fourth (unsuccessful) Academy Award nomination for Best Actor, while Bricusse and Williams were nominated for Best Score of a Musical Picture. America's press reception, however, was far less fulsome, sparing the leads but pouring such scorn on the direction and score that MGM cut several musical numbers before its US general release. Pauline Kael, while accepting the 'charm of the story', (infamously) lambasted 'an overblown version of James Hilton's tearstained little goldmine of a book, with songs where they are not needed (and Leslie Bricusse's songs are never needed)' (*New Yorker*, 8 November 1969). The film found advocates in the British press, Alexander Walker arguing that 'Anderson's revolutionary *If....* may be more in fashion, but there's still a place for filmgoers who only want a nostalgic When' (*Evening Standard*, 27 November 1969). The vast majority, though, agreed with Ian Christie that it 'all seems terribly dated' (*Daily Express*, 25 November 1969): Margaret Hinxman (cogently) rationalised that 'A social revolution has swept away, not the reality of a posh Brookfield-type school, but the less-lettered public's awe and affection for it' and, 'lacking instant devotion', the new film 'failed to find a substitute' (*Sunday Telegraph*, 30 November 1969).

Buffering these opposed depictions of boys' public school experience was *The Prime of Miss Jean Brodie* (Ronald Neame, 22 February 1969), set in a 1930s prestigious girls' school that shared Ross' historical periodisation but supported Anderson's deep-seated critique of the enduring ills of a British education. Muriel Spark's 1961 breakthrough novel, based on her own pupil experiences in Edinburgh, had been successfully dramatised by American Jay Presson Allen: when Twentieth Century Fox acquired the screen rights, Allen re-adapted her play, with Maggie Smith taking the lead. Surprised at the award of an 'X' certification, the studio's appeal for a wider audience revealed little change at the BBFC since *Boys Will Be Boys*: its secretary John Trevelyan accepted that, while free of the sex and violence normally associated with 'X' films, the BBFC 'was concerned with the corruption of children by a teacher, and Maggie Smith's performance was so powerful that we felt genuine concern about the possibility of young girls being influenced by the philosophy of life that she presented to her pupils' (*BBFC Correspondence*, 21 April 1969). Recipient nonetheless of a royal premiere, the first 'X' certificate film so chosen, the film follows Jean Brodie who scandalises her more hidebound colleagues at the private Marcia Blaine School for Girls by ignoring the prescribed curriculum and pampering her favourite pupils, Sandy (Pamela Franklin), Monica (Shirley Steedman), Jenny (Diane Grayson) and new arrival Mary McGregor (Jane

Carr). When Brodie's open admiration for fascism leads Mary to her death in the Spanish Civil War, she is denounced by Sandy, providing head-mistress Miss Mackay (Celia Johnson) with the long-sought evidence to dismiss her nemesis.

The first British school film to focus on an eponymous female practi-tioner, *Jean Brodie* offers a complex character study of the teacher as the-atrical *performer*—Monica's praise for Brodie making history 'seem like cinema' is corrected by Sandy: 'no, more like Shakespeare'. Her openly hyperbolic gestures and delivery, coupled with the frisson of complicity—'prop up your books in case of intruders'—is not only diegetically effective on her impressionable pupils but evidently, by extradiegetic extension, on generations of audience members since *Jean Brodie* is often adjudged as the female companion-piece to Donat's *Goodbye, Mr. Chips*, an influential and inspiring example of the charismatic teacher film: Jo Keroes notes how 'Jean Brodie appeals to a popular belief that the truly memorable teacher is the one who cultivates our individuality and helps us to discover our tru-est, best, and most original selves, especially as she explicitly sets herself in opposition to the notion of the teacher as one who merely imparts infor-mation' (1999: 36). The opposing stance is repeatedly advocated by the 'dowdy provincial' Miss Mackay who insists that 'culture is no compensa-tion for lack of hard knowledge' and curtly dismisses pupil discussions of the consumptive Violetta from *La Traviata*, claiming, in upstanding public school fashion, that 'if she'd been brought up properly, she'd be out on a hockey field breathing deeply'. Within a generic context, intertextual reso-nances add to Brodie's affection-earning carnivalesque: when Miss Mackay finds Monica crying in class, Brodie's retort that they have been studying the moving Battle of Flodden (and not her love affair with Hugh 'who fell in Flanders Field') is as nimble-witted as Will Hay's Agincourt impro-visation in *Good Morning, Boys*; she debunks the Hitchcockian psychol-ogy underlying hierarchical delays in punishment, imperiously countering Mackay's summons for 4.15 p.m. with 'she thinks to intimidate me by the use of quarter hours?' That meeting, the first of three strategic confronta-tions between the 'progressive' teacher and 'conservative' headmistress, successfully dramatises another generic staple, but here offers staging posts in a reverse trajectory to *Goodbye, Mr. Chips*, incrementally exposing its articulate defendant not to be the widely adjudged charismatic role-model but, in Sandy's words, a 'dangerous and unwholesome' influence on the young girls she claims are her vocation. Despite her proudly proclaimed (if trite?) etymological definition of education as 'to lead out what is already there', Brodie is shown as working to mould Edinburgh epigones, indoc-trinated extensions of her own 'European' views. Objective truth resides solely with the dominant teacher who sweeps away Jenny's suggestion that the greatest Italian painter is da Vinci: 'The answer is Giotto. He is my favourite.' Her self-aggrandising eccentricities seem less innocuous when praising Mussolini and Franco, political affiliations that (over-)signify the dangers of the classroom demagogue, rendered explicit when Sandy calls the Brodie set her 'faithful *fascisti*, marching along'. Self-knowledge is sorely lacking: Brodie may contrast herself to the Marcia Blaine staffroom, 'dedicated to the status quo', a term she defines as 'staying the same to the point of petrification', but her own stiff, affected manner—she 'always strikes attitudes', Sandy observes—is eventually revealed as not just per-formative but character-driven; long convinced that she is enjoying her 'prime', Brodie addresses her next set of first-formers in exactly the same manner, promising to put 'old heads on young shoulders' and elevating them to the 'crème de la crème'. Experiencing life vicariously through her favourite pupils, be it making one of her 'gels' a proxy lover in the bed of married Art teacher Teddy Lloyd (Robert Stephens) or a fascist fighter in Spain, her cult of personality may initially inspire but, unfettered, poten-tially culminates in exploitation, totalitarianism, even death. Socially this explores at an individual level the late-1960s 'revolutionary' dangers that *If....* treated at the institutional; cinematically it establishes a trope *inter alia* revisited in works such as *Dead Poets Society* (Peter Weir, 1989), and *Die Welle/The Wave* (Dennis Gansel, 2008).

Brodie's contradictory feminism—her rallying call that women can 'serve, suffer and sacrifice' as well as any male, but only in the cause of a 'dedicated man' like Franco recalls Miss Whitchurch—is matched by the (female-authored) film's gender depictions. Several of Brodie's cultural references, notably her praise for D.H. Lawrence and Marie Stopes, can be read as tangential reinforcements to her right-wing views, but equally serve as reference points for a free-thinking 'new woman', one who prefers (wealthy) music teacher Gordon Lowther (Gordon Jackson) as a lover than a husband and seeks that pupils such as Jenny should enjoy love affairs free of 'the common moral code'. However, while Lloyd's 'bohe-mian' lifestyle and pupil affairs go unpunished, not so Brodie's unconven-tional presumptions. Firstly, her opposition to Miss Mackay is eroded, both at a personal level, when Lloyd crushingly rejects Brodie as 'a frustrated spinster' and 'schoolma'am'—she retorts with a defiantly non-gendered, but imminently redundant 'I am a teacher!'—and also at a pedagogical level, when her Franco-inspired encomium is repeated near-verbatim in Mackay's end-of-year pledge that the school's training will provide its pupils with 'courage and gallantry.' This elision of difference—working as much to categorise private schooling as to prick Brodie's individuality—is not alone the 'necessary destiny' for abjuring traditional (passive) gender roles and Brodie must, in New Wave style, be punished, not with a literal death, but with betrayal and dismissal, Sandy becoming her calculating 'assassin'.

Jean Brodie was entered, alongside *If....*, for the 1969 Cannes Film Festival. In its crowning achievement, Smith won the 1969 Academy Award for Best Actress, while Rod McKuen's (rather incongruous) 'Jean' was nominated for Best Song—awards and nominations reversed at the Golden Globes. Having originally made a small profit on its $2.8 million production budget, Smith's Oscar victory occasioned a further $2 million in box-office takings. UK reviews were, unlike Brodie herself, restrained but predominantly supportive. Most, as ever, laboured the film's inferiority to the source novel and Allen's theatre version: for Jay Dawson 'the result, predictably, is a dramatisation of a dramatisation, a succession of *scenes-à-faire* and telling monologues which provide a field day for the principal performers at the expense of that elusive irony that gave the original story much of its distinction' (*MFB*, April 1969: 75). Several UK reviewers ventured to 'criticise the divine Maggie Smith who makes of [Brodie] such as figure of comedy (almost a revue sketch of a prissy-accented, unconventional Scottish spinster) that your average schoolgirl—the craftiest creature in existence—would have sized her up and sniggered behind her back before her first class was over' (*Sunday Telegraph*, 2 March 1969). America, though, uniformly eulogised the central performance: Vincent Canby, for whom Smith 'is simply great', also praised the 'hard, constricted faces of anonymous girls and teachers, little Stones of Scone, painted white with small black pits for eyes. They are not the sort of faces that are likely to be found around Mr. Chips' (*New York Times*, 3 March 1969). They might, though, have found a place alongside Travis in College House.

NOTES

1. The ideological tensions of this 'tripartite' system are evident in the Crown Film Unit's explanatory documentary *Children's Charter* (Gerard Bryant, 1945).
2. A first for British cinema: the BBFC allowed the word for its economic evidencing of class difference. *Evening News*, 21 October 1948.

3. *Torment* was Ingmar Bergman's first filmed screenplay.
4. The extract, in the Browning version, reads: 'And, through desire of one across the main,/A ghost will seem within the house to reign./And hateful to the husband is the grace/of well-shaped statues; from—in place of eyes/ Those blanks—all Aphrodite dies.' Robert Browning, (2009 [1877]) 'The Agamemnon of Aeschylus', in *Complete Poetic and Dramatic Works*. Maryland: Wildside Press: 835.
5. Jeffrey Richards posits that authors who depicted the lives of public school masters as happy and fulfilled, Hilton, Hay and R.F. Delderfield, were heterosexual; those who depicted teacher lives as empty and arid, E.M. Forster, Walpole and Rattigan, were homosexual: 'It is evident that, with the school as a metaphor for society, they are exploring their own feelings of repression, rejection and dissatisfaction' (1988: 264).
6. Harper and Porter categorise 1950s British cinema as offering 'residual' and 'emergent' film types, 'old and new ways of presenting the world and pleasing audiences' (2003: 1).
7. Scottish Protestant reformer Knox's polemical work of 1558 attacks female (Catholic) monarchs, notably Mary I and Mary Queen of Scots, arguing that rule by females is contrary to natural law and the Bible's revealed religion. See R. M. Healey et al. (1994) 'Waiting for Deborah: John Knox and Four Ruling Queens'. *Sixteenth Century Journal*, 25, 2: 371–86.
8. This relocation offered a contemporary resonance of colonial hubris: 'There was a grand scheme for growing groundnuts in Tanganyika, to provide cheap vegetable oil for Britain—though that was a swift and embarrassing failure. For a while it seemed that the Raj would be transplanted, in fragmented form, to Africa.' Andrew Marr (2007) *A History of Modern Britain*. London: Macmillan: 40.
9. For instance, the recent headline: 'The REAL St Trinian's: Headmistress of girls' school where pupils ran riot... is suspended.' *Daily Mail*, 5 September 2013.
10. The affair between Secretary of State for War John Profumo and 19-year-old Christine Keeler, arguably a contributory factor in Labour's 1964 victory, is dramatised in *Scandal* (Michael Caton-Jones, 1989).
11. Andrew Sarris famously described *A Hard Day's Night* (Richard Lester, 1964) as 'the *Citizen Kane* of jukebox musicals'. *Village Voice*, 27 August 1964.
12. On Sherwin's long-overlooked contribution, see Charles Drazin (2008) '*If.... Before If....*' *Journal of British Cinema and Television*, 2, 2: 318–34.
13. The director later revealed that the headmaster's surrounding discourse was taken almost verbatim from ex-Eton housemaster J.D.R. McConnell (1967) *Eton: How it Works*. London: Faber and Faber. 'So some of the more idiotic things spoken by the headmaster are real' (Anderson 2004: 118).

14. *If....* is 'literally' a textbook example of unconventional narrative. See Allan Rowe, 'Film form and narrative'—Case Study 3, *If....*—an alternative text', in Jill Nelmes (ed.) (1992) *An Introduction to Film Studies.* London: Routledge: 116–9.

15. I.Q. Hunter (2013) borrows the line to summarise the nation's film industry: 'British cinema for all her triumphs remains awkwardly stranded between art and populism, a nubile Cinderella...sparsely clad and often interfered with.' *British Trash Cinema.* London: Palgrave Macmillan: 1.

16. The quote comes from Tennyson's 'The Third of February 1852', a patriotic address to 'lovers of political honesty and friends of freedom'. Hugh Walker (2011[1910]) *Literature of the Victorian Era.* Cambridge: Cambridge University Press: 448.

17. Jeffrey Richards discusses what he (surprisingly) termed 'one of the finest films the cinema has produced' in a section entitled 'The Cinema of Empire' (1973: 58).

References

Ackroyd, P. (1979) *Dressing up, Transvestism and Drag: The History of an Obsession.* Norwich: Thames.

Allen, S. (2010) 'A French Exchange: Education as the Cultural Interface in British Comedies'. *Journal of British Cinema and Television*, 7, 3.

Anderson, L. (2004) *Never Apologise: The Collected Writings.* London: Plexus.

Armes, R. (1975) *A Critical History of British Cinema.* London: Secker and Warburg.

Babington, B. (2002) *Launder and Gilliat.* Manchester: Manchester University Press.

Baker, R. (1994) *Drag: A History of Female Impersonation in the Performing Arts.* London: Cassell.

Barber, M. (1994) *The Making of the 1944 Education Act.* London: Cassell.

Barr, C. (1977) *Ealing Studios.* London: Cameron and Tayleur.

Board of Education (1943) *White Paper Educational Reconstruction*, Cmd. 6458. London: HMSO.

Bourne, S. (1996) *Brief Encounters: Lesbians and Gays in British Cinema 1930–1971.* London: Cassell.

Brown, G. (1977) *Launder and Gilliat.* London: BFI.

Butler, J. (1993) *Bodies that Matter: On the Discursive Limits of Sex.* London: Routledge.

Cadogan, M. and P. Craig (1986) *You're a Brick, Angela! The Girls' Story 1839–1985.* London: Victor Gollancz.

Darlow, M. and G. Hodson (1979) *Terence Rattigan: The Man and his Work.* London: Quartet Books.

Durgnat, R. (1970) *A Mirror for England: British Movies from Austerity to Affluence*. London: Faber and Faber.

Gathorne-Hardy, J. (1979) *The Public School Phenomenon*. Harmondsworth: Penguin.

Geraghty, C. (2000) *British Cinema in the Fifties: Gender, Genre and the 'New Look'*. London: Routledge.

Harper, S. and V. Porter (2003) *British Cinema of the 1950s: The Decline of Deference*. Oxford: Oxford University Press.

Hay, I. (1914) *The Lighter Side of School Life*. Edinburgh: Ballantyne Press.

Hedling, E. (1998) *Lindsay Anderson: Maverick Film-maker*. London: Cassell.

Higson, A. (1994) 'A Diversity of Film Practices: Renewing British Cinema in the 1970s', in B. Moore-Gilbert (ed.) *The Arts in the 1970s: Cultural Closure?* London: Routledge.

Keroes, J. (1999) *Tales Out of School: Gender, Longing and the Teacher in Fiction and Film*. Carbondale: Southern Illinois University Press.

Lambert, G. (2000) *Mainly About Lindsay Anderson—A Memoir*. London: Faber and Faber.

Landy, M. (1991) *British Genres: Cinema and Society, 1930–1960*. Princeton NJ: Princeton University Press.

Leach, J. (2004) *British Film*. Cambridge: Cambridge University Press.

Low, R. (1985) *Filmmaking in 1930s Britain*. London: George Allen and Unwin.

McFarlane, B. (ed.) (1992) *Sixty Voices: Celebrities Recall the Golden Age of British Cinema*. London: BFI.

Medhurst, A. (1984) '1950s war films', in G. Hurd (ed.) *National Fictions: World War Two in British Films and Television*. London: BFI.

Murphy, R. (1992) *Sixties British Cinema*. London: BFI.

Petley, J. (2000) 'The pilgrim's regress: the politics of the Boultings' films', in A. Burton, T. O'Sullivan and P. Wells (eds) *The Family Way: The Boulting Brothers and British Film Culture*. Trowbridge: Flicks Books.

Quigly, I. (1982) *The Heirs of Tom Brown: The English School Story*. London: Chatto and Windus.

Rattigan, N. (1994) 'The last gasp of the middle class: British war films of the 1950s', in W. Wheeler Dixon (ed.) *Re-Viewing British Cinema, 1900–1992*. Albany: State University of New York Press.

Richards, J. (1973) *Visions of Yesterday*. London: Routledge and Kegan Paul.

Richards, J. (1984) *The Age of the Dream Palace: Cinema and Society in Britain 1930–1939*. London: Routledge and Kegan Paul.

Richards, J. (1988) *Happiest Days: the public schools in British fiction*. Manchester: Manchester University Press.

Richards, J. and A. Aldgate (1983) *British Cinema and Society 1930–1970*. Oxford: Blackwell.

Russell Taylor, J. (1975) *Directors and Directions*. London: Eyre Methuen.

Searle, R. (1959) *The St. Trinian's Story*. London: Perpetua Books.

Shafer, S. (2003) *British Popular Films 1929–1939: The Cinema of Reassurance*. London: Routledge.

Sherwin, D. (1996) *Going Mad in Hollywood—and Life with Lindsay Anderson*. Harmondsworth: Penguin.

Sinker, M. (2004) *If....* London: BFI.

Slide, A. (1985) *Fifty Classic British Films, 1932–1982: A Pictorial Record*. New York: Dover Publications.

Sussex, E. (1969) *Lindsay Anderson*. London: Studio Vista.

Sutton, D. (2000) *A Chorus of Raspberries: British Film Comedy 1929–1939*. Exeter: University of Exeter Press.

Sutton, P. (2005) *If....* London: I.B. Tauris.

Walker, A. (1974) *Hollywood England: The British Film Industry in the Sixties*. London: Michael Joseph.

Wells, P. (2000) 'Comments, custard pies and comic cuts: the Boulting brothers at play', in A. Burton, T. O'Sullivan and P. Wells (eds) *The Family Way: The Boulting Brothers and British Film Culture*. Trowbridge: Flicks Books.

CHAPTER 4

The Post-War State School Film (1945–70)

1   THE RIGHT STUFF

For the 95 per cent of the British population not sent to public school, the Elementary Education Act of 1870 first made provision for educating all children aged five to 13, though it took an 1880 Act to make it compulsory and 1891 before early years education became free of charge. Arthur Balfour's Education Act of 1902 set a clear division in education systems at the age of 11 and led to a rapid expansion in the building of secondary schools. So, by the early years of the new century and the early years of cinema, Britain finally had a coherent national educational system, though one still class-riven and 'largely confined to the provision of a minimum standard' (Williams 1961: 137)—and lengthily devoid of fiction film representation. The 1944 Education Act's extension of a full and free education had quickly become a 'bipartite system' given the reluctance of LEAs to invest in expensive technical colleges and was thus adjudged as perpetuating the nineteenth century's class-bound system of education: the grammar school with its promise of a university place and professional career became the goal for the aspirational middle class; the secondary modern became the 'sink' for the restricted working class.

The first British fiction film fully set in a state school, 55 years into the medium's existence, came in the northern circuit programme filler *School for Randle* (John E. Blakeley, October 1949), Lancashire music hall comic Frank Randle's seventh film for the Mancunian Film Corporation, then the only working studio outside of London and the South East. Randle

© The Editor(s) (if applicable) and The Author(s) 2016
S. Glynn, *The British School Film*,
DOI 10.1057/978-1-137-55887-9_4

was a rough proletarian antidote to respectable fellow-son-of-Wigan George Formby, yet big enough a draw to sell a film (in the north) on his name—here punning on Sheridan's 1777 comedy of manners *The School for Scandal*. Randle plays 'Flatfoot' Mason, former music hall artiste and now caretaker at Lynhurst's High School for Boys and Girls. His teenage daughter, Betty (Terry Randall), previously given up for adoption, runs away from the school to follow her dream of treading the boards, but is rescued by Flatfoot who traces her to the seedy 'Cuties and Capers' touring revue where—with fellow caretakers and Mancunian regulars Dan Young and Alec Pleon disguised as the Chinese 'Three Who Flungs' acrobatic act—he persuades Betty to come home and resume her studies. In a finale narratively recalling *Tell England*, but poles apart in class and register, Betty proves her worth and her birth father's judgement by winning the inter-school swimming gala alongside her budding beau Ted (Johnny Singer). Before then the caretakers three blunder around the school, reciting *Hamlet* in the boiler room, 'helping' the cook to make rabbit pie, and training Betty and Ted in the pool. This unreconstructed knockabout humour marries with an evident wariness at post-war moves towards co-education: not only does the mixed-school setting tone down Randle's habitually lecherous and drunken persona, but when paternalistic Flatfoot is warned off by staff, unaware of his blood-ties with Betty, for being too attentive, his subsequent reserve triggers her absconding. Segregated in separate buildings for lessons, the playful boy-girl 'extra-curricular' rivalry is also censured as, in parallel scenes, Betty and Ted are warned by their respective teachers to stay away from the opposite sex. There is no displacement here of burgeoning sexuality as a foreign, French practice, and the film hints at transgressive play with Betty's embryonic new career but, in a reversal of *The Romantic Age*'s dynamic, Randle's 'responsible' central narrative role ensures a hegemonic male control of female self-fulfilment.

Randle was marginal, northern fare—a safe starting point, perhaps. The mainstream *It's Great To Be Young!* (Cyril Frankel, 30 May 1956), scripted for Marble Arch Films by *Top of the Form* co-writer Ted Willis, starred John Mills as Mr Dingle, a grammar school History and Music teacher trying to mediate between a repressive new headmaster, Mr Frome (Cecil Parker), and the pupils who want to play 'modern music'. When the head, discovering Dingle's clandestine efforts to help his pupils buy instruments for a forthcoming national competition, forces his resignation, head boy Nicky (Jeremy Spenser) organises a pupil strike, a gym occupation, and support from neighbouring schools. Realising his own intransigence, Frome offers to resign instead, only for Dingle to condemn the adolescent imitation of industrial practices as 'sentimental rubbish', asking 'Since when had one man been more important than the whole school?' The impressed head reinstates Dingle, the pupils cheer, carry both men shoulder high, and the happy, compromise ending allows Dingle to lead his school into the closing concert. In précis, this mid-1950s youthful rebellion triggered by popular music could suggest *Rock Around The Clock* (Fred F. Sears, 1956) reformulated for the British screen: alas, no. Though given a selective state school setting, it is hard to distinguish *It's Great to be Young* visually or sonically from prior public school fare, with Angel Hill Grammar situated in 'traditional' ivy-bedecked buildings, filled with masters sporting gowns and mortarboards, white-flannelled cricketers on extensive school grounds and well-mannered pupils declaiming 'keep cave, you chaps' or 'thanks awfully' and defending their strike action as 'only standing up for fair play'. Mills is an unworldly Will Hay-style man-child, running in the corridors, easily distracted from his History lessons and innocently initiating subversion through his passion for music. Generic hybridity, however, is crucially just off the beat: vaunted in the trade press as a 'Jolly, fast-moving Technicolor collegiate-musical-comedy-drama' (*Kinematograph Weekly*, 31 May 1956), the film does not move fast enough, entering production just as Elvis Presley entered the pop charts and, though Frome instructs a noisy corridor to 'disguise the fact that you're hooligans', these are not the troublesome tenement teenagers of emergent 'social problem' films such as *I Believe in You* (Basil Dearden, Michael Relph, 1952) and *Cosh Boy* (Lewis Gilbert, 1953), but culturally advantaged grammar school children whose demands for a school orchestra are an aspirational parent's dream in their appeal to high art and disciplined self-improvement. Raymond Durgnat saw 'a progressive effect' in the way the film 'stand[s] up, against strong traditional prejudices, for co-education, for all this modern leniency in schools' (1970: 57–8), but with Dingle admitting his guilt in defying school discipline and accepting his punishment, the film concludes, like *The Guinea Pig*, with the rule of authority vindicated, antiphonal voices absorbed and community restored. *It's Great to be Young* was a financial success, entering the year's UK box-office top ten, but contemporary critical reception was more parsimonious. While the *Daily Herald* lauded, in carnivaleque style, 'a British comedy full of whizzo wheezes and wacko capers that parents will pinch their kids' pocket money to go and see' (1 June 1956), Isabel Quigly more bluntly considered the Angels and their mentor 'quite nauseating' (*Spectator*, 8 June 1956). Mediating such extremes, Paul Dehn saw the pupils as 'falling between two stools' since 'some of the children seem to have popped grotesquely from the pages of the twopenny comics. Others are manifestly intended to seem as plausible as present-day Tom Browns.' He termed the film 'a roaring musico-realistico-farcico failure' (*News Chronicle*, 1 June 1956), but it would prove an enduring Pied Piper narrative.

Carry On Teacher (Gerald Thomas, 25 August 1959), the third state school comedy, was also the third film in the burgeoning Carry On franchise. The ensemble cast, including Kenneth Williams, Charles Hawtrey, Hattie Jacques and Joan Sims, was beginning to cohere, but the film's lead, television and radio star Ted Ray, was sufficiently coveted for his part to be written expressly for him by Norman Hudis. Ray plays popular (acting) headmaster William 'Wakie' Wakefield, who after 20 years' service at Maudlin Street School, London, hopes a successful inspection will earn him the permanent headship of a newly built 'super school'. However, the pupils so effectively undermine procedures that Wakefield is about to cane the ringleaders when he discovers their behaviour is motivated to keep him at Maudlin Street: moved by their intentions, he agrees to stay. With American cinema increasingly exploring teenage angst, *Carry On Teacher* kept the British school film coy and cosy: while Robert Ross terms its 'rose-tinted social document' as 'more Billy Bunter and Greyfriars than James Dean and the juvenile court' (1996: 21), it more specifically mines indigenous school *film* traditions, beginning with Searle-like cartoon miscreants for its poster and credit sequence, through its Wetherby Pond inspection-for-promotion plot steal, back to the Will Hay provenance of Charles Hawtrey who, tables turned, is now the hapless teacher battling bespectacled schoolboy nemesis George Howell. The film is generically consistent in its carnivalesque depiction of mature, organised pupils versus a childish, inefficient teaching staff, though here the pupils add a co-educational sexual awareness, asking knowing and awkward questions on underage sex and 'wedding beds' in Shakespeare. To the fore in staffroom juvenilia is the in-fighting between Hawtrey's Music master Mr Bean and Williams' English master Mr Milton, their excessive artistic temperaments motivating their Carry On camp personae as they bicker over the school's *Romeo and Juliet* production—and intimating how, unlike a vocational Mr Chips, teaching can serve as a substitute for unfulfilled career ambitions. Underpinning such antics are broadly sketched dialectics on educational and sexual politics. Milton, like Gilbert in *The Browning Version* an adherent of 'the modern psychological method', is 'down with the kids' in his casual clothing and cogently liberal in his attitudes towards discipline: 'Extraordinary theory, you bend a child double in order to give it an upright character!' Such progressive attitudes are lampooned, however, in visiting educational psychiatrist Alistair Grigg (Leslie Phillips), impractical author of 'Contemporary Juvenile Behaviour Patterns'. In the opposite camp Jacques' Miss Short, the deputy head termagant of cane-wielding authority, battles alongside Sims' Miss Allcock, a staunch advocate of practical experience before fashionable theories, to right male educational wrongs and save the school for the feminist cause.

Responding to *It's Great to be Young*, Raymond Durgnat had requested 'a more radical topic… Why not, after all, a secondary modern *If….*' (1970: 58): it does not happen here. The pupils' secure syndicalism may suggest an anticipation of *soixante-huitard* attitudes, but everywhere the film again works to preserve the status quo and restore long-established social and economic structures—thus continuing the consensual conclusions of Thomas' *Carry on Sergeant* (1958) and *Carry on Nurse* (1959). And so, while John Hill bemoaned how, in *It's Great to be Young*, 'The "problem" of youth becomes a crisis merely of authority, internal to the middle class, and requiring little more than some inter generational understanding for a solution' (1986: 104), here the pupil body, gathered beneath the head's window to chant 'We want Wakey!', indicates how, in its early state school film context, the 'problem' is equally elided from working-class youth experience. *Kinematograph Weekly*, exercising its penchant for pedagogical puns, affirmed that '*Carry On Teacher* brilliantly passes the box-office Eleven Plus' and should 'enable exhibitors to earn enough to give their own offspring a college education!' (20 August 1959). It did, succeeding commercially on both sides of the Atlantic. America's *Variety* liked the teaching variety, 'eccentric characters who are nicely assorted and all have plenty of "fat" without being on the screen long enough to become tedious' (2 September 1959). Britain's response customarily fell along political lines: the *Daily Worker* appreciated its 'good strong basic humour and working-class values. The school background and staffroom discussions ring as nearly true as they are meant to' (5 September 1959); a worried *Daily Mail* decried humour 'occasionally prep school suggestive, indicating that the current film censors are either unexpectedly indulgent or very innocent' (5 September 1959). The *Times* spoke for all persuasions in finding Ray (in what would prove his only Carry On appearance) 'somewhat subdued as the headmaster—the memory of Will Hay… will not be banished' (4 September 1959).

2   THE WRONG WOMAN

With the historical watershed of the 1956 Suez crisis confirming the end of Britain's status as a world power, more serious post-war depictions of the schoolteacher, previously a metonym for national pride and power, revealed a similar struggle to maintain control of their domain. In tandem with distant and difficult international reassessment came discernible high-street evidence of consumerism, high-profile teenagers with disposable income and, swiftly here for them to consume it, high-school-inflected American youth culture. *The Blackboard Jungle* (Richard Brooks, 1955), ostensibly a standard Hollywood piece in its portrayal of a single sympathetic adult, teacher Richard Dadier (Glenn Ford), bridging the gap between truculent youth and uncomprehending authority, but ramped into the cultural stratosphere by the last-minute use over its credits of Bill Haley and the Comets' 'Rock Around the Clock', was released in the UK in September 1955, with 20 minor cuts and an 'X' certificate. Though barred to its depicted audience (the 'X' certificate, introduced in 1951, could only be shown to over-16s), the film's success was ultimately catalytic in bringing the British school film out of its comic cocoon and into the gritty combative arena of inner-city secondary modern education, paving the way for a 1960s 'state school trilogy', each featuring similarly discordant, discarded pupils but married to very British concerns, the potentially inflammatory results of a middle-aged male teacher having to confront an infatuated female pupil.

A genteel forerunner can be found in *Personal Affair* (Anthony Pelissier, 20 October 1953), set at an ivy-covered grammar school in the fictional 'stuffy' English country town of Rudford. Adapted by Lesley Storm from her play *A Day's Mischief*, the film, produced by Two Cities with Gene Tierney brought in to improve overseas marketing, relates the infatuation of 17-year-old schoolgirl Barbara Vining (Glynis Johns) with her 'Ode to Chloe'-reciting Latin teacher Stephen Barlow (Leo Genn), labelled 'one of the dedicated people': when Barbara, confronted by Barlow's wife Kay (Tierney), goes missing, suspicion falls on the luckless teacher, causing him to be ostracised by the community, lose his job and jeopardise his marriage before Barbara's contrite return three days later. The film revisits the dangers to family life of teenage female sexuality raised in *The Romantic Age* and the broad social unease at co-education broached in *School for Randle*—headmaster Mr Griffith (Michael Hordern) warns Barlow how 'in a mixed school, an "experimental" school of this nature, even a slight indiscretion is a serious matter', while melodramatic shots of the major players' faces looming out of storm clouds and rushing water intimate the 'unnatural' potential in superimposing such educational and emotional arrangements. Though Barlow admits only to a vague 'state of love' in the classroom air and Mr Vining (Walter Fitzgerald) clings to the idea that his daughter is still a child, it is pointedly not male suppression but female sexuality, burgeoning as with Barbara, or repressed as with her maiden aunt Evelyn (Pamela Brown) whose Miss Haversham-like bitterness fuels the teacher–pupil rumours, that ultimately constitutes the disruptive force within a school, family and whole-town context. Replicating such unwitting misogyny, UK critics trumpeted *Personal Affair*'s matinee appeal: 'Queue up for your little weep, ladies. This is a fine film' (*Daily Mirror*, 23 October 1953). America found it 'an earnest and plausible study' but all too British in its 'decent, eventually tedious delivery' whereby 'the situation is kept too well in hand, everyone tries to be too chin-up and the scandal is too refined' (*New York Times*, 23 October 1954). It would prove a long struggle to break free of that refinement.

2.1   Section Prize Winner: Spare the Rod *(1961)*

Spare the Rod, a successful novel by (Burnage Grammar-educated) Michael Croft published in 1954, the same year as Evan Hunter's source text for *The Blackboard Jungle*, drew on its author's experience as a supply teacher to tell the tale of a new recruit's struggles at a badly-equipped East London secondary modern school. Unpopular within the teaching profession for its dispiriting depiction, Croft's novel underwent its first attempted film adaptation later that year, but collapsed because of the censor's demands for stringent script deletions and the warning of an inevitable 'X' certificate. Fearful of the effect the film would have on parents, teachers and educational authorities, a Board spokesman even warned that 'there'll be riots in the classroom if this is made' (Michael Croft, *Observer*, 4 June 1961). A second attempt came in 1956, now with full cognisance of Brooks' US adaptation (reprints already advertised Croft's novel as 'the English equivalent of America's *The Blackboard Jungle*'), but it again floundered, for the same reasons. Third time lucky, *Spare the Rod* was again tendered for BBFC consideration in 1960, during ex-schoolmaster John Trevelyan's more liberally minded tenure as Board chairman.[1] With Victor Lyndon producing, a key change in tack saw the film presented as a star vehicle for wholesome family entertainer Max Bygraves: Croft had wanted Trevor Howard for his semi-autobiographical lead but Bygraves, with an East End upbringing similar to that described in the novel, was so keen to realise the adaptation that he sank his life savings of nearly £50,000 towards Bryanston Films' production costs. Leslie Norman, 'the council schoolboy who became a major in the war' (McFarlane 1997: 441) and best known for directing *Dunkirk* (1958), was entrusted with the director's chair for this council school tale of intergenerational warfare. Finding Croft's treatment too heavy, Norman commissioned a new screenplay from John Cresswell which 'lightened' the load by adding an attempted schoolgirl seduction and a *Blackboard Jungle*-inspired class riot. Shot predominantly at Shepperton Studios, location work included Hammersmith's Corona Stage School since London County Council refused filming in any of its schools lest 'parents and teachers might think the sort of school to be shown on the screen is typical of one of ours' (*Bryanston Newsletter*, 4 May 1961). Finally granted the commercially requisite 'A' certificate, *Spare the Rod*, marketed as 'the Film they Tried to Stop', premiered at the Odeon, Marble Arch on 18 May 1961 and went on general release on 19 June, nearly seven years after its first submission to the BBFC.[2] The (belated) film relates how ex-naval instructor John Saunders accepts an East End teaching post at Worrell Street School. Though surrounded by staff advocating fulsome use of the cane, Saunders' preference for winning pupil confidence achieves some success with his previously uncontrollable final-year cohort, even surviving an attempted seduction by one of his pupils, Margaret (Claire Marshall), but a loss of class control makes him resort, reluctantly, to caning three boys, unjustly in the case of the academically promising Harkness (Richard O'Sullivan). When long-serving disciplinarian Arthur Gregory (Geoffrey Keen), locked all night in the school lavatory, blames and starts violently caning Harkness, Saunders intervenes, occasioning a class riot and the demand that he resign. Ready to leave the profession altogether, the gratitude shown by his pupils gives Saunders second thoughts.

The pre-credit sequence to *Spare the Rod* shows the near-paradigm shift from the socio-geographical context of public school films such as *The Guinea Pig*. Instead of train journeys to country piles with pastoral accompaniment, a brash jazz score follows a set of un-uniformed children across a busy street, obstructing traffic and gesturing at drivers, before continuing their bullying of younger pupils in the playground of their Edwardian-housed secondary 'modern'. Its run-down facilities are everywhere foregrounded on Saunders' arrival: the doorknob to the headmaster's office comes off in his hand, the chair he sits on collapses and his classroom's broken sash cord sends the window crashing down. The greeting of headmaster Jenkins (Donald Pleasence) is equally demoralising, enquiring why he has come into teaching—'you shouldn't be tired of life at your age'—and informing him that his new class of 15-year-olds are 'all duds, throw-outs, all of them' with many only here because the approved schools are full. Classics are not on this curriculum, nor specialists to deliver it: Saunders must take on classes in Mathematics, English, History, Geography—and Science, for which he looks vainly though the school's sole relevant resource, an outdated Children's Encyclopaedia. In this spartan setting, the film quickly sets up the customary staffroom dialectic. Jenkins' trusted lieutenant, the embittered woodwork master Gregory, advises Saunders to 'keep them down. Don't give them an inch' and his serial caning, even for running into lunch, offers a chilling but clearly effective tool of short-term control. Saunders, a mature 'modern educationalist' fresh from training college, looks instead to elicit pupil support, offering his class a vote on school monitors (an aborted failure, with pupils confused by his liberal stance) and, acting on the advice of colleague Alec Murray (Peter Reynolds), introducing project work that feeds into their current interests and opens their horizons to future travel (an inspection-evaluated success). It is a hard struggle, though, against engrained indifference: leaving school one evening, Saunders and his progressively-minded colleague Ann Johnson (Betty McDowell) reject Gregory's condemnation of teaching as 'a mug's game' with 'short pay, hard work and no thanks for it'; their argument in favour of 'teaching the future generation to do better than we did' may be two against one, but as they pass the school gates an infant group's skipping song— 'Mine's a cheerless occupation,/All this gloom and desolation'—already sounds supportive of Gregory's jaundiced worldview. It is, in truth, a rare moment of relative subtlety. Broadly polemical in its pedagogical discussions, schematic in its narrative development and conformist in Norman's directorial style, *Spare the Rod* remains nonetheless laudably earnest in intent and displays a genuine interest in the way such pupils' background lives can explain if not excuse their school behaviour. Murray, supplementing his teaching with evening barman work, knows of several parents' drunken neglect of their children: 'bad stock and filthy homes in most cases', he terms them. Saunders sees this for himself when duped into visiting Margaret's dingy single-roomed tenement-block home, curtailed when her parents, home from the pub, lash out at the unwanted visitor. A hang-over from the source text, the war is still a blight on young lives, especially Harkness, who confides in war-serving Saunders memories of his now-deceased father's nightmares, who became a 'broken man' after being a prisoner of war in Singapore.

While locatable as a belated addition to the 'social problem' cycle of late-1950s British filmmaking and a cinematic cousin to *Violent Playground* (Basil Dearden, 1958), *Spare the Rod* most evidently parallels *The Blackboard Jungle* with Bygraves in the Glenn Ford role of an ex-serviceman new recruit whose reforming zeal starts to yield results in a tough working-class school. Both are caring and charismatic teachers, averse to corporal punishment and keen to make their teaching relevant: much as Dadier used a cartoon of 'Jack and the Beanstalk' to engage his pupils' critical faculties, Saunders relates Shakespeare's *Julius Caesar* to Hitler and his assassins to gangsters, enthusing the class by acting out the murder scene as a mass scrum on the classroom floor. Both men face severe obstructions in their liberal agenda: while Dadier is assaulted by male teenage violence, *Spare the Rod* replays the British genre's fear of female teenage sexuality with Margaret's clumsy advances. And both films climax in classroom riots. Here the attempted seduction proves the turning point, with all progress undone in the following morning's lesson where the class mood has hardened—has their teacher failed his test by refusing Margaret or by naively falling into her trap?—and the confused Saunders (sublimating sexuality into violence?) resorts to the caning against which he has vehemently argued (Fig. 4.1). His efforts to reaffirm his progressive credentials by tackling the sadistic Gregory also backfire, again signalling the abandonment of negotiation for brute force, an example his pupils immediately follow by going on the rampage. Authority must be reasserted, and the pattern of *It's Great To Be Young* is repeated with the head demanding the non-conformist master's resignation. The right or wrong of the incident is irrelevant, Jenkins explains: 'When you opposed Gregory, you identified with the pupils against authority. They'll expect you to remain loyal to them. When you're compelled to oppose them in the future, they'll kick your teeth and your principles right down your throat.' The explanation has merit, and is fully supported by the previously supportive district inspector.

Spare the Rod thus offers a damning dystopian view of Britain's secondary modern education system, a visual affirmation of the ill and work-weary Jenkins' résumé that there are 'not enough schools, not enough teachers of the right sort; too many children of the wrong sort'. All, though,

Fig. 4.1   To Beat or Not to Beat, that is the question

is inverted with a last-minute warm-glow conclusion. As Saunders, like Donkin in *Housemaster*, takes a final walk around the school, he hears the pupils in assembly singing 'Jerusalem'; as he clears out his desk the hymn's sentiment to 'not cease from mental fight' makes him pause; the wronged Harkness comes in to offer thanks, a cigarette and a Merry Christmas; as he crosses the school playground, the children gather affectionately around 'the hero of Class II', an evident contrast to the fighting and chaos of the opening scenes; Margaret apologises for having been 'a bad girl'; enlightenment falls even on Gregory who decides against beating a pushing pupil, prompting Jenkins' gloss that it is 'never too late to learn'. To add to the new-found gender and generational harmony, a black schoolgirl, Olive (uncredited), suddenly appears with her racially mixed parents to thank Saunders for her academic improvement. With Saunders again 'confused'—the assumption is that, like Dadier, he will remain in the profession—John Hill cogently compares the ending to Douglas Sirk who admitted his trademark melodramatic conclusion 'makes the crowd happy, but to the few makes the aporia more transparent' (Halliday 1971: 132). For Hill, *Spare the Rod* offers a similar final overloading: 'To "the crowd",

as Sirk suggests, this may provide contentment; to "the few" it undoubtedly confirms the liberal gloom' (1986: 105–6).

Contemporary critical opinion did not bear this out, however. The *Daily
Worker* thought 'it has many weaknesses, but an overriding strength—the
courage and sincerity to expose, as no other film has, the rottenness of slum
conditions and the state of many of our modern secondary schools'; by
contrast, the crowd-pleasing *People* awarded 'Nought out of ten!' to a film
that 'should never have been made' since 'the facts of school life are grossly
distorted' and, worse still, 'To foreigners this picture would give the impression that we are still living in the dark ages of *Oliver Twist*' (21 May 1961).
The majority, though, thought the rod had been spared to a fault, with
Isabel Quigly regretting 'a basic sentimentality that only just steers clear of
the heavenly choir' (*Spectator*, 26 May 1961), and critics who had rallied to
the film's cause in a 1960 magazine debate now sorely disappointed: Derek
Hill ('The Habit of Censorship', *Encounter*, July 1960) bemoaned how
the adaptation 'introduces melodrama and excitement which have nothing
to do with the original', and placed the blame with the director, 'clueless
at controlling a bunch of actors who act with a capital A' (*Tribune*, 26
May 1961); William Whitebait ('This Censorship', *New Statesman*, 30 July
1960) similarly decried 'ladling in the melodrama' as 'Delinquency with
a capital D starts to rampage' (*New Statesman*, 19 May 1961). Opinion
was also divided as to Bygraves' performance: for the *Observer* 'in the very
act of groping for a solution to the technical problems that his part poses,
[Bygraves] finds an earnestness and sincerity which are entirely appropriate'
(21 May 1961); the *Sunday Telegraph* felt such 'an engaging comedian...
would be no great shakes as a teacher—would hardly last an hour, in fact,
in this particular school' (21 May 1961). *Films and Filming* stayed within
cinematic yardsticks: 'Inevitably this will be compared with *The Blackboard
Jungle*. On almost every point the British picture gives a more honest,
more human reflection of the depressingly inadequate way Western communities are looking after their unruly young' (July 1961).

Inadequate educational provision and the advances on a mature male
teacher by an infatuated female pupil would reach their tortuous nadir
in *Term of Trial* (16 August 1962). Based on James Barlow's novel, the
adaptation's New Wave credentials are evident not just in its 'X' certificate, the first British school film thus categorised, but in its personnel
links to the movement's debut work, *Room at the Top* (Jack Clayton,
1959): it was produced by James Woolf and Romulus Films, directed

by (Stonyhurst-educated) Peter Glenville, Woolf's alternative choice to Clayton, while Glenville-recommended Simone Signoret again played the female lead. Even theatre doyen Laurence Olivier had 'kitchen sink' cinema credentials from playing Archie Rice in *The Entertainer* (Tony Richardson, 1960). Olivier here plays Graham Weir, an unhappy teacher at the co-educational East Secondary Modern School in the poorer section of an unnamed northern industrial town. He is berated by his ex-barmaid French wife, Anna (Signoret), both for their childless marriage and for Graham's inability to rise in the profession, the latter due to serving a sentence as a conscientious objector during the war, a stance which brings equal despite from his colleagues. One pupil, 15-year-old Shirley Taylor (a debutante 18-year-old Sarah Miles), responsive to Weir's kindnesses, becomes infatuated and, in a hotel on the way back from a school trip to Paris, begs the teacher to sleep with her (Fig. 4.2). When Weir gently refuses, a humiliated Shirley accuses him of assault: tried and convicted, his final impassioned speech to the bench draws a confession from Shirley that

Fig. 4.2   Weir and French love

she was lying. Though the case is dismissed, only Anna believes him to be innocent: Graham tells her that Shirley's accusation was true, making Anna for once admire his courage, thus salvaging their marriage.

Term of Trial traces a similar narrative arc to *Spare the Rod*—bar the last-minute teacher salvation. Weir, like Saunders, believes in education as a means of social promotion, hence the offer to tutor Shirley privately; he too respects his pupils, his credo of non-violence making him forego the cane in an environment where the deputy head's advice, like Jenkins, is to 'belt the little beasts!' Unlike Saunders, though, Weir has no idealistic commitment to state schooling: the film is explicit that, though well-born and holding a good degree, Weir's wartime experiences render his untrustworthy for grammar, let alone public school teaching. As socially condemned as his charges to the 'jungle' of secondary modern education, the disillusioned Weir stoically avoids confrontation and finds solace in after-school drinking. For Raymond Durgnat Weir's behaviour throughout a film that shows how 'only a thin chalk line has been holding proletarian savagery at bay... betokens his confusion about teenagers. He can't understand that older schoolchildren are, biologically, adults' (1970: 44). He seems at times equally confused about which education system he is working in. An early scene at the Weir's house has Graham, Anna and Shirley seated around the family table drinking tea: for Graham the scene fulfils a benign familial compassion, the same enjoyed by young Arthur in Parry's *Tom Brown's Schooldays*. (Weir's attitude towards Shirley can be read as not just *in loco parentis* but pseudo-parental, with Shirley the surrogate child for his barren marriage.) With boys, the public school code would conclude a beating with a shake of hands, both sides understanding the need for deference to authority and the merits of stern discipline, but in *Term of Trial* such consensual 'man-making' values do not apply. When the sexual bullying of Shirley by 'the disgusting and sordid young savage' Mitchell (further debutant Terence Stamp) provokes Weir into losing his 'splendid record of non-violence', the severe caning leads not to reconciliation but retribution, Mitchell smashing Weir's car windscreen while his father and friends attack Weir in the town.[3]

Term of Trial is considered part of a British cinematic movement past its sell-by date: for Alexander Walker it gives a strong 'feeling of bits broken off from earlier, better British realist films' (1974: 160). Rather it is a film *about* a generational/pedagogical attitude nearing its end, Weir retaining the emotional restraint of an earlier age while Shirley and Co. are set to enjoy the 'swinging' 1960s. In *Spare the Rod* Murray's advice to run with pupil interest was countered with Gregory's blunt definition of those interests, 'sex': central to this shifting social ethos, *Term of Trial* repeatedly displays what Gregory defines. Mitchell is first seen passing around a pin-up during school assembly; when Weir visits Shirley's parents he is confronted, like Saunders, by bleak tenement blocks, but here with landings frequented by prostitutes; again like Saunders pupil sexuality undermines the progressive teacher's programme, with Mitchell's photo of Shirley in the toilet provoking Weir (also sublimating sex into violence?) to brandish the cane; when Shirley is rejected, she makes out with Mitchell in a train corridor, an express exhibition for Weir of the pleasures now denied him. Most explicitly, on his way to court, the Christian pacifist teacher wanders the streets and finds jukebox cafés with teenagers dancing, sex shops with youths peering through the windows and a lurid cinema hoarding again with adolescents leering. Weir's walk presents the middle-class nightmare of a culture being destroyed by modern decadence, its working classes obsessed with consumerism, sex and violence—qualities which *Term of Trial* itself does not conspicuously eschew. Here, extrapolated from Weir's pupils, are examples of Richard Hoggart's warning over contemporary youth: 'The hedonistic but passive barbarian who rides in a fifty-horse-power bus for threepence, to see a five-million dollar film for one-and-eightpence, is not simply a social oddity; he is a portent' (1959: 250). Weir's final speech to the court is thus not that of a man, haunted by fears of cowardice, finally standing up to defend himself, but a conscientious middle-class innocent declaiming the cultural debasement consequent upon the 'shiny barbarism' of an emergent mass culture. An exculpation of his personal and professional inadequacies, and implicitly of Shirley's socialised conflation of affection with sex, Weir calls it an 'exquisite irony that I should be condemned by a society that presumes itself more moral than I, a society endlessly titillating itself with dirty books and newspapers and advertising and television'. Worse still, when acquitted, Weir loses a promotion to the colleague who brazenly picked up a prostitute while in Paris, but gains a newfound respect from his pupils who believe that the old man 'got away with it'. That he can only survive by enacting the culture's fantasy of sexual depravity exposes 'the "upside-down" values of a commercialised society' (Hill 1986: 108): it is, at least for the spooked bourgeoisie, a cruel carnivalesque.

Who, then, is at fault? In court Weir claims, redolent of Stephen Barlow's platonic defence in *Personal Affair*, that 'What I felt for [Shirley] was the love of an unworthy man for a quality—innocence, tenderness, love… Sex was not in my mind for that child.' It was in the child's mind, though, and *Term of Trial* is, finally, unmistakably a New Wave film in its reactionary, indeed misogynistic female representations. The clearest example of the movement's ideological closure comes in *Room at the Top* with the car-crash death of Signoret's sexually active Alice, her 'necessary destiny' for straying from the expected passive gender role. In *Term of Trial* Weir is presented as the victim not just of a society losing its moral compass, but especially of libidinous and vindictive women, the selfish, shallow wife and the underage, ungrateful pupil. Anna's mature sexuality—she is constantly attired in low-cut dresses and décolleté lingerie—conflates emasculating taunts with passionate 'make up' embraces (rendering its study of a teacher's dysfunctional marriage another 'straight' reworking of *The Browning Version*), while Shirley's teenage sexuality pruriently elides with scholastic worth: Roy Fisher et al. persuasively argue that 'The film appears to vindicate the discrimination against girls and the working classes that characterised the UK education system of the time. It suggests that working-class children cannot take advantage of the opportunity of a good education and are too debased to be able to benefit' (2008: 98). Rather than a mind to be developed to intellectual or even emotional maturity, the film itself presents Shirley as primarily a sexual being, with her sexuality dangerous to men and ultimately antiphonal to secondary education.

Term of Trial performed well in competition: Glenville was nominated for the Golden Lion at the Venice Film Festival, with Olivier and Miles nominated for BAFTAs. Contemporary press reviews were less impressed, though for Penelope Gilliatt 'The evocation of the school is one of the most potent things in the movie. The cold brown radiators and the seedy cloakrooms and the miserable Anglican hymns send a chill through one's bones' (*Observer*, 19 August 1962). Opinion was divided over whether a grand thespian could embody a downtrodden teacher: for Paul Dehn 'Olivier's long speech from the dock is a piece of inarticulate agonising as unforgettably delivered as the best of his Shakespearean soliloquies' (*Daily Herald*, 18 August 1962); for Thomas Wiseman 'His noble looks, his commanding personality and his natural authority are against him. He can play a king but he cannot play a mouse' (*Daily Express*, 18 August 1962). Most baulked at the closing moral, Felix Barker asking 'will women agree with Simone Signoret that they would prefer a husband who has been tempted by a young girl to an amoral coward?' (*Evening News*, 16 August 1962).[4] American critics were also underwhelmed by 'this British rehash of *Blackboard Jungle* with minor *Lolita* undertones': Bosley Crowther bemoaned the final 'cheap fiction snapper' as out of keeping with the rest of the film and offered a carnival conjecture: 'It's as though they hoped to save it with a wry joke—a sort of Rabelaisian ending. But they don't' (*New York Times*, 31 January 1963).

This section concludes with another film featuring music in a new town grammar school. It is, though, at least in provenance and publicity, far removed from the quaint charms of *It's Great to Be Young*. *The Yellow Teddybears* (Robert Hartford-Davis, 12 July 1963) is an early work from the stable of Tony Tenser and Michael Klinger, godfathers of the low-budget film with controversial themes. Having first treated venereal disease in *That Kind of Girl* (Gerry O'Hara, 1963), their co-named Tekli Productions turned to teenage female sexuality. Tenser found his theme in a tabloid exposé of pupils at an all-girls' school in North London who showed they had lost their virginity by wearing Robertson's Jam yellow 'golliwog' badges. His initial outline, named 'The Yellow Gollywog', was rejected by the BBFC for fear of unwanted publicity or even racist associations with the actual school.[5] With a change of titular insignia, the outline's reworking by Derek and Donald Ford aimed for a commercially viable yet 'sociological' study balancing underage sex and teenage rebellion with parental and authority figures to voice society's moral stance—a mix of exposure and education. A similar contrast was effected on the musical score: the Wimbledon Girls Choir delivered high cultural capital with Shakespeare's 'A Lover and His Lass', while the title track and cameo band appearance, potentially a debut film outing for a burgeoning quartet called the Beatles—they baulked at singing others' songs or losing copyright on their own compositions—was performed instead by (non-charting) fellow Merseybeat group the Embers. An inevitable 'X' certificate in the UK, even after minor cuts, the American release was less ambiguously retitled *The Thrill Seekers* and *Gutter Girl*. The film follows a clique of sixth-form girls at Peterbridge New Town Grammar (a composite of Peterborough and Stevenage?) who proudly wear yellow teddybears in their lapel to signal their sexual activity. The group's leader, Linda Donaghue (Annette Whiteley), is pregnant by window-cleaner and part-time pop-singer Kinky Carson (Iain Gregory). A prostitute friend, June (Jill Adams), arranges an abortion, but it is prevented by Linda's father (Victor Brooks), furious that his daughter's behaviour has jeopardised his council election chances: Linda flees to London and an uncertain future. In parallel runs the story of Linda's young Biology teacher Anne Mason (Jacqueline Ellis), engaged to Art master Paul Brinner (John Bonney).

When she overhears the significance of the teddybears, Anne lectures the class, asserting her right to advise by confessing that she too is not a virgin. When Mr Donaghue blames the school for teaching sex to his daughter, Anne is called before the board of governors: rather than apologise she berates a system that fails to teach the difference between lust and love. She storms out of the meeting, and her job.

The publicity surrounding *The Yellow Teddybears*—British posters foregrounding schoolgirls in uniform or in the shower, America leading with the tagline 'What they learned isn't on any report card!'—suggests a typical Tekli product: Tenser was later hailed as 'the Irving Thalberg of the exploitation movie' (McGillivray 1992: 129). However, lying on the 1963 cusp of the demise of 'legitimate' social problem films and the rise of 'sexploitation' (Hunt 1998: 98), *The Yellow Teddybears* is much less show than tell, foregoing schoolgirl sex and foregrounding an examination of sex education in schools. Occasional titbits for censors and sensation-seekers are present, principally in a sleazy, youth-corrupting party scene organised by June where drunken teenagers grope each other or play a game of musical striptease (in the British version cut down to bras and underskirts). The school swimming gala is less a *Tell England* demonstration of sporting prowess than a chance to show female bodies, in swimwear and then, through frosted glass, without. The majority of the film, however, earnestly—even ponderously—discusses the 16-year-old girls' ill-informed explorations of sex. Though differing from *Spare the Rod* and *Term of Trial* in its utopian new town setting of identikit lawns, detached houses and spaciously displayed knick-knacks, there is little change in adolescent female behaviour—the habitual schoolgirl crush is here a minor-key infatuation by a pupil with Anne's fiancé—nor in contributory parental neglect, not now drunken pub sessions but Linda's parents' weekends in Deauville. *The Yellow Teddybears* thus joined its own (laudable) clique, alongside *My Teenage Daughter* (Herbert Wilcox, 1956), *Beat Girl* (Edmond T. Gréville, 1960), *The Wild and The Willing* (Ralph Thomas, 1962) and *The Party's Over* (Guy Hamilton, 1963), in showing that delinquency and promiscuity are not the sole prerogative of working-class youth—nor is sexual ignorance. Peterbridge's 16-year-olds, variously described as 'only a baby' by parents or 'just little kids' by staff—one pupil precociously notes how 'the whole topic of sex seems to bring out the child in every one of us'—are shown to be 'confused' with their growing sexuality, or in Linda's case 'scared to death': with abortion not legalised until 1967, her use of Kinky's ineffective 'home made cure' tablets recalls the unsuccessful gin-and-hot-bath remedy from *Saturday Night and Sunday Morning* (Tony Richardson, 1960). Linda knows the stigma of unwanted pregnancy—'It's like you've got leprosy and they're afraid it's catching'[6]—and a fear of contamination pervades the film: Linda's father intends to send her away, her school will not accept her back, and it twice motivates Anne, mouthpiece for the film's counterbalancing (though rather preachy) moral message. Explaining to her class the difference between sex and true physical love, she reveals a Graham Weir-like—though domestically gendered—attitude towards the new consumer society when angrily asking 'What sort of world are you girls living in? Is it a world where sex is given out like soap coupons?'—kitchen sink, indeed. Her use of artistic simile fares little better: having sex just for kicks and to wear a teddybear is 'degrading, it's like taking a Picasso and using it as a fire-screen!' When the scandal breaks and Anne is called before the school board, led by lawyer Harry Halburton (the genre's ubiquitous Raymond Huntley), she can, again like Weir, devote the film's denouement to a denunciation of the hypocrisies of 'a society where sex has become an adjective: they read every day about the love lives of their idols'; where 'exploitative advertising' tells them that 'if they wear the right brassiere they'll get a boyfriend with a Jaguar'; and where 'promiscuity has become socially acceptable: it's getting caught out that isn't'. Redolent of the implicit message as far back as *Young Woodley*—a motherly prostitute warns Linda that fleeing to London will not bring her 'loving friends with tea and sympathy'—Anne explicitly berates a school curriculum which prides itself on finally allowing technical instruction on reproduction into Biology lessons but refuses still to place this information in a concomitant emotional context: 'It's your fear and their inexperience that makes the misery', she contends. It is a brave, narratively privileged but ultimately futile stance met largely with impolite incomprehension: 'you ask for charity, we ask for chastity', the mediating Halburton affirms. Anne departs, accompanied by Paul but denied the validation afforded to John Saunders as her pupils, eager to depart, simply fail to notice her.

'Should the teacher be responsible for giving sex instruction to teenage girls?' ran the moral-dilemma heading in *The Yellow Teddybears'* pressbook. To arrest the accusation of sensationalist exploitation, the producers sought endorsements from within the teaching profession: during filming the script was shown to and approved by the secretary of the National Union of Teachers (*Daily Cinema*, 10 July 1963); then, in a special preview at Birmingham's Cinephone cinema, 'over 120 pupils attended the screening and joined in an open discussion with a panel consisting of a headmaster, a doctor, a clergymen, a sociologist, a marriage guidance counsellor, and 17-year-old Annette Whiteley, the star of the film', after which 'the City Education authorities and headmistresses of grammar and secondary modern schools voted that their senior pupils should see this film' (*Kinematograph Weekly*, 21 November 1963). Thus a story 'ripped from the headlines' made headlines itself: *Daily Telegraph*—'Schoolgirls see X Film'; *Daily Mail*—'The Girls Who Took an X-Lesson at the Cinema Yesterday'; *Birmingham Post*—'Schoolgirls Have X-film Lesson on Life!' (all 16 November 1963). Even Trevelyan 'praised the "educated experiment" of showing this "X" certificate film to students' and noted how '*The Yellow Teddybears* deals with the special difficulties of sex which young people—especially girls—are faced with today. Any performance which stimulates discussion with adults and helps the understanding of the problem is to be encouraged' (*Kinematograph Weekly*, 21 November 1963). Such publicity—huge for an independent release—was exactly what Tekli had hoped for and *The Yellow Teddybears* made a healthy profit across the UK independent circuit. Rather like the film's diegetic denouement, however, balanced discussion was not forthcoming: Blackburn and Chester councils simply banned the film, while the national press lambasted 'an embarrassingly inept attempt to investigate the mind and mores of sexually promiscuous teenagers' (*Daily Herald*, 13 July 1963), scorned its 'amateur performances, cliché ridden dialogue, stock characters, halting direction' (*Evening News*, 11 July 1963), and seemed almost disappointed at 'a film that sets out to be daring but is curiously old-fashioned' (*Daily Worker*, 13 July 1963). The *Times* offered it up (harshly) as 'a likely contender for the title of the year's funniest film' (11 July 1963).

3   TINSEL AND REALISM

The UK government's 1963 Newson Report, aka 'Half Our Future', having examined the education of 13-to–16-year-olds 'of average or less than average ability', uncovered serious neglect, including London secondary moderns sitting 15-year-olds on primary school furniture and staff changing as often as once a term. By the early 1960s a grammar school as featured in *The Yellow Teddybears* enjoyed 'three times the resources of the average secondary modern, and usually the pick of the best teachers' (Sandbrook 2005: 422), while Peter Laurie declared that 'To have been consigned to the limbo of the secondary modern is to have failed disastrously, and very early in life' (1965: 141). In July 1965 the Labour government had called on local authorities to end the existing divisive system and move towards the establishment of non-selective comprehensive schools: two films, however, a mirror image to the concurrent cinematic treatment of public schools offered up by *Goodbye, Mr. Chips* and *If….*, explored how little had been done to arrest this educational exclusion.

To Sir, With Love (1967), based on Guyanese E.R. Braithwaite's semi-autobiographical novel of 1959, was scripted, directed and produced by (Portsmouth Grammar-educated) US émigré James Clavell. As an entrée for American audiences, Sidney Poitier, in 1955 a juvenile delinquent giving Glenn Ford a hard time but now at the peak of his popularity as an accessible black star, was cast as 'Sir', a pedagogical 'poacher turned gamekeeper' teaching self-respect to a class including 18-year-old Scottish pop star Lulu. The film was funded by Columbia Pictures, its vice president Mike Frankovich trusting star and director with a modest £640,000 budget for a script the studio considered 'too soft, too sweet, too sentimental' (Harris 2008: 204–5). Thus, while a British film by dint of employing a predominantly British cast and crew, *To Sir, With Love*'s financing, however small, came from and therefore its profits, however great, went to an American company. In this, it followed the trend for much 1960s British cinema: as with the James Bond and Beatles films, *To Sir, With Love* may have been quintessentially British in its iconography and ideology, but its economics were entirely American (Walker 1974: 289–310). As was its premiere: sat on for over a year by a US studio unsure how to market such workaday British fare, it opened in California on 14 June 1967 before coming home to London for an Mile End Road European premiere on 3 September. The film follows Guyanese Mark Thackeray who, unable to find UK employment as an engineer, accepts an interim teaching post at London's East End 'sink' North Quay Secondary School. Like Saunders and Weir before him, Thackeray faces up, with new Music teacher Gillian Blanchard (Suzy Kendall), to tyrannical or time-serving colleagues, insolent male and provocative female pupils. In established generic mode Thackeray initially flounders until, finding a sanitary towel burning on the class stove, his angry outburst provokes an epiphany: like Saunders he scraps the textbooks and declares a new curriculum, demanding courtesy, cleanliness and class-time discussions of 'life, survival, love, death, sex, marriage, rebellion… anything you want'. Add in musical photo-montage excursions to central London, and Thackeray's progressive programme not only wins over class rebel Denham (Christian Roberts) to a sense of civic responsibility and converts the downtrodden, atomised staff to a new sense of communality, but it also prompts the appreciative Lulu, backed by the Mindbenders at the school-leavers' dance, to sing him a five-week US number one single—the title track becoming Billboard's top-selling single of 1967. When offered a post with a Midlands engineering firm, Thackeray tears up his job offer and determines to continue with the career for which he clearly has a calling.

The plot and casting of *To Sir, With Love* may have promised to bring the blue-collar earthiness of *The Blackboard Jungle* to London's East End, but the generic hybridity of a school film with music replicates, far more than *The Yellow Teddybears*, the worldview of *It's Great to be Young*, conservative at gendered, racial, class and pedagogical levels. It begins with Don Black and Mark London's title song, a romantic rather than sexualised paean to a teacher whose work can be interpreted as a professional and moral guide in the rites of passage into adulthood. The singer, though, can only manifest this appreciation by offering her heart, endorsing her prescribed range of identities: 'While a schoolboy could presumably "reward" his teacher by achieving success in later life, the schoolgirl is defined solely in terms of her romantic relationships' (Fisher et al. 2008: 100). The film is similarly restricted in its approach to race, foregoing the source text's exposé of racial prejudice, all the more hurtful 'because it had been perpetrated with the greatest of charm and courtesy' (Braithwaite 1959: 42). Instead, though cynical colleague Theo Weston (Geoffrey Bayldon) dismisses his teaching success as 'voodoo' and Denham seeks to rile Sir with questions about bare-breasted African women, Thackeray maintains his calm dignity and tolerance and his class duly follow suit: when the mother of a mixed-race boy dies, the class, initially baulking at delivering a wreath for fear of neighbourhood condemnation, all appear for the funeral as Sir smiles proudly. If interracial remorse is thus socially realised, romance is not as, completing the decade's 'state school trilogy', Poitier's character handles the *de rigueur* pupil infatuation from Pamela Dare (Judy Geeson) with gentlemanly care, performing with her 'some sort of awkward chicken dance, in a presumably involuntary reinforcement of his distance from black stereotypes' (Goudsouzian 2004: 260) (Fig. 4.3): meanwhile staff colleague Gillian, aware of the difficulties for interracial couples, remains just another admirer of her skilled teaching colleague. Thus miscegenation, a key theme of Braithwaite's novel, is erased, with Poitier's 'safe' image again deflecting white anxieties off the (literally) untouchable and unimpeachable moral exemplar.

Fig. 4.3   Hey, teacher! Leave those kids alone!

Like *Spare the Rod* and *Term of Trial*, the film expounds educational improvement as the acceptance and assimilation of middle-class values. The stance initially confuses Thackeray's class: recounting his former jobs as a cook and janitor, a pupil objects 'but you talk posh an' all!' His book-binning is not the prelude to a 1960s liberal agenda, nor an embrace of working-class shiny barbarism: his position is entirely conservative and Weston's antiphonal voice singularly rings true in disparaging their new lessons as an experiment only in 'suburban formality'. Thackeray stands as a buttoned-down symbol of bourgeois norms, his role that of a mission-ary to the lost tribes of dockland, marking an inversion of the imperial colonial mentality and public school code as *To Sir, With Love* applies a veneer of post-colonial gentility onto the British class system, with former Cockney rebels moulded to await their menial jobs with equanimity. For Jim Leach Thackeray 'becomes one of Althusser's decent teachers whose efforts cannot really change the system' (2004: 196): Jim Pines is less forgiving, adjudging his perpetuation of assimilated white middle-class values—Thackeray forsakes his native patois to learn 'proper' English—as a social and pedagogical 'emasculation' (1977: 117). However, the film's biggest alteration, perhaps even betrayal, is to the educational experience underpinning the source text. Braithwaite had joined a cane-free 'experimental school' based on 'disciplined freedom', democratically run with the pupil voice central to all decision-making (Fielding 2005). This communality is again erased as *To Sir, With Love* portrays its educational innovations as entirely the brave and solitary work of interim Mark Thackeray. Concepts of fidelity aside, this reorientation outstrips even *Goodbye, Mr. Chips* in its hagiographical depiction of the inspirational teacher. Early on a struggling Thackeray stares into the sun through the window of his empty classroom, arms spread out along the sill: in silhouette he is not so much a charismatic secondary teacher as a second Christ on the cross, a Saviour from afar nobly sacrificing his own shot at middle-class respectability to redeem young strays with their hereditary sins of bad grammar and poor personal hygiene. No wonder Braithwaite later expressed his 'hatred' for the film adaptation ('To Sir, With Love Revisited', BBC Radio 4, 24 August 2007).

Not so the paying public. If *Spare the Rod*'s censorship tribulations showed a concept ahead of its legislative time, and *Term of Trial*'s well-worn kitchen sink tropes were stylistically passé, then *To Sir, With Love*, though based on a novel relating early post-war experiences, fully reflected the 'Swinging London' zeitgeist and performed strongly at the UK box office. Further still, alongside Poitier's inclusive casting, the 'Cockney sparrer' dialect and overplayed shots of Red London buses, colourful markets and miniskirts—a kind of Swinging Sixties 'Pop porn'—all indicate more than one eye on the American market where *To Sir, With Love* surprised all with a theatrical take of close to $20 million, making it the eighth-ranked film for 1967 and the third-best grossing British film of the entire decade in the USA.[7] Film critics were far less generous, however. UK reviews at best patronised *To Sir, With Love* as 'good old-fashioned sentimental nonsense' (*Times*, 7 September 1967): Ian Christie, for instance, acknowledged 'The film means well' but found that 'its sugar-coated, rose-tinted solution to our educational problems is just so much pi R squared in the sky' (*Daily Express*, 8 September 1967); Nina Hibben, unimpressed by 'its snobbery towards the children' and 'oversentimentalising of the teacher', more bluntly termed the film 'an appalling phoney' (*Morning Star*, 9 September 1967). It garnered more American reviews than any previous British school film, and while Andrew Sarris contended that the pupils 'come on less like stragglers in a slum school than like a well-drilled troupe from a British high school for the performing arts' (*Village Voice*, 7 December 1967), most gravitated to Poitier and the problematic image of 'Mr. Chocolate Chips' (Goudsouzian 2004: 262): Stephen Farber, for instance, condemned a 'foolish, offensively simple-minded movie' where Poitier played 'the suburban audience's dream of a well-adjusted Negro' with 'no desires, no passions, no weaknesses' (*Film Quarterly*, 22, Winter 1968: 57), while the *New Yorker* informed Columbia that 'If the hero of this Pollyanna story were white, his pieties would have to be whistled off the screen and his pupils blamed for cringing' (17 June 1967). Cringe-worthy or not, *To Sir, With Love* has remained a US school film favourite.[8]

3.1　The State School Film Victor Ludorum: Kes (1969)

The decade's depictions of Britain's state school sector ended not with a saccharine 'whitewash' but with a coruscating condemnation of 'the colossal wastage of kids' resulting from 'a national school system that educates them only for failure' (Loach, quoted in Stephenson 1973: 48–9). *Kes* is, for this writer, the key state school film, decrying the secondary modern system through the story of a 15-year-old 'Easter leaver' in his final term, ending his education without skills or qualifications: (the raising of the school-leaving age to 16, promised in 1943, would only be effected in 1972/3). The film's origins lie in British television. Tony Garnett (Central Grammar, Birmingham), a prominent BBC producer for the socially engaged but warily tolerated 'Wednesday Play', had read *The Blinder*, the 1966 debut semi-autobiographical novel about a talented working-class schoolboy footballer written by miner's son and former comprehensive school PE teacher Barry Hines (Ecclesfield Grammar). Garnett sought to commission a screenplay but Hines declined, wanting to concentrate on his next novel. This became *A Kestrel for a Knave*,[9] a story inspired by Hines' brother Richard who had kept a hawk in the family garden shed. While still in manuscript form the book was optioned by Garnett, not for the BBC, which he had left due to its obstructive bureaucracy, but for his own independent production company, named Kestrel Films after this debut project. The subsequent production history proved similar to that endured by *If....*: an initial arrangement with America's National General Corporation collapsed, reputedly over (erroneously calculated) projected filming budgets, and the film was only rescued by the last-minute intervention of director Tony Richardson, who brokered funding from Anglophile Hollywood major United Artists by offering cross-collateral with his own current project, the *Lolita*-like *Laughter in the Dark* (1969). This led to the production being credited as a Woodfall Film and, though essentially the result of financial expediency—apart from offering the title *Kes*, Richardson remained 'hands off'—this structuring created an apposite artistic link with Britain's social realist tradition since Woodfall, set up by Richardson and playwright John Osborne, had nurtured several seminal New Wave films, including the borstal-set *Loneliness of the Long Distance Runner*.

Garnett's established collaborator was Ken (then Kenneth) Loach (King Edward VI Grammar, Nuneaton): a miner's grandson and a determinedly left-wing interventionist director, Loach joined the BBC as a trainee director in 1963 and progressed to the 'Wednesday Play' strand where, with Garnett producing, he filmed the stylistically innovative and controversial *Up the Junction* (1965) and the nationally discussed exposure of homelessness *Cathy Come Home* (1966). From his debut feature film *Poor Cow* (1967), Loach retained, for *Kes*, John Cameron and Chris Menges, promoting them respectively from musical director to score composer, and from camera operator to director of photography. Cameron's spare, 20-minute score for strings and soaring alto-flute would soften the visual impression and anchor the bird-training scenes in a folk-inflected pastoral tradition; Menges, who in contrast pre-flashed the film stock to tone down any 'poetic' or picturesque potential, was to prove an especially significant partner, helping Loach achieve a more naturalistic, mise-en-scène-led, and less formalist, montage-driven filming style—a move, in short, from Brecht to Bazin. This more withdrawn camera position, allowing the actors greater improvisatory space, fed into the film's casting strategy. Loach picked several entertainers from the Northern Club circuit, including Lynne Perrie and Freddie Fletcher, performers not moulded in the Olivier thespian tradition. Alongside these were non-professionals, Barnsley residents playing approximate versions of themselves: central here was the young lead Billy Casper, a part that, after seeing close to 200 local hopefuls, Loach entrusted to 13-year-old David Bradley, completing a triumvirate of miner descendants. In similar vein, the headmaster of the nearby Ashton School, Bob Bowes, played Billy's unsympathetic head Mr Gryce, while Bradley's real-life form-teacher Trevor Hesketh was cast as the pompous Mr Crossley. More lastingly, *Kes* offered, as the tyrannical PE master, a debut role for Brian Glover, a teacher friend of Hines and semi-professional wrestler—his audition consisted of breaking up a playground fight. Colin Welland was the only experienced actor, though his casting rested on four years' experience as a teacher in northern England. The eponymous kestrel was played by three birds named after the shoe chain, Freeman, Hardy and Willis: in keeping with the necessary authenticity, all were trained by Hines' brother, Richard.[10] Hines' source novel had been set in the writer's native Barnsley: Loach ensured that *Kes* replicated this firm sense of place by filming on location in the same town's streets, homes, clubs, betting shops, markets and surrounding fields on a seven-week shoot during the 1968 school summer holidays. The film thus captured the topography of tightly-knit mining communities with the grime and machinery of the colliery adjacent to unspoilt countryside, while the school scenes were shot at the recently built St Helen's School, Athersley South (demolished in 2011) where Hines had taught and which was currently attended, either as pupils or teachers, by several cast members, including Bradley. *Kes* eventually came in £10,000 under budget, at £155,000. However, after Loach and Roy Watts had completed their editing in early 1969, United Artists were unsure how to handle a film with no stars, a downbeat ending and uncompromising Yorkshire accents.[11] The Rank chain, with exhibition ties to United Artists, saw little box-office potential and, despite a well-received screening at the London Film Festival in November 1969, refused *Kes* a circuit release. They did, though, allow United Artists to offer it to the rival ABC chain who, equally disconcerted by the film's vernacular, took the unique step of placing its premiere in Doncaster on 25 March 1970, before opening exclusively in the North of England—a cultural match to the film's depiction of an educational apartheid (and a symmetrical match to *School for Randle*'s exhibition reach). *Kes* finally opened in London at the small arthouse Academy Cinema in May, a full year after its delivery to Rank and close on two years after filming wrapped. Healthy attendances and highly favourable press coverage prompted ABC finally to exhibit the film in its own London cinemas in August 1970. It received only limited distribution in the USA, with some revoicing of the lead characters, effected unbeknownst to Loach or Garrett.

In its raw (or reworked) Yorkshire dialect, *Kes* relates the story of Billy Casper, who lives with his libidinous mother (Perrie) and loutish miner brother Jud (Fletcher)—the father having fled some years ago—in a council house on a new estate in an unnamed northern mining town. At school he is bored and unresponsive but he enjoys his rare 'bird nesting' sorties into the country. One day he finds a kestrel's nest and takes one of the fledglings. He keeps the bird in the garden shed and, with the aid of a stolen book on falconry, trains 'Kes' to fly free and return for food. Totally absorbed in the bird, he pays even less attention in class and is constantly in trouble, though English master Mr Farthing (Welland) takes some interest in him and his hobby. When Billy spends the money Jud gave him to put on a winning horse, his furious brother exacts revenge by killing the bird and throwing it in the dustbin: Billy, heartbroken, runs off to bury Kes.

While the bird gives its name to the film and the falconry scenes are memorably tender in their near-lyrical depiction of Billy's communion with nature, the exposure of the fate awaiting Britain's Eleven Plus-failing working-class majority makes *Kes*, as Derek Malcolm notes, 'one of the most remarkable films about education, or the lack of it, ever made' (*Guardian*, 22 June 2000). Director and producer were both insistent on education's ideological function to perpetuate existing class relations: for Loach, 'for all the liberal aspirations of trying to draw things out and not push them in, the objective role of the secondary modern is to produce a certain amount of unskilled labour' (*Times*, 20 March 1970); for Garnett 'The subtext... was really the seventy per cent of the kids of this country thrown onto the scrap heap at fifteen, which is a very sad situation, not in economic terms, but in human terms... This little lad is really one of those, so we thought it would be a good idea to do a film about that' (1970: n.p.). To see Billy as 'representative', individuating a national crisis in education, may appear counter-intuitive—not many schoolboys independently raise a kestrel. However, he is carefully placed as 'ordinary' in the early focus on his morning activities—doing a paper round, talking to the milkman, making his way to school—and especially in the criticism he draws from every authority figure he encounters: the newsagent recounts how 'They're all alike off that estate'; 'These kids, I don't know, they're just all the same', moans the chip shop owner. (Less forgivably, his headmaster will also treat him as representative of a sullen and useless 'generation that never listens'.) The path mapped out for Billy, and his peers, is made clear from the opening scene: waking his brother in the single-pillowed bed they share, Billy is resentfully reminded by Jud that in a few weeks he too will be working down the pit. Though Billy declares his determination not to follow suit, the cramped mise-en-scène suggests they share, not just a bed, but a future. Montage then reinforces the idea, following Jud through sunlit woodland, accompanied by the bucolic Cameron score: he is walking, though, to the colliery and as the metallic clanging of his pitshaft lift recedes, it is replaced by the morning hymn and pupils singing at the school: the overlapping soundtrack and image juxtaposition not only link the brothers spatially but also the pre-determined process of education and employment—the school leads straight to the mine. Even Billy's apparent moments of escape, as when he breaks his paper round to sit on a grassy hillside and read Desperate Dan in *The Dandy* (a sign of the system's cultural infantilisation), are ominously recontextualised as a wider shot reveals two collieries and their smoking chimneys below: as played out this is less a New Wave 'psychologised' elevation of the main characters from their surroundings (Higson 1996) than an 'historicised' anchorage to the industrial reality that imposes continuously on their lives and, in all senses, prospects. At other moments the film privileges Billy's point of view: not always to his advantage, as when he steals from his employer, the milkman and a second-hand bookshop. However, the publicity image of Billy flicking a 'V' sign does not feature in the film which portrays not an active rebel confronting repressive authorities but a resourceful survivor who uses his social intelligence to fashion a private space in an uncaring world. As in previous state school films' home visits, *Kes* explores Billy's difficult family environment, consistent for the malicious bullying of his brother (the taunts of schoolmate MacDowall (Robert Naylor) suggest he is a half-brother) and the neglect of his mother—the absence of a strong paternal presence more securely links *Kes* to New Wave forebears. When the film follows both to the local pub, its scenes of noisy desperation modify *Spare the Rod*'s condemnation of parental 'bad stock from filthy homes': Mrs Casper's neediness and disappointment with her lot are painfully evident in her faltering attempts to make new boyfriend Reg (Joe Miller) take their relationship more seriously, while Jud's boozy assertion of his contentment cannot mask a deep frustration. As much as their mutual contempt, leavened with colourful if clichéd banter—'You chuck your bloody money round like a Scotsman with no arms'—the mother and son's poverty binds them inextricably together, even on a Saturday night out: Billy is caught in the middle.

His situation is no better at school, with numerous incidentals revealing adult disregard for his potential and that of his peers: the morning assembly bible reading from Matthew 18—'see that you do not look down on one of these little ones'—recalls *If....* in its dramatic irony. Two extended scenes illustrate the pervasive brutalising culture, again with a layering of wry comedy. The first shows, like *To Sir, With Love*, the most openly bullying teacher to be the PE master, here Mr Sugden (Glover) who, in *Kes*' sole scene of ludic non-realism, caricatures every games teacher who never made the grade (the sporting equivalent to Messrs Bean and Milton in *Carry on Teacher*) as he leads his class onto the football field to the strains of BBC's *Sports Night* signature tune and, with pretention-pricking scores appearing on screen—*Manchester United 0 Spurs 1*—acts out his fantasy of being the United striker Bobby Charlton (another miner's son). Sugden's simultaneous abuse of his position as both player and referee, awarding himself a twice-taken penalty and sending off the opposing captain, accompanied by the pompous and hypocritical admonition that 'We'll play this game like gentlemen', both intertextually ridicule the genre's long tradition of school games as 'character-building' and textually reveal Billy and his classmates as impotent prey to their teachers' solipsistic eccentricities. The changing-room scenes that bracket the football farce depict a more openly sadistic Jud-like strain to Sugden's instruction.[12] The pre-match attempt to humiliate an evasive kit-less Billy by making him wear oversize shorts backfires as Billy turns Sugden's orders into a comedy set, pulling the shorts into exaggerated shapes and positions. It is a rare victory, Billy obeying yet openly mocking orders, much to the amusement and approval of his peers, and an indication of his astute 'knavery', aware of the extent to which he can challenge adult authority. It is a pyrrhic victory, though, as Billy's post-match attempts to skip a shower are met by a brutal slap to the face, its effect the more telling for coming just three short shots after Billy's comic climbing on the goal posts. The subsequent forcing of Billy into the showers with the water turned to cold draws protests from the boys— unlike Billy, the teacher has gone too far—but he can do so with impunity, the pupils too deadened to rebel: despite the identical shower-room injustice, this still will not realise Durgnat's hoped-for 'secondary modern *If....*'. The second extended school scene takes place at the study of headmaster Gryce, outside which stand five habitual-offender fifth-form boys. Billy's observation that Gryce likes to make them wait for their punishment reveals a psychological cruelty that would have been familiar to Frears and Hitchcock. Another boy's rejoinder that 'he can keep me till four o'clock, I'm not bothered: I'd rather the cane than do lessons' conveys—with less psychological subtlety—the shared experience of a meaningless curriculum and bluntly indicts a nation's education system whose failings are then fully enacted. When a younger messenger boy arrives, he is forced to hide the group's cigarettes: exemplifying the 'food chain' of bullying, Billy holds his neck to force him to comply. Once inside Gryce launches into a Graham Weir-like diatribe on the moral malaise of modern youth with 'their music and their gear': he relates how past pupils will stop him in the street 'and we'll laugh about the thrashing that I gave them' while all the current generation give is 'a honk from a greasy, pimply-faced youth sitting at the wheel of a big second-hand car'. The empty rhetoric of an oft-repeated haranguing—the head (actor Bowes as much as character Gryce) stares out of the window as he recollects the wording—occasions only barely contained laughter from the fifth-formers. But then, on checking everyone's pockets and ignoring the youngest's protestations of innocence, he canes all six. As with Sugden, the proximity of comedy and punishment increases the shock value of the adult violence: the indiscriminate punishment underlines the alienation between pupils and headmaster and undermines the legitimacy of the entire school system. With Gryce admitting it will act as no corrective, the scene closes with a close-up on the young messenger, sobbing out a heart-rending 'yes, sir': with the sting of his hand, one could conjecture that it is not discipline but disillusion that has been branded. Gryce is exposed as pompous and uncaring, a secondary modern Wackford Squeers, unchanged in attritional attitudes since the *Nicholas Nickleby* of Alberto Cavalcanti and, before him, Alf Collins.

In this context, Billy's training of the kestrel is not just a (metaphorical) representation of the imagination and potential of his social class for escape and autonomy; it also and especially offers a dialectic display of educational models, with Billy's tender 'gentling' of the small bird a stark contrast to the state's violent taming and training of a small boy, its moulding to a dominant concept of orderliness and quiet class acceptance. In contradistinction to the regressed Sugden and repressive Gryce, *Kes* ostensibly endorses the pedagogical 'Murray method' outlined in *Spare The Rod*, to find and run with pupil interests. Billy's attention to the bird leads first to teaching himself the techniques of falconry, via his stolen manual. Others so frequently decry Billy as near-illiterate that he comes to profess it himself: however, over footage of his careful coaxing of Kes, the film's sole voiceover has Billy determinedly if haltingly narrating the training methods from his book, complete with its complex and arcane terminology, counter-evidence that this is no 'numbskull' but a neglected child with a fertile, if untended inner life able to achieve self-set targets; here is no mere 'fodder for the mass media' as Gryce terms it, nor another pawn for the pit face as proposed by the government-backed Youth Employment Officer (Bernard Atha), but a talent that could—and in a caring society would—be nurtured, be 'gentled'. When Farthing (another generic staple in being the school's sole liberal and sympathetic teacher) threatens detention to 'coax' a distracted Billy into talking of his passion during a lesson centred on 'fact and fiction', the rapt attention and engaged questions he receives becomes an isolated occasion where the young pupils can demonstrate their creativity and enthusiasm. There is some mild teasing, but all understand and empathise with Billy's motivations in an epiphanic moment emphasised by rare close-ups on Billy and several classmates as he excitedly describes the first time he flew Kes without a leash. Together Kes and Farthing lead a disenchanted youth through books to public articulacy (Fig. 4.4).

The knowledge that the teacher's attention is too little too late, and the immediate reverting to type of his peers, with Billy again bullied by MacDowell during break—significantly on top of a coal slag heap—only serve to pinpoint the message highlighted by the preceding scene's Dickens-invoking blackboard sentence: that teenagers like Billy, whose potential *Kes* so fully demonstrates, are betrayed not only by their neglectful home life but also, and especially, by indifferent school authorities looking only to prepare them for adult-life 'Hard Times', for Gradgrindian 'facts' and uniformity rather than gentled 'fiction' and individuality. When Billy is rescued by Farthing from his tormentor, he succinctly articulates the failings of the system and its teachers: 'They're not bothered about us and

Fig. 4.4 Hobby talk: 'lift off' for an English lesson

we're not bothered about them': as an informal exit interview, it stands as a frustrated but heartfelt correction to Gryce's lip-serving condemnation. *Kes* concludes by linking Billy's more formal final session with the uncaring careers officer to Jud's revenge on his beloved bird—each intended to remove horizons beyond the mining community. Hines' source novel had ended with Billy, prior to burying Kes, breaking into the disused Palace Cinema and creating a vengeful film fantasy with 'Billy as hero. Billy on the screen. Big Billy', using his kestrel, 'Kes on his arm. Big Kes. Close up. Technicolor', to attack a terrified Jud on the moors (Hines 1968: 159). Deemed unrealisable (and probably too self-consciously meta-cinematic), Garnett and Loach were nonetheless pressurised to provide a more uplifting ending, such as Billy, with Farthing's help, finding a job away from the pits: a betrayal, Garnett avers, of their intention to raise questions about 'the system' rather than individuals (1970: n.p.). Even so, one could question whether the last scene's burial of Kes can only signify a metonymic death of childhood innocence and/or defeat for Billy's adult ambitions, crushed not just by family discord but by environmental determinism—a working class internalisation that perpetuates oppression as successfully as any public school indoctrination. Filmed in mid to long shot, with no musical signposting or discernible response from actor Bradley, the scene works to preclude intellectual or emotional closure, its resultant ambiguity allowing a reading that, as with Mick Travis, privileges a newly determined and articulate Billy who will not be trapped within the dominant ideology or undermined by a single violent act.

On its delayed release, *Kes* 'gradually asserted itself through judiciously chosen television clips and word-of-mouth publicity' (Walker 1974: 380) and turned in a satisfactory UK profit—it made no impression in America. It also won two BAFTAs, Bradley for Promising Newcomer, Welland for Supporting Actor, and the 1971 Writers' Guild of Great Britain award for Best Screenplay. Eulogising press reviews contributed to the film's eventual dissemination: for the *Sunday Express* critic 'It offers the most resonant echo of one's own childhood memories I have ever experienced in the cinema' (22 March 1970), while the *Daily Telegraph* considered *Kes* 'as, artistically, one of the most accomplished films of its kind in the whole of British post-war production' (20 March 1970). Most agreed that the adult roles were 'good without being outstanding, but the children, and especially David Bradley, as Billy, live their parts with total belief' (*MFB*, April 1970: 74). Educational themes were foregrounded: Margaret Hinxman stressed how 'every frame of film is a telling comment on an overburdened mass education system which has only the time and patience to cope with stereotypes' (*Sunday Telegraph*, 22 March 1970), while David Robinson emphasised 'the inescapable pressure of background: the inadequacy of a school which for all its fine buildings and Welfare State amenities is quite deficient in human contacts or human respect' (*Financial Times*, 29 May 1970). For Paul Barker, 'Just as Cathy personified the homeless, Billy Casper personifies the "Newson children"—those secondary school children who will leave early and fill most of the country's jobs': he stressed, though, (unlike Billy) that 'it is wrong just to fault the teachers. This is what parents and employers largely want of the staff in such schools. They want the children assembly-belted into leading decent, orderly, wage-earning lives' and argued that, despite its distribution difficulties, 'at the very least, all education committees should see it, compulsorily' (*New Society*, 20 November 1969). The film's cinematic (if not educational) influence has increased with its reputation: the scene where Billy skulks past a girls' dance lesson pinpoints *Kes* as a bleak forefather to *Billy Elliot* (Stephen Daldry, 2000); in Frears' cane-laden *Typically British*, Alan Parker unequivocally declared *Kes* 'the best film made in Britain since the war'; 1999's BFI poll voted *Kes* the seventh greatest 'culturally British' feature film of the twentieth century, a state school victory ahead of *If....* and *Goodbye, Mr. Chips*. The same body's 2005 international poll of the 'Top 50 Films to see by the Age of 14', a listing to inspire parents and educators to treat film as a serious art form, placed just one British effort in its alphabetically listed Top 10—*Kes*, cock o' t'estate.

4   APPROVED SCHOOL

For those unable to sustain a mainstream state education, alternative systems were available. The first institution to separate under-21 offenders from older convicts was established in 1902 at Borstal prison, Kent. The brief of subsequent 'borstals', combined with 'industrial', 'reformatory' and 'training' schools from 1933 under the label of 'approved schools', was to be educationally corrective before punitive, and their routine of discipline and authority, dorms and exercise, uniforms, houses and 'headmasters', was expressly moulded on the boarding public school—with equally secure locks on the doors. The theory was that subjecting delinquent youths to public school methodology would inculcate self-discipline, a sense of pride and future employability. British cinema began exploring/exploiting these institutions amidst the moral panic centred on the nation's youth (itself a metaphor for fears of rapid social change) that immediately followed the Second World War. First house points went to *Children on Trial* (Jack Lee, August 1946), an early public service 'story documentary' from the Central Office of Information, which follows both male and female 'slum-reared' teenage delinquents to enlightened approved schools from which they emerge as fully rehabilitated 'decent citizens'. A reassuring paean to post-war youth social work, the film combines actuality footage with scripted scenes for its amateur cast: the headmaster of Liverpool Farm School, John Vardy playing himself, advises his new arrival that, if cooperative, the new environment will be 'not a prison but a pleasant sort of school'. It was ambivalently received at home, praised for its social engagement but criticised for simplifying a complicated debate. Washington authorities, however, studied it as a potential model to tackle America's delinquency problem (*New York Times*, 10 November 1947).

Gainsborough Studios next tackled the borstal experience in a pair of single-sex films. *Good Time Girl* (David MacDonald, 29 April 1948) was a loose but accomplished adaptation, by Muriel and Sydney Box with Ted Willis, of Arthur La Bern's novel *Night Darkens the Street*, itself inspired by the infamous Cleft Chin murder of 1944.[13] The film, first presented to the Home Office in July 1947, caused great concern, less for its resemblance to recent headline events than for its graphic depiction of a female approved school. This created repeated correspondence at 'the highest level', with unprecedented intervention in a single film's content by a Home Secretary, then Chuter Ede, who wrote directly to J. Arthur Rank requesting radical changes to the borstal sequences. Violence amongst the inmates was duly trimmed and two moralising court scenes added to top and tail a film that, nonetheless, was banned by Hertfordshire County Council.[14] Thus, *Good Time Girl* begins with Juvenile Court Chair Miss Thorpe (Flora Robson) regaling Lyla (a young Diana Dors) with a cautionary tale to dissuade her from leaving home. We then follow the descent into crime of 16-year-old Gwen Rowlands (future Mrs Crocker-Harris Jean Kent) who, framed for a jewellery theft, is sent to an approved school for the maximum three-year term. Her experiences therein harden her to crime and violence as, befriending the 'mummy' Roberta (Jill Balcon), she begins a reign of terror and, when the customary riot ensues, makes her escape. From here it is rapidly 'Downhill', Gwen's hardened attitude leading her into a gangland lifestyle which culminates in the murder of Red (Dennis Price), the only man who cared for her. There is no redemption here, just 15 years imprisonment as an accomplice, though Lyla finishes suitably chastened and contrite.

A bracing British noir, *Good Time Girl* also succeeds as a British school film because it provides a full contextualisation for the borstal experience, offering before-referral causes and, significantly, after-release effects. The 20 (of 90) minutes set in borstal serve as the film's fulcrum, showing to devastating effect the institution's corrupting impact on an unwilling but essentially good-hearted inmate: the plum-voiced principal (Nora Swinburne) smugly moralises on 'the salvaging of those youngsters whose natural growth has been marred by bad upbringing, bad companions, or plain bad luck', but Gwen, just such a youngster yet already alienated by the severity of her sentence (handed down by the obliviously patronis-ing Thorpe), fights back and, learning to 'play the system' by offering a surface conformity to gain official approval while bullying fellow inmates to gain security and status, leaves her school not 'corrected' but cunning and cruel. The Home Office was rightly worried at a film which skew-ers the counter-productive results of middle-class exercises in pious do-goodery—even the required moral framework merely furthers our siding with the rejection of bourgeois philanthropy and gender conformity by a working-class girl whose original 'crime' was merely wanting to have a good time. Though Muriel Box had visited approved schools and read Royal Commission reports on the borstal system, *Good Time Girl* was vili-fied as exploitative, the *Daily Mirror* damning 'another of those unsatisfac-tory, unsavoury pictures which depend on sordid brutality for box-office appeal' and labelling it 'A story which should never have been filmed' (30 April 1948). Its sole Red-like defender, the *MFB*, praised how, 'apart from perfect direction, fine photography and good acting, the story makes one think and argue', though it (naively) wondered: 'Is this an indictment against Juvenile Courts and the way in which approved schools are run?' (May 1948: 59). Indeed it was, and it scared the Establishment more than any subsequent treatment.

Lessons learnt, its tamer male partner constituted Gainsborough's final social problem 'quota' feature. *Boys in Brown* (Montgomery Tully, 23 January 1950), adapted from Reginald Beckwith's play with Richard Attenborough, fresh from *The Guinea Pig*, now the sitting duck amidst a set of overaged borstal 'boys' including future *If....* co-producer Michael Medwin, relates how getaway driver Jackie Knowles (Attenborough), sentenced to three years in (another unnamed) borstal, falls easy prey to peer pressure and the manipulations of scheming Alfie Rawlins (Dirk

Bogarde) until, making a break for freedom during the inmates' performance of (the habitual) *Julius Caesar*, he seriously injures a master. Like Jimmy himself, the film's intentions and execution seem rather at odds. Stylistically *Boys in Brown* was the first full-length feature to use Rank's short-lived Independent Frame (Winston Dixon 1994: 41–52), a meticulously planned back-projection process ostensibly in tension with a project advocating liberality and sensible limits to social control. Though the accompanying press release stressed that 'the film sets out to give a true picture of life in a Borstal Institution', narratively it follows generic school film emphases in privileging dramatic action sequences, a perfunctory montage of the boys at work revealing little of their 'character-building' daily grind. Undermining any progressive programme, Jimmy's crimes (unlike Gwen's) appear more the result of personal weakness than of social context while the borstal system is doubly implicated: internally it exacerbates the lot of gullible Jimmys by throwing them in with the genuinely malevolent—only two of the eight escapees show any remorse; externally, its stigma—no-one wants to be an 'Old Borstalerian', a housemaster notes—ruins the chances for recidivists like Bill Foster (Jimmy Hanley) of finding decent employment thereafter. These narrative traits are unconvincingly contradicted, both morally and mathematically, by the 'message statement' from the liberal governor (Jack Warner) that, given a raw material of 100 per cent failures, neither Eton nor Harrow could equal his record of turning out 50 per cent successes. The final scene, where Warner surveys the recreation yard's 'wheat and chaff' and defines the need to discover what causes the latter, arguably articulates a significant absence rather than offering a summative conclusion. Less controversial than its 'sister' film, *Boys in Brown* still met with mixed reactions, either praised as a 'fairly exciting entertainment' that 'credibly abstains from exploiting its serious subject in a sensational way' (*MFB*, December 1949: 211), or else dismissed as a 'slow, uneven "Dead End Kids" romantic melodrama' (*Kinematograph Weekly*, 15 December 1949).

4.1 Section Prize Winner: The Loneliness of the Long Distance Runner *(1962)*

The parallels and polarities between Britain's approved and public schools were most explicitly realised in Alan Sillitoe's adaptation of his Hawthornden Prize-winning 1959 short story, the monologue of a disillusioned borstal boy fighting against the system. Produced by Tony

Richardson for Woodfall, it was originally slated as the debut feature for Lindsay Anderson, who was preparing a first draft when Richardson took over directing duties. Much like Anderson with *If....*, Richardson brought his own biography to the project: he attended Ashville College public school and, again like Anderson, attained a head prefect position, before heading off to Wadham College, Oxford, stage directing and film criticism; less ambivalently, however, Richardson stated how 'it's impossible to write anything bad enough about English public schools' (1993: 66). Sillitoe, without the fee-paying education but with an equal hatred of the class system, named the film borstal's rival public school 'Ranleigh', one letter different to the oppressive Raleigh bicycle factory in Nottingham where, having failed his Eleven Plus, he started work aged 14.[15] With the ballast of New Wave regular Walter Lassally as cinematographer, plus school film stalwart (and Richardson's father-in-law) Michael Redgrave as the borstal governor-headmaster, newcomer Tom Courtney was cast as the sullen and defiant long distance runner. Richardson's intentions to research and film at a genuine borstal were thwarted by authorities more astute on directorial intent than Cheltenham's headmaster would later prove. Instead, the borstal-set scenes were shot in the spring of 1962 at Ruxley Towers, a Victorian mock castle militarised during the war and loosely name-checked in the film. As with *If....*, the film's themes and language dictated an 'X' certificate, and censorship restrictions were relatively minor (Aldgate 1995: 99–101). *Loneliness* was released in Britain on 21 September 1962 and a fortnight later in the US, where it was retitled *Rebel With a Cause*. The film follows the experiences of aimless teenager Colin Smith (Courtney) who, caught for theft, is sent with his pal Mike (James Bolam) to Ruxton Towers Borstal Institution. Redgrave's upper-class governor, an ex-runner for whom athletics is a cornerstone of his rehabilitation programme, fosters Colin's talent for cross-country running and visualises him winning their inaugural race against nearby Ranleigh and ultimately competing at the Olympics. During his practice runs, Colin reflects on his father's ugly death, his mother (Avis Bunnage) swiftly installing a new 'fancy man' and a dispiriting trip with his girlfriend Audrey (Topsy Jane) to Skegness. On Sports Day Colin leads the race until, a few yards off the finishing line, he stops and waves through his public school rival, Gunthorpe (James Fox). The price of his victory over 'the head' is a return to his old job in the workshops, stripping down gas-masks.

Loneliness is a key work of the British New Wave and a polemical film against the forces working to subjugate working-class youth. Equally resistant to the mouldings of authority figures such as the pompous governor and the temptations of consumerism parodied in his mother's compensation-fuelled shopping spree, one must consider Colin Smith happy. His emaciated stature and cramped home environment and career prospects evoke a future Billy Casper, and yet, in its portrayal of a British rebel with/out a cause, Richardson's film can more readily be seen, at both narrative and stylistic levels, as a reform school 'run through' for the displaced Anderson's *If*..... In his opening address to the newest arrivals the governor repeats the trite Kemp-like exhortations customary of the genre: 'If you play ball with us, we'll play ball with you. We want you to work hard and play hard.' The speech's hollowness and the system's latent brutality are exposed by the subsequent treatment of Stacey (Philip Martin), Colin's Jute-like antithesis: introduced as 'proud of being the leader of Drake House', Stacey's rapid replacement by the better runner as the governor's 'blue-eyed boy' results in his fighting with Colin and absconding, only to be caught and (savagely) beaten by the warders amid ironic cross-cutting to enthusiastic singing of 'Jerusalem'. On Sports Day, where changing-room banter centred on corporal punishment highlights the fundamental similarities between Ranleigh and Ruxton, Smith's pre-race handshake with his class enemy parallels Travis' post-beating hand-shake with Rowntree, each later revealed as a perfunctory playing by the rules. Both films have strong parallels when openly escaping regulations and reality: Colin and Mike's café excursions with girls in a purloined Ford Prefect echo Mick and Johnny's stolen motorcycle seductions; and much as *If*.... ostensibly concludes with wish-fulfilling gunfire, Colin tells his fellow inmates early on how, if granted a free wish, he would 'get all the coppers, governors, army officers and members of parliament, and I'd stick them up against this wall and let them have it'. Thus a similar meta-phorical imperative is writ large: 'The reformatory in which he finds him-self comes to represent for Colin Smith the hostile society at large' (Slide 1985: 106). There are also stylistic parallels, with Richardson's (social) realism similarly problematised by European influences. The structure of *Loneliness* offers a response to Jack Warner's closing question from *Boys in Brown* as the runner's extensive flashbacks of family life, fascistic police and old-school-tie governor potentially explain if not exculpate his current predicament. The flashback, however, often equated with Brechtian alienation, is also a cinematic representation of subjective truth (Hayward 1996: 123) and, much as *If*.... conflated reality with fantasy, so *Loneliness* employs the stylistic traits of the contemporary French *nouvelle vague* to effect disorientating switches between 'subjective' and 'objective' points of view—Dilys Powell confessed her inability to decide whether she was witnessing 'what the central figure sees... or fact' (*Sunday Times*, 30 September 1962). Richardson's voguish use of varied speeds and rapid montage has drawn enduring opprobrium: William Horne finds the opening borstal sequence, where the boys' undressing suddenly speeds up, 'wholly misconceived since it undermines the integrity of the dramatic reality by gratuitously distorting space and time' (1999: 114). The scene is explicable however, if viewed as a subjective interpolation, the exaggerated rapidity externalising the effect on their behaviour of the appearance of muscular master Roach (Joe Robinson): similarly, after Colin and Mike turn down the television volume, the speeding up of the presenter's image offers the boys' (impeccably New Wave) perspective on his inane irrelevance, while the Chaplinesque acceleration of their escape from the baker's shop shows how their thieving is done 'for a laugh' rather than from financial necessity. The reformatory setting and final freeze frame have encouraged explicit comparisons with *Les Quatre Cents Coups/The 400 Blows* (François Truffaut, 1959), seldom to the British director's advantage: Penelope Houston argued that, 'where Truffaut's style grew out of his theme, Richardson's looks like the result of a deliberate act of will, so that the bits and pieces remain unassimilated' (1963: 121). This is debatable: a scene, similar to *Les Quatre Cents Coups* but differently motivated, shows new housemaster Brown (Alec McCowen) trying out on Colin his 'new-fangled' psychological theories; where Truffaut never showed the interviewer—there is no need as the professional child psychologist is calm and self-assured—Richardson moves the camera hurriedly back and forth to expose a naïve and outwitted adult debutant unwisely offering the shrewd miscreant a cigarette, his well-intentioned over-familiarity as doomed to defeat as the older disciplinarians with their culturally uncomprehending concerts of bird-call experts and classical musical ensembles.

Colin's motivations remain as resistant as those of Mick Travis to any one definitive interpretation. He is labelled 'like his father', a tradeunionist strike-leader, and the son's refusal to 'play the game' struck a contemporary political chord, deeply upsetting the BBFC advisor who thought the film 'blatant and trying Communist propaganda', called Colin 'a good hero of the British Soviet' and expressed incredulity at his refusal of Newbolt's ideal: 'what the objection is to an honest-to-goodness prize openly and honestly competed for and judged, I can never see myself' (Audrey Field, *BBFC Examiners Report on Loneliness*, 3 January 1962).

Colin's rebellion, however, is more muddled than Marxist: recalling his father's statement that 'the workers should get the profits', he tellingly continues 'but I don't know where to start'. He learns, though, where his race should finish and, sensing that to win would endorse the patriotic ideology that sport enacts for the borstal/public school culture, Colin has no desire to progress to represent the 'honest-to-goodness' land that betrayed his father and imprisoned him: thus he rebels, not with a late-1960s bullet to the head but a (new) wave of the hand, a winning working-class withdrawal of labour (Fig. 4.5). Or does he? Anderson saw his Crusaders as 'traditionalists': Alexander Walker calls Colin 'a case-hardened conservative' who 'retains a vested interest in the status quo characteristic of the petty proletarian thief' (1974: 127). He is certainly unlike his mother—or the youths at the end of *Term of Trial*—in his determinedly anti-consumerist stance: on reluctantly receiving his share of the factory payout he goes up to his father's room and symbolically sets fire to a one pound note. His later more costly symbolic gesture is, for all the nearby baying crowds, similarly lonely, an individualist action at odds with the collectivist ideas he constantly spouts at borstal. Running grants Colin a welcome respite from class cohorts, a private communion with

Fig. 4.5 Not playing the game: 'a good hero of the British Soviet'

England's green and pleasant land, and a means of protest consigning him to its dark satanic mills.

Though Colin threw the race, Courtney won a Most Promising Newcomer BAFTA and unanimous praise—'no glamour boy but what a performance he puts up', enthused Alexander Walker (*Evening Standard*, 27 September 1962). Otherwise, reviews were predominantly negative. Peter Harcourt decried the usual literary shortcomings: 'there is an externality about the film's whole conception, so that unlike the story, it has neither a style nor a pulse of its own' (*Sight and Sound*, 32, 1, Winter 1962–3: 19), while the *MFB* expressed a common revulsion at Richardson's French-style 'restless tricksiness' and 'a great deal of childishly unacceptable caricature'—though it conceded that 'the public school types are absolutely believable, done with untypical generosity' (November 1962: 148). Most shared the BBFC's concern at the didactic sympathy extended to irresponsible working-class youth, Leonard Mosely condemning the film as 'not so much a dirge for the Establishment as a lament for a layabout' (*Daily Express*, 27 September 1962), while *Time* bemoaned a work where 'the hero is too palpably prolier-than-thou, his case is too obviously rigged', and how a 'specious pleading for the British proletariat ominously suggests that the battles of World War III may be lost on the playing fields of her Majesty's reform schools' (26 October 1962). *O tempora, o mores!* they might have added.

NOTES

1. On Trevelyan's tenure and approach, see James C. Robertson (1989) *The Hidden Cinema: British Film Censorship in Action 1913–1972*. London: Routledge: 119–126.
2. On Croft et al.'s protracted negotiations with the censors, see Aldgate 1995: 13–29.
3. The Smiths, whose 'The Headmaster's Ritual' recounts lead singer Morrissey's abusive punishments at secondary modern school, sought Olivier caning Stamp as the single's cover image. Both actors objected. David Bret (2004) *Morrissey: Scandal and Passion*. London: Robson Books: 8.
4. The view has, unsurprisingly, hardened with time: Jaci Stephen finds the film 'bizarre in its approach to what it thinks women want…She'd rather

live with a pervert who goes around assaulting underage schoolgirls than one who's legal, decent, honest and truthful. Fine.' *Evening Standard*, 11 August 1989.

5. A third factor advanced for the name change is that 'Robertson's refused permission for their trademark to be besmirched'. McGillivray 1992: 54.

6. Broadcaster Joan Bakewell recalls that pregnancy for a grammar school girl remained 'the worst conceivable crime—she was expelled before she could contaminate the rest of us'. Cited in D. Kynaston (2007) *Austerity Britain 1945–51*. London: Bloomsbury: 66–7.

7. To Sir, with Interest: Poitier, having agreed a basic $30,000 fee in exchange for 10 per cent of the film's overall gross, received one of film history's most significant payoffs. Harris 2008: 328.

8. In 2012 *To Sir, With Love* was ranked at number 27 in 'The 50 Best High School Movies', ahead of *Gregory's Girl*, *Get Real* and *Harry Potter and the Goblet of Fire*: *The Breakfast Club* (John Hughes, 1985) topped the predominantly American listing. Michelle Kung, *Entertainment Weekly*, 22 September 2012.

9. The title references the feudal ranking of hunting birds whereby, while an emperor would have an eagle, the lowest-ranking servant or 'knave' was only permitted a kestrel.

10. The film's production history, featuring cast biographies prior and subsequent to *Kes*, are recorded in Simon W. Golding (2005) *Life After Kes*. Bridgnorth: GET Publishing.

11. Several United Artists executives claimed that they could understand Hungarian better than the film's dialect. Ken Loach, *La Semaine de la Critique*, 15 April 2013.

12. John Hill (2011) suggests that 'a sense of "imprisonment" hangs over the majority of characters, most of whom, including the teachers, appear to be "trapped" in unfulfilling roles. In this respect, the gym teacher, Mr Sugden… possesses a degree of similarity to Jud.' *Ken Loach: The Politics of Film and Television*. London: Palgrave Macmillan: 114.

13. This murder of a London taxi-driver is discussed in George Orwell, 'Decline of the English Murder', *Tribune*, 15 February 1946, and dramatized in *Chicago Joe and the Showgirl* (Bernard Rose, 1990).

14. The film's BBFC file is empty. On the 2006 release of relevant Home Office documents, see James C. Robertson (2006) '*Good Time Girl*, the BBFC and the Home Office: a Mystery Resolved'. *Journal of British Cinema and Television*, 3, 1: 159–163.

15. Suggestive of Richardson's influence, the cross-country race in Sillitoe's source text had featured other borstal institutions.

REFERENCES

Aldgate, A. (1995) *Censorship and the Permissive Society: British Cinema and Theatre 1955–1965*. Oxford: Oxford University Press.

Braithwaite, E.R. (1959) *To Sir, With Love*. London: Bodley Head.

Durgnat, R. (1970) *A Mirror for England: British Movies from Austerity to Affluence*. London: Faber and Faber.

Fielding, M. (2005) 'Alex Bloom, Pioneer of Radical State Education'. *Forum*, 47, 2–3.

Fisher, R., A. Harris and C. Jarvis (2008) *Education in Popular Culture: Telling Tales on Teachers and Learners*. London: Routledge.

Garnett, T. (1970) 'The interview: Tony Garnett'. *Afterimage*, 1.

Goudsouzian, A. (2004) *Sidney Poitier: Man, Actor, Icon*. Chapel Hill: University of North Carolina Press.

Halliday, J. (1997) *Sirk on Sirk*. London: Secker and Warburg.

Harris, M. (2008) *Scenes from a Revolution: The Birth of the New Hollywood*. London: Canongate.

Hayward, S. (1996) *Key Concepts in Cinema Studies*. London: Routledge.

Higson, A. (1996) 'Space, Place, Spectacle: Landscape and Townscape in the "Kitchen Sink" Film', in A. Higson (ed.) *Dissolving Views: Key Writings on British Cinema*. London: Cassell.

Hill, J. (1986) *Sex, Class and Realism: British Cinema 1956–1963*. London: BFI.

Hines, B. (1968) *A Kestrel for a Knave*. London: Michael Joseph.

Hoggart, R. (1959) *The Uses of Literacy*. Harmondsworth: Penguin.

Horne, W.L. (1999) 'Greatest Pleasures', in J.M. Welsh and J.C. Tibbetts (eds) *The Cinema of Tony Richardson: Essays and Interviews*. Albany: State University of New York Press.

Houston, P. (1963) *The Contemporary Cinema*. Harmondsworth: Penguin.

Hunt, L. (1998) *British Low Culture: From Safari Suits to Sexploitation*. London: Routledge.

Laurie, P. (1965) *The Teenage Revolution*. London: A. Blond.

Leach, J. (2004) *British Film*. Cambridge: Cambridge University Press.

McFarlane, B. (1997) *An Autobiography of British Cinema*. London: Methuen/ BFI.

McGillivray, D. (1992) *Doing Rude Things: The History of the British Sex Film, 1957–1981*. London: Sun Tavern Fields.

Pines, J. (1977) *Blacks in Films*. London: Studio Vista.

Richardson, T. (1993) *Long Distance Runner: A Memoir*. London: Faber and Faber.

Ross, R. (1996) *The Carry On Companion*. London: B.T. Batsford.

Sandbrook, D. (2005) *Never Had It So Good: A History of Britain from Suez to the Beatles*. London: Little Brown.

Slide, A. (1985) *Fifty Classic British Film, 1932–1982: A Pictorial Record.* New York: Dover Publications.

Stephenson, W. (1973) '*Kes* and the Press'. *Cinema Journal*, 12, 2.

Walker, A. (1974) *Hollywood England: The British Film Industry in the Sixties.* London: Michael Joseph.

Williams, R. (1961) *The Long Revolution.* London: Chatto and Windus.

Winston Dixon, W. (1994) 'The Doubled Image: Montgomery Tully's *Boys in Brown* and the Independent Frame Process', in W. Winston Dixon (ed.) *Re-Viewing British Cinema, 1900–1992.* Albany: State University of New York Press.

PART IV

The Final Years Programme (1970–)

CHAPTER 5

The Contemporary School Film (1970–)

1 Fright School

The comforts of Ross' *Goodbye, Mr. Chips* spawned no re-evaluative lineage; instead a clutch of murderous public school-set films were 'greenlit' by the internecine *If.....* The first, *Walk a Crooked Path* (John Brason, July 1970), a convoluted but capable crime film set in a boys' boarding school, shows the deteriorating childless marriage of staid long-serving senior housemaster John Hemming (Tenniel Evans) and his wealthy but ambitious—and strong-drinking—wife Elizabeth (Faitih Brook) to be further exacerbated when he is passed over for the position of headmaster. When Hemming is subsequently accused of assault by sixth-former Philip Dreaper (Clive Endersby), poisonous school gossip makes Elizabeth drive drunkenly away to a fatal car crash. Though Hemming is cleared and has plenty of female interest, he still hands in his resignation: the 'assault' is revealed to be a plan, engineered by teacher and pupil, to encourage Elizabeth's suicide and inherit her money. Hemming seeks to retain Dreaper's company, but the pupil's financial demands lead to an acrimonious split. While *Walk a Crooked Path* can appear to be cashing in on the violent public school atmosphere of *If....*, it emerged from a series of production problems beginning in 1966. The final version of a twice-abandoned project may recall *Mr. Perrin and Mr. Traill* with its machinations of bored and isolated masters' wives and *The Browning Version* for its late emotional awakening, but the most apposite school film comparison is

© The Editor(s) (if applicable) and The Author(s) 2016   171
S. Glynn, *The British School Film*,
DOI 10.1057/978-1-137-55887-9_5

with *The Children's Hour* (William Wyler, 1961) where pupil accusations that their teacher is gay again prove unwittingly accurate. Here the 'reveal' explains the plan to remove Elizabeth as subconsciously oriented: when Nancy (Patricia Haines), the games master's wife who expects to succeed Elizabeth, hears Hemmings describe a past holiday swimming naked with other boys, she realises his newly awakened sexuality and, horrified, abandons him. The melodramatic denouement, with Hemming alone in his ill-gotten house as the image shifts to black and white, fed Stephen Bourne's condemnation of 'a truly reprehensible and depressing film' which 'appears to be a warning to gay men in 1970 to watch out, especially those who think they may have found "freedom" after the passing of the 1967 [Sexual Offences] Act' (1996: 223–4). The trade press—with a far different *parti pris*—also found it all 'a somewhat depressing affair' and wondered 'if one can accept this as a remotely possible condition in a better class school' before sympathising with 'the long-suffering husband' who 'could almost be excused his actions with such a nagging and depressing wife' (*Kine Weekly*, 18 July 1970).

1.1   *Section Prize Winner:* Unman, Wittering and Zigo *(1971)*

Unman, Wittering and Zigo (13 June 1971), produced by and starring David Hemmings, was filmed at St David's College, Llandudno with interiors at Reading Blue Coat School. The film follows idealistic John Ebony (Hemmings) who, quitting his advertising job to realise his desire to teach, moves with wife Silvia (Carolyn Seymour) to take up his first—temporary—post at Chantry (founded 1678), a public school for 300 boys. He is put in charge of the unruly Lower 5B—the film's title lists the last names on the roll-call—after their previous master, Mr Pelham, fell to his death at the nearby coastal cliffs, reputedly having lost his way in the fog. On his first day, when Ebony threatens the disruptive class with Saturday detention, the 16 boys (the seventeenth, Zigo, is permanently absent) calmly inform him that, should he continue in this vein, they will murder him as they murdered his predecessor. Soon believing their threats, the fearful Ebony submits to his pupils' rules, a '*modus vivendi*' whereby, in return for his safety, he will fake their exam results and place their horseracing bets. On learning from the headmaster (Douglas Wilmer) that he will be replaced at the end of term—'we always like to have Old Chantrovians on the staff'—Ebony determines to resist the boys' demands: they retaliate by attempting a mass rape of Silvia, forcing the constantly-bullied Wittering

(Colin Barrie) to begin. When he proves incapable, Silvia escapes: the next morning Wittering is found dead at the foot of the cliffs.

It is again tempting to view this school-set psychological horror-thriller through the prism of Anderson's film: from the orchestrated murder of staff down to signalling Zigo's absence with an O in the register and thus evoking Vigo and his *Zéro de Conduite*, here, potentially, is *If....* retold from the masters' point of view. Such readings must again be tempered by the film's lengthy origins, a 1965 television play adapted by (Lancing-educated) Giles Cooper from his original radio production, premiered on BBC's Third Programme on 23 November 1958. The adroit plotting and achieved direction by John Mackenzie, a former teacher then assistant director for Loach and Garnett at the BBC, scotches the view that Cooper's plays 'are so conceived as to be virtually unthinkable in terms of any medium but radio' (Russell Taylor 1963: 26): for instance, Ebony's narrative containment is skilfully mirrored in a mise-en-scène frequently foregrounding polite pupil malevolence (Fig. 5.1). While the Ebonys' isolated coastal cottage, their awkwardness in a hidebound environment and the communal sexual attack on Silvia pinpoint *Unman, Wittering and Zigo* as a cloistered variant on the concurrent *cause célèbre Straw Dogs* (Sam Peckinpah, 1971), and Hemmings' role as a naïve but determined murder investigator offers coastal intimations of his earlier *Blow Up* (Michelangelo Antonioni, 1966), school film connections still resonate strongly. Sexual tension in the squash court chimes with the assault of Mrs Dadier (Anne Francis) in *The Blackboard Jungle*; the world-weary cynicism of colleague Cary Farthingale (Anthony Haygarth), a self-proclaimed 'connoisseur of failure', is a darker rerun of Birkland in the similarly cliffside-set *Mr. Perrin and Mr. Traill*—and arguably just as corrupting of Ebony's idealism as his class's terror-tactics; Lower 5B's complete materialism and haughty authority—six expect university scholarships with minimum preparation—might precociously equate with the prefects in *If....*, though the inverted class dynamic ('authority is the child of obedience' and all Chantry pupils are called 'men', the head proudly states), the penchant for gambling and the brazen declaration by the prime worker of betting odds that he is an archdeacon's son are all, at least in tone, more Will Hay than Whips and Scum.

Cooper's play was adapted for cinema by Simon Raven. A 'promiscuous chronicler of upper-class life', notably in his *Alms for Oblivion* novel sequence, Raven had been expelled from Charterhouse for 'serial homosexuality' (David Hughes, *Guardian*, 16 May 2001), and Martin Jones senses 'his demonic signature' in the interpolated scenes where, seemingly

Fig. 5.1   Mise-en-scène as *modus vivendi*

triggered by the oneiric vision of two exhausted pupils caressing each other on the gym floor, Ebony has a nightmare where he is stripped naked in the woods and carried away by his class, all dressed in their standard white PE shirts and shorts (2012: 248). Like earlier public school fare, *Unman, Wittering and Zigo* is open to 'multiple expositions': the dream sequences permit, as with *If...*, a wider blurring of the fantastic and the actual (is Ebony paranoid?), while the post-nightmare brutal love-making with his wife suggests a Hemming-like sexual ambivalence in Ebony—the fallout from their awkward dinner at the headmaster's house suggests all is not well with the marriage and, at the film's conclusion, he ignores Silvia's ultimatum and stays with his suddenly infantilised class in their panicked search for Wittering. The latter's suicide note may disclose him as the acceptance-seeking 'ringleader' for Pelham's murder, but it fails fully to answer Ebony's final dismayed 'What made them do it?' The perennial severity and isolation of public school life offers an implicit motivation but latent also, as with *Young Woodley*, are 'the tensions and ambiguities of homosexual desire' (O'Connor 1998: 22). Pelham, as the headmaster remarks (in obituary style), was 'unmarried'; choirboy Wittering is complimented by Silvia for his 'lovely voice' and 'adorable' cherubic appearance, while the set-up rape threat—'you'll be so ashamed, feel so dirty, so disgusted with what's happened to you'—can be interpreted as more purposefully a test failed by Wittering, finally 'outed' by his excited heterosexual classmates and unable to live with the shame.

Unman, Wittering and Zigo received lukewarm reviews, with many criticising the ending as rushed and unresolved—for *Variety* 'it asks a great deal of credence' (31 December 1970). Patrick Gibbs thought the film abandoned the play's 'serious examination of the mutually destructive teacher–pupil relationship' for 'a slightly superior example of the horror genre' (*Daily Telegraph*, 24 September 1971), while Alexander Walker (with different ideas to mine of what is real) regretted a lack of uncertainty 'whether the menacing events may not all have been happening inside the fevered imagination of the Hemmings character' and concluded that the film, 'like some kinds of teaching, only succeeds in killing the imagination' (*Evening Standard*, 24 September 1971). Focusing on the reality, David McGillivray noted how, amongst the 'genuine-looking, crumpled-collared staff and an array of ink-stained pupils who are not patently fresh from the stage school, [Ebony] is easily recognisable as a teacher struggling to discipline a class of delinquents, and David Hemmings' performance succeeds in communicating the feeling of desperation that inexperience fosters' (*MFB*, October 1971: 206); Christopher Hudson by contrast found it 'a silly and repulsive film, throbbing with obsessional public school fantasies' (*Spectator*, 25 September 1971). Grossly unfair criticism for a minor gem of school-set horror.

Alongside the Grand Guignol of *Unman, Wittering and Zigo* came tentative explorations of a Great British *giallo*.[1] The ground was prepared with *Assault* (Sydney Hayers, 11 February 1970), based on Kendal Young's suspense novel *The Ravine*, where the rape and then murder of two 16-year-old pink-miniskirt-uniformed schoolgirls in woodland surrounding exclusive Heatherdene School leads Art teacher Julie West (Suzy Kendall), witness to the murder, to offer herself as bait by promising to reveal the killer's portrait. While mostly setting up a line of potential murderers in standard procedural fare, *Assault* offers an intermittent self-awareness of its exploitative strategies and narrative lineage, both domestic and continental. When the headmistress' harangued pornography-collecting husband confesses to the crimes, his exculpation by case-psychiatrist Greg Lomax (James Laurenton) as a peeping tom who 'wants sex without contact' implicates the film's male audience in its scopophilia and (crudely) anticipates Laura Mulvey's influential psychoanalytical analysis of the 'male gaze' and female sexual objectification in cinema (1975). The reveal that the assailant is Dr Bartell (Anthony Ainley), director of the hospital caring for the first and safely catatonic victim (Lesley-Anne Down), overlays the salacious schoolgirls-in-peril trope with a then-prevalent British exposé of older authority figures as 'psychopathic killers... preying on miniskirted birds' (Newman 2002: 79). However, more relevant to Kendall's casting than the demure Gillian from *To Sir, With Love* was her recent work in Dario Argento's *The Bird with the Crystal Plumage* (1970), now considered a globally influential landmark in the Italian *giallo* (Schneider 2007: 19–20). Taking her car to search for the second missing girl, Julie can only decipher through the rain the black-gloved killer leaning over his victim, his eyes shining bright red in the car's tail-lights: her subsequent testimony that he resembled the devil has her laughed out of court but pinpoints emergent *giallo* iconography more than the critics' pejoratively perceived 'B picture formulas' (*Financial Times*, 12 February 1971).[2]

This overseas generic influence was next developed under the patriotic banner of Hammer horror with *Fear in the Night* (Jeremy Sangster, 9 July 1972). Another *If....*-eased project with a convoluted gestation reaching back to Sangster's 1963 script, the film follows mentally fragile newlywed Peggy Heller (this time *To Sir, With Love*'s Judy Geeson) who accompanies teacher husband Robert (Ralph Bates) to his country school cottage. Before and after her arrival at the school, deserted for autumn half-term, she is attacked, with suspicion falling on the school's one-armed head-master-owner Michael Carmichael (Peter Cushing). The plot, intricate enough for the head's wife Molly (Joan Collins) to meta-comment on its deviousness, reveals the school as a façade, equipped to humour Michael unhinged by a fatal fire five years previously, with long-time lovers Molly and Robert manoeuvring Peggy into killing him so they can inherit his 'Stockbroker Tudor' school and grounds. Instead, Michael manoeuvres Robert into shooting Molly and then hangs him from a tree: a deranged Peggy walks down the drive as Michael's tapes of morning prayers echo from the school.

While *Fear in the Night* is British to the core in its studio provenance, wider influences are again evident: the opening bathroom attack recalls *Psycho* (Alfred Hitchcock, 1960) and the school context exposes the plot's indebtedness to Henri-Georges Clouzot's 1955 suspense classic *Les Diaboliques/The Fiends*, here given a *giallo* touch with another black-gloved stalker. Nonetheless, Sangster's film plays intertextually with the expectations of indigenous school film fare, both for character and location. Cushing's grey-haired round-spectacled appearance recalls loser-in-love Vincent Perrin, though their parallel trajectory here sees initial atrophy morph into a more achieved psychotic violence with his rival eliminated, while the three teddy bears sitting bedside now signify not Peterbridge's lost virginity but Peggy's child-like vulnerability. When Michael first meets Peggy and takes her to the gym, generically the optimum site for violation, the mise-en-scène places between them a wall-hung noose, intimating the mortality to come/already shown (the film having a flashback structure). In its most successful suspense sequence, the seemingly indestructible Michael—gunfire only shatters his glasses, creating a key advertising image—stalks Peggy through the school's empty corridors which echo with disembodied youthful laughter: a similar pursuit in *Personal Affair* had a self-serving motivation, but here, more damning than in previous realisations, the very animus of the (British) boys' public school seemingly reveals and revels in its deep misogyny. Despite its creative flashes, *Fear In the Night* failed to impress the public or critics, only David Pirie enjoying its 'quaint but enjoyably old-fashioned flavour' (*MFB*, August 1972: 161). 'Old school', perhaps: it would prove the final Hammer thriller, and Sangster's last direction.

Italianate *giallo* was followed by Catholic guilt. The Catholic Church, the country's first providers of schools and universities, had disappeared with the Reformation, its education going underground or across the Channel: the oldest extant UK Catholic schools date from this time, notably St Edmund's, Ware, founded at Douay (1568), Stonyhurst, at Saint-Omer (1593), and Downside, again at Douay (1607), all returning to England following the French Revolution and remaining a significant presence thereafter (Barnes 1926).[3] With a similarly tortuous history, Catholic schooling finally came to the British screen in *Absolution* (Anthony Page, December 1978). The film is traceable back to post-*If....* 1970 when playwright Anthony Shaffer (St Paul's, London) promised a psychological thriller set in a boys' Catholic public school: the project languished, however, until picked up in 1978 by Bulldog Productions on the recommendation of Richard Burton who long coveted the lead role. In supporting parts, notable state sector transfers included *Kes'* David (now Dai) Bradley and Brian Glover, plus a debut film role for banjo-picking comedian Billy

Connolly. Though London premiered in December 1978, *Absolution*'s struggles continued, shelved in the UK until November 1981 and in the US until 1988, four years after Burton's death—financial litigation the proffered explanation. The film (eventually) showed how, at St Anthony's Roman Catholic public school, the rigid Latin and Religious Knowledge schoolmaster-priest Father Goddard (Burton) favours Benjamin Stanfield (Dominic Guard) as a model scholar with priesthood potential, but is unsympathetic to the physically handicapped Arthur Dyson (Bradley), enthusiastic but cloying. 'Benjie', tiring of his reputation, teases Goddard in confession with repeated tales of sexual high jinks and the murder plus woodland burial of Scottish drifter Blakey (Connolly). Powerless to act due to the inviolable seal of confession, Goddard twice investigates and finds, in shallow graves, first a scarecrow then Blakey's body. When Benjie confesses his intent to murder Arthur and Goddard finds his leg-brace protruding from a shallow grave, the enraged priest beats Benjie to death with his spade, only to hear his voice mocking him as he prays in the chapel. The pupil who appears, though, is Arthur, who murdered Blakey and mimicked Benjie's voice since the first confession prank. He leaves the tormented Goddard screaming at the altar.

Another generic hybrid, the initial pacing of *Absolution* suggests a coming-of-age film, until the false confessional scenes propel it towards a tense murder-mystery. The premise of a priest forced by confidentiality to stay silent over a murder had previously been employed in *I Confess* (Alfred Hitchcock, 1953), while Shaffer had replayed a false death in *Sleuth* (Joseph L. Mankiewicz, 1972). Nonetheless, the Catholic setting here allows for variations on the school film genre's familiar patterning, with washroom battles and refectory breakfast leading to a mass and Goddard blessing the sacrament. Thereafter, as pupils, rehearsing for Gilbert and Sullivan's *Patience,* wander the campus in full military regalia—'in good voice, Colonel?' Goddard asks of one—the defunct imperial purpose of the British public school is gently lampooned, while the Catholic Church's more persistent missionary function is signalled by the Zulu spear adorning Goddard's study. Pedagogy and plot, however, fully conform to generic tradition. Goddard is an erudite but aloof disciplinarian in the Crocker-Harris mould, his dry discussions of Caesar's *Gallic Wars* and humiliation of a genuinely inquisitive Dyson contrasted with a younger priest's English lesson where Dyson, centre-stage declaiming '*Et tu, Brute?*' as his classmates fall on him, repeats John Saunders' approach to Shakespeare in *Spare the Rod*. Offering an intensely emotive performance, like Olivier in *Term of Trial*, Burton successfully conveys Goddard's inner turmoil: a teacher reading love poetry is a common conduit for pupil infatuation (cf. *Personal Affair*), but here Goddard's recitation to Benjie of Gerard Manley Hopkins' 'The Leaden Echo and The Golden Echo' has a restrained sexual tension all emanating from the teacher. Benjie's awareness of these repressed homosexual desires and the encouragement to tease Goddard via the confessional come from whisky-fuelled woodland discussions with Blakey and girlfriend Louella (Sharon Duce), a biker couple recalling *If....* as catalysts for (sexual and scholastic) rebellion while, manipulated into murder, Goddard's final crucified stance is at least more textually appropriate than Thackeray's in *To Sir, With Love*. As with its lead, though, the film found no absolution: Paul Taylor expressed the majority view that it had endured 'a justifiably long shelf-life' being 'a dire slice of clever-clever narrative trickery' and 'a mechanistic exercise in spotting the guilty Catholic' (*MFB*, December 1981: 239). America's *Variety* similarly decried 'a dull, gloomy, nasty, contrived market misfit, apparently designed to ride on Richard Burton's shirttails. Or in this case his cassock' (31 December 1981). The public response suggested Amen to that.

Horror thereafter receded from a British school setting. An interim gentler goading of a teacher occurs in *Waterland* (Stephen Gyllenhaal, 21 August 1992), for Janet Maslin 'a ghost story told by the ghost himself, a gaunt, ravaged Englishman whose wounds go almost unimaginably deep' (*New York Times*, 30 October 1992). A UK–US co-production, Peter Prince's adaptation of Graham Swift's 1983 multigenerational Fenland gothic novel strips back the sinuous and ruminative narration to show how, in 1974 and with a reverse momentum to the opening lesson in *If....*, History teacher Tom Crick (Jeremy Irons) responds to the belligerent questioning by pupil Matthew Price (Ethan Hawke) of his subject's relevance by abandoning the French Revolution textbook and telling instead his East Anglian family's inbred elixir-driven history from the First World War onwards. Crick's new approach has the merit of refocusing attention on individuals' small stories marginalised by the canon's grand narratives, in the process problematising the very notion of 'history'; it has the demerit of exposing pupils to graphic accounts of his teenage sex life. A maudlin male variant on Jean Brodie, Crick's cutting the curriculum similarly annoys the school's head, Lewis Scott (John Heard), who intimates it may be time for Tom, and his subject, to leave—a mooted 'merger thing with Social Studies' makes Crick realise, in the pupils' vernacular, that he is 'history'. The film's decision to put the pupils in an open-topped bus on a school trip to Crick's virtual homeland is, depending on the viewer's threshold for reality, either foolish or Fellini-esque in rendering the past more theme park than foreign country, but the commercial pragmatism of relocating the classroom to Pittsburgh, Pennsylvania incontrovertibly dilutes a thematically necessary topographical rootedness: when Crick announces during his Crocker-Harris-style farewell assembly that the 'disease of the Fens' has made him tell stories where 'there was always a fog of horror, of sadness or despair', his word must largely be accepted. This misplaced *Waterland* was adjudged 'a talented but terminally parched piece of literary cinema' (*Variety*, 31 October 1992), and even, 'with every moment milked for pseudo-significance, the kind of film that gives artiness a bad name' (*Sunday Times*, 23 August 1992).

The lengthy school-shaped hole in British horror was eventually filled by the Anglo-French-funded *The Hole* (Nick Hamm, 20 April 2001). After Hamm's ten-year struggle to realise teenager Guy Burt's novel *After the Hole*, pre-publicity focused on the seven-figure fee paid to Thora Birch, fresh from *American Beauty* (Sam Mendes, 1999): retrospective publicity would note a first significant role for Keira Knightley. The film centres on Liz Dunn (Birch) who persuades fellow Brabourne pupils, American hunk Mike (Desmond Harrington), rugby hero Geoff (Laurence Fox) and glamour girl Frankie (Knightley), to hide out for the weekend in a disused war bunker rather than join a Geography field trip to Wales, only for them to be permanently locked in. The film adds an investigating psychologist Philippa Norwood (Embeth Davidtz) and *Rashomon*-style alternative versions of events underground. The first is recounted by sole-survivor Liz, a smart but mousy outcast: her evidence frames her friend Martin (Daniel Brocklebank) for locking them in, citing his gay jealousy of her crush on Mark. Norwood knows this version to be fantastical, and Martin's different summary of Brabourne life exposes Liz, the object of his unrequited affections, as a popular and manipulative figure who acted alone. When confronted with Martin's testimony, Liz recalls the grisly reality of the last three weeks and reveals her impulsive passage to fully realised sociopathy (the 'hole' in her mentality): as well as reacting advantageously to increasing underground mayhem she finally kills Martin and plants on him the incriminating bunker key. While her first 'invented' version exaggerates a conventional trajectory with partying teens swapping generic ghost stories, the final 'true' take on the friends' disintegration is equally intertextual: Michael Thomson thought the 'dark, grisly adventure' appropriate 'if the "Famous Five" had been egotistical or unhinged' (bbc.co.uk/films [accessed 9 June 2015]) while for Kim Newman 'Birch acts like a vampish reincarnation of the teenage bullies in *Carrie* [(Brian De Palma 1976)]' (*Sight and Sound*, 11, 5, May 2001: 52). Within the British school film genre, Liz Dunn offers a distaff continuation of Philip Dreaper and Arthur Dyson, pupil manipulators of adults and audiences, while her credible 'outing' of Mike and Geoff's rugby-scrum homoeroticism adds a familiar subtext to the bunker's sexual tensions.

The Awakening (Nick Murphy, 11 November 2011), a BBC Films presentation, again explores a 'hole' where school-life memories should be. Set in 1921, it follows Florence Cathcart (Rebecca Hall), a campaigning author who exposes phoney spiritualists exploiting credulous victims tormented with post-war guilt. When brusque war-wounded Latin master Robert Mallory (Dominic West) invites her to his Cumbrian boarding school Rookford (motto 'Semper Veritas') to investigate how a sickly pupil was reputedly frightened to death by a disfigured ghost-child, Florence accepts, expecting to uncover individual deception or group hysteria (cf. *The Falling*). Reversing the momentum of *The Hole*, the film's sceptical rationalism cedes once we learn that Florence is here at the behest of school matron Maud (Imelda Staunton): revelations follow of Florence's suppressed memories of Rookford as her childhood home and her father's pre-suicide shooting of her family, including her half-brother, the Munch-like screaming boy that only she and Maud, the boy's mother, can see. Unfavourably compared to horror fare such as *El Orfanato/The Orphanage* (Juan Antonio Bayona, 2007) and berated for its contrived ending, 'as harshly unenlightening as a blow to a schoolboy's knuckles' (*Washington Post*, 17 August 2012), it is precisely as an (abusive) school film that *The Awakening* works best, revisiting Edwardian public school values manifested at an intergenerational and (inter)national level. Rookford's teachers, hollowed out by the First World War, constitute another level of the walking dead: Mallory painfully stammers his way to a consolatory relationship with Florence while sadistic master Malcom McNair (Shaun Dooley) justifies the cane by insisting that 'these boys must be stronger—stronger than us!' Telling England anew 70 years on, the film invites a psychological gloss with the cod-Freudian title of Florence's forthcoming book, 'The Interpretation of Ghosts', and primal tensions root adult trauma not only in long-hidden childhood abuse by the father, but in a complex matrix extendable to the heartless discipline and bullying of a boys' public school education and its concomitant war-hungry patriarchal culture.

Another school bearing secrets features in *Never Let Me Go* (Mark Romanek, 13 October 2010), adapted by Alex Garland from Kazuo Ishiguro's 2005 Booker Prize-shortlisted novel. Set in an alternative post-war Britain where genetic (before nuclear) advancements have created a life expectancy exceeding 100 years - organ donations permitting, the film is narrated by professional 'carer' Kathy (Carey Mulligan), who looks back on her 1970s schooldays and troubled love triangle with fellow pupils Tommy (Andrew Garfield) and Ruth (Keira Knightley). With its tended grounds, tidy dormitories, wooden-floored assembly hall, and fussy headmistress Miss Emily (Charlotte Rampling) constantly reminding her charges that they are 'special', Hailsham initially matches any middle-ranking British boarding school. Yet details gradually disconcert: guards patrol the gates and delivery men avert their eyes, while the pupils wear electronic wrist tags, sing and applaud in worrying unison, and betray no parental influence, or surnames. An eerie amalgam of Brookfield and borstal, Hailsham, we discover, provides a hermetic environment where pupils are carefully prepared for their adult roles, numerous euphemisms revealing them to be clones, (palely beautiful) British stock reared to be 'farmed' as compulsory organ donors, with three or four donations leading to 'completion' by their mid-twenties. Though physical fitness is paramount, Hailsham forego-goes sport for art, a state-funded experiment (later abandoned) to discern 'human' characteristics in these mass-produced children. Romanek repeat-edly holds the frame after pupils have exited, visually emphasising their ephemerality and unimportance: as with *The Awakening*, here are the living dead. Beyond its ostensible bioethical dystopia, the film, like its source text, has received allegorical interpretations ranging from our inability to escape the human lifespan (Ishiguro) to our 'cognitive dissonance' over third-world clothing industries (Romanek) (Miller 2011: 38–9). A greater unity of response has criticised the clones' lack of fight: for many, 'the plot suffers, as it did on the page, from how accepting these lambs are of their impending slaughter' (*Telegraph*, 10 February 2011). However, *Never Let Me Go* has no interest in forging a rebellion against evil overlords, as in *Logan's Run* (Michael Anderson, 1976) or indeed *If....*—at best it follows a cloned couple's naïve if touching hope that true love will delay the inevitable. Instead the film underlays its low-resolution sci-fi tropes with an investigation of the centrality of education to an ideology: though made with transatlantic backing by an American director from an Anglo-Japanese author's novel, here is a forensic study in how successfully British schooling inculcates a sense of national duty, an understated and unquestioning altruism. Peter Bradshaw saw the film as 'a dreamlike parable of Britishness—a particularly miserable Britishness... which submits numbly and uncomplainingly to authority' (*Guardian*, 10 February 2011), and Hailsham's highly effective hegemony ensures that Kathy, Tommy and Ruth, as much as a Tom Brown or Roddy Berwick, are fully moulded products of their educational environment, indoctrinated to accept their part in an apparently unchanging social order, be it here an abused underclass proudly serving in mints for the coining of organs.

The seriously ambitious *Never Let Me Go* met with decidedly mixed reviews: *Empire* considered it 'a beautifully realised adaptation of a profoundly affecting novel' (7 February 2011), the *Daily Express* 'a suffocating self-important bore that makes you wish a hasty end for the characters' (14 February 2011). Those characters inhabited a state-run boarding school, and British state school horror first surfaced, as ever in comic mode, with *Tormented* (Jon Wright, 22 May 2009), a belated effort at the US-owned high school slasher movie.[4] The only previous UK production to take a stab at the subgenre, *Slaughter High* (George Dugdale et al., 1986), had deemed an American setting so essential that, though filmed in Westminster with a British cast including 36-year-old Caroline Munro as teen 'prom queen' Carol, it set itself Stateside at Doddsville High and employed variable US accents for its self-aware ten-year-reunion 'revenge of the nerd' storyline. The confidence finally to situate a slasher film in a suitably dissolute British secondary school was boosted by the success of E4 television's drug-and-sex-drenched teen drama *Skins* (7 series, 2007–2013) which followed Bristol teenagers through their Roundview College sixth-form career (replacing the cast every two years). *Tormented* shows its indebtedness to *Skins* by drafting in former cast-members Larissa Wilson and April Pearson who join Alex Pettyfer, recent star of *Stormbreaker* (Geoffrey Sax, 2006), as members of the caustic in-crowd at (the still transatlantic named) Fairview High grammar school who cyber-bully fat and friendless Darren Mullet (Calvin Dean, a deliberate double for James Corden from *The History Boys*?): his resultant suicide is ignored until the cool kids receive text messages from beyond the grave and start dying in increasingly gruesome circumstances. With one potential murderer named Jason after *Friday the 13th*'s slasher franchise and copying Munch's *The Scream* in art class, *Tormented*'s ostensible mix of self-reflexivity with slaughter apes the slasher-reviving *Scream* (Wes Craven, 1996), but more original than the serial murders (a hair-raising end to bedroom hankypanky replays a trope from *Slaughter High*) is its depiction of the school characters, whose collection of sub-groups and vitriolic bitching—'you twisted dyke slut'—accurately updates the cut-throat ethos of *Heathers* (Michael Lehmann, 1988) for the favoured Facebook generation. One seriously effective scene amidst the blood and bile, where head girl Justine (Tuppence Middleton) accesses the clique-devised website and sees the horrific banality of Darren's persecution, offers a brief but chilling example of the new technology-enhanced culture of virtual bullying (and helped earn the film a '15' certificate). Fairview's staff are not spared the film's satirical edge, from the feckless headmaster (Peter Amory) whose anti-bullying campaign amounts to placing laminated posters around the campus, to the foul-mouthed games teacher, knowingly named Gordon Ramsey (Geoff Bell), who bemoans the killer sparing the lesser members of his rugby team and all but joins in the traditional bullying technique of flushing the class nerd's head down the toilet. Though some still questioned the viability of a home-grown slasher movie—the *Telegraph* found that *Tormented* 'comes across like a Rada production of *Scream*' (21 May 2009)—the indigenous jokiness was adjudged generically advantageous and the film 'consistently funny in a painful way' (*Empire*, 21 May 2009).

Tormented was also praised for offering 'a slightly more three-dimensional characterisation of teenagers—vicious and self-absorbed as they may be—than hoodie-wearing, contemporary bogeymen' (*Sight and Sound*, 19, 6, June 2009: 80). The latter are in plentiful evidence in writer-director Johannes Roberts' *F* aka *The Expelled* (27 August 2010), made for just £150,000 and set in Wittering College, another tough North London comprehensive. Here Robert Anderson (David Schofield), a harassed, overworked teacher, is head-butted by a pupil and, rather than being supported by the school authorities, is forced to take three months' leave to avoid being sued for the humiliation of giving the boy's work a grade 'F' for 'fail' instead of the school-approved 'RS' for 'resubmission'. On his return, Anderson is a broken man, a divorced alcoholic obsessed with the growth in teenage violence and Wittering's lax security. One evening, when on detention duty with his estranged pupil-daughter Kate (Eliza Bennett), his fears are realised as the school is attacked by a band of faceless hoodies who stalk and kill its late-working inhabitants. Shot with an oppressive green-tinged lensing and an Argento-influenced soundtrack of choral nursery rhymes and echoing whispers, *F*'s educational anarchy and unseen assailants drew comparisons with contemporary overseas fare such as *Ils/Them* (David Moreau and Xavier Palud, 2006), while its frequent recourse to the four-screen closed-circuit console of the school's security room explicitly set up associations with post-Columbine anxieties.[5] However, in its British school film context *F* exactly replays the anxieties over undisciplined youth culture enacted 50 years earlier by Graham Weir in *Term of Trial*—the male pupil antagonist, the domestic breakdown and problematic relationship with a female pupil are all repeated tropes while the mockery of his colleagues and hostility of parent-pleasing head Ms Balham (Ruth Gemmell) offer precise staffroom parallels. *F* was indifferently received, Wally Hammond reiterating 'the problem with realism in a British setting—the film can read, at times, like a frightfest episode of *Grange Hill* [(BBC, 31 series, 1978–2008)]' (*Sight and Sound*, 20, 11, November 2010: 58). But *is* it 'realism'? While Weir's walk to court externalised his class fears, Anderson's enervated state of mind and the hoodies' spectral depiction allow a reading that the whole event is internal, with the no-longer-passive barbarians a projection of his professional paranoia. If allowed, this subjective element (*pace* Alexander Walker) places the film affectively closer to *Unman, Wittering and Zigo* than Roberts' avowed reworking of *Assault on Precinct 13* (John Carpenter, 1976). This mitigation of an F-for-fascistic socio-political perspective—that Anderson's vigilante is less Tom Brown than *Harry Brown* (Daniel Barber, 2009)—is not extendable to *Unhallowed Ground* (Russell England, 25 April 2015) where six public school army cadets on end-of-term surveillance duty are assailed by working-class criminals and the irate ghosts of murdered old boys. *Tormented* with toffs, 'as a genre exercise it's merely underachieving', thought the *Guardian* (12 June 2015): as a class survey it is unpleasantly reactionary.

2   CO-ED CARNIVALESQUE (MOSTLY)

The 1970s comic school film begins, as it had in the 1960s, with a television sitcom 'spin-off'. *Please Sir!* (LWT 1968–1972), inspired by *To Sir, With Love* and set in London's beleaguered inner-city Fenn Street Secondary Modern School, starred John Alderton as the fresh-faced newly-qualified teacher Bernard 'Privet' Hedges, and followed his early struggles and later empathy with his unruly class, 5C. After three highly successful series, a film version was created for LW International and the Rank Organisation. *Please Sir!* (Mark Stuart, 10 September 1971) sends 5C to Woodbridge rural recreation camp and a fortnight of mischief, mishaps and pitched battles with the refined pupils of Boulter's School. When 5C learn that their presence is due to Hedges' advocacy, they turn over a new leaf and emerge victorious with the highest number of good conduct marks, while Hedges bonds with Penny, the local barmaid who, after early antipathy, has come to see his true qualities.

A similar re-evaluation occurred in the British film industry which had long looked upon television as the enemy: by the start of the 1970s it had become a saviour. With American money no longer coming in (due partly to Ross' *Goodbye, Mr. Chips*) and UK cinema admissions dropping below four million a week, the huge success of television sitcoms—many drawing regular audiences of nearly ten million homes—provided a ready market to exploit, and around 30 low-budget spin-off films appeared between 1969 and 1980. *Please Sir!* was typical in opening out the series' enclosed cadre, a move which habitually weakened the comic focus, though here it at least contributed to the source text's overarching narrative in presenting Hedges' first meeting with Penny—the two had married in the 1970 Christmas special. It also (just about) retains the television series' interpersonal dynamics, mainly because of the initial sourcing *from* British school film tropes. Surrounding the dedicated novice, alone attuned to the pupils' 'monosyllabic pop culture grunting', is a superannuated staffroom, evident in the *Carry On Teacher*-style tensions between ineffectual headmaster Morris Cromwell (Noel Howlett) and formidable disciplinarian deputy Doris Ewell (Joan Sanderson), with others prematurely cynical and defeatist, such as Maths and Science master Mr Price (Richard Davies) for whom, like a softer version of *Spare the Rod*'s Arthur Gregory, youth has a 'bouquet like an open sewer'. The linchpin of the school's functioning, as in *School for Randle*, remains its caretaker, the self-serving ex-Desert Rat Norman Potter (Deryck Guyler), while Hedges' class contains the expected rebel ringleader, Eric Duffy (Peter Cleall), the girl with a crush on teacher, Maureen Bullock (Liz Gebhardt), and the academic struggler, Dennis Dunstable (Peter Denyer), written off by all staff bar the caring newcomer. As in *Term of Trial* a troubled social hinterland is (briefly) revealed as contributory to academic deprivation: leaving her tenement flat Sharon Eversleigh (22-year-old Carol Hawkins) argues with her mother over her latest 'uncle', while Dennis is reportedly regularly beaten by his drunken and illiterate father. Here, though, the film's relocation to the 'carnivalesque' Rural Centre predicates an ultimately positive evaluation of Fenn Street, especially in contradistinction to the 'toffee-nosed red-blazered gits' of Boulter's Grammar. When Dennis, fiercely protected by his peers, is mocked by a Boulter's bully, class warfare—or at least a canteen food fight—ensues; this class unity, in all senses, extends to healthy intergenerational respect with Hedges born aloft after helping Dennis foil his father and remain at camp. *Please Sir!* more closely followed its spin-off peers in taking advantage of the 'A' certificate to include more 'colourful' and risqué material than permitted in its television version (when only 2 per cent of homes had colour sets)—publicity posters featured a 5C 'bottoms up' from the nubile Sharon, frilly knickers displayed as she writes on the blackboard—while retaining a conservative stance on gender/sexual politics: Sharon cries 'rape' to purloin a Boulter boy's fieldwork, Hedges is determinedly pursued in Joyce Grenfell-style by drab and doe-eyed Miss Cutforth (Patsy Rowlands), while even Penny wants Hedges to 'order and force me to come to dinner with you'. Fenn Street is co-educational but not yet equal opportunity. *Please Sir!* was also standard spin-off fare in earning impressive commercial returns, sandwiched between *Mutiny on the Buses* (Harry Booth) and *Up Pompeii* (Bob Kellett) at number 19 in 1972's box-office top 20. It even boasted a Lulu-light tie-in single, Cilla Black's 'La La La Lu' backing 'Something Tells Me' to a top three UK chart position. Such successful industrial interpenetration did not spare the film the habitual (if harsh) critical beating: 'In a comedy class of its own—and I do mean the dunces' section—*Please Sir!* is a roll-call of all that's worst in British low-brow comedy: it is pointless, witless, crude and grossly overacted codswallop', wrote Arther Thirkell, not untypically (*Daily Mirror*, 19 November 1971).

Leaving the country rather than visiting the countryside was the plot-line for *Sunstruck* (James Gilbert, January 1973), a vehicle for ex-Goon Harry Secombe. Inspired by the real poster (shown early in the film) of a teacher on Bondi Beach wearing shorts with academic garb, financed by New South Wales' state government to encourage UK teacher emigration, *Sunstruck* follows shy single schoolmaster Stanley Evans (Secombe) from the Welsh Valleys to Australia where, instead of sun and fun, he is seconded to the dead-end town of Kookaburra Springs. There he brings to book his unruly class by forming a competition-winning school choir and, like Hedges, finds true love with local girl Shirley (Maggie Fitzgibbon). Publicised as 'Goon Down Under', and throwing into the snake-ridden cultureless outback as many Australian and Welsh cultural stereotypes as possible in 90 minutes, the film, decried as 'a crude and sentimental comedy' (*MFB*, March 1973: 59), did not perform well. [Nonetheless, the 1976-set *Hunky Dory* (Marc Evans, 2 March 2012) would again equate Welsh education with group singing as Minnie Driver's vivacious drama teacher unites her disaffected South Wales comprehensive pupils with a glam rock musical based on *The Tempest*. A formulaic if lo-fi 'let's put on the show right here' piece, it would again underwhelm, Tim Robey adjudging it 'well meaning' but 'one to be filed under "poignant failure"' (*Telegraph*, 2 March 2012)].

2.1   Section Prize Winner: Gregory's Girl (1981)

In the 1980s a financial synergy with television and the treatment of education beyond England became more pronounced features of the British school film. *Gregory's Girl* (23 April 1981), written and directed by ex-documentarist Bill Forsyth (Knightswood Secondary, Glasgow), was set in and around Abronhill High, a comprehensive school (demolished in 2014) in Cumbernauld new town, outside Glasgow. Made after a three-year search for finance on a shoestring budget of £200,000, half-funded by Scottish TV alongside an NFFC contribution, many of Forsyth's cast were members of the Glasgow Youth Theatre who had appeared in his debut feature *That Sinking Feeling* (1980). The main strand of Forsyth's slightly-plotted sophomore film concerns the inept pursuit by gauche 16-year-old goalkeeper Gregory (John Gordon Sinclair) for Dorothy (Dee Hepburn), the attractive blonde girl who has replaced him as striker in the school's failing football team. With its drug-free playground, its toilets a site not for head-dunking bullies but teenage entrepreneurship, its teaching staff amiable eccentrics complicit with the pupils rather than their class enemy, *Gregory's Girl* exhibits the academic 'gentling' so lacking in *Kes*. A small scene encapsulates its tone and tactics: the headmaster initially appears authoritarian in his anomalous academic gown, and portrays a Wetherby Pond-like fear of unisex football when solemnly questioning first-team coach Menzies (Jake D'Arcy): 'the showers… think you can handle it?'; he betrays his soft centre, however, by playing the school piano during a chaotic lunch-hour and when two pupils gaze in bewilderment, his rejoinder, 'off you go, you small boys', reveals the male of all ages and positions in this world as irredeemably unworldly. The casting in this minor principal role of 'comedian's comedian' Chic Murray, veteran since 1934 of variety and surreal radio shows, links with the Will Hay tradition, and like *Boys Will Be Boys*, Forsyth's film is most openly carnivalesque—and resolutely unsentimental—on the games field. In its/her overturning of accepted sporting roles, Gregory's Girl quietly but pointedly subverts not just pupil–teacher roles, as when Dorothy dictates to ineffectual Menzies the team's training schedule, and inter-school rivalries, with both sides gathering to hug her after scoring a goal, but also, and especially, traditional notions of 'masculinity' and 'femininity'. This continues in the curriculum where the girls work diligently at their metalwork benches while the boys devotedly construct (and later trade) choux pastry. *Gregory's Girl* is throughout structured around similar inversions and reversals as characters refuse to comply with expected social roles, its ludic play with a plurality of identities and what Forsyth termed 'the fantastic nature of ordinary life' (*New Musical Express*, 27 October 1984) joyfully evident in the repeated sightings, with no final 'reveal', of a pupil dressed in a penguin costume. While co-education brings no peace to the hormonally challenged boys who channel their sexual neuroses into a knowledge of camera shutter speeds or proposed hitch-hiking expeditions to Caracas, the girls are grounded, self-assured and control the emotional and sexual landscape: Gregory's ten-year-old sister Madeleine (Allison Forster) has a 'steady' boyfriend, much to her brother's indignation; two girls looking down on the playground knowingly measure out the difference between boys and men at two fingers; and the film concludes with a relay of girls leading Gregory to Susan (Clare Grogan), *their* selection as his more appropriate partner. Gregory's courage in inviting her to 'dance on the ground' (his innocence removes any double-meaning) leads the film, if not to a complete upside-down world, then to a 90-degree turn as they contentedly hand-jive into the moonlight while lying on the gravity-securing grass (Fig. 5.2). This personal fluidity links with national identity as *Gregory's Girl* similarly overturns traditional presentations of 'Scottishness', differing from *Sunstruck* et al. in eschewing expected cinematic signifiers of nationhood, here notably 'tartanry, kailyard and Clydesidism' (McArthur 1982: 66). In a setting no different to the modernist new towns of *The Yellow Teddybears* or *Get Real*, the film speaks with a Scottish accent[6] but does not labour a discrete notion of Scotland through a reductive binary opposition to English culture. Growing up is international, be it in Abronhill or South America.

Gregory's Girl was a commercial sensation, its unexpected American success helping it take over £25 million at the international box office (125 times its hard-earned budget), and prompting a White House screening at Ronald Reagan's request (*Evening Standard*, 11 October 1982). It won a BAFTA for Original Screenplay, and nominations for Best Film, Director and Newcomer (Sinclair). The *Sunday People* was representative in finding it 'quite the most charming effort to come out of a British studio for years' (14 June 1981), while Alexander Walker singled out how 'school

Fig. 5.2   The Cumbernauld carnivalesque

is observed at an angle to life that always surprises us. Our expectations are forever being reversed' (*Evening Standard*, 11 June 1981). Indicative of the successful avoidance of an 'essentialising' construction of Scottish identity, the director and his work were feted in Britain and America with (lofty) cross-channel comparisons: for the *Observer* 'the mood is reminiscent of Renoir' (14 June 1981), while, for John Pym, a warm-up exercise from Dorothy and Menzies 'reminds one, for a second, of those other dreamers in *Bande à Part* [/*Band of Outsiders* (Jean-Luc Godard, 1964)] dancing, inconsequentially, in one of the cinema's most privileged moments' (*MFB*, June 1981: 114); for *Variety* Forsyth's 'friendly, unmalicious approach recalls that of René Clair' (31 December 1981), while Vincent Canby adjudged the film 'one of the cheeriest unsentimental reports on the human condition since François Truffaut's *Small Change* [/*L' Argent de Poche* (1976)]' (*New York Times*, 26 May 1982). Its reputation and representative status grows apace: number 30 in the BFI top 100, a clip of Hepburn from the film featured in the 2012 London Olympics' opening ceremony, broadcast into 900 million homes worldwide.

Such enduring praise was not forthcoming for Forsyth's sequel, *Gregory's Two Girls* (15 October 1999), produced by Channel Four Films alongside Scottish Arts Council lottery funding. Derek Malcolm had felt of

Gregory's Girl that 'The film's perhaps too gentle ironic point seems to be that the games we play in life are those we played at school. Nothing changes, only our perception of them' (*Guardian*, 11 June 1981). Such perceptions matter, though, with Greg Underwood (Sinclair again) now a 35-year-old English teacher back at his old school, and now from a different generation to his 'girl'. His adult romantic fantasies register as much less innocent, centred on football-playing sixth-former Frances (Carly McKinnon),[7] as does the film's humour—his excuse when they are caught in the park comes out not as the rehearsed 'watching badgers' but as not seeing 'Frances' beaver': meanwhile teacher Bel (Maria Doyle Kennedy), mature, intelligent and independent, inexplicably sees her place as at gormless Greg's side. Arguably equal to the regressive sexual politics, Forsyth foists on Greg (an outdated) political idealism, reading the *New Internationalist* and watching Noam Chomsky videos: off-syllabus lectures to his class on radical action, hypocritically urging them not to 'spectate, but participate', eventually lead him to help a committed Frances and (to Greg's annoyance) her boyfriend in destroying the hi-tech torture equipment being exported to South America by old schoolfriend Fraser (Dougray Scott). Forsyth's homecoming from Hollywood coincided with a millennial 'new wave' in radical Scottish filmmaking (Petrie 2000: 214–15), but this film exposed the 'founding father' as having forsaken his subversive punch. Cumbernauld and its school losing their white-washed modernity aptly amplifies Greg's flaky grey stagnation, but 1981's generalised sense of place is here replaced with contextualising tours around an ossified 'Heritage Scotland' and explicit discussions of hopes for Scottish independence, all of which, once Greg sublimates his inappropriate sexual desires into an engagement with politics and with Bel, allegorically over-signify, 'ensuring that his personal maturation reflects a vision of national (or, in fact, global/local) coming-of-age under globalisation' (Martin-Jones 2009: 32). Such site-specific straining for significance was, for Antonia Quirke, 'a bit like walking in after a revolution, when all the place-names have been changed' (*Independent on Sunday*, 17 October 1999). Comparable film names had certainly changed: instead of French auteurs Peter Bradshaw noted 'an uneven romp with all the plausibility of a Children's Film Foundation feature or an old Scooby Doo episode' (*Guardian*, 15 October 1999). Anne Billson (rightly) dismissed it as 'duff stuff, and an insult to the memory of the original film' (*Sunday Telegraph*, 17 October 1999).

Between Gregory's two films came *Heavenly Pursuits* (1 July 1986), financed by Film 4 and directed by Forsyth's former associate Charles Gormley (together they co-founded Tree Films in 1972 to make industrial documentaries). The film follows Vic Matthews (Tom Conti), an individualistic teacher at the Blessed Edith Semple School in Glasgow: while his colleagues pray for miracles to confer sainthood on the blessed Edith, Vic works unorthodoxly with his class of academic strugglers, fights to keep failing pupil Stevie (Ewen Bremner) from being transferred to a special school, and tries awkwardly to impress new Music teacher Ruth Chancellor (Helen Mirren). She is an active Catholic opposed to his radical teaching style while Vic is resolutely atheistic and unaware of his inoperable brain tumour, which disappears when he saves a pupil in a forty-foot fall from the school roof. All changes as his pupils' work, especially Stevie's, simultaneously improves, and soon the press are reporting the 'miracles' of Vic's physical and Stevie's academic improvements. An amiable amalgam of *Absolution* and *The Class of Miss MacMichael*, Gormley's film, indulgent with religion's pressure on a school ethos, instead rebukes press intrusion, which here emotes away Vic's effective teaching strategies (such as presenting Mathematics through gambling odds), and arrests the academic breakthrough of Stevie who is rushed to a retreat to escape the media glare. Love conquers all (sadly) as gentle social critique cedes to romantic comedy: but, as Tom Milne noted (pre-*Gregory's Two Girls*), 'with its generous affection for human frailties, there's more than a touch of Bill Forsyth about *Heavenly Pursuits*' (*MFB*, January 1987: 21).

Like John Gordon Sinclair, John Cleese featured in two films treating British secondary education. In *Monty Python's The Meaning of Life* (Terry Jones, 22 April 1983), the Python team's swansong return to the sketch format of their television *Monty Python's Flying Circus* (BBC, 4 series, 1969–1972), the school-set sequence, entitled 'Growth and Learning', is neither co-educational nor comprehensive but is quintessentially carnivalesque. In its traditional boarding school setting the Python cast make no attempt to look anything other than late-30 somethings infantilised in their shorts and blazers. Satirising both the ethos and etiquette of (generic) public school life, the chaplain (Michael Palin) conducts a nonsensical church service, while headmaster Humphrey Williams (Cleese) lectures the boys with an Arnoldian solemnity on the imperial significance of the resident cormorant, 'presented by the Corporation of the Town of Sudbury to commemorate Empire Day', and enumerates with the pedantry of a young Chipping the labyrinthine school rules which dictate the correct peg for hanging clothes. His subsequent lesson upturns the genre's standard tropes of pupil behaviour and interest: when the lookout warns the hard-working class that Williams is approaching, they leap into the expected unsupervised behaviour while the lesson itself, an explicit but lifeless discourse on sex education complete with practical demonstration by Mr and Mrs Williams (Patricia Quinn) on a fold-down four-poster bed, leaves the boys as disengaged as a Classics class from Crocker-Harris. The scene has been employed by cultural theorist Slavoj Žižek to illustrate, with echoes of Eco, a Lacanian 'inverted presentation of the "normal"' where 'enjoyment itself, which we experience as "transgression", is in its innermost status something imposed, ordered' (2002 [1991]: 9–10). More inversion follows as Biggs (Terry Jones), caught laughing, is 'punished' by being picked for the afternoon's rugby match where the school team is mercilessly beaten (to a pulp) by the masters. A graphic match cuts from the brutal 'education' of the rugby pitch to the wasted trees and trenches of the First World War and the 'Fighting Each Other' sequence where Biggs' mission to take out German guns cedes to social proprieties with high tea and presents from his devoted Tommies: the edit skewers the debilitating matrix of proletarian subservience, public school playing field training and the 'Pax Britannica' ethos as surely as *Tell England*.

Cleese re-presented headmagisterial inversion in the Michael Frayn-scripted *Clockwise* (Christopher Morahan, 14 March 1986). Cleese plays Brian Stimpson, headmaster of Thomas Tompion Comprehensive and proud to be the first such principal invited to address the public schools' Headmasters' Conference. A furiously paced farce, *Clockwise* begins with the meticulously organised Stimpson high in his office in all-seeing surveillance, barking orders over the public address system at any deviation, by pupil or teacher, from procedure or punctuality (Tompion was the 'father of English clock-making'): it ends, after numerous transport disruptions and desperate remedies, with him on stage stammering incoherently at a bewildered and condescending audience; it moves, in short, from a Michel Foucault panopticon to a Basil Fawlty breakdown.[8] Just as sympathies grow for Stimpson's implacable, if increasingly unhinged determination, the public school body he so desperately seeks to impress reveals its vanity and venality: one participant boasts that his school employs 'the same accountants as Mick Jagger'; another discusses plans to offer Arabic and 'have the school mosque ready by Ramadan'. Stimpson sins not in aspiring beyond his station but for travelling with a false educational ethos: his turmoil-creating inability to choose between left and right on the station platform is not just a personal but a political failing, and his final, fancies-fled haranguing of his supposed HMC superiors allows a fully carnivalesque conclusion. Though it fared poorly at the box office, *Clockwork* was favourably reviewed—'the comedy treat of the year', wrote Alan Frank (*Star*, 15 March 1986); Paul Attanasio noted a national metaphor in a film that 'hilariously illustrates' how 'the characteristically British attention to punctilio is a thin wall shored against chaos' (*Washington Post*, 25 October 1986).

School and soccer returned in Channel Four Films' *Fever Pitch* (David Evans, 4 April 1997), Nick Hornby's adaptation of his 1992 autobiography. A life measured out in Arsenal matches was diluted for cinema into the accessible tropes of romantic comedy, with Hornby substitute Paul Ashworth, a laidback but well-liked English teacher in his mid-30s at a North London comprehensive, portrayed by 'Mr Darcy heartthrob' Colin Firth. As with *Heavenly Pursuits*, the love interest is provided by an attractive new teacher initially resistant to the maverick male's charms. Sarah Hughes (Ruth Gemmell)'s football-hating feminist and strict disciplinarian nonetheless determines, after a lift home and the sight of Paul/Firth in his Gunners boxer-shorts, to understand this second male fixation. She quickly learns that Paul is not just obsessed by his football fanaticism, making his under-14 team practise Arsenal's infamous arms-raised offside trap, but infantilised by it: when an accidental pregnancy increases the emotional stakes, Sarah concludes that she has been 'impregnated by a 12-year-old'. Firth's performance successfully captures what Hornby called the 'dour, defensive, argumentative, repressed' nature of the Arsenal fan (1992: 46): he may have a perm and pupil popularity but his awkward, understated stance with women puts him in the same backline with Donkin, Chips and Perrin. Critics bemoaned a 'small screen sensibility' whereby 'visually *Fever Pitch* is stuck somewhere between *Grange Hill* and *Gregory's Girl*' (*Sight and Sound*, 7, 4, April 1997: 42). However, its major failing lies in (deviating from the book by) imposing on the unending round of football fandom (and teaching) a definitive climax: in a male (or rather 'lad') wish-fulfilment ending, all is saved by Michael Thomas' last-gasp goal as post-match street celebrations with a newly-converted Sarah absolve Paul of his adult responsibilities in both the private and professional sphere: two-nil to the Arsenal.

Football boots yielded to hockey sticks with the (twice-unexpected) reopening of St Trinian's. There seemed scant getting of wisdom when Launder and Gilliat returned after a 14-year hiatus for a final fling in *The Wildcats of St. Trinian's* (Launder, December 1980), the latest girls avoiding schoolwork by unionising and going on strike. The flavour of Ronald Searle's illustrations had long departed, his habitual cartoon-framed credit sequence here replaced by an opening that interweaves school song-singing younger girls with sixth-formers 'raunchily' disco-dancing. Casting ties are also effectively severed with Flash Harry now Joe Melia in a wardrobe of supposedly trendy 'talking' t-shirts. The expected character types such as headmistress Olga Vandemeer (Sheila Hancock), one-eyed, hair askew and prioritising her Dutch chocolates above school control, the obligatory Chemistry lab explosions, even the shapeless, sharp-nosed fourth-form girls are all marooned without the period tone and context—instead, the repressed anarchic 1950s energy becomes a soft porn display of Page Three stocking-and-suspender upper-school girls posing for fetishists whose fantasies had long since hardened.[9] Kidnapped Arab pupils and Flash Harry 'disguised' as a Chinese takeaway owner add a strain of xenophobia, uncomfortable even for 1980, while the theme of industrial relations with the Ministry's concerted attempts to quash the girls' 'wildcat' strike, potentially topical given the May 1979 victory of Margaret Thatcher's Conservative Party and their determination to remove the union power behind the previous year's Winter of Discontent, only triggers intertextual recollections of school films that did it better and with greater social relevance. Derek Malcolm called it 'without doubt one of the worst films I have ever seen. Please, please, don't do anything like it again. Ever' (*Guardian*, 18 December 1980). 26 years after *The Belles of St. Trinian's, Wildcats*, its first box-office failure, closed the franchise...

Until 27 years later when St Trinian's 2.0 hit cinemas. Filmed at the relaunched Ealing Studios, the UK Film Council Lottery-funded reboot, *St. Trinian's* (Barnaby Thompson, Oliver Parker, 21 December 2007), offered a loose retelling of *The Belles'* and *Blue Murder's* narrative of financial dire straits and winning a school quiz competition alongside, all the way from *Good Morning, Boys*, plans to steal a priceless painting from the National Gallery. It also revived the originals' casting strategy, with Rupert Everett, a prime mover behind the remake, looking to fill Alastair Sim's sling-backs and sturdy brogues as art-loving headmistress Camilla Fritton and shady art-collector sibling Carnaby. Though s/he enjoyably hams a pantomime dame take-off of Camilla, the Duchess of Cornwall, the reboot largely eschewed adult eccentricity and carnivalesque impersonations to reflect a saturation market-tested youth audience and its interests: celebrity/stunt casting brought in supermodel Lily Cole and polemical comic Russell Brand (here being neither as Flash Harry), while out went the originals' two-tiered pupil body for a contemporary cross-section of Britain's teenage demographic with posh totty, chavs, geeks, emos and first-formers. High-tech 'mischief' is sporadically evident with pranks posted on YouTube and webcams on hockey sticks but, too fashion-conscious to bear smudged faces or laddered tights, the noughties girls portray an outdated ersatz 'girl power' rather than genuine subversion—a sentiment intensified as a final school song singalong with (ersatz Spice Girls) Girls Aloud evacuates any sense of teen transgression. Here is a site for recognition, not rebellion, with a surfeit of intertextuality including a school adorned with images of Sim's Fritton and labelled 'Hogwarts for pikeys', while endless Jane Austen-led references to co-star Colin Firth's acting CV allow doubled laughter at exalted objects—the targeted painting is here Vermeer's (and Firth's) *Girl with a Pearl Earring* (Peter Webber 2003)—while Camilla's meeting with Firth's new Education Minister/old flame Geoffrey Thwaites has him answer her 'Another time' with '*Another Country*', an apposite reference given I.Q. Hunter's placement of *St. Trinian's* alongside the 'hopeless revival of *Carry On Columbus* [(Gerald Thomas, 1992)]' as 'heritage films, of a sort, reclaiming bawdiness through pastiche' (2012: 168). The film received a caning from older, mostly male film critics who put Thompson-Parker up against Launder-Gilliat: *Variety* bemoaned 'the pic's shoddy technical package, sloppy direction' and put it 'on a par with the fourth outing, *The Great St. Trinian's Train Robbery*' (27 December 2007); the *Guardian* condemned 'a monumentally naff film... cheesy, dated, humourless and crass' which 'despite its continuous stream of up-to-the-minute pop culture references, has been updated only to about 1978' (21 December 2007)—so just about on a par with *Wildcats*.

Nonetheless, aimed squarely/hiply(?) at Britain's female 'tweenie' audience, *St. Trinian's*, made for £7 million, proved critic-proof as it took £12 million at the UK box office, a further £14 million overseas, and so ensured a swift sequel, *St. Trinian's 2: The Legend of Fritton's Gold* (Thompson, Parker, 18 December 2009) with most of the cast encoring. Not averse to shameless bandwagon jumping, an historical prologue on board a 1589 pirate ship sets up a present-day treasure hunt between the perennially impecunious St Trinian's and villainous woman-hater Sir Piers Pomfrey (David Tennant). Everett playing two Fritton ancestors briefly promises an Ealing-heyday re-run of Alec Guinness in *Kind Hearts and Coronets* (Robert Hamer, 1949), but the lineage quickly stops as attention returns to the modern-day pupils, further focus-grouped research rendering their dress-sense more discretely tribal, adding new cliques with Ecos and Day-Glo-obsessed Flammables (whose polyester sets the school ablaze) and upgrading the chavs to bling-wearing Rude Girls. More securely plotted—the final chase down the Thames in the reconstructed *Golden Hinde* effectively links back to the pirate prologue—and less self-indulgently referential, the sequel is more discernibly carnivalesque: Anthony Quinn saw this St Trinian's as 'less a school, more a fancy-dress carnival—where the headmistress, Miss Fritton, is leader of the revels' (*Independent*, 18 December 2009). Rekindling *Blue Murder*'s sexual pragmatism, *Fritton's Gold* allows further 'girl power' walks towards the camera but also gentle play with gender performativity: the girls' clue-searching in an all-male school (filmed at *If....*'s Charterhouse) necessitates disguising themselves as boys, so successfully that one St Trinian takes a shine to her/his classmate; a Globe Theatre take-over of the inevitable *Romeo and Juliet* has Thwaites and Fritton acting out the balcony and death scenes, with Everett thus a man playing a woman playing a boy playing a girl. The denouement, revealing the treasure to be a lost play, 'Queen Lear', and its author, Shakespeare aka Pirate Fritton, to be a woman, offers a dialogic subversion that potentially marries Bakhtin with the Bard.[10] The sequel was again critically scuttled, though Philip French, admitting to lowered expectations, voiced the majority preference for Mark 2: 'schoolgirls and those who like ogling schoolgirls will enjoy it' (*Observer*, 5 January 2010). Not enough, though: a break-even take of £7 million stalled the franchise.

This section ends as it began, with the television sit-com spin-off. *The Inbetweeners* (E4, 3 series, 2008–2010), an award-winning cringe comedy, followed four social misfits, romantic Simon (Joe Thomas), geeky Will (Simon Bird), vulgar Jay (James Buckley) and dopey Neil (Blake Harrison), through the purgatory of sixth-form life at Rudge Park Comprehensive. *The Inbetweeners Movie* (Ben Palmer, 17 August 2011), from Film4 Productions on a £3.5 million budget, became a 'breakout' hit, its immediate £13 million return setting a UK record for a comedy's opening weekend before landing total earnings of £58 million. Labelled 'Britain's delayed riposte to *American Pie* [(Paul Weitz, 1999)]' (*Screen International*, 28 April 2011), it succeeds principally because it is a *post-school* film: unlike members of the contrived sitcom travel club such as *Holiday on the Buses* (Bryan Izzard, 1973) and even, to a lesser extent, the retro-fitted *Please Sir!*, the four lads possess a natural momentum to take feature film flight, having impatiently eyed the big wide world from their interim and enclosed sixth-form existence. Beginning with their last day at school, the film takes the fumbling four off to Malia on Crete for a summer tour of 'sex, minge, fanny and booze', a logical extension of the sitcom's scatological coming-of-age narrative. Intended as bringing closure to the television series, its commercial success prompted the inevitable sequel. *The Inbetweeners 2* (6 August 2014), directed by series creators Damon Beesley and Iain Morris, relinquished motivational credibility with its gap year/university holiday premise sending the boys, like Harry Secombe, 'down under': it cranked up the knob gags, vomit and misogyny, added some gay panic, bagged the UK's record first-day comedy takings of £2.75 million and, with £33 million, became the best-selling domestic film of the year. Lapped up by 'lad' culture, Australian critic Margaret Pomeranz thought the franchise's style of humour explained 'the collapse of the British Empire' (*At the Movies*, SBS Australia, August 2011): the Corporation of the Town of Sudbury would, for one, have disapproved.

Cornwall may also seek independence after enduring the breakaway jokes in *The Bad Education Movie* (Elliot Hegarty, 21 August 2015), a spin-off from *Bad Education* (BBC3, 3 series, 2012–2014), co-written by Jack Whitehall who plays Abbey Grove Comprehensive's incompetent posh-boy History teacher Alfie Wickers, desperate to be 'down with the kids'. Despite topical jokes on hashtags and Mumsnet, and tasteless jokes on debagging and tea-bagging, this post-GCSE exam school trip to the South East narratively and thematically reruns the template of *Please Sir!*, even down to the persistent misogyny and the meeting with Alfie's old public school peers—one is called Dave, 'short for the Earl of Daventry'—whose nasty interactions highlight the compassion and collegiality of the (bluntly stereotyped) state school class and their constantly schooled teacher. Box-office returns showed a film failing to repeat *The Inbetweeners*' 'crass crossover' appeal: for the *Guardian* its 'comic touch makes Seth McFarlane seem like Ernest Lubitsch' (25 August 2015).

3   QUEER SCHOOL

The absence of systematic sex education had been broached, with questionable intent, in *The Yellow Teddybears*: by the early-1970s such programmes were more prevalent, though still tied to the Biology curriculum. The health risks raised by HIV and AIDS in the mid-1980s, coupled with the growing strength of the lesbian and gay movement, led to a polarisation of views on sex education, a flurry of Conservative government circulars and controversial legislation reaching a head with Section 28 of 1988's

Local Government Act, an amendment stating that local authorities 'shall not intentionally promote homosexuality' or 'promote the teaching in a maintained school of the acceptability of homosexuality as a pretended family relationship'.[11] There is no intent in this section to 'ghettoise' the queer school experience—it has been present at an encoded or tangential level throughout the genre's development—but only now does it become a school film's openly central focus.

Nighthawks (August 1978), for Helen de Witt 'Britain's first explicitly gay film set in the gay community' (n.d.), is also Britain's first explicitly gay school film, following the double life of Jim, by day a respectable East London comprehensive teacher, by night a cruiser of the capital's gay bars and discos. Conceived in the more liberal mid-1970s, it took four years for co-writers and directors Ron Peck and Paul Hallam to raise a modest, barely sufficient £60,000 from multiple 'collaborators' including Lindsay Anderson, Tony Garnett and the Gay Teachers Group, only to find that no school would permit the shooting of classroom scenes with a gay teacher. Ken Robertson, cast as Jim, was the film's only professional actor, while the experiences of his amateur school colleagues, fellow clubbers and serial partners were woven into the loosely plotted script.[12] *Nighthawks*' employment of a lo-fi quasi-documentary approach celebrates the freedom of Jim's encounters in London's (pre-AIDS) gay scene, but equally reveals an emotionally unsatisfying repetition of one-night stands—'I've put two sugars in. Sorry, I've forgotten your name'—and faltering short-lived relationships. Though gay sex had been decriminalised a dozen years earlier, Jim feels constrained to remain 'closeted' to parents and colleagues, only recounting his hopes and experiences to Judy (Rachel Nicholas James), a supply teacher at his school. In the film's penultimate and most powerful scene, Jim combines two classes to cover for an absent colleague. Having heard rumours that Jim is 'bent', the new class directly confront him: with the camera largely adopting Jim's position (so the pupils directly harangue the audience), he responds with openness and equanimity, factually answering their chaotic and prejudiced questioning—a five-minute semi-scripted mix of planted and spontaneous interrogation about wearing women's dresses and what he does in bed. For this he must answer to the headmaster, worried that parents (and authorities) will complain about classroom discussions of homosexuality.[13] Jim's pedagogical integrity in arguing cogently for breaking down ignorance and educating pupils about sex and sexuality does not lead to angry resignation as with Anne from *The Yellow Teddybears*, but nor does it register as affirmative action:

the film concludes with Jim resuming his nightly round of gay locales in search of that perfect partner, the camera lethargically scanning the crowd accompanied by the pounding and repetitive dance music that dominates the soundtrack. Breaking with previous stereotypical 'camp' or 'repressed' representations of homosexuality—the choice of a Geography teacher presumably signifies 'ordinariness'—*Nighthawks'* downbeat tone still polarised opinion within the gay and critical communities: Andrew Sarris championed a 'broodingly directed meditation' on gay life where 'an unbearable intimacy is created' (*Village Voice*, 30 July 1979); for Gilbert Adair an 'undoubtedly worthy' film failed principally because 'it presents its hero as such as miserable sod: anyone tempted towards his own sex would surely be deterred after watching Robertson's endlessly unsmiling face' (*Time Out*, 9 March 1979). Others found the film troubling because of Jim's professional rather than private interactions: for John Pym the closing class scene registered 'less as a moment of catharsis, and more as an example of how *not* to run a classroom discussion' (*MFB*, February 1979: 30), while Alexander Walker was shocked at the unscripted pupil reactions: 'what a horrifying generation of pubescent bigots our schools are rearing. Little faces of childhood already set in the ugly plaster of adult prejudice' (*Evening Standard*, 8 March 1979). Some might consider the scene, with Section 28 around the corner, precise and prescient.

While *Nighthawks'* initial theatrical release passed quickly but relatively free of censorship or legal interference, by late 1982 the domestic climate had so hardened that the *Star* newspaper singled out the film in an attack on Channel 4's purchasing policy, fulminating that 'it must not be shown on TV!' (30 December 1982). In such a political climate it is perhaps understandable that further explorations of the queer school experience should retreat to the other end of the social/cinematic spectrum. Almost another country compared to *Nighthawks*, Goldcrest's £1.6 million-budgeted *Another Country* (Marek Kanievska, 29 June 1984), revisiting high-end public school life in the 1930s, was adapted by (Winchester-educated) Julian Mitchell from his successful stage play, itself modelled on the early friendship between future Soviet spies Guy Burgess and Donald Maclean. The film has Moscow and wheelchair-bound Guy Bennett (Rupert Everett) recounting his final term at public school 50 years previously, notably his ambitions to 'be elected to the Gods' (i.e. become a senior prefect), his friendship with committed Marxist Tommy Judd (Colin Firth) and passion for a younger pupil Harcourt (Cary Elwes). Homosexuality, though rife in the school, is officially condemned, and when the interception of a love letter to Harcourt forces Bennett to with-draw his prefect candidature, he finally understands Judd's ideas on the injustice of privilege.

Another Country contributes to the 'white flannel' treatment of homo-sexuality in 1980s British film and television: following *Brideshead Revisited* (ITV, Charles Sturridge, 1981) and preceding *Maurice* (James Ivory, 1987), its presentation of young gay men in an upper-class Edwardian educational cadre safely distances a contentious queer past for a homo-phobic present in the generic cocoon of 'heritage' cinema.[14] A representa-tional reticence increases the safe sexuality: Bennett's reciprocated staring at cricket-playing Harcourt matches the sporting exchange that initiated the affair between Philips and Wallace in *If....*, but rather than put them into bed together *Another Country* stops at the aesthetic display of chaste cuddles during moonlight punting. As Bennett learns from the film's her-itage narrative, appearances are all, and *Another Country*, like *Maurice*, explores the Edwardian era's hypocritical abuse and exploitation of homo-sexuality—Bennett is beaten and humiliated by the same prefects happy to sleep with him. As a 1930s-*set* school film, Bennett's declarations of his gay sexual conquests and subsequent selling of state secrets are potentially readable as challenging the ethos of personal restraint and patriotic duty central to both national and generic identity in 1930s-*produced* British school films. However, John Hill notes that, 'while the plots of heritage films characteristically contain elements of social criticism, these are often undercut by the fascination of the films with the visually spectacular trap-pings of the past' (1999: 87), and *Another Country*'s opening out of the source play (set entirely in what Bennett terms 'dingy' interiors), plus its concomitant preoccupation with re-presenting the British public school's décor, dress and colourful ceremonials such as the CCF inspection, result in the ostensive critique of its authoritarianism being effaced by 'quality' filmmaking, the dominant ideology reasserted via mise-en-scène. The flash-back device adds a temporal contrast between the fetishised public school past and Bennett's present-day spartan Moscow apartment with only a cricket ball and school photographs as reminders of his expulsion from Eden/Eton: thus, rather than allowing a 'distancing' critique of sexual intolerance, the framing structure serves unwittingly to endorse it, adding a reactionary punishment for an act that elides Bennett's communism with being gay and renders his coming out less a political act than a national betrayal. While the film was a commercial success, and Mitchell, Everett, and Gerry Hambling's editing earned BAFTA nominations, the critical reception was divided. Alexander Walker found the view that 'the road to Moscow is paved with English hypocrisy and public-school vice' to be 'made plausibly persuasive in the stifling atmosphere created in a school where a spy system already operates and moral blackmail (backed by a big cane) is the norm' (*Evening Standard*, 7 June 1984); Gilbert Adair, however, lambasted the employment of one of 'England's most potent socio-cultural "mythologies"... the public school as an exotic microcosm' which here 'did not do much more than confirm the strange national prejudice that Marxism is, essentially, something that goes on at English public schools, like cricket and buggery' (*MFB*, June 1984: 173). America sensed the heritage tensions, Vincent Canby adjudging 'a well-acted, literate but insufferably smug little movie' to be 'not quite as anti-public-school as it pretends to be' (*New York Times*, 29 June 1984).

The heritage trend continued with *The Browning Version* (28 October 1994), Mike Figgis' avowed remake of Asquith's adaptation rather than the Rattigan source play. Starring Albert Finney as Crocker-Harris, produced by Ridley Scott for Paramount British Pictures and scripted by Ronald Harwood, the plot is largely unaltered, though the remake 'modernises' the 1951 adaptation, ostensibly placing the action in the present and adding graphic language such as 'shagging' and 'fucking' to describe the affair between Frank Hunter (Matthew Modine) and Mrs Crocker-Harris, renamed Laura (Greta Scacchi). Continuing the trend for (American-funded) UK heritage spaces, Figgis' establishment shots of Abbey School (Sherborne again) are here reinforced by a museum-aesthetic medium-shot attention to interior design—Crocker-Harris' classroom, unlike in Asquith, is adorned with personalising objects, pictures and plentiful bookcases. In this cadre, though, the school loses temporal specificity: teachers discuss computers but none are on display, while the unaltered role for Fletcher (David Lever) still allows a gentleman amateur in cricket; (an even less credible anachronism has a teacher being dismissed on health grounds without compensation). Signalling evolution in both education and film finance, staff replacement Gilbert (Julian Sands) is now a Modern Linguist, while love interest Hunter is American, diegetically adding a cultural invasion to Crocker-Harris' personal betrayal. The displacement of blame from the 'crocked' teacher to the changing times offers heritage film nostalgia, with this Crocker-Harris 'a good teacher whose qualities are not appreciated by his pupils and colleagues, who all regard Classics as irrelevant to a modern curriculum' (Leach 2004: 198). Finney, stalwart of the Angry Young Men that long banished Rattigan to obscurity, had since modified his priapic persona with gay-centred films such as the Harwood-scripted *The Dresser* (Peter Yates, 1983) and *A Man of No Importance* (Suri Krishnamma, 1994), an identification which, for Marcia Landy, 'reinforces the gay subtext that runs through the play and adaptation' (2013: 81). It is hard, though, to equate such cinematic 'baggage' with the monolithic portrayal here on show: this is not Redgrave's febrile, anguished master; there is scant evidence of a sexualised bond between teacher and gift-giving Taplow (Ben Silverstone—whose *Get Real* casting could allow a retrospective gay inflection); and his final speech registers less as a personal coming out than a pedagogical elegy for the decline of Classics and the lofty aims of a humanistic education: 'how can we mould civilised beings if we no longer believe in civilisation?' The resultant standing ovation confers heroic status and wins new respect from his wife, confirming that, though Asquith's explicit sardonic reference is removed, this conservative Major-era remake of *The Browning Version* is unambiguously the domain of *Goodbye, Mr. Chips*. Hindered by US distribution problems, the film failed commercially and, though nominated for the 1994 Cannes Film Festival Palme d'Or, was domestically decried: Quentin Curtis (rightly) felt that 'watching the film will be like seeing a close friend being mugged' (*Independent on Sunday*, 30 October 1994).

Close male friendships first came to grammar schools in *Get Real* (Simon Shore, 14 May 1999), eventually adapted with Lottery funding by Patrick Wilde from his 1992 play *What's Wrong with Angry?*, a small-scale polemical piece on the need to repeal Section 28 and lower the age of consent from 21—its January 1994 reduction to 18 still criminalised gay sixth-formers. Set in Basingstoke new town, the film follows Steve Carter (Silverstone), a shy, intelligent and bullied 16-year-old pupil who cruises in public toilets where, to his surprise, he encounters conflicted class 'jock' John Dixon (Brad Gorton). A relationship starts but, when caught together in the school changing-room, John beats up Steve to maintain his group status. On winning a local newspaper essay prize, Steve anonymously substitutes a different piece on growing up gay called 'Get Real' before admitting his sexuality at the school's Prize Day. Part of a post-Thatcherite/New Labour gay re-enfranchisement, *Get Real* is a feel-good/wish-fulfilment coming-of-age coming-out story, similar in theme to *Beautiful Thing* (Hettie MacDonald 1996) and *Queer as Folk* (Channel 4, 2 series, 1999–2000) and sharing their tart dialogue—'every time I see his Head Boy badge I wish it was an invitation'—and trendy album-released soundtracks—Steve's toilet cruising is scored to The

Troggs' 'Love is All Around'. Alongside its pony-tailed teachers and 'Cool Britannia' pretentions, however, *Get Real* still mines long-standing school film tropes: Steve's after-hours cottaging is located in the woods, a staple site for 'beastly sex'; *Romeo and Juliet* is the habitual English set text, pertinent here for classroom discussions of lovers' honesty with friends and family; a Sports Day celebration of John's athletic prowess reaches back to *Tell England*; Steve's climactic soul-bearing and (muted) standing ovation is 'straight' out of Asquith's *The Browning Version*. Even the spaces open for the gay couple evoke both David Hockney's California, kissing in John's outdoor swimming pool, *and* the heritage of Forster and *Another Country*, their heart-to-heart discussion, framed by a red-brick viaduct's archway, rendering queer suburbia 'no less contingent on the classical past than its Victorian and Edwardian literary antecedents' (Williams 2006: 116). A cult success in the UK, *Get Real* occasioned 'pilgrimages' to Basingstoke and a plethora of fan fiction.[15] Picked up by the newly formed Paramount Classics, it was a 'breakout' hit in America, earning $1.15 million and gushing comparisons with John Hughes' 1980s high school movies—a far cry from its agit-prop beginnings. More soberly, Roger Ebert referenced the recent Colorado shootings (whose teenage perpetrators were reputedly taunted about their sexuality) and hoped that 'Movies like *Get Real* might help homophobic teenagers and adults become more accepting of differences' (*Chicago Sun-Times*, 14 May 1999). In Britain José Arroyo thought the film would 'find great favour with schoolteachers who want to get a discussion going but are afraid to expose their students to more challenging material' (*Sight and Sound*, 9, 5, May 1999: 48).

3.1   Section Prize Winner: The History Boys (2006)

One teacher keen to get a discussion going was Hector, lead character in *The History Boys*, a work placing both staff and pupils in the queer spotlight and the second film collaboration, following *The Madness of King George* (1994), of (Manchester Grammar-educated) National Theatre director Nicholas Hytner and writer Alan Bennett. After fame with the satirical revue *Beyond the Fringe* (1960–4) and numerous stage, radio and television sketches, Bennett's first full-length theatre piece, *Forty Years On* (1968), had used a minor public school, the metonymic Albion House, to review the country's post-1918 history through a school play within a play—and to generate gay-inflected *double entendres* such as 'I wish I could get my hands on the choir's parts'. Bennett returned to a school closer to his own Leeds Modern Grammar 35 years on in a play Hytner feared would prove 'too esoteric for a large audience' (2006: vii): instead *The History Boys* became the best-selling show ever produced by the National Theatre and winner of both Olivier and Tony Awards for Best Play. Its domestic success prompted a film version, which retained the original Lyttelton Theatre cast but reformulated its staffroom characterisations. With the BBC and UK Film Council contributing to a £2 million budget, filming was squeezed into thirty days in July–August 2005 before the play transferred to America, with school scenes shot at Watford's Boys' and Girls' Grammar Schools: it was released on 13 October 2006 in the UK and on 22 November in the States, just as the Broadway run closed. The film is set at Cutler's Grammar School, Sheffield, in 1983 where eight top 'A' level working-class pupils are staying on to try for Oxbridge scholarships. They are well grounded in History by Mrs Lintott (Frances de la Tour) and in language and literature by General Studies teacher Hector (Richard Griffiths), though his hands wander when pupils ride pillion on his motorcycle. The boys are more disconcerted when their status-conscious headmaster (Clive Merrison) hires recently graduated supply teacher Irwin (Stephen Campbell Moore) to coach them expressly for the exam: his encouragement to employ unorthodox attention-earning essay techniques gradually gains their approval. When Hector's sexual fumblings land him in trouble, the knowledge held by class gigolo Dakin (Dominic Cooper) of the headmaster's own peccadilloes with his secretary ensures the threatened dismissal is rescinded. Learning of Irwin's inflated qualifications, Dakin blackmails him too, into providing oral sex, though the deal is forgotten when Hector dies in a road accident. In a coda Mrs Lintott sketches out the boys' later careers, and Irwin's success as a television pundit.

The History Boys knows its history of the British school film. The added uncouth gym teacher Wilkes (Adrian Scarborough) is straight from *Kes*; Mrs Lintott notes of the headmaster that 'if this was a 1940s film he'd be played by Raymond Huntley'; Irwin exposes the exculpating memorialisation of the (undertrained public-school) carnage of the First World War, and advises his pupils to study Carry On films as potential interview fare—they 'have no intrinsic artistic merit' but 'acquire an incremental significance if only as social history'. Through its own study of such social history, who owns it and what it teaches us, *The History Boys* joins a line of school films that explore, through dialectical exponents of the profession, the very purpose of education—Hector's humanistic view that it is a moral and emotional preparation for life versus Irwin's results-oriented advocacy that it is a vehicle for career advancement. Their positions enact contemporary struggles as the Conservative government sought to render the secondary curriculum more vocational, assessible and thus accountable: while Irwin is the slickly goal-oriented Thatcherite educational entrepreneur, the headmaster bemoans Hector's lack of method: 'There's inspiration, certainly, but how do I quantify that?... In the current educational climate that is no use!'[16] Except for two Oxbridge montages, brief motorbike sorties and a monastery trip, *The History Boys* is entirely set at Cutler's and its classroom focus, as prominent as anywhere in the genre, reveals less the film's stage origins than the dramatics of much teaching methodology. Hector is often considered a 'brilliant, theatrical English master' (Philip French, *Observer*, 15 October 2006), an inspiration in the Mr Chips mould, but his pedagogy has demerits beyond a penchant for petting: his avowed hope that his pupils will remember him and his teaching in later life and, like a parcel, 'pass it on', contains the danger that the profession becomes a matter of self-projection before the provision of cultural/vocational guidance. That ultimately he fails, his pupils unheeding his credo and progressing to lucrative careers in construction or tax law, while one, Lockwood (Andrew Knott), dies serving in the forces, adds a parallel, not to Chips but to that other pedagogical *grande dame*, Jean Brodie. Not only are both studiedly different from the norm, ranging from their distinctive two-wheeled transport, through their linguistic self-stylisation, to a 'passionate' refusal to abide by any syllabus; like Brodie Hector's broadening of minds translates into dictating his (pre-1950s) cultural tastes; ultimately both are emotional fantasists, Hector glossing over his sexual advances as 'gestures of benediction' differing in degree if not in kind from Brodie's manipulations of her younger girls. Similarly, the film's early emotional weight lies with Hector, though this evens out as Irwin, more sympathetically characterised than on stage, reveals his emotional vulnerability. Irwin's early refusal of Dakin's advances seems, in the Bennett universe, less a teacher's morally calculated avoidance than an emotionally crippling inability to seize life: pointedly the film scene that the pupils enact for Irwin to guess comes from *Brief Encounter* (David Lean, 1945), the benchmark for British middle-class repression—he identifies it straight away, the first step towards his salvation, as the film's theme shifts from Oxbridge to sex education.

In 1990 Bennett wrote *102 Boulevard Haussmann*, a BBC play on Marcel Proust: *The History Boys* is another Proustian work, not in its search for time past but rather for the late explosion of gay sexuality. In the final pages of Proust's *A la Recherche du Temps Perdu/Remembrance of Things Past*, a number of characters unexpectedly come out as being gay: Malcolm Bowie terms the ending a 'comic millennium' for homosexuals (cited in May 1983: 40). With Hector joined by Irwin and Dakin, while even the godly Scripps (Jamie Parker) expresses his jealousy of Dakin 'being up for it', *The History Boys* offers a similar conclusion for a new millennium, a wish-fulfilment queer fantasy far outstripping *Get Real*. The school/film cadre is insistently gay: Hector's whole-wall classroom collage features Oscar Wilde, Bette Davis and several photos of Charles Laughton, a clear soul-mate for the hefty, histrionic homosexual; a shower scene fetishises the torsos of Dakin and Scripps; Dakin and Irwin literally hide in the closet from their straight-as-a-die headmaster; the Smiths' 'This Charming Man' plays on the soundtrack alongside Gracie Fields' 'Wish me luck as you wave me goodbye/Not a tear but a cheer, make it gay'; cultural figures from A.E. Housman to Michelangelo and Caravaggio are explicitly cited as 'nancies', while Irwin is informed that Auden 'snogged his pupils'; the Fountains Abbey visit broaches discussion of monastic socialisation and 'same-sex stuff'; even Mrs Lintott's first name is Dorothy. The most fantastical elements arguably lie in the school's complete absence of homophobia, and the aggressively heterosexual Dakin's matter-of-fact acceptance of his attraction to Irwin, so less psychologically plausible than the agonising of *Get Real*'s school stud John Dixon—to redeploy an assessment from Hector, 'it's flip: it's glib'. The film's sympathy for Irwin grows once he admits that, sexually, he is 'in the same boat' as Hector, whose brothel-based French subjunctive lesson may be a comic delight (his improvisation on the headmaster's sudden entry again recalling Jean Brodie—and Will Hay) but is indicative of his similar deferral of (sexual) experience to what could be but not what is (Fig. 5.3). As in the classroom Hector is no role-model: an 'unexpected wife' preserves a social façade, while his strongly defended view that there is a moral dimension to teaching sits uneasily alongside his motorbike gropings. Posner (Samuel Barnett), never offered a lift since he is too young in appearance for the adult-fixated (and thus, for Bennett, condonable) Hector,[17] presents a more open, honest sexual performativity. He directs to Dakin a rendition of Rodgers and Hart's 'Bewitched, Bothered and Bewildered', restoring the original gay intent of Hart's lyrics—'I'll sing to him/Each spring to him/And worship the trousers that cling to him'. In what Bennett has termed 'the heart of the play' (2006: xxi), Posner attends a tutorial with Hector where they discuss

Fig. 5.3 Ooh là là—le français... dans une maison de passe

Thomas Hardy's 'Drummer Hodge'. Like Father Goddard's recitation of Hopkins in *Absolution*, Hector's moving analysis reveals as much of teacher-pupil desires, here for the absent Dakin, as it does of the poet's use of compound adjectives: 'Un-kissed. Un-rejoicing. Un-confessed. Un-embraced.' The scene illustrates Hector's contention, less helpfully used on the headmaster to justify his 'handling the boys' balls', that, as in the intense pupil-mentor relationships of the Renaissance era, 'the transmission of knowledge is itself an erotic act'.[18] When Hector breaks down in class, the unhappy Posner—'I'm a Jew, I'm small, I'm homosexual, and I live in Sheffield: I'm fucked'—is the only pupil to come forward and comfort him: he is Hector's sole 'heir' and will pick up the parcel as an un-fulfilled gay schoolteacher.

The film was a commercial success, with a worldwide gross of $13.4 million, while Griffiths and de la Tour earned BAFTA nominations. As with Asquith's *The Browning Version*, critical attention focused on *The History Boys'* merits as a recent adaptation. Most saw a diminishment: Peter Bradshaw, titling his review 'Blackboard bungle', thought it 'a stagey and oddly contrived movie' with 'the kind of elaborate, highly worked dialogue that is exhilarating in the theatre, but rather unreal-sounding on the big screen' (*Guardian*, 13 October 2006). Its fuller sexual emphases were noted: for Tony Rayns the source play was 'gay-friendly but not overtly gay in its orientation… In close-up, on celluloid, it seems very gay indeed' (*Sight and Sound*, 16, 11, November 2006: 59). For Matthew Bond, this was clearly presumptuous for a selective state establishment, with 'an awful lot of homosexuality for such a small group of characters. Especially at a grammar school' (*Mail on Sunday*, 15 October 2006).

In Mrs Lintott's one moment centre stage she rails against the removal of her gender from her subject: 'What is history? History is women following behind with the bucket.' Women also follow behind in the queer school film treatment: beyond the confines of borstals or pornography, three recent films finally explore the permutations of schoolroom Sapphism.

The first explicit British film treatment of lesbianism, *The Killing of Sister George* (Robert Aldrich, 1968), was scripted by Lukas Heller. His daughter, Zoë, wrote the bestselling and Booker-nominated novel *Notes on a Scandal*, published in 2003 and quickly optioned for film treatment by the same production team behind *The History Boys*. Indicative of a more 'prestige' undertaking, *Notes on a Scandal* (2 February 2007) was directed by (Sherborne-educated) National Theatre director Sir Richard Eyre and adapted by Patrick Marber, with music by Philip Glass and a blue-chip cast featuring Dame Judi Dench and Cate Blanchett. Barbara Covett (Dench), nearing retirement as a lonely head of History in the *de rigueur* difficult North London secondary modern, keeps a diary which serves as the film's venomous voiceover. Disdainful of her environment, she slowly succumbs to the charms of beautiful and idealistic new Art teacher, Sheba Hart (Blanchett), and pursues her friendship. When Barbara witnesses her colleague in a compromising position with 15-year-old pupil Steven Connolly (Andrew Simpson), she feels she has the power to coerce Sheba into intimacy, and offers her support. A scandal breaks, hitting the press headlines: Sheba, forced to leave home, moves in with Barbara, but finding the diary, is appalled by her obsessive attention and (though later given a prison term) returns to her husband Richard (Bill Nighy). Barbara befriends a young woman reading about the affair.

Notes on a Scandal caused a scandal of its own, though not for Sheba's professional abuse of trust. The portrayal of Barbara as a vindictive stalking lesbian caused consternation in LGBT circles, especially amongst teaching staff: members of Schools Out UK felt that 'such characters reinforce prejudices against gay staff in schools' and 'make it increasingly difficult for gay teachers to come out at school' since 'there is this feeling that if a gay schoolteacher talks about their relationship at school, it is bringing sex into the classroom' (*Times Educational Supplement*, 2 February 2007).[19] Such reactions evidence little advance in socio-educational attitudes since *Nighthawks*. While sensitive to such viewpoints, three points could be made in mitigation of the film's approach to Barbara's sexuality. Firstly *Notes on a Scandal* offers a plague on all persuasions, with heterosexuals hardly presented as beacons of moral virtue: Sheba is the convicted abuser, committing statutory rape with a minor in her care, while her older university-lecturer husband has callously walked out on his first family. Secondly, while the film clearly signals Barbara's lesbianism—visually (and stereotypically) foregrounding her tweed suits and bad haircut, narratively referencing other relationships with women—and establishes her angry loneliness and mental instability, it makes no explicit connections between her sexuality and psychosis: her bitter aggressivity derives at least in part from her profession, the deadening duty of teaching generations of disruptive and disenchanted teenagers. Extrapolating from the classroom, one can infer Barbara's repressed nature as the (admittedly extreme) product of a homophobic society. Her family and supposed friends exacerbate rather than ease her situation: her sister's timid avoidance of explicit references, preferring terms like 'friends', undermines her emotional support, while Sheba's disgust and frenzied attack on reading the diary render Barbara the victim, evoking, not terror at her lesbianism, but pity for the way society has made her feel that her sexuality is unacceptable. Thirdly and above all, though, the British school film has proven itself less obsessed than other media by transgressive school sex—the diegetic moral outrage from the tabloids is signalled as overblown while Sheba's final daubing of Siouxsie Sioux-style make-up 'explains away' her actions as a pitiable pining for her art school youth. Rather, its enduring obsession has been with securing class divisions, and Barbara is ultimately punished not for her lesbian attractions but for the more serious crime of housing ideas above her social station: it is in this context that her blatant surname Covett contrasts with Sheba's vulnerable Hart. Barbara's diary entries reveal her pretensions and, fiercely despising her underclass pupils, she is driven, the film posits, by a fatal attraction to Sheba's easy 'bourgeois bohemia' and a desire to have some of her 'class' rub off on her. She gets it terribly wrong, turning up to an informal lunch invite dressed to the nines: for this and other social faux pas she is demonised, and Eyre's transformation of a shrewd spectator of life to avenging shrew is so melodramatically realised with the harsh lighting of Dench's face that it blanches out any psychological subtlety in the actress' subsequent portrayal. Sheba, by contrast, a briefly errant ingénue, is permitted to float back to her well-appointed upper-middle-class life, while the film's treatment of Steven is no better than Sheba's, sidelining him once his purpose has been served. Nonetheless *Notes on a Scandal*, made for $15 million, took close to $50 million globally and, amongst a host of international honours, received Academy Award nominations for Blanchett, Dench, Marber and Glass, plus BAFTA nominations for Dench, Marber and Best Film. Though there were dissenting voices—'When redemption is too easily earned, it's hard for the audience not to feel cheated' (*Sight and Sound*, 17, 2, February 2007: 68)—the film won largely positive reviews: for Peter Bradshaw 'the spirits of both Nabokov and Hitchcock are invoked in this delectable adaptation' (*Guardian*, 2 February 2007); *Empire* magazine (under the heading 'Dame Judi Dench Plays a Psycho Lesbian!') termed the film 'intelligent, classy and skin-crawling: you won't see a better acting masterclass this year' (February 2007).

Despite such encomia, school-set lesbianism also retreated to a privileged and safely historicised environment. *Cracks* (Jordan Scott, 4 December 2009), an all-female gothic melodrama, based on the South African-set novel by Sheila Kohler but relocated to a fictional island off the coast of England in 1934, centres on a group of pupils at the elite St Mathilda's boarding school who idolise their diving instructor and old girl Miss G (Eva Green) for her beauty and tales of exotic adventures. Di Radfield (Juno Temple) is the teacher's pet and group leader but her position is usurped by new Spanish girl Fiamma Coronna (Maria Valverde), until the latter exposes Miss G's tales of travel as second-hand. During an alcohol-fuelled midnight party, Miss G takes a passed-out Fiamma to her room and molests her, an act Di witnesses. Back in favour, Di accuses the new girl of seducing her teacher and a woodland pursuit ends with Miss G letting the asthmatic Fiamma die: the girls leave the diving team and Miss G is dismissed. *Cracks*—the title is jargon for schoolgirl 'crushes'—offers scenic, slow-moving montages of traditional boarding school practices: sport, dormitory feasts and parcels from home. In particular, it employs its lush island isolation to ramp up the harsh interdependent power struggles of school life: new favourite Fiamma suggests to Di, 'Maybe if I were kinder to [Miss G], she would be kinder to you.' It also explores the Brodie-esque personal need and pedagogical vacuity that 'inspirational teaching' can mask as Miss G revels in her charges' adulation and surreptitiously offers them contraband literature and counsel on the primacy of desire. The sexual nature of her obsession with the new arrival aligns lesbianism with psychosis more openly than *Notes on a Scandal* and, though the glamorous floaty woman is now the gay predator, once the outward poise 'cracks' it again reveals the compulsive fantasist beneath: Miss G's isolation from her colleagues is shown as their choice not hers, while even her fashionable clothes are exposed as homemade. Nonetheless, *Cracks* replays an educational exculpation: prepared by a shopping trip that ends in blind panic, a final scene shows Miss G, having rented a small room on the island's village, carefully selecting five personal possessions for her bedside table—the same maximum number permitted to Fiamma on arrival. Miss G, comes the reveal, is cripplingly institutionalised, no more able to survive outside of school than Roddy Berwick in *Downhill*. Class, though, remains paramount: the teacher identifies with self-assured aristocrat Fiamma as a worthy equal in cosmopolitan sophistication, but grows increasingly resentful as the girl's genuine worldliness exposes her hermetic stance and purloined travelogues; like Barbara she socially overreaches and suffers accordingly. *Cracks* sent critics into a frenzy of comparisons: Philip French found it a 'faintly ridiculous, sexually overheated mixture of *Jane Eyre*'s Lowood Institution for wayward orphans, Miss Jean Brodie's Edinburgh Acadamy and St. Trinian's' (*Observer*, 6 December 2009); Anthony Quinn thought it 'like Mallory Towers meets *Black Narcissus* [Michael Powell, Emeric Pressburger (1947)]' (*Independent*, 4 December 2009).

Quinn, like many, also saw *Cracks*' eerie and eroticised atmosphere as reminiscent of *Picnic at Hanging Rock* (Peter Weir, 1975): a more fully Weir-like mystery with supernatural overtones was played out in *The Falling* (24 April 2015). Written and directed by Carol Morley and BFI-funded for £750,000, the expansion of Morley's 2006 short *The Madness of the Dance* debuted at London's 2014 LGBT Festival. Set in a remote Oxfordshire boarding school in 1969, its early scenes follow the relationship between promiscuous Abigail Mortimer (Florence Pugh) and chaste Lydia 'Lamb' Lamont (Maisie Williams). At home Lydia's brother Kenneth (Joe Cole) schools them in occult forest beliefs; at school Abbie argues with Lydia, has a seizure and dies. With the school in mourning, Lydia faints, an event which spreads amongst the other girls and young Art teacher Miss Charron (Morfydd Clark), its epidemic nature leading the school to the brink of closure. Paralleling *Cracks* in its scenes of lakeside reverie and wide-eyed Wordsworth recitations, the fraying central relationship is evidently more than a passing 'crack' for Lydia who, falling in love with her best friend, falls in with the physical symptoms of her illness and becomes the centre of school attention. The subsequent fainting fits/shared rapture/communal collapse are pregnant with metaphorical potential, variously signifying mischievous teenage rebellion, genuine unspeakable grief, and, most powerfully, an adolescent sense of bodily discomfort—further encoded with quasi-subliminal flash-cuts related to each loss of consciousness. The wider film equally varies in generic and tonal emphasis: its early folk-horror, symbolising the threshold of sexual awakening, shifts into the study of a potential demon child with Lydia's despair potentially unleashing lay-lined occult energies, before ending bathetically as another gothic melodrama, full of poisonous overdetermined family revelations. Lydia's move to get closer to her lost friend by seducing Abbie's last lover, be it her own beatnik brother, may offer the thrill of transgressive release, but tracing the film's school-set mysteries to claustrophobic home-life rape and incest (in documentarist style) is reductively explicit. The period setting also facilitates visual and vocal over-emphasis: the tail-end of the Swinging Sixties is foregrounded both in the girls' short skirts, especially Abbie's, embodiment of the new permissiveness—'He had a car. What can I say?'—and their discussions of orgasms and 'doing it', conducted with unearned sophistication. Against the (habitual) threat to school/social order of this burgeoning female sexuality, the adults remain in their kitchen-sink conservative Britain, with Lydia's beehive-hairdoed mother (Maxine Peake) watching black-and-white television, while chain-smoking headmistress Miss Alvaro (Monica Dolan) labours the point on which is the more misunderstood generation. The film is also openly, rampantly intertextual: beyond its explicit references to Peter Weir, clearest in the rage for black umbrellas, Abigail's name connotes Arthur Miller's 1953 exploration of psychogenic illness in *The Crucible* (filmed by Nicholas Hytner in 1996), while the school's closeted setting evokes Ken Russell's *The Devils* (1971). In a school generic context, while hidebound staff reactions recall Marcia Blaine and the brooding psycho-sexual undertones replay contemporary *giallo*-inflected fare like *Assault*, the film tangentially adds to the number of school-set musicals: Tracy Thorn's folk-influenced score adds an eerily discordant ambience, the chamber pieces of Abbie's xylophone-led Alternative School Orchestra articulate an adolescent imaginary, while the fainting manifests itself as a form of dance, its balletic back-bends and arm-arching expressing not a submissive womb-wandering 'hysterical contagion', as the school doctor terms it, but an empowering politicised female collective, their elaborate slow-motion fainting during a fusty Women's Institute talk on accidents in the home an irreproachable rejection of the supportive housewife role for which they are being prepared. Here, with gyrations rather than guns, the film stands as a female companion to the more patriarchal rebellion of *If....*, a thematic comparison strengthened by its temporal setting (with echoes of second wave feminism), through to Lydia's explicit condemnation of her teacher Miss Mantel (Greta Scacchi) to break their inertia: 'Kill the system, it's killing you!' The trade journal *Screen International* correctly assessed *The Falling* as 'a film that will resonate with some but leave others exasperated' (11 October 2014). For Geoffrey Macnab 'a beautifully made and very subtle affair that combines melodrama, rites of passage and supernatural elements in an utterly intriguing way' (*Independent*, 24 April 2015), David Jenkins found it 'a very woolly, precious and nonsensical drama which flits and flails to its own off-tempo beat without a care in the world' (*Little White Lies*, April 2015). The depiction of carefree same-sex school-set relationships seemingly remains beyond the pale.

4   APPROVED AND SPECIAL SCHOOL

After the sentiment of *Boys in Brown* and the sociology of *Loneliness of the Long Distance Ruuner*, the post-1960s borstal treatment would become tabloid-bait for its sensationalism. A *cause célèbre* of television censorship, *Scum* was commissioned for the BBC's 'Play for Today' strand in 1976: scripted by Roy Minton and directed by Alan Clarke, a television social realist in the Ken Loach mould, the finished product was considered too shocking—its violent critique of the system not justifiable as legitimate social comment—and indefinitely shelved.[20] In January-February 1979, when the BBC script rights lapsed and with £250,000 funding from independent producer Don Boyd, Clarke reshot *Scum* for theatrical release, keeping most of the original cast, adding graphic language and violence, alienating Minton and gaining an 'X' certificate. Eschewing sociological pretentions in a 'sensationalist marketing campaign' (Barber 2013: 157), *Scum* (28 September 1979) follows three new arrivals to an English borstal where the officers encourage the boys' violence-based hierarchy. Carlin (Ray Winstone) is determined to stay out of trouble, but his retaliation to the humiliating attacks of Banks (John Blundell) make him the new 'daddy'. When the staff stand by while Banks rapes fellow new arrival Davis (Julian Firth), Carlin leads the boys in a full-scale riot which is brutally suppressed.

There is no remnant of the original corrective altruistic public school model in *Scum*, but plentiful evidence of a regressive Flashman-esque breeding ground for bullying and buggery, with the 'daddy', granted privileges for keeping control, equivalent to 'some kind of perverse "head boy"' (Wilson and O'Sullivan 2004: 43). The film registers its social realist lineage in an early homage to *Loneliness*, a close-up survey of young faces on a minibus moving down to focus on their cuffed wrists, while the drab colour palette (though regularly enlivened by bloodshed) consistently references a monochrome New Wave aesthetic. Much, though, is different. David Thomson saw the borstal in *Scum* as 'a universal metaphor, a place for the invisible members of society' (*Film Comment*, 29, 3, 1993: 80), and the fate awaiting Carlin's fellow newcomers foregrounds the experience of those marginalised in the New Wave and earlier periods' focus on the white heterosexual male. Black inmate Angel (Alrick Riley) suffers, from peers and staff, immediate violence and racial taunts, while the rape of the sensitive and therefore 'queer' Davis in the allotment's potting shed is a violent retort to the notion of rural respite enjoyed by Colin in *Loneliness*. Rather than Carlin, whose doorway framing as he beats the Block B leader references the taciturn John Wayne of *The Searchers* (John Ford, 1956), fellow inmate Archer (Mick Ford) is the insidious Colin Smith-style rebel, creating maximum inconvenience with claims to vegetarianism and atheism, and explicitly articulating the film's criticism of borstal, and incarceration in general, when he notes that 'the punitive system does not work' and asks the elderly warder Duke (Bill Dean) 'how can anyone build character in a regime based on deprivation?' Sian Barber sees Archer as 'a worthy successor to Mick Travis' (2013: 152), but there is no (even temporary) youthful victory here: the forces of Duke rather than 'the Duke' win out as, anticipating Thatcherism's suppressive policies, *Scum* (literally) rams home how 'the system... divides and rules the working class' (W.S. Gilbert, *Observer*, 29 January 1980). Archer apart, both inmates and warders are un(der)educated, and the temporal avoidance of contextualising flashbacks or voiceovers renders the borstal a totalising institution, denying inmate individuality and forging, as with Biles in *If....*, a complicity of behaviour between the young and their 'mentors', notably when the warders label Davis, with self-realising homosexual overtones, a 'mardy-arse'. This control is also spatially reinforced through the film's stylistic claustrophobia, focusing on cramped cell spaces and narrow corridors with even solitary inmates invariably hemmed in by flanking 'screws'. Unlike *Loneliness*, the camera is largely static, a mimetic tool of surveillance that controls the mise-en-scène as thoroughly as Independent Frame, only here with full thematic correlation. Dave Rolinson additionally notes how Clarke 'frames Borstal trainees in the bottom third of the frame, just as they are locked firmly into the bottom third of society' (2005: 78). The visually privileged dilapidated décor and the inmates' mechanical activities such as shovelling coal in snow emphasise less public school than workhouse values as *Scum* depicts the borstal system's ideological descent from Doctor Arnold to Dotheboys Hall. Scantily reviewed (especially in comparison to the coverage of its production history), Hugh Herbert termed it 'a piece of pure exploitation, interrupted occasionally by social messages put across in a way that makes you squirm with embarrassment' (*Guardian*, 20 September 1979), while for Felix Barker 'the over-kill is counter-productive' in 'a film which is so extreme that it ruins any good it might have achieved' (*Evening News*, 20 September 1979). Not its commercial good, though: with its offer of 'banned' material, *Scum* generated over £800,000 in its first year of release, and a lengthy afterlife as a 'lad mag' cult film regular.

Boyd would later claim that the debate around *Scum* hastened the Criminal Justice Act (24 September 1982) which abolished the UK borstal system and replaced it with youth custody centres ('Scum', BBC Radio 4, 4 November 2009). It certainly hastened the commissioning of 'sister' film *Scrubbers* (1982), a sole venture into social realism for the George Harrison-funded HandMade Films. An original treatment by Minton—who again later disassociated himself from the film—was reworked by *The Romantic Age*'s *femme fatale* Mai Zetterling for her first English-language direction. In spite of its 'authentic' wall-to-wall expletives, the film was awarded, uncut, the 'AA' certificate denied to *Scum*, BBFC Secretary James Ferman hoping (like *Good Time Girl*'s Miss Thorpe) that Zetterling's three months of research into female borstal life would constitute a salutary lesson for teenagers contemplating a life of crime. Its tale of two re-captured borstal girls, lesbian orphan Carol (Amanda York) let down by her faithless lover, and single mother Annetta (Chrissie Cotterill) fighting her way only to greater estrangement from her daughter, repeats several narrative elements from *Scum* and shares its drive to present a graphic depiction of the ugliness of borstal life, here with added face-flung excreta. There is again little diegetic thought given to education, though the inmates perform a play, not *Julius Caesar* for once but 'Hell Hole Bitches', a sanctioned cathartic/carnivalesque attack on the borstal system. It does not succeed: the punitively repetitive work shifts, during which the girls share their tales of male abuse, ferment their revenge attack on the male officers. To its credit, *Scrubbers* offers flashes of a credible mordant humour, while repeated scenes of the girls at bedtime talking through their cells' iron bars, singing songs or passing cigarette butts, successfully convey a sustaining sorority spirit. However, stereotypical characterisations such as the butch lesbian Eddie (Kate Ingram), the stilted slow-motion scrap between Annetta and Carol, sedative-induced wide-angle camera distortions and heavy-handed symbolism—a caged bird fluttering as its cell owner slashes her wrists—clash disconcertingly with Zetterling's social realist aspirations. *Scrubbers* found only sporadic national exhibition and, though winning the Press Jury prize at the Festival of Women's Films, received mixed reviews: 'alternatively overplayed and trivialised, pile-driving and prurient' was the sentence from the *Financial Times* (11 September 1982); the *Daily Mail*, though, found *Scrubbers* 'a more powerful, compassionate movie than *Scum*, made with passion, blazingly well-acted and it troubles the conscience, which is no bad thing' (11 September 1982).

The situation of *Scum* inmate Woods (John Fowler), illiterate and needing Archer to decipher his letters from home, indicates the potential educational continuum between reform and special educational needs (SEN). Under the 1944 Education Act, children with such needs were mostly categorised by medically-defined disabilities and placed in special schools. The 1978 Warnock Report radically changed the conceptualisation, introducing an educationally evaluated 'statement' of needs, and an 'integrative' or 'inclusive' approach, based on common educational goals for all children, so that by the turn of the century, while the proportion of children with SEN was calculated by the House of Commons at 18 per cent, only one per cent of children were still placed in special schools (House Commons Education and Skills Committee 2006: 11–12).

Two British films set in special schools bestride the 1981 Education Act consequent to the Warnock Report. The *Class of Miss MacMichael* (Silvio Narizzano, May 1979) follows Conor MacMichael (Glenda Jackson), a dedicated teacher of 'maladjusted children' at Selkirk School in a deprived inner-city London district. Her efforts to improve school conditions, such as converting a disused shed into a craft centre, are continually frustrated by the authoritarian headmaster, Terence Sutton (Oliver Reed), who despises the pupils and cares only for impressing local fund-donating dignitaries. Though set in an alternative educational establishment, there is nothing new in *The Class of Miss MacMichael* which plays like a Lulu-less distaff rerun of *To Sir, With Love* with MacMichael the good-Samaritan teacher whose belief in her pupils, all set for borstal or prison unless someone gets through to them, brings her into conflict with the school's uncaring hierarchy. There is the usual mix of social exposé, the pupils suffering various socio-sexual ailments including a girl parentally forced into prostitution and a boy who constantly exposes himself—cue peer group retaliation with a mousetrap; of sentimentality, with MacMichael's class surreptitiously cleaning and 'decorating' her flat when she falls ill; of heated polemical arguments between teacher and headmaster; of sporadic pupil violence, notably Gaylord (Riba Akabusi), whose destructive rages Conor (alone) believes need medical attention; and finally its humour, sharing the pupils' raucous jokes allowing Miss to show whose side she is on. With its reformist inspiration crucially undermined by acting inconsistencies, not from its inexperienced teenage cast but from the clash between Reed's overplayed music hall villain and Jackson's thrusting earnestness, the film was pilloried in the press: 'More like *Carry On Comprehensive* than anything else, the film is a chaos of vague intentions', wrote Nigel Andrews (*Financial Times*, 4 May 1979), while Philip French decried 'possibly the worst, most thoroughly irresponsible film on an important subject to have emerged from a British studio in recent years' (*Observer*, 6 May 1979).

By the mid-1990s the British film industry was as underfunded as the state education system. *Clockwork Mice* (23 June 1995)—the title references wayward children ready to hurtle off in any direction—was made by Vadim Jean, one of a 'brat-pack' of young British directors determined to circumvent lengthy apprenticeships by making films on shoestring budgets (Murphy 2000: 1–2). Dedicated to 'all those involved in special educational needs', the film follows Steve (Ian Hart), a new teacher at Parkwood's residential school for children 'statemented' with emotional and behavioural difficulties (EBD). While his arrival sets the pulse racing of colleague Polly (Catherine Russell), Steve fails to find common ground with his class until the challenge to withdrawn 14-year-old problem pupil Conrad James (Rúaidhrí Conroy) of a race around the school brings in enough kids for Steve to form a cross-country club. However, the death of Conrad's father prompts the boy to a series of increasingly dangerous running stunts, culminating in his rail-track death as he tries to escape his teachers. Every British film set in an approved or special school features boys and girls 'on the run', an explicit condemnation of the establishments supposed to educate and 'improve' them. Here a cameo part for John Alderton, promoted from *Please Sir!* to headmaster, may promise a comic approach, but knowledge of his late replacement for James Fox, coupled with James Bolam playing disillusioned teacher Wackey, indicates a casting strategy looking to establish a generic genealogy with the more sombre *Loneliness.* Picturesque long shots of figures pacing sunlit fields intertextually reference Colin Smith, while intratextually visualising the poetry with which Steve tries to inspire his classes—'We run because we like it/Through the broad bright land'.[21] The motif is overstretched, however, especially in a lengthy musical interlude which indicates that, while running serves as a catch-all metaphor for self-improvement, *Clockwork Mice* lacks any exploration, not just of training and technique, but of how, as part of a school curriculum, the discipline of distance running can foster a beneficial sense of ambition and achievement. Contemporary influences are also sometimes off the pace: though distinctly down-market, its inspiring single teacher and pupil demise securely place the film in the school of *Dead Poets Society*, while stylistically it borrows from *Chariots of Fire* (Hugh Hudson, 1981), even though slow-motion shooting during Steve's first race with Conrad contradicts the narrative point that speed is a means to school and social status. The critics adjudged it overall a close-run success: for Derek Malcolm it 'deserves an honourable mention in the classroom drama genre' but 'don't expect the subtleties of *Kes*' (*Guardian*, 22 June 1995).

5   Magic School

The British school film could be labelled essentially an inward-looking genre, exploring or exploiting an indigenous education system for a predominantly domestic audience. Such a charge cannot be levelled at the films comprising this final section, the eight adaptations of J.K. Rowling's Harry Potter literary phenomenon which, amongst its myths and monsters, offers a summation of the school genre as it follows a year group through its troubled secondary education, charts a range of teaching methodologies and, more broadly, retraces the genre's inherent Romance of Empire from zenith to dismantlement. While doing so, the Harry Potter films currently constitute globally the second highest-earning film series ever with receipts of $7.7 billion, while all eight Harry Potter films feature in the Top 50 'All Time Worldwide Box Office Grosses' (*Box Office Mojo* [accessed 21 November 2015]).[22] In 2011 the series received from BAFTA the carefully-worded Michael Balcon Award for 'Outstanding British Contribution to Cinema'.

5.1   Section Prize Winner: Harry Potter and the Philosopher's Stone (2001)

The story of the success of J.K. Rowling and her Harry Potter novels is well documented—poverty-line single-mother sitting in a local café and writing the prophetic opening-chapter sentence: 'He'll be famous—a legend… there will be books written about Harry—every child in our world will know his name!' (1997: 15). Their translation into film began late in 1997 when a manuscript of Rowling's first novel was picked up by the office of producer David Heyman who brokered the 1999 sale to Warner Bros. of film rights to four Harry Potter novels, reputedly for £1 million. Thus began, after the late-1930s of *A Yank at Oxford* and *Goodbye, Mr. Chips* and the late-1960s of *If…*. and *Goodbye, Mr. Chips*, a third thirty-year wave of US investment in the sumptuous iconography and social iniquities of British education. However, retaining primary artistic input, the author of what had meanwhile become an international publishing sensation stipulated that all principal cast members be British. With Rowling's broader insistence on textual fidelity, the careful adaptation process for an equally possessive public, estimated at 100 million readers, became a UK version of Margaret Mitchell's 1936 *Gone With The Wind*, ranging from the widely publicised casting process, through the money lavished on recreating the novels' physical world, to the extension of normal film length to include all necessary incidents. With Hayman installed as series producer, Britain's Stuart Craig as production designer and Steve Kloves as series scriptwriter, a roll-call of directorial A-listers were mooted to helm the opening film, including Steven Spielberg, Terry Gilliam, Alan Parker and Peter Weir, until Warner announced in March 2000 the appointment of Chris Columbus, citing his successful back catalogue of family films such as *Home Alone* (1990) and *Mrs Doubtfire* (1993), but essentially trusting an impersonal filmmaker to serve the material. Columbus' script for *Young Sherlock Holmes* (Barry Levinson, 1985), also featuring two boys and a girl fighting the supernatural in a British boarding school, was used throughout a seven-month search and thousands of open auditions which eventually secured the junior leads, Daniel Radcliffe as Potter, Rupert Grint as Ron Weasley and Emma Watson as Hermione Granger, while the adult cast included school film experience with (now Dame) Maggie Smith and Ian Hart as Professors McGonagall and Quirrell, plus minor roles for John Cleese (Nearly Headless Nick), Richard Griffiths (Vernon Dursley) and Leslie Phillips (voicing the Sorting Hat). Filming occupied September to December 2000 at Warners' Leavesden Studios, Hertfordshire, with location shooting including Alnwick Castle and Harrow School. Post-production, again Britain-based, continued until the summer of 2001 and consumed almost half of the $125 million budget. Following a string of teaser posters, trailers and a $150 million promotion deal with Coca Cola, its Leicester Square London premiere, on 4 November 2001, took place in a cinema externally redecorated to look like Hogwarts. *Harry Potter and The Philosopher's Stone* (America substituted *Sorcerer's Stone*, fearing 'philosophy' would alienate the public) introduces us to orphaned Harry, reared by his cruel aunt (Fiona Shaw) and uncle (Griffiths) until, on his eleventh birthday, he is informed of his magical heritage and whisked off to Hogwarts School of Witchcraft and Wizardry and Gryffindor House where, in a series of adventures alongside his fellow first-years Ron and Hermione, he excels at Quidditch, solves the mystery of the titular stone to thwart Voldemort and consequently, as announced to John Williams' soaring score, earns sufficient points for Gryffindor to win the school cup.

Stone is a safely realised film, from its achieved fidelity to the source text (perhaps understandable given the popular outrage to editing out even minor characters such as the spectral Professor Binns), to its (more problematic) feel-good nostalgia, with conservative school/social values cloaked in state-of-the art special effects. The first Potter film's journey into magic is equally a journey into Britain's past and its generic/heritage culture (thus earning it this study's section prize). School and its attendant class consignment are immediately delineated with Harry destined for the local *Kes*-like 'sink' comprehensive, Stonewall High, while the Dursleys' spoilt son Dudley (Harry Melling) enjoys Smeltings, the low-grade local public school that a Hay or Sim would lead. Both institutions are shown up as infinitely inferior to Hogwarts with its architectural grandeur and its idyllic (Scottish) countryside setting. Here is 'a mixed-sex multira-cial Eton for magicians', a magic-mirror world with top-class food and no mod cons, for Rob White 'a public school without bullying or sexual tension, a childhood where abusive adults can be outwitted' (*Sight and Sound*, 12, 1, January 2002: 44). A carnivalesque spirit certainly attends the first-years' perilous rite-of-passage quest, but White errs on the peer group dynamics, since the opening Potter book—and therefore film—closely follow the school story narrative arc and character templates set down by Hughes' *Tom Brown's Schooldays* and its cinematic adaptations. Both Harry and Tom are initially unprepossessing 11-year-olds sent away to a forbidding boarding school (Hogwarts/Rugby); each gains a best friend to support them (Weasley/East) and a fierce but understanding headmaster to mould them (Professor Dumbledore (Richard Harris)/Dr Arnold), while a third companion ensures a broader narrative dynamic and social/sexual propriety (Hermione/Arthur); each prospers less in class than on the sportsfield (Quidditch/rugby); *pace* White, each is victimised by an arrogant bully and his henchmen (peer-group Draco Malfoy (Tom Felton)/sixth-former Flashman) but still works to protect those equally bullied (Neville Longbottom (Matthew Lewis)/George); and finally, after wavering from the right path, each wins the day with unshakable loyalty and enduring bravery (Fig. 5.4).

The 'energising myth' of imperialism deeply embedded in early children's literature (Kutzer 2000: 66) similarly informs Hogwarts, for all its contemporary co-educational and (quasi-token) multi-ethnic school intake: Harry's early shunning for being a serpent-speaking Parselmouth connotes, alongside the Satanic, an imperial discourse of Parsee fakirs and snake charmers, while the 'otherly' turbaned Professor Quirrell proves the danger to national security, his cultural concealment allowing the Dark

Fig. 5.4   Spot the difference: Harry Potter/Tom Brown

Lord back into Britain and its halls of learning. The cinematic/national nostalgia for an age of global importance kicks in at King's Cross Station: the Hogwarts Express bisects a landscape shorn of modern technology, while Diagon Alley is deeply Victorian, its cape-wearing (and racist featured) goblin-bankers and wizened shopkeepers with their waistcoats and half-moon glasses comparable in design and decorum to Tom Brown's various arrivals at Rugby. Thereafter, the house and prefect system, the staff with their academic gowns and eccentric teaching styles, the Great Hall meals and dormitory nights, the central sporting set piece, all replay and revalidate British public school tropes consistent with insulating and socialising a white, empowered elite to replay the ideological traditions sullied since *If.....* Though the series always intended to darken and progressively problematise the position of Hogwarts, its opening upbeat instalment still has its moments of fear and grief, as when Harry sits before the magic-mirror, his reflection flanked by his murdered parents; overall, though, the young wizard is too protected, by fame and friendship, innate skill and inherited accoutrements, for the sheer terror that can attend starting a new school fully to manifest itself. Harry Potter is no Guinea Pig and Gryffindor no College House: instead, *Stone* created a child-driven rise in British boarding school applications.[23]

Though another critic-proof undertaking, the first film in 'the Harry Potter franchise' received predominantly positive reviews: in the aftermath of 9/11, a British school film was again held up as offering positive social messages, Philip French applauding how 'Harry Potter affords hope of magical powers available to the brave, the decent and the resourceful in our own anxious times' (*Observer*, 18 November 2001); Roger Ebert, who expressed similar hopes for *Get Real*, declared *Stone* 'an enchanting classic' that 'will be around for a long time, and make many generations of fans' (*Chicago Sun-Times*, 16 November 2001). Some (privately educated) critics found mimesis to equal the magic, Anthony Lane confessing that, while Hogwarts would be 'the sheerest invention' for most, 'to those who attended British boarding schools it feels like grinding neo-realism— a blast, either hallowed or horrific, from an all too insistent past' (*New Yorker*, 19 November 2001). Many, though, found the novel's presence too insistent and that Columbus, 'in choosing to be true to the words, has made a movie by the numbers' that 'isn't inept, just inert' (*Time*, 1 November 2001). Elvis Mitchell thought 'the Sorting Hat has more personality than anything else in the movie', but still admired Felton's Draco who 'has the rotted self-confidence of one of the upperclassmen from Lindsay Anderson's *If....*' (*New York Times*, 16 November 2001); Lisa Schwarzbaum, amongst many, noted Maggie Smith 'purring with vocal references to her prime as Miss Jean Brodie' (*Entertainment Weekly*, 15 November 2001). Such intertextuality was undoubtedly incidental to the film breaking UK and US opening day and weekend records en route to $975 million box office takings worldwide (£66 million UK), placing it, at the time, behind only *Titanic* (James Cameron, 1999) as the most successful commercial film ever. However, though nominated for three Academy Awards, Original Score, Art Direction and Costume Design, and seven BAFTAs including Best British Film, it won nothing—zero points to Hogwarts.

Midway through *Harry Potter and the Chamber of Secrets* (3 November 2002) Dobby the House Elf warns that 'History is to repeat itself'. It effectively summarises the sophomore film's *modus operandi*: the same director, cast and crew and the same full and faithful transfer to the screen. Considered a superior novel, allowing more action and less backstory exposition, Harry's second year at Hogwarts centres on the (unknown) heir of school co-founder Salazar Slytherin opening the titular Chamber and unleashing a basilisk that petrifies several school inhabitants. Amidst the adaptation's newly immersive handheld camerawork and smoother CGI monsters that overtake the inter-house competition (and strive to keep pace with Peter Jackson' concurrent *Lord of the Rings* venture), the second instalment begins to problematise the privilege and potential arrogance concomitant with its boarding school setting, installing a more socially conscious sub-plot that, while foregrounding a metaphorical representation of racial otherness, still exposes the villains' varying prejudices, all 'pureblood' pontification and Aryan blondness, against human/Muggle-born wizards like Hermione or lower-class fare like Ron with his second-hand textbooks. By comparison, Harry's temporary ostracism, another reworked Tom Brown trope, remains explicit before empathetic (exposing Radcliffe's limited acting range), with the pain such loneliness engenders more affectingly conveyed in Robert Stevenson's 1940 film version. *Chamber*'s wealth of supporting actors permits a wider if caricatured examination of pedagogical types, notably the 'charismatic' Gilderoy Lockhart (Kenneth Branagh) whose self-aggrandising set-texts cannot mask his classroom incompetence, while the lesson from Professor Pomona Sprout (Miriam Margolyes) on the properties of mandrakes plants a metaphorical seed of burgeoning sexuality amongst its pre-teen alumni. An enlarged Hogwarts, its endless corridors interspersed with lecture halls and science labs, and a plusher Quidditch stadium suggest (alongside a healthy capital investment programme) a first move from *Stone*'s flashy theme-park aesthetics towards darker labyrinthine dynamics redolent of Mervyn Peake's Gormenghast. While many found *Chamber* 'darker, funnier and finer than its predecessor' (*Guardian*, 4 November 2002), it was still criticised as 'basically an on-screen illustration of the book, not a proper "movie" by any structural cinematic definition' (*Empire*, December 2003). Another opening weekend record breaker, *Chamber* finally fell slightly short of *Stone*, taking $879 million worldwide (£55 million in Britain) and collecting (only) three BAFTA nominations.

Harry Potter and the Prisoner of Azkaban (23 May 2004) saw the series move to an 18-month production cycle with Columbus, now executive producer, replaced by Mexican director Alfonso Cuarón. Best known for the raunchy road movie *Y Tu Mamá También* (2001), Cuarón had boarding school film experience with *A Little Princess* (1995), a New York transposition of Frances Hodgson Burnett's children's classic. The cuts and conflations necessitated by the source novel's greater length excised most classroom scenes, including the magic potion lessons from Professor Severus Snape (Alan Rickman), but, with its diet of Dementors before detention, *Prisoner* succeeds *cinematically* because its special effects are harnessed to advancing character and plot rather than dazzling with show-stopping impact. This is evidenced in the Privet Drive preface where Harry, entering his terrible teens, is discovered under the bedcovers playing with his wand (Cuarón's visual pun?) before causing contemptuous Aunt Marge (Pam Ferris) to inflate and float into the suburban sky. The film's multiple bodily transformations serve effectively as metaphors for adolescence, with the pupil leads' childhood wonder ceding to a gangly grace as hormones hit Hogwarts and Harry's embodiment of the fantasy of omnipotence is counterbalanced by the nightmare of orphanhood. The neo-imperial motifs of invasion and militarised frontiers contribute to the film's equally darker narrative, with Harry's studies overshadowed by the escape of eponymous prisoner Sirius Black (Gary Oldman), Voldemort's acolyte and Harry's potential assassin. The foreboding generated by Black's delayed entry is augmented by the décor: like *Assault* and *Fear in the Night* the film is predominantly set in the school's surrounding woodland where Cuarón's sombre palette evokes nature's terrifying power, while even the compulsory Quidditch takes place in torrential rain and is quickly, violently ended by invasive Dementors (the Empire striking back) as the study of a Tom Brown wizard is enveloped in Dickensian gothic.

Hogwarts itself is now more mountainous and mirrored, its internal chiar-oscuro contributing to a disconcerting noir mise-en-scène. The classroom scenes are brief but, the template gelling, much of *Prisoner*'s humour is again generated by the steady run of replacement teachers. The chaos resulting from gamekeeper Rubeus Hagrid (Robbie Coltrane)'s Care of Magical Creatures class offers a warning against employing untrained teachers, while Emma Thompson replays Branagh's broad comic turn as Sybill Trelawney, the scatty myopic Professor of Divination. More tonally and thematically important is David Thewlis' Professor Remus Lupin, Lockhart's tweedy replacement as Defence against the Dark Arts teacher who, in one typically unorthodox lesson, challenges his pupils to conjure up their worst fears which they then dispel with humour: re-dressing Professor Snape as an Old Mother Riley grandmother and putting giant spiders on roller-skates exemplifies the film's wider mix of horror and slapstick, its juxtaposition of *The Hole* with Will Hay. Lupin's paternalistic approach also allows an exploration of the problematic emotional bond that can develop between pupil and teacher: the absence in Harry's life of caring adults, exac-erbated by Michael Gambon's less reassuring Dumbledore, accentuates the importance of his friendship with Lupin, whose quiet Chipping-style conversations allow Harry to reconnect with his painful past (and advantageously modulate the film's pace), and thus render the resolution more distressing when Harry's safety is threatened by Lupin's werewolf transformations, here more readily readable as a metaphor for socially mis-understood illnesses such as AIDS rather than paedophilia or 'passing' as a racialised other—though his resignation to pre-empt parental complaints situates enduring adult prejudice amidst school potions. *Prisoner* also reg-isters the differing rates of gender maturation: Ron remains nonplussed by the burgeoning romantic interest from Hermione, changing from annoying class swat to an impatient young woman, a prime plot-mover braver than the boys as when delivering an uppercut to Malfoy—she rightly holds central position in publicity posters since this is Hermione's film. Now generally considered the most achieved and visually inventive contribu-tion to the series, David Gritten thought that 'finally, here is a film that does justice to Rowling's soaring imagination' (*Telegraph*, 28 May 2004); for Peter Rainer it was 'the most powerfully entrancing children's film in years' with 'an emotional resonance for older audiences that was lacking in its predecessors' (*New York Magazine*, 7 August 2004). Continuing the series' commercial–critical inverse ratio, *Prisoner* was to prove the lowest-grossing film of the series, pulling in $797 worldwide (£46 million UK), though it earned Academy Award nominations for Original Score and Visual Effects.

Harry Potter and the Goblet of Fire (18 November 2005) brought a first British director to the project, Mike Newell. Alongside a back catalogue including *Four Weddings and a Funeral* (1994) and the (less successful) private school-set *Mona Lisa Smile* (2003), Newell's own education at St Albans, Hertfordshire led Heyman to enthuse that the latest director 'combines a professorial presence with that of a public-school boy [who] can totally empathise with boarding-school life and has an intuitive sense of the youthful rebellion that you often find in these institutions' (cited in McCabe 2011: 120). With the 734-page novel twice as long as *Azkaban*, Kloves and Newell's serious compression removed all aspects not directly related to Harry's narrative progression (the 157-page Quidditch World Cup prologue is over in under five minutes) while retaining the increasingly menacing tone: growing with its fan base *Goblet* became the first Potter film to be awarded a BBFC '12A' certificate (and an MPAA 'PG-13' rating) for its dark themes, frightening imagery and fantasy violence. In this instalment Harry, though underage, is selected by the titular Goblet to compete in the Triwizard Tournament, occasioning peer group jealousy, especially from Ron. Inter-house broadens to international—but still imperially Eurocentric—school competition as Hogwarts welcomes the Bulgarian boys of Durmstrang Institute and, continuing a generic lineage of cross-channel interactions, the sophisticated French girls of Beauxbatons Academy of Magic. The three challenges, retrieving a golden egg from fire-breathing dragons, rescuing a colleague from a dark lagoon and negotiating a maleficent maze transplanted from *The Shining* (Stanley Kubrick, 1980), lead Harry into a duel with the long-awaited Voldemort (Ralph Fiennes) and the death of fellow competitor and Hogwarts golden boy Cedric Diggory (a pre-*Twilight* Robert Pattinson).

The early British school film predominantly eulogised boarding school life, while its second half more regularly problematised school's ability to shield and shape its charges: the same trajectory holds for the Potter film series. 'Dark and difficult times lie ahead', Dumbledore informs Harry early on, and the fourth film tips over into the less enjoyable hinterland of wizardry and magic with a sustained struggle between Hogwarts' civilised traditions and the void of Voldemort. The central tournament, tied to the Tom Brown ethos with its *Victor Ludorum*, contributes to rendering Hogwarts less closed and less certain, while adult frailty is increasingly apparent with Dumbledore revealed not as an omniscient Arnoldian paterfamilias but an old man unsure of the future and unable to protect Harry. Though most class time is again excised, ex-teacher Brendon Gleeson's Alastor 'Mad-Eye' Moody, a mature entrant to the profession, exemplifies the straight-talking 'tough love' pedagogical persuasion, preparing his charges for adult life by appraising them unequivocally of ubiquitous evil. Other staff members appear only fleetingly: McGonagall teaching a terrified Ron the rudiments of ballroom dancing illustrates that extracurricular activities do not always successfully soften a stern classroom persona. The scene illustrates how *Goblet* becomes more emotionally affecting (and scarier for the boys) when the Yule Ball approaches and Harry and Ron, lacking the dark arts to conjure a first date, flounder in confusion and resentment. Hermione's impatient attendance with Durmstrang's finest, Victor Krum (Stanislav Ianevski), again demonstrates the discrepancy between the sexes' emotional and intellectual development, but equally signals a regression from the position of power and agency Hermione attained in *Prisoner*: now the passive object of love interest and sexualised by her ball gown, she is repositioned to traditional gender roles both in action and appearance, a conformism that finally attracts the attentions of Ron.[24] Harry's maladroit courting of Scottish-accented Cho Chang (Katie Leung) intimates a Gryffindor variant on *Gregory's Girl*, though the Prom Night setting more overtly mines a two-decade tradition from American teen movies. The pupils' growing pains are mirrored by staffroom romance as the French influence discernible in *Good Morning, Boys* and *A French Mistress* returns to 'loosen up' British reserve with Hagrid finding a woman he can look up to in Beauxbatons' headmistress Madame Olympe Maxime (Frances de la Tour). Most critics put the film a close second to *Azkaban*: 'The gloom and doom may be less poetically realised, but the combination of British eccentricity, fatalism and steady-on pluck remains irresistibly intact', wrote the *New York Times* (17 November 2005). While specific British school film tropes remained—for Peter Bradshaw the uniformed French pupils 'made me think of the misses once instructed by Miss Jean Brodie' (*Guardian*, 18 November 2005)—most now found, despite the British direction, US influences to the fore, Roger Ebert one of many adjudging the Ball section as 'almost in the spirit of John Hughes' (*Chicago Sun-Times*, 17 November 2005). Global success duly came: *Goblet* was the highest-grossing film of 2005, eventually bringing in $897 million worldwide (UK £49 million), second only to *Stone* in the series' takings. It received an Academy Award nomination for Art Direction and became the first Potter film to win a BAFTA, for Production Design—victory, if not, perhaps, Dumbledore's promised 'eternal glory'.

Harry Potter and the Order of the Phoenix (11 July 2007) was again British-directed, now by state-educated (St Helen's, Merseyside) David Yates, previously known for television series such as *State of Play* (BBC, 2003) and *Sex Traffic* (C4, 2004): his CV suited what Heyman termed 'a political film not with a capital P' centred on 'teen rebellion and the abuse of power' (*Variety*, 9 July 2007). With Kloves on battery-recharging sabbatical, Michael Goldenberg's 'trimming' of the longest (and least successful) Potter volume (766 pages) removed the Quidditch match entirely in its reduction to 138 minutes, the shortest thus far of the series, though filming needed a two-month summer 2006 hiatus so that Radcliffe and Watson could sit their respective A-level and GCSE examinations.

While the opening broomstick-swoop of London landmarks was as blatant an appeal to foreign audiences as the photo-montaged day trip in *To Sir, With Love*, the new creative team thereafter favoured a grey-black palette and a tone of deliberate unease. Fifth-form Harry, 'so angry, all the time', is immediately in trouble, only escaping expulsion (for illicit use of magic helping the increasingly Bunter-esque Dudley Dursley) with the intervention of a subsequently distant Dumbledore. Hogwarts is also in trouble, placed in wizard-world 'special measures' by the sinister Ministry of Magic that refuses to believe the contention that Voldemort has returned. It imposes a new Defence against the Dark Arts teacher, Professor Dolores Umbridge (Imelda Staunton), also handing her a deputy head brief to bring Hogwarts back 'on message'—the series' most explicit statement yet of school as an ideological arm of the state. A party apparatchik par excellence in her pink-knit twin-set, Umbridge instigates a softly-spoken rule of terror, bullying staff and pupils, placing an eight-inch exclusion zone on cross-gender contact, replacing practical magic instruction with 'Ministry-approved' rote-learning, and finally usurping Dumbledore to assume complete school control. Her pronouncement that 'Progress for the sake of progress must be discouraged' is intratextually dangerous for a film largely marking time, though her repressive 'troubleshooting' brooks the dramatically required pupil dissent: in a low-voltage moment of Vigo-like mischief the Weasley twins (James and Oliver Phelps) set off fireworks in the OWL (Ordinary Wizard Level) examination; Harry's more concerted response, assembling and training an underground rebel band knows as 'Dumbledore's Army', is filmed by Yates with an intensity that installs Potter and a reactivated Hermione as potential successors to Mick Travis and the café-girl from *If.....* Unlike Anderson, however, Yates' broad metaphorical range—Heyman compared the narrative to Germany 1939 and 'a world on the verge of war' (McCabe 2011: 150)—is at the expense of the precise texture of school life: though the scholastic domain remains deeply regressive, *Phoenix* conveys little sense of an academic year's rhythm, contains few classroom scenes and jettisons the crucial emotional matrix of interpersonal bonds and inter-house rivalries. Harry famously has his first kiss but, purpose served, love-interest Cho is unceremoniously dropped from the action, excluded even from the final confrontation with Voldemort at the Ministry of Magic, a fascistic monument under London's Whitehall whose banner-festooned décor is redolent of the finale to *Pink Floyd—The Wall* (Alan Parker, 14 July 1982) where, if only in a brief live-action/animation fantasy sequence, the pupil body again fights back against an oppressive school system, all to the liberating accompaniment of 'Another Brick in the Wall Part 2'. In *The Wall* Young Pink (Kevin McKeon) is publicly humiliated by the Teacher (Alex McAvoy) for writing poetry in class (the lyrics to Pink Floyd's 'Money'): Umbridge similarly exemplifies the creativity-crushing, sadistic pedagogue, at one point slapping Harry across the face and forcing him to write lines—an unjust 'I must not tell lies'—with a quill that bloodily scratches out the words on his hand. Overall, though, the emotional focus of *Phoenix* rests with family before school dynamics, Sirius Black's hatred of his relatives' 'true-blood mania' further contributing to the most Orwellian of British school films. Praised for its dramatic coherence and adjudged the first film to improve on its source text, Wally Hammond had mixed feelings on Yates' 'no nonsense approach' which 'keeps the scenes and action moving' but 'leaves no time for games—please, sir, can't we play just a little Quidditch—and the excision of scenes of lolling chat in study rooms will disappoint fans of Bunter and Tom Brown worldwide' (*Time Out*, 9 July 2007). Peter Bradshaw admired the scene with Harry's lines punishment: 'a painfully real case of schoolteacherly bullying. I haven't been so uncomfortable since the beating scene in *Kes*' (*Guardian*, 13 July 2007). The abusive Umbridge clearly served as a multipurpose embodiment of political evil: America thought her 'aims and methods inject a bit of McCarthyism into Hogwarts' (*Washington Post*, 9 July 2007), while, for UK critics, 'inevitably, we think of the Communist take-overs in post-war Eastern Europe' (*Observer*, 15 July 2007); perhaps scariest in a school context, Sukhdev Sandhu saw her as 'a National League Tables inspector' (*Telegraph*, 13 July 2007). All-purpose allegories did not affect box-office takings: $940 million (UK £50 million) placed it second for Potter profits and the sixth highest-grossing film in history, while its IMAX takings of $35 million remain (as of 2015) the world record for a live-action release.

Increasingly incomprehensible as 'stand-alone' ventures, by *Harry Potter and the Half-Blood Prince* (David Yates, 15 July 2009) the British school film had returned to its *Dotheboys Hall* roots as a 'cinema of attractions', its narrative fragments dependent on prior intertextual knowledge. The sixth instalment also forewent messenger owls and house elves for school security checks, messy romantic entanglements and encounters with mortality, as Harry obsesses over a mysterious school textbook previously belonging to the eponymous Prince. Roughly half of *Half-Blood Prince* explores teen romance (with added love potions) while a neglected Hermione smoulders with frustration. In a series context, relaxing the mythopoeia for social comedy normalises the magic-wielding pupils and renews empathy for their battles to come. It also allows a focus on the pathos and potential homoeroticism in Harry's male mentors, with Rowling's on-set revelation that Dumbledore is gay (McCabe 2011: 189) arguably coded when his opening observation of Harry flirting, in long-standing generic tradition, with a London waitress is framed by a station hoarding reading 'Tonight make a little magic with your man'—the slogan establishes post-Mulvey both a male and female gaze for the 'Chosen One'. The film's other half is a demonic detective story, Harry hunting down an assassin in a darker, emptier Hogwarts: to achieve this Horace Slughorn (Jim Broadbent) is encouraged to return as Potions Professor and bring with him crucial information about Voldemort's pupil past. The single social-climbing Slughorn provides a further pedagogical type, the self-aggrandising collector of star pupils (including now the famous Harry), a bon viveur who distorts Katherine Chipping's 'revolutionary' idea of inviting pupils to dinner so that he can drop the names of famous former-charges into the conversation and bask in the reflection of their successes—or, as with Tom Riddle/Voldemort, retreat in shame at their, and thus his, failings. Potions apart, lessons are again on hold, though Quidditch returns: rather than a rugby-like preparation for warfare, its moody participants here render the game of thrusting broomsticks and safeguarded hoops a more overt sexual metaphor than the series' pervasive but non-climactic magic. *Half-Blood Prince* had its admirers—for Claudia Puig it was 'witty, spectacular and one of the best' (*USA Today*, 14 July 2009)—but for many 'Every term at Hogwarts is Groundhog term. They're all starting to look the same' with Yates succeeding Columbus as the patronised 'safe pair of hands' (*Guardian*,

17 July 2009). Ever-immune to critical reservations, *Prince*'s takings of $934 million (UK £51 million) placed it second for 2009 to James Cameron's *Avatar*. It was the only Potter film to receive an Academy Award nomination for Cinematography.

Harry Potter and the Deathly Hallows Part 1 (David Yates, 19 November 2010) has Voldemort seizing control of the Ministry of Magic with a resultant rise in show trials, jackboots and fascistic propaganda ('When Muggles Attack!'). Barred from Hogwarts, Harry, Hermione and Ron spend three months on the run amidst the English countryside, incrementally attaining the independence denied them by a cocooned boarding school education as they seek out the Horcruxes—the seven pieces of Voldemort's soul that grant him immortality. 'These are dark times, there is no denying', intones Minister Rufus Scrimgeour (Bill Nighy): except that all previous instalments *did* deny it, leavening the fantasy's danger with comic relief. Not now: an exiled innocent bound by a sense of duty, Harry is a wizard version of Roddy Berwick, sinking deeper into a practical and emotional morass, rebuking the murdered Dumbledore for a lack of direction, awkwardly dancing with an upset Hermione (to Nick Cave's lugubrious 'O Children') when a jealous Ron storms off. In this 'intimate instalment' bodily transformations again feature: the Polyjuice Potion's creation of seven decoy Harrys, making Hermione wear Harry's glasses and putting the 'Chosen One' into Fleur Delacour's bra, lightly revisits *Prisoner*'s notions of gender performativity. More geared to the tensions of late adolescence, the trio's disguise as browbeaten adult functionaries to infiltrate the Ministry predicts the exhausted future awaiting even the bravest and smartest school-leavers. With the habitual tropes of a train to school, new teachers, uniforms, Quidditch and Christmas replaced by a surfeit of MacGuffins—alongside horcruxes are resurrection stones, Gryffindor swords and the eponymous death-conquering articles (beguilingly explained with animated shadow puppetry)—*Hallows 1* constitutes a waiting game, a phoney war for two ill-prepared young men that restores agency to the practical woman who, it seems, must care for both of them. The film again had its advocates—Lisa Schwarzbaum adjudged it 'the most cinematically rewarding chapter yet' (*Entertainment Weekly*, 17 November 2010)—but Lou Lumenick was typical in finding it 'beautifully shot but a soulless cash machine' that 'delivers no dramatic payoff, no resolution and not much fun' (*New York Post*, 18 November 2010). Such criticism mattered not as *Hallows 1* justified splitting the final Potter volume as it secured a worldwide gross of $960 million (UK £53 million), and received Academy Award nominations for Art Direction and Visual Effects.

The final film in the series, and in this study, *Harry Potter and the Deathly Hallows Part 2* (David Yates, 7 July 2011), eschewed its predecessor's character dynamics and lengthy exposition for an action-filled depiction of the incremental defeat of Harry's nemesis, Voldemort, albeit (perversely) at a faintly over-rushed pace, its 130 minutes running time the shortest of the series. With the Potter brand spread across a lucrative matrix of cross-media platforms, the stunning early set-piece in the Gringotts bank vaults, where treasures multiply Midas-like and then tumble if touched, offers an appropriately chaotic cine-social metaphor for late capitalism, while the swooping rail ride to get there enacts it, operating as a synergistic complement to the recently opened Wizarding World of Harry Potter theme park (Orlando, Florida, 2010). The quest for the last horcrux brings Harry and his fellow resistance fighters back to school for the final battle. Neville's announcement that 'Hogwarts has changed' is evident from the opening scene where new headmaster Snape has pupils marching rank-and-file through a misty courtyard like borstal boys in brown. The reunion of loyal staff led by McGonagall and a pupil body led by Harry in Henry V mode creates a siege situation for the school, surrounded by hooded Dementors in a phantom version of *F*. There are moments of partial relief, the pupils casting aside their uniforms for their Leavers' Day coupled with the realisation (like much of the loyal audience) of their imminent rite of passage into adulthood. That passage explores school not merely as a training ground for but in itself a site of imperial endeavour: both for staff, as evidenced in McGonagall's delighted conjuring of Hogwarts' stone statues into life as a defensive army; and for pupils, with the previously bullied Neville's heroic gesture in defying Voldemort. This and his phlegmatic 'well, that went well' when sent careering to a near-fatal fall offer minor-key complements to Harry's more sustained exemplar of the public school virtues of group solidarity, physical courage and the understated fulfilment (or failure) of duty.

The decisive to-the-death battle in *Deathly Hallows 2*, arguably underwritten in the source novel, converges thematic, emotional (and musical) threads from the entire series, reunites staff and revisits key Hogwarts locations, including the Quidditch stadium and Great Hall, before spectacularly reducing them to ruins reminiscent of a bombed-out wartime cathedral. It also re-problematises the public school code. Like *Tell England*'s Edgar Doe, Harry feels both physically and intellectually unprepared for the epic task demanded of him: as he asks Hermione, 'When have any of our plans actually worked? We plan, we get there, all hell breaks loose.' In similar questioning vein, the film's progressive nuancing of its Manichean good-versus-evil stand-off, providing the destructive Voldemort with a humanising vulnerability and positing that all, even self-sacrificing Harry, possess aspects of evil darkness, divisively blends the public school code with ambitions of world dominance, causally connecting a Tom Brown-style privileged education with the adult reality of western imperialism. This nationally-inculcated belligerence is replicated at a personal emotional level: when He-Who-Must-Not-Be-Named orders Snape's death in order to command the Elder Wand, the revelation of the Professor's unyielding hatred for Harry's father illustrates the life-lasting effects of school bullying as clearly as the reunion scene in *I'll Never Forget What's 'Isname*. Though beginning with childhood charms and a middle-class clamour for a fee-paying education, the Harry Potter series finally exposes, through Snape's long-hidden and conflicted motivations, the potential emotional stunting of uncorrected peer aggression within a boarding school environment. The revelation revives an issue close to the pupil body, discerning which adults ultimately deserve their trust, and pity. A Crocker-Harris for Hogwarts, Snape's cauterised sentimental education marries with the film's wartime environment: Andy Medhurst recast 1950s British war films like *The Cruel Sea* and *The Dam Busters* as 'films about repression, rather than as hope-lessly repressed films' (1984: 38), a reading relevant to the late-heroic Severus who joins Harry in being shaped, but more inwardly scarred, by a love maintained beyond death. Nonetheless, for all these revelations and reservations, the hegemonic function of school as a nation's 'imagined community' is ultimately reasserted. The film's coda, set 19 years in the future, has Harry, Hermione and Ron (all en route to mid-life anonymity in sensible clothing) waving off their children at King's Cross Station. Mawkish in the novel, the scene here succeeds both intertexually and con-textually: the passing of the baton/wand to another generation replays the genre's hereditary elitism most notably enacted in the generations of Colleys from *Goodbye, Mr. Chips*; it also bids farewell to the childhood and adolescence of the three principal actors which, under constant scrutiny, were largely devoted (albeit for enough riches to fill Gringotts vaults) to visualising the Potter phenomenon and a life of secondary education.

Hallows 2 prompted myriad reflections on a near-twenty-hour cinematic phenomenon. Philip French conceded its cultural import, noting that 'the films and the books have become for many young people and their parents a crucial part of their experience of this century' (*Observer*, 17 July 2011); Anthony Quinn emphasised the commerce: 'You might say it has been a small industry in itself: the British film industry' (*Independent*, 15 July 2011). *Hallows 2* was overwhelmingly adjudged a fitting finale, commonly placed second only to *Prisoner*, with Radcliffe seen as finally playing the part, gaining a self-assuredness that 'makes him resemble a genuine leader rather than a well-meaning school prefect' (*Telegraph*, 14 July 2011). Breaking records for advance ticket sales, midnight and IMAX takings, *Hallows 2* raced to a final gross of just over $1.3 billion worldwide (UK £73 million), placing it top financially for 2011, top of the Potter series and of all children's book adaptations. It received Academy Award nominations for Art Direction, Make Up and Visual Effects and won the Visual Effects BAFTA. The series thus finished with seven Oscar nominations but no award, while 28 BAFTA nominations yielded only two awards. To the end the industry saw it as schoolkid stuff: *Finite Incantatum*.

NOTES

1. The 'typical' Italian *giallo* features a mysterious black-gloved psychopathic killer who stalks and murders a series of beautiful women; supernatural elements are sometimes present. For a theoretical reading of the genre, see M.J. Koven (2006) *La Dolce Morte: Vernacular Cinema and the Italian Giallo Film*. Maryland: Scarecrow Press.
2. *Assault* remains a relatively demure cousin to the London-filmed Italian *giallo What Have You Done to Solange?* aka *Terror in the Woods* (Massimo Dallamano, 1972), where pupils from the capital's St Mary's Catholic School for Girls are stabbed in the vagina, a stark visual metaphor for teenage sexual punishment.
3. As of 2016, 130 UK independent schools have a Catholic character, while the Catholic Education Service oversees the annual schooling of 850,000 pupils in its 2300 state schools, 10 per cent of all maintained places. http://www.brin.ac.uk/news/2011/roman-catholic-schools-in-england-and-wales/ [accessed 04 January 2016].
4. On the subgenre, see Sotiris Petridis (2014) 'A Historical Approach to the Slasher Film'. *Film International*, 12, 1, March: 76–84.
5. The Columbine High School massacre, 20 April 1999, prompted, alongside *Bowling for Columbine* (Michael Moore, 2002), a US subgenre of school-shooting soul-searching films, notably *Heart of America* (Uwe Boll, 2002), *Zero Day* (Ben Coccio, 2003) and *Elephant* (Gus van Sant, 2003).

6. In some regions a 'toned-down' accent: *Gregory's Girl* was re-recorded by original cast members for its American release.

7. The film's release corresponded with high-profile proposed legislation to criminalise sexual relationships between teachers and sixth-formers—it became law in 2003's Sexual Offences Act. Jonathan Romney's review noted that 'a schoolteacher lusting after his pupils isn't considered a terribly amusing topic these days'. *New Statesman*, 18 October 1999.

8. On the theory that all hierarchical structures, not just prisons but schools, hospitals and factories have evolved to resemble a panopticon by prioritising an 'unequal gaze', see M. Foucault (1977) *Discipline and Punish: The Birth of the Prison.* London: Allen Lane. A 2000 BFI survey voted Cleese's hotel-set comedy *Fawlty Towers* (BBC, 2 series, 1975, 1979) the best British television series of all time.

9. Most (in)famously, throughout the 1970s John Lindsay made short porn films on schoolgirl themes, including *Classroom Lover* (1970), *Jolly Hockey Sticks* (1974) and *Boarding School* (1976). See David Kerekes (2000) 'Jolly Hockey Sticks! The Career of John Lindsay, Britain's "Taboo" Filmmaker of the Seventies', in Jack Stevenson (ed.) *Fleshpot: Cinema's Sexual Myth Makers & Taboo Breakers.* Manchester: Headpress.

10. On the carnivalesque and gender, see D.M. Bauer and S. Jaret McKinstry (eds) (1999) *Feminism, Bakhtin and the Dialogic.* Albany: State University of New York Press.

11. On Section 28 and 'the policing of sexuality', see C. Chitty (2002) *Understanding Schools and Schooling.* London: Routledge: 136–142. For a wider examination of Thatcherite homophobia, see A.M. Smith (1994) *New Right Discourse on Race and Sexuality: Britain, 1968–1990.* Cambridge: Cambridge University Press: 183–239.

12. Peck places the film into its historical and personal context in *Nighthawks II: Strip Jack Naked* (1991).

13. Peck similarly had to answer to the press which, for an article treating the exploitation of minors in pornography, ran the headline: '12-year-old children have appeared as actors in a shock film about a homosexual schoolteacher'. Harry Bonner, *Sun, 8* April 1978.

14. A wealth of literature examining this cinematic examination of the wealthy begins with Andrew Higson (2003) *English Heritage, English Cinema: Costume Drama Since 1980.* Oxford: Oxford University Press.

15. Nearly 60 continuations of the story are available at http://www.bensilverstone.net [accessed 20 September 2015].

16. On the Conservative Party's move 'to abandon the post-war welfare consensus and embrace social and educational policies based on nineteenth-century free-market anti-statism', see C. Chitty (2004) *Education Policy in Britain.* Basingstoke: Palgrave Macmillan: 47.

17. 'Hector laying hands on the boys would be totally different if they were much younger, but these are all 17-, 18-year-olds… I think they are

actually much wiser than Hector. He is the child.' *Daily Telegraph*, 21 June 2004.

18. Bennett adapts the quote from George Steiner's 2003 investigation of how 'eroticism, covert or declared, fantasised or enacted, is interwoven in teaching, in the phenomenology of mastery and discipleship'. *Lessons of The Masters*. London: Harvard University Press: 26.

19. Schools Out estimates that, of 25,000 lesbian, gay or bisexual teachers in Britain, 99 per cent say they are too afraid to come out. For the counter-argument that lesbian depictions have advanced sufficiently to allow the occasional 'classic negative stereotype', see Julie Bindel, 'We can take stereotypes'. *Guardian*, 29 January 2007.

20. It would first be shown on Channel Four in 1991 as part of a season on censorship.

21. Charles Hamilton Sorley, 'The Song of the Ungirt Runners'.

22. The top franchise is the broader 'Marvel Cinematic Universe' films.

23. The year's one per cent rise in British boarding school numbers, the first increase since the economic boom of 1987, was attributed to the profile-raising effect of the Harry Potter books and film. Tim Miles, *London Evening Standard*, 23 April 2002.

24. The process continued contextually, with the *Sun*'s 'countdown' to Emma Watson's 16th birthday submitted to the Leveson Inquiry into the culture, practice and ethics of the press. *Guardian*, 29 December 2011.

References

Barber, S. (2013) *The British Film Industry in the 1970s: Capital, Culture and Creativity*. London: Palgrave Macmillan.

Barnes, A.S. (1926) *The Catholic Schools of England*. London: Williams and Norgate.

Bennett, A. and N. Hytner (2006) *The History Boys: The Film*. London: Faber and Faber.

Bourne, S. (1996) *Brief Encounters: Lesbians and Gays in British Cinema 1930–1971*. London: Cassell.

De Witt, H. (n.d.) 'Nighthawks', BFI. http://www.screenonline.org.uk/film/id/548405 [accessed 14 October 2015].

Hill, J. (1999) *British Cinema in the 1980s*. Oxford: Oxford University Press.

House of Commons Education and Skills Committee (2006) *Special Educational Needs*, Vol 1. London: Stationary Office

Hornby, N. (1992) *Fever Pitch*. London: Victor Gollancz.

Hunter, I.Q. (2012) 'From window cleaner to potato man: Confessions of a working-class stereotype', in I.Q. Hunter and L. Porter (eds) *British Comedy Cinema*. London: Routledge.

Jones, M. (2012) 'Unman, Wittering and Zigo', in J. Upton (ed.) *Offbeat: British Cinema's Curiosities, Obscurities and Forgotten Gems*. London: Headpress.

Kutzer, M.D. (2000) *Empire's Children: Empire and Imperialism in Classic British Children's Books*. New York: Garland.

Landy, M. (2013) '*The Browning Version* revisited', in R.B. Palmer and W.R. Bray (eds) *Modern British Drama on Screen*. Cambridge: Cambridge University Press.

Leach, J. (2004) *British Film*. Cambridge: Cambridge University Press.

Martin-Jones, D. (2009) *Scotland: Global Cinema: Genres, Modes and Identities*. Edinburgh: Edinburgh University Press.

May, D. (1983) *Proust*. Oxford: Oxford University Press.

McArthur, C. (1982) 'Scotland and Cinema: The Iniquity of the Fathers', in C. McArthur (ed.) *Scotch Reels: Scotland in Cinema and Television*. London: BFI.

McCabe, B. (2011) *Harry Potter Page to Screen: The Complete Filmmaking Journey*. London: Titan Books.

Medhurst, A. (1984) '1950s war films', in G. Hurd (ed.) *National Fictions: World War Two in British Films and Television*. London: BFI.

Miller, H.K. (2011) 'Remaining days'. *Sight and Sound*, 21, 3, March.

Mulvey, L. (1975) 'Visual pleasure and narrative cinema'. *Screen*, 16, 3, Autumn.

Murphy, R. (ed.) (2000) *British Cinema of the 1990s*. London: BFI.

Newman, K. (2002) 'Psycho-thriller, qu'est-ce que c'est', in S. Chibnall and J. Petley (eds) *British Horror Cinema*. London: Routledge.

O'Connor, S. (1998) *Straight Acting: Popular Gay Drama from Wilde to Rattigan*. London: Cassell.

Petrie, D. (2000) *Screening Scotland*. London: BFI.

Rolinson, D. (2005) *Alan Clarke*. Manchester: Manchester University Press.

Rowling, J.K. (1997) *Harry Potter and the Philosopher's Stone*. London: Bloomsbury.

Russell Taylor, J. (1963) *Anger and After: A Guide to the New British Drama*. Harmondsworth: Penguin.

Schneider, S.J. (ed.) (2007) *100 European Horror Films*. London: BFI.

Williams, R. (1961) *The Long Revolution*. London: Chatto and Windus.

Williams, M. (2006) '"Come and have a bathe!" Landscaping the queer utopia', in R. Griffiths (ed.) *British Queer Cinema*. London: Routledge.

Wilson, D. and S. O'Sullivan (2004) *Images of Incarceration: Representations of Prison in Film and Television Drama*. Winchester: Waterside Press.

Žižek, S. (2002 [1991]) *For They Know Not What They Do: Enjoyment as a Political Factor*, 2nd ed. London: Verso.

PART V

Conclusion

CHAPTER 6

The School Film: A British Genre

1 PLENARY

In their pioneering *Film History: Theory and Practice*, Robert Allen and Douglas Gomery categorise 'the major avenues of film historical investigation' as the aesthetic, technological, economic and social (1985: 37). Invariably interconnected, each avenue is relevant in differing measure to the work of historiography on offer here: indeed, the course of the British school film offers common threads for a British film school course. Viewed as aesthetic film history, *The British School Film* by methodology functions primarily as a genre study, exploring distinct narrative patterns and a secure iconography while exposing the protean nature of such an entity, cutting across traditional categorisations of British cinema, venturing into 'low' comedy and exploitation modes, social realism and heritage cinema, hybridising with genres ranging from horror to musical comedy. Approaching the aesthetic avenue from a different direction, several British 'auteurs' are shown to have turned their camera at least once to a school film, thus contributing to a British 'directorial autobiography' (Sarris 1968: 30). Of directors with monographs on their work a register would record as present Anderson, Asquith, Boulting John, Boulting Roy, Clarke, Figgis, Forsyth, Gilliat, Hitchcock, Launder, Loach, Richardson (and Zampi); their school work, in this study's aesthetic judgement, would range from the 'Pantheon' (Anderson and Loach) to 'Less than Meets the Eye' (late Launder and Figgis). Though more tangential, technological developments in British cinema can also be traced: early school films postulate silent cinema's 'descriptive talker', illustrate developments in the use of intertitles, show awkward then achieved transitions from silent to sound cinema; middle years offer the failed technological experiments of Independent Frame, while the recent Potter films highlight indigenous state-of-the-art computer-generated imagery (CGI). As economic film history, a full gamut of production, exhibition and reception strategies are exemplified: the genre's financing stretches from the proto-crowdsourcing of *Nighthawks*, through (the majority) independent production houses, with Hollywood investment phases culminating in the multi-million tentpole Harry Potter series; its exhibition patterns advance from the earliest cinema of attractions, through 'B' movie second features and royal premieres to 3D IMAX blockbusters, with marketing ploys ranging from charity-targeted Narkover mementoes to saturation Hogwarts merchandising; box-office returns range from franchise world records and independent 'breakout' hits to US losses terminating UK investment, while critical reception moves from ignored provincial fare, through media campaigns securing a national release (for *Kes*) to BAFTA and Academy Award winners, with press evaluations utilising the full markscheme, from conferring canonical status on *If....* down to placing *Wildcats of St. Trinian's* on a final warning, with the majority adjudged, at best, of middling ability— the ubiquitous 'could do better'.

The more sustained readings essayed here, though, marry British school films' aesthetic strengths and weaknesses with their (often-contested) meanings as a major vehicle of social film history. Such a claim, with advocates ranging from Althusser to Žižek, is dependent on three important contentions: that schools are integral motors in the national imagination; that schooling has an important ideological function and symbolic weight concerning the nation's welfare and prospects; and, crucially, that school-centred films reflect or 're-present' these concerns. Formulated on the cusp of the twentieth century, both the mass secondary education system and the mass entertainment cinema industry were pivotal means for promulgating conceptual frameworks of normative behaviour and historical import. Histories of the nation, its education and its cinema are again invariably interconnected, with the British school film allowing a socio-historical study of attitudes towards the nation's education over the past hundred years. A development plan would show that, with the means of production long lying with a public schooled Establishment, the first half of the twentieth century saw this (largely English) elite in ideological discussion with itself, with an (unpopular) post-Great War trilogy of reformist films that explored the inadequacies of such an education in personal, interpersonal and professional contexts swiftly countered by three (more popular) war-anticipating films that defended the national benefits of public schools for inculcating a 'code' of leadership and service. Here, as always, the escapist function of cinema was understood and encouraged, comedy's consistent financial returns matched by its carnivalesque discourse, an authorised 'safety valve' ultimately reinforcing the dominant ideology. The Second World War and its concomitant social changes proved a cinematic watershed: firstly by re-examining public schools in films with a more persistently critical slant, initially through its 'anti-Chipping' personifications of teaching staff—before the whole edifice was gunned down in *If....*; secondly by finally bringing to the screen the majority's educational experience, though even its 'hard-hitting' 1960s trilogy of inner-city secondary modern films failed fully to indict an unfair, underfunded state system by focusing instead on 'inspirational' teachers whose determination to prepare work-fit adults supported existing social paradigms rather than perpetrating a more egalitarian national image— before the whole ideology was glaringly exposed in *Kes*. Thereafter, the centre cannot hold: the ceremony of innocence is not so much drowned as stalked and slashed, flung from a cliff, hung from a tree, buried in a hole, put in borstal, cloned, rebooted and openly, insistently psychoanalysed.

The parameters of this study do not attempt an intervention in precise disciplinary fields such as childhood studies, pedagogical theory or educational policy: instead it argues that, as commercial and ideological entities, school films serve as and serve up shorthand exemplars for preferred and perceived patterns of behaviour. Take the central role of the teacher: school films have little time for the reality of lengthy lesson preparation or marking, nor do they recognise the repeated imposition on staff of statutory frameworks. Instead, generic paradigms grant teachers full agency over their charges and, when not dwelling on the staffroom as a prolongation of the pupil domain where friendships and romance vie with hierarchical bullying and back-stabbing careerism, a cinematic teacher taxonomy would discern a 'Famous Five' of classroom archetypes: the dedicated public school linchpins such as Donkin and Mr Chips who learn to inspire; the antiphonal desiccated 'lifers' who retreat into intimidation and self-loathing such as Perrin, Crocker-Harris and, arguably, Severus Snape; the social realists such as Saunders and Thackeray (even Hedges) transforming their inner-city charges into decent self-confident citizens; the dangerous romantics, charismatic 'loose cannons' that go too far on impressionable minds, like Jean Brodie, and members, like Hector; finally the comic incompetents, eccentric, unqualified or both, generic constants of the carnivalesque from Will Hay's headmaster through to Alfie Wickers' embodiment of a bad education. Brodie is an evident rarity in this listing: though most teachers in the British education system have long been female (currently only one in four full-time state schoolteachers is male—Department of Education, *Statistical First Release*, November 2013: 7), this is not reflected in the British school film. Largely absent until St. Trinian's, female teachers are presented as troubling custodians of authority, the 'unnaturalness' of their status explicitly signalled by female impersonations from Sydney Howard to Rupert Everett, by termagants such as Miss Short and Dolores Umbridge, or more recently by psychotic lesbianised teachers such as Miss G and Barbara Covett. They are, 'at best', sexualised figures defined not by their classroom talents but their romantic relationships with male colleagues, a trope stretching from the foregrounded glamour of Helen Mirren back to the fairground gaucheness of Cicely Courtneidge. The male teacher is the genre's default protagonist, a perennial figure of cane- (or wand-) wielding justice, the 'correct' moulder of proto-disruptive adolescence for a future of social service. His role as a surrogate father is regularly embedded in this broader patriarchal discourse, offered as a touching dynamic in a public school cadre with *éminences grises* like Chipping and Dumbledore, accepted as more troubling in co-educational contexts with 'romantic aged' masters like Stephen Barlow and Graham Weir.

   Whatever their status, each male teacher archetype has, over time, availed himself of the cane. The entrée for Stephen Frears' personal history of British cinema (and purloined for this study), the (sado-masochistic) school trope of beating errant youth into conformity is so fundamental that it has been labelled 'the English Vice' (Gibson 1974) and applied to wider patterns of national behaviour. Terence Rattigan, a key contributor to the genre, attempted a broader definition in his penultimate play *In Praise of Love* (1973): 'Do you know what *le vice anglais*—the English vice—really is? Not flagellation, not pederasty—whatever the French believe it to be. It's our refusal to admit to our emotions' (1985: 247). While equally relevant to staff (e.g. Crocker-Harris), the lasting mark of schooling on the pupil body here comes to the fore. More than the mechanics of lesson structure and learning styles, the British school film has repeatedly explored the adolescent's sentimental education, the struggle to emote, to find a voice, a place, an identity in school and, by extrapolation, in the world beyond. From Tom Brown reaching Rugby through to Harry Potter's Hogwarts arrival, the school film has re-presented the formulation of peer groupings, with lasting friendships matched by ever-present bullying—the latter (sadly) long tacitly tolerated for its 'character-building' function. The genre's exploration of male sexuality had to await on-screen co-education explicitly to depict its concerns over heterosexual male teen passions, as with Terence Stamp's 'savage' Mitchell in *Term of Trial*: homosexuality has more lengthily registered and empathised, from the deeply encoded Lydia in *Young Woodley* and heritage safe distance of *Another Country* to the honesty of *If….* and coming out speeches of *Nighthawks* and *Get Real*. By contrast, burgeoning female sexuality has been a constant source of quasi-terror and demonised as corrosive to a fully functioning society, from 'little minx' waitresses leading decent public schoolboys *Downhill* and away from Dumbledore, via Arlette's vengeful finishing school seductress to the career-threatening crushes facing (and exculpating) state schoolteachers such as Saunders and Weir. Doubly damned, lesbian desires have only recently found less vituperative (if veiled) treatment in the poetic realism of *The Falling*. Such rarity—indeed tokenism—is far more manifest in issues of ethnicity: the British school film, as with Harry Potter's 'blink-and-you-miss-it' romance with Cho Chang, remains steadfastly white in focus, bar pointedly in its approved school treatments. Beyond even such sexual and racial marginalisation, the genre reveals itself as most unyielding in its depiction of social class, with schooling consistently revealed as related to upper-middle-class hegemony (public schools), to acceptable class mobility (grammar schools) and to the reproduction of class subservience (secondary modern schools). Significantly, these institutions appear in British cinema in this chronological order, with the class system shown to be directly re-produced in the unequal opportunities afforded by its schooling systems. These hierarchical values still insinuate themselves into the fragmented post-*If….* landscape: remove the class-controlling eye/I, and seemingly we are left with *F*.

2   INDIVIDUAL ASSIGNMENTS

Ideologically freighted, the school film constitutes part of the DNA of British cinema and society: this of necessity holds equally for individual film viewers, whose small psychological stories together constitute the grand social narrative. In one of many Potter-inspired press ruminations on the genre's longevity, Philip Hoare, noting the truism that 'almost everyone goes to school', reiterates the experience's individuated universality: 'School is a place of initiations, discoveries, loneliness, sociability, tests and failures, full of dramatic possibility—where friends are made (and betrayed), and all too easily enemies, where bullies and victims abound, where rules of appalling artificiality circumscribe our every move, just waiting to be broken, and where a few teachers loom large in our consciousness as ogres or objects of worship. Schools are places of protection from the adult world—and prisons from which we escape into the adult world. They are places where we grow up—or fail to' ('Lessons in How to Live', *Telegraph*, 9 November 2002). School is ultimately a personal affair and, whether successfully raised to adult estate or suffering an arrested development, the British school film endures because it allows us all individual points of recognition or comparison; it prompts recollections of the happiest days of our life or our most hellish, un-rejoiced moments; it provides an index of what would or could have happened to us *if....*

Class dismissed.

References

Allen, R.C. and D. Gomery (1985) *Film History: Theory and Practice*. New York: McGraw-Hill.

Gibson, I. (1974) *The English Vice: Beating, Sex and Shame in Victorian England and After*. London: Gerald Duckworth and Co.

Rattigan, T. (1985) *Plays: Two*. London: Methuen Drama.

Sarris, A. (1968) *The American Cinema*. New York: Dutton.

Filmography: A Century of School Films

Absolution (Anthony Page, 1978)
Another Country (Marek Kanievska, 1984)
Assault (Sidney Hayers, 1970)
The Awakening (Nick Murphy, 2011)
The Bad Education Movie (Elliot Hegarty, 2015)
The Belles of St. Trinian's (Frank Launder, 1954)
Blue Murder at St. Trinian's (Frank Launder, 1958)
Bottoms Up! (Mario Zampi, 1960)
Boys In Brown (Montgomery Tully, 1949)
Boys Will Be Boys (William Beaudine, 1935)
The Browning Version (Anthony Asquith, 1951)
The Browning Version (Mike Figgis, 1994)
Carry On Teacher (Gerald Thomas, 1959)
Children on Trial (Jack Lee, 1946)
The Class of Miss MacMichael (Silvio Narizzano, 1978)
Clockwise (Christopher Morahan, 1986)
Clockwork Mice (Vadim Jean, 1995)
Cracks (Jordan Scott, 2009)
Decline and Fall (...of a Birdwatcher) (John Krish, 1968)
Dotheboys Hall (Alf Collins, 1903)
Downhill (Alfred Hitchcock, 1927)
Escapade (Philip Leacock, 1955)
F (Johannes Roberts, 2010)
The Falling (Carol Morley, 2015)

© The Editor(s) (if applicable) and The Author(s) 2016   247
S. Glynn, *The British School Film*,
DOI 10.1057/978-1-137-55887-9

Fear in the Night (Jimmy Sangster, 1972)
Fever Pitch (David Evans, 1997)
A French Mistress (Roy Boulting, 1960)
Fun at St. Fanny's (Maurice Elvey, 1956)
Get Real (Simon Shore, 1998)
The Ghost of St. Michael's (Marcel Varnel, 1941)
Girls, Please! (Jack Raymond, 1934)
Good Morning, Boys (Marcel Varnel, 1937)
Good Time Girl (David MacDonald, 1948)
Goodbye, Mr. Chips (Sam Wood, 1939)
Goodbye, Mr. Chips (Herbert Ross, 1969)
The Great St. Trinian's Train Robbery (Frank Launder, Sidney Gilliat, 1966)
Gregory's Girl (Bill Forsyth, 1981)
Gregory's Two Girls (Bill Forsyth, 1999)
The Guinea Pig (Roy Boulting, 1948)
The Happiest Days of Your Life (Frank Launder, 1950)
Harry Potter and the Chamber of Secrets (Chris Columbus, 2002)
Harry Potter and the Deathly Hallows—Part 1 (David Yates, 2010)
Harry Potter and the Deathly Hallows—Part 2 (David Yates, 2011)
Harry Potter and the Goblet of Fire (Mike Newell, 2005)
Harry Potter and the Half-Blood Prince (David Yates, 2009)
Harry Potter and the Order of the Phoenix (David Yates, 2007)
Harry Potter and the Philosopher's Stone (Chris Columbus, 2001)
Harry Potter and the Prisoner of Azkaban (Alfonso Cuarón, 2004)
Heavenly Pursuits (Charles Gormley, 1986)
The History Boys (Nicholas Hytner, 2006)
The Hole (Nick Hamm, 2001)
Housemaster (Herbert Brenon, 1938)
Hunky Dory (Marc Evans, 2012)
I'll Never Forget What's 'Isname (Michael Winner, 1967)
If.... (Lindsay Anderson, 1968)
The Inbetweeners Movie (Ben Palmer, 2011)
It's Great To Be Young (Cyril Frankel, 1956)
Kes (Ken Loach, 1969)
The Life and Adventures of Nicholas Nickleby (Alberto Cavalcanti, 1947)
The Loneliness of the Long Distance Runner (Tony Richardson, 1962)
Monty Python's The Meaning of Life (Terry Jones, 1983)
Mr. Perrin and Mr. Traill (Lawrence Huntington, 1948)
Never Let Me Go (Mark Romanek, 2010)

Nighthawks (Ron Peck, 1978)
Notes on a Scandal (Richard Eyre, 2006)
Old Mother Riley, Headmistress (John Harlow, 1950)
Personal Affair (Anthony Pelissier, 1953)
Pink Floyd—The Wall (Alan Parker, 1982)
Please Sir! (Mark Stuart, 1971)
Please Teacher (Stafford Dickins, 1937)
The Prime of Miss Jean Brodie (Ronald Neame, 1969)
The Pure Hell of St. Trinian's (Frank Launder, 1961)
The Romantic Age (Edmond T. Gréville, 1949)
School for Randle (John E. Blakeley, 1949)
Scrubbers (Mai Zetterling, 1982)
Scum (Alan Clarke, 1979)
South Riding (Victor Saville, 1938)
Spare the Rod (Leslie Norman, 1961)
St. Trinian's (Oliver Parker, Barnaby Thompson, 2007)
St. Trinian's 2: The Legend of Fritton's Gold (Oliver Parker, Barnaby Thompson, 2009)
Sunstruck (James Gilbert, 1972)
Take My Life (Ronald Neame, 1947)
Tamahine (Philip Leacock, 1963)
Tell England (Anthony Asquith, 1931)
Term of Trial (Peter Glenville, 1962)
Things Are Looking Up (Albert de Courville, 1935)
To Sir, With Love (James Clavell, 1967)
Tom Brown's School Days (Robert Stevenson, 1940)
Tom Brown's Schooldays (Rex Wilson, 1916)
Tom Brown's Schooldays (Gordon Parry, 1951)
Top of the Form (John Paddy Carstairs, 1953)
Tormented (Jon Wright, 2009)
Unhallowed Ground (Russell England, 2015)
Unman, Wittering and Zigo (John Mackenzie, 1971)
Vice Versa (Maurice Elvey, 1916)
Vice Versa (Peter Ustinov, 1947)
Walk a Crooked Path (John Brason, 1970)
Waterland (Stephen Gyllenhaal, 1992)
Wildcats of St. Trinian's (Frank Launder, 1980)
The Yellow Teddybears (Robert Hartfort-Davis, 1963)
Young Woodley (Thomas Bentley, 1930)

SELECT BIBLIOGRAPHY

Ackroyd, P. (1979) *Dressing up, Transvestism and Drag: The History of an Obsession*. Norwich: Thames

Aldgate, A. (1995) *Censorship and the Permissive Society: British Cinema and Theatre 1955–1965*. Oxford: Oxford University Press

Allen, R.C. and D. Gomery (1985) *Film History: Theory and Practice*. New York: McGraw-Hill

Allen, S. (2010) 'A French Exchange: Education as the Cultural Interface in British Comedies'. *Journal of British Cinema and Television*, 7, 3

Althusser, L. (1971) *Lenin and Philosophy and other Essays* (trans. Ben Brewster). New York: Monthly Review Press

Anderson, L. (2004) *Never Apologise: The Collected Writings*. London: Plexus

Armes, R. (1975) *A Critical History of British Cinema*. London: Secker and Warburg

Babington, B. (2002) *Launder and Gilliat*. Manchester: Manchester University Press

Baker, R. (1994) *Drag: A History of Female Impersonation in the Performing Arts*. London: Cassell

Bakhtin, M. (1984a [1963]) *Problems of Dostoevsky's Poetics* (trans. Caryl Emerson). Manchester: Manchester University Press

——— (1984b [1965]) *Rabelais and his World* (trans. Helene Iswolsky). Bloomington: Indiana University Press

Bamford, T. (1974) *The Rise of the Public School*. London: Nelson

Barber, M. (1994) *The Making of the 1944 Education Act*. London: Cassell

Barber, S. (2013) *The British Film Industry in the 1970s: Capital, Culture and Creativity*. London: Palgrave Macmillan

© The Editor(s) (if applicable) and The Author(s) 2016   251
S. Glynn, *The British School Film*,
DOI 10.1057/978-1-137-55887-9

Barnes, A.S. (1926) *The Catholic Schools of England*. London: Williams and Norgate

Barr, C. (1974) ' "Projecting Britain and the British Character": Ealing Studios'. *Screen*, 15, 1, Spring

——— (1977) *Ealing Studios*. London: Cameron and Tayleur

——— (1999) *English Hitchcock*. Moffat: Cameron and Hollis

Bennett, A. and N. Hytner (2006) *The History Boys: The Film*. London: Faber and Faber

Board of Education (1943) *White Paper Educational Reconstruction*, Cmd. 6458. London: HMSO

Bourne, S. (1996) *Brief Encounters: Lesbians and Gays in British Cinema 1930–1971*. London: Cassell

Braithwaite, E.R. (1959) *To Sir, With Love*. London: Bodley Head

Braudy, L. (1992) 'From the World in a Frame', in G. Mast, M. Cohen and L. Braudy (eds) *Film Theory and Criticism: Introductory Readings*, 4th edn. New York and Oxford: Oxford University Press

Brown, G. (1977) *Launder and Gilliat*. London: BFI

Bulman, R.C. (2004) *Hollywood Goes to High School: Cinema, Schools and American Culture*. New York: Worth Publishers

Burke, C. and I. Grosvenor (2008) *School*. London: Reaktion

Burton, A. (2002) 'Death or Glory? The Great War in British Film', in C. Monk and A. Sergeant (eds) *British Historical Cinema*. London: Routledge

Butler, J. (1993) *Bodies that Matter: On the Discursive Limits of Sex*. London: Routledge

Cadogan, M. and P. Craig (1986) *You're A Brick, Angela! The Girls' Story 1839–1985*. London: Victor Gollancz

Cartmell, D. and I. Whelehan (2010) *Screen Adaptation: Impure Cinema*. London; Palgrave Macmillan

Comolli, J-L. and P. Narboni (1977 [1969]) *Screen Reader: Cinema / Ideology / Politics* (trans. Susan Bennett). London: Society for Education in Film and Television

Crawford, P. (2002) *Politics and History in William Golding: the World Turned Upside Down*. Columbia: University of Missouri Press

Dalton, M.M. (1999) *The Hollywood Curriculum: Teachers and Teaching in the Movies*. New York: Peter Lang

Darlow M. and G. Hodson (1979) *Terence Rattigan; The Man and his Work*. London: Quartet Books

De Witt, H. (n.d.) 'Nighthawks', BFI. http://www.screenonline.org.uk/film/id/548405 [accessed 14 October 2015]

Deeney, J. (2000) 'When Men Were Men and Women Were Women', in C. Barker and M. B. Gale (eds) *British Theatre Between the Wars, 1918-1939*. Cambridge: Cambridge University Press

Duguid, M. (n.d.) 'Downhill', BFI. http://www.screenonline.org.uk/film/id/437747 [accessed 10 October 2015]

Durgnat, R. (1970) *A Mirror for England: British Movies from Austerity to Affluence*. London: Faber and Faber

——— (1974) *The Strange Case of Alfred Hitchcock*. London: Faber and Faber

Eco, U. (1984) 'The Frames of Comic Freedom', in T. Seboek (ed.) *Carnival!*. Berlin: Mouton Publishing

Edensor, T. (2002) *National Identity, Popular Culture and Everyday Life*. Oxford: Berg

Ellsmore, S. (2006) *Carry on Teachers! Representations of the Teaching Profession in Screen Culture*. Stoke-on-Trent: Trentham Books

Elsaesser, T. (1993) 'Images for Sale: The "New" British Cinema', in L. Friedman (ed.) *British Cinema and Thatcherism*. London: University of London Press

Fielding, M. (2005) 'Alex Bloom, Pioneer of Radical State Education'. *Forum*, 47, 2–3

Fisher, R., A. Harris and C. Jarvis (2008) *Education in Popular Culture: Telling Tales on Teachers and Learners*. London: Routledge

Fiske, J. (1987) *Television Culture*. London: Routledge

Garnett, T. (1970) 'The Interview: Tony Garnett'. *Afterimage*, 1

Gathorne-Hardy, J. (1979) *The Public School Phenomenon*. Harmondsworth: Penguin

Geraghty, C. (2000) *British Cinema in the Fifties: Gender, Genre and the 'New Look'*. London: Routledge

Gibson, I. (1974) *The English Vice: Beating, Sex and Shame in Victorian England and After*. London: Gerald Duckworth and Co.

Giroux, H.A. (2002) *Breaking in to the Movies: Film and the Culture of Politics*. Oxford: Basil Blackwell

Glancy, H. M. (1999) *When Hollywood Loved Britain: The Hollywood 'British' Film 1939-45*. Manchester: Manchester University Press

Gledhill, C. (2008) 'Genre', in P. Cook (ed.) *The Cinema Book*, 3rd edn. London, BFI

Goudsouzian, A. (2004) *Sidney Poitier: Man, Actor, Icon*. Chapel Hill: University of North Carolina Press

Grant, B.K. (2007) *Film Genre: From Iconography to Ideology*. London: Wallflower

Halliday, J. (1997) *Sirk on Sirk*. London: Secker and Warburg

Harper, S. (1997) '"Nothing to Beat the Hay Diet": Comedy at Gaumont and Gainsborough', in P. Cook (ed.) *Gainsborough Pictures*. London: Cassell

Harper, S. and V. Porter (2003) *British Cinema of the 1950s: The Decline of Deference*. Oxford: Oxford University Press

Harris, M. (2008) *Scenes from a Revolution: The Birth of the New Hollywood*. London: Canongate

Hay, I. (1914) *The Lighter Side of School Life*. Edinburgh: Ballantyne Press

Hayward, S. (1996) *Key Concepts in Cinema Studies.* London: Routledge

Hedling, E. (1998) *Lindsay Anderson: Maverick Film-maker.* London: Cassell

Higson, A. (1994) 'A Diversity of Film Practices: Renewing British Cinema in the 1970s', in B. Moore-Gilbert (ed.) *The Arts in the 1970s: Cultural Closure?* London: Routledge

―――― (1995) *Waving the Flag: Constructing a National Cinema in Britain.* Oxford: Oxford University Press

―――― (1996) 'Space, Place, Spectacle: Landscape and Townscape in the "Kitchen Sink" Film', in A. Higson (ed.) *Dissolving Views: Key Writings on British Cinema.* London: Cassell

―――― (2002) 'Cecil Hepworth, *Alice in Wonderland* and the Development of the Narrative Film', in A.Higson (ed.) *Young and Innocent? The Cinema in Britain 1896–1930.* Exeter: University of Exeter Press

Hill, J. (1986) *Sex, Class and Realism: British Cinema 1956–1963.* London: BFI

―――― (1992) 'The Issue of National Cinema and British Film Production', in D. Petrie (ed.) *New Questions of British Cinema.* London: BFI

―――― (1999) *British Cinema in the 1980s.* Oxford: Oxford University Press

Hilton, J. (1934) *Goodbye, Mr Chips.* London: Hodder and Stoughton

―――― (1938) *To You, Mr Chips.* London: Hodder and Stoughton

Hines, B. (1968) *A Kestrel for a Knave.* London: Michael Joseph

Hoggart, R. (1959) *The Uses of Literacy.* Harmondsworth: Penguin

Hornby, N. (1992) *Fever Pitch.* London: Victor Gollancz

Horne, W.L. (1999) 'Greatest Pleasures', in J.M. Welsh and J.C. Tibbetts (eds) *The Cinema of Tony Richardson: Essays and Interviews.* Albany: State University of New York Press

House of Commons Education and Skills Committee (2006) *Special Educational Needs,* Vol 1. London: Stationary Office

Houston, P. (1963) *The Contemporary Cinema.* Harmondsworth: Penguin

Hunt, L. (1998) *British Low Culture: From Safari Suits to Sexploitation.* London: Routledge

Hunter, I.Q. (2012) 'From window cleaner to potato man: Confessions of a working-class stereotype', in I.Q. Hunter and L. Porter (eds) *British Comedy Cinema.* London: Routledge

Jones, M. (2012) 'Unman, Wittering and Zigo', in J. Upton (ed.) *Offbeat: British Cinema's Curiosities, Obscurities and Forgotten Gems.* London: Headpress

Kardish, L. (1984) 'Michael Balcon and the Idea of a National Cinema', in G. Brown and L. Kardish, *Michael Balcon: The Pursuit of British Cinema.* New York: Museum of Modern Art

Kember, J. (2013) 'Professional Lecturing in Early British Film Shows', in J. Brown and A. Davidson (eds) *The Sounds of the Silents in Britain.* Oxford: Oxford University Press

Keroes, J. (1999) *Tales Out of School: Gender, Longing and the Teacher in Fiction and Film*. Carbondale: Southern Illinois University Press

Kristevea, J. (1980) *Desire in Language: A Semiotic Approach to Literature and Art*. New York: Columbia University Press

Kutzer, M.D. (2000) *Empire's Children: Empire and Imperialism in Classic British Children's Books*. New York: Garland

Lambert, G. (2000) *Mainly About Lindsay Anderson—A Memoir*. London: Faber and Faber

Landy, M. (1991) *British Genres: Cinema and Society, 1930–1960*. Princeton NJ: Princeton University Press

———— (2013) 'The Browning Version revisited', in R.B. Palmer and W.R. Bray (eds) *Modern British Drama on Screen*. Cambridge: Cambridge University Press

Laurie, P. (1965) *The Teenage Revolution*. London: A. Blond

Leach, J. (2004) *British Film*. Cambridge: Cambridge University Press

Leitch, T. (2002) *Encyclopedia of Alfred Hitchcock*. New York: Checkmark Books

Low, R. (1951) *History of the British Film, 1914–1918*. London: George Allen and Unwin

———— (1985) *Filmmaking in 1930s Britain*. London: George Allen and Unwin

Mack, E.C. (1938) *Public Schools and British Opinion, 1780–1860*. London: Methuen

Martin-Jones, D. (2009) *Scotland: Global Cinema: Genres, Modes and Identities*. Edinburgh: Edinburgh University Press

May, D. (1983) *Proust*. Oxford: Oxford University Press

May, J. (2013) *Reel Schools: Schooling and the Nation in Australian Cinema*. Bern: Peter Lang

McArthur, C. (1982) 'Scotland and Cinema: The Iniquity of the Fathers', in C. McArthur (ed.) *Scotch Reels: Scotland in Cinema and Television*. London: BFI

McCabe, B. (2011) *Harry Potter Page to Screen: The Complete Filmmaking Journey*. London: Titan Books

McFarlane, B. (ed.) (1992) *Sixty Voices: Celebrities Recall the Golden Age of British Cinema*. London: BFI

———— (1997) *An Autobiography of British Cinema*. London: Methuen/BFI

———— (1999) 'Jack of All Trades: Robert Stevenson', in J. Richards (ed.) *The Unknown 1930s: An alternative history of the British cinema, 1929–1939*. London: I.B. Tauris

McGilligan, P. (2003) *Alfred Hitchcock: A Life in Darkness and Light*. New York: Regan Books

McGillivray, D. (1992) *Doing Rude Things: The History of the British Sex Film, 1957–1981*. London: Sun Tavern Fields

Medhurst, A. (1984) '1950s War Films', in G. Hurd (ed.) *National Fictions: World War Two in British Films and Television*. London: BFI

Mietzner, U., K. Myers and N. Peim (eds) (2005) *Visual History: Images of Education*. Bern: Peter Lang

Miller, H.K. (2011) 'Remaining Days'. *Sight and Sound*, 21, 3, March

Morrison, D. (n.d.) 'Tom Brown's Schooldays (1916)', BFI. http://www.screenonline.org.uk/film/id/575267/ [accessed 28 August 2015]

Mulvey, L. (1975) 'Visual Pleasure and Narrative Cinema'. *Screen*, 16, 3, Autumn

Murphy, R. (1992) *Sixties British Cinema*. London: BFI

——— (ed.) (2000) *British Cinema of the 1990s*. London: BFI

Musgrave, P. W. (1985) *From Brown to Bunter: Life and Death of the School Story*. London: Routledge and Kegan Paul

Neale, S. (1980) *Genre*. London: BFI

Newman, K. (2002) 'Psycho-thriller, qu'est-ce que c'est', in S. Chibnall and J. Petley (eds) *British Horror Cinema*. London: Routledge

Noble, L. (1939) 'Goodbye, Mr. Chips! and farewell, England!'. *Sight and Sound*, 8, 29, Spring

O'Connor, S. (1998) *Straight Acting: Popular Gay Drama from Wilde to Rattigan*. London: Cassell

Orwell, G. (1970 [1940]) 'Boys Weeklies', in *The Collected Essays, Journalism and Letters*, 1. Harmondsworth. Penguin

Petley, J. (2000) 'The pilgrim's regress: the politics of the Boultings' films', in A. Burton, T. O'Sullivan and P. Wells (eds) *The Family Way: The Boulting Brothers and British Film Culture*. Trowbridge: Flicks Books

Petrie, D. (2000) *Screening Scotland*. London: BFI

Pines, J. (1977) *Blacks in Films*. London: Studio Vista

Quigly, I. (1982) *The Heirs of Tom Brown: The English School Story*. London: Chatto and Windus

Rattigan, N. (1994) 'The last gasp of the middle class: British war films of the 1950s', in W. Wheeler Dixon (ed.) *Re-Viewing British Cinema, 1900–1992*. Albany: State University of New York Press

Rattigan, T. (1985) *Plays: Two*. London: Methuen Drama

Renov, M. (ed.) (1993) *Theorising Documentary*. London: Routledge

Richards, J. (1973) *Visions of Yesterday*. London: Routledge and Kegan Paul

——— (1984) *The Age of the Dream Palace: Cinema and Society in Britain 1930–1939*. London: Routledge and Kegan Paul

——— (1988) *Happiest Days: The public schools in English fiction*. Manchester: Manchester University Press

Richards J. and A. Aldgate (1983) *British Cinema and Society 1930–1970*. Oxford: Blackwell

Richardson, T. (1993) *Long Distance Runner: A Memoir*. London: Faber and Faber

Rivette, J. (1985 [1957]) 'Six Characters in Search of Auteurs: A Discussion about French Cinema', *Cahiers du Cinéma*, 71, May, in J. Hillier (ed.) *Cahiers du*

Cinéma: The 1950s – Neo-Realism, Hollywood, New Wave. Cambridge MA: Harvard University Press

Rolinson, D. (2005) *Alan Clarke.* Manchester: Manchester University Press

Ross, R. (1996) *The Carry On Companion.* London: B.T. Batsford

Routt, W.D. (1994) 'Some early British films considered in the light of early Australian production'. *Metro,* Summer

Rowling, J.K. (1997) *Harry Potter and the Philosopher's Stone.* London: Bloomsbury

Russell Taylor, J. (1963) *Anger and After: A Guide to the New British Drama.* Harmondsworth: Penguin

—— (1975) *Directors and Directions.* London: Eyre Methuen

—— (1978) *Hitch: The Life and Times of Alfred Hitchcock.* London: Faber and Faber

Sandbrook, D. (2005) *Never Had It So Good: A History of Britain from Suez to the Beatles.* London: Little Brown

Sarris, A. (1968) *The American Cinema.* New York: Dutton

Schneider, S.J. (ed.) (2007) *100 European Horror Films.* London: BFI

Searle, R. (1959) *The St. Trinian's Story.* London: Perpetua Books

Seaton R. and R. Martin (1978) *Good Morning Boys: Will Hay, Master of Comedy.* London: Barrie and Jenkins

Shafer, S. (2003) *British Popular Films 1929–1939: The Cinema of Reassurance.* London: Routledge

Sherwin, D. (1996) *Going Mad in Hollywood—and Life with Lindsay Anderson.* Harmondsworth: Penguin

Silver, C. (2003) 'King and Country', in M. Mandy and A. Monda (eds) *The Hidden God: Film and Faith.* New York: Museum of Modern Art

Sinker, M. (2004) *If…..* London: BFI

Slide, A. (1985) *Fifty Classic British Films, 1932–1982: A Pictorial Record.* New York: Dover Publications

Smith, M. (1995) 'The War and British Culture', in S. Constantine (ed.) *The First World War in British History.* London: Edward Arnold

Sorlin, P. (1980) *The Film in History: Restaging the Past.* Oxford: Basil Blackwell

Stam, R. (2004) 'The Theory and Practice of Adaptation', in R. Stam and A. Raengo (eds) *Literature and Film: A Guide to the Theory and Practice of Film Adaptation.* Oxford: Blackwell

Stephenson, W. (1973) '*Kes* and the Press'. *Cinema Journal,* 12, 2

Sussex, E. (1969) *Lindsay Anderson.* London: Studio Vista

Sutton, D. (2000) *A Chorus of Raspberries: British Film Comedy 1929–1939.* Exeter: University of Exeter Press

Sutton, P. (2005) *If…..* London: IB Tauris

Threadgold, T. (1989) 'Talking about Genre: Ideologies and Incompatible Discourses'. *Cultural Studies,* 3, 1, January

Truffaut, F. (1978) *Hitchcock*. London: Paladin
Turim, M. (1989) *Flashbacks in Film: Memory and History*. London: Routledge
Walker, A. (1974) *Hollywood England: The British Film Industry in the Sixties*. London: Michael Joseph
Warburton, T. (1998) 'Cartoons and Teachers: Mediated Visual Images as Data', in J. Prosser (ed.) *Image-Based Research: A Sourcebook for Qualitative Researchers*. London: Falmer Press
Ward, P. (2005) *Documentary: The Margins of Reality*. London: Wallflower
Wells, P. (2000) 'Comments, custard pies and comic cuts: the Boulting brothers at play', in A. Burton, T. O'Sullivan and P. Wells (eds) *The Family Way: The Boulting Brothers and British Film Culture*. Trowbridge: Flicks Books
Williams, A. (1984) 'Is a Radical Genre Criticism Possible?'. *Quarterly Review of Film Studies*, 9, 2
Williams, M. (2006) ' "Come and have a bathe!" Landscaping the queer utopia', in R. Griffiths (ed.) *British Queer Cinema*. London: Routledge
Williams, R. (1961) *The Long Revolution*. London: Chatto and Windus
Wilson, D. and S. O'Sullivan (2004) *Images of Incarceration: Representations of Prison in Film and Television Drama*. Winchester: Waterside Press
Winston Dixon, W. (1994) 'The Doubled Image: Montgomery Tully's *Boys in Brown* and the Independent Frame Process', in W. Winston Dixon (ed.) *Re-Viewing British Cinema, 1900–1992*. Albany: State University of New York Press
Žižek, S. (2002 [1991]) *For They Know Not What They Do: Enjoyment as a Political Factor*, 2nd edn. London: Verso

INDEX

© The Editor(s) (if applicable) and The Author(s) 2016
S. Glynn, *The British School Film*,
DOI 10.1057/978-1-137-55887-9

CPI Antony Rowe
Eastbourne, UK
March 10, 2019

Gaidheal gu Chul

Rugadh Dòmhnall Grannd an Camus-chros an sgìr Shléibhte anns an Eilean Sgitheanach an 1903.   Dh'oileanaicheadh e an sgoil Dhùisdail, an àrd-sgoil Phort-rìgh, agus an Oil-thaigh Ghlaschu, far an tug e a mach inbhe *M.A.*   An déidh-làimhe choisinn e *Ed.B.* an Oil-thaigh Ghlaschu agus *B.A.* bho Oil-thaigh Lunnainn. An déidh bliadhna an Colaisde an Luchd-teagaisg an Cnoc-Iordain, chaidh e a theagasg an sgoil Cheann-loch-gilb an 1926.

An 1930 chaidh Dòmhnall a theagasg sgoile an Glaschu, far an do chuir e seachad an còrr de a bheatha gus an do chaochail e air a' cheud là de'n Ghearran 1970.   An 1936 phòs e Mairearad NicAonghais, de theaghlach a bhuineas do Shléibhte agus Eàrar an Cnòideart.

Theagaisg Dòmhnall an àireamh sgoilean air feadh Ghlaschu, agus dh'éirich e ceum air cheum gus an d'rinneadh àrd-mhaighistir-sgoile dheth.   Anns an inbhe sin bha e air ceann trì sgoilean móra, *Washington Street, Eastbank,* agus *Broomhill.*   Leig a dheth uallach a dhreuchd an 1968.   Bho 1951 gu 1954 bha e mar an ceudna a' teagasg nan clasaichean Gàidhlig an Colaisde Chnoc-Iordain.

'Na òige choisinn Dòmhnall cliù air a' bhlàr-iomain.   Bha e air ceann sgioba camanachd Oil-thaigh Ghlaschu agus chluich e an sgioba-iomain Sgitheanaich Ghlaschu. Fad shia bliadhna fichead b'e rùnaire, agus bho 1960 gu 1963 ceann-suidhe, Comunn Sgitheanach Ghlaschu.   Fad ùine mhóir bha e an ard-chomhairle agus comhairlean eile A' Chomuinn Ghàidhealaich.   Bho 1962 gu 1964 b'e fear-deasachaidh mìosachan A' Chomuinn, *"An Gàidheal,"* agus bho 1966 gu 1968 b'e ceann-suidhe A' Chomuinn.   Bha e 'na cheann-suidhe air Aitreabh nan Gàidheal an Glaschu bho 1958 gu 1960. Bha e 'na rùnaire, agus mu dheireadh 'na cheann-suidhe, ann am Meur Albannach Còmhdail nan Ceilteach. Bha e 'na bhall-comhairle aig an Urras Ghàidhealach, agus bha làmh aige ann an Comunn Oiseanach Oil-thaigh Ghlaschu, Céilidh nan Gàidheal, Comunn Ceilteach Ghlaschu, agus Comunn Gàidhlig Ghlaschu, agus, faodaidh e a bhith, an comuinn eile air nach 'eil lorg agamsa.

B'iomadh mòd aig an robh e 'na bhritheamh Gàidhlig. Gu tric aig mòd nàiseanta no mòd ionadail bhiodh e 'na fhear-stiùraidh air còisirean chloinne, a' mhór-chuid dhiubh 'nan Goill a dh'ionnsaich bhuaithe-san ùidh a ghabhail ann an ceòl nan Gàidheal.

Nach bu leòr sin uile a chum gach là de'n t-seachdainn a lìonadh? Ach bha Dòmhnall Grannd mar an ceudna 'na bhàrd comasach agus 'na fhear-sgrìobhaidh ealanta, mar a chithear anns an leabhar-sa. Aig a' mhòd nàiseanta an Dun-éideann an 1935 chrùnadh e mar bhàrd. An 1951 b'esan a choisinn a' cheud duais air son bàrdachd Ghàidhlig ann an co-fharpaisean Comhairle Ealdhain Bhreatainn. Aig Féill-dhràma Ghlaschu fhuair e dà uair a' cheud duais air son na dealbh-chluich Ghàidhlig a b'fheàrr, agus aon turus a' phrìomh dhuais mar an cluicheadair a b'fheàrr. Dheasaich e àireamh leabhraichean grinne Gàidhlig, le dealbhan, air son na cloinne, fo iùl A' Chomuinn Ghàidhealaich.

Fìor dhuine tàlantach nach d'rinn caomhnadh air fhéin, b'e sin Dòmhnall Grannd! A' cheud uair a choinnicheadh tu ris, shaoileadh tu gum b'e a bha ann duine sàmhach, sòlaimte, car diùid, ach le barrachd eòlais air mhothaicheadh tu gu robh fo'n aogasg sin inntinn bhreithneachail, gheur-chuiseach, eirmseach, le cridhe blàth agus le làimh chuideachail. 'Na dhealas agus 'na dhìchioll as leth nan Gàidheal agus na Gàidhlig bha e sònraichte.

Fhad is a bhios a' Ghàidhlig 'ga leughadh agus an leabhar seo air mhaireann, bidh cuimhne air Dòmhnall Grannd. Am measg a luchd-eòlais bidh ionndrainn air fad iomadh là.

TOMAS M. MACCALMAIN.

CLAR INNSIDH

SGEULACHDAN

Tir an Aigh

AM MEASG NAN CUDAIGEAN

Bha sgioba iasgaich againne cho math ri gin an Camuschrann.
Bha sin air a dhearbhadh an da dhòigh, an snas leis an do
làimhsich sinn am bàta, agus an t-iasg a bhiodh againn a'
tighinn dhachaidh. Chan innseadh sgiobachan nam bàtaichean
eile riamh dé na fhuair iad, ach bha a' chùiltearachd sin an
còmhnuidh 'na dhearbhadh dhuinn nach d'fhuair iad uiread ruinne.

Cho math 's gan cleitheadh na fir àireamh an éisg, cha b'
urrainn do na boireannaich a chumail aca fhéin, agus mar sin
gheibheamaid forfhais air an là-'rna-mhàireach. An corra uair
a rinn iad an gnothach oirnn, bha an triùir againne riaraichte gum
b'ann le seòrsa de bhuidseachd a fhuair iad làmh-an-uachdair,
agus bha an smuain sin 'na shòlas nach bu bheag dhuinn.

Chan 'eil math dhomhsa bhith ro abartach mu'n chùis, oir cha
robh mi aig an am ud ach 'na mo bhalach, an déidh tighinn gu aois
a bhith air mo mheas mar aon de'n sgioba mi fhìn. Bha deagh
bhàta againn co-dhiùbh ; bhuineadh i do Eachann Mór fhéin,
duine sgairteil aig an robh mór-chliù mar sheòladair is mar iasgair.
Bha e air Astràilia a ruigheachd iomadach uair. Chuir e Rudha
na h-Adhairc fodha barrachd is aon uair. Ciamar a dh'fhàg sin
e na b' fheàrr air iasgach shaoithean an Loch Chamuschrann,
chan aithne dhomh, ach chan 'eil teagamh nach tug a chuid
siubhail àite-sònraichte dha am measg iasgairean a' bhaile.

Mar sin b' e urram mór a bh' ann dhomhsa a bhith am bàta
Eachainn. Gu dearbh b' e sòlas do-thuigsinneach a bhitheadh
ann a bhith am bàta sam bith aig an aois ud. Nach e mo chridhe
a bheireadh an leum as, is mi ri obair na bochdainn ud, a'
bhuachailleachd, nuair a chithinn Eachann a' tighinn is na

12

fuaidreagan aige fo achlais, is a theireadh e, "A bheil thu a' tighinn ? "

Bha nì àraidh a' foillseachadh gum b' e Eachann am prìomh sheòladair anns a' bhàta againne—b' ann aige a bhiodh na slatan. Anns na bàtaichean eile chitheadh tu fear mu seach an dràsd 's a rithisd a' fàgail an ràimh agus a' gabhail speil anns an deireadh. Cha robh sin a' tachairt uair sam bith anns a' bhàta againne.

A nise, chuireadh an t-eadar-dhealachadh so friamh a' chòmhstri am bàta sam bith, oir b' e suidhe aig na slatan riamh an t-saothair a b' inntinniche na bhith fad an fheasgair air na ràimh.

Tha mi cìnnteach gun canadh am misionaraidh còir rium gu bheil feum anns a h-uile seòrsa obrach, agus gu bheil urram co-cheangailte ris an obair as ìsle. 'S dòcha gu bheil am fear a tha 'na thàmh a' smaoineachadh gur e fhéin as fheàrr air an stiùir. Tha sin a' ciallachadh, tha mi cìnnteach, nach deanadh am fear a tha 'na thàmh feum an t-saoghail air an stiùir. Bitheadh sin mar a bhitheadh, gun eas-urram sam bith a thoirt do'n mhisionraidh, bha mise an uair ud, agus tha fhathasd, dhe 'n bheachd gum bu chòir am fear a tha 'na thàmh greis fhaighinn air an stiùir, agus am fear a tha ag iomramh greis fhaighinn aig na slatan. Dh'fhàg am misionaraidh agus Eachann Mór tìr nam beò o chionn iomadh bliadhna, agus tha mi cìnnteach nach cuir mo bheachdan faoine-sa dragh orra tuilleadh.

A' cheud turus a chaidh mise a mach am bàta Eachainn Ruaidh, bha mi ro bheag airson iomramh. Bha mi 'nam ghiobal anns an deireadh agus greim agam air aon de na fuaidreagan. Gheall Calum Peutan dhomh, car le faoineis, mar gum b' e a ghnothach-san a bh' ann, nam beirinn air iasg gu faighinn dhomh fhìn e. Fhuair mi da liùtha bhrèagha, agus cha d' rinn mo chompanaich an aon mhearachd a rithisd.

Tìr an Aigh

Dà bhliadhna eile agus leig Domhnull Uilleim seachad an t-iasgach buileach. Dh'fhàs e fhéin no a bhean ro dhripeil mu obair na cruite, gus mu dheireadh an do sguir e a thighinn. Bha mise mar sin air m' àrdachadh an inbhe agus bha ràmh agam dhomh fhìn. An rud a bu chudthromaiche, bha m' earrann a' dol dhachaidh uiread ri càch. Mhair so seachdainn no dha. Bhon a chaidh leam cho math, carson nach deanainn na b' fheàrr ? Carson nach fhaighinn tac aig na slatan ? Gòrach 's mar a bha mi, cha robh mi a' dol a dh' iarraidh cead air Eachann Mór. Ach aon là, chuir mi mo chomhairle ri Calum Peutan. Bha sinn a' tighinn a mòine an Tota Chloiche. " Ni e deagh oidhche iasgaich a nochd," arsa mi fhìn. " Thu fhéin is d' iasgach," fhreagair Calum, " chan 'eil nì 'na do cheann ach iasgach."

A nise thainig e 'nam cheann-sa uair no dhà gum faodadh Calum sgur dhe 'n iasgach mar a rinn Domhnull Uilleim. Chuireadh sin a' mhì-shealbh air a' ghnothach uile gu léir. " Cha toigh leibh an t-iomramh," arsa mise, car mar gum bitheadh co-fhaireachadh agam ri Calum. " Carson nach fhaigheamaid greis an urra aig na slatan ? " Bha dùil aig Calum gum b' ann as mo chiall a bha mi. Bha aon aobhar agus da aobhar aige. B' ann le Eachann Mór am bàta ; bha e 'na sheòladair barraichte ; bha e èasgaidh aig na slatan ; bha e ris an obair fad nan ochd bliadhna a bha Calum còmhla ris. Ach cha robh Calum cho gorm. " 'S tu fhéin," ars esan, " a tha ag iarraidh greis aig na slatan."

A dh'innseadh na fìrinn, dh'iarradh Calum air mo sgàth-sa rud nach iarradh e air a shon fhéin, agus aig a' cheann thall, dh'aontaich e gun deanadh e oidhirp am feasgar sin fhéin nam faigheadh e leisgeul idir.

14

Sgeulachdan

Bha feasgar iasgaich air leth ann, deireadh reothairt, pìos lìonaidh aig seachd uairean, aidhireag de ghaoith an iar-eas. Chuir sinn a mach am bàta bho chùl Sgeir nan Caorach. " Tha deagh sheòl-mara againn a nochd," arsa Eachann Mór, is e a' cur a mach a' cheud slat gu sgiobalta aig ceann Eilean an Sgadain. Bha na coig aige a muigh mun d' ràinig sinn Port a' Chalaidh, agus chuir e a mach na fuaidreagan aig Sgeir na Ceàrdaich.

Thog e dà smalag aig Leac an Dùna agus aig Bogha na Seana Chreig bha iad a' gabhail cho math is gun tug sinn sgrìob eile oirre.

Cha robh so ro ghealltanach. Mar a b' fheàrr an t-iasgach 'sann a bu duilghe a bhitheadh e do Eachann Mór na slatan fhàgail. Chan e nach fhaodadh iomraichean raga móran millidh a dheanamh air an iasgach nam biodh mìorun fo 'n aire ; cha robh dad dhe 'n spiorad sin annamsa, gun tighinn idir air Calum. Dh'fhaodainn-sa gun teagamh buille a chall nam biodh an t-iasg a' leum air na slatan, agus thionndaidheadh Eachann le spochadh, " Cumaibh rithe, 'illean, cumaibh rithe."

Chaidh sinn timcheall Rudha an Tuirc agus ràinig sinn an Fhaoilinn. Cha b' fhada gus an robh an t-am againn tilleadh dhachaidh. Bha crochadh na poite againn mar tha agus greis iasgaich romhainn fhathasd.

Chunnaic sinn bàta Ean Ruaidh aig Rudha an Tuirc. Bha spàglaich neo-iomchuidh a' dol air adhart. " Dé an ùpraid a th' orra sud," arsa Eachann gu sgaiteach. " Tha Iain Ruadh a' dol a dh'iomramh " arsa Calum. " Mur a toir e 'n aire, bithidh e thar na cliathaich," arsa Eachann.

Bha sinn air ais aig ceann an Oib agus corra fhear a' leum air maghar fhathasd. " Dé tha ceàrr air ur làimh," arsa mise ri Calum, is mi cho mór as mo sheòltachd fhìn. " O, gheàrr mi ris an speal i," fhreagair Calum, ach bithidh i ceart gu leòr." " Gabhaidh mise an dà ràmh," arsa mise, rud a dh'fhiachainn ris cuideachd, nam b' e 's gun cuireadh am Freasdal a leithid 'nam char. Chaidh sud troimh chraiceann Eachainn Mhóir fhéin. "So," ars' esan ri Calum "tiugainn a nuas is thoir dhomh fhìn an ràmh." 'S gann a chreidinn gun robh e fìor. Rinn Calum beagan gorachail 'na sgòrnan, mar nach biodh e deònach a bhith air àrdachadh gu a leithid so a dh' inbhe. Bha mi dìreach a' smaointeachadh gun cumadh e air ro fhada a' diùltadh nuair a chunnaic mi a ràmh a' tighinn a steach agus Calum ag éirigh 'na sheasamh. "Glan," thuirt mise rium fhìn, "thig mo sheal-sa aig na slatan an ùine ghoirid, an ath-oidhch', 's dòcha, có aig a tha fios."

Bha an là a' ciaradh agus bha mise an dòchas gun tigeadh iasg an rathad Chaluim mum fàsadh e ro anmoch. Cha mhór nach do dh'éigh mi nuair a thòisich an t-slat a b'fhaide muigh a' crith agus a' bragadaich air beul a' bhàta.

Thog Calum i le sitheadh uamhasach. Leig e as i nuair a chunnaic e iasg air an ath té, agus air an ath té a rithisd. Chùm mi orm le buille shocair coltach ris an fhear stòlda a bha mu'm choinneamh. Thill Calum gu'n cheud shlat, ach bha an t-iasg air falbh dhith. Thog e an dara té. Cha chailleadh e am fear so. Chaidh an t-iasg seachad os ar cionn agus chuala sinn an sgleog a rinn e air an uisge air thoiseach oirnn.

"'Se rionnach a th'ann," arsa Eachann Mór, "gabh air do shocair e." Cha b'e an t-àgh a chuir rionnach an àite saoithein rathad Chaluim. Thog e slat eile. Bha na driamlaichean a nise air suaineadh. Cha robh dòigh air an toirt as a chéile.

Mu dheireadh thug e slat is driamlach is iasg a stigh, a' gabhail air a shocair. Bha e ag ionnsachadh mar tha. Ach cha d'rug an làmh cheàrr air an driamlach a' cheud turus. Chunnaic mi sealladh de rionnach a' dol seachad air mo lethcheann agus air an rathad air ais dé rinn e ach laighe gu socair air gualainn

16

Eachainn. Bha sàmhchar mhì-nàdurra anns a' bhàta. Cha do shaoil mi riamh roimhe gun robh am bàta cho cumhang. Aig a' cheann thall tharruing Calum an driamlach agus thuit an rionnach am broinn a' bhàta. Cha robh aige fiù is an dubhan a thoirt as. Air son nan slatan eile cha robh air ach breith orra ceart còmhla agus an slaodadh a steach do'n bhàta.

Ma bha na driamlaichean air an toinneamh roimhe bha an truaighe buileach a nis orra. " So " arsa Calum, " 's fheàrr dhuit fhéin am pasgadh, Eachainn."

Dh'éirich Eachann gun aon fhacal agus chaidh e sìos gu'n deireadh. Cha deachaidh na slatan a réiteachadh an oidhche ud ; b'fheudar fuireach gu solus latha.

Bha sinn a muigh ag iasgach a rithisd, sinn a bhá. Bha mi riamh de'n bheachd, agus cha chuir duine as mo bharail mi, gun do thoill Calum aon oidhirp eile co-dhiùbh leis na slatan.

A BHEIL A' CHOIR MAR A CHUMAR I?

'S tric a chuala sinn mu luach nan sean-fhacal. Gheibh an neach a sgrùdas na sean-fhacail Ghàidhlig gu h-àraidh luach a shaothrach, oir annta tha freumh a' ghliocais agus smior na fìrinn. Bitheadh sin mar a bhitheas, có am fear uair no uaireigin nach eil air a shàrachadh leis an neach a bheir dhut sean-fhacal a fhreagras a h-uile suidheachadh, gun ghuth gu bheil na sean-fhacail gu tric calg-dhìreach an aghaidh a chéile.

Faodaidh tu a bhith an cuideachd far a bheil feadhainn a' bruidh-eann a null 's a nall mu cheisd chudthromach air choireigin, abair ceisd mar so, am bu chòir dhuinn a bhith na bu chàirdeile ris na Ruisianaich na tha sinn? Tha cuid a' cumail amach gum bu chòir dhuinn cuireadh a thoirt do thuilleadh dhe na Ruisianaich tighinn a choimhead oirnn, agus cuid eile an aghaidh sin. Tha an còmhradh a' dol air adhart gu socair. Gun teagamh chan abradh tu gu bheil an luchd-labhairt a' dol a chur móran soluis air na cùisean air a bheil iad a' bruidhinn, agus chan 'eil an còmhradh a' dol a chur gnothaichean an t-saoghail mhóir an òrdugh. Ach tha iad 'gan toileachadh fhéin gun a bhith a' cur dragh air duine eile.

So far an tig fear nan sean-fhacal air adhart. "Cha tig," arsa esan, "muir-tràigh gun mhuir-làn 'na déidh." Tha stad obann air a' chòmhradh. Chan 'eil an còrr ri ràdh. Sgapaidh a' chuideachd, a h-uile fear a' coimhead mar gum bitheadh nàir air, aon chuid airson a bhith a' cur seachad a leithid de dh'ùine a' bruidhinn, no a chionn nach do smaointich e fhéin air a leithid de cho-dhùnadh dha'n chòmhradh.

Is dé a tha fear nan sean-fhacal a' ciallachadh air an turus so le a sheanchas? 'S cìnnteach gu bheil "muir-tràigh gu muir-làn" a' ciallachadh daingneachadh càirdeis. Ceart gu leòr, ach

nam b' e lasachadh càirdeis a bu mhath leis, bha e cheart cho
furasda dha an sean-fhacal a thionndadh mar so: "Cha tig
muir-làn gun mhuir-tràigh 'na déidh.

Shaoileadh duine gum bitheadh mi-rùn air fhoillseachadh an
aghaidh neach a bheir còmhradh gu crìch anns an dòigh so, ach
chan ann mar sin a tha. 'S ann a tha a chliù air a mheudachadh
gu mór a measg a chàirdean. Nam faigheadh e mar a thoill e,
cha bhitheadh càirdean idir aige.

Nach iomadh duine a bh' air a chlaoidh leis an fhear aig am
bi an duan "Tha a' chòir mar a chumar i." Ma tha so a'
ciallachadh dad idir, tha e ag ràdh gu bheil gnìomh no cleachdadh
sam bith ceart ma tha daoine 'ga dheanamh gu cunbhalach.
Dh'fhaodadh an ràdh so a bhith air bilean aon sam bith de na
slaightirean mu'n cuala sinn an eachdraidh; chan fhàgadh sin
e ach 'na dhroch chomhairle gu bhith air a cur mu choinneamh
sluagh an latha an diugh. Cha leigeadh duine sam bith a leas
fiachainn ri casg a chur air euceartan Mhgr. N., no Mhgr. H., no
Mhgr. K., 'nam latha fhéin le bhith ag ràdh riù: "Cha bu chòir
dhuibh sin a dheanamh," oir fhreagradh gach fear aca gu ladarna,
"Tha a' chòir mar a chumar i." Ma ghabhas sinne cuideachd
ris an t-sean-fhacal so, tha sinn aig a' cheann thall ag aontachadh
còmhla riù nach 'eil a leithid de rud ris a' chòir idir ann.

Tha comharraidhean àraidh air sean-fhacail dhe'n t-seòrsa so.
Tha iad goirid. Tha facail annta a tha a' tòiseachadh leis na
h-aon litrichean, mar a tha "Chòir, chumar." Bhitheadh an sean-
fhacal so a cheart cho pongail nan abradh neach, "Tha a' chòir
mar a chithear i" no "Tha a' chòir mar a chanar i," no rudeigin
dhe'n t-seòrsa sin. B' e a' cheud rud a chuir mi-fhìn an aghaidh nan
sean-fhacal, co-dhiùbh a dh'fhàg mi car amharusach mu'n fheadhainn
a bhitheadh 'gan cleachdadh, gun cuala mi gu tric 's mi 'nam
bhalach "Ceann mór air duine glic is ceann circ' air amadan." Bha so

Tìr an Aigh

a' còrdadh rium-sa taghta, oir bha mi a' toirt a chreidsinn orm
fhìn gun robh an ceann agam dhe'n fheadhainn a bu mhotha—
a measg nan sgoilearan. Cha do mhair mo shòlas fada. Thàinig cuideigin (bliadhnachan
an déidh sin bha amharus agam gun robh cinn caran beag aig
clann an duine so) agus 's e so a chuala mi, " Ceann mór air duine
glic, is mar as trice air amadan."
Cha robh nì na bu bhuailtiche na sud air droch-nàdur duine,
no balaich, a dhùsgadh. Dé am feum a bh'ann a ràdh gun robh
dà roinn an t-sean-fhacail so calg-dhìreach an aghaidh a chéile.
Ma bha e a' ciallachadh " Tha ceann mór mar as trice air amadan,
ach faodaidh tu fhaotainn fìor chorra uair air duine glic," carson
nach canadh iad sin ?
B' e a' bhuil a bh'ann dhomhsa agus tha mi cìnnteach do iomadh
balach eile aig an robh ceann os cionn a' chumantais gun d'fhalbh
sinn a' cnuasach am b' e uisge air an eanchainn no nì dhe'n t-seòrsa
a dh' aobharaich meudachd a' chlaiginn. Air an làimh eile chan
'eil teagamh nach toireadh an sean-fhacal anns an dreach so
misneachd do luchd nan ceann beaga, ach có a theireadh gum
b' e rud feumail a bh'ann dha'n càirdean 's dha'n dùthaich gum
faodadh iad-san a thoirt a chreidsinn orra fhéin gun robh iad na
bu ghlice na bha iad.
Tha sean-fhacal eile ann a dh'fhaodar a thogail mar eiseamplair
air a' mhilleadh a tha an seòrsa so a' dèanamh. So agaibh i,
" 'S i a' mhuc shàmhach as motha a dh'itheas." Tha am fear a
their so a' cur 'nad cheann ma chi thu duine sàmhach gum faod
thu a bhith cìnnteach gu bheil peacannan dìomhair air choireigin
air a shiubhal.
Cha tig air ach casaid a thogail 'na aghaidh mar a leanas agus
theagamh gun téid againn air na freagairtean aige a mheas, ma tha
dad de reusonachadh cothromach idir 'na chomas.

20

Ceisd—A bheil mucan air an roinn 'nan dà sheòrsa, mucan sàmhach agus mucan straighleach ?

Freagairt—Gun tuilleadh eòlais air mucan, chan urrainn domh a ràdh.

Ceisd—A bheil aobhar sam bith agad a chreidsinn gu bheil iad air an roinn anns an dòigh so ?

Freagairt—Chan 'eil.

Ceisd—Ged a bhitheadh cuid de mhucan na bu shàmhaiche na feadhainn eile, am bitheadh e coltach gun itheadh an fheadhainn sin barrachd air càch ?

Freagairt—Nam bitheadh ùine agam agus cothrom air leabhraichean ionnsaichte a sgrùdadh, dh'fhaodadh gum faighinn aobhar a chuireadh iongnadh ort.

Ceisd—Ach ged a chuir thu so as leth nam mucan sàmhach, cha d'fhuair thu aobhar fhathasd ?

Freagairt—Cha d'fhuair.

Ceisd—Ged a bhitheadh na thuirt thu fìor mu ainmhidhean an leanadh e bho sin gum bitheadh e fìor mu'n chinne-daonda ?

Freagairt—'S dòcha nach leanadh.

Ceisd—A bheil e 'na chleachdadh aig daoine a bhith a' beachdachadh air mucan ag itheadh ?

Freagairt—Chan 'eil aig móran dhiùbh.

Ceisd—Mar sin 's e fìor chorra dhuine a bheachdaicheadh, agus 's e fìor, fìor chorra dhuine a leanadh eiseamplair nam muc.

Freagairt—'S e.

Ceisd—Mur ith an duine sàmhach barrachd na càch, an e gu bheil an sean-fhacal a' cur teachd-geàrr air choireigin eile as a leth ?

Freagairt—Faodaidh gu bheil.

Ceisd—Ach chan 'eil dearbhadh agad gu bheil an duine sàmhach nas buailtiche do a leithid sin de mhì-stuamachd na bhitheadh duine deas-bhriathrach ?

FAISNEACHD CHALUIM BHUIDHE

Aon là fliuch as t-samhradh an uiridh 's mi air chuairt anns an Eilean Sgitheanach, fhuair mi cead rùtachd ann an ciste anns an robh seann phaipearan agus seann leabhraichean. Bha e furasda fhaicinn gun robh iomadh là bho nach tug duine sùil orra roimhe. Cha do ghabh mi an toiseach móran suim dhe na chunnaic mi, a bharrachd air an ùidh a bhitheadh aig duine sam bith ann an seann rudan. Ach an ceann greise laigh mo shùil air pasgan de dhuilleagan a bha air am fuaghal ri chéile le snàth geal ann an dòigh car cearbach. Agus ann an deagh làmh-sgrìobhaidh air an taobh a muigh bha beagan fhaclan ann an Gaidhlig.

Chuir so gu rannsachadh mi agus bha agam trì fichead duilleag 's a coig, an deidh dhomh an cùnntas, oir cha robh àireamh orra. Cha robh sgrìobhadh ach air an dara taobh dhe gach duilleig, an taobh ceart. Thainig a' cheud duilleag air falbh bho chàch nuair a laimhsich mi i, agus nuair a thug mi fainear gu robh nithean sònraichte ri am faicinn oirre, thionndaidh mi an fheadhainn eile gu faicilleach.

Shaoil leam gun robh litreachadh nam facal car neònach. Co-dhiùbh a b' e so an gnàthas litreachaidh a bh' ann aig an am a chaidh na paipearan a sgrìobhadh, no nì a thainig bho neònachas an sgrìobhadair fhéin, cha robh fios agam aig an ám, agus chan 'eil mi móran nas glice fhathasd.

Cha robh na duilleagan uile de 'n aon mheudachd. Chaidh cuid dhiùbh a réir coltais a ghearradh a pìosan na bu mhotha. Bha na duilleagan am bitheantas mu ochd òirlich gu leth am fad agus mu shia òirlich an leud. Cha robh sreathan-sgrìobhaidh air a' phaipear idir.

Le beagan saothrach agus móran tuairmse chuir mi seòrsa de

chiall air na faclan, agus an ceann seachdainn bha mi an déidh a dhol troimh 'n chuid mhór dhe 'n làmh-sgrìobhainn. Bha sreath an sud 's an so air nach b' urrainn dhomh breithneachadh tùrail sam bith a chur. Bha cuideachd feadhainn dhe na duilleagan air sracadh aig na h-oirean, agus mar sin bha an àiteachan leth-facail agus uaireannan facal slàn air chall. Air trì dhe na duilleagan gu h-àraidh bha sgallan buidhe mar gun d' rachadh stuth air choireigin a dhòrtadh orra. Bha an sgrìobhadh air na duilleagan so na bu tighe agus na bu làidire na bha e air càch, ach gu mì-fhortanach bha an làmh-sgrìobhaidh agus an litreachadh air na duilleagan agus air an fheadhainn eile a bha faisg orra na bu duiliche an leughadh na bha iad air gin sam bith eile.

Air taobh-duilleig a h-aon-deug bha sgall mu thri òirlich gu leth an leud. Thug mi an aire gun robh mu cheathramh de thaobh-duilleig a naoi nach b' urrainn domh a chur an Gaidhlig a thuigeadh duine sam bìth. Bha mu leth de thaobh-duilleig a deich mar sin agus bha taobh-duilleig a h-aon-deug, 's e sin an té air an robh an sgall, gun fheum uile gu léir. Bha dara leth taobh-duilleig a dhà dheug thar mo bhreithneachaidh agus gu h-iongantach, mu cheathramh de thaobh duilleig a trì-deug mar sin. An deidh sin dheanainn oidhirp chuimseach dhe 'n chuid eile gus an d' ràinig mi taobh-duilleig a sia ar fhichead, agus bha an duilleag so agus an fheadhainn a bha faisg oirre, air am milleadh air a' cheart dòigh. Bha a' cheart nì fìor mu thaobh-duilleig dà fhichead 's a h-ochd, an treas té air an robh an sgall.

B' e nì iongantach a bha an co-fhreagradh nan duilleagan sònraichte so agus an droch sgrìobhadh a bh' orra. Dh' fhiach mi ùine mhór ri aobhar fhaotainn carson a bha an da rud a' tighinn còmhla, ach dh' fhairtlich orm. Cha mhotha a thug duine eile dhomh aobhar leis am b' urrainn dhomh a bhith riaraichte. Thuirt

Tìr an Aigh

aon sgoilear Gàidhlig rium gu dearbh, ma 's e stuth air choireigin a dhòirt an sgrìobhadair air na duilleagan so, gum faodadh gun do chuir e uiread de dhorran air 's gun do chaill e comas sgrìobhadh cothromach a dheanamh. Dh' aontaich mi gum faodadh sin a bhith 'na dheagh aobhar air son milleadh na duilleig bhuidhe agus an fheadhainn as déidh sin, ach dé a dh' aobharaich milleadh nan duilleagan roimh 'n duilleag bhuidhe ?

Ach do-dhiùbh, cha shàraich mi sibh leis a' chòrr a sgrìobhadh mu chumadh nan duilleagan, ach innsidh mi beagan mu na bha sgrìobhte orra.

An toiseach bha an tiotal car mar so: " *Fàisnearnachd Chaluim Bhuige, air a sgrobadh le a mhac ann am Port Tiri anns an Eilean Sgiotach, mar a chall e o bheallan feu agus o a cho-cheird an deidh a bhauis.*" 'S e sin an Gàidhlig an la-an-diugh, " Fàisneachd Chaluim Bhuidhe, air a sgrìobhadh le a mhac ann am Portrìgh anns an eilean Sgitheanach, mar a chual e e o a bhilean (bheul ?) fhéin agus o a chàirdean (choipirean ?) an deidh a bhàis."

Tha e soilleir gur e bàs Chaluim Bhuidhe agus nach e bàs a mhic a tha air a chiallachadh an so.

Faodaidh mi beagan a ràdh an so mu chlaonadh eile a tha ri fhaicinn an litreachadh nam facal. Tha cuid dhe na litrichean mar gum bitheadh air an cur sios cas mu sheach, mar a tha " Culam " an àite " Calum." Gus na chuir sgoilear Gaidhlig solus dhomh air an litreachadh éibhinn so, chuir e dragh nach bu bheag orm, ach aon uair 's gun deachaidh an gnothach a mhìneachadh dhomh, bha e móran na b' fhasa cuid dhe 'n sgriobhadh a thuigsinn. Tha ainm fada Beurla agus ainm Gearmailteach cuideachd air an t-suidheachadh a tha ag aobharachadh an atharrachaidh so, ach 's e an t-ainm Gaidhlig as fheàrr a bheir mise air " Iomlaid Casadach." Tha iad ag ràdh gun robh na màthraichean an déidh

Bliadhna Thearlaich a' fiachainn ri toirt air a' chloinn sgur de bhruidhinn na Gaidhlige, gu h-àraidh ma bha saighdearan an airm dheirg faisg air làimh. Mar sin, bha na buillean a bha a' chlann a' faighinn anns an druim a' cur lididhean nam facal air iomrall orra.

Tha mac a' Chaluim Bhuidhe so mar sin a' cur sios mar as fheàrr a theid aige air nithean a chual' e athair ag ràdh agus cuid eile a dh' fhàgadh air athair. Cho-éignich a chàirdean e, tha e ag ràdh, so a dheanamh. Thachair cuid dhe 'n fhàisneachd aig Calum Buidhe ri linn a mhic fhéin, mar a b' fhiosrach e, agus mar sin cha robh e mì-choltach gun tachradh e uile.

'S e nì feumail a th' ann, tha e a' smaointeachadh, gum bitheadh na gnothaichean a dh' innis fiosraiche mar so ro-làimh air an cur sios air paipear, chum 's gum faod daoine ullachadh a dhèanamh fa chomhair nan tachartasan a tha romhpa.

Tha so 'gar toirt gu oidhirp a dheanamh air bliadhna an sgrìobhaidh a dhearbhadh, ma ghabhas e deanamh. Thuirt Calum Buidhe gun tuiteadh craobh mhór Sgèaboist an ceann dà bhliadhna. A réir an ughdair thachair so an taobh a stigh de chealla-diag bho 'n am a chomharraich athair. A nise, tha fhios aig na h-uile, gun tuirt an t-Ollamh Somhairle MacIain, 'na leabhar air a thurus a dh' ionnsaigh nan eilean, nach robh craobh ri fhaicinn anns an eilean Sgitheanach. Ach thuirt a charaid Boswell ris gun cual' e le cìnnt gun robh craobh chuimseach mór faisg air Portrìgh cóig bliadhna roimhe sin. A nise tha fhios againn air bliadhna turus an Ollaimh Mhic-Iain agus mar sin faodaidh sinn an sgrìobhadh so a chàradh anns an dara leth de 'n ochdamh linn deug.

Chan 'eil mise a' dol a ràdh gun robh Calum Buidhe 'na fhios-aiche cho math 's a bha a mhac ag agairt. Chan urrainn dhuinn a nise a bhith cìnnteach dé cho iomlan 's a bha e, oir chan 'eil fhios againn dé na nithean a thainig gu teachd. Tha e duilich

Tìr an Aigh

a ràdh co-dhiùbh dé cho geur-sheallach 's a dh' fheumas fiosaiche a bhith ma 's urrainn dhuinn a shuidheachadh an fhiach e a bhith air a dhleasadh mar fhiosaiche idir. Ach ma tha fhios againn gun tainig cuid de 'n fhiosachd gu teachd mar tha, tàirnidh sin ar n-aire a dh' ionnsaigh nan tachartasan nach tainig gu buil fhathasd.

Ach thoireamaid sùil air an fhàisneachd fhéin. "An diugh," arsa Calum Buidhe, "cha leig na Sasunnaich leinn ar n-éideadh Gaidhealach a chur oirnn, ionnan 's gu bheil móran dhinn air ar lathadh leis an fhuachd. Ach seallaidh na Sasunnaich do na Gaidheil fhathasd ciamar as còir dhaibh an t-éideadh Gaidhealach a ghiùlan."

Agus ann an àite eile. "A dhaoine mo chridhe, air sgàth nan Stiùbhartach bha sibh a' gleachd còmhla ris na Frangaich an aghaidh nan Sasunnach 's nan Gearmailteach. Ach an ùine gun a bhith fada bithidh sibh air taobh nan Sasunnach 's nan Gearmailteach an aghaidh nam Frangach, agus an déidh sin bithidh sibh a' cuideachadh nan Sasunnach 's nam Frangach an aghaidh nan Gearmailteach.

"Ach cha bhi cogaidhean ann gun sgur agus dé nì sibh an uair sin? Feumaidh sibh ur dùthaich fhàgail a cheart cho cìnnteach. Bithidh móran agaibh toilichte an tìrean céin agus móran deònach tilleadh. Thill cuid bho na cogaidhean. Ach cha bhi gu fortanach an aon iargain air ur mic gu tilleadh."

AN SGIOBAIR AIR TIR

Thainig an sgiobair dhachaidh. Anns a' Ghlaic Uaine cha b'e sgiobair a theireadh iad ris, ach " An Caiptean." Nuair a thuirt ball dhe'n Chomunn nach robh an sin ach facal Beurla, cha ghabhadh Domhnall an t-Srath' ris a muigh no mach. " Tha dithis no triùir de sgiobairean againn anns a' bhaile so," arsa Dòmhnall, " ach chan 'eil ann ach aon Chaiptean. Cha robh na sgiobairean ud ach air sgothan iasgaich, no sgothan samhraidh, no's dòcha puthairean guail." Cha robh de eòlas aig Dòmhnall fhéin air seòladaireachd ach gann na dh'innseadh dha toiseach bàta seach a deireadh, ach cha do chuir sin maille 'na chainnt. Cha robh na sgiobairean ach a' pollaireachd a measg nan sgeirean bho òb gu òb, a' cumail sròn a' bhàta air cnoc, agus a' toirt a chreidsinn air an sgioba, agus 's dòcha orra fhéin, gu robh iad a' leughadh na combaist.

B'e " An Caiptean " a bh'aca air, sean is òg, agus air sgàth na sìthe, feumaidh sinn a bhith leagte ris an droch Ghaidhlig.

Thainig an Caiptean dhachaidh gu clachan a sheann eòlais. Phàidh e a' chìs gu dòigheil aig an laimrig. Rinn fear a' chidhe othail gu leòr gun teagamh mu'n da sgillinn, barrachd, bha an Caiptean a' smaointeachadh, na chual' e bho'n fhear do'n tug e dà cheud not airson cead seòlaidh troimh an Suez Canal. Ach thug e sùil air a' chidhe agus chuir e a làmh 'na phòcaid. " So dhuit " ars' esan, " ma chuidicheas e an cidhe a chàradh, b'olc dhomhsa a bhith 'ga chaomhnadh ort."

" Cha toigh leam a choltas," arsa fear-a-chidhe a' coimhead suas ri aodann a' Chaiptein, mar gun sealladh e dha co-dhiùbh gun robh beagan eòlais aige air droch shìde. " Tha na faoileagan a' dol tuilleadh is dàna air talamh tioram."

27

Tìr an Aigh

Ach cha b'ann air faoileagan no droch shìde a bha aire a' Chaiptein. Anns a' bhus chaidh e thairis gu mionaideach air a h-uile ceum troimh 'n tainig e bho'n a b'fheudar dha drochaid bàta mór na smùide fhàgail air son na h-uaire mu dheireadh. Cha robh e aig an ám ud faisg air aois obair a leigeil dheth ach eadar teas na h-àird an ear agus fionnaireachd na h-àird an iar ghabh e a' cheud tinneas a bh'aige 'na bheatha, agus mun gann a fhuair e thairis air, chuir luchd-seilbh nam bàtaichean f'a chomhair gum bu chòir dha sgur a dh'obair.

Cha robh so idir ri càil a' Chaiptein agus cha do shaoil e gun robh e mar fhiachaibh air a bhith modhail riutha mu'n chùis. Bha deagh bharail aige air fhéin. Chaidh e gu muir nuair a bha e glé òg agus le a dhìchioll fhéin, gun mhóran ionnsachaidh no cuideachadh bho dhuine eile, dhìrich e bho ìre gu ìre gus an d'rainig e an drochaid. Fad na h-ùine so rinn e deagh chruinneachadh dha fhéin de dh'ionmhas an t-saoghail. Chaidh leis gu math cuideachd ann an innleachdan eile a bhitheas aig daoine saoghalta, no faodaidh e bhith, daoine glice, gu bhith a' leasachadh am maoin. A' seòladh troimh 'n Mhuir Mheadhonaich bhitheadh aon sùil aige air a' chairt-iùil, agus sùil eile air fiosan cabhagach mu phrìsean àraidh an Lunnainn. Feumar gun robh na sùilean biorach, oir cha deachaidh bàta mór na fichead mìle tunna riamh air iomrall, agus bha i an comhnaidh aig a' phort aig am a' cheud muir-làn.

Shaoil leis mar sin nach robh an so ach an droch dhiol, agus b'e a' bhuil a bh'ann gun do ghabh e a chead leis a' bhàta mhór.

Ged a bha an Caiptean 'na sheòladair barraichte, bha e eadar-dhealaichte bho gach seòladair eile ann an seagh àraidh. Tha e air aithris umpa-san gu bheil bean aca anns gach port, ach bha e fìor mu'n Chaiptean, a réir barail a chàirdean co-dhiùbh, nach robh bean aige an gin idir.

Chan e gun robh e 'na chleachdadh aige a bhith a' seachnadh nam boirionnach. A h-uile turus a bhitheadh speil aige air tìr, nam bitheadh e idir faisg air làimh, bheireadh e baile Ghrianaig air, far an robh a' chuid mhór de a chàirdean mu dheas, agus dheanadh e céilidh an sud 's an so. Gheibheadh e fàilte anns gach taigh, mar a gheibheadh seòladair Gaidhealach sam bith an déidh a bhith fada an dùthchannan céin'. E a bhith cuideachd 'na fhleasgach agus anns an ainm e a bhith car pailt de stòras an t-saoghail, dé an còrr a dh'iarradh tu ; dé an còrr a dh'iarradh mnathan Gaidhealach Ghrianaig ?

Ged a bha an Caiptean cùramach, cha robh e mosach. 'S minig a chòrd e ris dithis no triùir de na h-igheannan a thoirt leis do chuirm-chiùil no do thaigh-cluich'. Ach dh'fheumadh dithis a bhith aige co-dhiùbh ; anns na bliadhnaichean sin chan fhacas riamh e an cuideachd aoin té. 'S feudar gur iomadh uair, 's e faicinn fear an sud 's an so 'ga thréigsinn, a smaointich e air pòsadh, ach ma smaointich, cha robh an cuan an ear fada a' cur sin as a bheachd.

Nuair a sguir e a sheòladh, bha cùisean air atharrachadh. Ged a b'e sin a mhiann, cha robh comas teichidh ann tuilleadh ; bha an cuan an ear fada air falbh. Ach a réir coltais, cha b'e teicheadh a bha 'na bheachd, oir chaidh e a dh'fhuireach a Ghrianaig, far am bu mhotha an cunnart.

Bha gu leòr an sin a bha déidheil (agus faodar a ràdh, comasach) air comhairle a thoirt air anns an t-suidheachadh ùr anns an robh e. Thairg nighean a bhràthar gum fàgadh i an obair a bh'aice fhéin agus gun tigeadh i còmhla ris a chumail taighe dha. Ach, rud a tha a' foillseachadh nach robh an Caiptean dad na bu mhaoile air tìr na bha e air muir, thuirt e rithe, mas e cumail taighe a bha a dhìth oirre, gum bu chòir dhith a dhol a chumail taighe dha h-athair fhéin, a bha 'na sheann duine bochd a bha feumach air aire.

Tìr an Aigh

B' i an té a bha a' saoilsinn gu h-àraidh gum b'e a dleasdanas an Caiptean a chur for a sgéith, Bean Chaluim Mhóir, air am bitheadh e a' tadhal gu math tric. Bha i a' fuireach leis an duine agus aon nighinn am bràigh a' bhaile, agus thuirt i rithe fhéin gun robh fhios aice air an dearbh bhoirionnach a dheanadh deagh bhean do'n Chaiptean. B' i an té a bha 'na beachd Mairi Sheumais, té nach robh uamhasach sean no uamhasach òg, aig an robh seòrsa de chàirdeas fad as ris a' Chaiptean fhéin. Bhitheadh i an taigh Chaluim gu math tric. "Bu bhochd a rud" ars' a' bhean ri Calum, "gum bitheadh an duine còir ud air fhàgail gu a chead fhéin am measg na bhitheas as a dhéidh de bhoironnaich, is e cho tur aineolach air an dòghannan fad a bheatha. Chan 'eil fhios có a ghoirealais nighinne a dh'fhaodadh greim a dheanamh air air sgàth a chuid airgid."

Cho fad 's a chitheadh Bean Chaluim, bha gach cùis a' dol gu math Bha an Caiptean agus Màiri a' tachairt gu math tric anns an taigh, agus ged a thuirt Calum nach robh esan a' smaointeachadh gun robh Màiri cho iarratach air a phòsadh 's a bha Bean Chaluim, cha do nochd Màiri mì-ghean sam bith do'n Chaiptean.

Thàinig deireadh an fhoghair agus bha e a' tighinn faisg air oidhche mhór Gaidheil a' bhaile, an cruinneachadh bliadhnail. Chunnaic Bean Chaluim a cothrom. Rachadh an Caiptean do'n talla mhór agus bheireadh e Màiri Sheumais leis. Leig an Caiptean fhaicinn dhaibh gun robh e am beachd a dhol do'n chuirm, ach cha robh guth air Màiri no té eile a thoirt leis gus mu chealla-deug roimh 'n ám, agus có do'n tug e cuireadh do'n chruinneachadh ach do Shìne, nighean Chaluim Mhóir. Feumar aideachadh nach tàinig an leithid so an ceann Shìne riamh. Rinn i leisgeul leibideach air choireigin mu dheidhinn gnothaich eile air an robh a h-aire air an fheasgar ud.

Cha bu rud sam bith annas Shìne taca ris an tàmailt a bh'air a

màthair, nuair a chual i mar a thachair. Am b'e so na bh'aice
an déidh a sothrach ? Saoil thusa an robh an Caiptean a' smaoint-
achadh gur ann a' sireadh duine dha 'n nighinn aice fhéin a bha ise ?

Cha tug an Caiptean móran cothrom dhith gu dearbhadh dé
am fìor-rùn a bh'aice. Chan fhac e cruinneachadh no cruinneachadh air a' gheamhradh ud. An taobh a stigh na seachdainn'
thog e air agus bha e air an rathad chun nan eilean.

Chùm am bus air gu dìchiollach, a' tulgadh 's a' leum 's a'
seachnadh nan sloc a bu mhotha air rathad mór an righ. Thainig
an Caiptean a mach aig tigh a pheathar. Bha i 'ga choinneachadh
agus thug e an aire gun robh na faoileagan air a' chnoc. " Droch
chomharradh," arsa fear-a-chidhe. "Droch chomharradh cia air ?"
arsa an Caiptean ris fhéin. " Air droch shìde no air droch fhortan ?
Geasagan, geasagan ! "

Cha robh an Caiptean fada aig an taigh nuair a chunnaic muinntir
a' bhaile nach robh e am beachd fuireach fada còmhla ri a
phiuthar. Fhuair e bean, té nach robh dad na bu shine na Sìne
Chaluim Mhóir. Bha móran crathadh cinn a measg nan Glaiceach,
ach ghuidh iad uile sonas dha'n chàraid.

Thainig is dh'fhalbh bliadhna eile agus aon latha breagha
earraich bha othail mhór an taigh a' Chaiptein. Chuala e sgiamhail
agus cha b'e sgiamhail nam faoileagan. Bha oighre anns a'
chreitheil. Thainig na Glaicich 'nam buidhnean beaga is aoidh
orra a dh'amharc air an leanabh. " 'S e sgiobair a bhitheas anns
an fhear so " arsa bean Iain Ruaidh. " Chan e idir " arsa Dòmhnall
an t-Srath', abartach mar bu dual, " ach Caiptean."

Bha na faoileagan ag itealaich gu socair sàmhach a muigh os
cionn na linne. Chunnaic an Caiptean iad is e a' toirt sùil a
mach air an uinneig, agus có a chuireadh coire air nan saoileadh
e gun robh so 'na chomharradh math air deagh shìde, agus air
deagh chrannchur d' a fhéin 's d' a theaghlach.

31

AITHISG BHLIADHNAIL AN RUNAIRE

So an t-iomradh a thug Rùnaire Comunn Gallda Dhuisdeil Mhóir agus Dhuisdeil Bhig—no an t-iomradh bu mhath leis a thoirt—do na buill aig a' cheud choinneimh bhliadhnail—agus an té mu dheireadh.

"A mhnathan agus a dhaoin' uaisle, tha e a' toirt toileachaidh, gu dearbh *fìor* thoileachadh, dhòmhsa, a bhith a' cur mu'r coinneamh mo cheud aithisg bhliadhnail mar rùnaire Comunn Gallda Dhuisdeil Mhóir agus Dhuisdeil Bhig, Aonaichte.   Tha mi cìnnteach gun aontaich sibh uile gum bu mhath an ceum a ghabh na fògaraich a dh'fhàg Duisdeal Mhór, agus Duisdeal Bheag, nuair a chuir iad air chois an comunn ùr so an uiridh.

Tha cuimhne agaibh mar a bha na Gàidheil eile ud, mas e Gàidheil a th'annta, ag ràdh ruinn gun robh comuinn gu leòr anns a' bhaile so mar tha. A bheil iad a' smaointeachadh gun dì-chuimhnich sinn mar a rinn iad ruinn aig an céilidhean-san, a' coimhead oirnn uaireannan mar choigrich ; agus uaireannan eile, feumaidh mi aideachadh, mar naimhdean ?   Ciamar a b'urrainn muinntir Dhuisdeil a bhith riaraichte leis a' bhiadh—an dà chuid biadh spioradail agus biadh làitheil—a bha acasan aig an cuid coinneamhan ?   B'ann dìreach 'na am a fhuair sinn cothrom a bhith a' cruinneachadh mar so, gu bhith a' seinn òrain Dhuisdeil— òrain a tha fada os cionn òrain eile am bàrdachd 'san ceòl, agus a bhith a' gabhail da chupa tea agus da bhonnach mhilis an àite aon chupa agus aon bhonnach mar a tha aca aig na coinneamhan a dh'ainmich mi.

Nach minig a bha sibh air ur claoidh ag éisdeachd ris a' Ghaidhlig leibidich a bh'aca.   Rinn sinne anns a' chomunn so, gnothach mór ann a bhith a' cumail fuaran na cànain glan réidh mar bu chòir dhith a bhith.   A nise, tha mi a' dol a dh'innseadh dhuibh rud a chòrdas ruibh.   Bha mi a' dol a sgriobhadh òrain

do'n chomunn so. Cha robh de dh'ùine agam ach na chuir
crioch air a' cho-sheirm, ach an uair a dh'innseas mi dhuibh
gun tug mi ceithir-la-deug air, aontaichidh sibh gum feudar gu
bheil e math. So agaibh e—

> " Deagh shlàinte Dhuisdeil Mhòir
> Deagh shàinte Dhuisdeil Bhig.
> Ni sibhse othail mar as còir
> Is cumaibh càch gun diog."

Nach e an t-àgh a chuir 'nar rathad Ceann-suidhe cho comasach
'sa tha againne 'nar ceud dol-a-mach ? Tha fhios agaibh uile
dé'n t-ainm a choisinn e dha fhéin mar òraidiche, agus thoireamaid
meal-an-naidheachd dha mar a rinn e an gnothach air fear-na-
cathrach aig a' chruinneachadh bhliadhnail. Ghabh fear-na-cathrach da fhichead mionaid is a tri, ach ghabh ar Ceann-suidhe leth
mionaid a bharrachd. Sin agaibh ùine, tha sinn an dòchas, a
ghleidheas an t-àite mullaich fad iomadh bliadhna.

Bha seachd coinneamhan aig na buill fad an t-seisein — a
dha a' cluich chairtean ; céilidh ; céilidh is cairtean ; cairtean is
céilidh ; cairtean is dannsa, agus an cruinneachadh bliadhnail. Cha
robh e 'na chleachdadh thuige so a bhith a' cluiche chairtean aig
a' chruinneachadh bhliadhnail, ach bha innleachd ùr againne am
bliadhna a tha fìor ghealltanach. Thug sinn cothrom do fheadhainn
a bhith a' cluich chairtean ann an seòmar ri taobh an talla mhóir.
Cha b' urrainn dhuinn ach seòmar beag a thoirt dhaibh
am bliadhna, ach tha mi toilichte a ràdha nach do chuir an ùpraid
anns an talla mhór dragh sam bith orra. 'S dòcha, an ath bhliadhna,
gum biodh e glic an cruinneachadh bliadhnail a chur do'n t-seòmar
bheag agus na cairtean a chur do'n t-seòmar mhór.

Sin, matà, mar a tha sinne a' deanamh ar dìchill, an tomhas
beag, gu bhith leantainn dlùth ri cliù ar sìnnsrean an Duisdeal.

33

B

Tìr an Aigh

An co-fharpuis nan cairtean, eadar comuinn Ghlaschu, fhuair a' bhuidheann againne an dara duais. Nan robh barrachd de chothrom aca air cluich roimh-làimh, cha b'e an dara duais a bhitheadh aca. Bheothaich an fheadhainn a tha a' deanamh am beòthachd air cluich chairtean beagan mì-rùin anns na coinneamhan againne mar an coinneamhan eile, ach nuair a thainig e gu sabaid, thug sinn dhaibh cho math 's a fhuair sinn. 'S gnothach duilich a th'ann nach 'eil na fir cho ealanta ris na mnathan air an obair ghrinn so ; bhitheadh e iomchuidh sgoil-fheasgair chairtean a chur air chois gu beagan teagaisg a thoirt dhaibh. Bho nach robh móran aig an aon chéilidh a bh'againn, is dòcha gum bu chòir duinn cairtean a chur 'na àite an ath turus.

Tha sinn fada an comain a' phaipeir ainmeil sin. " Tìm nan Eilean " airson a' chòmhraidh thòcairich a bh'ann mun chruinn-eachadh bhliadhnail againn, agus gu h-àraidh a chionn gun do chuir iad sios àireamh air an àrd-ùrlar na bu mhotha na bha aig comunn sam bith eile ; chuir fear-nan-naidheachd aca sios móran a'nmean de fheadhainn nach robh air an àrd-ùrlar idir—nì a tha a' foil!seachadh an duine coibhneil glic a th'ann.

An lorg nan riaghailtean air a bheil an comunn so air a stéidheachadh, thug sinn seachad suimean airgid air a' bhliadhna so mar a leanas :—

Comunn Gàidhlig Dhun-éidinn (N.Z.)	£20
Mòd Vancouver	£10
Obair-coille Lochlainn	£5
Dachaidh Seann Daoine Dhuisdeil	£2
Gairm	£1

Dhiùlt sinn cuideachadh sam bith a thoirt do Chomunn Streupair-eachd a' Chuilthinn, a chionn gun do mhaoidh an t-ionmhasair againn aon uair eile gun tilgeadh e bhuaithe riaghladh an ionmhais

34

nan toireamaid dhaibh £25, mar a b'àill le cuid. Tha mi deimhin gu bheil rudeigin de mhathas ann an raigead an ionmhasair, nam bitheadh ùine aig duine coimhead air a shon.

Tha sinne cho dealasach ris na comuinn eile ann a bhith a' sealltainn do dh'òganaich 's do chaileagan mar a chaitheas iad na feasgair a th'aca saor, agus mar sin, chuir sinn air chois Buidheann Baidmeantan Dhuisdeil. Thaisbean iadsan do bhuidhnean eile mar bu chòir do'n chleas so a bhith air a chluich le cluicheadairean barraichte Dhuisdeil. Chuir sinn air bonn cuideachd Buidheann Ruidhlearan Dhuisdeil, Buidheanan Dràma Dhuisdeil, agus Cròilean an Dà Sheallaidh. Dh'iarr cuideigin buidheann iomain a bhith air a stéidheachadh cuideachd, ach shocraicheadh dàil a chur an so gus am fiosraich sinn tuilleadh mun chleas neònach so.

Fhuair an comunn so cuireadh iad fhéin a cheangal an dàimh ri comuinn mhóra eile, coltach ri Comunn nan Cruithneach, Comunn nan Crònan, Co-chomunn nan Comunn, agus mar sin air adhart. 'Se ar riaghailt-seòlaidh-ne sinn féin a cheangal ri comunn sam bith nach eil cheana ceangailte rinn. 'Se bhuil a th'ann gu bheil sinn ceangailte a mhàin ri Co-chomunn nan Comunn. Phàidh iadsan a' chìs a dh'iarr sinn, dà ghini: agus phàidh sinne dhaibhsan a' chìs a dh'iarr iadsan, aon ghini. Tha mi an dòchas gum bi ar beachdan an còmhnaidh farsuinn gu leòr gu ceadachadh dhuinn dàimh a bhith againn ri comunn sam bith air na cùmhnantan sin.

Tha fhios agaibh uile nach d'fhuair a' choisir a chuir sinn do'n Mhòd mhór an Dumfries a' cheud duais ris an robh dùil againn. Faodaidh mi a ràdh, gun uaill no guth mór, nach robh duais sam bith eile math gu leòr airson seinneadairean Dhuisdeil. Tha fhios agaibh cuideachd mar a thachair anns an rannsachadh a bh'againn an déidh a' Mhòid, mar a chuir muinntir Dhuisdeil Mhóir a' choire air muinntir Dhuisdeil Bhig, ag ràdh gun robh blas Gàidhlig Chelbhinside air an seinn, agus mar a bha muinntir

Tìr an Aigh

Dhuisdeil Bhig a' cumail a mach gun robh muinntir Dhuisdeil Mhóir a' coimhead air na breitheamhan an àite sùil a chumail air an fhear-iùil.

Le rùn tuilleadh còmhstri agus as dòcha sileadh fala a sheachnadh tha a' chomhairle a nis a rùnachadh gum bi dà chomunn ann an ath bhliadhna—Comunn Dhuisdeil Mhóir agus Comunn Dhuisdeil Bhig. B'ann fialaidh a bha muinntir Dhuisdeil riamh, agus chan 'eil e 'na annas dhuinne gun do rinn iad còrdadh càirdeil mu roinn iommhas a' chomuinn so, gun a dhol gu lagh m'a dheidhinn. Mar sin, bithidh an crùn a bh'aca air fhàgail air a roinn, 2/9d do Dhuisdeal Mhór agus 2/3d do Dhuisdeal Bheag.

Faodaidh mi innseadh dhuibh gu bheil a nise dà òran agam deas, òran do gach comunn. Cluinnibh an t-séisd:—

Oran Dhuisdeil Mhóir:—

Suas le Duisdeal Mhór
Sìos le Duisdeal Bheag
An strì no sìth am fagus oirnn
Cha tainig iad 's cha tig.

Oran Dhuisdeil Bhig:—

Suas le Duisdeal Bheag
Sìos le Duisdeal Mhór
Ge b'e raon 'sam fiach iad ruinn
Bheir sinne dhoibh an leòr.

Bu mhath leibh, tha mi cìnnteach, fios a bhith agaibh dé an comunn a tha mise mi fhìn a' dol a leantainn. Matà, ghabh mi cuireadh a fhuair mi gu àite a ghabhail mar cheud rùnaire comuinn ùir a tha gu bhith air a stéidheachadh an ath bhliadhna, Comunn Gallda Chamuschrois."

TIODHLAIC NOLLAIG

Latha Nollaig air tighinn mu dheireadh is Pàdruig Beag mu chomhair an diomhaireachd mhóir. Cha robh fhios aige ro mhath air a' mhadainn so co-dhiùbh a bu chòir dha a bhith sona no tùrsach.

Ged nach robh Pàdruig ach 'na naoi bliadhna seachad bha seòrsa de fhaireachadh aige gum b' e bròn a bha ceart is daoine 'ga fhaicinn. A leithid sin a dhaoine air ais 's air adhart chan fhaca e riamh roimhe. Bu chòir dha a bhith tùrsach gun teagamh is ise a bha coibhneil ris 'na laighe sa' chadal bhuan. B' e sin a dh' iarradh Iseabail, piuthar a mhàthar, air co-dhiùbh, agus bu shuarach an rud e ged a leanadh e a seòl-se aig a leithid de àm.

Chan e gun robh e gu math sam bith snuadh a' bhròin a bhith air d' aghaidh ma bha aighear 'nad chridhe. An robh e a' toirt a chreidsinn air fhéin gun robh e duilich? Cha robh. Bha e 'ga h-ionndrain gun teagamh, 's ann dha a thigeadh. Gu dearbh nan cumadh e air an rian sin cha b' fhada gus am bitheadh e fhéin a' caoineadh cho math ri piuthar-a-mhàthar.

Cha robh e a' dol a chaoineadh. Cha b' e mulad idir a thainig an uachdar oir b' e an sealladh mu dheireadh a fhuair e dhith sealladh ciùin sona, fiamh air a h-aodann nach fhaca e bho chionn sheachdainnean fhad 's a bha i air a léireadh le euslaint.

Cha b' e so a' cheud turus a thainig am bàs gu math dlùth do Phàdruig. Bha fìor-chuimhne aig nuair a chaill e a' cheud mhàthair a bh' aige, ged nach robh e buileach trì bliadhna nuair a thachair e. B' e sud an aois a thuirt iad ris fada an déidh sud.

Cha robh a' cheud mhàthair ach bochd mar a bha móran timcheall oirre an sràidean caola a' bhaile-mhóir. Bha an sòlas-an fhéin aig gach teaghlach a dh' aindeoin sin agus iad a' deanamh an dìchill gu bhith cho adhartach ris na daoine m' an timcheall.

Tìr an Aigh

Ged nach robh cuimhne réidh aig Pàdruig air mar a thachair 'na cheud dachaidh chan 'eil teagamh nach d' fhàgadh claisean 'na inntinn nach rachadh a lionadh gu siorruidh. Ciamar a thachair aig am na Nollaig is gun e fhathasd trì bliadhna a dh' aois? Bha na giobaill eile a' faotainn rudeigin bho phàrantan no luchd-daimh, agus bha Pàdruig cho dàna 's gun dubhairt e sin ri a mhàthair. Mar nach bitheadh a' bhochdainn dona gu leòr, thainig an tinneas 'na car. An robh e 'ga mhealladh fhéin, no an do gheall e dhi fhad 's a bha i 'ga aithneachadh, gun toireadh esan tiodhlaic Nollaig dhi cho luath 's a choisneadh e airgiod air a shon fhéin?

Ma gheall cha do sheas e dearbhadh. Dh' fhuasgail am bàs e bho choimhlionadh a' gheallaidh mun gann a ruith a' bhliadhna gu ceann.

Cha robh sin ach saoghal eile. Thugadh Pàdruig air falbh as a' bhaile mhór agus fhuair e dachaidh ùr. Ghabh Mairi banntrach Alasdair cùram dheth, agus ged nach robh i dad na bu shaidhbhire an gnothaichean an t-saoghail na bha an té a dh' fhalbh chan 'eil teagamh nach robh i saidhbhir an dòighean eile.

Thug muinntir na Glaic Uaine an aire cho piollach truagh 's a bha Pàdruig nuair a thainig e. Is gann a chumadh an deise ùr a bh' air, làidir tiugh 's gun robh i, am falach an gainne feòla air a bhodhaig. Thuirt iad riutha fhéin gum b' e an t-àgh a chuir an rathad e, agus gu h-àraidh an rathad Banntrach Alasdair. Bha fhios aca nach bitheadh móran air fhàgail aig ceann na seachdainn dhe na tasdain a bha i a' faotainn o'n Stàit airson Pàdruig a chumail.

Cha robh Pàdruig mì-thaingeil. Cha b' ann le briathran a nochd e a thaingealachd, ach le aghaidh aoidheil agus ceum aotrom. Cha robh an còrr a dhìth air Màiri banntrach Alasdair. Chaidh

Pàdruig do'n sgoil agus lean soirbheachadh ris an sin mar an ceudna.

Cha robh a' chlann eile mì-choibhneil ris, oir cha b' e so a' cheud dìlleachdan a chunnaic iad a' tighinn do'n Ghlaic Uaine. Bha balach an sud 's an so, agus corra chaileag cuideachd, a' tréigsinn seann eòlaich agus a' cumail astigh air a' choigreach. Rinn cuid spliachd dhe na bloighean Beurla a bh' aca agus moit orra gum b'urrainn daibh bruidheann ri Pàdruig 'na chànain fhéin. Chan e gu leigeadh iad a leas sin, oir bha Pàdruig ag ionnsachadh na Gaidhlig na bu luaithe na bha iadsan ag ionnsachadh na Beurla.

"Tha balach tapaidh an sud agaibh," arsa am maighstir - sgoile ri Màiri banntrach Alasdair aon latha Sàbaid is iad a' tighinn dhachaidh as an eaglais, "na bith c'àit' an d' fhuair sibh e." "Tha e sin," fhreagair Mairi, "cha deanadh mac na b' fheàrr."

Cha d' fholaich Màiri bhuaipe fhéin no bho Phàdruig sgeul nam bliadhnachan bho thoiseach. Is minig a bha iad a' còmhradh air a' mhàthair a chaill e. Theagamh gun do dhaingnicheadh am meas air a' chéile anns an dòigh sin na bu treasa na ghabhta dèanamh air dòigh sam bith eile.

Dh' fhàs na sgoilearan eòlach air Pàdruig; bha e mar aon dhiubh fhéin. Cha robh an latha buileach leis, oir dhùisg 'fhileantachd farmad an àite no dha. B' e Calum Mac-an-aba am prìomh-sgoilear mun tainig Pàdruig; b' fheudar dha a nise an inbhe ud a leigeil bhuaithe. An rud nach deanadh Calum astigh anns an sgoil, dh' fhiach e ri a dheanamh air an raon-chluiche. Cha do dhearmad e cothrom Pàdruig a chur air a dhruim-dìreach anns gach gleachd a bhitheadh ann.

Bha so na b' fhurasda do Chalum na bu chòir dha bhith, oir cha robh nàdur a' ghearain am Pàdruig. Cha mhotha a bha Mairi comasach air a chòir a sheasamh. Bha i strì ris a' chroit moch is anamoch agus nach b'e sin, a réir mar a thuirt na nàbaidhean, a thug an gaiseadh innte mu dheireadh. Cha robh Màiri idir gu math.

Cha do chùm an lighiche ainmeil fada i. Thuirt e rithe tilleadh dhachaidh agus gach cùis a réiteachadh eadar i fhéin 's a teaghlach. Cha robh sin ach a' chomhairle a bha aige, smaointich Màiri, do gach duine anns an h-suidheachadh so, gun fhoighneach dé an teaghlach a bh' ann no an robh teaghlach idir ann.

Bha Iseabail piuthar Mairi, aig an taigh 'na h-àite agus gu fortanach, ma bha sgeul air fortan, bha i comasach agus deònach fuireach còmhla ri Màiri. Bha Mairi aoidheil ris na h-uile. Shaoileadh tu gum bu mhath leatha a dhearbhadh nach robh i a' cur a' choire airson a cor air duine beò. Bha an latha a' giorrachadh. Mar a lughdaich an solus anns an speur, dh' fhalbh an solus a sùilean Mairi beag is beag. Bha fhios aig Iseabail agus aig na coimhearsnaich nach maireadh i fada.

Bha Pàdruig a' mothachadh gun robh a mhàthair glé thinn. Ma thuig e dé a bha anns a' bhàs cha do ghabh e air e. B'e rud a bh' ann a bha tachairt do fheadhainn eile.

Bha an Nollaig dlùth agus othail am measg nan sgoilearan fa chomhair a' chuiridh bhliadhnail a bha a' feitheamh orra gu taigh na baintighearna aig ceann shuas an loch. Bha Pàdruig còrr is naoi bliadhna a nise agus air teachd gu'n inbhe a leigeadh leis a dhol gu'n chuirm airson na ceud uair. Neo-air-thing sgeul dha-san agus do'n fheadhainn òg eile bho na sgoilearan móra a bha thall 's a chunnaic mu'n ghreadhnachas a bha romhpa.

Cha chuireadh nì, eadhon tinneas a mhàthar, an cruinneachadh so a smaointean Phàdruig. Thainig an latha roimh Nollaig agus thuirt Mairi ri Iseabail tràth dhe'n latha, "Bi cìnnteach a nise gun teid Pàdruig gu'n treut a nochd." Cha duirt Mairi móran an déidh sud.

40

Bha cuirm na Nollaig cho math 's a bha an t-ainm. Bha Pàdruig cho cìnnteach 's a b' urrainn aon de aois a bhith nach fhac e a leithid riamh agus nach robh e an comas duine nì na b' fheàrr a shealltainn dha gu bràth tuilleadh. Thainig Bodach na Nollaig agus shìn e do Phàdruig poca shaoiteas agus neapaicinn pòcaid. Bha na h-uile riaraichte agus thainig deireadh na cuirme. Chruinnich còmhlan beag na Glaic Uaine agus ghabh iad an ceum dhachaidh.

Sios an rathad còmhla ri Pàdruig bha Calum Mac-an-aba agus dithis no triùir eile. Bha cagnadh gu leòr air rudan milis ach thug Calum an aire nach do bhlais Pàdruig air a chuid fhéin. " Dé tha thu a' dol a dheanamh leis na saoiteas ? " arsa Calum ri Pàdruig. " Tha mi a' dol 'gan toirt dhachaidh gu mo mhàthair," fhreagair Pàdruig. " 'S tu nach eil," arsa Calum, is càch a' stad a dh' éisdeachd, " chan e do mhàthair a th' innte co-dhiùbh. Tha fhios againne glé mhath cia as a thàinig thu." " Tha mi coma," arsa Pàdruig, a' deanamh greim na bu dain gne air na bha 'na dhòrn, " tha mi a' dol 'gan toirt dhachaidh co-dhiùbh." Mhothaich am fear eile le mì-thlachd nach robh Pàdruig air a leòn cho mór 's a bha dùil aige.

Thòisich Calum a rithisd. " Cha toir thu dhachaidh iad. Thoir aonan dhomhsa." Leis a sin spion e am poca a làmhan Phàdruig agus sud na saoiteas sgapte air an làr mu'n timcheall. Dh' fhàg Pàdruig Calum a' cruinneachadh nan saoiteas agus thug e ris na buinn. Bha an neapaicinn aige fhathasd.

Bha dithis dhe na coimhearsnaich astigh còmhla ri Iseabail. Bha e furasda gu leòr do Phàdruig coiseachd gu fiataich agus bruidhinn air a shocair mar a bha iadsan a' deanamh. Nach b' e sin an cleas a bh' aige a nise bho chionn sheachdainnean.

" Dé th' agad an sin ? " arsa Iseabail. Sheall Pàdruig dhi an neapaicinn-pòcaid agus thuirt e, " 'S ann dha mo mhàthair a

41

tha e." Chaidh e fhéin is Iseabail asteach do'n t-seòmar gu socair. Bha Mairi 'na sìneadh 's a sùilean dùinte. Cha duirt aon seach aon guth. Chuir Pàdruig an neapaicinn fo na meòirean os cionn an aodaich agus chaidh iad amach air ais.

Bha Pàdruig air a chois tràth an là-'rna-mhàireach. Bha barrachd na b' àbhaist air ais 's air adhart, na h-uile gu stòlda, ged nach robh feum air stòldachd an diugh. Bha Mairi far nach cuireadh stroighlich an t-saoghail dragh oirre tuilleadh.

Thug Iseabail Pàdruig asteach 'ga faicinn. Shaoil leis gum fac e fiamh air a h-aodann nach fhac e riamh roimhe, agus bha an neapaicinn paisgte 'na laimh dheis. Dh' innis Iseabail gun d' rinn Mairi seòrsa de dhùsgadh feadh na h-oidhche. Sheall Iseabail an neapaicinn dhi agus thuirt i, " So agad tiodhlaic Nollaig bho Phàdruig." Thainig an aoidh sin air a h-aodann agus dhùin i a sùilean airson an uair mu dheireadh.

Bha Iseabail a' caoineadh. " Chan 'eil so ach Nollaig thruagh dhutsa, a Phàdruig a luaidh," arsa ise. Cha duirt Pàdruig guth ach b' e an sòlas, agus cha b' e am bròn, a fhuair làmh-an-uachdair 'na chridhe.

" BLIADHNA UR IS BEATHA UR "

" Cha toigh leam fhéin an solus ùr seo, Oidhrig," arsa Ean Ruadh is goillean aige a' lasadh na pioba. " Tha e ro-shoilleir airson taigh-ceilidh. 'Se an t-seann lampa fada a b' fheàrr." " Ma ta," fhreagair Oidhrig " nam bitheadh agad ri a glanadh 's ri cumail air dòigh mar a bh' agamsa cha chanadh tu sin. Tha an solus seo a fìor-chòrdadh riumsa."

" Seall fhéin an sgioblachadh gun tùr a th' ort an sin ann an oiseanan far nach fhaiceadh tu nì le solus na lampa," thuirt Iain. " Cha mhisde sinn sin dad," arsa Oidhrig. " Am maireach, latha na bliadhn' ùire, is feumaidh an taigh a bhith réidh, glan." " Latha na bliadhn' ùire ! Dé am feum a th' aig latha na bliadhn' ùire air an reiteachadh sin seach latha sam bith eile ? Chan fhaigh duine fiù fois gu smoc a ghabhail anns an taigh seo." " Fois, a sheòid " arsa Oidhrig, " mas e fois a tha dhìth ort thoir taobh shios an taigh' ort. Ma tha an solus a' cur dragh ort bheir sinn dhuit coinneal, bho nach eil crùisgein againn. Gu dearbh 's mi tha sgìth dhe'n phiob dhubh sin agad. Chan fhaigh mi fàileadh an tombaca dhe na cuirteannan gu siorruidh. Seall a nise, aig toiseach na bliadhna eile nach gabh thu fhéin bòid gun sguir thu a smocadh ? Agus an tombaca aig a' phrìs aig a bheil e ! "

" Ma sguireas mise a smocadh " arsa Iain, " sguiridh mi air latha ciallach. Chan 'eil latha na bliadhna ùire nas freagarraiche air son sgur no toiseachadh air smocadh na latha sam bith eile.

Gus a cheisd seo a dhùnadh, thainig Iain air tac eile. " Saoil có bhitheas againn an nochd ? ? " " O, tha mi cìnnteach gum bi an fheadhainn is àbhaist " fhreagair Oidhrig, " Alasdair is Seonaid as an taigh ud thall agus dòcha cuideigin as an iochdar. Aon rud cha tig an duine cunnartach ud, Domhnall, mac brathair d' athar,

43

as an Druim-ghlais co-dhiùbh," ars' Oidhrig. "O gu dearbh cha tig" thuirt Iain, "Bha iongnadh gu leòr air na nàbaidhean nach d' thainig e mu 'n am-sa an uiridh, an déidh a bhith tighinn cho cunbhalach airson cia-meud-bhliadhna? . . . . Deich co dhiùbh, no còrr.

Duine cunnartach, an d' thuirt thu? Chan 'eil duine 'san Druim-ghlais cho dòigheil ris an diugh, mar as math is aithne dhuit."

An sin fhéin chualas tartar aig an dorus agus thainig Seònaid Uilleim a steach. "Thig air adhart, a Sheònaid is dean suidhe" arsa Iain. "Cha leig mi leas duan iarraidh ort." "O 's iomadh gin a chuala mi" thuirt Seònaid, "agus a dh' ionnsaich mi cuideachd ach 's gann a chluinneas tu duan Calluinn aig firionnach fhéin an diugh."

Le seo chualas ceum a rithisd agus có a nochd a stigh ach Seumas an Iochdair. "Seo an dearbh dhuine a tha a dhìth oirnn" arsa Ian Ruadh. "Siuthad, a Sheumais, gabh do dhuan mun tig thu a steach." "Dé gheibh mi air a shon?" dh' fhoighnichd Seumas. "Coma leat" arsa Oidhrig, "chi thu sin mu falbh thu."

Thoisich Seumas 's an t-seasamh bonn:—

"Duan, duan a' ghille thruaigh a' siubhal sios is suas
Cha léir dhomh lias 's cha d'fhuair mi diar
'S mi muigh ri reothadh cruaidh
Ach tha mi nis 'san fhàrdaich cheairt
'S ann oirbhse ni mi luaidh
'S ma bheir sibh bonnach Calluinn dhomh
Chan ionndrainn sibh bhur duais."

"Glé mhath gu dearbh" arsa Iain. "Chan 'eil am fear ud uamhasach sean" ars' Oidhrig. "Suidh, suidh, 's gabh smochd" thuirt Iain, "bheir mi fhéin dhuit làn na pìoba."

" Tapadh leibh " arsa Seumas " seo an smoc mu dheireadh
dhomhsa. Tha mi a' dol a sgur dhe'n phìob am maireach." " Huh,
sin agad duine glic dhuit " as Oidhrig. " O a dhuine bhochd "
arsa Iain, " nach ann ort a thainig an dà latha ! "

Leis an seo thainig bràthair Seònaid, Alasdair Uilleim a steach.
Gun bhleid no brosnachadh ghabh e a dhuan gu socair:—

" Chaidh mi chùlaig an uiridh gu baile beag a' bhruthaich
   Ged chaidh mi nunn gu mall cha mhór nach d'fhan mi thall."

" 'S tu am fear as ait' a chì sinn ;
   Thuirt na càirdean nuair a thill mi
   Dé a dh' eirich dhuit 's a' bhruthach
   A chur aiteas air do ghnùis ? "

" Có a their nach dean mi fuireach
   Ann am baile beag a' bhruthaich
   Airson calluinn is bliadhn' ùir ?
   Ach ma tha an taigh seo fialaidh
   Le bonnach calluinn bi mi riaraicht'. "

'Cuiridh mi geall gum b' e Seumas a rinn am fear sin dhuit "
thuirt Ean Ruadh. " Chan e gu dearbh " as Alasdair " chan 'eil
aige-san ach ramalaigean. Cha toir duine bàrr air an fhear ud a
nochd, mur a toir Domhnull Sheumais Mhóir " arsa Alasdair.

" Mas ann mar sin a tha, cha teid bàrr air a nochd " thuirt
Iain. " Suidh Alasdair 's gabh do smoc." " Seo an smoc mu
dheireadh agamsa " asa Alasdair, " tha mi dol a sgur dheth am
maireach."

An ainm an àigh " lean Ean Rudh air " nach e fir a' bhaile seo
a th' air a dhol bhuaidhe buileach. Bòidean na bliadhn' ùire !
Chan fhad a mhaireas iad."

"Tha mi fhéin a' dol a sgur a dh' itheadh buntata air a a' bhliadhna
air thoiseach," arsa Seònaid Uilleim. " A bheil gu dearbh ? " arsa

Oidhrig. "Tha dùil agad fàs caol gu leòr airson fasanan J. D. Williams. Ach tha eagal ormsa gu bheil thu sia miosan ro fhada gun toiseachadh."

Chualas guth Sheumais. "Tha thu a' toirt 'nam chuimhne Mairi piuthair m' athar. Thuirt ise nach robh i a' dol a dh' itheadh ach càl air a' cheud latha dhe'n mhios as déidh siud. Bha i cho math ri a gealladh. Cha do dh' ith i ach càl air a' cheud latha dhe'n ath mhios, ach cha robh guth air an seòrsa trasgaidh ud air a' chuid eile dhe'n mhios."

"Ma ta" arsa Ean Ruadh, "is smùid aig air a' phìob mar gum bitheadh e a' toirt dùbhlain do na bha làthair. "Innsidh mise dhuibh dé thachair do fhear a rinn bòidean aig am na bliadhn' ùire."

Shocraich na céileadairean iad fhéin aig an teine, teine mór mòna, aon rud nach robh an cunnart dol a fasan, is an gual a' phrìs a bha e. "Bha cuid agaibh" thuirt Ian, "a' foighneachd mu Dhomhnall Sheumais Mhóir, mac bràthair m' athar anns an Druimghlais. Ach tha cuimhne agam air nuair a bha e 'na bhalach. Bha dùil agamsa gun robh clann a' bhaile seo olc; (chan 'eil mi a' coimhead ortsa a Sheumais) ach cha robh peasan 'nam measg riamh coltach ri Domhnull. Bhitheadh spòrs againn uile air Oidhche Shamhna, ach bha leithid Oidhche Shamhna aig Domhnull dha fhéin an dràsda 'sa rithisd fad na bliahdna. A nise, ged a bha e 'na thoirmeasg, cha robh cron ann mar sin agus cha robh neach air an robh barrachd meas aig beag is mór. Bhitheadh cuid is truas aca ri a mhàthair is i air a fàgail 'na bantraich le dithis ghillean.

Ach an fheadhainn a bha a stigh air a' chùis, bha fhios aca nach robh i a' faicinn cron an t-saoghail an Domhnall, agus gum b'e fada a bu mheasaile aice na a bhràthair, Calum, gille stòlda modhail. Thug Alasdair Uilleim fanear san dol seachad gum bu tric a thachair a cheart rud ann an teaghlach. Coimhead am mac stròigheil, mar a rinn e, agus an othail a rinn athair ris nuair a thill e. "Nach e sin" arsa Seumas an Iochdair, "ta nan robh mise an àite bràthair a' mhic stroigeil, bha mi air deagh fhùicean a thoirt air airson fuireach air falbh cho fada." "Siuthad, siuthad, a Sheumais" lean Ean Ruadh air, "thoir thusa an aire nach bi thu fhéin air taobh a muigh an doruis nuair a bhitheas ròic an laoigh bhiathta air a' bhòrd."

Tha cuid de'n bheachd gur fheàrr do dhaoine gach droch-bheairt a th' unnta a chur an céill nuair a tha iad òg, a' creidsinn gum faigh am bodhaigean cuidhte is e mun tig iad gu aois. A reir Ean Ruaidh, cha b' ann mar sin a thachair do Dhomhnall còir. Dh' fhalbh a mhàthair agus cha b' fheàirrd e sin ged nach do chùm i móran rian air fhad 's a bha i an tìr nam beò. "Nan robh e air pòsadh" arsa Oidhrig. "Cha do phòs" arsa Iain, "dh' fhuirich e an sud air a' chroit comhla ri Calum."

"Có a phòsadh fear dhe'n t-seòrsa sin?" arsa Seonaid Uilleim. "'S iomadh té sin" fhreagair Ean Ruadh, "ach iad a dh' fhaotain a' chothroim. 'S iad na boirionnaich a bha measail air." "Gheibh foighidinn furtachd 's gheibh trusdar bean," sean-fhocal mar bu dual bho Sheumas an Iochdair anns an robh géiread fhaclan gun mhóran brìgh.

"O cha b'e trusdar a bh' ann idir," bho Ean Ruadh. "Droch bhall 's docha. Bha tomhas de dhroch nàdur ann da-rìreadh no ma b' fhior cuideachd. Bha e leisg gun teagamh sam bith. Leigidh e le Calum eirigh a fhrithealadh air a' chrodh a h-uile maduinn 's e fhéin a' cadal orra. Gun teagamh rachadh e corra latha a dh' iarraidh cliabh mòna, ach b'e na cruachan a b' fhaisge a b' fheàrr leis na a' mhòine aige fhéin. Cha chreid mi gun canadh tu meirle ris—cha robh ann ach seòrsa de spòrs a bh aige dha fhéin."

"Cha b'e spòrs a theireadh tu ris nam b'e do mhòine fhéin a

bh' ann " arsa Seònaid Uilleim. " O chan 'eil fhios agam " arsa Iain " bha iad uile cho eòlach air. Bha e a' toirt aobhar bruidhne dhaibh 's gan cumail air an dòigh. 'Se glé bheag a bha a' talach mu'n mhòine ged nach canadh iad sin ri aodann."

" Nach bochd nach robh leth-ghloic dhe'n t-seòrsa sin againn anns a' Ghlaic Uaine " arsa Alasdair Uilleim. " Nach' eil Seumas an Iochdair againn " arsa Seònaid. " Air do shocair " arsa Seumas " a bheil thu a' cur as mo leth-sa gur e mòine chàich a tha mi a' losgadh ? Ach ma nì e spòrs sam bith dhuibh, tha mise deònach air toiseachadh air a' mhòine agaibh am maireach. Tha mi coma co-dhiùbh a their sibh leth-ghloic rium no nach abair an deidh sin."

" Cha teid mi leibh le leth-ghloic nas mo na chaidh mi le trusdar " arsa Ean Ruadh. Co-dhiùbh siud mar a bha Domhnull gu mu dha bhliadhna an ama-sa. Tha cuimhne agaibh air fhaicinn an seo an Oidhche Chulaig ud. Nuair a dh' fhàg e seo bha a cho togarrach, aighearrach 'sa chunnaic sibh riamh e. Ach dh' eirich rud-eigin dha eadar sin is la-'rna-mhaireach.

B'e Calum a mhothaich do an neònachas an toiseach agus cha bu bheag an t-eagal a chuir e air. Dé rinn Domhnull ach eirigh aig sia uairean 'sa mhaduinn agus tarruing a thoirt air obair a stigh 's a muigh.

A nise, cha do chord seo ri Calum idir. Bha e a' reusonachadh ris fhéin gum bu chòir dha a bhith toilichte leis an atharrachadh a thainig air Domhnull, ach bha na faclan molaidh a' stad 'na amhaich, agus air gum b'e càineadh air an tòisicheadh e 's ann a dh' fhan e sàmhach uile gu léir. Tha Calum a nise, tha mi cluinntinn a' bruidhinn air an taigh fhàgail aig Dhomhnull dha fhéin. Agus a bheil fhios agaibhse, bha muinntir an àite a cheart cho diombach de Dhomhnull 'sa bha Calum, nuair a chunnaic iad mar a thachair.

" Ach dé air an t-saoghal a thug an t-atharrachadh air Domhnull ann an ùine cho goirid ? " dh' fhoighnich Seònaid Uilleim. " Litir a fhuair e bho dheas, bha cuideigin ag ràdh " arsa Oidhrig. " 'S dòcha gum b'e taibhse a chunnaic e air an rathad dhachaidh," thuirt Seumas an Iochdair. " Chan e na taibhse " arsa Ean Ruadh " tha thu fhéin a' dol a sgur a smocadh A Sheumais, 's chan fhac thu taibhse no taibhse. Cha d' thainig air dìreach ach na bòidean a bhitheas daoine a deanamh mu am na bliadhn' ùire."

" Se a' cheisd as cudthromaiche ormsa " arsa Alasdair Uilleim " dé thug air an t-sluagh tionndadh 'na aghaidh." " Ma ta " fhreagair Ean Ruadh " chan 'eil sin cho duilich a thuigsinn 'sa shaoileadh tu."

" An d' thug thusa an aire gu bheil e a' deanamh feum mór do dhaoine ma tha fear 'nam measg a tha iad a' smaointeachadh a tha nas miosa na iad fhéin ? Tha e a' toirt barail mhath dhaibh orra fhéin. A bharrachd air a bhith 'na chuis-abhachdais do dhaoine aig nach' eil cuir-seachad a' bhaile-mhóir. Tha e a' cordadh riu a bhith faicinn duine mar seo a'deanamh cuid dhe na h-euchdan cunnartach a bu mhath leo fhéin a dheanamh, nam bhitheadh am misneachd 's an cothrom aca. Nuair a chaill Domhnull, ma ta, a chàil do'n dol-air-adhart chunnartach ud, chaill e a chàirdean aig a cheart am."

" Agus innsidh an duine innleachdach agamsa dhuibh, tha mi deimhinn " arsa Oidhrig, " gum b'e bòidean a rinn Domhnall Sheumais Mhóir aig am na bliadhn' ùire a dh' fhàg an diugh gun charaid e anns an Druim Ghlais."

" A nise," thainig Iain, " cha toigh leam duine eile a bhith a' cur faclan 'na mo bhial. Cha d' thuirt mi sin idir, ach tha mi ag ràdh ruibh gu bheil leithid Dhomhnuill Sheumais Mhoir nas luachmhoire do bhaile na shaoileadh sibh air a' cheud shealladh."

" Tha mi'n dòchas " arsa Seònaid Uilleim " nach eil Seumas an seo a' dol a thoirt leum as mar a rinn Domhnall Sheumais Mhóir. Mo thruaighe am baile-sa ma chailleas sinn ar cuis-àbhachdais."

49

Tìr an Aigh

" 'S aithne dhomhsa feadhainn " arsa Seumas " nach cuireadh droch fheum air leum a thoirt asda agus mar bu luaithe 'se b' fheàrr."

" Deanadh iad mar a thogras iad " arsa Ean Ruadh " fhad 's nach iarr iad ormsa sgur a smocadh Latha na Bliadhn' Uire no latha eile."

"AN GAMHAINN"

Bha muinntir na Glaic Uaine cho còirte am measg a' chéile 's a gheibheadh tu anns an Eilean Leitheann. Cha robh iad uile gu léir iomlan agus 's ann mar sin a bu mhath leinn iad, oir 'nuair a chì sinn daoine a' fàs iomlan bithidh eagal oirnn nach bi iad fada comhla ruinn anns an t-saoghal seo. Mar sin, na cuireadh e annas oirnn ged a chitheamaid feadhainn an dràsda 's a rithisd anns a' Ghlaic Uaine aig am bitheadh farmad ri a chéile. Bha dìreach uiread de dh' fharmad air am feadh 's a dh' fhàg iad car saoghalta coltach ruinn fhìn. Nam bitheadh iad na bu choimhlionta, bhitheamaid mi-chomhfhurtail 'nan cuideachd. Air an laimh eile, nam bitheadh iad na bu mhiosa, cha bu mhath leinn ar càirdean a bhith faicinn gu robh gnothuch sam bith againn riutha.

Gun teagamh chan 'eil am farmad fhéin cho olc 's a shaoileadh tu, oir tha an sean-fhacal ag radh gur e am farmad a nì an treabhadh. A nise cha robh an treabhadh riamh air a mheas cho luachmhor is a tha e an diugh, agus ged a b' e farmad fhéin a phrìs, có a theireadh gu robh e tuilleadh is daor aig a sin?

Mar a nì farmad air an treabhadh, ni e air rudan eile. Anns a' Ghlaic Uaine gu sònruichte chuir e adhartas air na gamhna, adhartas anns a h-uile doigh, an àirde, am fad, an leud, agus gu h-àraidh an dreach. Ma tha sibh dhe'n bheachd nach urrainn dreach a bhith air gamhainn, nach 'eil aon ghamhainn ach mar ghamhainn eile agus iad uile mì-dhreachmhor, tha eagal orm gu bheil raointean farsuing am mac-meanmain muinntir na Glaic Uaine nach do shiubhail sibh riamh. Leigibh ruith le bhur n-inntinnean car tacain agus tuigidh sibh an luach a bha na Glaicich a' cur air na gamhna. Bha iad a' meas cuid dhiubh bòidheach, cuid meadhonach, agus feadhainn eile car mì-thlachdmhor. Ach

51

Tìr an Aigh

an gnùis a h-uile gamhainn bha rudeigin tùrail suidhichte a bha
a' cur luach air anns an àite mar ainmhidh aig an robh toinisg—
chan e beathach faoin coltach ri caora no creutair gun eanchainn
mar a tha cearc. Chan fhaca duine riamh coltas faoineis air
aodann gamhainn, oir dh' fheumadh duine a bhith fìor éibhinn
mu'n abramaid m'a dhéidh "Bheireadh e gàire air gamhainn."

Bha cothrom gu leòir aig na Glaicich air eòlas a bhith aca
air na gamhna, an cruth, an gnè, is an dol-air-adhart. Bha móran
an crochadh air a' ghamhainn agus nithean cudthromach gu tric
a' feitheamh air am a reic. Bhrògan ùra do'n fhear bheag a' dol
do'n sgoil, ad ùr do bhean an tighe air son a' chomanachaidh,
prìs a thuruis do'n òganach a' feitheamh gu an-fhoiseil gu tighinn
dachaidh as a' Cholaisde. Mar sin bha an croitear air a mheas
an tomhas mór 'na dhuine cothromach no eu-cothromach a réir
nan gamhna a bha e a' cumail. Dh' fhaodadh iomadh failnigeadh
eile a bhith air a ghabhadh cleith, ach bha na gamhna an siud am
fiadhnuis a' bhaile, agus ma bha iad piollach, truagh, cha ruigeadh
e leas a bhith fiachainn ri toirt a chreidsinn air càch gur e croitear
tapaidh a bha ann.

Cha robh aig Ean Ruadh ach aon ghamhainn. Reic iad a' bhó
bhàn toiseach a' gheamhraidh agus bha a' bhó ruadh cuideachd a
nis a' fàs sean. Bha an gamhainn math da-rìreadh, gamhainn
boirionn cuideachd, agus bha Oidhrig, bean Iain a' dol 'ga cumail.
Oir ged thubhairt mi gu'm b' e gamhainn Ean Ruaidh a bh' ann,
cha d' rinn mi sin ach air sailleamh modha ; cha robh eòlas no
suim aig Iain air crodh, agus cha robh duine a thuig sin na b'
fheàrr na Iain. Bha e aig a chosnadh a h-uile samhradh air
bàtaichean Chluaidh agus b' i sin an obair a thigeadh ri a chàil.
B' e a bha dìchiollach a' cumail an luchd-turuis air an dòigh—ged
nach robh iad cho feumach air an uair ud is a tha iad an diugh.

Ma bha Iain aineolach air spréidh, cha b' e sin do dh' Oidhrig

e, agus cha bu bheag an uaill a rinn i as an fhiosrachadh a bh'
aice. B' ann aice riamh a bhitheadh na gamhna a b' fheàrr, agus
cha robh fear na bliadhna seo dad air dheireadh. Aig ám na
féille b' i a bu dòcha a' phrìs a b' àirde fhaighinn, rud a bh' air
tachairt cho tric a nise 's nach robh dùil aig sluagh a' bhaile ris a'
chòrr. Ciamar a bha i 'ga dheanamh? Cha robh fios. Bha
móran seanchais air ola nan trosg is ola nan ròn, min choirce is
min ìnnseanach. Ma bha na gamhna a' faotainn a' bhìdh sin, cha
b' ann gu follaiseach. 'Nuair a bha iad 'nan laoigh, 's docha gu
robh iad a' faotainn barrachd bainne na laoigh eile. Co-dhiubh,
bha na boirionnaich a' tighinn as a' bhuaile aon fheasgar agus
na laoigh aig na balaich air thaod mar a b' àbhaist. Bha an
comhradh air laoigh is air bainne.

"Tha feadhainn an diugh" arsa Peigidh Thearlaich, "a' toirt
a' bhainne do na laoigh an àite a thoirt do an cuid cloinne." "Ma
tha" arsa Oidhrig, "tha a' chlann agamsa cho fallain 's a tha
anns a' bhaile, co dhiùbh a tha cion bainne orra gu nach 'eil.
Thoir thusa dhaibh gu leòr de bhuntàta is sgadan is càl duilisg,
is cha bhi cùram orra." Thug iad uile sùil a null rathad Chaluim
Bhig, gille Ean Ruaidh, théid-cha-téid aige fhéin is an laogh mór,
agus cha b' urrainn daibh gun fhaicinn gu robh Calum a cheart
cho sgairteil, ris an laogh fhéin.

Ma bha Oidhrig iomraiteach anns a' Ghlaic mar bhana-chroiteir,
bha Alasdair Sheumais Mhóir a cheart cho fada an rathad eile.
Bha e daonnan aig an tigh is a' fuireach le a phiuthair. Cha robh
aca ach aon bhó, agus bha sin fhéin 'gan cumail a' dol, an seòrsa
dol a bh' ann. Chan fhaca tu coltas cabhaig air an dithis ud
latha dhe'n bhliadhna, ach bha móran ag ràdh gu robh iad aig a'
cheann thall a' cheart cho math dheth ri càch. As t-fhoghar mar
bu trice chruinnicheadh muinntir a' bhaile am feur an cabhaig,
ged nach robh e an còmhnuidh cho tioram 's a bu mhath leo. An

Tìr an Aigh

déidh sin thigeadh lathaichean matha, agus chuireadh Alasdair crioch air an obair mar gun robh fhios aige gum bitheadh an aimsir seo air a buileachadh air leis an Fhreasdal. Mar a thuirt Domhnull an t-Srath, "Nach minig a chuala sibh gum faigh an drèibh a latha fhéin ! "

Cha robh bó Alasdair ach beag ach ged a bha i beag bha i righinn. Toiseach an t-samhraidh 'nuair a rachadh na bà-laoigh a mach 'na mhonadh, bhitheadh iad a' sabaid gus am fàsadh iad eòlach. B' i bó Alasdair, beag 's gun robh i, aig am bitheadh an còmhnuidh an dara urram. Cha ruig mi leas innseadh dhuibh gu'm b' i bó Oidhrig a bhitheadh air thoiseach, a' mhàthair mar an laogh. B' i an t-sabaid seo an deagh spòrs leis na balaich, ach gheibheadh iad an deagh chàineadh nan cluinnteadh gun robh iad 'ga ceadachadh.

Mu dheireadh thàinig Oidhche Shamhna, nuair a theirear gamhna ris na laoigh. Dh' fhàs gamhna na Glaice mór làidir, gu h-àraidh gamhainn Bean Ean Ruaidh. Thainig Ean Ruadh dhachaidh as a' bhaile mhór agus thuirt Oidhrig ris gun cumadh iad an gamhainn gu mart a dheanamh dheth, agus gun ceannaicheadh iad gamhainn eile an ath bhliadhna, rud a cheadaicheadh dhaibh a' bhó ruadh a reic an ceann bliadhna no dha. Bha Iain deònach gu leòir aonta a chur ri gnothuch sam bith a chuireadh Oidhrig f'a chomhair.

Aig toiseach an earraich dh' fhàgadh na gamhna a muigh air son na ceud uaire anns a' mhonadh mhór. An ceann ceithear-la-deug rinneadh deasachadh gus an crodh a chur a nunn gu bhith seachdainn anns a' mhonadh bheag, a reir riaghailt a' bhaile. Tràth 's a' mhaduinn fhad's a bha Oidhrig a' bleoghann a' mhairt dh' fhalbh Iain a dh' iarraidh a' ghamhna agus 'nuair a fhuair e beothach a shaoil leis a bha coltach ris, dh' fhuadaich e a nunn e do'n mhonadh bheag. Có bha roimhe thall ach Peigidh Thear-laich. " Dé an gamhainn a th' agad an sin ? " arsa Peigidh, " Nach 'eil an gamhainn againn fhìn ? " arsa Iain. " Chan e gu dearbh " arsa Peigidh, " thàinig an gamhainn agaibhse a nall comhla ris a' chrodh againne. Siud agad e air a' chnoc ud shuas. Innsidh mise dhut dé an gamhainn a th' agad an sin. Tha gamhainn Alasdair Sheumais Mhóir." Nuair a chitheadh tu an da ghamhainn taobh ri taobh, cha robh iad idir ao-coltach ri a chéile, ged a bha gamhainn Oidhrig na bu mhotha agus ceann air cho féin-spéiseal ri taobh ceann iriosal a' ghamhna eile. " Stad thusa gus an cluinn Oidhrig seo " arsa Peigi. Cha robh Iain sios no suas agus dh' innis e fhéin do Oidhrig 'nuair a ràinig e an tigh mar a thachair. Am feasgar sin fhéin bha na boirionnaich a' tighinn dhachaidh as a' bhuaile. " An cuala sibhse, a nigheanan," arsa Oidhrig, " mar a rinn an duine agamsa an diugh   An gamhainn ceàrr a thoirt leis, agus nam b' e gamhainn eile a bhitheadh ann ach gamhainn Alasdair Sheumais Mhóir ! " " Sin agadsa an fheadhainn a tha tuilleadh is fada air Galldachd " arsa Peigi Thearlaich, " tha iad a' call am beagan tùir a th' aca."

Co-dhiubh, chaidh a' mhearachd bheag seo air di-chuimhne agus thainig ám na féille. Bha i ann air Di-ardaoin agus bha dùil aig Iain falbh a Ghlaschu an ath Dhi-luain. Bho'n a bha làrach na féille mu ochd mìle as a' Ghlaic, b' ann do dh'Iain a b' fheudar a dhol do'n fhéill a cheannach gamhna.

Bha Alasdair Sheumais Mhóir e fhéin a' dol a reic a ghamhna. Bha Uilleam Bàn mac bràthair athar, a' fuireach faisg air làrach na féille. Mar sin thug Alasdair leis an gamhainn feasgar Di-ciadain agus dh' fhuirich e an oidhche sin an tigh Uilleim. Bha fhios aig Uilleam glé mhath nach robh an Alasdair ach duine socharach agus thuirt e ris gun toireadh e fhéin an gamhainn a dh' ionnsaidh na féille a chum a reic dha. Bha Alasdair deònach gu leòir.

B' ann an siud a bha an sluagh. Neo-air-thaing othail air

gach taobh agus an reic 's a' cheannach a' dol air adhart gun diobradh. Thachair Ean Ruadh air Uilleam, agus dh' aithnich e gur e gamhainn math a bh' aige. Cha b' fhada gus na chòrd iad air còig punnd Sasunnach, prìs air leth math anns an latha a bh' ann. Bha dàil bheag an siud 's an seo a' coinneachadh ri càirdean ach bha cabhag dhachaidh air Iain ach am faiceadh Oidhrig an gamhainn eireachdail a cheannaich e.

Bha ciaradh air an fheasgar 'nuair a ràinig e an tigh. Cha bu léir do dh' Oidhrig an gamhainn ro mhath ach b' fheudar dhith aideachadh gu robh cumadh foghainteach air. " Coig puinnd Shasunnach," arsa Iain, " is e a nise a' fàs car spracail, " cha b' fheàrr a nasgaidh e." Bha coltas air a' ghamhainn cuideachd a bhith glé chòir, oir cha do ghluais e nuair a cheangail iad anns a' bhuaghal e. " Shaoileadh tu gu robh e an seo riamh " arsa Oidhrig.

Maduinn la-iar-na-mhaireach, bha Oidhrig air a bonn gu math tràth agus a mach a dh' fhaicinn a ghamhna. Cha b' fhada gus an do thill i agus i ag éigheach ri Iain. " Trobhad an seo, cha mhor nach canainn-sa gur e an gamhainn againn fhìn a tha an siud." A mach a ghabh Iain agus eadar a' bhoil a bh' air Oidhrig agus na ceisdean a bha i a' tilgeil air, bha e toilichte lethsgeul fhaighinn falbh as a rathad, suas am monadh a dhearbhadh an robh an gamhainn aca fhéin air fàireadh.

Bha e air falbh mu uair a thìde agus thill e is gamhainn aige co-dhiù. Cha luath 's a chunnaic Oidhrig e, dh' eubh i na creachan a rithisd. " A bhumailear, sin agad gamhainn Alasdair Sheumais Mhóir — càit' an d' fhuair thu e ? " " Fhuair " arsa Iain, " shuas air cul a' Chnuic Bhàin." " Ach stad ort " arsa Oidhrig, " nach robh Alasdair air an fhéill leis a' ghamhainn ? " Gu grad thàinig solus ùr 'na shuilean. " Tha fhios agam a nise dé a thachair. Thug Alasdair leis an gamhainn againne do'n fhéill agus cheannaich thusa e air coig puinnd Shasunnach. Ach an do dh' aithnich thu Alasdair fhéin idir, ged nach aithnich thu na gamhna ? " Thàinig an sgeul am follais beag is beag, mu Uilleam Bàn is mar sin, agus cha robh i fada a' ruith air a' bhaile. Có a thigeadh a nall gu tigh Ean Ruaidh ach Alasdair fhéin.

"Seo do ghamhainn" arsa Oidhrig, "bha mi'n dùil gu'n do reic thu e." "Bha mi fhìn sin gu seo" arsa Alasdair. "Tha mi glé dhuilich mar a thachair. Dé a nì sinn ? " "Tha mise an seo" arsa Oidhrig "le mo ghamhainn fhìn, ach a dhìth coig notaichean. Tha thusa an sin le do ghamhainn fhéin cuideachd agus coig notaichean a bharrachd 'na do phòcaid. Tha a nise an fhéill seachad agus cha d' fhuair sinne an gamhainn a bha sinn ag iarraidh." "Nach cùm sibh an gamhainn agamsa ? " arsa Alasdair, "'s cinnteach nach 'eil e cho truagh 'nuair a chaidh an duine agaibh fhéin dà uair agus mise aon uair, iomrall eatorra." "Ma ta 's mi nach gabh" arsa Oidhrig. "Cha chuirinn-sa am beothach suarach sin 'san aon bhàthaich ris a' ghamhainn agamsa. Thoir dhomhsa mo choig notaichean agus thoir leat do ghamhainn as a seo."

B' ann mar sin a thachair. Cha do chuir an gnothach cùram sam bith air Alasdair. An ceann seachdainn thainig dròbhair rathad a' bhaile. Bha cuid ag radh gu robh an drobhair air chùl sgeul nan gamhna . . . . Co-dhiùbh a bha gu nach robh, chan 'eil teagamh sam bith nach tug e coig puinnd 's a deich air gamhainn Alasdair—deich tasdain a bharrachd air na thug Ean Ruadh air a ghamhainn fhéin air an fhéill.

" TIR AN AIGH "

Tha e coltach gu robh oidhche mhór aca le litrichean an taigh Ean Ruaidh Di-haoine seo chaidh. Chan e gu robh mise an taigh Ean Ruaidh an oidhch' ud, ach fhuair mi sgeul nan litrichean bho Dhomhnull Bharabhaig an dé.

Cha robh duine eile anns a' Ghlaic Uaine a' faighinn uiread de litrichean ri Domhnull Bharabhaig fhéin. Fhad's a bha e a' fuireach mu dheas, chuir e eòlas air móran dhaoine inbheach is de sgoilearan, agus air dha a dhachaidh a dheanamh anns an Eilean Ghoirid, chum an fheadhainn ud orra a' sgriobhadh d'a ionnsaidh air gach cuspair fo'n ghréin. Tha mi cinnteach gu dearbh nach deanadh iad sin mur a bitheadh tlachd aig Domhnull fhéin ann a bhith a' sgriobhadh gu math tric do'n ionnsaidh-san.

Mar sin aig na céilidhean an tigh Ean Ruaidh, cha robh ni air an talamh air nach toireadh Domhnull barail chudthromach, barail a bha air a steidheachadh air nì a thuirt am Fear-Parlumaid ud, no rud-eigin a thuirt am fear-dreuchd ud eile.

Ach co-dhiù bha a' chuideachd cruinn feasgar Di-haoine an tigh Ean Ruaidh mar a b' àbhaist. Thainig an còmhradh gu a bhith air an iasgach is air na lathaichean a dh' fhalbh. " Tha cuimhne agamsa," arsa Ean Ruadh, " 'nuair a choisicheadh tu bho bhàta gu bàta anns an acarsaid, ach chan fhaic duine againne sin a rithisd." " 'S docha," arsa Peigi Eoghainn, car mar gu'm bitheadh i a' magadh, " gu'n d' fhuair Domhnull Bharabhaig litir mu'n iasgach." Cha d' rachadh móran seachad air Peigi, agus chunnaic i gu'n do thadhail am posta air Domhnull an lath' ud mar a b'àbhaist.

"Mata." arsa Domhnull air a shocair, " 's iomadh duine a labhras an fhìrinn gun fhios da. Fhuair mi litir mu'n iasgach, 's mi fhuair, dìreach an diugh fhéin, agus chan e aon litir a mhain ach sia, seachd, ochd litrichean." Leis a sin thug e a mach deagh phasgan as a phòcaid. "Nach d' thuirt mi riut?" arsa Peigi. "Coma leat, cluinneamaid dé th' aig Domhnull ri ràdh," arsa Ean Ruadh.

Shocraich a' chuideachd iad fhéin agus chaidh Domhnull troimh na litrichean gus an d' fhuair e té fhada ghorm, le paipear tiugh a rinn brag 'nuair a dh' fhosgail e i ris an t-solus.

"Sin agaibh té a fhuair mi bho Bhord an Sgadain," arsa Domhnull. Thòisich e air leughadh gu socair, ciallach, oir bha e ag eadar-theangachadh mar a bha e a' dol air adhart.

Uasail, na bitheadh cùram oirbh anns a' Ghlaic Uaine mu'n iasgach. Bithidh féill gu leòir air sgadan fhathasd. Creididh an sluagh na tha sinne ag innseadh dhaibh mu'n bhiadh shultmhor a tha am buntata is sgadan, oir tha muinntir Bord an Sgadain, an deidh toiseachadh air sgadan itheadh iad fhéin. Mar sin bho seo a mach 's ann a bhitheas moit air mnathan 'nuair a gheibh na nàbaidhean àileadh an sgadain o na tighean aca—chan e nàire, mar a bh' orra thuige seo, agus eagal orra gu'm bitheadh fhios aig daoine gu'm b'e seo am biadh suarach a bh'aca. Cuiridh seo neart agus ùrachadh air luchd-obrach. Mar cheud cheum a chum seo a thoirt gu buil tha sinn a' cur suas an t-suaicheantais seo fad is farsuing air sràidean Dhùn-Eidinn, "Suas le sgadan, sios le sgìos." Leigidh mi fios dhuit mu na ceuman eile a tha fo ar n-aire. Is mise, Do sheirbhiseach, ro-iriosail, A. S. Bord an Sgadain.

"Glé mhath," arsa Seumas a' Ghobha. "Cùm ort, dé an ath litir a th' agad?" "Tha an ath té an seo," arsa Dòmhnull, "bho dhotair a b' aithne dhomh anns a' bhaile mhór. Seo mar tha i a' dol:

"An innis thu dhomhsa a bheil dòigh agam air cosnadh fhaotainn anns an sgìr agad fhéin no an sgìre eile is aithne dhuit. Tha iad ag innseadh dhomhsa gu bheil sluagh na Gaidhealtachd

59

Tìr an Aigh

a' fàs cho làidir, fallain a nise 's nach'eil ach glé bheag aig dotairean ri dheanamh 'nam measg. Riamh bho na thilg sibh uaibh iuchraichean nan croganan, agus a thill sibh gu biadh bhur n-athraichean, agus a sguir sibh de na mhathachadh Ghallda a chur air na croitean, tha sibh a' dol o neart gu neart. Bu mhath leamsa a' chuid eile de mo bheatha a chur seachad 'nar measg. Ciamar a theid mi timchioll air ? "

" Cha leig e leas fiachainn ri tighinn a seo co-dhiùbh arsa Bean Ean Ruaidh, " cha tig an latha a gheibh sinn cuidhteas an fhir a th' againn."

Cha do chuir siud móran maille air Domhnull, oir bha a' chuideachd ag iarraidh tuilleadh de na litrichean.

" Seo agaibh té bho'n Fhear Parlumaid againn " arsa Domhnull, " a' dol mar seo: 'Fhir-siorrachd chòir, tha mi toilichte gu'n do thog thu na puingean ud na do litir. Chan 'eil eagal sam bith ormsa gu'n abair duine a rithisd nach 'eil na Gaidheil a' deanamh na's urrainn daibh air an son fhéin. Feumaidh an Riaghaltas aideachadh an ùine ghoirid nach e mhain gu bheil na Gaidheil a' saothrachadh a chum am math fhéin, ach gu bheil iad 'ga dheanamh a chùm math na feadhna nach 'eil 'nan Gaidheil idir. Tha mise a' gealltainn dhuibh gun tuilleadh dàlach, gun cuir an Riaghaltas helicopterean agus goireasan eile a dh' ionnsaidh na Gaidhealtachd fad na bliadhna gun a bhith a' feitheamh ri ám an t-sneachda mhóir.

Dh' ainmich thu rathaidean mora. A nise, mur 'cil mi air mo mhealladh, a charaid, bha sibh fhéin ag iarraidh nan rathaidean mora chumail cho cumhang lubach a 's gu'n cumadh sibh coigrich air falbh. Có eile a chuir na h-upagan uamhasach an teis meadhon nan rathad agus a chladhaich na claisean air gach oir ? Faodaidh gu robh sin glé phongail aon uair, ach tha latha eile air tighinn.

Tha sibh a nise a' breithneachadh gu bheil soirbheachadh mór an cois luchd-turuis. Gu dearbh, faodaidh sibh an diugh luchd-turuis a chur gu feum air nach do smaointich sibh thuige seo. Nach leig sibh leotha a dhol an sàs an obair nan croitean ? 'N uair a dh' iarras iad cead oirbh, faodaidh sibh leigeil oirbh nach 'eil sibh ro-dheònach an saorsa a thoirt dhaibh, air eagal gu'm bi dùil aca gu'n lùghdaich sibh prìs am bùird. Ma bhitheas sibh seòlta gu leòir, cha bhi agaibh ach am feur a bhuain ; nì na coigrich an còrr.

Mur a bi aimsir feòir ann, carson nach bitheadh iad ag iasgach ? Ma dh' fhàsas sibh sgìth de iasg mara, cuiribh a dh' ionnsaidh nan aibhnichean iad. Anns an dòigh sin coisnidh an luchd-turuis chan e mhàin biadh is annlan dhaibh féin ach dhuibhse cuideachd.

Gu mi-fhortanach chan 'eil móran de luchd-turuis a' dol an rathad an ám buain na mòna, ach a bheil aobhar air an t-saoghal ann carson nach tairgneadh iad dhachaidh i ? 'S ann a bhitheadh an spòrs agus an dìbhearsoin dhaibh. Chan 'eil ùin' agam dad a ràdh air na puingean eile an drasda. Is mise, do fhear-parlumaid dealasach, A.B.C., *M.P.*' "

" Gu dearbh, bu dual do leithid a bhi briathrach," arsa Alasdair an Dùin.

" 'S ann bho mhinistear Gallda a tha i seo," arsa Domhnull ; 'A Charaid Chòir, nach mi tha toilichte a chluinntinn gu bheil uibhir de Ghaidheil òga ag ullachadh airson dreuchd na ministrea-lachd. Tha feum mór orra air a' Ghaidhealtachd fhéin, gun teagamh, mar a thuirt thu, ach tha mi an dòchas 'nuair a bhitheas sibhse buidheach, gu'm bi aireamh chuimseach dhiubh air fhàgail gu tighinn a measg sluagh aingidh, borb nam bailtean mu dheas. Bha e dual do d' chinneach-sa searmoinichean ainmeil àrach agus a chur a mach. Fiach gu'n cùm thu ort 'g an co-éigneachadh a chùm gu'n tig iad a shoillseachadh ar dorchadais an seo. Leis na beannachdan. L. Mc. L. DD.'.

Tìr an Aigh

"Seo agaibh aon eile, bho bhall de Chomhairle an Fhoghluim, an turus seo":

A Mhaighstir, chan 'eil mi a' smaointeachadh gu bheil gnothuichean anns na sgoiltean cho mi-mhisneachail 's a tha thu ag ràdh. Tha mise deimhinn gu'n tuig na pàrantan fhathasd nach 'eil cleachdadh na Gaidhlig a' dol a chur moille sam bith an adhartas an cuid cloinne. Feumaidh sinn a' Ghaidhlig a chumail beò, chan ann a mhàin air a sgàth fhéin, ach a chionn gur e luchd na Gaidhlig as fheàrr a bhruidhneas a' Bheurla. Tha thu fhéin a' faicinn an diol a tha an fheadhainn aig nach 'eil ach Beurla leatha fhéin a' deanamh oirre an diugh.

Chan 'eil mi ag radh idir gu'm bu choir dhuinn sgur de'n Fhraingeis anns na h-àrd sgoilean. Tha fhios gu'm bitheadh i feumail nam fàsadh neach sgìth de leughadh na th' againn de leabhraichean Gaidhlig agus de leabhraichean Beurla. 'Se fìor àbhachdas a th' ann cuideachd faclan Fraingeis a thilgeil air Frangach bochd ma bheir thu cuairt a null do'n Fhraing. Is mise, Le deagh mheas, X.Y. Fear Comhairle.

"Seo, ma tha, litir eile," arsa Domhnull, "bho rùnaire a' Mhòid Ionadail:"

'A Charaid, tha mi toilichte gu'm bi a' choisir agaibh aig a' Mhòd am bliadhna. Ach tha barrachd toileachais orm gu bheil uibhir a' fiachainn co-fharpaisean a' bheul-aithris. 'Se seo a' cheud bhliadhna a dh' fheumas sinn na seinneadairean a chur anns an talla bheag, agus a' bheul-aithris agus na dealbhan-cluiche a chur anns an talla mhór. Tha sin 'na mhisneachd mhór dhuinne a tha a' fiachainn ris a' chànain a chumail beò agus tha sinn fada an comain muinntir na Glaic Uaine airson a' chuideachaidh a thug iad dhuinn anns an doigh seo. Bha thu a' bruidhinn air a' bhreitheamh Eadailteach ris nach do chòrd na h-I's agad an uiridh.

Na bitheadh cùram sam bith ort ; cha bhi e againn gu siorruidh tuilleadh, fhad's a bhitheas mise 'na mo Rùnaire co-dhiùbh.

Ach nach mi a tha mór as an da Shasunnach anns a' Ghlaic a chur air bonn Comunn-cuimhne Dhonnchaidh Bhàin. Nach math an rud gu'm bi aon oidhche fhéin agaibh 's a' bhliadhna gu bhith a' seinn òrain a' bhaird. Tha thu ag innseadh dhomh gu'n d' thug an triùir Ghlaiceach a chuir air chois Comunn Raibeart Burns a' bhon-uiridh suas an gnothuch buileach. Nach math gu robh uiread sin fhéin de ghliocas air a bhuileachadh orra 'nan seann aois ! Chan 'eil aca a nise ach iad fhéin a cheangal ri Comunn Dhonnachaidh Bhain, agus bheir sinn maitheanas iomlan dhaibh. Do cho-oibriche anns a' Ghaidhlig, Iain a' Ghlinne'.

" Ach seo agaibh litir cho annasach 's a fhuair mi uile gu léir," arsa Domhnull. " Litir bho Cheann-suidhe Comhlan Iomain nan Eileanan Siar. Agus cha chùm mi fada tuilleadh sibh ; seo agaibh an té mu dheireadh."

'A Ghlaicich Ionmhuinn, bu mhath leam gu'm bitheadh fios agad mar a tha an iomain a' soirbheachadh anns na h-eileanan seo bho na thoisich sinn air. Gu dearbh chan 'eil aithreachas air duine gu'n do leig sinn seachad na cleasan a bha againn roimhe—mar a bha ball-coise, goid a' chruin, cricket, falach-fead, rugby is an leithidean sin. Tha adhartas mór ri fhaicinn air iomadh dòigh. Tha na balaich na's làidire agus na's cuimire 'nam bodhaigean na bha iad riamh. Tha na suilean aca na's bioraiche—cha mhór gu faic thu speuclannan air duine dhiùbh an diugh. Tha cuimhne agad fhéin air an fheadhainn a bha ris a' bhall-coise, na casan cuagach a bh' aca, 's na làmhan agus na gàirdeannan aca ach gann a' fàs idir, 's gun fhios aca dé a dheanadh iad leotha.

Chan ann mar sin a tha o na thoisich iad air an iomain. 'S iad na boirionnaich fhéin a dh' innseas sin dhuit. Chan 'eil aon dhiùbhsan an diugh a dh' iarras na h-eileanan fhàgail agus a dhol gu tir-mór, mar a b' àbhaist daibh, a shireadh gillean tapaidh nan caman ; tha gu leòir dhiùbh aca aig an tigh.

Feumaidh mi aideachadh gu'n d' fhuair cluicheadair no dha gearradh le caman an dràsda 's a rithisd, ach dé is fhiach sin ? 'Se gearraidhean glana, dìreach a th' annta a leighiseas an ùine glé ghoirid gun dragh sam bith : cha b' ionnan 's na breaban 's na leòin a b' àbhaist daibh fhaotainn an ám cluich a' bhall-coise.

'Se aobhar-misneachd mhór a th' ann dhuinn cuideachd a bhith a' faicinn mar a tha comhairlean de gach seòrsa 'gar cuideachadh le bhith a' ceannach chaman agus gach airneis eile dhuinn.

Le taing agus buidheachas. Eileanach'.

Bha Domhnull ullamh. " Cha chreid mise," arsa mi fhéin, " nach d' thug thu oidhche dhaibh. Dé a thuirt iad 'nuair a bha thu ullamh ? " " O, cha d' thuirt móran," arsa Domhnull, " fiù Peigi Eoghainn fhéin : cha mhór gu robh guth aice 'nuair a dh' innis mi dhaibh gu'm b'e mi-fhìn a sgriobh na litrichean."

" Thu fhéin," arsa mise. " A chiall beannaich thu, an saoil thu fhéin gu robh sin ceart—an car a thoirt á do chàirdean anns an dòigh sin ? " " An car a thoirt asda ! " asa Domhnull. " Nach bi thu sàmhach. A bheil cuimhn' agad idir gu'm b'e Di-haoine seo chaidh latha na gogaireachd ? "

"A' BHANAIS"

"Bu chòir dhuit pòsadh ille." Bha an duan seo aig Cailean Mór ris a h-uile fleasgach anns a' Ghlaic Uaine. 'S iomadh fear a ghabh a chomhairle cuideachd, agus cha do stad e aig comhairle idir, b'e nach do stad. Thaghadh e bean fhreagarrach do dh' fhear sam bith, agus dheanadh e gach fiosrachadh a bha feumail dhuit. Ma bha fear ann aig nach robh de mhisneachd na chuireadh a' cheisd ris a' mhaighdinn, cha leigeadh sin a leas bacadh a chur air ; dheanadh Cailean sin cuideachd.

Bha Cailean dìchiollach air sailleamh nan seann fhleasgach gu h-àraidh. Aig an fheadhainn a b' òige cha robh e ach 'na chùis-bhùrta. B'e banntrach a bh' ann fhéin. An déidh dha a bhean a chall, thoisich e air mnathan a shireadh do fheadhainn eile. Uaireannan aig ceilidhean mur a bitheadh e an làthair, bhitheadh na Glaicich a' meòrachadh air dé a thug air a bhith mar seo.

"Cailean Mor," arsa Domhnull an t-Srath, aon de na h-oidhcheannan an tigh Eachainn Bhàin, " dé tha ceàrr air ? " Mata, innsidh mise dhuibh. Tha fhios aig an t-saoghal nach robh Cailean agus a' bhean a' tighinn a réir a cheile. 'Se an aon toileachadh a th' aige a nise a bhith a' faicinn feadhainn eile a' fulang mar a rinn e fhéin." Cha do ghabh a' chuideachd ris a seo idir, oir bha iad ro-eòlach air seanchas Dhomhnuill, an sgoilear sgaiteach a chuir seachad uiread de a shaoghal air Galldachd.

"Bha mise cho eòlach air teaghlach Chailein ri duine anns a' bhaile," arsa Eachann Ceisdear, " agus chan fhaca mi dad a' tighinn eatorra riamh. Tha mise a' smaoineachadh gu bheil Cailean ri mholadh airson mar a tha e a' cuideachadh dhaoine eile anns an dòigh seo. Bu mhath leis dìreach an deanamh cho sona 's a bha e fhéin."

Cha mhotha a dh' aontaich iad uile ris a' Cheisdear, oir cha thogadh esan guth mór no droch fhacal mu dhuine sam bith. Air a' cheann thall cha robh a' mhór-chuid a' faicinn air shiubhal Chailein ach failigeadh a tha ri fhaicinn an iomadach fear eile — 'se sin a bhith a' gabhail gnothach ri móran rudan ris nach 'eil gnothach aca.

A dh' aindeoin lionmhorachd nam barailean, cha robh duine a chuireadh casg air an obair a bha Cailean a' deanamh. An lorg a chuid obrach bha na bainnsean, agus dé an leth-sgeul a b' fheàrr airson subhachais a gheibheadh na Glaicich na banais ? Dh' fhaodadh a' chàraid òg (no is dòcha a' chàraid shean) a bhith mì-choltach gu leòir ri amharc orra, ach ma bha gu leòir ann ri itheadh 's ri òl oidhche na bainnse, cha bhitheadh a' chuideachd fada a' dichuimhneachadh gu robh càraid an làthair.

B'e Cailean fear nam bainnsean ma tha. Cha robh cìs no duais a dhìth air. Bha e riaraichte le bhith a' smaointeachadh gu'n robh deagh bharail aig muinntir a' bhaile air mar neach aig an robh buadhan agus cumhachd àraidh air choir-eigin.

Air an dara croit a nunn seachad air Cailean bha aig am ar sgeòil fear Calum Dhonnchaidh, a' fuireach leis fhéin. Fhad 's a bha Marsailidh, piuthar Chaluim, beò, cha tigeadh boireannach faisg air. Chan 'eil fhios an d' thainig riamh 'na chridhe suil a thoirt air té sam bith, ach tha fhios againn co-dhiubh nach bitheadh Marsailidh fada a' cur a leithid sin ás a bheachd. Bha ise coltach ri càch, eòlach air cleasan Chailein Mhóir, agus thug i an deagh aire nach fhàgadh i e fhéin is Calum leotha fhéin nam b' urrainn dhise a leasachadh. Cìnnteach 's gu robh Cailean as fhéin, bha e 'na bu ghlice na gu'n canadh e am fianuis Marsailidh: "Bu chòir dhuit pòsadh, a Chaluim."

Dh' fhalbh Marsailidh. Shaoileadh tu a nise nach leigeadh Calum a leas feitheamh ri comhairle bho Chailean Mór no bho dhuine eile. Ach a réir coltais cha robh dad de chabhaig air Calum gu pòsadh.

Nach bu ghlan an cothrom seo do Chailean Mór ! An déidh sin cha robh an latha leis mar a bha e an dùil. " Carson nach 'eil thu fhéin a' pòsadh ? " fhreagair Calum Cailean aon latha. " Mise," arsa Cailean. " Bha mise pòsda mar tha. Tha mi gu math socair a nise comhla ri Peigi agus an duine. Chan e sin dhuitsa e. Tha thu ceart gu leòir an dràsda, ach stad gus am fàs thu sean. Siuthad, abair gu bheil thu deònach, agus is aithne dhomh fhéin a' cheart té air do shon." " O," arsa Calum airson na ficheadamh uair, " chan fhiach dhomhsa pòsadh tuilleadh. Tha mi toilichte gu leòir mar a tha mi."

Aig deireadh an fhoghair a' bhliadhna sin fhéin ghabh Calum fuachd, agus eadar gach fliuchadh a bh'ann a' siubhal as déidh a' chruidh bha e an ceann seachdainn air an leabaidh ann am fiabhrus. Ghabh na nàbuidhean oidhche ma seach 'ga chaithris. A dh' innseadh na fìrinn cha robh duine cho trang ri Cailean Mór a' cur air doigh có thigeadh a nochd is có thigeadh an ath-oidhch', có a rachadh 'na mhoinidh no có a rachadh an tobar.

Ged bu bheag a bha de choltas air aon uair, thainig feabhas air Calum. Bha Cailean agus na coimhearsnaich uile, air an doigh. "A Chaluim, a charaid," arsa Cailean ris aon latha, " tha thu a' tighinn air adhart. Ach bitheadh seo 'na rabhadh dhuit. Dh' fhaodadh latha tighinn 'nuair nach bi muinntir a' bhaile deònach an aire a thoirt dhuit. Tha fhios gun aidich thu a nise co-dhiubh gur e bean a tha dhìth ort ? "

" Air do shocair ma ta," arsa Calum. " Tha thu ag ràdh gu bheil té agad 'san amharc dhomhsa, ach dé an dearbhadh a tha agad gu'n gabhadh i gnothuch riumsa ? " Thug Cailean an aire gun ghuth a ràdh gu'n robh toiseach aig Calum air géilleadh. Bha e a' dol a chonnspoid mu'n chùis agus bha sin fhéin 'na adhartas.

Chum Calum air, " Seall boirionnaich na Glaic Uaine fhéin. Tha Ciorstaidh Anna ro-shean agus Seonag a' Bhraighe ro og. Mairi an Oig, cha chuirinn cùl rithe-se, ach mar a gabhadh i mi, bhitheadh a h-uile duine 's a' bhaile a' magadh orm."

Bha Cailean deiseil. " O tha thu air an tac cheàrr uile gu leir, a charaid. Na bi a' bruidhinn air boirionnaich a' bhaile seo. Bheir mise nunn thu do'n Druim-ghlais, agus gheibh sinn Sìne Ean Mhóir dhuit. Nì i deagh bhean croiteir, theid mise an urras, agus chan 'eil i grannda idir, ma's e 's gu bheil suim agad an snuadh no'n cumadh. Tha mi gu math eòlach air a h-athair agus air a mathair, agus tha mi deimhinn gu'n toir iad Sìne dhuit gu togarrach."

Dh' fhaoidte nach b'e seo an teisteanas a b' fheàrr a ghabhadh toirt air boirionnach, ach ma thug Calum an aire cha do leig e dad air. Bha dà rud a dhìth air Calum, cinnt gu'n rachadh leis, agus dearbhadh nach cluinneadh duine eile guth air na bha 'na rùn gus am b' fheudar dhaibh. Bu mhath a bha fhios aig Cailean air seo, agus cha robh e fada a' dearbhadh do Chalum gu'n tachradh gach nì a réir a mhiann.

" Saoil an gabhadh i mi," arsa Calum. " Chan 'eil mise ach gliogach air mo chasan fhathasd an dcidh an tinneis. 'S fheàrr dhuinn fuireach gu samhradh co-dhiùbh.

" 'S iomadh rud a dh' fhaodas tachairt roimh shamhradh," arsa Cailean. " Chan 'eil math dàil a dheanamh. O'n a tha thu a nise air toiseachadh air a' bhròs a rithisd, chan fhada gus am bi thu cho làidir 's a bha thu riamh. Bithidh sinn deiseil air son na cuairt an ceann deich latha no cealla-diag co-dhiùbh."

" Bha latha ann," arsa Calum, " agus cha chuireadh seachd

mile gach rathad mise a null no nall. Bha mi òg làidir an uair sin, gun chùram de'n t-seòrsa seo air m' inntinn."

Fad nan lathaichean as deidh sin chum Cailean Mór sùil air Calum, agus mur a fàsadh esan treas cha b'e cion bròis is bainne is uibhean a bu choireach. Gach latha choisich e beagan na b' fhaide bho'n taigh. Bha e a' fàs laidir, shaoileadh tu, ge b' oil leis, agus cha robh lethsgeul ann tuilleadh. "Faodaidh tu cliabh mòna a thoirt dhachaidh latha sam bith," arsa Cailean. "Ma tha sinn a' dol a chur a' ghnothuich seo air dòigh roimh 'n Bhliadhn' Uir, feumaidh sinn a bhith sgiobalta.

Thainig an latha a chuireadh air leth airson an turuis. Am beul na h-oidhche dh' fhàg gach fear a thigh fhéin agus choinnich iad air an rathad àrd mu mhìle bho'n bhaile. Chan fhaca suil iad a' falbh agus nan rachadh leotha gu math bhitheadh iad air ais mu'n eireadh muinntir a' bhaile. Cha do chuir ceum a' mhonaidh sianadh air Calum, is deagh chuaille bata 'na dhòrn. Cha robh dad aige ri ghiulain co-dhiubh, ach an t-searrag dhe'n Talasgar a bha 'na phòcaid.

Cha robh Calum ro bhriathrach air an rathad agus dh' fhiach Cailean Mór ri a chumail o a bhith a' cnuasachadh air aobhar an turuis. Gu fàbharach bha an aimsir ciùin, tioram, agus rainig iad an Druim-ghlas an deagh àm.

"Theid mise a steach an toiseach, a Chaluim, mar a thuirt mi riut," arsa Cailean Mor. Chi mi ciamar a tha gnothuichean agus thig mi mach 'gad iarraidh. Ach chan 'eil math dhuit am botul a thoirt a steach leat an toiseach co-dhiubh. Fàgaidh sinn an seo e an àite tearuinte." Stad iad faisg air cruachan mòna ri taobh an rathaid astar beag bho thigh Ean Ruaidh. Thug Calum fàd a aon de na cruachan, agus chuir e am botull gu cùramach 'na àite.

Dh' fhalbh Cailean agus cha b' fhada gus am faca Calum

Tìr an Aigh

deàrrsadh soluis a' sealltuinn gu'n d' fhosgail dorus Ean Ruaidh. Chùm Calum faisg air na cruachan air sgàth an fhasgaidh agus air eagal gu'm faicteadh e le duine de mhuinntir an Druim-ghlais a dh' fhaodadh a bhith a' spaisdearachd air an rathad mhór aca fhéin.

Cha robh Calum ach aonaranach. Mheòraich e air an t-suidheachadh neònach anns an robh e. Uair no dha thainig 'na cheann a chasan a thoirt leis air an rathad dhachaidh. Cha b'e am meas a bh' aige air Cailean Mór a chùm e far an robh e, ach fios a bhith aige nach deanadh teicheadh ach a dhraghanan a mheudachadh. Bha e a nise a' fàs car fuar 'na sheasamh an déidh coiseachd. An sin smaoinich e air a' bhotull. Carson nach toireadh e tarruing air ? B'e am fuachd an leth-sgeul a ghabh e dha fhéin, ach có aig a tha fios nach e cion misneachd an t-aobhar a bu làidire. Agus cha robh Cailean Mór a' tilleadh. Chuir Calum a làmh far an do shaoil e am botull a bhith, ach botull cha robh ann. Saoil an ann aig a' chruaich cheàrr a bha e. Bha iad cho coltach ri cheile anns an dorchadas. Chuir e cuairt air cruaich eile. Cha bu mhor a b' fheàirrde e sin. Cha robh feum air, ach toiseachadh air na cruachan a thoirt as a cheile.

Chuir e na foid sios car cùramach an toiseach ach mar a b' fhaide a lean e, b' ann a bu chruaidhe a chaidh e ris, gus mu dheireadh nach mór nach robh uiread de mhòine air an talamh 's a bha anns na cruachan.

Bha Calum cho dian a' rannsachadh 's nach mór nach robh Cailean Mór ri a thaobh mu'n d' thug e an aire dha. " Dé is ciall d'a seo ? " arsa Cailean. " Tha am botull Talasgair air chall," fhreagair Calum, a' cumail air mar a bha e roimhe. " Dean air do shocair," arsa Cailean, " a bheil thu a' dol a dh' fhoighneachd mu dheidhinn Shìne idir ? " " O! tha gu dearbh," arsa Calum. " ciamar a chaidh dhuit ? " " Cluinnidh tu sin " arsa Cailean. " Tha Sìne a' dol a phòsadh ach cha tusa a tha i a' dol a phòsadh ach mise. A' cheud fhacal a thuirt mi mu phòsadh, thog iad ceàrr mi, agus cha do smaointich iad riamh nach mi fhéin a bha ag iarraidh Shìne airson posaidh. Mu'n d' fhuair mi cothrom an cur as am barail chaidh an seanchas cho fada 's nach leigeadh an nàire leam an fhìrinn innseadh dhaibh. Tha mi duilich air do shonsa, a Chaluim." " O, tha sin ceart gu leòir," arsa Calum, 's e a' fiachainn ri chleith gu'n robh e cho toilichte is a bha e a' faireachduinn."

" Feumaidh sinn greasad dhachaidh a nise," arsa Cailean, " air neo cha bhi sinn a staigh roimh mhaduinn." " Chan 'eil mise a' falbh a seo gus am faigh mi am botull " arsa Calum. " Faodaidh mi tilleadh gun mhnaoi, ach chan 'eil mi a' falbh as aonais an Talasgair. Co dhiùbh, feumaidh sinn do dheoch-slàinte òl."

Thoisich an rùtachd a rithisd agus mu dheireadh thall thainig Cailean Mór air a' bhotull. Rinn iad ma b' fhior, sgioblachadh air a' mhòine agus an sin bha aon deoch slàinte ann agus 's dòcha a dha no trì. Mu'n am a thug iad an rathad dhachaidh orra, cha robh uiread de chùram orra co-dhiubh a bhitheadh iad tràth no anmoch.

An ceann beagan sheachdainnean thainig banais Chailein Mhóir agus Sine Ean Ruaidh agus b'i sin a' bhanais. Cha robh duine a b' urrainn coiseachd anns an da bhaile nach robh aice. Chan fhacas riamh uiread de chearcan aig cuirm, agus de'n Talasgar cuideachd. Cha robh an corr guth aig muinntir an Druim-ghlais air diol an cuid chruachan mòna.

Chuir muinntir na Glaic-uaine romhpa gu'm bitheadh banais an seo nach cualas riamh a leithid, oir có aig a bha fios cuin' a bhitheadh banais eile aca, is fear nam pòsaidhean a nise pòsda e fhéin ?

71

AN T-EACH BAN

" Gu dearbh 's iomadh uair a thuirt mi ris," arsa Seumas, " nach fhaca mi duine riamh cho rag ris." Bha Seumas ag innseadh dhomh mu Dhòmhnull a bhràthair, is e an déidh togail air gu deas an latha roimhe siud. Chuir seo iongnadh nach bu bheag air muinntir na Glaic-uaine, gus an cual iad mar a thachair. Dh' fhalbh Dòmhnull an cabhaig, agus cha robh fois aig duine anns a' Ghlaic-uaine gus an d' fhiosraich iad aobhar na cabhaig. Bha mi fhéin cho eòlach ri duine 'san àite air an dithis ud, ach cha robh dad de dhùil agam gu'n cluinninn sgeul cho neònach 's a chuala mi an lath ud.

Bha a h-uile duine a' smaoineachadh 'nuair a leig Dòmhnull dheth obair agus a thàinig e dhachaidh a dh' fhuireach còmhla ri a bhràthair, nach fhalbhadh e tuilleadh. Cho fad 's a bha fhios, bha an dà bhràthair, is iad le chéile gun phòsadh riamh, còirte gu leòir comhla. Ged a bha fathunn an dràsda 's a rithisd air beagan còmhstrith a bhith eatorra, bha iad a' tighinn ri chéile gu dòigheil. An t-àm a bha Seumas leis fhéin, cha robh aige ach taigh ròpach. Airson sin, bha iad ag ràdh gu robh e fìor-mhath air còcaireachd is air fuine. Cha toireadh boirionnach 's a' bhaile bàrr air air dèanamh aran corca.

Air an làimh eile, cha robh suim aig Dòmhnull air an obair seo. Bha esan gun teagamh sgiobalta 'na phearsa, agus dh' fheumadh gach nì air feadh an tighe a bhith sgiobalta aige mar an ceudna. 'S iomadh uair a chuir e dorran air Seumas, is e a' sìor chur badan aodaich is seithrichean is soithichean gu h-òrdail 'nan àite fhéin. " Dé am feum a tha anns an sgioblachadh seo ? " arsa Seumas. " Aite fhéin aig a h-uile rud agus a h-uile rud 'na àite fhein," fhreagair Dòmhnull. " Ud," arsa Seumas, " chan 'eil cuimhne agam an diugh càit a bheil ni. Bha mi móran na b' fheàrr dheth 'nuair a bha a h-uile rud riamh còmhla am mèadhon

72

an ùrlair agus ma bha dad a dhìth orm cha robh agam ach mo làmh a shìneadh agus bha e an siud deiseil rium."

Cha b'e trod a bha seo ach seòrsa de tharruing as. Cha b'e seo a chuir Dòmhnull air imrich cho obann a dh' ionnsaidh na h-àirde deas. Thuig mise glé mhath gur e rud-eigin móran na bu chud-thromaiche a bh' ann, agus fhuair mi an sgeul gu léir an lath ud a thadhail mi air Seumas.

B'e Di-sathurna a bh' ann, an latha an déidh do Dhòmhnull falbh. Bha mise càirdeach do na bràithrean ; bha sinn anns na h-iar oghaichean, tha mi smaointeachadh. Co-dhiùbh eadar an càirdeas a bh' ann agus an t-astar (mu sheachd mìle) eadar ar dachaidhean, bha an t-seann nòs a' suidheachadh gun rachamaid a choimhead air a chéile da uair 's a' bhliadhna. Nan deanamaid e na bu trice na sin, bheireadh e a' cheart uiread de oilbheum 's a bheireadh e nan rachamaid ann na b' ainneamha.

Co-dhiùbh, b'e seo aon de na tursan agamsa, agus bha eagal orm 'nuair a chuala mi gu'n robh Dòmhnull an déidh falbh, gu'n d' thàinig mi aig am car mì-shealbhach, ach cha do leig Seumas ris an dòigh 'sam bith nach robh e toilichte m' fhaicinn. Gun teagamh bha mi air bhioran gus an cluinninn mar a thachair, agus bha mi glé thoilichte gu'n cuala mi an sgeul gu ceann gun mhóran ceasnachaidh a dhèanamh. Gu dearbh bha Seumas na bu deònaiche air a h-innseadh nan gabhadh e bhith, na bha mise air a cluinntinn. A réir Sheumais, cha robh an Dòmhnull ach duine saoghalta, fear a bha a' smaointeachadh gu'n robh beatha an duine gu léir fo bhuaidh riaghailtean faicsinneach an t-saoghail. B'e sgoilear a bh'ann. Fad àireamh bhliadhnachan fhritheil e air clasaichean nam feallsanach anns an Oil-thigh. An déidh sin chuir e an céill do'n t-saoghal gu'm b'e duine òrdail reusanta a bh' ann fhéin, fear nach creideadh gu'm b' urrainn ni tachairt mur a toireadh eanchainn dha urras air a shon. Bha e fad dà fhichead bliadhna

Tìr an Aigh

a' teagasg ann an sgoil Ghallda, agus ré na h-uine sin rinn e a dhìchioll gus a' cheart sheòrsa reusonachaidh a bh' aige fhéin a ghintinn an inntinnean a sgoilearan.

"Chuala tu mu mhinistear maide," arsa Seumas. "Mata, cha robh ann an Dòmhnull ach maighstir sgoile cloiche."

'Nuair a thàinig Dòmhnull a dh' fhuireach 's a' Ghlaic Uaine cha do sguir e a dh' fhiachainn ri adhartas a thoirt air muinntir a' bhaile. Uair no dhà leig na coimhearsnaich an céill do Sheumas nach robh searmonachadh Dhomhnuill a' tighinn uile gu léir ri an càil, ach chuir Domhnull roimhe nach robh e an còmhnaidh a' dol a dh' aontachadh leotha an aghaidh a bhràthar fhéin. Ged a bha beagan an drasda 's a rithisd a' tighinn eatorra, is iomadh uair a bha moit air Seumas gu robh a leithid de bhràthair briathrach, ealanta aige.

Cha robh nì a' foillseachadh an eadar dhealachaidh a bha eadar an da bhràthair na b' fheàrr na na connspoidean a bhitheadh aca gu tric mu shamhlaidhean, mu bhòcain, mu thaibhsichean, mu eich-uisge, is an leithid sin. Bha Seumas, coltach ris a' chuid eile de mhuinntir na Glaic Uaine a' creidsinn annta gu daingeann, ach cha bhitheadh gnothuch aig Dòmhnull riutha a muigh no mach. "Eich Uisge," arsa Dòmhnull, "faoineas!" "An dà shealladh." "Buamastaireachd! A bheil an dà shealladh agad fhéin? Chan 'eil. An aithne dhuit duine aig am bheil e? Chan aithne. O cha leig thu leas innseadh dhomh mu bhodach an t-saibheir. Chuala mi tric gu leòr mar tha e. Na dhì-chuimhnich mi mar a thachair do Mhàiri an Oib an oidhche roimhe?" Gu casg a chur air briathran Dhòmhnuill agus an sgeul a ghiorrachadh, tha e coltach gu'n d' thàinig Màiri seo dhachaidh o bhith air chéilidh an tigh an t-saoir, agus a h-anail na h-uchd agus a h-aodann cho geal ris an anart agus i ag ràdh gu'm faca i samhladh air lot Alasdair Chrubaich. Ge b'e air bith dé a bh' ann, bha Màiri an impis a dhol a cochull a cridhe. Ach cha robh fhios aice nach robh ann ach each bàn a bha aig Alasdair Crubach airson toirt dhachaidh na mòna. Fhuair Alasdair iasad dheth o mhac bràthair athar anns an Druim Uaine. Cha robh e soirbh Màiri a chur as a barail.

"Coimhead fhéin sin," arsa Dòmhnull. "Each bàn—cha robh ann ach each bàn. Innis thusa dhomhsa duine a tha ag ràdh gu'm fac e taibhse agus cuiridh mi geall riut nach robh ann ach each bàn. Cha tachair rud sam bith gun aobhar, ma chleachdas duine foighidinn gu sealltuinn air a shon." Bha am facal mu dheireadh aig Dòmhnull mar a b' àbhaist, ged a bha a bharail fhéin aig Seumas, 's ann aige a bha.

Aon oidhche mu chealla-deug an déidh do Mhàiri an Oib an an t-eagal uamhasach a ghabhail, bha Seumas agus Dòmhnull air an rathad dhachaidh as a' bhùthaidh mhóir. Theireadh cuid gu'n robh barrachd ùidh aca anns an taigh-sheinnse taobh na bùthadh na bh'aca anns a' bhùthaidh fhéin. Dh' fhaodadh sin a bhith a thaobh Sheumais mu'n d' thàinig Domhnull dhachaidh, ach cha robh Dòmhnull ach ga mheas 'na amaideas a bhith a' tadhal air an tigh sheinnse idir. Nam faigheadh Seumas ruith a stigh an dràsda 's a rithisd gun fhios da, cha robh an còrr ann.

Co-dhiùbh bha an oidhche seo car dorcha, ach cha robh tàire sam bith aig na seòid cumail air an rathad. Le sùil a chumail air bàrr nam preasan a bha a' fàs air gach taobh, bha e furasda gu leòir dhaibh cùrsa dhìreach a stiùireadh.

Dìreach 'nuair a bha iad a' dlùthachadh air geata Alasdair Chrùbaich stad Seumas an làrach nam bonn. Chuir e làmh le gréim teann air guaillainn Dhòmhnuill agus thuirt e le guth tùchanach: "Seall siud." Thug Dòmhnull sùil agus gu dearbh bha rud-eigin ann, cumadh glas eadar iad agus leus air ìochdar lot Alasdair Chrùbaich. Bha ceann aige, agus bodhaig, agus

casan. " Seadh, dé th' ann ? " arsa Dòmhnull, " Tha an t-each a
chunnaic Màiri an Oib, each bàn Alasdair Chrùbaich. Gu
dearbha, 'ga fhaicinn 'na sheasamh an siud cho stòlda anns an
t-solus seo, cha chuirinn a' choire air duine faoin ged a shaoileadh
e gur e cumadh duine a bh' ann. Ach thig thusa a null comhla
riumsa agus cha bhi mise fada a' dearbhadh dhuit gur e each a
th' ann." " Nach tu a chaidh as do chiall ! " arsa Seumas. " Gu
dearbh 's mi nach téid. Theid sinn a nunn air a' ghàrradh air an
taobh eile agus gabhaidh sinn an rathad àrd dhachaidh." " Seo
fear nach 'eil a' dol a theicheadh," arsa Domhnull. " 'S fhada o
bha mise a' feitheamh ri cothrom de'n t-seòrsa seo. Tha mise
deimhinn gur e each a tha siud. Agus stad ort, gus a dhearbhadh
dhuit gur e each a th' ann, tha mise a' dol 'ga mharcachd dhachaidh."
" Ma tha, dall ort," arsa Seumas, agus gun an còrr sùil a thoirt
an rathad an rud a bh' ann, dhìrich e an gàrradh agus thug e a
chasan leis a nunn an rathad àrd.

Cha do chuir seo Dòmhnull a null no nall, mar a thigeadh
do dhuine rianail reusanta. Thionndaidh e ris an each agus b'e
sin an t-each. Ghabh Domhnull a nùnn troimh na preasan agus
'nuair a ràinig e thall, b'e each a bh' aige ceart gu leòr, each
gun sgian gun fhiamh. Sheas e an toiseach gu còir socair, agus
choisich e gu ciùin gu taobh na bruaiche 'nuair a rug Dòmhnull
air mhuing air agus a threòraich e a nunn gu'n a' bhruaich e, is e
a' bruidhinn ris fad na tìde leis na faclan a bha e a' smaointeachadh
a bu chòir do dhuine a chleachdadh ri each. Cha robh Domhnull
comharraichte mar mharcaiche 'nuair a b' òige bha e, ach mas
e marcachd a bha a dhìth air, cha b' urrainn dà beothach na bu
shoitheamha fhaighinn na am fear ud. Sheas e ris a' bhruaich gus
an do shreap Dòmhnull le móran spàirn air a mhuin agus ged
a ghreimich Dòmhnull air a mhuing air eagal tuiteam dheth, cha
leigeadh e fhéin a leas e. Dh' fhiach e ri ceann an eich a

76

thionndadh an rathad a bha e ag iarraidh a dhol agus cha robh feum air a' chòrr.

Bha dùil aig Dòmhnull gu'n leumadh an t-each thairis air clais an rathaid agus rinn e greim na bu daingne air 'amhaich, ach 's ann a ghabh e a mach rathad a' gheata gun mhoille 'na cheum. " 'S fheudar nach do dhùin Alasdair an geata an nochd," arsa Domhnull ris fhéin. Chaidh an smuain seo as a chuimhne mar a thàinig i, agus bha aire Dhòmhnuill gu h-iomlan air an ainmhidh ghrinn a bha fodha. Bha iad a nise a' dèanamh deagh astar, ach bha iad a' siubhal cho socair 's gu'n saoileadh Domhnull gur gann a bha casan an eich a' bualadh an làir idir. Shìn e air mar gu'm bitheadh a' ghaoth. " Gu dearbh " arsa Dòmhnull ris fhéin, " 'se each air leth a tha seo, no is e marcaiche air leth a th' annamsa is gun fhios agam air thuige seo."

Cha robh ùine aige leudachadh air na smuaintean sin, oir siud e air a lot fhéin. Stad an t-each dìreach mar a dh' iarr e air shios fo'n tigh, leig e le Dòmhnull tearnadh, agus ann am priobadh, mu'm b' urrainn do Dhomhnull co-dhunadh co-dhiùbh a mholadh e e an Gàidhlig no am Beurla, bha e air falbh cho luath 's cho sàmhach 's a thàinig e, dìreach as an t-sealladh. Bha Dòmhnull air a dhòigh. Mìle gu leth an seachd mionaidean. Cha robh siud dona, thairis air atharnaich is claisean is bruaichean. Dh' fheumadh e foighneachd de Sheumas am b' urrainn daibh fhéin each a cheannach. Leis a sin có a chunnaic e ach Seumas fhéin a' tighinn 'na leth ruith. Chuir iad fàilte air a cheile gu sùnndach, Dòmhnull làn de'n each mhìorbhuileach aig Alasdair Crubach, agus Seumas car mar gu'm bitheadh nàire air gu'n do thréig e a bhràthair ri aghaidh cunnairt. Bha e toilichte Dòmhnull fhaicinn slàn fallain, ged a thug e an aire air an rathad suas gu'n tigh gu'n robh coiseachd Dhòmhnuill car na bu spàgaiche na b' àbhaist: cha robh sin 'na iongnadh. Chaidh iad mu thàmh agus an la-iar-na mhàireach bha Dòmhnull air a chois gu math tràth agus an déidh dha soithichean a' bhreacaist a ghlanadh, thug e tigh Alasdair Chrùbaich air. 'S dòcha gu'n robh 'na bheachd iarraidh air Alasdair a lethsgeul a ghabhail airson an t-each a thoirt leis, no theagamh nach robh e ach a' sireadh cothroim air a' bheothach iongantach seo fhaicinn ri solus latha.

Cha robh fhios aig Seumas dé bha 'na bheachd, ach 'nuair a thill Dòmhnull an ùine gun a bhi ro-fhada, thug Seumas an aire nach robh e ach ann an droch shùnnd, gun ghuth, cha mhór, aige ri radh. "Am faca tu Alasdair?" arsa Seumas. "Chunnaic," fhreagair Dòmhnull. "Am faca tu an t-each?" "Chan fhaca." "C' ait a' bheil e?" arsa Seumas. "Anns an Druim-Uaine," fhreagair Dòmhnull. "Dé tha thu 'g ràdh?" arsa Seumas, is e a' faireachadh an fhuil a' fàgail a ghruaidhean. "Thug mac bràthair athar Alasdair dhachaidh an t-each a bhòin-de," arsa Domhnull. Thuig Seumas nach robh an còrr còmhraidh ri càil Dhòmhnuill agus dh' fhuirich e sàmhach.

"Sin mar a bha," arsa Seumas rium fhéin, "agus dh' fhalbh e gu deas an dé." "Saoil an tig e air ais tuilleadh?", arsa mise. "O thuirt mise ris," arsa Seumas, "gu robh e di-beathte còmhla riumsa uair sam bith. Ach mar a thuirt mi riut, bha e cho fada 'na bharail fhéin, is dùil aige gu robh fios aige air gach ni fo'n ghréin. Chan 'eil cothrom air ; mur a bi agam ach mi fhéin a' cur a' bhuntata, cha bhi ann ach mi fhéin 'ga itheadh."

TAOBH LOCH ARCAIG IS LOCH NIBHEIS—
IOMRADH AIR CUAIRT 'S NA FRITHEAN

Nach tric daoine ag iarraidh rathaidean móra, ach smaointicheamaid tiota air na frith-rathaidean. Có am fear cabhagach nach d'fhairich uaireigin tàladh a' cheum a tha sios an siud troimh'n fhraoch is a' dol a sealladh timchioll cnuic ? Dé a chitheadh tu mu'n ruigeadh tu a cheann, ma tha ceann aige ? Nithean iongantach, tìr a' gheallaidh, 's docha Tir-nan-Og ?

Am b' iad siud na smaointean a bh'air siubhal mo charaid Iain ann an Gleann-garaidh, is a shùil a' laighe air an rathad chaol gu Ceann Loch Uthairne ? Tha Iain, fhios agaibh, air a bheannachadh, no air a mhallachadh ma thogras sibh, le càr. Beannachd ma tha cabhag oirbh, ach mallachd ma tha sibh a' creidsinn gu bheil luchd nan càraichean a' call cothrom nan cas agus ma leanas iad orra nach bi casan idir aca.

Cha chreid mi gu robh eagal air Iain mu na casan, ach co-dhiubh air dha tilleadh as an eilean an uiridh thuirt e, " Ciamar a chòrdadh e riut coiseachd timchioll Chnòideart ? Bheir sinn leinn na gillean."

Dhomhsa cha bu ruith ach leum, ma thuigeas sibh nach ann gu litireil a tha mi a' bruidhinn. An làithean m'òige bha Cnòideart mu' m choinneamh a h-uile latha a dh'éirinn. Ach smaointeachadh air coiseachd ann an dùthaich thall thar cuan mór na Linne Shléibhtich, cha b'e a bh'againn ri dheanamh, eadar crodh is eile 's gach bodaraigeadh dhe'n t-seòrsa.

Am bliadhna, ma ta, bha cuairt Chnòideirt gu bhith agam. Thuirt na càirdean gum bitheadh an turus taitneach, ach bha teagamh air aodann cuid, is fiamh a' ghàire air cuid eile.

Thug mi fhìn is Iain tarruing air Cnòideart gach uair a thachair sinn ; mu dheireadh thuig na h-eòlaich gu robh sinn a cheart d'a rìreadh. Bha earbsa mhór againn anns na gillean, am fear againn sia-deug, agus gille Iain ceithir-deug a dh'aois. Cha robh sinn a' dol a chur cudthrom mì-chuimseach orra, ach bha iad eòlach air campaichean 's gach obair theantaichean is còcaireachd a tha co-cheangailte riutha.

Chuireadh latha air leth, Di-luain, an dara latha fichead dhe'n Iuchar. Cheannaich na Granndaich teanta a chumadh dithis, agus Clann Aonghais a leithid eile. Bha brògan móra is màileid is poca-cadail r'am faotainn. Chualas móran mu ladarnas nam bodach. " Dùil aca," asa Seidhic, " gu bheil iad òg fhathasd." " Tha an cuthach orra," asa Peigidh Alasdair.

Cuthach ann no as chaidh na brògan móra fhiachainn uair no dha agus sheas na casan riutha gu h-iongantach.

Mu dheireadh thainig an latha mór. Chaidh na màileidean a stodhadh anns a' chàr agus ghabh sinn beannachd aotrom leis an luchd-daimh.

Sios gu Loch Laomainn neo-air-thaing coisichean, a' chuid mhór 's na meòirean an àird ag iarraidh an togail. Ghabh sinne seachad orra le gne de nàire. Cha b'ann mar siud a bhitheamaidne nuair a gheibheamaid fo uidheam coiseachd.

Beagan dàil am buithnean a' Ghearasdain agus a' chiad ghreim os cionn an rathaid anns a' Ghleann Mhór. Dh'fhàg Iain an càr an cùram tuathanaich ann an Gearr-Lòchaidh.

Le beagan spairn chaidh na màileidean an àird agus thog sinn oirnn suas taobh Loch Lochaidh. B'e aon de na comhairlean a fhuair sinn — o fhuair sinn móran chomhairlean — gum bu chòir dhuinn deanamh coltach ris na saighdearan, leth-cheud mionaid coiseachd agus deich mionaidean analach 's an uair. Ach thuirt fear miobhail gum b'e deich mionaidean coiseachd agus fois a b'fheàrr a thigeadh ruinne.

A' cheud uair a stad sinn, leig sinn dhinn na màileidean. Sinn a bha aotrom, car a' dol mu seach. Cha robh cabhag oirnn ; bha am feasgar briagha is bha sinn an deagh shùnnd.

'Nuair a thionndaidh an rathad gu'n iar bha fiughair againn ris "a' mhìle dhorcha" agus ri sealladh air Loch Arcaig. An seo rug bhan oirnn agus, rud a chuir beagan iongnaidh oirnn, thairg fear-na-cuibhle ar togail. Thug sinn uile sùil air Iain agus 'nuair nach d' rinn e maille, siud sinn agus an airneis an cul a' bhan.

Bha an draibhear agus an té a bha ri 'thaobh aoidheil agus fiosrachail. Chuir e iongnadh oirnn an rathad a bhith cho math is na tighean cho tearc. Dh'innis e dhuinn gu robh ochd mile deug caora air a' mhonadh seo, dùthaich Loch Iall. Sgeul a chualas gu tric, lionmhorachd chaorach is gainne sluaigh.

Thall air taobh eile an locha bha Coille Ionar-mhailidh, bunnan glasa na seann Choille Albannaich. B'i a' Bheurla chruaidh a bh'againn, ach nuair a dh'fhaighnich sinn an robh rathad aithghearr eadar an Tom Dhonn agus Loch Arcaig (is sinn a' smaointeachadh air ar tilleadh), thuirt e gu robh, thairis air Coir an Daga, rathad cruidh bho shean. Thug Coire an Daga snodha gaire air a' bhoirionnach, mar gum bitheadh i a' gabhail a lethsgeil airson Gaidhlig a bhruidhinn ris na Deasaich. 'Nuair a fhreagair mise anns a' Ghaidhlig, sinn a bha còirdte.

Thug a' bhan da mhìle sinn suas taobh an locha. Chùm sinn oirnn gus an d'fhuair sinn àite airson nan teantaichean. Bha na balaich a' leigeil fhaicinn cho gleusda 'sa bha iad 'gan cur suas, agus leig sinne leotha. Thug ciùinead an fheasgair seann eascaraid guineach nar car, na cuileagan meanbha. Comhla ri rabhadh m'an deidh-san, fhuair sinn botuil de stuth a chuir, tha mi 'smaointeachadh, seòrsa de thuainealaich orra co-dhiubh. Gu dearbh bha glùinean geala nam bodach gu math feumach air.

Cha robh a' cheud oidhche fo chanbhas ro anshocrach agus

bha a shòlas fhéin aig gach tràth-bidh. Feasgar Di-mairt rinn sinn ceann Loch Arcaig dheth. Chùm sinn oirnn da mhìle suas Gleann Deasairigh mu'n do stad sinn.

Bha sinn a' fàs eòlach air na màileidean agus bha itheadh a' bhidh 'gam fàgail na b'aotruime. Cho luath 's a rachadh biadh ainmeachadh bha Iain a mach leis a' chnogan feòla. 'Nuair a thachair seo an dara agus an treas uair thainig e thugamsa nach b'e uile gu léir an coibhneas a dh'fhàg Iain cho còir ; ach an t-eòlas gu robh e ag aotromachadh na màileid. Duine léirsinneach ; dh'aidich e air eagal céis làn siabuinn-seubhaidh a thoirt leis, gun do chuir e a dhara leth a mach ann an soitheach mun d'fhàg e. Co-dhiubh rinn sinn còrdadh gun dàil mu thoirt gnothuichean as na màileidean turus mu seach.

Bha campa Ghlinn-Deasairigh na b'àirde agus cha robh sgeul air meanbh-chuileagan. Beanntan móra air gach taobh. Romhainn air aon diubh bha sgiathan de cheò gu math iseal. " Cha toigh leam siud," asa fear aig tigh Ghlinn-Deasairigh Iochdraich, is sinn a' cur ceisd air 'san dol seachad. Cha do ghabh sinn móran suim de a bhriathran aig an am, ach chuimhnich sinn uair is uair orra roimh dheireadh na seachduinne.

'Nuair a dh'fhàg sinn maduinn Di-ciadain bha uisge mìn ann. Cha robh an ceum, far an robh ceum, ach corrach. Mar a bha sinn a' dìreadh bu truime a dh'fhàs an t-uisge. An toiseach bha mise cho faicilleach ri càch c'àit an cuirinn mo chas ; aon uair 's gun do lion an t-uisge na brògan, cha robh feum air faiceall— mu chasan fliucha co-dhiubh.

Bha am map ag innseadh mu na sguran àrda os ar cionn ged nach leigeadh an ceò is an sian leinn am faicinn. Air an laimh dheis bha Sgur na Cìche, trì mìle is ceithir cheud troidh. Fliuch 's mar a bha sinn cha b'urrainn duinn gun seasamh a dh'amharc air na h-easan eireachdail a bha a' taomadh a nuas air gach taobh.

Bha sinn a nis a' tearnadh agus mu dheireadh thainig Loch Nibheis am follais. Bha an t-uisge cho cunbhalach 's gun robh cùram oirnn mu chur seachad na h-oidhche. Dh'fhàs an ceum na bu leatha agus an àiteachan bha e air a neartachadh le ballachan ìseal cloiche. Chuala sinn gum b'ann ri linn an t-Sinilear Wade a ghearradh a chuid ud dhe'n rathad.

Thainig sinn gu Abhainn Coire na Cìche, a' ruith bho Loch Cuaich gu Loch Nibheis. Bha an staran an lath ud fo'n tuil. Gu faiceallach thug sinn a mach an taobh eile mean air mhean, agus bha sinn mór as na gillean, ged nach do ghabh sinn dad oirnn.

Chunnaic sinn da thigh shios faisg air a' Chladach agus chaidh sinn gu'n fhear a b'fhaisge. Bha triùir a staigh, luchd-siubhail coltach ruinn fhìn, a' gabhail seilbh air tigh falamh airson na h-oidhche. Bha an taigh eile falamh cuideachd ach bha e car as ar rathad. A' gabhail comhairle fear dhe'n triùir a bha 'stigh chùm sinn air adhart gu tigh falamh eile, mu mhìle air thoiseach, thuirt esan, ach eadar a h-uile bogalaich a thachair oirnn, shaoil leinn gu robh e na b'fhaisge air a tri.

A bharrachd air sin bha abhainn bhras eile, abhainn Carnach, eadarainn agus an tigh. Cha robh air fhàgail dhe'n t-seann drochaid ach na cliathaichean agus b'fheudar dhuinn coiseachd suas astar math mun do thàr sinn a nunn, greim daingeann aig gach fear air làimh an fhir a b'fhaisge.

Dh'fhosgail sinn dorus taigh Charnaich gun chead iarraidh. Bha ceithir seòmraichean seasgair ann. Dh'aithnicheadh duine air an uidheam-rùsgaidh agus gu h-àraidh air an ùrlar gum b'e caoraich, agus pailteas dhiubh, a bh'ann mu dheireadh. Reitich sinn aon cheann agus cha b'fhada gus an robh teine briagha de sheann fhiodh againn. Neo-air-thaing nigheadaireachd is tiormachadh an uair sin. Theagamh gu robh an tiormachadh na bu choimh-lionta na an nigheadaireachd. Aon rud cha robh cion uisge oirnn ;

cha robh dòigh air tuilleadh fliuchaidh a sheachnadh ach a dhol a mach cas-ruisgt' g'a iarraidh. Cha robh an t-ùrlar ach cruaidh ach chuir sinn sios caob dhe'n stuth ùr ud a thoill na pocannan-cadail as an leth-oir.

An la'rna-mhaireach, Di-ar-daoin, bha an t-uisge cho trom 's a bha e riamh. Dh'fhan sinn gun deidh mheadhon-latha ach a faiceamaid an togadh e air. Cha do thog ach bha sinn deònach Inbhir-Idh ruigheachd an lath ud. Bha gu leòir againn de bhiadh chnogan is annlann eile, ach cha d'thug sinn leinn de dh'aran ach na dh'fhoghnadh gu Inbhir-Idh.

Ghabh sinn an rathad a b'fhaide gu Inbhir-Idh timchioll a' chladaich. Bha aithreachas oirnn a rithisd nach do ghabh sinn an rathad a bu ghiorra a mach am monadh agus sios Gleann Meadail, ach bhac eagal a' cheò sinn. A reir a' mhap bha ceum rathad a' chladaich bho Chaolas-Chnòideirt mu leitheach slighe, ma bha cha d'amais sinne air ro thric.

Cha deachaidh sinn fada bho Chàrnach 'nuair a b'fheudar dhuinn coiseachd troimh allt ; bha sinn eòlach air a' chleas sin mun robh an latha seachad. Mu dha mhìle bho Chàrnach chunnaic sinn an ceathramh tigh falamh, aig Camus Ruairidh. Cha robh adhartas furasda eadar raineach is bogalaich is bearraidhean. Chaidh sinn seachad air tigh Caolas-Chnòideirt gun mhóran cuideachaidh no fiosrachaidh fhaotainn air ciod a bha romhainn.

Goirid an deidh sin rainig sinn togalach fhiodha ri oir an locha, an t-àite far an robh iad a' cruinneachadh a' mhiotail sin, Mica, an am a' chogaidh. Bha torran beaga dheth timchioll agus rathad cuagach suas am bruthach air am bitheadh na h-eich bheaga 'ga ghiulain a nuas chun a' chidhe bhig a bha shios fodhainn. Sguir an obair seo an déidh a' chogaidh.

Rinn sinn greim bìdh an seo. Bha sinn an sin suas is sios gus mu dheireadh thall an d'thainig Ob Inbhir-Idh m'ar comhair. Bha sinn a nise gu math àrd agus b'e tearnadh a bu duilghe na dìreadh. B'e seo Creag an Dotair far na chaill " an Dotair Bàn " a bheatha aon oidhche dhorcha a' tighinn a Caolas-Chnòideirt. Chuir e ri ar cliù an Inbhir-Idh 'nuair a chual iad gun d'rinn sinn an gnothuch air Creag an Dotair, ged a bha solus latha againn.

A' ruigheachd Inbhir-Idh chuir sinn romhainn tilleadh gu deas rathad Mhalaig an la-iar-na-mhaireach. Bho ar cairdean an Inbhir-Idh fhuair sinn gabhail ruinn gu coibhneil, suipeir 'nan tigh fhéin an toiseach, tigh-cadail dhuinn fhìn le teine guail ris an d'rinn sinn sogan airson blàiths is tiormachadh aodaichean, agus braiceast maduinn Di-haoine.

Bha a' mhaduinn seo fiadhaich a bharrachd air a bhith fliuch. A' coiseachd gu'n laimrig, astar mu mhìle, bha an t-aodach a thiormaich sinn cho curamach cho fliuch 'sa bha e riamh. Agus mar nach robh ar leòir againn de uisg' an adhair, fhuair sinn a nis ar cuibhrionn de uisge an locha.

Bha am bat-aiseig mu fhichead slat bho'n chidhe agus dithis ag iomramh triuir aig gach turus a mach ann an geòla bheag. Chaidh Iain agus na gillean a mach air an dara turus. Bha mise a measg nan coignear a bh'air am fàgail an turus mu dheireadh, agus thug na seòid leotha comhla sinn.

Bha beul na geòla glé fhaisg air an uisge agus cha d'rachadh agamsa fiù suidhe anns an deireadh air eagal gum fliuchainn a chuid sin dhe'm bhodhaig a bha thuige seo cuimseach tioram. 'Nuair a sheas cuid aig cliathach a' bhàta mhóir rinn a' gheòla an rud a bha i 'bagairt a dheanamh fad na h-ùine, chaidh i fodha aig an deireadh. Bha taidhir cuibhle thar na cliathaich os mo chionnsa, agus chaidh agam air greim a dheanamh oirre le aon làimh, rud a bha feumail, oir bha an sàile a' ruigheachd nan aisnean. Bha othail gu leòir air mo làimh dheis, ged nach b-urrainn domh fhaicinn. Cha robh ùine ann airson aithreachais a thaobh a' mhaileid a chumail orm. Thainig fear 'gam chuideachadh agus bha mi shuas, mi fhìn 'sa' mhaileid 's an cot-uachdair 's na brògan móra. Bha càch shuas romham. Cha bu fhliuichead riamh gu seo e, ach bha e furasda gu h-àraidh do Iain, fealla-dha a dheanamh dheth 'nuair a bha e seachad.

Bha an t-aiseag cho salach 'sa chunnaic mi riamh. An deidh gearan mhodhail a dheanamh am Malaig fhuair sinn àite beag far na chuir sinn dhinn aodach fliuch agus a chuir sinn oirnn aodach leth-thioram. Anns an trean cha robh sinn uamhasach tioram ach cha robh sinn an droch shùnnd.

Bha sinn an Drochaid Spidhein aig tri uairean ach bha e uair 'sa mhaduinn nuair a rainig sinn Glaschu. Ach 'se tha sin sgeul eile.

" Cha chreid mi nach d'fhuair sibh leasan," asa Seidhic. Fhuair gu dearbh, barrachd is aon leasan—mu ghiulain, can, màileid air do dhruim ann an geòla.

Ach ma bhitheas sinn beò slàn an ath shamhradh, có a their nach toir sinn oidhirp eile air cuairt Chnòideirt !

DEALBHAN-CLUICHE

"MOD MHIC AN TOISICH"
Dealbh-chluich an tri seallaidhean

Luchd-cluiche:

Fionnlagh Mac-an-Tòisich.
Mairi Alasdair Iain.
Peigi Bean Alasdair.
Alasdair Ean Ruairidh.
Murchadh Greum.
   (Am maighstir-sgoile).
Diorbhail Ghreum.
Rùnaire a' Mhòid.
Iarla Loch Nis.

A' chiad sealladh.
Seòmar an taigh Alasdair Ean Ruairidh.
Feasgar. Mairi 'na suidhe air an t-seise.

FIONNLAGH: (*A' cumail an t-snàth*). Cha bhi fada againn ri feitheamh a nise, a Mhairi a ghràidh. Cuin' a tha thu a' dol a chur air leth an latha mhóir ?

MAIRI: Aon uair 's gu'm faigh sinn tigh, Fhionnlaigh, a luaidh. Feumaidh sinn tigh fhaotainn an toiseach.

FIONNLAGH: Feumaidh, feumaidh. Ach cha bhi sinn fada feitheamh tuilleadh. Chi sinn dé thachras air an t-seachdain-sa tighinn.

MAIRI: Ma theid gu math leinn, toisichidh sinn air a chur air dòigh, agus an déidh sin, Fhionnlaigh . . . .

FIONNLAGH: 'S ann an sin a bhitheas an latha, latha na bainnse . . . .

MAIRI: O Fhionnlaigh . . . .

FIONNLAGH: (*A' cronan*) Ho mo Mhairi Laghach.

MAIRI: Tha thu math air seinn, Fhionnlaigh. Bu chòir dhuit a dhol gu na Mhòid.

FIONNLAGH: (*A' magadh*). Bu chòir gu dearbh ! Gheibhinn a' cheud duais, tha mise creidsinn.

MAIRI: C' arson nach fhaigheadh tu a' cheud duais ; a' cheart da rìreadh a tha mi.

FIONNLAGH: An nise, a nise, a Mhairi. Chan 'eil móran nach fhiachainn air do shon, ach seinn aig a' Mhòd, sin agad aonan dhiubh.

MAIRI: Nì thu seo air mo shon-sa Fhionnlaigh. Tha thu dìreach an deagh am ; tha tri seachdainnean agad fhathasd.

FIONNLAGH: Tri seachdainnean ! Na dhì-chuimhnich thu dé a bha sinn a' dol a dheanamh leis na tri seachdainnean sin ?

MAIRI: O, a' deasachadh tighe. Faodaidh sinn an da chuid a dheanamh.

FIONNLAGH: Dìreach sin. Cluinn mise a' seinn 's mi ag obair air peantadh.

MAIRI: C' arson nach bitheadh. 'Se sùnnd seinn a bu chòir a bhi ort ri leithid a dh' obair.

FIONNLAGH: Nan canadh tu sùnnd bainse gu dearbh ;

MAIRI: A nise, cha bhith guth air banais gus am bi am Mòd seachad.

FIONNLAGH: Cha chuala mi riamh a leithid. Dé am feum a dheanadh e dhomhsa ged a gheibhinn duais aig a' Mhòd, rud nach fhaigh ?

MAIRI: Nì e feum dhuit — agus urram ;

FIONNLAGH: Ciamar ?

Tìr an Aigh

MAIRI: Smaointich air na céilidhean 's na cruinnichidhean a chuireadh iad air chois dìreach air son do chluinntinn.

FIONNLAGH: 'S iad nach cuireadh. Agus mur a faighinn duais, 's docha nach pòsadh tu idir mi.

MAIRI: O Fhionnlaigh, phòsainn-sa thu ged nach bitheadh smid ciùil 'na do cheann.

FIONNLAGH: Siuthad ma ta, gabhaidh mi thu air d' fhacal.

MAIRI: O cha teid thu as mar sin idir. Bu mhath leamsa gu'n cluinneadh feadhainn eile cho math 's a tha thu air seinn.

FIONNLAGH: Tha siud gu leòir dhe do bhrosgul.

MAIRI: Chan e brosgul a th' ann idir, Fhionnlaigh. Cuiridh tu d' ainm air adhart an diugh fhéin.

FIONNLAGH: O mar a tha mi leat. Nach bochd nach do sguir mi aig bruidhinn chiallach, an àite ramalaig de dh' òran.

MAIRI: Ramalaig de dh' òran! Ramalaig de dh' òran. A bheil cuimhn' agad dé an t-òran a bha thu seinn?

FIONNLAGH: O bha, stad ort, "Ho mo Mhàiri Laghach."

MAIRI: Seadh agus mise a' smaointeachadh gu'm b' ann ormsa a bha d' aire 'nuair a bha thu 'ga sheinn.

FIONNLAGH: Có air a bhitheadh m' aire ach ortsa, a Mhairi. Ach 'se aon rud a th' ann a bhi a' seinn 's gun an seo ach sinn fhìn, ach rud eile seasamh air àrd-ùrlar a' Mhòid.

MAIRI: Na cuireadh àrd-ùrlair a' Mhòid dragh sam bith ort. Suidhidh mi fhéin shios mu d' choinneamh agus seinnidh tu an t-òran mar gu'm bitheadh tu 'ga sheinn dìreach dhomhsa. Cha bhi umhail agad do dhuine beò anns an talla ach mi fhìn.

FIONNLAGH: Glé shoirbh sin a ràdh, a Mhairi, a luaidh. Cha bhi e cho soirbh a dheanamh.

MAIRI: Bithidh e soirbh gu leòir, chi thusa.

FIONNLAGH: Chi mi . . . .

MAIRI: O, tha thu deònach. Nach 'eil sin glan!

FIONNLAGH: Cha dubhairt mi . . . .

MAIRI: Thuirt thu agus cha bhi a' chaochladh ann. Stad gus an innis mi dha m' athair 's dha mo mhàthair e.

FIONNLAGH: (*Ag amharc air fhéin anns an sgàthan*). A' seinn aig a' Mhòd! A' seinn aig a' Mhòd.

ALASDAIR: (A' tighinn a steach). A' dol a sheinn aig a' Mhòd! Fhionnlaigh?

FIONNLAGH: Airson dad a chuala sibh 'se Mairi as coireach. Seo agaibh i fhéin. (*Mairi a' tighinn a steach le tea air treudha, agus a màthair 'ga leantuinn*).

MAIRI: Bha mi ag innseadh dhaibh, Fhionnlaigh.

PEIGI: A' dol a sheinn aig a' Mhòd. Saoil nach 'eil gu leòir air d' inntinn, Fhionnlaigh.

FIONNLAGH: 'Se sin a bha mise ag ràdh.

MAIRI: De bith dé bha thu 'g ràdh, tha thu a' dol a sheinn aig a' Mhòd.

ALASDAIR: Chan ann a h-uile latha a bhitheas Mòd aig Mac an Tòisich. Nach tu fhéin a bhitheas spaideil le féileadh beag air àrd—ùrlar a' Mhoid!

FIONNLAGH: An saoil thu? Chan 'eil féileadh agam.

PEIGI: Chan urrainn Mac an Tòisich a dhol gu Mòd gun feileadh-beag.

MAIRI: Cha leig thu leas féileadh, Fhionnlaigh, mur a togair thu fhéin; seinnidh tu a' cheart cho math ann am briogais.

PEIGI: Chan abair mi sin idir. Tha fhios gu bheil na breith-eamhnan a' coimhead air coltas nan seinneadairean.

ALASDAIR: 'S docha gu bheil iad a' coimhead air an aodann gun sùil a thoirt air an aodach. Dé do bharail fhéin, Fhionn-laigh?

FIONNLAGH: 'Se mo bharail-sa gur e leth-bhotul a b' fheumaile do sheinneadair na féileadh.

Tìr an Aigh

ALASDAIR: O chan e. Ciamar seo a thuirt bard Loch Nis:
Le gloinne shlàn gun gabhainn-sa
Sia ceathramhnan 's a fonn dhuibh
ach òlam té a bharrachd dhiubh
Is chumainn ceòl a chaoidh ruibh.

FIONNLAGH: Chan 'eil sibh air a-shon.

ALASDAIR: Chan 'eil. Chan fhaigheadh tu seachad air an dithis aig an dorus co-dhiùbh leis.

MAIRI: Coma leat. Cha leig thu leas féileadh beag no leth-bhotul.

PEIGI: Mura leig, dé a' chomhairle a bheireadh tu air, a Mhairi.

MAIRI: Tha mise ag ràdh ris ma chumas e a shùil ormsa 'nuair a bhitheas e seinn, nach teid e iomrall.

ALASDAIR: Cha dean sin an gnothuch.

MAIRI: Carson nach dean ?   Tha e aoidheil agus tha e ceòlmhor. Nach dean sin an gnothuch.

ALASDAIR: Cha dean.

PEIGI: Innis thusa dhuinn ma ta, Alasdair dé as còir dha dheanamh.

FIONNLAGH: Fuireach aig an tigh. Sin as còir . . . .

ALASDAIR: Innsidh mise dhuibh dé as còir dha dheanamh.

MAIRI: Seadh ma ta?

ALASDAIR: 'S còir dha eòlas a chur air na daoine cearta.

FIONNLAGH: Cha ghabh mi gnothuch riutha.

MAIRI: Uisdibh athair, có chuir sin 'nur ceann ?

PEIGI: Chan 'eil mi a' creidsinn guth dheth.

ALASDAIR: Có dhiubh a chreideas gu nach creid, siud mar a tha.

MAIRI: Có na daoine cearta sin air a bheil sibh a' bruidhinn ?

ALASDAIR: O . . . . uil . . . . . feadhainn mar a tha Iarla Loch Nis . . . .

PEIGI: O, duine urramach, còir.

MAIRI: 'Se gu dearbh.

FIONNLAGH: Chan aithne dhomh idir e. Có e?

ALASDAIR: Iarla Loch Nis. O tha e 'na Fhear-Cathrach air Comhairle a' Mhòid . . . .

FIONNLAGH: An e sin uile . . . . ?

ALASDAIR: O chan e. Tha e a' tadhal air a' Mhòd a h-uile bliadhna. Tha a dhealbh anns na paipearan—naidheachd.

PEIGI: Agus tha daoine a' tighinn a mach 'ga fhaicinn.

ALASDAIR: O, tha, gu h-àraidh na boirionnaich. Dheanadh iadsan rud sam bith nam faodadh iad fiù beantainn ri iomall aodaich.

FIONNLAGH: A nise dé an gnothach a th' aig seo ri duaisean aig a' Mhòd?

ALASDAIR: O tha. Nam faigheadh tusa eòlas air Iarla Loch Nis, dh' fhaodadh tu a bhith coma co-dhiubh bhitheadh aoidh no dreun ort, no co-dhiubh a dheanadh tu seinn no sgiamhail.

PEIGI: A nise Alasdair, tha thu a' dol tuilleadh is fada. A bheil thusa ag innseadh dhomhsa gu bheil iad a' foighneachd de Iarla Loch Nis có a bu chòir a' cheud duais fhaighinn?

ALASDAIR: O chan 'eil iad a' foighneachd dheth mar sin . . . . ach nan sealladh esan dhaibh . . . . 's docha gun bhruidhinn idir . . . . gu robh ùidh aige ann an seinneadair àraidh, abair Fionnlagh an seo, cha b' urrainn daibh a' cheud duais a dhiùltadh dha.

FIONNLAGH: Carson?

ALASDAIR: Cha bhitheadh e modhail . . . . agus cha bhitheadh e glic.

MAIRI: A bheil sibh a' smaointeachadh gu bheil sin onoireach?

ALASDAIR: Faodaidh nach 'eil air doigh, ach tha e a' cumail a' Mhòid a' dol.

Tìr an Aigh

FIONNLAGH: Mas ann mar sin a tha e air a chumail a' dol, tha cho math dha sgur. Seo aon fhear nach gabh gnothach ri Iarla Loch Nis no ri . . . .

ALASDAIR: Fhionnlaigh a charaid, tha thu car doirbh do riar-achadh. Cha ghabh thu gnothach ri Iarla Loch Nis, chan fhaod thu leth-bhotul a bhith agad, agus chan 'eil thu ro-chìnnteach mu'n fheileadh-bheag.

PEIGI: (A' dol a mach). Gheibh mise am féileadh beag an toiseach.

ALASDAIR: Cha dean am féileadh coire, ach tha seòl eile agamsa nach do dh' ainmich mi fhathasd.

MAIRI: Thoiribh dhuinn e, mata.

ALASDAIR: Theid sinn a choimhead air mo charaid, am maighstir-sgoile.

FIONNLAGH: Dé a ni esan?

ALASDAIR: Tha e air a bhith 'na bhritheamh aig a' Mhòd bhon as cuimhne leam, agus tha mi cìnnteach gu'm bi e'm bliadhna a rithisd ann.

MAIRI: An saoil sibh gu'm bitheadh sin ceart?

ALASDAIR: O chan 'eil sinn a' dol a dh' iarraidh air Fionnlagh a chur air thoiseach, mar a tha thusa an dùil.

MAIRI: Dé tha sibh a' dol a dh' iarraidh, ma ta?

ALASDAIR: Iarraidh sinn cuideachadh air leis a' Ghaidhlig, leasan no dha mu na h-ll-s, fhios agad.

FIONNLAGH: Nach fhaod e a bhith amharusach m'ar timchioll?

ALASDAIR: Ged a bhitheadh, chan e amharus as motha a bhitheas air, ach moit gu bheil sinn a' toirt dha an urraim tha dligheach mar sgoilear Gaidhlig.

PEIGI: (A' tighinn a steach leis an fhéileadh). Seo agad a nise, Fhionnlaigh. Ciamar a theid e riut? (Ga chur air a bhialaibh).

MAIRI: Tha e car fada ach gabhaidh e togail.

ALASDAIR: Ceart gu leòir. Thoir thusa leat e, Fhionnlaigh.

FIONNLAGH: Tapadh leibh.

PEIGI: Paisgidh mi e gum bi thu falbh.

ALASDAIR: Chuir sinn rud eile air doigh 'nuair a bha thu shios, a Pheigi.

PEIGI: An do chòrd sibh mu rud-eigin mu dheireadh?

ALASDAIR: Chòrd; Tha mi fhìn is Fionnlagh a' dol a thadhal air a' Ghreumach, anns an tigh sgoile.

PEIGI: Air a' Ghreumach. Tha an Greumach ceart gu leòir ach (*car eadar fealla-dha is da rìreadh*) cuimhnichibh air an nighinn ud a th' aige, is e a' fairtleachadh air duine fhaotainn dhith.

ALASDAIR: Thu fhéin 's do spòrs, a Pheigi. 'S ann ri a h-athair a tha an gnothuch againne.

PEIGI: O ge ta, bi air d' fhaiceall roimh'n nighinn mhóir ud aige, Fhionnlaigh.

FIONNLAGH: Chan 'eil nighean dhomhsa ach Mairi.

MAIRI: 'S ann agam a tha fios, Fhionnlaigh.

PEIGI: Thuirt mi fhéin a cheart rud ri d' athair.

ALASDAIR: Agus bha e fior, nach robh?

PEIGI: Bha, bha. Ach ma theid sibh a' choimhead air a' Ghreumach, dé a nì esan air ur son.

ALASDAIR: Tha e gu bhi 'na bhritheamh aig a' Mhòd, nach 'eil.

PEIGI: Tha, ach tha barrachd is aon bhritheamh ann. Tha britheamh ciùil ann cuideachd nach 'eil?

ALASDAIR: O tha, tha fhios agam air sin. Ach mas e an aon ablach de Shasunnach a bhitheas an mar as àbhaist cha thog e a ghuth an aghaidh a' Ghreumaich.

FIONNLAGH: Tha earbsa mhór agaibh anns a' Ghreumach seo, ach dé a' chìnnt a th' agaibh gu'n còrd a' Ghaidhlig agamsa ris ?

ALASDAIR: Cha chòrd an dràsda, ach faodaidh tu fiachainn ri bruidheann coltach ris-san, aon uair 's gu'n cluinn thu e.

FIONNLAGH: Chan fhiach. Chan atharraich mise mo Ghaidhlig air sgàth britheimh air thalamh ; chan 'eil Gaidhlig ann nas fheàrr na a' Ghaidhlig agam fhìn.

MAIRI: Na can sin, Fhionnlaigh. Cha mhisde duine sam bith da sheòrsa Gaidhlig.

PEIGI: Nì aon seòrsa an gnothach dhomhsa. Fagaidh mi agaibh fhéin e. (*A' sgioblachadh nan cupanan agus a' dol a mach*).

ALASDAIR: Faodaidh tu sin, a Pheigi. Na cuireadh nighean a' Ghreumaich cùram sam bith ort.

FIONNLAGH: Mur 'eil e cur dragh oirbh ach sin, tha mise deònach a dhol far an togair sibh.

MAIRI: Ceart gu leòir, Fhionnlaigh.

ALASDAIR: Gasda. Leigidh mi fhéin fios a dh' ionnsaidh a' mhaighstir-sgoile am maireach agus theid sinn le cheile a choimhead air roimh dheireadh na seachduinne.

An Dara Sealladh
Seòmar ann an tigh-còmhnuidh na sgoile : Feasgar.
Murchadh Greum, am maighstir-sgoile 'na shuidhe a' darnaigeadh agus Diorbhal a nighean a' dol a shuidhe a leughadh leabhair.

DIORBHAL: O, tha mi sgìth. (A' suidhe).

AN GREUMACH: Thu fhéin 's do sgìos. Dé dh' fhàg sgìth an nochd thu ?

DIORBHAL: Thiormaich mi na soithichean.

AN GREUMACH: Tiormachadh shoithichean. Feumaidh tu barrachd is sin a dheanamh mun toir duine sùil ort, a Dhior-bhail.

DIORBHAL: Nach tric a chuala mi sin.

GREUM: Is tric a thuirt do mhàthair chaomh nach maireann riut.

DIORBHAL: Agus sibh fhéin o'n dh' fhalbh i. Ach innsibh dhomh cuin' a tha e a' tighinn ?

GREUM: Tha dithis a' tighinn.

DIORBHAL: O tha fhios agam air a sin. Cuin' a tha Fionnlagh . . . . Fionnlagh Mac an Tòisich a' tighinn ?

GREUM: Am fear a tha dol a sheinn aig a' Mhòd ? Bu chòir dha fhéin 's do Alasdair Ean Ruairidh a bhith an seo uair sam bith a nise.

DIORBHAL: Fionnlagh seo, de seòrsa fear a th' ann ?

GREUM: Duine foghainteach, tha mi tuigsinn. Chan e gu faca mise an duine riamh. Tha deagh bharail aig Alasdair air, 's foghnaidh sin dhomhsa.

DIORBHAL: Tha e ag iarraidh cuideachadh leis a' Ghaidhlig, nach 'eil.

GREUM: Tha, tha. 'Se sin a tha iad uile ag iarraidh.

DIORBHAL: Carson nach fhaigheadh e cuideachadh le seinn a bharrachd air Gaidhlig.

GREUMACH: Có a bheireadh sin dha ?

DIORBHAL: Bheirinnsa.

GREUM: Obh, obh. Leasanan seinn. Thusa ?

DIORBHAL: Seadh, leasanan seinn a h-uile feasgar eadar seo 's am Mod.

GREUM: A bheil thu samointeachadh gun tréig e an té a th' aige cho ealamh sin ?

DIORBHAL: Cha b'e a' cheud fhear. Ma shaoileas e gun toir sibhse a' cheud duais dha, 's ann a chuireadh e iongnadh oirbh dé a nì e.

Tìr an Aigh

GREUM: An ann mar seo a tha, a Dhiorbhail. Geallaidh mise a' cheud duais dha ma ghabhas e leasanan seinn uatsa . . . .

DIORBHAL: O cha d' thuirt mi sin idir, athair.

GREUM: Agus an déidh dha leasanan seinn fhaotainn uatsa, bhitheadh e cho fada 'nad chomain 's gun iarr e ort a phòsadh-ho-ho-ho.

DIORBHAL: Bitheadh sibhse a' gaireachdaich. Dh' fhaodadh sibh a bhith air a chur na bu laghaiche na rinn sibh gun teagamh.

GREUM: Bi sàmhach. Seo agad iad. Tog ort 's dean rud-eigin. Thigibh a steach. Ciamar a tha thu Alasdair ? (*Tha Diorbhal a' togail stocainn agus a' tòiseachadh air fighe*).

ALASDAIR: Tha mi gu math, taing. Agus thu fhéin ; Seo an duine òg, Fionnlagh Mac an Tòisich.

GREUM: O gu dearbh, Mac an Tòisich. Seo am fear a tha 'dol a sheinn aig a' Mhòd.

ALASDAIR: 'Se.

GREUM: Ho, ho, chan ann a h-uile latha a bhitheas Mòd aig Mac an Tòisich.

ALASDAIR: (*A' deanamh lasgan*). Nach 'eil sin fhéin math. Mòd aig Mac an Tòisich. Cha do smaointich thu air siud Fhionnlaigh.

FIONNLAGH: Uh-uh-uh.

GREUM: Agus seo agaibh an nighean agam, Diorbhal.

ALASDAIR: O thachair sinne roimhe.

DIORBHAL: Thachair, thachair. Tha mi toilichte ur faicinn a Mhgr. Mhic an Tòisich.

GREUM: Deanaibh suidhe. Dé as urrainn dhomh a dheanamh air ur son ? Beagan Gaidhlig ri dhol thairis air . . . . no . . . . ?

FIONNLAGH: 'Se ma's e bhur toil e ; Tha Alasdair 's mi fhéin dhe'n bheachd gur i a' Ghaidhlig as luachmhoire na an ceòl . . . .

ALASDAIR: Agus nach cluinneamaid Gaidhlig na bu choimhlionta na chluinneamaid agaibhse.

GREUM: Dìreach sin. Tha mise gu bhith 'nam bhritheamh aig a' Mhòd am bliadhna rithisd.

FIONNLAGH: O ma tha, cha robh còir againn air tighinn a seo idir 's docha.

ALASDAIR: Carson, air eagal gu'n cuireadh iad leth-bhreith as leth a' bhritheimh !

GREUM: Na bitheadh cùram oirbh. Chan abair mise ri duine gu robh sibh an seo. Cha dean e coire sam bith dhuibh ; 'S docha gun dean e feum dhuibh, 'se sin, ma ghabhas sibh mo chomhairle.

FIONNLAGH: Dé sin ? Gabhaidh sinn do chomhairle gun teagamh.

GREUM: Chan 'eil móran ceàrr air do Ghaidhlig, a Mhic an Tòisich, cho fad 's a chi mise, ach bheirinnsa a' chomhairle ort leasanan seinn a ghabhail.

ALASDAIR: Cuin' a ghabh thu uibhir de ùidh anns an t-seinn a Ghreumaich ?

GREUM: Uel, tha Comhairle a' Mhòid a' toirt an àite as àirde do'n cheòl a nise.

ALASDAIR: A bheil ? Cuin' a thachair seo ?

GREUM: Thachair 'nuair a rinneadh Fear-Cathrach de Iarla Loch Nis.

FIONNLAGH: Iarla Loch Nis ! Iarla Loch Nis ! Cha chluinn mi ach Iarla Loch Nis.

DIORBHAL: Cha toigh leibh Iarla Loch Nis, a Mhgr. Ic an Tòisich ?

Tìr an Aigh

FIONNLAGH: Chan 'eil ni agamsa 'na aghaidh. Chan fhaca mi'n duine riamh, ach 's coltach leamsa gur e a tha a' riaghladh a' mhòid seo.

DIORBHAL: Duine gasda. Tha mise glé eòlach air.

FIONNLAGH: Agus bho nach 'eil mise eòlach air, cha leig mi leas fiachainn ri seinn aig a' Mhòd.

GREUM: Leigidh. Nach d' thuirt mi riut gu'm bu chòir dut leasanan seinn a ghabhail?

FIONNLAGH: Leasanan seinn. O thuirt. An toir sibhse leasanan seinn dhomh an àite leasanan Gaidhlig?

GREUM: Cha toir, ach bheir Diorbhail an seo dhuit iad.

ALASDAIR: O cha chreid mi gu leig thu leas leasanan seinn, Fhionnlaigh.

FIONNLAGH: Cha leig. Bithidh iad ro-dhaor co-dhiubh.

DIORBHAL: Cha bhi. Cha bhi iad daor idir. Gu dearbh bheir mi dhuibh a nasgaidh iad.

GREUM: Sin agad a nise cothrom dhuit. Thig thusa an seo airson leasanan seinn, agus mo làmhsa dhuit gu'm faigh thu duais aig a' Mhòd.

ALASDAIR: Chan 'eil ùine aige, a Ghreumaich.

GREUM: 'S ann aige a tha.

FIONNLAGH: Cosg ùine gun fheum. 'S ann a réir an t-seann nòs a bhitheas mise a' seinn.

GREUM: Coma leam dé an nòs a th' agad. Tha mi ag aithneachadh air do ghuth gu bheil feum agad air leasanan. Trobhad an seo. Seinn Doh. Nach d' thuirt mi riut? Tha e ro fhada. Cuiridh Diorbhail sin ceart.

DIORBHAIL: Cuiridh, agus bho'n a tha sibh an seo, tòisichidh sinn an nochd fhéin.

GREUM: Tiugainn ma ta Alasdair agus seallaidh mi dhuit leabhar a fhuair mi an latha roimhe.

FIONNLAGH: O nach faod mo charaid fuireach.

DIORBHAIL: O chan fhaod. Chan urrainn dhomh leasan a thoirt dha na h-uile duine a nasgaidh.

ALASDAIR: Cha bhi sibh ro-fhada ma ta, o'n is e seo a' cheud oidhche. Tha sinn car anmoch co-dhiubh.

FIONNLAGH: O cha bhi sinn fad' idir.

DIORBHAIL: Cha bhi sinn uamhasach fada.

DIORBHAIL: Am faod mi Fionnlagh a ràdh riut?

FIONNLAGH: Faodaidh, ma thogras tu, a Bha . . . Bha . . .

DIORBHAIL: O can Diorbhail rium. Tha e soirbh a ràdh.

FIONNLAGH: A Dhiorbhail.

DIORBHAIL: O, tha an guth agad cho ceòlmhor. 'S toigh leam 'nuair a chanas tu " Diorbhuil." Can a rithisd e.

FIONNLAGH: A nise, tha mise a' dol a dh' fhaotainn leasan.

DIORBHAIL: O gheibh thu leasan gun teagamh. A bheil thu déidheil air dannsadh, Fhionnlaigh? 'Se ainm grinn a th' ann am Fionnlagh. An toigh leat dannsadh, Fhionnlaigh?

FIONNLAGH: 'S toigh. Ach dé a th' aig dannsadh . . . .

DIORBHAIL: Tha sin glan. 'S toigh leamsa dannsadh cuideachd.

FIONNLAGH: Chan 'eil mise a' dol a dhannsadh. Tha mi a' dol a sheinn aig a' Mhòd.

DIORBHAIL: Can " A Dhiorbhail."

FIONNLAGH: A Dhiorbhail.

DIORBHAIL: Cha chuala mi duine riamh 'ga ràdh mar sin. Ach Fhionnlaigh, tha dannsadh gus a bhith anns an talla bheag Di-haoine. Bha e uamhasach math an uiridh.

FIONNLAGH: A bheil thu dol ann?

DIORBHAIL: Chan 'eil fhios agam fhathasd.

FIONNLAGH: An robh thu ann an uiridh?

DIORBHAIL: Cha robh, ach cha chreid mi nach bi mi ann am bliadhna . . . .

Tìr an Aigh

FIONNLAGH: Tha mi'n dòchas gu'm bi, a Dhiorbhail.

DIORBHAIL: O nach tu tha laghach, Fhionnlaigh.

FIONNLAGH: Ciamar? Tha an ùine a' dol seachad agus feumaidh mi fhéin is Alasdair falbh an ceartuair.

DIORBHAIL: Dé a' chabhag a th' ort? Faodaidh Alasdair falbh ma thogras e ach cha leig thusa leas cabhag a bhith ort.

FIONNLAGH: Feumaidh mi falbh 'nuair a bhitheas an leasan seachad.

DIORBHAIL: Ceart gu leòir. Se an rud a bha mi a' dol a dh' fhoighneachd dhiot: A bheil thusa a' creidsinn ma tha duine ag iarraidh rud eigin le uile dhùrachd, gu'm feum e tachairt?

FIONNLAGH: Dé na rudan air a bheil thu a' smaointeachadh? Dol gu dannsadh is a leithid sin?

DIORBHAIL: Seadh ... Dannsadh, gun teagamh, is companaich, is dachaigh .... is rudan mar sin.

FIONNLAGH: O tha, tha mise 'creidsinn gu'm faigh feadhainn rudan dhe'n t-seòrsa mas e rudan reusanta a th' ann.

DIORBHAIL: Tha mise a' creidsinn a' cheart rud, Fhionnlaigh. Tha sinn a' creidsinn an aon nì le cheile.

FIONNLAGH: Ma ta, tha mise ag iarraidh aon rud an dràsda, agus 'se sin leasan air seinn.

DIORBHAIL: Bheir mise dhut leasan air seinn: Tha seinn a' tighinn bho ghuth-labhairt agus tha labhairt a' tighinn bho fhaireachadh. Fairich thusa gaol blàth a' tighinn beò 'na do chridhe agus cuiridh e chan e mhain solus 'na do shùilean ach srann 'na do ghuth. Aon uair 's gu bheil an guth drùiteach, tiamhaidh cha leig thu leas cùram a bhith ort mu'n t-seinn. Aon uair 's gu bheil thu air do ghluasad anns an doigh seo, seinnidh tu ge b' oil leat fhéin, agus seinnidh tu air a' leithid de dhoigh 's gu'n éisd daoine riut ge b' oil leotha fhéin.

FIONNLAGH: Cha chuala mi sin riamh roimhe.

DIORBHAIL: Sin agad a' cheud leasan ma tha. Chosgadh e gini do dhuine sam bith eile, ach cha chosg e sgillinn dhuitsa, Fhionnlaigh.

FIONNLAGH: Chan fhuilear dhomh barrachd is aon leasan.

DIORBHAIL: Na bitheadh cùram ort. Bheir m' athair-sa dhuit ceud comharradh airson Gaidhlig no ceithear fichead 's a h-ochd deug co-dhiubh. Tha e rithisd cho eòlach air Iarla Loch Nis.

FIONNLAGH: Na ainmich an duine sin a rithisd.

DIORBHAIL: Ceart gu leòir. Ach tha mi deimhin gu faigh thu a' cheud duais. Bithidh mise aig a' phiano latha a' Mhòid agus seasaidh tusa far am faic thu mi fad na tìde agus cumaidh mi ceart thu.

FIONNLAGH: O chan urrainn dhomh sin a dheanamh. Feumaidh mi mo shùil a chumail air . . . .

DIORBHAIL: Cumaidh tu do shùil ormsa. Chan urrainn duit a' cheud duais a sheachnadh, agus a bheil fhios agad dé nì sinn as déidh sin ?

FIONNLAGH: Dé ?

DIORBHAIL: Cuidichidh tusa mise le Gaidhlig agus cuidichidh mise thusa le seinn agus bithidh sinn a' seinn comhla.

FIONNLAGH: C' àit' am bi sinn a' seinn ? Aig a' Mhòd ?

DIORBHAIL: Aig a' Mhòd agus an àiteachan eile.

FIONNLAGH: Dé cho fad 's a tha thu a' smaointeachadh a mhaireas sin ?

DIORBHAIL: Cho fad 's a thogras sinn fhìn. Gu bràth faodaidh e bhith.

ALASDAIR: (*A' deanamh fuaim aig an dorus*). A bheil guth air a dhol dhachaidh an seo a nochd ?

FIONNLAGH: Tha. Feumaidh sinn falbh.

Tìr an Aigh

GREUM: An d' fhuair thu leasan?

DIORBHAIL: Fhuair, fhuair. Agus bithidh leasan eile againn an ath oidhch' 's dòcha, Fhionnlaigh.

ALASDAIR: An ath-oidhche!

GREUM: Faodaidh tu tighinn an seo cho tric 's a thogras tu.

FIONNLAGH: Chan urrainn dhomh tighinn am maireach ach thig mi an earar.

ALASDAIR: A bheil thu cìnnteach?

FIONNLAGH: Tha tha. Oidhche mhath leat a Dhiorbhail.

DIORBHAIL: Oidhche mhath, Fhionnlaigh.

ALASDAIR: Dé tha seo? A dhuine chridhe! Oidhche mhath leibh.

GREUM: Oidhche mhath leibh.
An Treas Sealladh
Mòd Loch Nis. An t-àrd-urlar. MADUINN.
Fionnlagh agus Diorbhail aig a' phiano.

DIORBHAIL: A nis Fhionnlaigh, cuimhnich air na thuirt mise riut, agus gheibh thu a' cheud duais.

FIONNLAGH: B' fheàrr leam nach robh mi air tighinn idir. Cha toigh leam a bhith an comain duine sam bith. Cuin' a bhitheas iad a' toiseachadh?

DIORBHAIL: Cha bhi iad fada tuilleadh. Cha d' thainig Iarla Loch. O cha d' thug mi cuimhne. Chan fhaod mi an duine sin ainmeachadh.

FIONNLAGH: Gabh mo lethsgeul. (A' dol a nunn).

MAIRI: Tha thu a' dol a sheinn, a dh' aindeoin na thuirt mi riut an raoir.

FIONNLAGH: Tha. 'S tu fhéin a chuir 'na mo cheann an toiseach e, a Mhairi.

MAIRI: An saoil am faigh thu duais?

FIONNLAGH: Chan 'eil fhios agam. Bha thu fhéin gu math cìnnteach aon uair, chan e mhain gu faighinn duais ach gu faighinn a' cheud duais.

MAIRI: Ma ta, tha mi coma a nise co dhiubh a gheibh thu duais no nach fhaigh, tha mi coma ged nach seinneadh tu idir.

FIONNLAGH: Feumaidh mi seinn a nise, air sgàth . . . .

MAIRI: Air sgath có ?

DIORBHAIL: (Ag eigheach a nunn riutha). Greas ort, Fhionn-laigh. Tha an t-am aig an té sin falbh. Chan 'eil gnothach aice a bhi a bhos an seo co-dhiubh.

MAIRI: Tha h-uile gnothach agamsa a bhith Fhionnlaigh ?

FIONNLAGH: Tha, tha.

DIORBHAIL: Tha Fionnlagh a' dol a sheinn agus tha e a' dol a dh' fhaighinn na ceud duais. Agus 'se mise a rinn seinneadair dheth. Na cuir thusa troimhe cheile e.

AN RUNAIRE: Tha sinn a nise a' cumail oirnn far an do sguir sinn an raoir. Co-fharpuis a tri deug agus co-fharpuiseach da fhichead 's a seachd. Bha dùil againn gum bitheadh Fear Cathrach na Comhairle, Iarla Loch Nis, an làthair an diugh airson facal brosnachaidh a thoirt dhuinn, ach tha aige ri falbh air a' phleuna an diugh gu Lunnuinn agus 's docha nach bi tìde aige tadhal. Mar sin 's fheudar dhuinn tòiseachadh as aonais. Co-fharpuiseach da fhichead 's a seachd, Fionnlagh Mac an Tòisich.

AN RUNAIRE: Tha Iarla Loch Nis air tighinn agus bheir e a nis dhuinn na facalan brosnachaidh mar as àbhaist agus mar is math is aithne dha. Feumaidh sinn a' cho-fharpuis a stad gus am bi an òraid seachad. Iarla Loch Nis.

RUNAIRE: Iarla Loch Nis (applause).

Tir an Aigh

AN T-IARLA: (A' tighinn air adhart agus a' leughadh far paipeir). A cheardan agus a bhan-cheardan. (Tha e a' toirt sùil air Fionnlagh). A chàirdean agus a bhana-cheardan. Có am fear a tha seo a' cumail air a' seinn agus mise a' labhairt?

AN RUNAIRE: Seo co-fharpuiseach da fhichead 's a seachd. Bruidhnidh mise ris.
(Ri Fionnlagh). Dé as ciall d'a seo? A bheil fhios agad có tha seo air am bheil thu cur eas-urraim? So Iarla Loch Nis, Fear Cathrach na Comhairle.

FIONNLAGH: (A' sgur a sheinn). Tha mise coma có th' ann. Bha e mi-mhodhail dha tòiseachadh air bruidhinn mu'n robh an t-òran agamsa ullamh.

AN T-IARLA: Mi-mhodhail gu dearbh. O-h-h-h, a bheil fhios agad gur e mise Fear-Cathrach na Comhairle agus gu faod mi do bhacadh fo sheinn idir aig a' Mhòd?

FIONNLAGH: Mo thogair. Dé as motha ormsa 'ur bacadh? Sguiridh mi le mo chead fhéin.

DIORBHAIL: (A' tighinn air adhart) (Ris an Iarla). O na cuiribh air falbh buileach e. Bha e a' dol a dh' fhaotainn na ceud duais.

AN RUNAIRE: An robh gu dearbh? Có a dh' innis dhuitsa gu robh e a' dol a dh' fhaotainn na ceud duais?

DIORBHAIL: (A' tighinn ga h-ionnsuidh fhéin). O cha d' innis duine. Iarr air an Iarla do lethsgeul a ghabhail agus seinnidh tu 'nuair a bhitheas e ullamh.

FIONNLAGH: Leth-sgeul. Ta 's mi nach iarr airsan.

IARLA: Cha gheibh thu duais uamsa gu buileach. Faicidh mise sin, da fhichead 'sa seachd.

FIONNLAGH: Mo thogair. Faodaidh sibh bhur duaisean a chumail. Trobhad, a Mhairi. Seo an aon duais a tha a dhìth ormsa.

"AN EAGLAIS EILE"

Luchd-cluiche
Am Ministear
Iseabail
(Bean a' Mhinisteir).
Alasdair
Cailleach
(Màthair Alasdair).
Bean a' Mhaoir
An t-uachdaran.

(Latha breagha grianach samhraidh. Am ministear is a bhean a' gluasad am measg beagan de airneis tighe am muigh air lianaig — bord, beinge, seithrichean, badan aodaich leapa is aodach latha, poitean, cumain, coire, mios, soithichean).

MINISTEAR: Bheir sinn a' chuid as fheàrr dhiubh seo a nunn do'n mhansa.

ISEABAIL: Bheir; chan 'eil iad gu móran feum do dhuine sam bith tuilleadh.

MINISTEAR: Bu cho math dhaibh a bhith air am fàgail a stigh.

ISEABAIL: B' eadh. Ach thug mo mhàthair air Alasdair an toirt am mach; a' smaoineachadh gu'n cheann mu dheireadh gu'n deanadh i an gnothach air a' mhaor.

MINISTEAR: Chan 'eil e furasda deanamh an gnothach air a' mhaor.

ISEABAIL: Chan 'eil. Cha dean e ach teine a chur ri seo mar a rinn e air a' chòrr.

MINISTEAR: Bu chòir do'n mhaor fhéin a bhith air ais a nise. Saoil ciamar a chaidh aige air do mhàthair is Alasdair a chur air bord na luinge.

ISEABAIL: Cha dùraichdinn sùil a thoirt an rathad a bha i. Bithidh iad ri aghaidh a' chuain mhóir a nise. Dé an ùine a ghabhas e mu ruig iad Aimearaga?

MINISTEAR: Tri no ceithir a sheachdainnean, ma mhaireas an sìde.

ISEABAIL: Agus tha thu 'smaointeachadh gun teid gu math dhaibh air an taobh thall.

MINISTEAR: Nach 'eil fhios gun teid. Tìr mór farsaing fa'n comhair, talamh àitich gu leòr, seach a bhith strìth ri criomagan Bhaile Chrò.

ISEABAIL: Ach cha toireadh tu sin a chreidsinn air mo mhàthair. Bha i cho mór 'na barail fhéin.

MINISTEAR: Nach i a bha! 'S ann a bha i air dòigh ri a moladh air a shon. Bha mi-fhìn car duilich air a son cuideachd. Ach 'nuair a thig e gu h-aon 's gu dha, thug am maor rabhadh gu leòr dhaibh.

ISEABAIL: Thug, mun do chuir e teine ris a h-uile tigh 's a' bhaile. Ach chaidh e ro fhada 'nuair a chuir e teine ri tigh mo mhàthar is fhios glé mhath aige gu robh i fhathasd gun éirigh. Dh' fhaodadh e a bhith air a losgadh gu bas. Dé chanadh tu m' a dheidhinn an uair sin?

MINISTEAR: Cha chreid mi gu robh cron cho mór sin air aire. Bha cabhag air is fhios aige gum feumadh an long mhór seòladh roimh mheadhon-latha.

ISEABAIL: Is a h-uile duin' eil' aca air bòrd.

MINISTEAR: Seadh. Bha fhios aige glé mhath, tha mi cìnn-teach, gum bitheadh do mhàthair deònach gu leòr tighinn am mach 'nuair a dh' fhairicheadh i teas an teine os a cionn.

ISEABAIL: Deòin ann no as, cha robh an còrr ann ach gun d' thainig i mach ann an am. Mur a b' e Alasdair a bhith faisg oirre, bha i an dràsda 'na guaillean.

MINISTEAR: Nach fhaca mi e 'ga slaodadh a mach agus an déidh sin sios do'n chladach. Tha mi cìnnteach gun do shlaod e a steach do'n gheòla i cuideachd. Gu dearbh 's math dhi Alasdair a bhith aice.

ISEABAIL: O, 's math. Mur a bitheadh i cho rag bhithinn fhìn 's i fhéin còirdte fhathasd. 'S e thusa a bhith cho mór air taobh an Uachdarain . . .

MINISTEAR: Agus 'nuair a phòs sinn, bha sin gu leòr.

ISEABAIL: Gnothach duilich.

MINISTEAR: 'S e, 's e, ach ma chuir mise taic ris an Uachdaran, cha b' ann gun aobhar.

ISEABAIL: O, chan 'eil fhios a'm. Cha robh an t-Uachdaran ach a' sealltainn ri a bhuannachd fhéin.

MINISTEAR: Ciamar?

ISEABAIL: Tha e an dùil 'fhortan a dheanamh air caoraich aon uair 's gun sguab e air falbh an fheadhainn a bha 'san rathad air.

MINISTEAR: Coma leam dé tha 'san amharc aige, ma shoirbhicheas an sluagh 'nan dachaidhean ùra.

ISEABAIL: Seadh, ma shoirbhicheas. Thig iomadh cruaidh-chàs 'nan car roimhe sin, agus có aig' a bhios a' choire?

MINISTEAR: Aig an Uachdaran, tha mi cinnteach. Ach cuimhnich, tha lagh na rioghachd air a thaobh.

ISEABAIL: Agus tha an rioghachd làidir.

MINISTEAR: Ach cruaidh 's gu bheil an t-Uachdaran, 's e am maor as miosa. Rinn easan iomadh rud air nach robh fhios aig an uachdaran idir.

ISEABAIL: Leithid a bhith a' cur thighean 'nan teine. Chan urrainn do'n mhaor sin a chleith bho'n Uachdaran, no bho 'n t-saoghal. Tha craosan daithte nan cabar air gach tigh am Baile Chro ag eigheach ris na neamhan airson dìoghaltais.

Tìr an Aigh

MINISTEAR: Chan ann dhuinne a thig e a bhith bruidhinn air dìoghaltas.

ISEABAIL: Co-dhiubh a dh' iarras sinn dìoghaltas no nach iarr, dé an toileachadh a th' ann tuilleadh a bhith anns a' bhaile aognaidh, fhàsail seo?

MINISTEAR: Na bitheadh cùram ort, Iseabail. 'S docha gum faigh sinne sgìre eile uaireigin.

ISEABAIL: Tha mi'n dòchas gum faigh, an ùine ghoirid.

MINISTEAR: Ach cuimhnich gur e facal an Uachdarain a sheasas an sin cuideachd. Agus cuimhnich gu bheil deagh mhansa, mo shìopain agus mo ghlìob agam-sa fhathast.

ISEABAIL: Dé as fheàirrde sinn sin ma bhitheas sinn tùrsach gach latha mu'n fheadhainn a dh' fhalbh.

MINISTEAR: Ud, tha an fheadhainn a dh' fhalbh ceart gu leòr, gu socair air uchd a' chuain, a' deanamh air tìr a' gheallaidh, is do mhàthair is Alasdair 'nam measg.
(*Alasdair a' Stàplaich a Nuas 'Gan Ionnsaidh*).

MINISTEAR AGUS ISEABAIL: Có tha seo? Alasdair! Cia as a thainig thu?

ALASDAIR: Stadaibh is innsidh mi dhuibh.

MINISTEAR: Cia as a thainig thu? Càit' a bheil do mhàthair?

ALASDAIR: Stadaibh is cluinnidh sibh, 'nuair a gheibh mi m' anail.

MINISTEAR: Siuthad, innis dhuinn. Dé a thachair?

ISEABAIL: Càit' a bheil do mhàthair? A bheil i ceart gu leòr?

ALASDAIR: Tha.

ISEABAIL: An d' fhalbh i air an luing?

ALASDAIR: Cha d' fhalbh, ach tha i ceart gu leòr. Ach innsidh mi mar a thachair ma gheibh mi cothrom.

MINISTEAR: Seadh, cùm ort.

ALASDAIR: Mar a tha fhios agaibh, chaidh mi fhìn 's mo mhàthair sios gu'n chladach leis a' mhaor.

ISEABAIL: Chaidh.

ALASDAIR: Tharraing am maor a stigh am bàta.

ISEABAIL: Am bàta agad fhéin?

ALASDAIR: Am bàta agam fhìn. Chaidh sinn innte. Cha robh mo mhàthair ag ràdh dad. Chaidh am maor sios gu'n deireadh agus thoisich e air a' chruaidh a tharraing a steach. Bha cabhag air ach cha robh mise a' dol g'a chuideachadh. Bha a' ghaoth air éirigh is am bàta a' tulgadh, agus dìreach 'nuair a bha a' chruaidh gu bhith stigh aige—siud e mach an comhair a chinn.

MINISTEAR: Am mach air a' mhuir.

ALASDAIR: Am mach air a' mhuir.

MINISTEAR: Gun duine faisg air.

ALASDAIR: Uel, cha robh mi faisg air, ach cha robh mi fada bhuaithe. Chan 'eil am bàt' agam-sa ro mhór.

MINISTEAR: Seadh.

ALASDAIR: Siud e mach an comhair a chinn agus as an t-sealladh.

MINISTEAR: Dé 'n sin a thachair?

ALASDAIR: Feumaidh gun do bhuail e a cheann anns a' chreig.

MINISTEAR: Ciamar a tha fhios agad air sin?

ALASDAIR: Cha d' thainig e an uachdar a rithisd.

MINISTEAR: Is dé a rinn sibh?

ALASDAIR: Cha robh nì a b' urrainn dhuinn a dheanamh. Ach 's fheudar gum fac iad anns an luing mhóir dé a thachair, oir chunnaic sinn geòla 'ga leigeil sios agus rinn i air cladach le ceathrar ag iomramh. Thuirt mo mhàthair gum b'e sin ar cothrom. Cha d' thug e tiota tilleadh gu tìr agus rinn sinn air a' choille bhig.

Tìr an Aigh

ISEABAIL: Is am faca sibh dé rinn am bàt' eile?

ALASDAIR: Chunnaic. Chithinn-sa iadsan ged nach fhaiceadh iad mise. Thog iad corp a' mhaoir as a' mhuir agus thug iad air tìr e. Chunnaic sinn té a' coiseachd sios 'gan ionnsaidh. Có bha seo ach bean a' mhaoir. Thug iad an corp suas do'n tigh.

MINISTEAR: Dé rinn iad an uair sin?

ALASDAIR: Thill iad gu'n chladach agus dh'iomair iad air ais do'n luing.

MINISTEAR: Cha d' thainig iad 'nur còir.

ALASDAIR: Cha d' thainig. Bha coltas cabhaig orra. Dh' fheumadh iad a bhith troimh 'n chaolas mun tionndadh an làn.

MINISTEAR: Bha sin 'na aobhar cabhaig gun teagamh.

ALASDAIR: Agus dh' fhaodadh aobhar eile a bhith ann. Leis an luchd a bh' aice, fir is mnathan is clann, anns an staid anns an robh iad, có a b' urrainn a bhith cìnnteach nach leumadh fear an siud 's an seo thar na cliathaich, a' deanamh oidhirp air tilleadh gu tìr.

MINISTEAR: Nam bitheadh an cothrom sin aca. Bhitheadh iad air an dùnadh sios aca gu h-ìseal.

ALASDAIR: Sheòl i co-dhiubh agus tha sinne an seo fhathasd.

ISEABAIL: Dé tha 'dol a thachairt a nise? Càit' a bheil mo mhàthair?

ALASDAIR: Dh' fhàg mi shios anns a' choille bhig i gus am faicinn ciamar a bhitheadh cùisean. 'S fheàrr dhomh a dhol g'a h-iarraidh.

ISEABAIL: Càit' am bi sibh an nochd?

ALASDAIR: O, bheir mi nuas an seo i. Caidilidh sinn anns an t-sabhal an nochd.

(Alasdair a Mach).

ISEABAIL: Ciamar a theid dhaibh a nise ?

MINISTEAR: O, gheibh Alasdair thairis air, tha e òg. Ach do mhàthair . . . .

ISEABAIL: Cha leig sinn a leas iarraidh oirre tighinn a dh' fhuireach còmhla ruinne.

MINISTEAR: Cha leig. Cha deanadh i roimhe e agus cha dean i idir a nise e.

ISEABAIL: Tha iad a' dol a chadal anns an t-sabhal.

MINISTEAR: Tha. 'S math an sabhal a bhi ann.

ISEABAIL: Bha am maor air teine a chur ris an t-sabhal còmhla ris a' chòrr, mur b' e am beagan feòir a th' ann.

MINISTEAR: Am maor. 'S duilich a chreidsinn nach 'eil e tuilleadh an tìr nam beò. Bithidh an cuthach air an uachdaran.

ISEABAIL: Saoil an tig e an rathad seo ?

MINISTEAR: Chan 'eil nì as cìnntiche. Chan 'eil fhios dé nì e le do mhàthair is Alasdair.

ISEABAIL: Càit' an teid iad ?

MINISTEAR: Bithidh greis mum bi iad a' cur bàta eile do Chanada.

ISEABAIL: Bithidh. Seo agad iad a' tighinn. 'S fheàrr dhomh-sa falbh mum faic i mi.

(*Alasdair Agus a Mhàthair a' Tighinn*).

MINISTEAR: Tha sibh ann, a bhean.

CAILLEACH: Tha. Tha mi an seo fhathast, ged nach robh dad de dhùil agaibh-se rium, an robh ?

MINISTEAR: Tha mi toilichte 'ur faicinn beò slàn.

CAILLEACH: 'S dòcha gu bheil, ach bha sibh an dùil gum bithinn-sa air falbh anns a' bhàta mhór còmhla ri càch. Ach cha bhi e cho furasda 's a tha sibh a' smaointeachadh. (*Ri Alasdair*). Thoir sùil air an tigh, Alasdair, ach saoil am faigh sinn oisean ann airson fasgadh na h-oidhche. 'S dòcha gu bheil an ceann shios dionach fhathasd.

Tìr an Aigh

ALASDAIR: (*A' dol a mach*). Ceart gu leòr, ach faodaidh sibh a leigeil as 'ur ceann.

CAILLEACH: Có bha a' cur nan gnothaichean seo troimh a chéile? An robh Iseabail an seo?

MINISTEAR: Bha i bhos mionaid. Cha chreid mi gun urrainn dhuibh fuireach anns an tigh mar a tha e.

CAILLEACH: Tha sibh ag ràdh rium.

MINISTEAR: Tha taighean a' bhaile uile air an aon dòigh.

CAILLEACH: Chan 'eil sin 'ga fhàgail dad nas fhasa dhomh-sa. Nach ann oirnn a thàinig e an tìr an t-soisgeil gum bitheadh cead aig daoine ar dachaidhean a chur 'nan smàl.
An cuala sibh mu bhur caraid, am maor? Sin aon fhear nach cuir teine ri an còrr thighean.

MINISTEAR: Chuala mi mu dheidhinn. Bha Alasdair 'ga innse dhuinn. Cha b' e caraid mór dhomhs' a bh' ann, ach 's e gnothach duilich a tha ann am bàs duine sam bith. Dh' fhàg e bean a bhitheas 'ga ionndrain.

CAILLEACH: Dìreach sin.

MINISTEAR: 'S iongantach mar a thachair. Cha do bhean Alasdair ris an doigh sam bith?

CAILLEACH: Dé tha sibh a' ciallachadh? An do bhean Alasdair ris!

MINISTEAR: Cha do bhean, cha do bhean. Co-dhiubh cha bhi sinn a' cur sios air fear nach maireann.

CAILLEACH: Duine eucorach, cruaidh. B' e sin mo bharail-sa air, agus chan 'eil mi 'dol 'ga atharrachadh. Tha e duilich leam seo a ràdh ruibh, anns an dreuchd a th' agaibh, ach thug e air falbh bhuam buileach mo dhochas is mo chreideamh ann am Freasdal Uile-Chumhachdach, Uile Thròcaireach.

MINISTEAR: Tha sinn uile feumach air tròcair.

114

CAILLEACH: Tha sinn uile feumach air, ach a bheil sinn 'ga mhealtainn?

MINISTEAR: Mata, mealaidh sibhse iomadh tròcair fhathasd.

CAILLEACH: Bu mhath leam sin a chreidsinn. Innsidh mi dhuibh — ma mhealas mi aon tròcair fhéin, leigidh mi fios dhuibh gun dàil.

MINISTEAR: Cha bhi fada agaibh ri feitheamh.

(*Alasdair air ais*).

ALASDAIR: Tha eagal orm nach rachadh againn air fuireach 'san tigh.

MINISTEAR: B' e sin mo bharail fhìn. Feumaidh mise falbh an dràsda. Thig mi a nall a rithisd.

CAILLEACH: O, nì sinn an gnothach doigh-eigin.

MINISTEAR: Am bi biadh agaibh?

ALASDAIR: Bithidh. Tha beagan air fhàgail an seo, agus theid mi dh'iasgach air Sgeir an Sgairbh feasgar. Bithidh iasg na mara saor againn fhathasd, 's cìnnteach.

MINISTEAR: Siuthadaibh mata. Chi sibh mar a theid dhuibh.

(*Am Ministear a' Falbh*).

CAILLEACH: Latha math leibh. Mas e siud buachaille nan caorach, mo thruaighe na caoraich. Chan e gu bheil caoraich aige a nise; 's e caoraich de sheòrs' eile a bhitheas aige a dh' aithghearr, caoraich mhaola Shasainn.

Dé tha thu a' dol a dheanamh a nise, Alasdair?

ALASDAIR: Togaidh mi teine. Seallaibh fhéin airson biadh am measg na tha sin.

CAILLEACH: Nach ann oirnn a thainig latha na bochdainn! Nuair a smaoinicheas mi air — an tigh snog a thog d' athair, 's e fhéin a bha moiteil as —

ALASDAIR: 'S dòcha gu robh sinn air a bhith na b'fheàrr air falbh còmhla ri ar càirdean. Tha an t-àite seo marbh.

Tìr an Aigh

CAILLEACH: Tha na càirdean air falbh gun teagamh, ach fhad 's a chi mise a' mhuir, na cnuic 's na glinn, Alasdair, cha bhi mi leam fhéin.

ALASDAIR: Cha mhór a nì iad sin gu ar cumail beò, a mhàthair.

CAILLEACH: A nise ma tha aithreachas sam bith ort-sa airson fuireach, cuimhnich gum faod thu falbh cho luath 's a gheibh thu cothrom.

ALASDAIR: Tha fhios agaibh nach fhàgainn-sa an seo sibh leibh fhéin.

CAILLEACH: 'S math sin a chluinntinn. Aig m'aois-sa tha e cho math crioch a chur air mo làithean far a bheil mi.

ALASDAIR: Ud, tha iomadh bliadhna romhaibh fhathasd. 'S docha gu faigh sinn fois a nise 's am maor air falbh.

CAILLEACH: Am maor —'san t-siorraidheachd mhór. Air a bhàthadh fo chomhair a thighe fhéin. 'S ann a bha bàthadh tuilleadh is math dha.

ALASDAIR: Cha chòir dhuibh a bhith bruidhinn mar sin mun cluinn duine sibh.

CAILLEACH: Có a chluinneas mi an seo tuilleadh — ach na faoileagan.

ALASDAIR: O chan abair mi sin idir. Cha ghabhainn annas ged a thigeadh an t-Uachdaran.

CAILLEACH: Ma thig, bithidh sinn deiseil, nas deiseile na bha sinn riamh ; chan 'eil a nise dad againn ri chall.

ALASDAIR: 'S dòcha gun cuir e coire oirnne airson bàs a' mhaoir.

CAILLEACH: Ciamar a nì e sin ma bhitheas tu air d' fhaiceall mar a bhruidhneas tu. Bha am maor 'gar toirt am mach, anns a' bhàta againn fhìn, ge b' e air bith có thug cead dha.

ALASDAIR: Cha robh cead a dhìth air. Có thug cead dha an tigh againn a chur 'na theine ?

CAILLEACH: An t-Uachdaran, tha mi cìnnteach. Ach cha robh cead a dhìth air. 'S e fhéin a bu mhiosa na'n t-Uachdaran.

ALASDAIR: Bha fhios aig a h-uile duine air sin.

CAILLEACH: Ach bha mi ag ràdh riut mar a thachair. Bha am maor an deireadh a' bhàta, am bata againne, nach 'eil sin ceart?

ALASDAIR: Tha, tha sin ceart.

CAILLEACH: Uel, bha e an deireadh a' bhàta, a' togail na cruadhach. Thug am bàta tulgadh aisde agus thuit e am mach air a' mhuir.
Chan 'eil an còrr air ach sin.

ALASDAIR: Chan 'eil.

CAILLEACH: Agus feumaidh gun do bhuail a cheann air sgeir, oir chan fhacas sgeul air tuilleadh.

ALASDAIR: Tha fhios gun do bhuail; chuala mi fhìn an sgailc.

CAILLEACH: Sgailc a chuir peiseanadh air, mac an fhir mhóir.

ALASDAIR: Sin dìreach mar a thachair.

CAILLEACH: Bithidh cuimhn' agad air sin ma tha.

ALASDAIR: Saoil an robh amharus air a' mhinisteir.

CAILLEACH: Carson a bhitheadh. Cumadh esan a shròn a gnothaichean dhaoin' eile. Carson nach 'eil e air falbh còmhla ri a chomhthional?
Có ris a tha e 'dol a shearmonachadh a nise?

ALASDAIR: 'S dòcha gum falbh e-fhéin is Iseabail fhathasd.

CAILLEACH: Chan fheàirrde a chliù fuireach. Dé am math a bhith bruidhinn, fear sam bith a theireadh ri muinntir a' bhaile gun tigeadh soirbheachadh mór 'nan car an Aimearaga Canadh e siud rium-sa!

ALASDAIR: Chuala mi fhìn air a' cheart phuing e.

CAILLEACH: Chuala, tha mi cìnnteach. Ach có tha seo?

Tìr an Aigh

ALASDAIR: Bean a' mhaoir. Dé tha i ag iarraidh?
(Bean a' Mhaoir a' tighinn).

BEAN A' MHAOIR: Tha latha briagh ann.

CAILLEACH: Tha gu dearbh, latha àlainn.

BEAN A' MHAOIR: A bheil sibh toilichte a bhi air ais?

CAILLEACH: Cho toilichte 's as urrainn do neach sam bith a bhith an suidheachadh dhe'n t-seòrsa.

BEAN A' MHAOIR: Tha mo shuidheachadh-sa air atharrachadh cuideachd.

ALASDAIR: An ann air sin a thainig sibh a bhruidhinn? Mu na mhaor . . . 's e gnothach . . . .

CAILLEACH: Chaill mise mo dhachaidh is mo chàirdean.

BEAN A' MHAOIR: Chaill mise an duin' agam, mar a tha fhios agaibh.

CAILLEACH: 'S fhad o chaill mise m' fhear pòsda fhìn. Chan fhac e mar a thachair an seo — nach e a chuireadh a' ghaoir 'na fheòil nan robh e beò.

ALASDAIR: Theid mise do'n tobar. Tha an tobar mar a bha e, tha mi'n dòchas.
(Alasdair air falbh).

BEAN A' MHAOIR: Tha, tha. Tha bliadhnachan o'n chaill sibhse 'ur ceile, ach b' ann an diugh a thachair sin dhomh-sa. Sibh-se an dithis mu dheireadh a chunnaic beò e.

CAILLEACH: B' e latha cruaidh a bha seo do mhóran. Dé 'ur barail air na thachair?

BEAN A' MHAOIR: Air na thachair. Nach bu choir bàs m'fhir gach gnothach eile a chur as mo chuimhne?

CAILLEACH: Ge ta cha teid iad as ar cuimhne-ne. Cumaidh tighean rùisgte air leud a' bhaile seo, agus ar tigh fhìn air aonan dhiubh, 'nar cuimhne iad.

BEAN A' MHAOIR: Chaill sibh 'ur tigh. Seo agaibh Alasdair a' tilleadh.

    (*Alasdair a' tighinn*).

Togaidh Alasdair tigh ùr dhuibh . . . .

CAILLEACH: Ma leigeas an t-Uachdaran leis.

BEAN A' MHAOIR: Togaidh Alasdair tigh ùr dhuibh, ach chan fhaigh mise m' fhear-pòsda air ais.

CAILLEACH: 'S e fhéin a bu choireach.

BEAN A' MHAOIR: Cha rachainn leis a' bharail sin uile gu léir.

CAILLEACH: Carson: Carson? Chan 'eil thu a' cur coire oirnne . . . air Alasdair?

BEAN A' MHAOIR: Chan 'eil . . . . . air Alasdair.

CAILLEACH: Có air, mata?

BEAN A' MHAOIR: Tha oirbh-se.

CAILLEACH: Orm-sa!

BEAN A' MHAOIR: Bha mise 'nam sheasamh anns an dorus 'nuair a bha an triùir agaibh anns a' gheòla, agus chunnaic mi dé a thachair.

CAILLEACH: Seadh. Dé a thachair?

BEAN A' MHAOIR: Bha am maor crom anns an deireadh. Bu sibhse a b' fhaisge air.

ALASDAIR: A bheil sibh cìnnteach nach mise a bh'ann?

CAILLEACH: Uisd Alasdair. Dé tha sin — mise a b' fhaisge?

BEAN A' MHAOIR: Chunnaic mi sibh 'ga sguabadh thar an deiridh, le 'ur n-uilinn, mar siud.

CAILLEACH: Tha sibh ag ràdh gum faca sibh sin?

BEAN A' MHAOIR: Chunnaic.

ALASDAIR: A bheil sibh cìnnteach? Mo mhàthair?

BEAN A' MHAOIR: Tha mi cìnnteach. Dé a th' agaibh ri ràdh a nise?

CAILLEACH: O, chuir e thuige cho mór mi. Cha robh mi agam fhéin. Smaointich mi nach bu mhisd' e deagh bhogadh.

BEAN A' MHAOIR: Ach na smaointich sibh gum bu mhath an airidh a chur gu bàs ?

CAILLEACH: O cha robh sin 'na mo bheachd. B' i a' bhuille a fhuair e air an sgeir a thug crioch air.

BEAN A' MHAOIR: Faodaidh sin a bhith, ach chan 'eil mi cìnnteach nach gabhadh cuirt lagha droch bharail de na rinn sibh.

CAILLEACH: Glé cheart mata. Mas mise a rinn e bu mhath an airidh air e. Is mise a chuir a mach air a' mhuir e. Innsibh sin do'n fheadhainn a thogras sibh, cùirt lagha, uachdaran, no eile.

ALASDAIR: Cha robh ann ach tubaisd.

CAILLEACH: Coma, seasaidh mise ri m' fhacal agus cha bhi duine tuigseach air feadh na tìre nach abair gum b' ann 'na am a rinneadh tomhas beag de cheartas — le stad a chur air gniomharan mallaichte a' mhaoir seo.

BEAN A' MHAOIR: Cha teid dioladh a' cheartais fhàgail 'nur lamhan-sa. Chan abair mi an corr an dràsda agus tha mi'n dòchas nach d' thuirt sibhse tuilleadh 's a chòir. Latha math leibh.

(*Bean a' Mhaoir a' falbh*).

ALASDAIR: Saoil an d'thuirt sibh tuilleadh 's a' chòir ?

CAILLEACH: Chan 'eil aithreachas sam bith orm.

ALASDAIR: 'S docha nach 'eil ; faodaidh aobhar a bhith agaibh air fhathasd. Càit' a bheil sibh a' dol ?

CAILLEACH: Tha mi a' dol a nunn do'n tigh, no — bu choir dhomh a ràdh — far an robh an tigh.

ALASDAIR: Na bithibh fada. Feumaidh sinn tòiseachadh air na gnothaichean seo a chur a steach do'n t-sabhal.

(*An t-Uachdaran a' tighinn*).

UACHDARAN: 'S tusa Alasdair MacLeoid.

ALASDAIR: 'S mi.

UACHDARAN: A bheil àit' agad far an dean mi suidhe ? Is mise an t-Uachdaran.

ALASDAIR: Tha fhios agam. Aite-suidhe ? Bha àiteachan suidhe gu leòr againn an dé, ach, mar a dh' fhaodas sibh fhaicinn, chaill sinn a' chuid mhór dhiubh.

UACHDARAN: Chuala mi rud-eigin mu dheidhinn sin. Bu mhath leam beagan cheisdean a chur ort mu na thachair an diugh.

ALASDAIR: Glé mhath, siuthadaibh.

UACHDARAN: Bha thu còmhla ris a' mhaor 'nuair a chailleadh e aig Sgeir nan Sgarbh —

ALASDAIR: Bha.

UACHDARAN: Có eile bha còmhla ruibh ?

ALASDAIR: Bha mo mhàthair.

UACHDARAN: Tha fhios agad gu robh e aig an am timcheall air an obair dhligheach a dhearbadh ris.

ALASDAIR: Tha fhios agam, gu robh e 'gar toirt am mach gu'n bhàta mhór, mas e sin a tha sibh a' ciallachadh — .. Co-dhiubh a b' e obair dhligheach a bh' ann no nach b' e, 's ann agaibh fhéin as fheàrr a tha fios ; sibh as eòlaiche anns an lagh na mise.

UACHDARAN: 'Nuair a rainig sibh an cladach, chaidh sibh a steach do bhàta ?

ALASDAIR: Chaidh.

UACHDARAN: Có bu leis am bàta ?

ALASDAIR: Bha i leam-sa.

UACHDARAN: An e bàta math a bh' innte ?

ALASDAIR: Bha i math gu leòr airson na bha mise a' deanamh leatha.

UACHDARAN: An robh i dionach ?

ALASDAIR: Bha i cuimseach dionach.

UACHDARAN: Cha deachaidh dad a dheanamh rithe gu a milleadh air doigh sam bith ?

ALASDAIR: Cha deachaidh, cho fad 's as aithne dhomhsa. Dé chuir sin 'nur beachd ?

UACHDARAN: Innsidh mi dhuit an ceartair dé tha 'nam bheachd. An do nochd thu mìo-rùn do'n mhaor air an rathad sios do'n chladach ?

ALASDAIR: Cha do nochd ; chan e gun do nochd mi móran deagh-rùn dha nas motha.

UACHDARAN: Ach bha thu a' faireachadh mìo-rùn d' a thaobh, faodaidh e bhith.

ALASDAIR: A nise chan 'eil mi a' dol a dh' innse dé bha mi a' faireachadh ; cha deanadh e feum dhuibh-se no dhomh-sa.

UACHDARAN: Theagamh gun innis thu ann an cùirt e, ma dh' iarrar ort.

ALASDAIR: Dé tha sin a' ciallachadh ?

UACHDARAN: Cluinnidh tu sin a dh' aithghearr.

ALASDAIR: Um . . .

UACHDARAN: Có chaidh a steach do'n bhàta an toiseach ?

ALASDAIR: Chaidh mise.

UACHDARAN: Agus có a lean thu ?

ALASDAIR: Lean mo mhàthair, mas math mo chuimhne.

UACHDARAN: Agus có a chaidh air bòrd an déidh sin ?

ALASDAIR: Uel, cha robh air fhàgail ach aon duine — am maor. Chan 'eil sin doirbh a chùnntas.

UACHDARAN: Bhitheadh toiseach a' bhàta ri tìr ?

ALASDAIR: Bha, agus an deireadh ri muir.

UACHDARAN: A nise chan e cùis-spòrs a tha seo idir.

ALASDAIR: Cha b' e cùis-spòrs a bh' ann dhuinne.

UACHDARAN: Ciamar a shuidh sibh? Có a chaidh do'n deireadh?

ALASDAIR: Chaidh am maor.

UACHDARAN: Carson a chaidh esan do'n deireadh?

ALASDAIR: Bha aige ris a' chruaidh a thogail.

UACHDARAN: Bha aige ri a togail. Carson nach togadh tu fhéin i?

ALASDAIR: Cha b' e sin mo ghnothach-sa. Nach b' e siud cuid dhe'n obair dhligheach airson an robh e air a phàigheadh — leibhse.

UACHDARAN: Tuigidh tu gur e am modh a phàigheas. Bha thusa faisg air a' mhaor 'nuair a bha e 'togail na cruadhach?

ALASDAIR: Feumaidh mi ràdh gu robh mi na b' fhaisg air na bu mhath leam.

UACHDARAN: Na b' fhaisg air na do mhàthair?

ALASDAIR: Bha sinn car a' cumail an aon astair bhuaidh'.

UACHDARAN: An robh e soilleir nach robh am maor ro eòlach am broinn bàta?

ALASDAIR: Bha, ach dé an còrr a gheibheadh sibh bho fhear a thug sibh as a' bhaile mhór?

UACHDARAN: Agus a dh' aindeoin sin, cha do smaointich thu air a dhol g'a chuideachadh?

ALASDAIR: Cha do smaointich mi air a leithid.

UACHDARAN: Dé a thachair 'nuair a thòisich e air tarraing na cruadhach?

ALASDAIR: Uel, cha robh mise 'ga fhaicinn.

UACHDARAN: Ciamar seo?

123

ALASDAIR: Bha m' aghaidh ri cladach is ris na bha mi a' fàgail as mo dhéidh.

UACHDARAN: An robh do mhàthair a' coimhead an aon rathad?

ALASDAIR: Chan 'eil mi cìnnteach, ach shaoilinn gum bitheadh.

UACHDARAN: Dé a thachair an uair sin?

ALASDAIR: Chuala mi eubh agus an sin plub.

UACHDARAN: Dé bha thu a' smaointeachadh a thachair?

ALASDAIR: Thainig e g'am ionnsaidh gu robh am maor am mach air a' mhuir.

UACHDARAN: Dé cho fad' 's a thug sin air tighinn g'ad ionnsaidh?

ALASDAIR: Cha d' thug e uamhasach fada.

UACHDARAN: An do thionndaidh thu 'nuair a chual' thu am fuaim?

ALASDAIR: Thionndaidh.

UACHDARAN: Dé chunnaic thu?

ALASDAIR: Chunnaic mi na tacaidean móra am brògan a' mhaoir.

UACHDARAN: Dé thachair an deidh sin?

ALASDAIR: Uel, bha dùil agam gun tigeadh e an uachdar a rithisd, agus 'nuair nach d' rinn e sin, chaidh mi sios do'n deireadh a shealltainn.

UACHDARAN: Dé a chunnaic thu an sin?

ALASDAIR: Chan fhaca ach uisge dorcha a' gheodha.

UACHDARAN: Cha robh sgeul air an duine.

ALASDAIR: Cha robh. 'S fheudar gun d' fhuair a cheann sgailc air an sgeir.

UACHDARAN: Dé rinn sibh an sin?

124

ALASDAIR: Chunnaic sinn bàta beag a' tighinn bho'n luing, agus dh' aontaich mi-fhìn 's mo mhàthair nach robh aobhar dhuinn fuireach na b' fhaide.

UACHDARAN: Cha do smaointich sibh air na daoin' eile a chuideachadh.

ALASDAIR: Cha do smaointich. Thainig sinn air tìr.

UACHDARAN: Càit' a bheil do mhàthair?

ALASDAIR: Tha i thall aig an tigh.

UACHDARAN: Can rithe gu'm bu mhath leam a faicinn.
(*Alasdair am mach, agus a' tilleadh le a mhathair*).

ALASDAIR: 'S aithne dhuibh an t-uachdaran.

CAILLEACH: 'S aithne. 'S dòcha nach aithne dha-san mise.

UACHDARAN: Chunna' mi sibh, tha mi cìnnteach, a' deanamh corra obair latha.

CAILLEACH: 'S iomadh obair latha a thug mi dhuibh 'nuair a b' fheumaiche mo chroit fhìn air. Chan 'eil fhios có nì an obair dhuibh a nise.

UACHDARAN: Gheibh sinn feadhainn a nì e . .

CAILLEACH: Gheibh, ach chan fhaigh sibh a nasgaidh iad.

UACHDARAN: 'S dòcha nach fhaigh. Chunnaic sibh mar a dh' éirich do 'n mhaor.

CAILLEACH: Chunnaic.

UACHDARAN: Bha sibh còmhla ri Alasdair anns a' bhàta?

CAILLEACH: Bha.

UACHDARAN: Agus càit' an do shuidh sibh?

CAILLEACH: Air an tobhta.

UACHDARAN: Agus càit' an do shuidh Alasdair?

CAILLEACH: Air an tobhta cuideachd.

UACHDARAN: Air an aon tobhta ruibh-se?

CAILLEACH: Seadh.

Tìr an Aigh

UACHDARAN: An deachaidh Alasdair an còir a' mhaoir?

CAILLEACH: Dé thuirt sibh?

UACHDARAN: An do bhuail Alasdair am maor?

CAILLEACH: An do bhuail . . . An do bhuail thu am maor, Alasdair?

ALASDAIR: Tha fhios agaibh nach do bhuail.

UACHDARAN: Tha sibh a' cur a' ghnothaich car aotrom.

CAILLEACH: Chan 'eil mise a' dol a chnàmhan mu bhàs an fhir a chuir teine ri tughadh an tighe agam.

UACHDARAN: An tughadh. B' ann leam-sa an tughadh; b' ann air an fhearann agam-sa a bhuain sibh an luachair airson an tughaidh.

CAILLEACH: Cha chuala mi riamh a leithid; chan eisd mi ris a' chòrr . . . .

(A' Chailleach a' dol a dh' fhalbh).

UACHDARAN: Deanaibh air bhur socair. Chan 'eil mi riar-aichte le bhur sgeul.

(Ri Alasdair). Iarr air bean a' mhaoir tighinn a nall an seo, agus, a chum gum bi fianaisean againn, iarr air a' mhinisteir agus a bhean tighinn a nall cuideachd.

UACHDARAN: 'S e call a tha ann am bàs a' mhaoir.

CAILLEACH: Call có dha?

UACHDARAN: Dhomh-sa is do'n bhaile.

CAILLEACH: Dé tha sibh a' smaointeachadh a their mise ris a sin? Call do'n bhaile! Is beag an call seo do'n bhaile an coimeas ris a' chall a thug e-fhéin air a' bhaile mun d' fhalbh e.

UACHDARAN: Nach sibh a bhitheas toilichte gun d' fhuair sibh cuidhteas e! Ach seo an te a dh'innseas an fhirinn dhuinn.

(Bean a' Mhaoir, am Ministear, is Alasdair a' tighinn).

126

MINISTEAR: Thainig sinn mar a dh' iarr sibh, uachdarain.

UACHDARAN: Thainig. Tha mise a' dol a chur ceisd no dha ri bean a' mhaoir agus bu mhath leam gun eisdeadh sibh ri a freagairtean. Chan 'eil mi riaraichte leis na chuala mi o'n dithis eile.

ALASDAIR: Chan 'eil e riaraichte !

MINISTEAR: Feumaidh sinn gabhail ri iarrtas an uachdarain.

CAILLEACH: Seadh, gabhaidh sinn ris. Tha mise deiseil.

UACHDARAN: Glé mhath. Càit' an robh sibhse, a bhean 'nuair a bha an duin' agaibh air a rathad sios do'n chladach ?

BEAN A' MHAOIR: Bha mi 'nam sheasamh aig dorus an tighe.

UACHDARAN: Aig dorus 'ur tighe fhéin ?

BEAN A' MHAOIR: Seadh.

CAILLEACH: Uel, cha robh tighean eil' ann aig an seasadh i.

ALASDAIR: Bha am mansa ann.

CAILLEACH: O bha, ach chuir am maor as do'n chòrr.

UACHDARAN: Am bi sibhse sàmhach le chéile. Fhuair sibh cothrom mar tha. Bha an duin' agaibh còmhla ris an dithis seo.

BEAN A' MHAOIR: Bha.

UACHDARAN: Is e a' dol g'an toirt am mach a dh' ionnsaidh na luinge.

CAILLEACH: O, chan ann ; is ann a bha e-fhéin an dùil falbh do Aimearaga, mas fhior.

ALASDAIR: Cha robh, bha tuilleadh feum air aig an tigh. Taighean an ath bhaile ri an cur 'nan teine, 's dòcha.

UACHDARAN: A nise, thuirt mi ruibh a bhith sàmhach. Seo mata a' cheisd a tha mi a' dol a chur ruibh agus thoiribh deagh aire ciamar a fhreagras sibh.

BEAN A' MHAOIR: Nì mi mo dhìchioll, uachdarain.

127

Tìr an Aigh

UACHDARAN: Am faca sibh duine a' beantainn ris a' mhaor anns a' bhàta ?

BEAN A' MHAOIR: Chan 'eil mise a' togail casaid an aghaidh duine sam bith.

UACHDARAN: Dé tha sin a' ciallachadh ? Cuiridh mi a' cheisd ribh a rithist. Cuimhnichibh air 'ur fear-pòsda do nach urrainn an diugh freagairt air a shon fhéin. Am faca sibh duine a' beantainn ris anns a' bhàta ?

BEAN A' MHAOIR: Le'r cead, thug mi dhuibh mo fhreagairt mar tha.

UACHDARAN: Bheir mise oirbh an fhìrinn innse.

BEAN A' MHAOIR: Chan fhiosrach mi gu'n d' innis mi breug sam bith.

UACHDARAN: Cha dean sin feum. Bheir mise oirbh gun abair sibh barrachd is sin.

BEAN A' MHAOIR: O, cha toir ; chan e tigh cùrtach a tha seo idìr.

UACHDARAN: An cluinn thu i, a mhinisteir. Dé ghabhas deanamh rithe ?

MINISTEAR: Tha eagal orm nach gabh ni.

UACHDARAN: (A' gabhail a mach). Cluinnidh sibh an còrr mu seo fhathast.

ISEABAIL: Dé nì e a nise ?

BEAN A' MHAOIR: Chan 'eil nì as urrainn dha a dheanamh. Ach tha nì no dha eile as urrainn domh-sa a dheanamh a chùm pàirt dhe na fiachan a dhioladh. A bhean, an tig sibh a dh' fhuireach comhla rium-sa, co-dhiubh gus am faigh 'ur mac àite nas fheàrr dhuibh.

CAILLEACH: An gabh seo creidsinn ? A mhinisteir, thuirt mi ribh-se nach robh dùil agam ri tròcair fhaicinn tuilleadh air thalamh.

MINISTEAR: Thuirt sibh sin.

CAILLEACH: Agus thuirt mi nam faicinn aon chomharradh fhéin air a leithid gun leiginn fios dhuibh.

MINISTEAR: Thuirt sibh sin cuideachd. A nise thoireamaid buidheachas do'n Tì Uile Thròcaiteach—An taic a chéil' tha mhil 's an gath.

E

" BUTH AIR IASAD "

Luchd-cluiche

Beitidh.

Rùnaire.

Murchadh.

Seònaid.

Cailean.

Eilidh.

Ministear.

BEITIDH: B'fheàrr leam gu robh sinn air ais anns an oifis againn fhìn.

RUNAIRE: Dé th' agad an aghaidh na h-oifis seo ? Tha i comhfhurtail gu leòr, nach 'eil ? Mur b'e Cleireach a' bhaile, cha bhitheadh àit' idir againn airson coinneachadh.

BEITIDH: Cha bhitheadh, tha mi cìnnteach. Chan ann air an oifis uile gu leir a tha mis, a' gearain, ach air an àite. An t-àite cho samhach—chan 'eil nì a' tachairt.

RUNAIRE: 'S cìnnteach gun cuir thu suas leis airson—stad ort—dé th' ann—ceithir latha eile. Tha do rùm 'san taigh-sheinnse comhfhurtail, nach 'eil ?

BEITIDH: O tha. 'S i fhéin a tha math air ceasnachadh.

RUNAIRE: I-fhéin ? 'S i bean an taigh-sheinnse tha thu ciallachadh ?

BEITIDH: 'Si.

RUNAIRE: Dé an ceasnachadh a th' oirre-se ?

BEITIDH: O—dé tha sinn a' deanamh an Camaseòrna, 's có tha 'g iarraidh iasaid, 's mar sin.

RUNAIRE: O, tha iad uile math air ceasnachadh 'san àite seo. Ach bithidh thusa cho faicilleach dé their thu 's as àbhaist dhuit.

BEITIDH: Bithidh, bithidh.

RUNAIRE: Seadh, mata. Ceithir latha eile — cha bhi sin fada. 'S ciamar a tha 'dol dhuinn ? Tha sinn ullamh leis an fhear a bha 'ceannach a' chruidh, nach 'eil ?

BEITIDH: Tha. Tha esan a' faotainn tri cheud not.

RUNAIRE: Agus am fear a tha 'g iarraidh an tractair.

BEITIDH: Tha.

RUNAIRE: Dé mu'n bhanntraich a tha 'cur mullach ùr air an tigh ?

BEITIDH: Tha ise 'tighinn air ais am maireach.

RUNAIRE: Glé mhath, is dé a th' air a' phrògram againn an diugh fhéin ?

BEITIDH: Nach 'eil dithis a' tighinn roimh choig uairean. Chan fhaca mi riamh àite cho marbh. Chan 'eil nì ri 'fhaicinn ?

RUNAIRE: Nì ri fhaicinn ! Càit' a robh thu 'nuair a thainig na busaichean ? Bha othail gu leòir ann an uairsin. Có a cheud duine 'tha tighinn ?

BEITIDH: Murchadh Cuimeineach, fear na bùtha sin thall. Cha bhi fad aige-san ri 'tighinn. Chan fhaigh thu fiù is dannsadh fhéin 'san àite thruaigh seo.

RUNAIRE: Dannsaidhean, dannsaidhean, chan 'eil ni 'na do cheann ach dannsaidhean. Nach e an nochd fhéin oidhche dannsadh Chamaseòrna ? Fear na bùtha — càit' a bheil am paipear aige-san ?

BEITIDH: Seo agaibh e.

RUNAIRE: Murchadh Cuimeineach . . . . . ?

BEITIDH: 'S e: fhuair e iasad an uiridh. Càit' am bi an dannsadh seo ?

RUNAIRE: 'S an talla bheag ud thall tha mi cìnnteach. Bu chòir dhuit dhol ann. Chan 'eil an Cuimeineach seo a' deanamh ro mhath.

131

Tìr an Aigh

BEITIDH: Chan 'eil. Seallaibh sin. Cha do phàigh e uile gu léir ach fichead not.

RUNAÌRE: Is dé a fhuair e an uiridh ? Coig ceud airson bùtha.

BEITIDH: 'S e, 's cha do phàigh e air ais dheth ann am bliadhna ach fichead. Ach cha bhi nì a dh'fheum anns an dannsadh seo—ruidhlidhean an t-seann t-saoghail, creid.

RUNAIRE: Na bi cho cìnnteach. Dé tha 'cumail an duine seo thall gun phàigheadh ?

BEITIDH: O, cha bhi móran a' ceannach bhuaidhe.

RUNAIRE: Uill, bha gu leòir a' ceannach aige 'nuair a thainig mise seachad an diugh. Dé th' againn a seo — Murchadh Cuimeineach, ainm fhéin anns a' bhùthaidh, a phiuthar ag obair còmhla ris, agus téile a' mhuinntir a' bhaile 'ga cosnadh aca.

BEITIDH: A nise, mun tig e, feumaidh mi cuimhneachadh air cupa-tea a' bhodaich.

RUNAIRE: Nach tric a thuirt mi riut gun a bhith 'bruidhinn mar sin mu'n Fhear Cathrach againn, Fear-Cathrach Bòrd an Urleasachaidh.

BEITIDH: 'S e am ' Bodach ' as fheàrr leamsa. 'S e as giorra.

RUNAIRE: Fichead not ann am bliadhna. Cha dean sin feum. Dé a nise ?

BEITIDH: Tha am Bodach 'na chadal.

RUNAIRE: Fear-na-Cathrach, nach d'thuirt mi riut. Tha e 'na chadal. Bithidh e sgìth an déidh na dinneir mhóir an raoir.

BEITIDH: Bithidh. Bithidh cupa tea deiseil 'nuair a dhùisgeas e. Tha sinn fhìn feumach air cupa cuideachd.

RUNAIRE: Tha tha, is có eile a tha 'tighinn an diugh a bharrachd air a' Chuimeineach ?

BEITIDH: Tha — chi sibh an sin e — Fear eile ag iarraidh iasaid.

RUNAIRE: Seo e . . . . . Cailean MacAmhlaidh.

132

BEITIDH: Greasaidh mi orm leis an tea.

RUNAIRE: Cailean MacAmhlaidh, ag iarraidh ceithir cheud airson bùtha ùr fhosgladh. MacAmhlaidh, 's ann a tir-mór a tha esan, ach buinidh a' bhean aige do'n bhaile seo fhéin.

BEITIDH: Saoil an toir sinn dha an t-airgead.

RUNAIRE: Chan 'eil fhios againn air sin fhathasd.

BEITIDH: Cha chòrd e ris an duin 'eile bùth ùr fhaicinn faisg air.

RUNAIRE: Faodaidh nach còrd, ach, chan 'eil e còrdadh ruinne nach eil e-fhéin a' paigheadh air ais an iasaid mar a gheall e.

BEITIDH: O, có bhitheadh a' bodraigeadh ri àite beag suarach dhe'n t-seòrsa seo. Cha toirinn sgillinn do dhuine seach duine aca.

RUNAIRE: O, na can sin. Tha na h-àiteachan beaga cho luachmhor aig a' Bhòrd ris na h-àiteachan móra.

BEITIDH: Tha fhios agam.
Seo agaibh an duine.

RUNAIRE: Fosgail an dorus —

BEITIDH: Cumaibh ur sùil air an tea.
Thigibh a steach.

RUNAIRE: Thigibh air adhart. Deanaibh suidhe.

MURCHADH: Chan 'eil a stigh ach sibh fhéin.

RUNAIRE: Chan 'eil. Mi-fhìn is Beitidh an seo. Tha Fear-na-Cathrach 'san t-seòmar chùil. Tha fhios agaibh carson a dh'iarr sinn oirbh tadhall.

MURCHADH: Tha. A nise tha mi 'deanamh mo dhichill. Pàighidh mi a h-uile sgillinn.

RUNAIRE: Cha leig sibh a leas a bhith 'coimhead air Beitidh. Tha i dìreach mar aon dhinn fhìn. Faodaidh sibh bruidhinn an seo gu saor.

MURCHADH: Chan 'eil cùisean a' dol ro mhath anns a' bhùth.

Tìr an Aigh

RUNAIRE: Nach 'eil, 's a leithid de luchd-turuis an rathad? Stadaibh, fhuair sibh coig ceud agus gheall sibh ceud 's a' bhliadhna a phàigheadh air ais a bharrachd air riadh.

MURCHADH: Gheall, ach . . . . . .

RUNAIRE: Cha do phàigh sibh fhathasd ach fichead. Feumaidh sibh deanamh nas fheàrr na sin.

MURCHADH: Leigibh leam gu deireadh an fhoghair.

RUNAIRE: Agus dé a tha 'dol a thachairt aig deireadh an fhoghair.

MURCHADH: Gheibh sibh ceithir fichead eile.

RUNAIRE: Cha bhi sin gu leòir. Bu chòir ceud gu leth a bhith pàighte roimh dheireadh na bliadhna.

MURCHADH: Cha dean mi 'n gnothach air sin, ach gheibh sibh uile e ri tìde.

RUNAIRE: Seadh ma ta, dé a tha sibh a' dol a phàigheadh? Cha dean ceithir fichead an gnothach. Cuimhnichibh gum faod am Bòrd a' bhùth a thoirt uaibh mur a pàigh sibh na suimean a gheall sibh.

MURCHADH: Ceart gu leòir, ach feumaidh mi bruidhinn ri mo phiuthar.

RUNAIRE: A nise, cuimhnichibh gur e sibh fhéin a chaidh an urras airson an airgid.

MURCHADH: Nì mi oidhirp air ceud a phàigheadh mata.

RUNAIRE: Ceud, um-m-m. Feumaidh mi seo a chur mu choinneamh Fear-na-Cathrach.

MURCHADH: Chunnaic mi thusa roimhe.

BEITIDH: Cuin'?

MURCHADH: An dé agus a bhòn-dé.

BEITIDH: Càite?

MURCHADH: A' tighinn a mach as an taigh-sheinnse. 'S ann a sin a tha thu fhéin is esan a' fuireach. Dé cho fada 's a tha sibh a' fuireach an Camaseòrna ?

BEITIDH: Ceithir latha eile 's tha sin gu leòr.

MURCHADH: Càit' a bheil an oifis mhór agaibh ?

BEITIDH: An Ionar-odhaich.

MURCHADH: Bithidh gille agad a sin ?

BEITIDH: 'S docha gu bheil.

MURCHADH: Tha dannsadh gu bhith an seo an nochd. Ciamar a chòrdadh e riut a dhol ann ?

BEITIDH: Chan urrainn domh a dhol ann leam fhìn.

MURCHADH: Theid sinn ann còmhla.

BEITIDH: Mise, còmhla ribhse ? Tha fhios gu bheil sibhse pòsda.

MURCHADH: Chan 'eil no pòsda. Tha mo phiuthar a' fuireach còmhla rium.

BEITIDH: Cumaidh ise sùil oirbh.

MURCHADH: O 's docha gun cùm, ach tha lassaichean gu leòr agam airson sin. Ach 's tusa as fheàrr leam.

BEITIDH: A nise, a nise.

SEONAID: Dé tha seo ? Có thusa, a nighean gun nàire ? (Ri Murchadh). A bheil guth agad-sa air a' bhùthaidh idir ? Greas ort is sinn feumach air cuideachadh.

MURCHADH: Tha mi 'tighinn.

SEONAID: Dé bha 'ga do chumail ?

MURCHADH: Bha mi a' bruidhinn ri Runaire a' Bhùird ?

SEONAID: Bha thu a' bruidhinn—direach a' bruidhinn. Na seachnadh tu 'n taigh-sheinnse, 's e b' fheàrr dhuit.

MURCHADH: Seadh, a Sheònaid.

SEONAID: Na seachnadh, cha bhitheadh a' bhùth agad cho fad air ais 's a tha i. Greas ort is daoine 'feitheamh.

Tìr an Aigh

MURCHADH: Tha sinn ceart gu leòr is Peigi air cùl a' chuntair.

SEONAID: Peigi—mar as lugha ni Peigi leatha fhéin, 's e 's fheàrr. Gun toinisg idir aice a' tomhas. Aithnichidh tu sin 'nuair a chi thu mar a tha daoine a' fiachainn ri frithealadh fhaotainn bhuaipe.

MURCHADH: Chan 'eil i cho dona sin.

SEONAID: 'S tu an aon duine a their facal math m'a timcheall, ge bith carson. Neo air thaing nach 'eil i math air cruinneachadh guscul. Agus tha i 'na deagh bhean-ghlùine, tha mi 'tuigsinn. Dé am math a bhith 'bruidhinn ! A bheil thu tighinn ?

MURCHADH: Feumaidh mi fuireach gus an till an Rùnaire. Bithidh mi null as do dhéidh.

SEONAID: Uel, bi modhail co-dhiùbh. Na faiceam an còrr de do ghòralais. 'S am ministear 'gad fhaicinn 's e cho faisg oirnn.

MURCHADH: Am ministear !

BEITIDH: Cuiridh siud an dannsadh as ur ceann.

MURCHADH: Cha d' thuirt mi sin idir. Gheibh mi tiocaid dhuit agus chi mi thu aig naoi uairean.

BEITIDH: 'Nuair a dhùineas an taigh-seinnse ! Tha eagal orm.

RUNAIRE: Bha mi 'bruidhinn ri Fear-na-Cathrach.

MURCHADH: 'S dé a thuirt e ?

BEITIDH: A bheil tea a dhith air ?

RUNAIRE: 'S fheàrr dhuit foighneachd dheth mu'n tea. (Ri Murchadh). Tha e 'g radh ma nì sibh ceud dheth roimh bhliadhn' ùir, agus coltas oirbh a bhith pongail, gum bi e riaraichte — ach feumaidh sibh a bhith faicilleach.

MURCHADH: Ceud . . . Ni mi mo dhìcheall.

RUNAIRE: Tha fhios agam nach bu mhath leis a' Bhòrd a' bhùtha a thoirt uaibh, gu h-àraidh air sgàth ur peathar, is i ag obair cho cruaidh.

MURCHADH: Obraichidh mise cruaidh cuideachd.

RUNAIRE: Glé mhath ma ta. 'S fheàrr dhuibh falbh an dràsda. Rachaibh dìreach dha'n bhùthaidh, 's i cho trang.

MURCHADH: Cuimhnich, naoi uairean.

BEITIDH: O seo an dithis eile.

MURCHADH: Có tha seo?

RUNAIRE: Thigibh a steach. Mgr. MacAmhlaidh nach e? 'S e.

MURCHADH: 'S tu fhéin a th' ann, Eilidh. Ciamar a tha thu?

EILIDH: Tha gu math.

CAILEAN: 'S aithne dhuit an duine seo.

EILIDH: 'S aithne.

MURCHADH: 'S fhad' o'n uair sin. Sinn a bha eòlach air a chéile.

EILIDH: Seo an duin' agam.

MURCHADH: Ur beath' an dùthaich. Ciamar a tha sibh?

CAILEAN: Agus sibh fhéin. Ach ri gnothach.

RUNAIRE: Ri gnothach gu dearbh. A' bhùth, a Mhgr. Cuimeineach.

MURCHADH: (Ri Beitidh). Am faic mi . . . . . ? Agus sibhse . . . . . O ceart gu leòr.

RUNAIRE: Deanamh suidhe a nise. Siud fear na bùtha — thuig sibh gur e bh' ann, tha mi cìnnteach?

CAILEAN: Chan aithne dhomh idir e. 'S ann leis a tha a' bhùth ud thall?

RUNAIRE: 'S ann 'sann. Dh'fhosgail e an uiridh i.

CAILEAN: Cha chòrd e ris bùth eile a bhith tighinn cho faisg air.

RUNAIRE: Cha bhi i cho faisg sin idir air. Suas ri mìle, nach bi, eadar a bhùth aige-san agus far am bi a' bhùth agaibh-se.

CAILEAN: Tha — 's e sin ma gheibh sinn i. Saoil am faigh sinn i.

Tìr an Aigh

RUNAIRE: Uel, chan 'eil mi faicinn carson nach fhaigheadh. Thug sibh ainm a' mhinisteir dhuinn mar urras.

CAILEAN: Thug; chan 'eil e eòlach ormsa ach b' aithne dha mo bhean o chionn fada.

EILIDH: Thuirt e gum bruidhneadh e air ar son.

RUNAIRE: Tha mi cìnnteach gun dean e sin. Ach b'e a bhruidhinn airson a' Chuimeinich cuideachd an uiridh, 'nuair a fhuair e fhéin a' bhùth.

CAILEAN: Fhuair an Cuimeineach iasad cuideachd.

RUNAIRE: Fhuair — ach chan 'eil gnothach aig duin' 'eile ri sin.

EILIDH: Gheall am ministear a bhith seo.

RUNAIRE: Gheall, agus thuirt Fear-na-Cathrach gu bheil a' chùis an crochadh air dé their am ministear. 'S e am ministear a bhruidhinn airson an duine eile, agus the Fear-na-Cathrach a' smaoineachadh gur ann aige as fheàrr a tha fios an deanadh da bhùtha feum.

CAILEAN: Bhitheadh iad astar bho cheile.

RUNAIRE: Bhitheadh, bhitheadh. Cha dhi-chuimhnich sinn sin, no puing sam bith eile.

EILIDH: Bithidh am ministear leinne ceart gu leòr.

RUNAIRE: O chi sinn ciamar a bhitheas. Duine coibhneil a th' anns a' Mhinistear, tha iad ag radh, ach duine cruaidh; cumaidh e sinn air an t-slighe cheairt co-dhiùbh.

EILIDH: 'S iongantach nach 'eil e 'tighinn.

BEITIDH: O 'se bhios an so.

RUNAIRE: Tha sibh air tighinn. Ciamar a tha sibh an diugh, a Mhgr. Caimbeul?

MINISTEAR: Tha mi slàn am bodhaig, taing do Ni Math.

RUNAIRE: Deanaibh suidhe. Tha fhios agaibh carson a tha sinn a' coinneachadh an seo.

138

MINISTEAR: Tha — tha Mgr. MacAmhlaidh an so ag iarraidh iasaid airson bùtha.

RUNAIRE: Tha dìreach.   'S docha gum bu chòir dhuibh am Ministear 's mi-fhìn fhàgail leinn fhìn airson beagan mhionaidean.

MINISTEAR: Cha leig iad a leas falbh air mo shon-sa.

RUNAIRE: Glé mhath.   Dé ur beachd air an dithis so ?

MINISTEAR: Chan aithne dhomh an duine, ach tha coltas gasda air, agus thainig a' bhean bho dheagh theaghlach.

RUNAIRE: Saoil sibh an deanadh iad soirbheachadh le bùtha ?

MINISTEAR: Uel, tha bùth an seo mar tha, ach . . . . .

RUNAIRE: Tha, ach bhitheadh an té ùr suas ri mìl' air falbh.

MINISTEAR: Bhitheadh — am Camasodhar — ach 's iongantach mur a toireadh i feadhainn air falbh.

RUNAIRE: 'S docha gun toireadh.   Ach gu tighinn gu gnothach, an saoil sibh am bitheadh e ceart iasad a thoirt do Mhgr. MacAmhlaidh ?

MINISTEAR: O, bhitheadh an t-airgead tearainte gu leòr co-dhiùbh.

RUNAIRE: Glé mhath.   'S e sin na bha dhìth orm a chluinntinn. Their mise sin ri Fear na Cathrach.

MINISTEAR: An dean sin a' chuis ?

RUNAIRE: Nì, ni ; ma tha sibhse air a shon, foghnaidh sin dhomhsa.   Ma tha mise air a shon, tha sin gu leòr do Fhear-na-Cathrach, agus an rud a their Fear-na-Cathrach an diugh, 's e their am Bòrd am maireach.

MINISTEAR: Faodaidh mise falbh, ma tha.

RUNAIRE: Faodaidh.   Tapadh leibh airson ur cuideachaidh.

RUNAIRE: Tha mi toilichte a Mhgr. Ic Amhlaidh gu bheil sinn deònach iasad a thoirt dhuibh.

EILIDH: 'S math sin.

Tìr an Aigh

CAILEAN: 'S math. Cuin' a dh'fhaodas sinn tòiseachadh ?

RUNAIRE: Cha bhi dàil mhór sam bith ann. Cho luath 's a choinnicheas am Bòrd.

MURCHADH: Dé seo a tha mi 'cluinntinn, a Rùnaire ? Cuideigin a' fosgladh bùth eile ?

RUNAIRE: 'S fheàrr dhuibhse ur n-aire a chumail air a' bhùth a th' agaibh.

MURCHADH: 'S fheàrr, 's fheàrr, ach a bheil e fìor gu bheil sibh a' toirt cead do bhùth eile a bharrachd air a' bhùth agamsa ?

RUNAIRE: Chan e sinne a tha toirt cead airson bùithnean idir.

MURCHADH: A nise tha fhios agaibh dé tha mi 'ciallachadh. Ma bheir sibhse iasad airson bùth eile, millidh sin a' bhùth agam-sa. A bheil sibh a' dol a dheanamh sin ?

RUNAIRE: A nise, chan 'eil e ceadaichte dhomh-sa na cùisean sin innse do fheadhainn eile.

MURCHADH: 'S dòcha gun innis an té og dhomh ciamar a tha cùisean.

RUNAIRE: Chan innis. 'S fheàrr dhuibh a bhith falbh.

MURCHADH: Innsidh tusa dhomh, Eilidh — air sgàth nan seann làithean. Ceart gu leòr. Ach innsidh sibhse dhomh a Mhgr . . . . . .

CAILEAN: MacAmhlaidh.

MURCHADH: A Mhgr. MhicAmhlaidh . . . . cuiridh mi geall . . . . gu bheil fhios agaibhse . . . . cuiridh mi geall gura sibh fhéin a' cheart duine.

CAILEAN: Tha sibh ceart. Tha bùth eile gus a bhith ann agus 's mis an duine a tha dol 'ga fosgladh.

MURCHADH: Tha an fhìrinn againn mu dheireadh.

RUNAIRE: Bithibh a' falbh, bithibh a' falbh.

140

MURCHADH: Cha bhi gus am faic mi Fear-na-Cathrach. Càit' a bheil Fear-na-Cathrach ? Tha e aig baile nach 'eil ?

RUNAIRE: Tha.

MURCHADH: Glé mhath. Gheibh sinn ceartas a nise. Canaibh ris gum bu mhath leamsa fhaicinn.

RUNAIRE: Chan fhaod e bruidhinn ruibh.

MURCHADH: Carson seo ?

RUNAIRE: Chan 'eil Gaidhlig aige.

MURCHADH: Chan 'eil Gaidhlig aige ! Mur eil, dé a th' aige ? Fraingeis, an e, no Gearmailtis . . . . . . ''

RUNAIRE: Chan e: chan 'eil aig ach Beurla.

MURCHADH: Beurla ! Nach b'e a bha 'n seo an uiridh 'nuair a fhuair mis' an t-airgead ?

RUNAIRE: B'e, a' cheart fhear.

MURCHADH: Bha Beurla gu leòr a' dol eadarainn an uair sin.

RUNAIRE: Bha.

MURCHADH: Uel, tha a' Bheurla agamsa a' cheart cho math fhathasd.

RUNAIRE: O tha, tha fhios agam air a sin. 'S dòcha tuilleadh is math. Chuala mi na guidheachan móra Beurla a bh' agaibh thall aig dorus an taigh-sheinnse. Ach cha dean ur Beurla feum sam bith an seo dhuibh.

MURCHADH: Ciamar ?

RUNAIRE: Thainig riaghailt ùr am mach.

MURCHADH: Dé an riaghailt ?

RUNAIRE: Nach fhaodar ach Gaidhlig a chleachdadh 'nuair a bhitheas am Bòrd is muinntir a' bhaile seo (no bailtean coltach ris) a' coinneachadh. Cuiridh a' Ghaidhlig rian air ur teangaidh. Cha bhi uiread de shaors' agaibh innte.

141

Tìr an Aigh

MURCHADH: Nach bi ! Stadaibh gus am faic sibh. Cha chuala mi riamh a leithid. Có a dh' aobharaich an riaghailt neonach seo ?

RUNAIRE: Dh' aobharaich An Comunn Gaidhealach.

MURCHADH: O, tigh na . . . . . .

RUNAIRE: A nis, a nise !

MURCHADH: Tigh na sad dha'n Chomunn Ghaidhealach.

BEITIDH: Obh, obh.

MURCHADH: Ach nì mise an gnothach oirbh, am Beurla no'n Gaidhlig ! An Comunn Gaidhealach !

RUNAIRE: Tha e a' falbh a dh'iarraidh a pheathar. Cha bhi ise cho soirbh a ceannsachadh.

EILIDH: Chan urrainn gu bheil i cho fiadhaich ri a bràthair.

RUNAIRE: 'S i as miosa, agus a' sior fhàs borb a h-uile latha. A' sior fhàs borb mar as sine a tha i.

CAILEAN: Chan 'eil eagal oirbh roimhpe.

RUNAIRE: Chan 'eil. 'S dòcha gum b' ann oirbh-se a bu chòir eagal a bhith. Boirionnach comasach. Boirionnach cunnartach.

SEONAID: Dé seo a tha mi 'cluinntinn ? Bùth eile 'ga fosgladh. An e seo fear na bùtha ùir ?

RUNAIRE: Chuala sibh sin o ur bràthair.

SEONAID: Chuala, ach bha deagh amharus agam air roimhe. Chan 'eil nì a thachras nach cluinn mise, fhad 's a bhitheas Peigi anns a' bhùthaidh againn.

RUNAIRE: Gabhaidh an t-àite seo da bhùtha.

SEONAID: Chan 'eil mi 'dol le sin. Dé an t-eòlas a th' agaibh air an duine seo, fear a th' air ùr-thighinn do'n àite ?

RUNAIRE: Faodaidh sin a bhith, ach b' fheàirrde cuid againn nach bitheadh uiread de eòlas aig daoine orra.

SEONAID: Tha mi 'tuigsinn, tha mi 'tuigsinn, ach ma theid
a' bhùth againne sios, 's ann as fhaide a bhitheas sinn a'
pàigheadh air ais an airgid. Cha chòrdadh sin ruibh. Na
gabhaidh gnothach ris an duin' ùr.

RUNAIRE: Chan 'eil dad ceàrr air an duin' ùr. A bharrachd
air sin tha muinntir an àite glé eòlach air a' bhean aige.

SEONAID: Muinntir an àite! An robh sibhse 'bruidhinn ri
muinntir an àite?

RUNAIRE: Cha robh, ach bha mi 'bruidhinn ris a' mhinistear.

SEONAID: Bha, ach cha chluinn am Ministear a h-uile nì a
tha tachairt. Tha sibh an dùil a dhol air adhart?

RUNAIRE: Tha.

SEONAID: Ceart gu leòr.

BEITIDH: Chan 'eil i sud air a dòigh.

RUNAIRE: Chan 'eil 's cha bhi.

BEITIDH: Saoil an tig i air ais.

RUNAIRE: Tha eagal orm gun tig.

CAILEAN: Chan 'eil i deiseil fhathasd.

RUNAIRE: Chan 'eil. Tha i bagairt fianais air choireigin a
thogail. Ach na bitheadh cùram oirbh. Tha ur cliù gun bheud
'san àite seo.

EILIDH: Chan 'eil mi cìnnteach. Saoil an fhiach e an dragh,
a Chailein, bhon a tha iad cho fada nar n-aghaidh?

CAILEAN: Feumaidh sinn a dhol air adhart a nise. Tha an
Rùnaire agus am Bòrd leinn.

RUNAIRE: Gun teagamh. Na cuireadh bòilich na té ud cùram
sam bith oirbh. Chan 'eil an suidheachadh fhéin cho math
an ceartuair.

EILIDH: Ge ta b'fheàrr leam fhìn . . . . . .

BEITIDH: Có tha seo? Mgr. Cuimeineach a rithisd.

Tìr an Aigh

RUNAIRE: 'Se. Chan ann as a' bhùthaidh a thainig e 'n turus seo, a réir coltais.

MURCHADH: Có tha seo? Càit' a bheil Fear-na-Cathrach? Tha mise 'g iarraidh Fear-na-Cathrach.

RUNAIRE: Na cuireadh e dragh ort, a Bheitidh. Leig leis. Chi sibh Fear-na-Cathrach am maireach.

MURCHADH: Am maireach. Chan 'eil gealladh againn air am maireach. 'S e sin a thuirt am ministear. Tha bùtha mhath agamsa agus dithis mhath a' frithealadh innte. An teid sibh as àicheadh sin?

RUNAIRE: Cha teid, cha teid. 'S fheàrr dhuibh a dhol a null do'n bhùth air eagal gum bi iad a' coimhead air ur son.

MURCHADH: 'S fheàrr, 's fheàrr. Theid mi null am maireach. An dean sin feum? Cha dean. Carson? Chan 'eil gealladh againn air am maireach.

RUNAIRE: A nise, bithibh a' falbh.

MURCHADH: Có am fear a tha seo? An duine aig Eilidh. Uel, uel. 'S tu fhéin a th' ann, Eilidh. Bha uair a bha mise glé eòlach air Eilidh. Nach robh? Ach chan aithnich i 'n diugh mi. Coma leat, tha mi-fhìn 'san té òg a' dol do'n dannsadh an nochd.

EILIDH: Tha 'n t-am againne falbh.

RUNAIRE: Fuirichibh far a bheil sibh.

MURCHADH: Seònaid a th' ann. Cha bhi bùth eile an Camaseòrna, a Sheònaid. Chi mise Fear-na-Cathrach. Beurla gu leòr agamsa.

SEONAID: Cùm thusa do theanga.

RUNAIRE: Dé thug an seo sibh a rithisd?

SEONAID: Cluinnidh sibh, a dh' aithghearr, dé thug an seo mi. A bheil sibh a' dol air adhart leis a' bhùth ùir?

EILIDH: Leigeamaid leotha.

144

CAILEAN: Na can guth 's na gluais.

SEONAID: An cluinn sibh, a Rùnaire, chan 'eil iad cho cìnnteach. Tha iad a' géilleadh.

RUNAIRE: Chan 'eil, no géilleadh. Carson a ghéilleadh iad?

SEONAID: Glé mhath, mata. Tha sibh a' faighinn aon chothrom eile, an gnothach a leigeil seachad.

MURCHADH: Tha mise ag iarraidh Fear-na-Cathrach.

BEITIDH: Feumaidh sibh fuireach far a bheil sibh.

SEONAID: Aon chothrom eile, tha mi a' toirt dhuibh aon chothrom eile.

RUNAIRE: Tha sibh deonach a dhol air adhart, nach eil, a Mhgr. MhicAmhlaidh?

EILIDH: A bheil . . . . .

CAILEAN: Tha.

SEONAID: Ceart gu leòr, mata. Fhuair sibh ur cothrom. A Mhurchaidh, iarr air a' mhinistear seasamh a stigh. O dé math a bhith 'bruidhinn riut-sa.

RUNAIRE: Carson a tha sibh ag iarraidh a' mhinisteir?

SEONAID: Cluinnidh sibh sin an deagh am.

RUNAIRE: Ceart gu leòr. Ur toil fhéin. Theid Beitidh 'ga iarraidh.

SEONAID: Siuthad ma tha.

BEITIDH: Tha e muigh air an starsnaich. Canaidh mi ris gu bheil sibh 'ga iarraidh.

MURCHADH: Theid mise còmhla riut.

SEONAID: Fuirich thusa far a bheil thu.

MURCHADH: Nam faicinn-sa Fear-na-Cathrach . . . . . .

RUNAIRE: Chan fhaic, ach tha sibh a' dol a dh' fhaicinn a' mhinisteir, tha e coltach. Ach carson — na bithibh a' foighneachd dhiom-sa.

Tìr an Aigh

SEONAID: Bithidh e soillear gu leòr an ceartuair. Tha rud-eigin agamsa ri innse a chuireas gaoir 'na ur cluasan.

RUNAIRE: 'S cìnnteach gur e diomhaireachd mhór a tha seo.

CAILEAN: Bu chòir dhaibh a bhith a' tighinn.

MURCHADH: Có tha 'tighinn?

SEONAID: Tha am ministear is thoir thusa an aire.

MURCHADH: O Tigh na . . . . . .

RUNAIRE: A nise, cuimhnichibh far a bheil sibh.

MURCHADH: Tigh Iain Ghrota dha na mhinistear.

MINISTEAR: Dé tha cearr air a h-uile duine an seo? Tha coltas anshocrach oirbh uile. Có a chuir 'gam iarraidh?

MURCHADH: Bha mise ag iarraidh Fear-na-Cathrach.

SEONAID: Chuir mise gur n-iarraidh.

MINISTEAR: Seadh ma ta. Dé tha sibh a' dol a ràdh?

SEONAID: Bha sibhse deònach an uiridh gun cuireamaid bùtha suas ri taobh a' mhansa.

MINISTEAR: Bha — bha mi smaoineachadh gu robh feum oirre, leis an obair ùir, 's an luchd-turuis. Agus tha mi dhe'n aon bharail fhathasd.

SEONAID: 'S a bheil fhios agaibh gu bheil bùth eile a' dol suas?

MINISTEAR: Tha, chuala mi sin, ach bithidh i pios math air falbh.

SEONAID: A bheil fhios agaibh có tha 'dol 'ga cur suas?

MINISTEAR: Tha—an dithis seo, nach iad, Eilidh NicAmhlaidh is an duin' aice.

SEONAID: A bheil sibh eòlach orra?

MINISTEAR: Uel, chuir mi eòlas air Eilidh nuair a thainig mi dha'n àite.

SEONAID: Chan 'eil sibh cho eòlach oirre 's a tha sibh a' smaoineachadh.

MINISTEAR: Ciamar? Dé tha sibh a' ciallachadh?

SEONAID: Seo dhuibh.
Leigidh sin fhaicinn dhuibh dé tha mi 'ciallachadh.

MINISTEAR: Gu faigheamaid trocair!

RUNAIRE: Dé tha ceàrr? Am faod mise am paipear sin fhaicinn? Chan 'eil nì aige ri dheanamh ruinne?

SEONAID: Nach 'eil, nach 'eil, a Mhinisteir! Dé ur barail-se?

MINISTEAR: Cha d' innis duine seo dhomh. Nach mi a bha air mo mhealladh!

CAILEAN: Dé an gnothach falachaidh a tha seo a mheall sibh cho mór? Nach fhaod sinn uile a chluinntinn?

MINISTEAR: Chan e seo an t-am dhomhsa airson innse. Nì mi anns an eaglais e latha na Sàbaid far am bi cothrom agam air amhchasan iomchaidh a thoirt an làthair a' choithionail.

CAILEAN: Leugh sibhse am paipear, a Runaire. A bheil gnothach sam bith aig a seo ruinne?

RUNAIRE: Chan 'eil mi 'smaointeachadh gu bheil.

SEONAID: Innsidh mise dhuibh uile e, mur innis duin 'eile.

CAILEAN: Siuthadaibh ma ta.

SEONAID: Tha mise an deidh a chluinntinn gu robh leanabh diolain aig a' bhean agaibh-se 'nuair a bha i gu math òg.

EILIDH: Tiugainn a mach a seo.

CAILEAN: Stadaibh. Dé tha seo? A bheil sibhse a' cead-achadh an dol air adhart seo, a mhinisteir?

SEONAID: Cha chuala sibh-se seo. Thachair e mu'n d'thainig sibh do'n àite.

CAILEAN: Chuir mise mo cheist ris a' mhinisteir.

MINISTEAR: Feumaidh gun do thachair e mu'n d'thainig mise dha'n àite. Cha chuala mi mu dheidhinn. Is càit' a bheil an leanabh a nise?

SEONAID: Chaochail e.

147

Tìr an Aigh

MINISTEAR: Chaochail. Tha sin ceart gu leòr. Innsidh mise dhuibh.

EILIDH: Cha d' innis mi dhut. Bha duil agam nach leiginn a leas. Dé am feum a dheanadh e ged a dh' innsinn? Ach bha còir agam air innse.

RUNAIRE: An ainm an àigh, dé an gnothach a th' aig seo ri obair a' Bhùird? Cuin' a thig daoine gu ciall? Dé tha sibhse a' dol dheanamh, a mhinisteir, bho'n is ann ribh is còir dhuinn a bhith 'g amharc.

MINISTEAR: Chan 'eil mi 'g ràdh gum bitheadh an aon bharail agam air a' bhoirionnach nan robh mi air seo a chluinntinn. Cha chreid mi gun cuirinn m' ainm ris an tagradh airson an iasaid.

RUNAIRE: Carson? Nach gleidheadh i bùth a cheart cho dòigheil ged a thachair seo dhi?

MINISTEAR: Chan e sin a' chùis uile gu léir. Cha bu mhath leamsa gnothach a ghabhail ri té nach do ghleidh i-fhéin gu cubhaidh.

RUNAIRE: Gu cubhaidh! Cha chuala mi riamh a leithid. Dé a thuirt an Slanuighear fhéin mu'n té a ghlacadh ann am peacadh, "Am fear nach do thuislich, tilgeadh e a' cheud chlach oirre." An do thilg duine clach? Cha do thilg aon duine.

SEONAID: Dé tha sibh a' dol a dheanamh a nis, a Mhinisteir?

MINISTEAR: Feumaidh mi meòrachadh air a' chùis an sàmhchair mo sheòmair.

RUNAIRE: Is a bheil comhairle sam bith agaibh deiseil dhuinn an dràsda fhéin?

MINISTEAR: Fàgaibh cùisean mar a tha iad an dràsda. Sìth gu robh maille ribh uile.

SEONAID: Fàgaibh cùisean mar a tha iad, sin mar a thuirt e.

148

CAILEAN: Nach ann oirbh bu choir a' mhoit a bhith !

MURCHADH: Deanaibh air ur socair, a Mhgr. MhicAmhlaidh. Innsidh mise rudeigin dhuibh nach còrd ribh.

SEONAID: Siuthad, a Mhurchaidh. innis dhaibh.

MURCHADH: Faodaidh mi seo innse a nise 's am ministear air falbh.

CAILEAN: Seadh.

MURCHADH: Bu mhise athair an leinibh a bh' aig Eilidh. Dé do bharail air a sin ?

EILIDH: Dé thug oirnn tighinn an seo ?

MURCHADH: Ciamar a tha sin a' còrdadh ribh ? Sin thu a nise, a Mhgr. MhicAmhlaidh, sin an seòrsa bean a th' agad, 's dùil agad gu robh i cho beusach. Siuthad, cuir air falbh i. Cha bhi bùtha no bùtha agaibh a nise.

CAILEAN: Tha siud gu leòr, a bhladhdaire mhosaich. Na can an còrr, mun cuir mi d' fhiaclan 'nad amhaich. Gabh a mach a seo, no cuiridh mi as na h-iarmailtean thu mu choinneamh do bhùtha fhéin.

SEONAID: Cha leig thu leas a bhith cho fiadhaich. Cuimhnich mar a rinn do bhean. Cha d' iarr i mathanas ort fhathast.

CAILEAN: Sibhse gu dearbh a' bruidhinn ! 'S olc a thig a leithid de chainnt bho bhial boirionnaich mu bhoirionnach eile. Sibhse a' cur sios air té aig an robh leanabh, 's gun oirbh ach farmad nach d' rachadh duine faisg no fàireadh oirbh fhéin. Searbh an gnothach gun d'thug sibh orm a leithid a ràdh.

SEONAID: Thig mo bhràthair-s' air ais . . . .

CAILEAN: Na ainmichibh an drongair sin, ur bràthair — fear a tha 'cosg anns an taigh-sheinnse a h-uile sgillinn a tha sibh a' toirt a steach anns a' bhùthaidh, an àite a bhith 'pàigheadh air ais an iasaid a fhuair e.

SEONAID: Có nach 'eil 'ga phàigheadh air ais ?

CAILEAN: Có ach ur bràthair — an duine tapaidh sin !

SEONAID: An cuala sibh siud, a Runaire ? Innsibh dha. An do phàigh mo bhràthair-sa thuige seo na fiachan a bh' air ?

RUNAIRE: Cha do phàigh.

SEONAID: Dé ? Phàigh e rudeigin, 's cìnnteach.

RUNAIRE: Phàigh — fichead not.

SEONAID: An àite . . . . . ?

RUNAIRE: An àite ceud gu leth.

SEONAID: Agus dh'innis sibh sin dha'n duine seo ?

RUNAIRE: Cha d' innis.

SEONAID: Dh' innis ise, ma tha.

RUNAIRE: Cha d' innis.

SEONAID: Có mata a dh' innis dha e ?

CAILEAN: Cha d' innis duine.

SEONAID: Is ciamar a fhuair e eòlas air ?

CAILEAN: Coma leibh-se.

SEONAID: Fichead not — mac an fhir mhóir. Stadaibh gus am faigh mise greim air.

RUNAIRE: Diolaidh iad peanas air a' cheile a nise agus bithidh ceartas riaraichte.

CAILEAN: Is coma . . . . .

RUNAIRE: Innsidh mi dhuibh dé nì sinn. A Bheitidh, trobhad an seo. Tha a' chuis air tighinn gu seo. Feumaidh am Bòrd a' bhùth a thoirt bho'n Chuimeineach. Cuiridh mise mu'n coinneamh gum bu choir a toirt dhuibh-se.

EILIDH: Cha ghabh sinn gnothach rithe.

CAILEAN: Cha ghabh.

RUNAIRE: 'S docha gu bheil sibh ceart. Tha mi 'tuigsinn mar a tha sibh a' faireachadh. Ach an ceann latha no dha ma thig sibh air ais, chi sinn dé ghabhas deanamh, an seo, no'n àiteigin eile.

CAILEAN: Tha sinn 'nur comain. Bithidh sinn a' falbh. Latha math leibh.

EILIDH: Latha math leibh.

RUNAIRE: Mar sin leibh agus cumaibh cuimhne air na thuirt mi.

RUNAIRE: Có a nise bha 'g ràdh nach robh nì a' tachairt anns an àite seo ?

BEITIDH: Có gu dearbh ! Sinn a tha feumach air cupa tea ! 'S fheàrr dhomh sealltainn an toiseach an do dhùisg am Bodach . . . . . .

RUNAIRE: A nis, an aire.

BEITIDH: An do dhùisg Fear-na-Cathrach.

"EADAR CUIRT IS COIMISEAN"

An t-àite: Rùm ann an taigh Thormoid, an Leitir-daraich.
An t-ám: An diugh fhéin.

Luchd-cluiche

Tormod MacNeill (Tormod Alasdair Eoghainn, croitear).
Seònaid Nic-Neill (nighean bràthair Thormoid).
Goirseal Nic-Cuinn (Banntrach Sheumais Mhóir, bana-chroitear).
Cailean Mac-Cuinn (mac do Ghoirseal).
An Ridire Seumas MacCalmain (Fear Cùirt-na-Dùthcha).
Morair Chamusiunaraidh (Fear Coimisean-na-Tire).

SEONAID: Séithear mór an seo ; séithear beag an siud . . . . .
    bithidh sibh fhéin anns an t-seithear mhór, uncail.

TORMOD: Cha bhi, cha bhi. Fàgaidh sinn an seithear mór
    aig a' chùirt, a luaidh.

SEONAID: A' Chùirt ! Chan 'eil a' Chùirt uile a' tighinn.
    Cha d' rachadh Cùirt ann an aon séithear co-dhiubh.

TORMOD: Na bi a' magadh, a Sheònaid. Tha an gnothuch
    nas cudthromaiche na sin. Tha fhios agad gu bheil Fear
    Gaidhlig na Cùrtach a' tighinn, agus tha e cho math ri Cùirt
    shlàn.

SEONAID: Seadh, seadh, ma ta. Fear-na-Cùrtach anns s'
    chathair mhóir . . . Agus a bheil sibh fhéin a' dol a sheasamh ?

TORMOD: Chan 'eil. Chan 'eil mi cho iriosal sin buileach.

SEONAID: Cuiridh mi an séithear beag an seo dhuibhse mata.

TORMOD: Nì sin an gnothuch.

SEONAID: Tha mi 'n dòchas gun tig e.

TORMOD: Thig e. Nach 'eil fhios gun tig e ! Dé bha 'dol
    'ga chumail ?

SEONAID: Mur a saoileadh e an t-astar fada airson gnothuch
    cho faoin.

TORMOD: Gnothuch faoin ! An abair thu gnothuch faoin ri goid ?

SEONAID: 'S e facal làidir a tha sin.

TORMOD: 'S e facal làidir, agus obair làidir, a bhith a' buain mo chuid feòir a h-uile bliadhna, agus a bharrachd air sin a bhith a' teadhradh nam beothaichean aice far a ruig iad a nall gu ceann a' chnuic.

SEONAID: 'S docha gun can a' Chùirt nach 'eil a' chrioch a' leantainn sios an cnoc.

TORMOD: 'S iad nach can. Bha crioch an siud bhon as cuimhneach leamsa. Bha, bho am Achd nan Croiteirean, agus bithidh i ann fhad 's a mhaireas neart 'na mo bhodhaig-sa a sheasas airson ceartais.

SEONAID: Tha ceartas glé mhath, ach saoilidh mise anns an latha a th' ann gum bu chòir do nàbaidhean a bhith còirdte.

TORMOD: Cha tig an latha a bhitheas mise còirdte ri Goirseal, a Sheònaid. Thug mise . . . . . .

SEONAID: Uil, tha i a' cur an fheòir gu deagh fheum. Coimheadaibh sibhse ann a sin, uncail, gun bhó gun fheum air feur.

TORMOD: Mur a togair mise bó a chumail, 's e sin mo ghnothuch fhìn.

SEONAID: O chan 'eil a' chuis a' stad aig a sin.

TORMOD: Ciamar ?

SEONAID: Mur a cuir sibhse feum air an fhearann a th' agaibh, faodaidh iad a thoirt do fheadhainn a chuireas feum air.

TORMOD: Cha leig a' Chùirt leotha am fearann a thoirt bhuamsa.

SEONAID: O, ge ta, chan ann aig a' Chùirt a tha am facal mu dheireadh.

TORMOD: Nach ann ! Chi sinn dé their Fear na Curtach 'nuair a thig e.

Tìr an Aigh

SEONAID: 'S e duine mór a th' ann am Fear na Curtach, ach tha buidhnean eile ann an diugh a bharrachd air Cùirt.

TORMOD: Seo cuideigin a' tighinn.

CAILEAN: *(Aig an dorus ag eigheach)*. A Sheònaid.

SEONAID: 'S e Cailean a th' ann. *(Seonaid a' dol gu'n dorus)*.

TORMOD: Nach d' thuirt mi riut gun am fear sin a leigeil an còir an tighe. Cha chuir duine dhe'n treubh aig Goirseal a shròn a steach air an dorus seo.

SEONAID: Cha tig e steach idir. Cha bhi mi tiota.

TORMOD: Goirseal! Leigidh mise fhaicinn dhith. Cha bhi i cho spracail 'nuair a chi i Fear-na-Cùrtach an seo. Thig a steach an seo, a Sheònaid, agus leig leis an ablach sin falbh dhachaidh.

SEONAID: *(A' tilleadh)*. Deanaibh air ur socair.

TORMOD: Cha dean. Nach do dh' earb mi riut gun mac Goirseil a' leigeil faisg no fàire . . . .

SEONAID: Dé a th' agaibh an aghaidh Chailein. Cha d' rinn e coire sam bith oirbhse.

TORMOD: Nach d' rinn! Mac Goirseil, tha sin gu leòr. Gun fiù fhios aige có . . . .

SEONAID: Chan 'eil còir agaibh sin a ràdh.

TORMOD: Dé?

SEONAID: Bha sibh a' dol a ràdh gun fhios aige có as athair dha. Tha e móran nas fheàrr . . . .

TORMOD: O seadh. Bha e ann an colaisde, mar a bha thu fhéin, agus dé rinn sin dha?

SEONAID: Ni e feum dha fhathasd.

TORMOD: Chi sinn. Ach dé thug an seo an dràsd e? Innis sin dhomh.

SEONAID: Thainig e a thoirt rabhaidh dhomh.

TORMOD: Rabhadh. Dé an rabhadh?

SEONAID: Chuir a mhàthair fios a dh' ionnsuidh a' Choimisein agus tha fear dhiubh a' tighinn.

TORMOD: An Coimisean! Dé thug oirre sin a dheanamh?

SEONAID: Tha i ag iarraidh tuilleadh fearainn.

TORMOD: Is càite a bheil i a' smaointeachadh a gheibh i sin?

SEONAID: Chan 'eil fhios agam. Anns a' bhaile seo, tha mi cìnnteach.

TORMOD: Tha i fàs nas ladarna a h-uile latha, ach stad gus an tig a' Chùirt. Cha bhi e fada a' sealltuinn dhith. Agus cuin' a tha dùil aice ris an duine seo?

SEONAID: Chan 'eil iad cìnnteach . . . . an diugh 's dòcha.

TORMOD: An diugh! Dé tha 'toirt air tighinn an diugh? O, tha mi tuigsinn. Dh' innis thusa do Chailean gu robh dùil agamsa ri Fear na Cùrtach.

SEONAID: Cha leiginn a leas innse. Nach do dh' innis sibh fhéin fad is farsuinn e!

TORMOD: Na'n saoilinn-sa, a Sheònaid, gu robh thusa a' gabhail taobh na gràisg ud!

SEONAID: Na bruidhnibh mar sin. Nan gabhadh, cha bhithinn an seo.

TORMOD: Cha bhitheadh, tha thu ceart. O 's math leam thu bhi còmhla rium, cha bhithinn ach aonaranach as d' aonais.

SEONAID: Ged a dh' fhalbhainn-sa, bhitheadh sibh ceart gu leòr.

TORMOD: Cha bhitheadh idir.

SEONAID: Bhitheadh.

TORMOD: Ciamar?

SEONAID: Dh' fhaodadh sibh pòsadh fhathasd.

TORMOD: Huh. Dh' fhàg mi am pòsadh ro fhada, tha eagal orm. Có a phòsadh mise co-dhiubh.

SEONAID: Phòsadh gu leòr.

Tìr an Aigh

TORMOD: Ainmich aon té.

SEONAID: Goirseal.

TORMOD: Goirseal !

SEONAID: Seadh.

TORMOD: An té aig a bheil gràin a cridhe orm, agus a' cheart uiread agamsa dhi-se.

SEONAID: O ge ta, chan 'eil gràin agus gràdh uiareannan fad' o cheile. Cha b'e a' cheud uair a dh' fholaich fuath an gaol.

TORMOD: Uil, a nise, a Sheònaid, dé an sgoil anns an cual thu na diomhaireachdan sin ?

SEONAID: Ann an sgoil an t-saoghail, le a bhith a' cumail mo shùilean — agus mo chluasan, fosgailte.

TORMOD: Seadh dìreach. Cha do dh' fhalbh thu fhathasd, agus cùm do shùilean — agus do chluasan — fosgailte an dràsda air son Fear-na-Cùrtach.

SEONAID: Cumaidh. Cha tig e gun fhiosda.

TORMOD: Stad ort, o'n a tha thu cho glic, ciamar a bhruidhneas mi ris an duine seo ?

SEONAID: Stad, seo an litir aige. Tha e ag ràdh, " Cùirt na Duthcha, bho'n Ridire Seumas Mac-Calmain, Fear-Gaidhlig na Cùrtach."

TORMOD: An dean " A' Chuirteir " an gnothuch ?

SEONAID: Cha dean.

TORMOD: Ciamar a nì " Fhir-Cùrtach ? "

SEONAID: Beagan nas fheàrr. Ach innsidh mise dhuibh. Theiribh "A Ridire " ris.

TORMOD: Glé mhath, ma tha. Ciamar a tha sibh, a Ridire ? Thigibh a steach, a Ridire. A bheil mo cholair dìreach ?

SEONAID: Cuiridh mise ceart e. Sin e.

TORMOD: An toir sinn drama dha ?

SEONAID: 'S dòcha gur e tea as fheàrr leis. Bithidh an da chuid deiseil againn.

(*Gnogadh aig an dorus*). Seo e.

(*Fear a' Choimisein agus Goirseal a' tighinn a steach*).

TORMOD: Thigibh a steach (*ri Goirseal*) — agus thusa. Ciamar a tha sibh, Fhir-na-Curtach ?

MORAIR: Chan e Fear-Cùrtach a th' annamsa.

TORMOD: O, gabhaibh mo leth-sgeul. Ciamar a tha sibh, a Ridire ?

MORAIR: Chan e Ridire a th' annamsa.

TORMOD: Thuirt mi, Fhir-na-Cùrtach, mar tha.

MORAIR: Thuirt, agus bha sibh ceàrr.

TORMOD: Feumaidh gur e . . . .

MORAIR: Is e mise Fear a' Choimisein, Coimisean na Tìre.

TORMOD: Dé thug a seo sibh, a Mhgr . . . . ?

MORAIR: Tha thu a' bruidheann ri Moraire Chamusiunaraidh, Fear-Gaidhlig Coimisean na Tìre.

TORMOD: Agus có th' agaibh còmhla ribh an seo, a Mhoraire . . . Chamustianavaig ?

MORAIR: Na bi ri fealla-dha. 'S cìnnteach gun aithnich thu do nàbaidh, Goirseal Nic-Cuinn.

TORMOD: Cha robh mi a' ciallachadh nach aithnichinn i.

MORAIR: Agus dé bha thu 'ciallachadh ?

TORMOD: Bha mi 'ciallachadh nach robh mi 'tuigsinn dé bha i 'deanamh an seo.

MORAIR: Thàinig i an seo, mata, a chionn gun d' iarr mise oirre tighinn. Tha mi cìnnteach gum faod sinn suidhe.

TORMOD: Suidhibh-se an siud, a Mhoraire.

SEONAID: Agus faodaidh Goirseal suidhe an seo.

TORMOD: Is dòcha nach dùirig i suidhe. Is fhada bho'n nach d'rinn i suidhe, no seasamh fhéin, anns an tigh seo.

157

MORAIR: Co-dhiubh, bitheadh sin mar sin, tha mise ag iarraidh ort, an ainm a' chrùin, cead a thoirt dhith fuireach an seo beagan mhionaidean a chùm gun cluinn sibh le chéile dé th' agam ri ràdh.

GOIRSEAL: (*A' suidhe*). Tapadh leat, a Sheònaid.

SEONAID: Ni mi cupa tea.

TORMOD: Uh . . . nì . . . cupa tea.

MORAIR: A bheil fhios agad gun d' rinn am boirionnach seo tagradh ri Coimisean na Tìre ?

TORMOD: Cha chuirinn seachad oirre e. Rinn mise tagradh cuideachd.

MORAIR: Ri Coimisean na Tire ?

TORMOD: Chan ann. Ri Cùirt na Dùthcha.

MORAIR: An d' fhuair thu freagairt ?

TORMOD: Cha d' fhuair fhathasd, ach cha chreid mi gum bi e fada.

MORAIR: Seadh, seadh, is e mo dhleasdanas-sa an dràsda beachd a' Choimisein a thoirt seachad.

SEONAID: Agus dé thachras ma bhitheas an da bheachd eadar-dhealaichte ?

MORAIR: Có seo . . . . do nighean ?

TORMOD: Chan e. Seònaid, nighean mo bhràthar.

GOIRSEAL: Nighean cho grinn 's cho tapaidh, a Mhorair, 's a th'anns a' bhaile. Gu dearbh 's e ionghnadh a th' ann leamsa gu bheil i fuireach cho fada còmhla ris a' bhurraidh seo.

TORMOD: Ta gu dearbh, cha b' ionghnadh thusa a bhith 'bruidhinn !

MORAIR: A nise tha siud gu leòr dhe'n trod.

SEONAID: Bithidh obair agaibh, a Mhoraire.

GOIRSEAL: Gheibh sinn breith a' Choimisein.

TORMOD: A mach leis ! Chan 'eil eagal sam bith agamsa roimh bhreith a' Choimisein.

MORAIR: So dhuibh mata (*a' leughadh*). Ri linn 's gu bheil a' bhana-chroitear, Goirseal NicCuinn, aireamh a ceitheir-deug an Leitir-daraich, deònach agus comasach tuilleadh fearainn àitich a ghabhail, a thuilleadh air na th' aice mar tha, agus ri linn gu bheil a' chroit sin ri a taobh a bhuineas do'n chroitear Tormod MacNeill, aireamh a tri-deug an Leitir-daraich, a' dol fàs le cion àitich, is e mo chomhairle-sa, Fear-Gaidhlig Coimisean na Tìre, gum bi am fearann a tha i ag iarraidh air a thoirt dhith, agus sin bho'n cheud latha de mhios an Lùnasdail !

TORMOD: Am fearann agamsa ! Cha tig an latha ! A dhaoine gun nàire ! Ag iarraidh tuilleadh fearainn ! Am fearann agamsa ! Tha feum gur e boirionnach a th' innte, no rachadh i dhachaidh is sùil ghorm oirre.

GOIRSEAL: O cha leig thu leas a bhith cur asad cho mór mu choinneamh boirionnaich. Nam bitheadh Cailean agamsa an seo tha fhios agam có air a bhitheadh an t-sùil ghorm. Dùil agad bho'n a tha beagan airgid agad 's nach leig thu leas car obrach a dheanamh air fearann gu bheil thu nas fheàrr na càch anns a' bhaile seo. Chan 'eil 's cha bhi, agus fhad 's a their lagh na rioghachd gu bheil fearann an àite gu bhith air a chur gu feum ceart, 's e lagh na rioghachd a bhitheas ann, agus cha chuir thusa no siochaire sam bith eile stad air.

MORAIR: Leig leis a nise. Mìnichidh mise an gnothuch.

SEONAID: (*A tighinn a steach le poit tea*). Suidhibh a nise 's gheibh sibh uile cupa tea.

Tìr an Aigh

TORMOD: Chan 'eil feum air mìneachadh. Cha ghabh no tea. Air falbh leis. Toirt bhuam mo chuid fearainn ! Dé tha sibh a' smaointeachach a tha mise 'dol a dheanamh ?

MORAIR: O cha toir sinn a' chroit uat air fad. Fàgaidh sinn earrann agad timchioll an tighe.

TORMOD: Am fàg gu dearbh ? Nach sibh a th' air fàs còir !

GOIRSEAL: Fàgaidh. Chan 'eil a dhìth ormsa ach an t-iochdar, sios bho'n chnoc bheag gun chladach.

TORMOD: A bhean gun nàire, nach ann agad a tha a' bhathais a' togail do ghuth a rithisd an taobh a stigh dhe'n fhàrdaich seo !

MORAIR: Cha bhi thu riaraichte leis a sin.

TORMOD: Cha bhi mise riaraichte le aon òirleach a thoirt seachad gu siorruidh.

MORAIR: Mur a dean thu le d'dheoin e, nì thu a dh' aindeoin e.

(Fuaim aig an dorus).

TORMOD: Có tha seo ? Mu dheireadh ! Am fear ris an robh mi feitheamh. Seo am fear a chuireas sibh uile 'nur n-àite fhéin. O sibh a th' ann. 'S mi tha toilichte bhur faicinn. Thigibh a steach, a Mhoraire . . . . .

RIDIRE: O chan e Moraire a th' annam idir, fhathasd. Ni Ridire an gnothuch an dràsda. 'S ann a tha làn tighe agaibh an seo !

TORMOD: Tha, a Ridire. 'S docha gun cuala sibh mu'n duine urramach seo, Moraire Chamustianavaig.

MORAIR: Camusiunaraidh, an t-àite san d'rugadh mi.

RIDIRE: Cha chuala, ach theagamh gu bheil e urramach airson sin.

TORMOD: Seònaid, nighean mo bhràthar, agus . . .

MORAIR: Goirseal NicCuinn, àireamh a ceitheir-deug.

RIDIRE: Tha fianuisean gu leòr againn co-dhiubh. A bheil sibh deiseil airson mo ghnothuich-sa ?

TORMOD: Tha gu dearbh.

RIDIRE: Seo map a' bhaile. A nis tha a' chroit agaibhse an siud agus a' chroit eile an siud.

TORMOD: Agus seo agaibh a' chrioch sios agus siud far a bheil i 'tighinn a nall.

RIDIRE: (*A' pasgadh a' mhap*). Theid sinn sios le cheile a dh' fhaicinn an àite.

MORAIR: Cha bhi sinne a' fuireach.

RIDIRE: Ach bu mhath leam ur faicinn 'nuair a thilleas sinn. (*Tormod agus Ridire a' dol a mach*).

SEONAID: Suidhibh. Gheibh sinn an tea a nise. (*Morair agus Goirseal a' suidhe*).

MORAIR: Tha an tea seo math.

GOIRSEAL: The Seònaid math air an tea, mar a tha i air a' chòrr.

MORAIR: An robh thu riamh air falbh bho'n taigh ?

SEONAID: Bha. Bha mi greis an colaisde anns a' bhaile mhór.

MORAIR: B' fheàrr leam gu robh thu agam an oifis a' Choimisein.

GOIRSEAL: 'S i a' cheart té air do shon.

MORAIR: An tigeadh tu còmhla rium ? Obair sheasgair agus deagh phàigheadh.

SEONAID: Dé a theireadh bràthair m'athar ?

GOIRSEAL: Cha dean bràthair d'athar ach cur suas leis. Dh'fheumadh tu falbh uaireigin co-dhiubh.

SEONAID: Falbhaidh mi, ma bhitheas e deònach.

MORAIR: Cuiridh mi-fhìn a' cheisd ris.

GOIRSEAL: Chan 'eil math dhuinn a bhith an seo 'nuair a thilleas iad.

161

F

Tìr an Aigh

MORAIR: No saoilidh iad gu bheil thu a' gabhail seilbh air an tigh a bharrachd air a' chroit.

(*Goirseal is am Morair a' dol a mach*)

(*Seonaid a' cur air falbh nan cupannan agus a' sealltuinn a mach aig an uinneig*).

Cailean a' tighinn a steach

SEONAID: O, cha robh còir agad air tighinn an dràsda.

CAILEAN: Tha e ceart gu leòr. Chunnaic mi d'athair agus am fear eile shios air a' chroit.

SEONAID: Ge ta, faodaidh iad tilleadh uair sam bith.

CAILEAN: Coma leat, bithidh mise air falbh mun tig iad.

SEONAID: Feumaidh tu sin. Tha m'uncal air a chur mu chuairt gu leòr mar tha, agus chan 'eil fhios dé a dheanadh e nam faiceadh e an seo thu.

CAILEAN: Cha deachaidh gnothuichean leis?

SEONAID: Cha deachaidh.

CAILEAN: Dé thachair?

SEONAID: Thuirt Fear mór a' Choimisein ris gun cailleadh e a' chroit.

CAILEAN: Cha chòrdadh sin ris, ach nach math a thuirt mi riut gum b' ann mar sin a bhitheadh.

SEONAID: Thuirt, ach tha earbsa mhór aige ann am Fear na Cùrtach.

CAILEAN: Tha eagal orm nach dean sin feum dha.

SEONAID: Tha rud eile nach dean feum dha.

CAILEAN: Dé tha sin?

SEONAID: 'Nuair a chluinneas e . . . .

CAILEAN: Dé a chluinneas e?

SEONAID: 'Nuair a chluinneas e gu bheil mise a' bruidhinn air falbh.

CAILEAN: A' falbh ! Càite ?

SEONAID: A' falbh le Fear a' Choimisein.

CAILEAN: Có leis ?

SEONAID: A' falbh a dh' obair an oifis a' Choimisein.

CAILEAN: Cuin' a chuireadh seo air dòigh ?

SEONAID: Dìreach mu'n d' thainig thu steach.

CAILEAN: Có a dh' innis dha mu do dheidhinn-sa ?

SEONAID: Dh' innis do mhàthair.

CAILEAN: Agus tha thu 'dol 'gam fhàgail-sa an seo ?

SEONAID: Cha mhair sin fada. 'S docha gu faigh thusa thu fhéin obair air Galldachd. O seo iad a' tilleadh. Cha robh guth againn orra. Seo, gabh a steach an siud 's na gluais gus am faigh thu cothrom.

(Cailean a steach do'n rùm bheag eile)
(Tormod agus Ridire na Cùrtach a' tighinn a steach)

SEONAID: Ciamar a chaidh dhuibh a nise ?

TORMOD: Cha chord seo cho math ri Goirseal.

SEONAID: Tha Ridire na Cùrtach dhe'n bheachd gu bheil sibh ceart, uncail ?

RIDIRE: O, chan 'eil teagamh sam bith nach d' thainig i nall seachad air a' chrìch, deagh chaob cuideachd. Chan fhuiling lagh na rioghachd a leithid sin de lamhachas-làidir.

TORMOD: Tha fadachd orm, a Sheònaid, gus am faic mi aodann Ghoirseil. Tuilleadh fearainn ! Bheir mise tuilleadh fearainn dhith !

SEONAID: A bheil fhios agaibh, a Ridire, gu bheil Moraire a' Choimisein deònach a' chuid mhór de chroit bràthair-m'athar a thoirt dhith ?

RIDIRE: Tha, bha bràthair d'athar ag innseadh sin dhomh.

SEONAID: Agus an cùm sibhse ri ur barail fhéin an aghaibh a' bharail-san ?

163

Tìr an Aigh

TORMOD: Nach 'eil fhios gun cùm. Tha a' Chùirt cho math ri Coimisean uair sam bith.

RIDIRE: Uel, is e mo dhleasdanas-sa criochan a' bhaile a ghleidheadh far na chàirich Achd nan Croiteirean iad anns a' bhliadhna ochd ceud deug ceithir fichead 's a sia.

TORMOD: Glé mhath, agus is còir sin innseadh do Ghoirseal cho luath 's a ghabhas deanamh.

RIDIRE: 'S còir.

TORMOD: A Sheònaid. Eubh air a' bhoirionnach sin tighinn a nall an seo mionaid, agus innsidh sinne dhith dé tha lagh na rioghachd ag ràdh.

SEONAID: Ceart gu leòr. Cha bhi dad a dhìth oirbh. Tha am botul an siud thall. Bithidh mi air ais an tiota. (*Seònaid a' dol a mach*).

TORMOD: Seo agaibh a nis, a Ridire. Bithidh drama againn mu'n tig iad. 'S math as fhiach e drama.

RIDIRE: Coma leam dheth. 'S e cupa tea a b' fheàrr leam-sa.

TORMOD: Ud, chan 'eil fhios agam a bheil tea air fhàgail. O, tha tea freagarrach gu leòr do mhuinntir Coimisein, ach shaoilinn gun gabhadh Fear Cùrtach rudeigin na bu làidire.

RIDIRE: Tha mi fior mheasail air tea. Ach leig leis, gheibh sinn i 'nuair a thilleas an té òg.

TORMOD: O, ma's e tea as fheàrr leibh, gheibh mise tea. Ach bha dùil agam gum faighinn fhìn lethsgeul air slàinte na Cùrtach òl.

RIDIRE: O, mas ann mar sin a tha, cuir dileag bheag bhìodach 's a' ghloinne 's nì sin an gnothuch. Cuir uisge gu leòr ann.

TORMOD: 'S e sin as fheàrr (*a' cur deur anns gach gloinne*). Gheibh mi uisge.

(*A' cluinntinn fuaim a muigh*)

Sguabaibh as e mar a tha e. Tha iad a seo.

(*An triùir eile a' tighinn a steach*)

Thigibh a steach. Agus sibhse cuideachd, a Mhoraire, ma tha sibh deònach éisdeachd ri rud nach còrd ruibh.

MORAIR: Dé tha fainear dhuit a nise?

TORMOD: Cluinnidh sibh. Agus, a Sheònaid, dean cupa tea dha'n Mhoraire.

MORAIR: Cha ghabh mi an còrr tea. Cha do dh' òl mi a leithid de thea riamh an aon latha. Mur 'eil dad agaibh nas fheàrr.

TORMOD: Chan 'eil, chan 'eil. Tha sinn ro stuama an Leitir-daraich.

SEONAID: Fàgaidh mi sibh, agus ma bhitheas dad a dhìth oirbh . . . .

GOIRSEAL: An cuidich mi thu, a Sheònaid?

TORMOD: Fuirich thusa an seo, a nàbaidh, gus an cluinn thu breith Cùirt na Dùthcha air a' cheisd, a' cheisd chudthromach, có a tha ceart mu'n chrìch a tha eadar a' chroit agadsa agus a' chroit agamsa.

GOIRSEAL: Tha mise riaraichte leis a' bhreith a thugadh mar tha air a' chùis.

TORMOD: Tha sin furasda a thuigsinn — gu bheil thusa riar-aichte leis a' bhreith a fhuair thu mar tha. Ach cha robh mise riaraichte leis, agus bho nach robh, fhuair mi breith eile, agus a nise tha mi ag iarraidh air an Ridire Seumas Mac Calmain, Gaidheal urramach air Cùirt na Dùthcha, a' bhreith sin a chur fa'r comhair.

RIDIRE: Ni mise sin, a reir mo dhleasdanais. Ri lìnn 's gun d'rinn an croitear Tormod Mac Neill, aireamh a tri-deug an Leitir-daraich, gearan ri Cùirt na Dùthcha an aghaidh na

Tìr an Aigh

bana-chroitear Goirseal Nic-Cuinn, aireamh a ceithir-deug,
Leitir-daraich . . .

MORAIR: Có ris a rinn e a' ghearain ?

RIDIRE: Dh' innis mi sin mar tha. Rinn e a ghearain ri
Cùirt na Dùthcha.

MORAIR: Cha sheas sin. 'S e Coimisean na Tìre as ùire.

RIDIRE: 'S i a' Chuirt as sine.

MORAIR: 'S e an Coimisean as urramaiche.

RIDIRE: 'S i a' Chùirt as cothromaiche.

MORAIR: 'S e an Coimisean . . . .

TORMOD: A nise, a nise. Seo an tigh agamsa agus feumaidh
sibh modh a chleachdadh.

RIDIRE: 'S i a' Chùirt . . . .

TORMOD: Fhuair sibhse, a Mhoraire, cead beachd a' Choimisein
a chur an céill. 'S cìnnteach gun nochd sibh a' cheart mhodh
ri daoine eile is a fhuair sibh fhéin.

GOIRSEAL: Cluinneamaid dé th' aige ri ràdh ma tha.

TORMOD: Facal glic mu dheireadh thall.

RIDIRE: 'S e an co-dhùnadh gun d'thainig mise, ma tha, gu
bheil a' chrioch mu choig slatan deug bho cheann a chnuic
mar a bha Goirseal Nic-Cuinn ag ràdh, agus gu robh i mar
sin a'tighinn an t-astar a dh' ainmich mi seachad air a' chrìch
dhlighich.

MORAIR: Coig slatan deug. Gheibh i barrachd is sin ma
tha i comasach air feum a dheanamh dheth.

TORMOD: Mur a bi sibh sàmhach an làthair na Cùrtach, a
Mhoraire, feumaidh mi iarraidh oirbh an tigh seo fhàgail.

RIDIRE: Coig slatan deug air croit an duin' eile, nì a . . . .

MORAIR: Nì a tha air a cheadachadh leis an Achd Ur.

RIDIRE: Nì a tha air a chronachadh leis an t-seann Achd.

TORMOD: O mar a tha mi leibh ! Nach fan sibh sàmhach.

RIDIRE: Tha a' Chuirt mar sin a' bacadh . . . .

MORAIR: Tha an Coimisean a' ceadachadh . . . .

RIDIRE: Tha a' Chuirt a' bacadh . . . .

MORAIR: Tha an Coimisean a' ceadachadh . . . .

TORMOD: O mar a tha mi . . . . eadar Cuirt is Coimisean !

RIDIRE: Tha mise a' bacadh Ghoirseil Nic-Cuinn o so a mach o thighinn seachad air a' chrìch a chomharraich mise an diugh leis na biorainean, comharradh Cùirt na Dùthcha.

MORAIR: Agus cuiridh mise a maireach biorainean mu choinneamh tigh Thormoid Mhic-Neill air am bi comharradh Coimisean na Tìre, agus bithidh cead aig Goirseal Nic-Cuinn am fearann a chur am feum suas gu sin.

TORMOD: Na cuireadh duine cas air a' chroit agamsa le biorainean a maireach no latha eile. Ma chuireas, bithidh fhuil air a cheann fhéin.

MORAIR: 'S e am polasman a gheibh sin dhuit ma bhitheas tu maoidheadh mar sin.

RIDIRE: Bheir mise an gnothuch na's fhaide. Bheir mi gu Tigh nan Cumantan e . . .

MORAIR: Bheir mise gu Taigh nam Morairean e.

GOIRSEAL: 'S dòcha nach leig sibh a leas. Bithidh duan eile aige an ceartuair.

TORMOD: Có tha a' maoidheadh a nise ? Dé tha a' dol a thachairt an ceartuair ?

GOIRSEAL: Cluinnidh tu sin. Bha thusa deònach fuireach an seo gun char obrach a dheanamh bho'n a fhuair thu airgiod do bhràthar . . . .

TORMOD: Dé ma bha ? Dé do ghnothuch-sa ri sin ?

GOIRSEAL: 'S dòcha nach e, ach theagamh nach bi thu cho deònach fuireach an seo 'nuair a chluinneas tu gum bi thu leat fhéin ann.

Tìr an Aigh

TORMOD: Carson a bhitheas mi leam fhìn?

GOIRSEAL: Bithidh a chionn 's gu bheil Seònaid a' falbh.

TORMOD: A' falbh! Càite?

GOIRSEAL: A' falbh a dh' obair an oifis a' Choimisein.

TORMOD: A Sheònaid. Trobhad. Chuala tu mar a thuirt i. A bheil e fìor?

SEONAID: Tha, uncail.

TORMOD: Cuin' a chuir thu seo air dòigh?

SEONAID: An diugh.

TORMOD: An diugh!

GOIRSEAL: Bha fhios agam nach còrdadh e riut.

TORMOD: Tha e còrdadh riut-sa, tha mi cìnnteach. An robh gnothuch agad ris?

GOIRSEAL: 'S dòcha gu robh cuideachd. Ach innsidh i fhéin dhuit. Agus nach 'eil Fear a' Choimisein fhéin an sin?

TORMOD: Có a thuìrt riut gu faigheadh tu obair?

SEONAID: Thuirt Moraire a' Choimisein.

TORMOD: Dé tha agaibh-se ri ràdh ris a seo?

MORAIR: Tha e ceart gu leòr. Tha i a' falbh còmhla rium-sa.

TORMOD: Carson?

MORAIR: Airson gu bheil nighean a dhìth oirnn an oifis a' Choimisein agus gu bheil i glé fhreagarrach. A bharrachd air sin, bha i fhéin ag iarraidh falbh.

TORMOD: An robh?

SEONAID: Uel, thuirt sibh fhéin gu robh cead agam falbh uair sam bith.

TORMOD: Thuirt, agus chan 'eil mi 'gad bhacadh. Ach aig a' cheart ám is olc do Choimisean a chaidh a steidheachadh air son daoine a tharruing a dh' ionnsaidh obair fearainn, no co-dhiubh an fheadhainn a tha ris an obair mar tha a chumail ann, is olc dhaibh a bhith 'gan toirt air falbh.

168

MORAIR: Tha thu ceart. 'S ann air son sin a steidhicheadh an Coimisean.

TORMOD: Airson an nighean agamsa, agus feadhainn coltach rithe, a thoirt air falbh?

MORAIR: Mu choinneamh aon duine a dh' fhalbhas, cuiridh sinn, 's docha, sianar air ais.

TORMOD: Ciamar seo?

MORAIR: Cha dean an Coimisean adhartas anns an obair a chuireadh roimhe mur a bi oifis aca an toiseach anns am bi daoine ealanta.

TORMOD: Dé bhur barail-sa air a seo, a Ridire? Dé am feum a nì e dhomhsa ged a bheireadh Cùirt croit shlàn dhomh ma tha Coimisean a' toirt bhuam nighean mo bhràthar. Tha mi cìnnteach gu bheil oifis agaibhse cuideachd, a Ridire.

RIDIRE: Tha, gu dearbh. Cha deanamaid móran feum gun oifis.

TORMOD: Tha mi cìnnteach gu bheil e a cheart cho feumail ri oifis a' Choimisein.

RIDIRE: Tha e sin.

TORMOD: 'S briagh nach robh sibhse a' sireadh luchd cuideachaidh on a thàinig sibh an rathad.

RIDIRE: Ma ta, on a dh' ainmich sibh e, tha ait' agam do dhuine ceart gu leòir.

TORMOD: 'S math nach 'eil nighean eile comhla riumsa, no bhitheadh sibhse 'ga h-iarraidh.

RIDIRE: Chan e nighean a tha dhìth orm, ach duine òg, easgaidh, sgoilear cuimseach.

TORMOD: Duine òg, easgaidh.

RIDIRE: Seadh, chan aithne do neach agaibh fear dhe'n t-seòrsa an rathad seo?

Tìr an Aigh

GOIRSEAL: Chan aithne.

TORMOD: Duine òg, easgaidh, sgoilear cuimseach, an d'thuirt sibh ?

RIDIRE: Thuirt, thuirt.

TORMOD: 'S aithne dhomh a' cheart fhear.

GOIRSEAL: Có ?

TORMOD: Cailean agad fhéin, an dearbh fhear.

GOIRSEAL: Cha bhitheadh e freagarrach ; co-dhiubh tha feum air aig an tigh.

TORMOD: Feum air aig an tigh ! Nach cluinn thu am boir-eannach ! An cuala tu idir na daoine fiosrach sin ag ràdh gu bheil obair oifis nas feumaile na obair croite !

MORAIR: A nise cha d'thuirt mise sin idir.

TORMOD: O chan 'eil e agam buileach ceart. 'S e bu chòir dhomh a ràdh mu'n dean obair croite adhartas gu feum obair oifis a bhith air a chùl. Nach 'eil sin ceart, a Mhoraire a' Choimisein ?

MORAIR: Tha.

TORMOD: Nach 'eil e ceart, a Ridire na Cùrtach ?

RIDIRE: Tha.

TORMOD: Agus mu choinneamh aon duine a bheir iad air falbh, a bhoirionnaich, cuiridh iad sianar air ais. A bheil e ceart agam ?

RIDIRE: Tha.

MORAIR: Tha.

GOIRSEAL: Chan 'eil mise ag iarraidh sianar.

TORMOD: Cha tig an t-sianar air ais an seo. Bithidh iad sgap-te air feadh na dùthcha.

GOIRSEAL: Tha mise coma dé thachras air feadh na dùthcha.

MORAIR: A nise cha dean sin an gnothuch. Chan fhaod sinn a bhith coma. Feumaidh sinn amharc seachad oirnn fhìn gu feum ar coimhearsnaich.

TORMOD: Dìreach sin. Tha mi tuigsinn. Agus a' cumail sùil air feum nan coimhearsnach tha mi ag ràdh riubh, a Ridire, gur e Cailean aig Goirseal an seo a cheart fhear a tha a dhìth oirbh.

RIDIRE: Chan fhaca mi an duine fhathasd.

GOIRSEAL: Bithidh e anns a' mhòine, no ri rud-eigin.

TORMOD: Cha bhi sinn fada 'ga fhaotainn.

RIDIRE: A bheil e eòlach air obair fearainn?

GOIRSEAL: Tha e . . .

TORMOD: Tha gu dearbh, chan 'eil nas eòlaiche.

RIDIRE: An e sgoilear math a th' ann?

GOIRSEAL: Bha e . . .

TORMOD: Sgoilear air leth.

RIDIRE: Tha e ciallach, stòlda 'na dhòigh?

TORMOD: Gu dearbh fhéin. Cho grinn, modhail, ri fear 'san dùthaich.

GOIRSEAL: Bha duan eile agad roimhe.

TORMOD: Siud mo bheachd-sa, a Ridire.

RIDIRE: Saoil am bitheadh e deònach an obair a ghabhail?

GOIRSEAL: Cha bhitheadh.

TORMOD: Chi sinn. Cha bhi sinn fada 'ga fhaotainn.

(*Seònaid a' tighinn a steach*)

TORMOD: Seall a null ach a faic thu Cailean agus iarr air tighinn a seo.

171

Tìr an Aigh

SEONAID: Cha chreid mi gu bheil e aig an tigh.

TORMOD: Seall thusa.

(*Cailean a' tighinn a mach*)

Gu siorruidh ! Seo e ! C'àit' an robh . . . . ?

SEONAID: Bha.

CAILEAN: Gabhabh mo lethsgeul, ma leigeas mi leas sin iarraidh a nise o'n a tha barail cho math agaibh orm.

GOIRSEAL: Agus mise ag ràdh gu robh thu 's a' mhòine.

TORMOD: Co-dhiubh. Tha e an seo a nise. Sin agaibh e, a Ridire, is e deiseil obair sam bith a thairgeas sibh dha a ghabhail.

RIDIRE: Bruidhnidh e air a shon fhéin. 'S tusa Cailean Mac Cuinn air an robh sinn a' bruidhinn ?

CAILEAN: 'S mi.

RIDIRE: Agus chuala tu mu'n obair a tha a' feitheamh air duine freagarrach an oifis na Cùrtach ?

CAILEAN: Chuala.

RIDIRE: Agus a bheil thu deònach a ghabhail os laimh ?

GOIRSEAL: A nise, a Chailein . . . . .

CAILEAN: Tha mi deònach.

RIDIRE: Ceart gu leòr.

TORMOD: Nach d'thuirt mi riubh !

GOIRSEAL: Cha chuala mi riamh a leithid. Coimisean a' toirt dhomh tuilleadh fearainn agus Cùirt a' toirt bhuam mo mhic !

TORMOD: A nise chan fhaod gearain a bhith ann. Tha fhios agad, mu choinneamh aon duine a th' air a thoirt air falbh . . .

GOIRSEAL: Tha, tha. Tha sianar air an cur 'nan àite.

MORAIR: Tha ar n-obair a nise deas.

RIDIRE: Tha, faodaidh sinn a bhith falbh.

172

MORAIR: Chi mi thusa a maireach, a Sheònaid, agus cuiridh sinn air dòigh cuin' a thòisicheas tu.

RIDIRE: Agus chi mise thusa, a Chailein.

MORAIR: Latha math leibh.

GOIRSEAL: Tha sibh a' falbh mar sin.

MORAIR: Tha, tha ar n-obair seachad.

RIDIRE: Thug sinn seachad ar breith.

GOIRSEAL: Stadaibh. Cha dean ur breith feum sam bith dhomhsa.

TORMOD: No dhomhsa. A Ghoirseal, faodaidh tu a' chroit agamsa a ghabhail uair sam bith.

GOIRSEAL: Chan 'eil mi ag iarraidh do chroit, no ceann a' chnuic bhig nas mo.

TORMOD: A' cur fios air Cùirt! B' fheàirrde mise fios a chur air Cùirt!

GOIRSEAL: Chan 'eil Coimisean dad nas fheàrr na Cùirt.

RIDIRE: Na canaibh sin. A bheil fhios agad dé a' chomhairle a bheireadh a' Chuirt ort a nise, a Thoirmoid Mhic-Neill?

TORMOD: Fhuair mise gu leòr de chomhairle na Cùrtach.

RIDIRE: Ach seo agad comhairle a chòrdas riut.

TORMOD: Seadh.

RIDIRE: Bu chòir dhuibh pòsadh.

TORMOD: Có, an dithis againne?

RIDIRE: Seadh.

TORMOD: Cha do smaointich mi air a' leithid.

MORAIR: Agus bheirinn-sa a' cheart chomhairle ortsa, a bhean.

GOIRSEAL: Pòsadh.

MORAIR: Dé eile?

GOIRSEAL: Cha do smaointich mi air a' leithid. Ach feumaidh cuideigin iarraidh orm an toiseach.

TORMOD: Mata, a Ghoirseal, on a dh' fhàg iad leinn fhìn sinn, dé do bharail?

GOIRSEAL: Agus bithidh an cnoc beag againn le chéile.

TORMOD: Bithidh, agus a' chroit agamsa.

GOIRSEAL: Nach math an t-strìth a bhith seachad.

SEONAID: 'S math leam gum bi sibh còmhla mu dheireadh.

CAILEAN: Bithidh sinne còmhla cuideachd, a Sheònaid.

RIDIRE: Ciamar seo? Tha thusa a' dol comhla riumsa a dh'obair an oifis na Cùrtach, nach 'eil?

CAILEAN: Tha.

RIDIRE: Agus tha Seònaid a' dol a dh' obair an oifis a' Choimisein.

CAILEAN: Tha, 's e sin a thuirt i.

SEONAID: Thuirt mi sin. A bheil dad ceàrr?

MORAIR: Chan 'eil. Ach tha oifis a' Choimisein an Lunnuinn, agus tha oifis na Curtach an Obair-eadhain.

CAILEAN: Agus bithidh sinne an t-astar sin bho chéile!

TORMOD: Bithidh sinne co-dhiu, a Ghoirseil, còmhla ann an Leitir-daraich.

GOIRSEAL: Agus chi iad a chéile 'nuair a thig iad dhachaidh airson na bainnse.

TORMOD: 'S dòcha nach fhiach dhaibh falbh gu'n déidh na bainnse.

MORAIR: Tiugainn, a Ridire. 'S e rud math a rinn an Coimisean an siud.

RIDIRE: 'S e rinn e a' Chùirt.

MORAIR: Chan e, ach an Coimisean.

AIR TIR AM MUIDEART

An t-àite: Baile fearainn am Mùideart

An t-am: Feasgar Lunasdail, 1746

Luchd-cluiche

Torcull Mac an t-Saoir
(Torcull an Tac Iochdraich).

Mairi, Bean Thorcuill.

Fionnaghal, nàbaidh.

Eilidh, nighean Thorcuill.

Saighdear: Caiptean.

Saighdear: Seirdsean.

Goiridh, mac Thorcuill.

(*An tacair 'na shuidhe taobh a' ghealbhain*
a' càradh lìn: a bhean a' sgioblachadh
fo chomhair dol a mach; seòmar an deagh uidheam
a réir nòs an latha).

TORCULL: O, thu fhéin 's na Stiùbhartaich, a Mhairi.
Faodaidh tu dìreach an leigeil as do bheachd tuilleadh.

MAIRI: 'S mi nach leig. Gheibh e cothrom eile fhathasd.
Stad thusa, thig e air ais.

TORCULL: Tearlach Stiùbhart, air ais ! O cha tig, gu bràth.
Rinn Culodair an gnothuch air. Thig e air ais, thuirt thu.
Huh, feumaidh e falbh an toiseach. Cha d' fhalbh e fhathast.

MAIRI: O, thig e air ais, a Thorcuill, 'se thig. Duin' òg san
saoghal air thoiseach air.

TORCULL: Og 's gu bheil e, cha toirinn-sa móran air a sheansa
an ceartuair.

MAIRI: Ciamar ? Cha bhoin duine dha.

TORCULL: Cha bhoin duin' againne dha. Dé 's fheàrrd e sin ?
Càit' a bheil e nochd fhéin, saoil thu ? Tha, bheir mi geall,

175

'na dhiol-deiric, fuar, fliuch, acrach, 'na chrùban am fròig air choireigin, no 'na throtan air monadh is tathann miol-chon an airm dheirg 'na chluais.

MAIRI. Nach 'eil truas agad idir ris ?

TORCULL: Nach 'eil fhios gu bheil truas agam ris ! Ach 'se truas aon rud agus coimhead airson càise bàn na gealaich rud eile. Truas, cha dean mo thruas-sa feum sam bith dha.

MAIRI: Chan 'eil fhios agad.

TORCULL: Tha fios is cinnt agam. Agus a' bruidhinn air truas, a Mhairi, bu chòir dhomhsa mo thruas a ghleidheadh airson mo mhic fhìn, Goiridh truagh, gun fhios càit' a bheil e an nochd.

MAIRI: Chi thusa Goiridh a' tighinn dhachaidh.

TORCULL: Tha mi'n dòchas gum faic. Nam faicinnsa Goiridh a' coiseachd a nall a sin an dràsd, a Mhairi, bhithinn coma, feumaidh mi aideachadh, ged nach fhaicinn an Stiùbhartach gu siorruidh.

MAIRI: Cha d'thug mise dùil mu Ghoiridh, s mi nach d'thug, ach mur a faic sinn tuilleadh e, cha bhi sinn ach coltach ri móran eile, a Thorcuill, a thug seachad an cuid s an cuideachd air sgàth aobhar a' Phrionnsa.

TORCULL: 'S mi a tha sgìth dhe na bhruidhinn sin. Am Prionnsa ! Am Prionnsa ! Thu fhéin 's na boireannaich eile — agus 's i Eilidh againn fhìn as miosa buileach — cha chreid mi fhìn nach do thuit sibh uile an gaol air a' Phrionnsa. Rinn sibh dealbh dheth ged nach fhaca sibh riamh e. Tha e na sheòrsa de iomhaigh 'nur cridheachan. Ach 'se mo mhac a bhitheas mise 'g ionndrain.

MAIRI: A bheil thu smaointeachadh, A Thorcuill, nach 'eil mise 'ga ionndrain cuideachd ?

TORCULL: Ma ta, s tu a thug air falbh, thu fhéin is Eilidh. Nan robh e air mo chomhairle-sa a ghabhail, bha e air fuireach aig an tigh.

MAIRI: Tha duin' is duine a' tilleadh.

TORCULL: Agus móran *nach* till.

MAIRI: Feumaidh foighidinn a bhith againn.

TORCULL: Cha leig thu leas sin a ràdh rium-sa. Mur a bitheadh foighidinn agam, cha bhithinn ris an obair seo. Nach 'eil an t-am aig Eilidh a bhith stigh?

MAIRI: O, cha ghabh i gu fois gus an cluinn i na tha ri chluinntinn mu mhuinntir a' Phrionnsa, 's mu'n arm dhearg.

TORCULL: Bu chòir dhi a bhith glic, té gun a slàinte mar a tha i.

MAIRI: Chi mis' i s bheir mi leam a steach i.

TORCULL: Siuthad, na bi fada. Ma chi thu Seumas Uilleim, can ris gu bheil am bàta deiseil aig gob na sgeire. Bheir e leis na slatan. Faodaidh sinn sgriob a thoirt leotha fhad s a bhitheas an lion an cur.

MAIRI: Feasgar math iasgaich ann, nach 'eil?

TORCULL: Cha b' urrainn a bhith na b' fheàrr. Toiseach lionaidh air, is aidhearag de ghaoith iar-dheas.

MAIRI: Chan fhaca mi do leithid, a Thorcuill. Thigeadh tu beò air a' mhuir.

TORCULL: Uel, chan 'eil fhios cuin' a theid sinn a mach a rithisd. Feumaidh sinn tòiseachadh air feur an achaidh mhóir a maireach.

MAIRI: Tha mise falbh (*a' cluinntinn nan ròcais agus a' stad 'san dorus*).
Nach mi a tha sgìth dhe na ghàgail sin. Droch chomharradh a bh' unnta riamh.

177

Tìr an Aigh

TORCULL: Droch chomharradh ! Geasagan an t-saoghail mhóir !

MAIRI: Chan e idir.

TORCULL: Dìreach geasagan. Daoine a' toirt rudan a chreidsinn orra fhéin, s gun iad fad an t-siubhail a' cluinntinn ach an rud a tha iad ag iarraidh a chluinntinn.

MAIRI: Seadh, seadh, fàgaidh sinn mar sin fhéin e ma tha.
(*A' Fosgladh An Doruis*)

TORCULL: Siuthad, a Mhairi. (*Mairi a mach. Torcull a' cumail air a' càradh an lìn agus a' gabhail òran beag ris fhéin*). (*Stararaich aig an dorus. Fionnaghal, Bean a' Phiobaire, a' tighinn a steach; coltas cabhaig oirre*).

FIONNAGHAL: Có tha stigh ?

TORCULL: Tha mise. Thig air d' adhart, Fhionnaghail. A bheil dad ceàrr ?

FIONNAGHAL: Nach mi a tha taingeil a bhith an seo ! Bha dùil agam nach tigeadh an latha 'ruiginn.

TORCULL: Carson, dé th' ort ?

FIONNAGHAL: Chan 'eil dad ormsa, ach tha gu leòr ceàrr, airson sin. Ciamar as urrainn dhuit fhéin suidhe sin cho stòlda ?

TORCULL: Dé tha ceàrr ?

FIONNAGHAL: Dé tha ceàrr ? Dé tha ceàrr ? An can thu guth idir ach 'Dé tha ceàrr ?' Dé tha ceart ? bu chòir dhuit a ràdh.

TORCULL: Ciamar ?

FIONNAGHAL: Ciamar ? Aon rud, an cuala sibh guth air Goiridh fhathasd ?

TORCULL: Cha chuala. An cuala tu fhéin ?

FIONNAGHAL: Cha chuala, ach nam bitheadh mo mhac-sa air falbh, cha deanainn suidhe socair, gun fhios agam co-dhiubh bha e beò no marbh.

TORCULL: Uel, chan 'eil cothrom agams air, Fhionnaghail. Cha leigeadh e leas falbh. Thuirt mise ris gum bu chòir dha fuireach aig an taigh.

FIONNAGHAL: Cha bu mhath an cliù sin ort. Mur a b' e a mhàthair, bhitheadh e aig an tigh fhathasd.

TORCULL: A mhàthair — agus a phiuthar, an creutair truagh.

FIONNAGHAL: Creutair truagh! Creutair truagh gu dearbh! Lag 's gu bheil i am bodhaig, 's i as treasa inntinn agaibh uile.

TORCULL: Nan cuireadh i gu feum ceart e! Neo air thaing inntinn is spiorad, na bith càit' an d' fhuair i e.

FIONNAGHAL: Càite? Càit' am faigheadh i e ach o fhuil a sinnsirean, dualchas a dùthcha, dìlseachd do shliochd nan Stiùbhartach, rìghrean dligheach Alba.

TORCULL: Nach ann ort a tha an cor an nochd, a bhanacharaid!

FIONNAGHAL: Cor, a bheil. Ma tha, 's docha gu bheil deagh aobhar air. Chuala tu mar a thachair?

TORCULL: Tha thu ciallachadh mu Chulodair. Chuala a h-uile duine sin.

FIONNAGHAL: Ach an cuala tu mar a thachair on uair sin?

TORCULL: Chuala beagan. Tha duine a' tighinn dhachaidh an siud 's an seo air taobh thall an locha, tha e coltach.

FIONNAGHAL: Tha, agus air an taobh seo cuideachd. Thainig Iain Sheumais Chaluim an diugh.

TORCULL: Am fear a dh' fhalbh comhla ri Goiridh againne.

FIONNAGHAL: 'S e. Tha fhios agam.

TORCULL: Cluinnidh Mairi a bheil sgeul aig' air Goiridh.

179

Tìr an Aigh

FIONNAGHAL: Chunnaic mi a' coiseachd a nunn i. Tha mi'n dòchas gu faigh i sgeul math mu Ghoiridh. Gu dearbh tha sgeòil gu leòr aig feadhainn eile a thill, s chan e 'n t-àgh iad.

TORCULL: Mu chruaidh-chàs is allaban.

FIONNAGHAL: Seadh agus nas miosa na sin. An aon sgeul aca uile. Sgeul air ain-iochd an airm dheirg agus gu h-àraidh air cion-trocair an trusdair mhóir . . . . .

TORCULL: Có tha sin?

FIONNAGHAL: Có ach an comandair aca, Buidsear Chumarlan. An cuala tu sin? Cha chuala. Ciamar a chluinneadh, ann a shin a' càradh do lìn taobh an teine?

TORCULL: Cha chuala.

FIONNAGHAL: An cuala thu nach 'eil iad a' cumail phriosanach, ach ga spadadh mar a thig iad anns an t-seasamh bonn? An cuala tu sin?

TORCULL: Cha chuala.

FIONNAGHAL: Agus feadhainn nach robh 'na seasamh idir, feadhainn, ar càirdean fhéin, a bha 'nan sìneadh leòinte air an raon, gun chomas gluasaid, 'gan stobadh le'm beigleidean le ordugh a' Bhuidseir Chumarlan. An cuala tu sin, a Thorcuill Ic an t-Saoir?

TORCULL: Cha chuala. Is duilich leam a chreidsinn gum bitheadh daoine cho ainiochdmhor nuair a chi mi a' ghrian 'san speur 's a chluinneas mi na h-eòin le'n ceòl.

FIONNAGHAL: Eòin le'n ceòl! 'S e na faoileagan a bhitheas tusa a' cluinntinn, gun umhail agad do na ròcaisean.

TORCULL: 'S dòcha gu bheil thu ceart, Fhionnaghail. Chan 'eil cluas agamsa ach dha na cheòl a chòrdas rium fhìn.

FIONNAGHAL: Glé mhath ma ta. Sin beagan dhe na chuala mise. Ach tha naidheachd nas cudthromaiche na sin agam dhuit fhathasd.

TORCULL: Nas cudthromaiche ! Dé an naidheachd a tha sin ?
Greas ort. A mach leis. Tha mi dol a dh' iasgach.

FIONNAGHAL: Naidheachd a bheir cothrom dhuit, a Thorcuill,
beagan dhe na fiachan a dhioladh. Beagan a phàigheadh air
ais airson na dh' fhuiling do dhaoine, 's dòcha airson na
dh' fhuiling do mhac fhéin.

TORCULL: Dé tha thu 'g iarraidh orm ? Saighdearachd ?
Tha mise ro shean airson saighdearachd tuilleadh.

FIONNAGHAL: Bha thu aig Sliabh an t-Siorraim, nach robh ?

TORCULL: Bha, ach 's fhada bho sin. Bha mi 'n uair sin
òg, amaideach.

FIONNAGHAL: Cha chan mi sin idir, a Thorcuill. Ach gu mo
naidheachd. Cha chuala tu fhathasd i.

TORCULL: Cha chuala. Tha thu air fàs cho briathrach,
Fhionnaghail. Siuthad, a mach leis.

FIONNAGHAL: Tha e-fhéin air tighinn.

TORCULL: E-fhéin. Có e-fhéin ?

FIONNAGHAL: E-fhéin. Tha fhios agad, am fear nach
ainmichear gu follaiseach. Am fear a fhuair àite spéiseil dha
fhéin nar n-aignidhean 's nar cridheachan.

TORCULL: Tha thu 'ciallachadh a' Phrionnsa ?

FIONNAGHAL: A nise, Thorcuill, bi cùramach, mar a thuirt
mi. A cheart fhear. Tha mi 'ciallachadh Tearlach Og
Stiùbhart, Rìgh dligheach Bhreatainn.

TORCULL: Cha d' rug iad fhathast air ?

FIONNAGHAL: Cha d' rug.

TORCULL: Gnothuch iongantach.

FIONNAGHAL: Cha d' rug 's cha bheir.

TORCULL: Thuirt thu gu bheil e air tighinn. Càit' a bheil e ?

FIONNAGHAL: Tha e air tighinn do'n bhaile seo.

TORCULL: Cuine a thainig e ?

Tìr an Aigh

FIONNAGHAL: Thainig o chionn uair a thìde. Tha e an dràsda an Uamh an Sgairbh.

TORCULL: Có tha còmhla ris?

FIONNAGHAL: Tha Coinneach Bàn agus Domhnall Ailein. Thainig Calum, an duin' agam-sa, còmhla riutha a h-uile ceum a nuas an gleann.

TORCULL: Saoil an dean e an gnothuch air teicheadh?

FIONNAGHAL: Uel, tha sin an crochadh ortsa.

TORCULL: Ormsa! Ciamar a tha seo a' tachairt?

FIONNAGHAL: Feumaidh tus a thoirt a mach 'sa' gheola bhig.

TORCULL: Mise!

FIONNAGHAL: Seadh.

TORCULL: Có thuirt sin?

FIONNAGHAL: Thuirt Calum 's an dithis eile.

TORCULL: Is càit' an toirinns' e?

FIONNAGHAL: A nunn gu taobh eile an locha, far a bheil sgoth Ean Ruairi 'ga fheitheamh.

TORCULL: Nach toir iad-fhéin a nunn e. Bheir mise dhaibh am bàta. Leigidh sinn seachad an t-iasgach.

FIONNAGHAL: Cha ghabh e earbsa duin' eile. Tha iad ag ràdh gur tus an aon duine a tha eòlach air boghachan is sgeirean an locha seo. A rithisd tha thu gun amharus ort, bho nach robh thu ri aghaidh catha. Is tha 'n tigh agad cho faisg air a' chladach. 'S tu a dh' fheumas a dheanamh.

TORCULL: Cha mhi.

FIONNAGHAL: 'Se do dhleasdanas e.

TORCULL: Carson a chuirinnsa mi-fhìn an cunnart mo bheatha? Cha d' rinn am fear seo feum sam bith dhomhsa, no do dhuin' eile. B' fheàrr dha a bhith air fuireach far an robh e na bhith tighinn a seo a thogail aimhreit.

FIONNAGHAL: O, na cluinneam a leithid.

TORCULL: Glé mhath dha na Frangaich a bhith 'ga bhrod-anachadh.

FIONNAGHAL: Thug iad cuideachadh mór dha.

TORCULL: Thug iad beagan dha, fhad 's a bhitheadh iad cinnteach nach bitheadh an t-sabaid air am fearann fhéin. Is dé thug iad dha aig a' cheann thall an déidh na gheall iad?

FIONNAGHAL: Chan 'eil iad ullamh fhathast.

TORCULL: Chan 'eil, tha mi cìnnteach. Innsidh mise rud eile dhuit, Fhionnghail, rud eile a tha na Frangaich a' deanamh.

FIONNAGHAL: Seadh?

TORCULL: Fiachainn ris a' chreideamh Phàpanach a steidheachadh san duthaich seo a rithisd.

FIONNAGHAL: Nach ann a sin a tha a' bhruidhinn. Sin a rud as miosa a th' agad an aghaidh an Stiubhartaich, gur e Pàpanach a th' ann.

TORCULL: Chan e, chan e idir. Cha robh còir agam air siud a ràdh, 's gur e Pàpanach a tha 'na mo bhean fhìn, 's 'na mo chloinn. Is cha d' rinn sin sgaradh eadarainn riamh.

FIONNAGHAL: Carson a dhianadh? Nach 'eil lan am againn sgur de dhol troimh a cheile mu eaglaisean.

TORCULL: Tha gu dearbh. 'S còir dhuinn cuimhneachadh gur e Criosduidhean a th' annainn uile.

FIONNAGHAL: Dìreach an rud a bha mi dol a ràdh. Bu chòir do na Criosduidhean a bhith còirdte is gu leòr de na h-ana-creidmhich a' feitheamh gu brath a ghabhail orra.

TORCULL: Tha sin soirbh dhaibh nuair a chi iad sinne ri leithid de dheasbud nar measg fhìn.

FIONNAGHAL: Cha do chòrd sinn mu Thearlach Stiùbhart, ach tha sinn air fàs uamhasach còirdte mu na h-eaglaisean.

TORCULL: Sinn a tha gu dearbh. Aon eaglais a bu chòir a bhith ann.

Tìr an Aigh

FIONNAGHAL: Aon eaglais, mar a thuirt thu, Thorcuill, an
eaglais againne. Mur a b' e Mairtinn Lutar . . . . . .
(Fuaim aig an dorus: Mairi air ais)

MAIRI: Tha thu ann, Fhionnaghail. An ann a' trod a tha sibh?

FIONNAGHAL: O, bha sinn gu math còirdte an ceartuair, ach
cha do mhair e fada.

TORCULL: A faca tu duine?

MAIRI: Chan fhaca. Chuala mi gun d' thainig Iain Sheumais
Chaluim, ach cha d' rainig mi iadsan. Chuir mi staigh na
laoigh còmhla ri Eilidh. Tha i fhéin a' tighinn. An cual
thu fhéin guth as ùr, Fhionnaghail? Sann agad as trice a
bhitheas na naidheachdan.

TORCULL: Mur a b' e Mairtinn Lutar . . . . . .

FIONNAGHAL: Chuala, naidheachd ùr agus naidheachd
annasach.

MAIRI: Seadh gu dearbh!

FIONNAGHAL: Siuthad, innis dhi, a Thorcuill.

TORCULL: Uel, tha Fionnaghal ag radh gu bheil e-*fhéin* an
seo.

MAIRI: E-fhéin! Chan e, chan e Tearlach Stiùbhart?

TORCULL: Bhuail thu air, a Mhairi.

MAIRI: Chan 'eil thu 'g ràdh rium? Càit' a bheil e, Fhionnaghala?

FIONNAGHAL: Tha e an Uamh an Sgairbh.

MAIRI: An Uamh an Sgairbh! Am Prionnsa ann an uaimh.

FIONNAGHAL: Seadh, sin far a bheil e, gun fhacal bréige,
agus glé thaingeil a bhith ann cuideachd.

MAIRI: Cho faisg sin oirnn! Am faca tu e, Fhionnaghala?

FIONNAGHAL: Chan fhaca. Ach siud far a bheil e, ceart
gu leòr.

MAIRI: Am faic thu e? Am faic sinn uile e?

184

FIONNAGHAL: Chan fhaic. Co-dhiubh tha mi'n dòchas nach fhaic, air a sgàth fhéin.

MAIRI: Carson a tha thu 'g ràdh sin?

FIONNAGHAL: Feumaidh e fuireach am falach.

MAIRI: Na faicinn e, is breith air làimh air!

TORCULL: O, mar a tha mi leibh, a bhoireannaich, an dàrna té nas miosa nan t'eile.

MAIRI: Dìreach cothrom fhaicinn.

TORCULL: Tha e mar leannan agaibh uile.

FIONNAGHAL: O, bitheadh tùr agad, a Thorcuill. Tha sinne ro shean airson leannanachd.

TORCULL: Siud mar a tha. Bu chòir do na fir farmad a bhith orra ris an fhleasgach òg mhaiseach seo.

MAIRI: (*Le gaire*). Thu fhéin air fear dhiubh sin, tha mi cìnnteach, a Thorcuill.

FIONNAGHAL: A nise tha sinn a' cosg ùine. Cha d' innis e an sgeul uile dhuit, a Mhairi.

MAIRI: Siuthadaibh, ma ta. An sgeul uile.

FIONNAGHAL: Tha iad ag iarraidh cuideachadh o Thorcull airson a thoirt a cunnart.

MAIRI: Tha e ann an cunnart, tha mi cìnnteach.

FIONNAGHAL: An suidheachadh cunnartach, agus a' fàs nas cunnartaiche a h-uile mionaid.

MAIRI: Chan 'eil fhios aig an fheadhainn eile .... far a bheil e?

FIONNAGHAL: Chan 'eil. Nam bitheadh! An dùthaich eadar seo is Ionar Lochaidh air a gànrachadh le saighdearan an Airm Dheirg.

MAIRI: Saoil a bheil feadhainn dhiubh tighinn a rathad seo?

FIONNAGHAL: Chan 'eil nì nas cìnntiche. Chunnaic an ciobair ruadh feadhainn dhiubh a' tighinn timcheall Cnoc an Eadraiginn an diugh fhéin.

185

Tìr an Aigh

MAIRI: Seadh, 's dé tha thu 'g iarraidh air Torcull a dheanamh?

FIONNAGHAL: O, chan e mise a tha 'ga iarraidh.

MAIRI: Có, ma tha?

FIONNAGHAL: O, an triùir a thug an t-Og Uasal a nuas an gleann, Coinneach Bàn, Domhnull Ailein, is an duin' agam fhìn.

MAIRI: Is dé a tha iad ag iarraidh air Torcull a dheanamh?

FIONNAGHAL: Tha gun toireadh e mach anns a' gheola e, gu taobh eile an locha, far a bheil an sgoth 'ga fheitheamh.

MAIRI: Agus nì thu sin, a Thorcuill? (*A feitheamh, gun ghuth bho Thorcull*).
Cha mhór sin a bhi 'ga iarraidh air fior Ghaidheal, coma leam de na barailean a th' agad.
(*Ri Fionnaghal*). 'S e urram a bhitheadh ann, Fhionnaghail, do Thorcull agus dhuinn uile.

TORCULL: A nise tha sibhse le chéile cho glic is cho math air cùisean dhaoin' eil a chur air dòigh. Carson nach toireadh fear dhiubh fhéin a mach e?

FIONNAGHAL: Chaidh sinn a steach anns na h-aobharan sin uile mar tha. Tha iad ag ràdh gur e Torcull as freagarraiche air a h-uile dòigh.

TORCULL: Tha sin glé mhath, ach carson a rachainn-sa a ghlacadh san ribe agaibh. Chùm mi as thuige seo.

MAIRI: Am fàgadh tu do rìgh dligheach, fear co-dhiùbh a dh' earb e-fhéin ri do mhuinntir, an cunnart a bheatha?

TORCULL: Rìgh dligheach. Tha mise toilichte gu leòr leis an rìgh a th' againn.

FIONNAGHAL: Le Gearmailteach?

TORCULL: Tha mi coma ged a b' e Turcach a bhitheadh ann.

MAIRI: O, Thorcuill.

TORCULL: Uel, 's e sibh fhéin a thog a' cheisd. Dé th'anns an Stiùbhartach? Gaidheal? Chan e.

FIONNAGHAL: Bha fuil nan Gaidheal na shinnsirean.

TORCULL: Cha robh riamh. A bheil Gaidhlig aige?

FIONNAGHAL: Chan 'eil fhios 'am.

TORCULL: Tha fhios agaibh glé mhath. Chan 'eil srad Gaidhlig aige. Fraingeis gu leòr, 's dòcha, is bloighean de Bheurla.

FIONNAGHAL: Ged nach gabhadh iad an Sasuinn idir e, dh' fhaodadh e bhith againn dhuinn fhìn an Duneideann, is gun ghnothach againn ris na Sasunnaich.

TORCULL: Chan fhaic sibh sin gu siorruidh. Coma leamsa có tha 'n Duneideann no'n Lunnainn, fhad sa dh' fhàgas iad mise an seo ag obrachadh mo chuid fearainn 'sa deanamh beagan iasgaich an drasda sa rithist.

(An dorus a' fosgladh is Eilidh a' tighinn a steach. bàn san aghaidh si casadaich gun lasachadh o seo air adhart).

EILIDH: An cuala sibh? Tha na saighdearan dearga tighinn.

TORCULL: Tha 'n t-am agad a bhi staigh, Eilidh.

EILIDH: Tha na saighdearan dearga tighinn.

FIONNAGHAL: O, tha fhios againn, Eilidh. Nach e sin a tha cur oirnn.

EILIDH: Nam b' urrainn dhomhsa rudeigin a dheanamh. Saoil có chuireas an teicheadh orra?

MAIRI: A nise, dé dheanadh tusa, a luaidh?

EILIDH: Chan 'eil fhios agaibh de dheanainn. Thoiribh-se dhomh aon chothrom.

FIONNAGHAL: An fheadhainn aig a bheil an cothrom, chan 'eil iad deònach a ghabhail.

EILIDH: Có tha sin?

Tìr an Aigh

MAIRI: Dé am math dhuit tòiseachadh a rithisd, Fhionnaghail?

EILIDH: Innsibh dhomh. Có nach gabh an cothrom?

FIONNAGHAL: D'athair.

EILIDH: Dé an cothrom a th' aige?

FIONNAGHAL: Fear uasal ar gràidh a theasairginn.

EILIDH: Có thuirt sibh? Chan 'eil e . . . .? Càit' a bheil e?

FIONNAGHAL: Tha e . . . gu math faisg air làimh.

EILIDH: Càite? Càite?

FIONNAGHAL: Dìreach thall an siud, an Uamh an Sgairbh.

EILIDH: Tha e air ais am Mùideart. O, nam faighinn aon sùil air, bhithinn sona.

FIONNAGHAL: Chan urrainn dhuinn smaointeachadh air a leithid an dràsda. Tha an duine an cunnart a bheatha.

EILIDH: (Na's ciùine). O tha.

FIONNAGHAL: Agus tha a bheatha 'sa shaorsa an crochadh air d'athair.

EILIDH: Mar sin, bithidh e ceart gu leòr, 's cìnnteach.

FIONNAGHAL: Cha bhi. Sin a' chùis.

EILIDH: Dé tha iad ag iarraidh oirbh a dheanamh, athair?

TORCULL: A nise, na tòisicheamaid air seo uile a rithisd.

EILIDH: Anns a' bhàta?

FIONNAGHAL: Seadh.

EILIDH: (Ri a h-athair). S cha dean sibh sin, athair?

TORCULL: A nise, Eilidh, chaidh sinn thairis air a h-uile puing mun d' thainig thus' a staigh.

EILIDH: O chaidh, tha mi cìnnteach. Uel, càit' a bheil e? An Uamh an Sgairbh. Ceart gu leòr. Bheir mise a nunn e.

TORCULL: Na bi cho faoin. Tha fhios agad glé mhath nach deanadh tus' an gnothach.

EILIDH: (*A' deanamh air an dorus*). Leigibh leam. The mise
math air iomaradh. Thuirt sibh fhéin sin rium. S ann
còmhla ribh fhéin a dh' ionnsaich mi e.

TORCULL: Bha thu làidir fallain an uair sin.

MAIRI: Leig as do cheann e, a ghaoil. Gheibh sinn dòigh air
choiregin eile air.

EILIDH: Theid mi ann 's cha chùm duin' air ais mi.

TORCULL: (*A' cur air a bhoineid*). Fan far a bheil thu.

MAIRI: (*Ri Torcull*). Dé tha thu 'dol a dheanamh?

TORCULL: O tha fhios agad glé mhath dé tha mi dol a
dheanamh. Dìreach mar a bha sibh ag iarraidh. Rinn sibh
an gnothach orm — an triùir agaibh.

EILIDH: (*A' dannsadh —'sa' casadaich*). Sinne 'ga chuideachadh.
sinne 'ga chuideachadh. Urram mór dhuibh an seo, athair.
Urram mór dhuinn uile.

TORCULL: O, dean air do shocair.

EILIDH: Canaibh ris uamsa gu bheil sinn uile air a thaobh
agus gum bi sinn a' feitheamh ris gus an till e. Urram mór!

TORCULL: Urram nach robh mis ag iarraidh.

FIONNAGHAL: (*Ag eirigh*). Deanamaid cabhag.

MAIRI: A nise, thoir an aire dhuit fhéin, a Thorcuill.

FIONNAGHAL: (*A' tionndadh*). Bithidh iad uile feumach air
biadh.

MAIRI: Deasaichidh mise biadh. Bithidh e deiseil.

TORCULL: Bithidh mi air ais air a shon ma gheibh mi cothrom.
Mur a faigh, na bitheadh dùil agaibh rium gu anamoch.

MAIRI: Dia gu robh maille ribh.
(*Torcull is Fionnaghal a mach*).

EILIDH: Saoil an teid ac' air?

Tìr an Aigh

MAIRI: Theid, theid. Na cuireadh e an còrr dragh ort. An cuala tu guth air Goiridh. Cha b' e a bu chòir a bhith air dheireadh.
(*A' cur air na poite*).

EILIDH: Cha chuala, ach thainig Iain Sheumais Chaluim. Tha mi cìnnteach nach urrainn dha tighinn a nall. Chaidh a leòn, tha iad ag ràdh, le beigleid sa' ghualainn.

MAIRI: Bheir mi-fhìn ceum a nunn. Cùm thusa sùil air a' phoit. 'S docha gun tig d'athair a steach mum fàg iad an cladach.

(*Mairi a Mach*).

Eilidh a' cur mu chuairt na poite agus a' toirt sùil a mach air an uinneig. A' clisgeadh ri bhith faicinn dithis a' tighinn gu'n dorus; a' dol a nunn agus a' cur an dealain air. Guth aig an dorus:

GUTH: Có tha stigh? *Gun fhreagairt fhaotainn:*

GUTH: A bheil duine staigh? (*Sàmhchair*).

GUTH EILE: Leig thusa leamsa. (*An dorus a' tighinn a steach le neart.*
Saighdear mor, seirdsean a' tighinn a steach còmhla ris. Fear eile, caiptean, as a dhéidh).

EILIDH: Dé tha sibhse ag iarraidh?

CAIPTEAN: Có leis an tigh seo?

EILIDH: Chan 'eil e leibh-se co-dhiubh.

SEIRDSEAN: 'S glic dhuit a bhith modhail ris a' chaiptean.

EILIDH: Cha robh sibh fhéin ro mhodhail mar a chuir sibh a steach an dorus. Ach dé an còrr a gheibheadh duine bho'n arm dhearg.

CAIPTEAN: Buinidh sinne do arm na rioghachd.

EILIDH: Tha sibh san arm dhearg. Gaidheil, is Gaidhlig agaibh? Bu chòir nàire bhith oirbh.

SEIRDSEAN: Carson nach bitheadh Gaidhlig againn? Tha a' Ghaidhlig gu math feumail dhuinn air an dleasdanas air a bheil sinn.

EILIDH: (*Gu neochiontach*). Dé an dleasdanas a tha sin?

CAIPTEAN: A' lorg an reubalaich, Tearlach Stiùbhart.

EILIDH: O gu dearbh! Chan fhaigh sibh an seo e.

SEIRDSEAN: Na bi cho cìnnteach. Dé th' anns a' phoit? Tha àileadh math aisde co-dhiubh.

EILIDH: Cha teid thusa 'na còir.

SEIRDSEAN: Chan 'eil thu dol a ghabhail sin uile leat fhéin, a bheil? Có dha a tha thu 'ga dheasachadh?

EILIDH: Coma leatsa.

CAIPTEAN: Leig leatha an dràsda.

SEIRDSEAN: Mi-fhìn, dìreach gu fannachadh leis an acras.

EILIDH: (*Gun smaointean*). Nam bitheadh mo bhràthair-sa a seo, cha bhitheadh sibh . . . .

CAIPTEAN: O gu dearbh. Tha bràthair agad, a bheil? Càit' a bheil esan?

EILIDH: (*A' tighinn 'ga h-ionnsuidh fhéin*). Chan 'eil a seo.

CAIPTEAN: Chan 'eil. Tha mi faicinn sin. Cha d' rachainn fad an urras nach robh e sabaid air taobh nan Stiùbhartach, saoil a robh?

EILIDH: Dé eile a dheanadh e? Cha d' thuirt mise gu robh e a' sabaid idir.

CAIPTEAN: Cha d' thuirt, cha d' thuirt. Cha mhór a th'aig air a shon a nise co-dhiubh. Có tuilleadh a tha fuireach còmhla riut? A bheil d'athair aig an tigh?

EILIDH: Tha mi-fhìn 's mo *mhàthair* a' fuireach a seo.

Tìr an Aigh

CAIPTEAN: O gu dearbh ! D'athair air falbh cuideachd !
Càit' a bheil do mhàthair ?

EILIDH: Tha i thall am baile.

CAIPTEAN: Theirig a nunn 'ga h-iarraidh.

EILIDH: Agus fàgaidh mi sibhse an seo leibh fhéin !

CAIPTEAN: Bidh an tigh ceart gu leòr.

SEIRDSEAN: (*A' cumaii sùil air a' phoit*). Saighdearan
onoireach a th' unnainne.

EILIDH: ('*Ga fhaicinn a' sealltainn air a' phoit*). Cha teid sibh
an còir na poite.

CAIPTEAN: Carson ? Có dha a tha thu 'ga cumail ?
Cha ghabh thu fhéin s do mhàthair na tha sin.

SEIRDSEAN: (*A' gaireachdainn*). 'S docha gur ann dha — dé
their sibh ris — dha na Phrionnsa Tearlach — a tha e.

EILIDH: (*Ag atharrachadh a h-inntinn*). Ceart gu leòr.
Gabhaibh na thogras sibh dheth. Sùgh feòla is min eòrna.
(*A' cur a mach da thruinnsear, is da spàin ; a' dol a nunn
gu'n phoit, a' cur cnap suith innte gun fhiosda, 'ga cur mun
cuairt*).
Seo dhuibh.
('*Ga toirt dhe'n teine agus a' cur lodar innte*).
Seo dhuibh. Tha mi'n dòchas gun còrd e ruibh. Greasaibh
oirbh mun tig mo mhàthair.

CAIPTEAN: Cha chòrdadh e rith-se.

EILIDH: Chan 'eil mi cìnnteach.

SEIRSDEAN: Nach tu a th' air fàs coibhneil ! Bheir an
sinilear mathanas dhut.

EILIDH: Mathanas ! Carson ? Dé rinn mi ?

CAIPTEAN: Siuthad, bi falbh.

(*Eilidh a mach*).

SEIRSDEAN: Tha mise a' dol a ghabhail taosg math dhe'n t-sùgh seo.

CAIPTEAN: Dean air do shocair.

SEIRSDEAN: Tha mi gu toirt thairis leis an acras.

(*A' cur a mach cuid anns na truinnsearan*).

CAIPTEAN: Thuirt thu gu robh àileadh math dhe'n t-sùgh seo.

SEIRSDEAN: Thuirt. Bha mi smaointeachadh gu robh.

CAIPTEAN: Chan 'eil mise 'ga fhaotainn cho math sin.

SEIRSDEAN: Nach 'eil? (*'Ga bhlasad*). Tha blas car neònach air ceart gu leòr, maorach, no iasg, no rudeigin.

CAIPTEAN: (*A' blasad*). Chan 'eil mise dol 'ga ghabhail co-dhiubh. Fàgaidh mi agad fhéin e. Seallaidh mi airson rudeigin eile. Bheirinn a' chomhairle ort gun a dhol ro dhàna air, a sheirdsein.

SEIRSDEAN: Ghabh mise na bu mhiosa na seo ri mo latha. Sluigidh mi sios an cabhaig e agus cha bhi fhios agam dé 'm blas a th' air. (*A' gabhail a chuid fhéin agus an déidh sin cuid a' chaiptein*).

CAIPTEAN: (*Ag eiridh agus a' coiseachd air feadh an t-seòmair*). Saoil a bheil fhios ac' air dad? Thug i tarraing air bràthair agus chaidh i dheth sin an cabhaig.

SEIRSDEAN: Cha bhi sinne fada a' toirt asda na tha fhios ac' air.

CAIPTEAN: Tha deagh bharail aig an t-Sinilear gur e seo an taobh a thainig an Stiùbhartach.

SEIRSDEAN: Saoil an gabh mi 'n còrr dhe na stuth seo. Cha chreid mi gun gabh. Tha mi 'faireachadh car neònach mar tha.

CAIPTEAN: Nach d' thuirt mi riut!

SEIRSDEAN: S coma. Bidh mi ceart gu leòr.

Tìr an Aigh

CAIPTEAN: Seall an leabhar. Daoine adhartach a tha san tigh seo le leabhar dhe'n t-seòrsa seo aca — Bìobull Gàidhlig. (*A' fosgladh an leabhair*). Ainmeannan ; seo agad ainmeannan an teaghlaich.

SEIRSDEAN: Dé tha e 'g ràdh ?

CAIPTEAN: Torcull Mac an t-Saoir ; rugadh e anns a' bhliadhna sia diag ceithir fichead sa coig.

SEIRSDEAN: Sin an t-athair.

CAIPTEAN: 'Se. Chan 'eil thu cho maol, a sheirdsein. Rud eile, 's fheudar gu bheil e beò fhathast.

SEIRSDEAN: Có tuilleadh ?

CAIPTEAN: Mairi Nic an t-Saoir, sia diag . . . . , sin a bhean. Goiridh Mac an t-Saoir, ainm a' mhic agus, an t-ainm mu dheireadh, ar banacharaid, Eilidh Nic an t-Saoir, an té a rinn am brot, a sheirdsein.

SEIRSDEAN: Am brot. Coma. Cha ghabh mi an còrr dheth an dràsda.

CAIPTEAN: Cumaidh sinn cuimhn' air na h-ainmeannan. 'S docha gum bi iad feumail.

SEIRSDEAN: Bithidh iad feumail. Cuiridh mi geall gu robh sibh ceart ag ràdh gu robh am fear òg an arm an Stiùbhartaich.

CAIPTEAN: Uel, cha deach i as àicheadh.

SEIRSDEAN: Ma tha sinn ceart 'nar beachd, faodaidh sinn an car a thoirt asda.

CAIPTEAN: Ciamar ?

SEIRSDEAN: Canaidh sinn riutha gu bheil am mac 'na phriosanach againn an Ionar Lochaidh, agus gu leig sinn as e ma dh' innseas iad dhuinn càit' a bheil an Stiùbhartach.

CAIPTEAN: Chuala mi thu ag ràdh an ceartuair gum b'e saighdearan onoireach a bh' unnainn.

SEIRSDEAN: Feumaidh sinn a bhith coltach ri càch. Chan 'eil a leithid de rud ri fhaotainn an cogadh ri saighdearan onoireach.

CAIPTEAN: Bruidhinn thusa air do shon fhéin, a charaid. Ach tha e nas soirbhe gun teagamh a bhith onoireach 'nuair a tha thu 'buinig. Tha sinne buinig.

SEIRSDEAN: Faodaidh gu bheil, ach cha d' rug sinn air a' reubalach mhór fhéin fhathasd.

CAIPTEAN: Cha d'rug. Ach tha dòigh eile air na daoine seo a thoirt a thaobh agus an cur a bhruidhinn.

SEIRSDEAN: A bheil? Dé th' ann?

CAIPTEAN: Nach cual thu mu'n éiric a tha an crùn a' gealltainn?

SEIRSDEAN: Chuala mi rudeigin. Ciamar a tha e 'g oib- reachadh? O, mo mhionach!

CAIPTEAN: Uel, nam bitheadh tu na b' fhaicilliche dé dh' itheadh tu.

SEIRSDEAN: Tha e seachad. Dé mu'n éiric seo—thuirt sibh ...?

CAIPTEAN: Tha an crùn a' gealltainn deich mìle fichead pùnnd Sasunnach ...

SEIRSDEAN: Dé!

CAIPTEAN: Deich mìle fichead pùnnd Sasunnach do neach sam bith a bheir seachad an Stiùbhartach.

SEIRSDEAN: Deich mìle pùnnd Sasunnach?!

CAIPTEAN: Deich mìle fichead pùnnd Sasunnach.

SEIRSDEAN: 'Se airgead uamhasach a tha sin.

CAIPTEAN: 'S e.

SEIRSDEAN: Cha robh fios agamsa gu robh uiread sin a dh' airgead aca uile gu léir an Lunnainn. Tha mise dol a dh' iarraidh àrdachadh tuarasdail orra ma tha iad gu bhith cho fialaidh sin timcheall air.

Tìr an Aigh

CAIPTEAN: O, tha airgead gu leòr aca an Lunnainn, ged nach tric a chluinneas tu iad a' cosg uiread air na cearnaidhean iomallach seo.

SEIRSDEAN: Am bitheadh dòigh againne air cuid dhe'n airgead seo a chosnadh?

CAIPTEAN: Cha bhitheadh.

SEIRSDEAN: Nam beireamaid air an Stiùbhartach?

CAIPTEAN: Ged a bheireadh, chan fhaigheadh tu sgillinn dheth. Chan fhaigh e ach fear dhe dhaoine fhéin ma bhrathas iad e.

SEIRSDEAN: Uel, tha mi smaointeachadh gur e rud bochd a tha sin. B' fheàrr leam gu robh mi air an taobh eile. Dé thuirt sibh a bh' ann? Deich . . . . . . ?

CAIPTEAN: Deich mìle fichead pùnnd Sasunnach.

SEIRSDEAN: Chan fhaigh sinne sgillinn ruadh, an déidh ar saothair, a' sealg an fhir seo.

CAIPTEAN: Tha thusa agus mise air ar pàigheadh air a shon.

SEIRSDEAN: A' tilgeil airgid air reubalach a bha sabaid 'nar n-aghaidh. Cha chuala mi riamh a leithid.

CAIPTEAN: Ge ta, cuimhnich nach d' thainig orra a thilgeil, mar a thuirt thu, air duine fhathasd. Tha an Stiùbhartach fhathasd ma sgaoil, agus 'se do dhleasdanas-sa breith air, duais ann no as.

SEIRSDEAN: O, gheibh iad duine a choisneas an t-airgiod ceart gu leòr. Bhrathadh iad siud duine airson deich tasdain, gun tighinn air . . . . . na bith dé bh' ann.

CAIPTEAN: Saoil thu?

SEIRSDEAN: O mar a tha mi le mo bhroinn! Dé an truaighe a bha sa' bhrot ud? Innsidh mise dhuibh. Gheallainn-sa an t-airgead dhaibh agus 'nuair a gheibhinn an rud a bha dhìth orm, cha toirinn dhaibh idir e.

CAIPTEAN: Tha leithid de rud ann ri ceartas, a sheirdsein.

SEIRSDEAN: 'S fheudar ceartas. le ur cead, coltach ri onoir, a chur a Thigh Ean Ghrota 'nuair a bhitheas sibh a' déiligeadh ris na fineachan fiadhaich.

CAIPTEAN: Na can guth. So iad a' tighinn.

(*Mairi is Eilidh a stigh*)

MAIRI: Có sibhse ?

CAIPTEAN: Tha mi cìnnteach gun d' innis ur nighean sin dhuibh.

MAIRI: Dh' innis, ach bu mhath leam fios a bhith agam có thug cead dhuibh tighinn a seo.

CAIPTEAN: Chan 'eil cead a dhìth oirnn, ach tha ùghdarras againn bho shinilear an iar-thuath gu bhith a' sgrùdadh gach tigh sa' ceasnachadh gach duine gus am faigh sinn lorg air an dearg eucorach, Tearlach Stiùbhart.

SEIRSDEAN: Tha fhios agaibhse far a bheil e ? O ! (*A' cur a làmh ri bhroinn*).

EILIDH: Dé tha ceàrr ?

SEIRSDEAN: Tha greim mionaich orm.

EILIDH: A bheil ? Gabhadh sibh-se cuid de'n t-sùgh, 'S dòcha gun dean e feum.

SEIRSDEAN: Ghabh mi tuille sa chòir dheth mar tha, tha mi 'smaointeachadh. Eisdibh-sa ris a' chaiptean ; tha rud no dha aige ri ràdh ribh.

CAIPTEAN: Ceart ma ta. Cuiridh mi mo cheisd ribh-se, a bhean. A bheil eòlas sam bith agaibh air gluasad an fhir sin a thog a' cheannairc, Tearlach Stiùbhart ?

MAIRI: Chan 'eil nì agam ri ràdh ruibh.

CAIPTEAN: Tha deagh aobhar againn a bhith 'creidsinn gun d'thainig e 'n taobh sa. A bheil sibh a' cumail a mach nach 'eil fhios agaibh air 'àite-fasgaidh ?

MAIRI: Mar a thuirt mi mar tha, chan 'eil mi cumail a mach nì.

Tìr an Aigh

SEIRSDEAN: Bheir sinn air falbh iad le cheile. O ! . . . .
 (*A' deanamh òrais*)

EILIDH: Siuthad. Nach tu tha tapaidh ! Feumaidh tu barrachd is brot a ghabhail mun dean thu sin.

CAIPTEAN: Chan 'eil sibh a' tuigsinn, tha eagal orm, brìgh na cùise. Ma tha aobhar againne a chreidsinn gu bheil sibh ag innse nam breug, no a' cleith na fìrinn' air dòigh sam bith tha e 'nar comas 'ur toirt a dh' ionnsaidh an t-sinileir, airson ceasnachaidh, agus mur a dean sin feum, gu cùirt nas àirde. A bheil sibh a' tuigsinn sin ?

MAIRI: Tha.

CAIPTEAN: Chan 'eil sibh deònach dad a ràdh ?

MAIRI: Chan 'eil.

SEIRSDEAN: Innsibh dhaibh mu am bràthair.

M./E: (*comhla*). Dé.

CAIPTEAN: Bi sàmhach. Na toiribh feairt airsan. An cuala sibh gu bheil àrd mhinistearan an rìgh deònach sùim mhór airgid a thoirt do dhuine sam bith a bhrathas an t-eucorach ?

MAIRI: Có an t-eucorach ?

CAIPTEAN: Có ach am fear a chuir air adhart an t-aramach anns an dùthaich. 'S math a tha fhios agaibh có e.

MAIRI: Sùim mhór airgid. Cha chuala mise guth air sùim mhór airgid.

CAIPTEAN: Tha mata, ma chuireas sibhse, no duin' eile, sinne air lorg a' Phrionnsa (tha sibh a' tuigsinn có tha mi 'ciallachadh a nise) — air dòigh 's gum faigh sinn greim air, bheir an crùn dhuibh deich mìle fichead pùnnd Sasunnach.

MAIRI: Deich air fhichead pùnnd Sasunnach !

EILIDH: Deich mìle pùnnd Sasunnach, a mhàthair. Tha pùinnd Shasunnach gu leòr aca seo ; daoine móra beairteach.

CAIPTEAN: 'S tusa a b' fhaisge a chaidh air, a nighean, ach chan 'eil e agad fhathast. 'Se thuirt mise, deich mìle fichead pùnnd Sasunnach.

MAIRI: Tha sibh a' tairgse sin ?

CAIPTEAN: Tha. Dé ur barail air a sin ?

EILIDH: (*gu tàireil*). Dé ar barail ?

MAIRI: Cha ghabhainn sgillinn dheth.

SEIRSDEAN: O, mo mhionach. Chan 'eil iad glic.

CAIPTEAN: Smaointichibh dé a b' urrainn duibh a dheanamh le a leithid seo de dh' airgiod. Cha bhitheadh duin' air Gaidhealtachd cho beirteach ribh, no móran air Galldachd nas mò.

MAIRI: Dé a dheanadh airgiod dhomh-sa, is mi air mo mheas nam Iùdas am measg mo chàirdean !

CAIPTEAN: Smaointichibh air an nighinn sin agaibh, 'si gu math feumach, cho fad sa chi mise, air iochd-shlàint, ma tha sin ann dha leithid.

EILIDH: Fàgaibh mis' as . . . . . .

CAIPTEAN: Dh' fhaodadh sibh a cur a nunn thairis gu bhith fo chùram nan lighichean as fheàrr a th' ann, daoine a dh' aisigeadh i gu slàint as ùr.

EILIDH: Na cluinneam an còrr.

MAIRI: A bheil sibh ullamh ?

CAIPTEAN: Tha, an dràsda.

MAIRI: Chuala tu siud, Eilidh.

EILIDH: (*Gu taireil*). Chuala.

MAIRI: An ceannaicheadh tu do shlàinte air prìs a' bhrathaidh ?

EILIDH: Nach ann aca a tha bhathais ! Có ris a tha iad a' smaointeachadh a tha iad a' bruidhinn ? Tha fhios agamsa dé dheanainn le'n cuid airgid. Thilginn orra sa bhus e.

MAIRI: Chuala sibh siud ?

Tìr an Aigh

CAIPTEAN: Chuala. Ach . . .

SEIRSDEAN: O, mar a tha mi! B' fheàrr leam . . . .

MAIRI: Siud agaibh mata ur freagairt dhuibh.

(An dorus a' fosgladh; Torcull a stigh an cabhaig, a' coimhead timcheall air le ionghnadh, 's a' deanamh gu tilleadh).

TORCULL: O, gheibh mi rithisd e.

CAIPTEAN: Có th' againn a seo? Fear an tighe, nach e?

SEIRSDEAN: Dean greim air mun teich e. Nan robh mise . . . .

CAIPTEAN: Uisd, a sheirdsein. Fear an tighe, nach e?

TORCULL: 'S e.

CAIPTEAN: Torcull Mac an t-Saoir, aois tri fichead sa h-aon.

TORCULL: Có dh' innis sin dhuibh.

CAIPTEAN: O, tha fhios againne air barrachd sa shaoileadh sibh.

(Torcull a' coimhead air Mairi).

MAIRI: Chan 'eil fhios ac' air nì.

CAIPTEAN: An cuala tusa, a Thorcuill Ic an t-Saoir, mu'n éiric a tha an rioghachd a' toirt do'n duine a shìneas an Stiùbhartach dhuinn?

TORCULL: Cha chuala, ach ged a chluinneadh . . . .

CAIPTEAN: Seadh?

TORCULL: Chan 'eil airgead a dhìth ormsa.

SEIRSDEAN: Duin' eile as a rian.

CAIPTEAN: Chan 'eil airgiod a dhìth ort!

TORCULL: Uel, tha agamsa na dh' fhoghnas dhomh a seo, tac is stoc, is bàta beag airson iasgaich — o tha, is bean, is clann . . . . co-dhiubh . . . . bha . . . . *(a' stad).*

CAIPTEAN: Ach 's e tha seo sùim mhór. Smaointichibh air na dheanadh sibh le deich mìle . . . .

TORCULL: A nise, caomhnaibh an dragh dhuibh fhéin. Thuirt mi ribh nach 'eil ùidh agam an airgiod.

SEIRSDEAN: O, nach iad a tha rag! B' fheàrr leam gu robh mise air a chomas. Ach nì mi oidhirp air bruidhinn riutha, le'r cead, a Chaiptein.

CAIPTEAN: Uel . . . .

SEIRSDEAN: (A' bruidhinn air éigin). Tha sibh an seo.

MAIRI: Dé tha am fear seo ag ràdh?

EILIDH: Na toiribh feairt air co-dhiubh.

SEIRSDEAN: Bha mac agaibh cuideachd.

TORCULL: Bha, bha.

SEIRSDEAN: A bheil fhios agaibh càit' a bheil e?

TORCULL: A bheil fhios agaibhse?

SEIRSDEAN: Tha fhios againne ceart gu leòr. Tha e 'na phriosanach againn an Ionar Lochaidh.

MAIRI: O . . . .

EILIDH: Breugan. Na eisdibh ris.

SEIRSDEAN: An t-uil' fhìrinn. Thoiribh a mach aireamh nam priosanach, a Chaiptein.

(An Caiptean a' toirt a mach paipear agus a' sealltainn air).

Leughaibh dhaibh e.

CAIPTEAN: Goiridh Mac an t-Saoir. Nach e sin ur mac?

TORCULL: 'S e. Càit' an d' fhuair sibh an t-ainm?

SEIRSDEAN: Tha an aois againn cuideachd. Siuthadaibh, innsibh dhaibh, a Chaiptein.

Tìr an Aigh

CAIPTEAN: Bliadhn' air fhichead.

TORCULL: Tha sin ceart, nach 'eil, a Mhairi?

(*Mairi a' cromadh a cinn*).

SEIRSDEAN: Glé mhath ma ta. Innsibh dhaibh, a Chaiptein. Nam bithinn sa an sùnnd ceart! Uel, tha e a measg feadhainn a dh' fhaodar a chur a sheasamh cùrtach an Dùneideann no Lunnainn. Tha fhios agaibh dé dh' fhaodas tachairt an sin.

MAIRI: Dé dh' fhaodas tachairt?

TORCULL: Chuala sinn mar a tha air tachairt do chuid mar tha.

EILIDH: Na eisdibh riutha.

SEIRSDEAN: Bi thusa sàmhach. Glé mhath. Innsibh-sa dhuinn càit' a bheil Tearlach Stiùbhart, agus ma theid leinn, bheir an Caiptean cead bhur mac a leigeil dhachaidh. Dé their sibh ri sin?

EILIDH: Cha chuirinn earbsa an duine seach duin' aca.

MAIRI: Ged a bhitheadh an fhìrinn aca, dé dha sin?

TORCULL: Chan 'eil mi cìnnteach. Goiridh, a bheatha air thoiseach air. Am bitheadh e ceart gun an cothrom a ghabhail?

(*An seirdsean a nise an droch chàs a' deanamh air an dorus*).

SEIRSDEAN: Tha mi gu bhith tinn.

EILIDH: Ma tha, cha bhi thu tinn an seo. A mach leat!

(*A' fosgladh an doruis chùil*).

TORCULL: Goiridh 'na phriosanach!

MAIRI: A Thorcuill. Bi faiciollach.

TORCULL: Dé thuirt mi ? Carson a chuireadh duine an leithid dé dh' imcheist ?

(*An dorus a' fosgladh is Goiridh a stigh*).

EILIDH: Goiridh !

MAIRI: Cia as a thainig thu ?

TORCULL: Tha thu sàbhailte ?

GOIRIDH: Tha, tha mi ceart gu leòr. (*A' cur a ghairdeanan timcheall a mhàthar air an dara taobh is Eilidh air an taobh 'le*).

EILIDH: Có aig a bha na breugan a nise ?

CAIPTEAN: Tha sibh uile air taobh nan ceannairceach. Na fàgadh duine an rùm seo gus . . . .

(*Eilidh a' deanamh sanas ri a h-athair agus Torcull a' teicheadh a mach. Caiptean ag eigheach*).

A sheirdsein ! (*An Caiptean a' leum gu'n dorus is Eilidh a' cur a cùlaibh ris an dorus 'ga chumail air ais. Caiptean ag eigheach a rithisd*).

A sheirdsein !

Tha sibh uile ciontach. Cuiridh mise tuilleadh shaighdearan a seo agus bheir iad air falbh uile sibh.

EILIDH: (*A' coimhead air a màthair*). Bithidh sinne deònach gu leòr falbh.

GOIRIDH: Ma leigeas sibh leothasan, falbhaidh mise còmhla riubh.

CAIPTEAN: Ceart gu leòr. Tha sinn deiseil.

EILIDH: Chan 'eil sibh deiseil fhathasd. 'S fheàrr dhuibh ur caraid a thoirt leibh. Chan 'eil sinne 'ga iarraidh an seo.

(*An Caiptean a' sealltuinn air Goiridh agus, car teagamhach, air an dorus chùil*).

Tìr an Aigh

GOIRIDH: Tha e ceart gu leòr. Cha theich mise idir.

(An Caiptean a' dol a mach s a' tighinn air ais leis an t-seirdsean. Coltas gu math glas air t-seirdsean, is e car gliogach air a chasan. Caiptean, seirdsean, is Goiridh a mach air an dorus aghaidh).

GOIRIDH: *(A' tionndadh).* A nise bidh cùisean ceart gu leòr.

MAIRI: Tha mi'n dòchas gum bi.

(Triuir a mach).

(Mairi agus Eilidh 'nan seasamh is an dorus leth fosgailte. Iad a' coimhead a mach is ag eisdeachd).

MAIRI: *(A' cluinntinn nan ròcais).*
Cha do ghabh iad siud mu thàmh fhathasd.

EILIDH: Chan 'eil coire 's na ròcaisean.

MAIRI: *(A' cluinntinn fuaim mar gum bitheadh plub nan ràmh).*
Dé tha siud?

EILIDH: Bàta m'athar. Tha iad air sàil.

MAIRI: Dia maille riutha.

EILIDH: Agus ruigheachd sàbhailt.

MAIRI: Uisd. Sguir na ròcaisean.

EILIDH: Agus dé an t-eun a tha siud? An guilbneach.

MAIRI: 'S e. 'S iad na h-eòin mara as fheàrr le d'athair. Ciamar a thuirt e fhein, "Tha duine an comhnaidh buailteach air a bhith cluinntinn an nì as àill leis a chluinntinn."

"AIR TREAN MHALAIG"

Luchd-cluiche

Mairi
Seumas
Iain
Mór

MAIRI: Nach e Loch Laomuinn fhein a tha eireachdail an diugh!

SEUMAS: A bheil sinn ach aig Loch Laomuinn fhathast?

MAIRI: Uisge an locha mar a' ghloinne agus na cnuic, iad cho gorm. Duilleach bòidheach nan craobh. Fosglaidh mi an uinneag rud beag eile. Iain, a nise, cùm do chasan sios dhe'n t-suidheachan.

IAIN: Cuin' a ghabhas sinn ar braiceast?

MAIRI: Tha e tràth fhathasd, Iain. Stad gus an ruig sinn a' Chrion-laraich. Siud agad crodh shios agus caoraich cuideachd. Seall.

IAIN: Ge tà tha an t-acras orm.

MAIRI: Innsidh mi dé a nì thu. Sìn thusa thu fhéin anns an oisean sin agus caidil agus 'nuair a dhuisgeas thu gheibh thu . . . . tea . . . . .

SEUMAS: Chaidlinn fhìn nam bitheadh sibh sàmhach. Sìn dhomh am paipear, a Mhairi. 'S mi a tha sgìth dhe'n trean seo.

MAIRI: Uch, 's toigh leam fhìn an trean gu Malaig. Tha mi a' faireachadh mar gum bitheadh cùbhraidheachd nan eilean 'ga mo chuairteachadh mar tha. Sin thu a nis Iain, bheir mi dhiot do bhrògan agus caidlidh tu gu snog. Cha chuir duine dragh ort.

IAIN: Agus an uair a dhuisgeas mi gabhaidh sinn ar braiceast.

MAIRI: Gabhaidh.

IAIN: Agus gheibh mi tea teth as a' fhlasc?

Tìr an Aigh

MAIRI: Gheibh gu dearbh.

IAIN: Agus ithidh sinn na sandwiches ?

MAIRI: Ithidh, ithidh. Siuthad a nise, na can an còrr. Caidil.

IAIN: Cia meud seòrsa sandwich a rinn sibh, a Mhamai ?

MAIRI: Uisd a nise, coma leat.

IAIN: Chuir sibh piosan dhe'n chirc air cuid dhiubh, nach do chuir ?

MAIRI: Chuir, chuir, caidil a nise.

IAIN: 'Se sin an seòrsa as fheàrr leamsa.

MAIRI: Ceart gu leòr. Dùin do shuilean a nise.

IAIN: Agus gheibh mi pios ceic cuideachd ?

MAIRI: Gheibh, gheibh.

IAIN: Agus brioscaid ?

MAIRI: Gabh gu fois a nise, a ghràidh, agus chi thu 'nuair a dhùisgeas thu.

IAIN: Tha mi a' dol a . . . . . (An guth a' fàs fann is e a' tuiteam 'na chadal). Sandwiches agus ceic agus . . . .

SEUMAS: A bheil sinn faisg air a' Chrion-laraich fhathasd a Mhairi ?

MAIRI: Chan 'eil fhathast. Chan 'eil seo ach tràth.
   (A' crònan " An Rathad chun nan Eilean ").

SEUMAS: Seall seo. Murt uamhasach eile. Dithis ann an tigh còmhla.

MAIRI: Obh obh.

SEUMAS: Ach b' ann an Sasunn a bha e. Chan 'eil sin cho dona.

MAIRI: Nach cianail thu ? (A' cumail oirre leis an òran).

SEUMAS: Agus coig mìle deug air a ghoid air beulthaobh banca. Sin agad naidheachdan dhut ?   Cuin' a bhitheas sinn anns a' Ghearasdan ?

MAIRI: Cha bhi gu deich uairean. Tha Iain beag 'na chadal mu dheireadh, an truaghan. (*a' bruidhinn gu socair, iseal*).

SEUMAS: B' fheàrr leam gu robh sinn ann am Malaig. Tha aon nì feumail gun d' fhuair sinn an t-àite seo dhuinn fhìn.

MAIRI: Tha. Bha dùil agam an toiseach gum bitheadh Mór Mhór còmhla ruinn. Am faca tu aig an steisean i ?

SEUMAS: Chunnaic ach thug mi an deagh aire nach fhac ise sinne.

MAIRI: A nise cha robh sin laghach dhuit.

SEUMAS: Laghach ! Tha an turus seo fadalach gu leòir mar a tha e, ach chuireadh Mór Mhór an truaighe buileach air.

MAIRI: Ma ta, air a leithid seo de thurus, bhithinn fhéin aoidheil ri Mór Mhór fhéin an diugh.

SEUMAS: Bleadar boirionnaich cho mór 's a chunnaic mi riamh! Gu dearbh fhuair mise mo leòir dhith an oidhche mu dheireadh a bha i stigh againn. Cha chluinn thu aice ach " Seònaid againne an siud, agus Seònaid againne an seo."

MAIRI: Boirionnach bochd a' fuireach leatha fhéin.

SEUMAS: Agus am faca tu mar a chaidh i ris an tea ? Cha mhór nach do chuir i crioch air na bh' air a' bhòrd. A' fuireach leatha fhein ! Co a . . . . . . ?

(*Fuaim aig an dorus agus Mór Mhór a' tighinn air adhart*).

MOR: (*A' bruidhinn le guth mór, làidir*). O tha sibh an seo. Chunnaic mi aig an steisean sibh ach bha a leithid de chabhag oirbh. Tha mise a' falbh a ghabhail mo bhraiceast. Chan 'eil sibhse a' dol sios ?

MAIRI: Chan 'eil. Tha e ro dhaor . . . .

SEUMAS: Ach cha bhi sinn 'gad chumail, a Mhór.

MOR: O tha e daor do chuid, tha mi cìnnteach. Ach mar a thuirt Seònaid againn fhìn rium an uiridh is i 'gam thoirt a

Tìr an Aigh

ghabhail braiceast anns an trean "Tud, a Mhór" ars' ise, "chan 'eil e 'tachairt ach uair 'sa bhliadhna."

MAIRI: O, ghabh sinne ar braiceast mu'n d' fhàg sinn. Ach 's dòcha gun gabh sinn cupa tea aig a' Chrion-laraich.

MOR: Seo Iain beag. A bheil e 'na chadal? 'Se cùis-eagail a th' ann an cloinn ann an trean. A bheil e 'na chadal?

SEUMAS: Tha e 'na chadal, 'se a tha. Tha sinn uile a' dol a dheanamh greiseag chadail an ceartuair.

MOR: O, tha e 'na chadal, a bheil? O, clann an latha diugh is iad cho miobhail. Chan 'eil nì a dh' iarras iad nach fhaigh iad. An cuala sibh mar a rinn peasan anns a' bhaile air Seònaid againne?

SEUMAS: Chuala, chuala. Thilg iad . . . . .

MOR: Bha Seònaid ag radh nan gabhadh iad am bata dhaibh na bu trice gun deanadh e feum dhaibh.

SEUMAS: Cha chuala mi gu robh duine cloinne aig Seònaid agaibhse.

MAIRI: Chan 'eil a Sheumais, ach tha fhios agad fhéin . . . . . .

IAIN: (A' dusgadh). Tha mi ag iarraidh mo bhreacaist.

MAIRI: Uisd a nise. Caidil greiseag eile.

MOR: O 'se nach caidil. Chan e cadal a th' air aire.

IAIN: Chaidil mi mar tha agus thuirt sibh gum faighinn tea agus . . . . .

MAIRI: Gheibh, gheibh thu tea. Seo agad Antai Mór. Thig is beir air làimh oirre.

MOR: Trobhad an seo, Iain. Nach toir thu pòg do Antai? (Iain a' cnàmhan).

SEUMAS: Tha e car dreamach, ach thig e thuige an ceartuir.

IAIN: Tha mi ag iarraidh mo bhreacaist.

MAIRI: Stad ort ma ta. Sìn a nall am baga, a Sheumais. Seo, beir air na cupannan. Gabhaidh tu fhéin cupa còmhla ruinn a Mhór ?

MOR: Gabhaidh, ma thogras sibh, air sgàth na cuideachd.

IAIN: C' àit' a bheil na sandwiches ?

MOR: Dé thuirt thu ? Sandwiches, facal Beurla. A bheil iad ag ionnsachadh Gaidhlig dhuit idir, 'ille ? Nam bitheadh sibh a' dol do'n Chéilidh coltach ri Seònaid againne gheibheadh sibh a' Ghaidhlig cheart air a h-uile facal.

SEUMAS: Dé a' Ghaidhlig cheart a th' air sandwiches ?

MOR: Nach 'eil sandwichearan ?

IAIN: Tha mise ag iarraidh na sandwiches eile.

MOR: Trì seòrsachan sandwichearan. Cha chreid mi nach 'eil ròic agaibh. Agus sandwichearan circe . . . . . !

SEUMAS: Dé tha sin, sandwichearan circe ?

MOR: Feòil-circe—circe. Tha sin furasda gu leòr ionnsachadh. Gu dearbh cha ruig mise leas breacaist no braiceast an déidh seo. Nam faiceadh Seònaid againne . . . . .

SEUMAS: Chan fhaic ge ta.

IAIN: Tha na sandwiches math.

MAIRI: Sandwichearan, a luaidh.

BARDACHD

CO LEIS AN DIOGHALTAS ?

Long nan Lochlannach air sàl
Có do 'n dàn riu 'm bliadhna strìth ?
C'àit an toir iad nuas na siùil ?
Chaidh an cliù air feadh gach tìr.

Gaoth a tuath 'ga greasad dion,
Seachad sios air Sealtainn chiar ;
Tha nis na h-Arcaibh air a cùl,
Chum i a sùil 'san àird an iar.

Dhìrich a' mhuir cho àrd ri beul.
Cha d'thug i géill do ghàir nan tonn,
Shnàmh i mar fhaoileig air a' chuan,
Ni bheireadh buaidh oirr' cha robh ann.

Bha curaidh threuna innt' a' tàmh,
Bu tric a sàs iad ann am blàr ;
Bha geilt air Albannaich gu mór ;
Oir thainig dóruinn leo a ghnàth.

Bha àit an sin nach fhac iad riamh.
An taobh an iar dheth leag iad seòl,
Chaidh iad air tìr air maduinn bhreagh,
Air eilean Sgiathanach a' cheò.

Leum an ceannard air an tràigh,
Fearghus dàna, lann 'ga dhion.
A mhac-san Iomhar as a dhéidh,
Is ceud fear treun, air creich am miann.

Bu fhleasgach ciatach Iomhar féin,
Mar dharach treun, mar ghiuthas àrd.
Dath an òir air falt a' chinn,
'S math do na chì air fiamh a' ghàir.

Bhuail oillt is uamhann luchd an àit,
Gun fhios dé 'n nàmhaid bha 'nan còir.
Sheall iad gu dùrachdach an àird
A' guidh' gum fàgteadh iadsan beò.

Ri taobh a' chladaich bha a' tàmh
Gaisgeach làidir, àrd an cliù:
Iain a b' ainm dha, ri a thaobh
Bha chéile chaomh 's a nighean chiùin.

Bu nighean Màiri b' àillidh' snuadh.
Dearg a gruaidh mar fhuil ruith beò ;
Dubh mar fhitheach tuar a ciabh ;
A cneas fior-gheal mar shneachda leo.

Ruith Fearghus is a mhac gu luath.
Am priobadh ghluais iad fad o chàch.
Sheas Iain air beulaobh a luchd-daimh ;
Thug Fearghus dha-san buille-bhàis.

Bu latha brònach sin do'n t-sluagh.
Am beag a fhuair as sàbhailt beò.
B' aoibhneach na Lochlannaich 's bu dhian.
Chaill iomadh Sgiathanach an deò.

Dh'fhan iad fad rèithe anns an tìr.
Ach 's ann air Iomhar tha mo sgeul.
B' ionmhuinn leis Màiri thar gach té,
Bu tric a beusan-se 'na bheul.

Tìr an Aigh

Thainig an t-am do 'n bhìrlinn triall
Bu bhrònach Iomhar 'n àm bhith falbh.
Dh' asluich e 'n òigh gun rachadh i
Dha féin mar mhnaoi a null thar sàl.

Ciamar ghabhadh i mar fhear-pòsd
Neach thug bròn dith féin 's d 'a sluagh?
Có leag a h-athair fuar air làr
Ach athair, an t-ard-thriath: truaigh nan truaigh.

Bha màthair fiosrach air a' chùis:
'S bu mhór a dùrachd cur an céill,
"Mas e 's gun teid thu leis a' phrionns',
Mo mhallachd a d'ionnsaidh bheir thu fhéin."

Bha smuaintean air fad oidhch' is là.
Mu dheireadh dh' fhàs a beachdan réidh.
'S an fheasgar Iomhar choinnich i,
Chuir i a h-inntinn dha an céill.

"Ma tha do ghràdh mar thubhairt thu
Tha fios gur dlùth an dearbhadh dhuinn.
Marbh thusa d' athair féin gun dàil,
'S do Lochlainn a maireach seòlaidh sinn."

Bha uamhas follaiseach 'na ghnùis
Ach cha do ghluais e i bho miann.
Chuimhnich i bàs a h-athar dha.
Dh aontaich e 'n tràth sin ris a' ghniomh.

Bha 'n oidhche ciùin 's gach nì air dòigh.
Bha dùil ri seòladh ris an là.
Luidh Fearghus sios an cadal trom
Gun amharus ann dé bha 'na dhàil.

Gu feallta dh' ealaidh Iomhar suas
Airsan bu chruaidh so thoirt gu crìch.
Thog e an sgian a bha 'na laimh
Diog cha d' fhàg Fearghus: chaidh e dhìth.

A muigh a' feitheamh sheas an òigh,
Ag altrum dòchais, neart do làimh,
An tiotadh bha e 'g ràdh ri taobh,
" Nis creididh tu, faodaidh bhith, mo ghràdh."

Ghlaodh Màiri, " Tha na fiachan pàight'.
Theid mise leat do d' thìr mu thuath."
Dhì-chuimhnich i a cunnart mór.
Chan fhac i có lean iad gu luath.

Bha mathair amharusach m' a déidh ;
Is chual i dé bha 'm beachd na h-òigh.
Dh' éisd an luchd-faire ri a sgeul.
'S an ceannard treun, cha robh e beò.

Ghlac iad an dithis ud gun dàil
Bàs obann b' àill leo thoirt roimh là.
Thuirt aon fhear, " Bheir a' chailleach binn "—
B'e sin an inntinn bha aig càch.

" Cuiribh an geòla iad le chéil,
'S am fuadach 's fheudar sa Chuan Sgìth,
Seòl na biodh aca, crann no ràmh."
Binn na màthar, fuath 'na crìdh.

An làr-r-na-mhaireach shéid a' ghaoth,
O'n ear aognaidh gu cruaidh, is olc 'na rùn.
Chaidh bàta beag a chur air dòigh,
A réir a' chordaidh bh' ac' air tùs.

Tìr an Aigh

Cha dubhairt Iomhar facal riu.
Bu chalm' a shùil, 's bu deas a cheum.
Ach ri a màthair ghlaodh an òigh,
Le glaodhaibh bròin 'n am éirigh gréin'.

Thionndaidh a màthair null a ceann.
Sheòl iad gu mall air ais gu tìr,
Chaidh 'm bàta a sealladh-san gu luath
Guth cha chualas air neach' bha innt'.

Chaidh làithean seach, is smuain a' fàs
Blàth aig càirdean air an tòir.
Bha iad, aig neach, "a measg nan ròn,"
Fear eile fòs, "an Tìr-nan-Og."

TURUS SAMHRAIDH

Sòlas sìor do neach air bhoil,
   le strìth is trod an t-saoghail chruaidh,
Triall le sunnd a tìr nan Gall,
   air turus samhraidh do'n taobh tuath.

Ceistean cuiridh eòlaich air,
   "Car son a shìneas tu ri tuath?
Am faic thu 'n diugh na càirdean ann?
   Ma chi thu glinn, am faic thu sluagh?"

Feithidh freagairt luath 'na bheul,
   "Ged a tha na taighean fàs,
Chi mi bhuam o iomadh cnoc
   muir is monadh mar a bha."

216

Comhairle bheir càirdean dha,
" Seachainn fuachd is sileadh trom.
Gabh a nunn gu tìrean céin
sgrìob a chuireas tu am fonn."

Ceum cha chairich e o bheachd :
car chan aom iad e o mhiann :
Guth air géilleadh cha bhi ann ;
freagraidh e le faclan dian :

" Séideadh stoirm is sileadh sruth,
guth air gearain cha tig bhuam.
Dhuibhse grian na h-àirde deas :
dhomhsa gaillionn an taoibh tuath."

Làidir leosan fuaim a ghuth :
chi iad solus ùr 'na ghnùis.
Co-ionnan cuideachd ri a dhreach
a chridh' a stigh a réir a chliù.

Bailtean breagha nunn thar sàil,
iomadh ionghnadh geallar dha.
Bothan beag as ionmhainn leis,
lùchairt lìomhach thar a chàil.

Moladh mór air muir is raon
's tric a chluinneas tu 'na bheul :
Ged nach d'rinn e uaill mu shluagh
chan ann air sluagh as lugh' a spéis.

Ionndrainn air a' chuid a dh'fhalbh
cha toir neach an seo air bàrr.
Tadhal tìr san robh iad beò
sòlas dhasan chan e cràdh.

Tìr an Aigh

Dorsan dùinte bitheadh ann,
   iomairean le luibhean làn,
Buaile far nach faicear bó,
   gàrradh-crìch' a' dol gu làr.

Truagh leinn tìr mar seo gu fìor,
   is cha chùm e aonta bhuainn.
Dhasan tha an t-àite làn
   liuthad smuain ag éirigh suas.

Aisling ait an i a chuir
   aoidh air aodann, saod 'na cheum?
Faileasan a' falbh as ùr,
   cruth nan daoin' a bh'ann an dé?

Cosnaidh cnuic is iochdair dha
   saorsa spioraid, tuilleadh treòir.
Gheibh e fois an tìr a bhreith
   nach d'fhiosraich e o làithean òig'.

Có a chuireas le guth mór
   cuimhne chealgach as a leth?
Cleachdadh bha aig cuimhne riamh
   math a thaghadh, olc a chleith.

Aobhar ionghnaidh cha bhi ann
   dealbhan dreachmhor bhith 'na shùil;
Na bliadhnachan mar ghloinne dhait
   cur loinn na h-òige air gach cùis.

Dealbh fad as air achaidh feòir,
   àile cùbhraidh thig 'na leum,
Saoghal ùr aig bun gach stàth,
   diasan feòir cho àrd ris fhéin.

Suainte mu gach smuain cho teann
nach tig an toinneamh as gu bràth:
Coltas té air feadh gach dealbh,
an té thug breith is àrach dha.

Bha sonas ceangailt' ri a ceum
cluasan biorach feitheamh fuaim.
Dubhar dha i bhith air falbh,
gath na gréin' i bhith mun cuairt.

Mios a' chéitein chuimhnich e
casan rùisgt' mu dheireadh thall:
Toileachadh troimh chom gu léir
a' dìreadh suas bho shàil gu ceann.

Toileachadh a dh'fhoillsich dha
talamh fhéin ag innseadh dhuinn
Fìrinn nach do thuig e òg,
doimhneachd dàimhe do a cloinn.

Greann a' gheamhraidh tarraing dlùth,
teachdaireachd roimh aimsir reòt':
Comhairle na talmhainn fial,
seasgair socair taic nam bròg.

Feasgar samhraidh fiathach thall,
siobadh slaite mach bho sgeir,
Companach le còmhradh ciùin,
saoghal romhpa réidh gun chnead.

Iasgach eile chuimhnich e
bàta beag a' ghluasaid mhìn;
A' mhoit a bh'air 'nuair mhol na fir
mar a dh' iomair e gun sgìos.

Tìr an Aigh

Aon uair eile bheachdaich e
    air ainm gach rudha, sgeir, is òib,
Lorgan lean ris domhain riamh
    mar a rinneadh iad 'na òig'.

Thuig e mar o shean an aoidh
    chuir 'na ghruaidhean rudhadh blàth
Ruigheachd dhachaigh le gad éisg
    slaodadh sleamhain sios gu làr.

Mar leig e air nach b'fhiach siud dad
    nach mór an dragh a thug e dha ;
Gidheadh bha 'chridhe làn de dh'uaill
    e air a mheas 'na dhuine fàs.

Coimeas caitheamh latha ri siud
    siubhal tràigh le sùil air tiùrr :
Ionghnaidhean a chumadh riut
    is ri gach neach a bh'ann bho thùs.

Cladach làn a h-uile ceum,
    feamainn air gach cumadh ann :
Maorach, ainmhidhean na tràigh,
    acainn luingeis nach bu ghann.

Doirbh an diugh a thuigsinn leis
    comas balaich aig an am :
Eallach connaidh air a dhruim
    b'fheudar tric gu robh e fann.

Gliocas bhliadhnachan mar sin
    chuir air òige solus ùr :
Iarraidh òganaich a ghnàth
    bhith mar fhireannach an cliù.

Seasaidh sònraichte measg chàich
   làithean eil' a mach 'na chuimhn',
Reothairt deanamh oitir lom,
   buain nam muirsgian beul an tuinn.

Sealladh anabarrach air tràigh
   nach fhaicear gann ach uair sa' bhliadhn';
Iongantas thug bàrr air sin
   'ga tadhal oidhche ghealaich bhreagh'.

Sgrìob a nunn do'n choille chnò,
   turus taitneach a bhitheadh ann ;
Cha b'fhad' gum bitheadh poca làn
   aig fear nach trusadh iad gu mall.

Sa mhonadh choimhdeadh e gu mion
   air làraich nam puill-mhòna shuas ;
Air éigin lorgadh e an t-àit,
   baic air fàs cho staoin gun bhuain.

'Na chuimhne las an aimsir ait,
   buain na mòna cùl an t-sléibh:
Chan iarradh fir no mnathan falbh,
   do chloinn e cha bu ruith ach leum

Rinn cuid le tuigse mhóir seach càch,
   glic eadhon thar am barail fhéin,
Aighear de na bhitheadh 'na dhragh,
   a' chlann 'nan cluich a' deanamh feum.

Am bu shòlasaich de'n là,
   suidh aig biadh aig ceann a' phuill.
Cuirm na b'fheàrr air thalamh riamh
   cha chuala duine is cha chluinn.

Tìr an Aigh

'S iomadh uair a dh'iarradh cead
biorainean a chur air doigh,
Uisg' an fhuarain thoirt a nall,
tein' a dheasachadh le fòid.

Glan a chuimhn' air teas na tì,
aran coirc is uibhean cruaidh,
Acras a' cur blas air biadh,
còcaire as àirde luaidh.

Mun tug e cùl ri tuath a rìs
chaill an àireamh bheag seo aon,
Aon a chaidh air turus buan
nach fhaodar chur an dara taobh.

Do'n tìodhlacadh chaidh fear ar sgeòil,
mar chaidh gach fear le cothrom slàint';
Cleachdadh cubhaidh a bhith cruinn,
beachdachadh air cumhachd bàis.

Briathran freagarrach mar chleachd:
sheas fear togail sailm a muigh:
Buaidh na seinn bha air an t-sluagh
na sreithean réidh bho bheul a' ruith.

Corp an caraid ghiùlain iad
gun chabhaig astar réir an nòs.
Dhearc na h-ainglean 's dh'aithnich iad
spéis 'ga nochdadh mar bu chòir.

Là na Sàbaid thog e air
do'n eaglais, rathad eòlach dha ;
Sàbaid Comanachaidh a bh'ann ;
choisich esan mar bu ghnàth.

Càr le muinntir eaglais tric
    fad an rathaid sìos gu luath:
Air adhart chùm e ceum air cheum
    cuideachadh cha d'iarr no truas.

Fhuair e àite-suidhe fhéin,
    Bìobull fuaraidh leis an aois
Theann na smuaintean air gu tiugh
    umpasan a bh'ann 's a dh'aom.

Ràinig fhaireachaidhean àird,
    'nuair a dh'éirich iad gu'n Bhòrd:
Thill iad, ar leis, a ris gu thaobh
    le'n aghaidh nèamhaidh a' tighinn beò.

Am fear-turuis thill fa-dheòidh,
    mac-meanmainn làn de dhealbhan ùr:
Doigh nan daoin' o'n tàinig e
    lean am feasd do aigne dlùth.

'S mór an sòlas dha mu dheas,
    bitheadh saoghal còir no cruaidh
Na chunnaic is na chual e greis
    'na thurus samhraidh do'n taobh tuath.

223

TURUS CHNOIDEIRT

Thug Iain còir an uiridh dhomh
Le fialaidheachd an cuireadh ud,
Gu falbhainn-sa air turus leis
A choiseachd timchioll Chnòideirt.

B'e 'n t-aobhar gun do dh'aontaich mi
Cho suilbhir ri a smaointean-san,
An dealbh a bha mi cuimhneachadh
Air Cnòideart làithean m'òige.

Is ged a dh'fhàg an òige sinn
'Sa thilg cuid oirnn ar gòraiche,
Bha mac an urra còmhla ruinn
Gillean tapaidh treuna.

Na canaibh gu robh dùil againn
Gun deanadh iad a' ghiùlain dhuinn
Le eallaich throma dhùbailte,
Sinn fhìn a' falbh gu h-aotrom.

Ach bha iad suas ri teantaichean
Is ri gach nì dhe'n trealaich sin.
Air còcaireachd 's air campaichean
Bha moit orra mu'n eòlas.

Is ann a bha an t-ullachadh
An deasachadh 'san cruinneachadh
Air brògan mór' is briogaisean
Is biadh na chumadh armailt.

Bha'n càr aig Iain luchdaichte,
Le gach goireas cruthaichte ;
Is ghabh sinn beannachd dhùrachdach
Gun deur air sùil, ri dàimhich.

Seachad taobh Loch Laomuinn sios
Bha aon nì a chuir ionghnadh oirnn
Na coisichean a dh'fhaodamaid
A thogail leinn nam b'àill leinn.

Ach dh'amhairc sinn le tnùth orra
'Nar sùilean bu chùis-bhùrta iad ;
Cha b'ann mar siud a shiùbhlamaid
Air sgrìob le brògan móra.

Am bùithnean mór a' Ghearasdain
Bu mhodhail ruinn na ceannaichean ;
Ged b'eibhinn leo an sealladh sinn
Cha'n fhacas fiamh a' ghàire.

Bha astar troimh 'n Ghleann Mhór againn
A' meas gur sinn bha foghainteach,
Ach cion a' chàr chuir dóruinn oirnn
Nuair dh'fhàg sinn e 'n Gearr-Lòchaidh.

Thog sinn oirnn na màileidean
Gu dearbh cha b'ann gun spàirn dhuinn e ;
A' dol mu seach gu tàmailteach,
B'fhasa leam cliabh-mòna.

Cha b'fhada gun do tharruing sinn
Gu'n iar air tòir an rathaid ud
Air an robh anns na mapaichean
An t-ainm a' Mhìle Dhorcha.

Shoillsicheadh ar dorchadas
Le tachartas ro-fhortanach
'Nuair stad a' bhan air thoiseach oirnn
'S a fhuair sinn tairgse dìreadh.

Tìr an Aigh

A' cur air chùl nam bòidean sin
A thug sinn 'nuair a thòisich sinn
Nach sireamaid an sòlas seo ;
Ghabh sinn ris an tairgse.

'San dòigh seo rinn adhartas
Da mhìle suas gun oidhirp dhuinn ;
Loch Arcaig nis mu'r coinneamh-ne
'Na laighe shios gu lh-àlainn.

Nuair lorg sinn àite freagarrach
Cha d'fhuaras duine teagamhach.
Bha sòlas nach bu bheag oirnn
A' gabhail fois na h-oidhche.

Is thug na balaich leasan dhuinn
Air teantaichean a dheasachadh
Air còcaireachd bha fhios againn
Nach toireadh iadsan bàrr oirnn.

Ach mallachd air na cuileagan
Bha fad an fheasgair cuide ruinn
Bha dorran air gach fear againn
Mu chraicionn bog nan glùinean.

An la-'r-na-mhaireach ràinig sinn
Gu ceann an loch gun fàiligeadh ;
Gu dearbh cha robh na màileidean
A nis cho doirbh ri'n giùlain.

Ràinig sinn Gleann Deasairigh
Is champaich sinn am feasgair sin
An àite àrd gu faiciollach
Gun meanbh-chuileag 'gar léireadh.

Ach b'iad sin fhéin a b'fhasa dhuinn
Na'n t-uisge trom gun lasachadh
A thàinig air an ath latha
'S a mhair gus an do thill sinn.

Is ged a rinn e drùdhadh oirnn
Cha b'urrainn duinn gun sùil thoirt air
Na beanntan àrda ùdlaidh ud
'S na still a nuas 'nan dian-ruith.

B'e 'n gnothuch tighinn gu aibhnichean,
An tuil 'na dheann le straighlich ann
Ach thàrr sinn làmh mu laimh a nunn
'S cha robh na balaich diùid.

Roimh oidhche rinn sinn Carnach dheth
Aig ceann Loch Nibheis sàbhailte ;
Bha seann taigh cìobair falamh ann
Far an d'fhuair sinn fasgadh oidhche.

Bha teine a bhruicheadh tarbh againn
Cha mhór cho luath 'sa ràinig sinn
Có fear nach deanadh gàire ruinn
A' faicinn meud ar feum air ?

Bha uisge la-'r-na-mhàireach ann
Cho cunbhalach 'sa b'àbhaist da.
Cha'n fhaodamaid-ne tàmh an siud,
Is thog sinn oirnn le dòchas.

227

Tìr an Aigh

Cha bu fhliuichead riamh dhuinn e
Gu'n am-sa 'nuair a stiallamaid
Troimh uillt a' mhonaidh fhiadhaich ud
Feadh bhogalaich is choilltean.

B'e 'n sealbh a thug gu fìrinneach
Thar Creag an Dotair cìnnteach sinn.
A' faicinn Ionar-Idh an siud,
B'e thog ar crìdh le sòlas.

'S a' bhaile seo bha càirdean
A thug aoidheachd dhuinn le bàighealachd.
Ach rùnaich sinn gum b'fheàrr an seo
An còrr de Chnòideart fhàgail.

Gu dearbh b'e 'n t-aiseag fiadhaich e
A' seòladh ris an iar an siud,
Am bàta air a riasladh nunn
Mu'n d'rinn sinn Malaig sàbhailt.

Abair thusa gàirdeachas
Mu dheas ruinn 'nuair a ràinig sinn ;
Iad uile ag ràdh nach tàrramaid
A ris air cuairt cho gòrach.

Ach ma bhios an t-slàinte againn
Is coltas side bàidheil air
Có their nach fhalbh sinn làth-eigin
A ris air Turus Chnòideirt.

AN UILE-BHEIST IS NA FOGHLUMAICH

An éisd sibh tacan ri mo sgeul?
Is guidhibh dhomh d'ur deòin,
Gum bitheadh agam còmhnadh bhàrd
A dh'fhalbh a tìr nam beò.
Is nì mi duan air Biasd Loch Nis,
'S air triùir de dhaoine còir,
An t-Ollamh Caol, an t-Uasal Maol,
'San Dotair Mac Iain Ghròt.

Is dòch gun cuala sibh mu thràth
Mu'n ainmhidh tric gu leòr,
Oir chunnaic móran dhaoine e
Nach deanadh breug 's iad beò.
Ach theagamh gu bheil feadhainn ann
Nach cuala fhathasd fòs
Mu'n Ollamh Chaol, mu'n Uasal Mhaol,
'S mu'n Dotair Mac Iain Ghròt.

Bu chiùin Loch Nis ré iomadh linn
Gun ghoil no gàirich thonn.
Bha neart nam beann 'ga dìon bho stoirm;
Cha b' ionnann 's cuan le greannd.
A dh'aindeoin sin bu tric a' ghaoth
A' greasad nuas gach gleann,
A mhilleadh sgàthan réidh an uisg'
Le cuairteig nach bu ghann.

Cha b' ainneamh breac a' leum le plub
Air feasgar ciùin an àird.
Cha b' ainneamh eala bhàn le céil'
Bho thaobh gu taobh a' snàmh.

Tìr an Aigh

Cha b' ainneamh fear an geòla chaoil.
A' sìneadh air dà ràmh.
Cha b' ainneamh eadhon bàt' na smùid
'S na làithean so a chaidh.

Bha uair nach robh ach sin 'san loch,
Cho fad 'sa b' fhiosrach leo.
Cha robh ri fhaotainn air Loch Nis.
Ach sàmhchair mar bu nòs,
Ach thàinig beothach mór ro threun,
'S na fir so air a thòir—
An t-Ollamh Caol, an t-Uasal Maol,
'S an Dotair Mac Iain Ghròt.

Cha b' aon fhear do'm bu léir a' bhiasd ;
Cha b'eadh, no dhà, no trì,
Cha tug mi feairt air feadhainn dhiubh
A bha dhe'n eaglais chlì :
Ach 'nuair a chuala mi an sgeul
Bho neach dhe m' eaglais fhìn,
Cha b' urrainn dhomh gun aideachadh
Gun robh an t-iomradh fìor.

Ach bha gach fear a' faicinn cruth
Nach faca neach de chàch.
Bha cuid a chunnaic adhaircean,
Cuid eile ceann maol bàn
Thuirt cuid gu robh i mìl' am fad,
Cuid eile slat no dhà ;
A h-astar uair cho luath ri fiadh,
I ris cha mhór 'na tàmh.

Bha sligean carrach air a druim
Cheart uiread ri do dhòrn,
Ach beagan làithean as a dhéidh
Bha i cho slìom ri ròn.
Air tùs bha 'druim 'na fhichead snaim
A rìs, a trì bu dòch.
Aon fhear 'ga faicinn stigh air tìr,
Smùid aic' air itheadh 'n fheòir.

'Se thuirt riumsa fear na sgeig
Nuair chual e brìgh mo sgeòil,
"Is math an stuth tha'n Inbhir-Nis
Ma chithear sud le seòid."
Ach 's neònach leam a ghabhail a steach
Gu robh iad uil 'ga òl,
Oir tha 'nam measg na h-éildearan
Nach blaiseadh deur ri 'm beò.

Ach tha e soilleir dhuinn có-dhiùbh
Gun d'rinn am beothach feum,
'S gun d'ràinig daoine taobh Loch Nis
Nach cuala roimh m'a déidh,
Their Sasunnaich, "'S ann air son so
A thog an sluagh an sgeul."
Tha Goill an dùil gu bheil gach neach
Cho breugach riutha féin.

Is nì cho iongantach 'sa bh' ann
Ri fhaicinn anns an tìr,
Mar thàinig biasdan eile beò
Gach seachdainn fad na tìd.

Tìr an Aigh

An loch nach cumadh biasd no dhà
Gu dearbh cha b' fhiach i nì:
Bha iad cho pailt ri sgadan sios
Loch Aillse gu Loch Fìn.

Cha chuala tus' a leithid riamh
De dh' ùpraid measg an t-sluaigh ;
An dara taobh a' mionnachadh
Gu robh rud ann a ghluais ;
Cuid eil' an aghaidh sin gu dion—
An cual thu dad cho truagh ?
O làithean an ath-leasachaidh
Cha robh ann cath cho cruaidh.

Gach neach a thuirt nach biasd a bh' ann,
Bha beachd aige dha fhéin ;
B'e iarratas gach fir gum biodh
A bheachd-san ùr gu léir,
'S gun cluinnteadh barail bhuaith-san
Ge beag bhiodh innt' de chéill,
Mar nach biodh ann ach faileas bheann
'Ga chluich fhéin ris a' ghréin.

Is ma bha mìle eanachainn
A' cnuasach air a' chùis,
Gu deimhin chluinnteadh mìle beachd,
Nan éisdeadh daoine riu.
Gach paipeir-naidheachd beag is mór
Làn bhiasdan fad na h-ùin:
Is sgrìobhadh eadhon leabhraichean
A tha nis àrd an cliù.

Bha daoine foghluimte 'nam boil
'S an inntinn ann an ceò ;
A dh'aindeoin sgrùdadh leabhraichean
Cha d' fhàs iad glic gu leòr,
Bha eòlas sònraichte aig triùir
Air biasdan marbh is beò—
An t-Ollamh Caol, an t-Uasal Maol,
'S an Dotair Mac Iain Ghròt.

Na biodh sìbhs' a' smaoineachadh
'Nuair thàinig a' bhiasd ùr
Gum b'aithne dhoibhsan dad seach càch,
Cha b'aithne, duine dhiùbh.
Ge mór an t-ionnsachadh a bh' ac'
Air biasdan allt is ciùin,
Bha'n triùir aca, 'nuair thachair so,
Air chall, gun solus iùil.

Ach 'se bu mhò thug dhoibh de dhragh
Dé 'n dòigh 'sam freagradh iad
Na ciadan dhaoin' a dh' fheòraich dhiubh
De *bha* sud, mur e biasd,
Mun robh iad fad a' meòrachadh
Bha falt gach fir dhiubh liath,
Chaidh fichead bliadhna air an aois
An taobh a stigh de mhios.

An t-urram aig an Ollamh Chaol
Gum b'e a thuirt ri càch,
" O, feumaidh sinn bhith onoireach
Is aideachadh gun dàil

Tìr an Aigh

Gun d'rinn a' bhiasd an gnothuch oirnn,
'S nach urrainn dhuinn an dràsd
Bhith idir cinnteach as a gnè—
Chan fheum sinn dad a ràdh."

Mun d' fhuair ach gann an t-Ollamh Caol
Na briathran as a bheul,
Ghrad thionndaidh air an t-Uasal Maol
Le campair is le feirg.
"Ge bith," ars esan, "dé ni sinn,
Cha nàraich sinn sinn féin,
Oir dé a shaoileas daoine dhinn
Le leithid sin de sgeul?"

Is dh' aontaich leis an Uasal Mhaol
An Dotair Mac Iain Ghròt.
Cha mhór nach d' ith iad eatorra
An t-Ollamh bochd gun ghò.
Mu dheireadh dh' iarr e maitheanas
Le osnaidhean 's le bròn,
Is gheall e dhoibh nach canadh e
Ri duine sud ri 'bheò.

Is bha an Dotair Mac Iain Ghròt
Ro-innleachdach seach càch:
Cha b' ann an sud a stadadh e,
Ach thuirt e gun dàil,
"Carson a bhuaireadh daoine sinn
Le ceist is ceist gun tàmh?
Nam marbhamaid a' bhiasd gun fhios,
Cha chluinnteadh ceist gu bràth."

234

Cho luath 'sa chual' an t-Uasal so
Dha cha bu ruith ach leum,
Le beagan spàirn cho-éignich iad
An t-Ollamh mar an ceudn'.
Ach b'fhas' a ràdh na chur an gniomh,
'S gun ghniomh bha cainnt gun fheum ;
'Nam fianuis chuir an Dotair còir
An innleachd mhór an céill.

Mar so gu seòlta dh'inns' e dhaibh
Mar dheanadh iad an gniomh:
Ars esan, " Gheibh sinn bàta math
Is tàirrnidh sinn a' bhiasd
Le lòchran mór air oidhche dhorch'
A chur do'n uisge sios."
Gu dearbh cha chreid mi fhìn nach robh
An Dotair as a rian.

Cha deanadh am an t-samhraidh feum,
Mar thubhairt an Dotair riu ;
Is dh' fheumadh foighidinn bhith ac'
Fad aon dà mhios co-dhiùbh.
Bha Biasd Loch Nis os cionn an uisg'
Gach seachdainn fad na h-ùin.
Is dòcha gu robh fhios aice
Glé mhath dé bha 'nan rùn.

Ach nuair a thàinig fad 'san oidhch'
Is Oidhche Shamhna dlùth
Bha othail air na foghlumaich
B'fhior shealgairean an triùir.

235

Tìr an Aigh

Bha làithean féille ac' a nis
'Nuair bha an colaisd dùint'
Ach smid cha d'innis iad do neach
Dé ris an robh an sùil.

Bha'n t-Uasal Maol le claidheamh trom
Le meirg air fàs ro ruadh ;
An Dotair fhéin le gunna mór
Le'n tug a shinnsir buaidh.
Bu shèimh seach iad an t-Ollamh Caol
Nach dòirteadh fuil gun truas,
Cha tug e leis do'n chogadh mhór
Ach sgonn de dharach cruaidh.

Aon latha ràinig Inbhir-Nis
Triùir ghiùlnach armaicht ghleusd,
Gu leòr de threalaich air an cùl
Ach duine cha tug géill.
Bu bheag bha amhrus sluagh an àit'
Air rùintean fuilteach geur
Nan sealgairean a mharbhadh biasd
A chosnadh fois dhoibh féin.

Gun mhoille fhuair iad tigh gu tàmh
Air taobh na locha dlùth.
Bha bàt' is acainn air an tràigh
Mar dheasaich iad air tùs.
B'e àite uaigneach a bha so,
Is fhuair iad fois 'nan triùir.
Bha e fìor fheumail dhoibh gun robh
Aon fheasgar ann glé chiùin.

236

Is beagan an déidh mheadhon-oidch',
   An saoghal paisgt an sìth,
Gu fiataidh mach a ghabh na seòid—
   Bha fois air muir 's air tìr—
Chuir iad am bàta anns an uisg';
   Gu socair shuidh iad innt.
Bha'n Dotair anns an, deireadh shios,
   Is càch le ràimh rith' sìnt.

Cha tric air gniomh cho iongantach
   A sheall na nèamhan shuas ;
An Dotair leis an lòchran laist',
   'Ga thumadh uair is uair ;
An dithis eile dìchiollach
   Ag iomramh null gu cruaidh,
An dùil air faicinn sud do'n bhéisd
   Gun tigeadh i gu luath.

Gu dearbh cha b' fhad' gun tàing i,
   Is cha bu chneasd a tuar.
B'iad cluasan biorach Mhic Iain Ghròt
   A chual an toiseach fuaim.
"Nach éisd sibh, 'illean," thubhairt e,
   Chan 'eil i fada bhuainn ;
Nis deanaibh fodha mionaid bheag:
   So agaibh uair na buaidh.

Mar dh'iarr e rinn a chompanaich,
   Is leagadh an da ràmh.
Gu h-obann chual' iad sloistreadh uisg'
   Cruth glas a' teachd gu dàn.

237

Tìr an Aigh

"Tha ceithir lùban air," ars' aon,
"Tha cóig air," arsa càch.
Ge mór bu mhath leo teicheadh as,
Cha teicheadh a bha 'n dàn.

Ged thug an Dotair Mac Iain Ghròt
An lòchran steach do'n bhàt,
Is ged a dh'iomair iad gu cruaidh
Bu bheag feum sin an dràsd
Ach c' àit' an robh na h-airm a nis
'San d'rinn iad uaill glé thràth ?
Cha robh guth idir ac' orra
Ged bha ann cunnart bàis.

An aghaidh ionnsaigh béisd mar sud
Bha airm gun fheum co-dhiùbh.
Cha d'fhuair iad eadhon sùil thoirt air
A cruth, mun robh i dlùth.
Mar shlige dh' fhalbh am bàta ro.mhp' ;
Na fir cha mhór sa ghrunnd.
Bu mhath an nì 'san uair sin dhoibh
Nach d' rinn i stad 'na cùrs.

Nuair dh' éirich iad gu bàrr an uisg'
Bha i deagh astar uap'.
Ghlac iad mar b'fheàrr a dh' fhaodadh iad
Na ràimh 's na clàir mu'n cuairt.
Bha iad ro-thaingeil a bhith beò
Ged bha an staid ro-thruagh,
Is dòchas aca faighinn as
Ri ùin' o'n chunnart chruaidh.

Ri éirigh gréine chunnaic iad
Nach robh iad fad o thìr
Bha aobhar ac' air buidheachas
Nach fhac iad biasd a rìs.
Cha b'fhad gum faca feadhainn iad
A theasairg iad 's a thill:
Cha d'éirich dad ach bogadh dhaibh,
Ged theab iad dol a dhìth.

Cha mhór a chuala riamh an sgeul.
Gu deas thill iad fadheòidh.
Tha fhathasd Biasd Loch Nis gu tric
Ri fealla-dha 's ri spòrs:
Cha chòrd aon nì na's feàrr rithe
Na'n dòigh 'san tug i bròn
Do'n Ollamh Chaol, do'n Uasal Mhaol.
'S do'n Dotair Mac Iain Ghròt.

COMHFHURTACHD

Mas e do chàil,
    air sgàth na sìth,
An t-srìth a chur
    A beachd gu tur,
Cha chuir ri d'chliù
    nach fiù leat gul.

Tìr an Aigh

Cha chuir ri d'chliù
An sùnnd a th'ort
Ri toirt na gréin',
'S an saoghal breun
Gun chéill mu'n cuairt
le bhruaillean fhéin.

Air saoghal breun
Nach tréig a dhoigh
An còir do thaic
A bhith cho tric?
Am bi do sgeul
Cho deurach sin?

A bheil an sgeul
Gu léir gun dreach,
A' teachd gu d'chluais
Mu'n bhagradh chruaidh.
Bho'n fhuair thu fios
Air sgrios bho shuas?

Tha fiosan clis
A nis 's a' ghaoith
Air claoidh is leòn
Is sluagh ri bròn.
Do shòlas fhéin
Air tréigsinn fòs.

240

Do shòlas fhéin
　Bha réidh a' fàs
A' gabhail céill
　Bho cheòl nan eun,
Ged léireadh cuid
　Le spuirean geur.

Ged léireadh cuid,
　Cha sguir an ceòl.
Ged leònadh pàisd
　Air sràid gu bàs
Is tràth a' chlann
　Le fonn mar bha.

Mar chithear clann
　Tha clann nan daoin
A' faotainn brath
　Mar thuirt Ni Math,
Gum fàg E ghnàth
　Am bàs gun ghath.

LUINNEAG

Có their rium le faclan faoin
Nach 'eil an so ach saoghal staoin ?
Aon sealladh thug mi air a sùil,
Sealladh nach teid a chaoidh air chùl.

Dòimhneachd 'na sùilean, dòimhneachd cuain,
Dòimhneachd nach siubhail mi chaoidh ri ùin.
Cho tric 's gun seall mi air a gnùis,
Gun leugh mi annta nithean ùr.

Bhuair iadsan mi air iomadh uair,
Buairidh iad cuideachd mi a so suas,
Cha duilich leam gach buaireadh ùr
So am buaireadh air an dean mi luaidh.

Có nis their rium le briathran faoin
Nach 'eil an so ach saoghal staoin ?
Aon sealladh thug mi air a sùil,
Sùil shoilleir, shìobhalt, shèimh, mo rùin.

ABOU BEN ADHEM

Le Leigh Hunt

(Air eadar-theangachadh)

Bha fear, Abou Ben Adhem, anns na
dùthchannan thall ;
cha robh a leithid ach tearc—b'e sin an call.
Bha Abou Ben Adhem, an duine còir,
an sàmhchair na h-oidhche ag aisling gun ghò.
Dhùisg e, is dé bha 'na ionad-tàimh,
an solus na gealaich, ach aingeal ri làimh !
Bha dealradh san t-seòmar mar lili fo bhlàth
is an t-aingeal a' sgrìobhadh an leabhar gun
tàmh.

Bha dreach an leabhair air dreach an òir.
Le suaimhneas an àite ghléidh Abou a threòir.
Chuir e ceist ris an tannasg. " Dé sgrìobh thu
an dràsd ? "
Fhreagair esan, " A mhuinntir do Dhia a thug
gràdh."
" A bheil m'ainm-sa air aon diubh ? " arsa
Abou gun dàil.
" Chan 'eil," deir an t-aingeal. Thuirt Abou
'na thràth,
le guth caran ciùin ach suilbhir a ris,
" Cuir sios mi mar fhear a ghràdhaich gun dìth
na càirdean mun cuairt air an eòlach mi."
Chuir an t-aingeal siud sios is dh'fhalbh e gu
luath.
Dhùisg an solus an ath-oidhche Abou o shuain.
Anns an leabhar bha 'n àireamh a dh'fhoillsich
gràdh Dhé.
Feuch ! Bha Abou Ben Adhem air thoiseach
gu léir.